MW00787819

GREEK GENRES AND JEWISH AUTHORS

GREEK GENRES AND JEWISH AUTHORS

Negotiating Literary Culture in the Greco-Roman Era

Sean A. Adams

BAYLOR UNIVERSITY PRESS

Cover and book design by Kasey McBeath
Cover image: Part of a frieze on the Arch of Titus in Rome, showing Jewish prisoners carrying artefacts from Jerusalem (litho). Private Collection/Look and Learn/Elgar Collection/Bridgeman Images

Library of Congress Cataloging-in-Publication Data

Names: Adams, Sean A., author.
Title: Greek genres and Jewish authors : negotiating literary culture in the Greco-Roman era / Sean A. Adams.

Description: Waco : Baylor University Press, 2020. | Includes bibliographical references. | Summary: "Examines how Second Temple Jewish writings appropriated and adapted Hellenistic generic conventions"-- Provided by publisher.
Identifiers: LCCN 2020017779 (print) | LCCN 2020017780 (ebook) | ISBN 9781481312912 (hardback) | ISBN 9781481312950 (pdf) | ISBN 9781481312943 (mobi) | ISBN 9781481312936 (epub)
Subjects: LCSH: Greek literature--Jewish authors--History and criticism. | Greek literature, Hellenistic--History and criticism. | Literary form--History--To 1500.
Classification: LCC PA3083 .A33 2020 (print) | LCC PA3083 (ebook) | DDC 880.9/8924--dc23
LC record available at https://lccn.loc.gov/2020017779
LC ebook record available at https://lccn.loc.gov/2020017780

Greek Genres and Jewish Authors has been made possible in part by a major grant from the National Endowment for the Humanities: Exploring the human endeavor. Any views, findings, conclusions, or recommendations expressed in this book do not necessarily represent those of the National Endowment for the Humanities.

Printed in the United States of America on acid-free paper with a minimum of thirty percent recycled content.

This work is dedicated to three of my most formative teachers and mentors.
Thank you so much for all of your support over the years;
I would not have been able to write this without you.

Bryan D. Wylie, *schulevater* (d. 2018)

Stanley E. Porter, *mastervater* (1956–)

Larry W. Hurtado, *doctorvater* (1943–2019)

CONTENTS

PREFACE

This project began with funding from the British Academy for a post-doctoral fellowship and was completed at the University of Glasgow. I am thankful for both institutions for their financial support, which allowed space for writing and reading (including research leave in 2018). I am blessed to have a supportive family and a great set of colleagues, both of which have had to listen to me talk about this subject for many years.

This work benefited from the comments and feedback of many colleagues, including the anonymous reviewers. Without your generosity this work would have been much poorer. Many thanks to: Jim Aitken, Francis Borchardt, Frank Dicken, Susan E. Docherty, Zanne Domoney-Lyttle, Seth M. Ehorn, Mark Elliott, Ayala Gorodzinsky, Lisa Hau, Matthew Hoskin, Sara Johnson, Craig Keener, Nathan Leach, Steve Mason, Sarah Nicholson, Jonathan Norton, Tessa Rajak, Elizabeth Shively, Timothy Sinclair, Joan Taylor, Benjamin Wright III. Special thanks to Marieke Dhont, who read multiple chapters, and to my doctoral student, Zachary Vickery, who compiled the bibliography. Thank you also to the staff at Baylor University Press, who worked very hard to make this volume possible.

Sean A. Adams
Glasgow, UK
October 2019

ABBREVIATIONS

In addition to the following, all abbreviations in this book are taken from Patrick H. Alexander et al., *The SBL Handbook of Style: For Biblical Studies and Related Disciplines* (2nd ed.; Atlanta: SBL, 2014), and T. Whitmarsh, *Oxford Classical Dictionary* (4th ed.; Oxford: Oxford University Press, 2012).

ACD	*Acta Classica Universitatis Scientiarum Debreceniensis*
AJEC	Ancient Judaism and Early Christianity
ANET	*Ancient Near Eastern Texts Relating to the Old Testament.* Edited by James B. Pritchard. 3rd ed. Princeton: Princeton University Press, 1969.
ANS	Ancient Narrative Supplementum
ASE	*Annali di Storia dell'esegesi*
AST	Apokryfy Starego Testamentu
AYBC	Anchor Yale Bible Commentaries
AYBRL	Anchor Yale Bible Reference Library
BAGL	*Biblical and Ancient Greek Linguistics*
BCRFJ	*Bulletin du Centre de recherche français à Jérusalem*
BCAW	Blackwell Companions to the Ancient World
BCNH	Bibliothèque Copte de Nag Hammadi
BCSM	Bloomsbury Classical Studies Monographs
BdA	Biblioteca di Adamantius
BET	Biblical Exegesis and Theology
BHL	Brill's Handbooks in Linguistics
BIS	Biblical Interpretation Series
BRLJ	Brill Reference Library of Judaism
CBR	*Currents in Biblical Research*

CCS	Cambridge Classical Studies
CHSC	Center for Hellenic Studies Colloquia
CM	Classica Monacensia
CO	Classica et Orientalia
CQS	Companion to the Qumran Scrolls
CSCT	Columbia Studies in the Classical Tradition
CTL	Cambridge Textbooks in Linguistics
DS	Demotische Studien
EC	*Exemplaria Classica*
ÉC	Études et Commentaires
ECCA	Early Christianity in the Context of Antiquity
ECHC	Early Christianity in Its Hellenistic Context
ELCH	Studies in English Literary and Cultural History
Exag.	*Exagoge*
FFRS	Foundations and Facets Reference Series
FGrH	*Die Fragmente der griechischen Historiker*. Edited by F. Jacoby et al. Leiden: Brill, 1923–.
FJB	*Frankfurter judaistische Beiträge*
GAP	Guide to Apocrypha and Pseudepigrapha
GMTR	Guides to the Mesopotamian Textual Record
HE	Historia Einzelschriften
I.Cret.	M. Guarducci (ed.), *Inscriptiones Creticae*, 4 vols., Rome 1935–1950
JA	Joseph and Aseneth
JAJ	*Journal of Ancient Judaism*
JAJSup	Journal of Ancient Judaism: Supplements
JCPS	Jewish and Christian Perspectives Series
JCTCRS	Jewish and Christian Texts in Context and Related Studies
JSJSup	Supplements to the Journal for the Study of Judaism
JSRC	Jerusalem Studies in Religion and Culture
JWCI	*Journal of the Warburg and Courtauld Institutes*
KP	*Der kleine Pauly*
LA	Letter of Aristeas
LCR	Longman Critical Readers
MPL	*Museum Philologum Londiniense*
MneSup	Mnemosyne, Supplement
NHMS	Nag Hammadi and Manichaean Studies
NLH	*New Literary History*
NTT	New Testament Theology
OLAC	Orality and Literacy in Ancient Greece
PAPM	Les oeuvres de Philon d'Alexandrie

PAST	Pauline Studies
PBM	Paternoster Biblical Monographs
PTA	Papyrologische Texte und Abhandlungen
RbPH	*Revue belge de Philologie et d'Histoire*
RFIC	*Rivista di filologia e di istruzione classica*
SANt	Studia Aarhusiana Neotestamentica
SAT	Sources of the Armenian Tradition
SBLPS	Society of Biblical Literature Pseudepigrapha Series
SCL	Sather Classical Lectures
SEPT	Septuagint Commentary Series
SGA	Studien zur Geschichtsforschung des Altertums
SGU	Studia Graeca Upsaliensia
SH	Studia Hellenistica
SJSHRZ	Studien zu den Jüdischen Schriften aus hellenistisch-römischer Zeit
SPHS	Scholars Press Homage Series
SSEA	Society for the Study of Egyptian Antiquities
STAC	Studies and Texts in Antiquity and Christianity
STCPF	Studi e testi per il "Corpus dei papiri filosofici greci e latini"
TCH	Transformation of the Classical Heritage
TCSup	Trends in Classics—Supplementary Volumes
TrC	Tria Corda
TUK	Texte und Kommentare
UCPH	University of California Publications in History
WGW	Wissenskultur und gesellschaftlicher Wandel

Classical Works

Arius Didymus	
Epit.	*Epitome of Stoic Ethics*
Basil	
Reg. Fus.	Regulæ fusius tractatae
C. Ord. Ptol.	Corpus des Ordonnances des Ptolémées
Demosthenes	
Or.	*Orations*
Diodorus Siculus	
Bibl.	*Bibliotheca historica*
Diogenes Laertius	
Vit.	*Vitae philosophorum*
Dracontius	
Rom.	*Romulea*

Epictetus
Disc. — *Discourses*
Eunapius
Vit. soph. — *Lives of the Philosophers and Sophists*
Galen
Aff. pecc. dig. — *De Propriorum Animi Cuiuslibet Affectuum Dignotione et Curatione*
Ars med. — *Ars medicinalis*
Dig. puls. — *De Pulsuum Differentiis*
Lib. prop. — *De Libris Propriis*
Herodian
Hist. — *History of the Roman Empire*
Hyperides
Or. — *Orations*
Iamblichus
Vit. Pyth. — *De Vita Pythagorica*
Julius Victor
Rhet. — *Ars Rhetorica*
Justin
Hist. — *Liber Historiarum Philippicarum*
Lucian
Podag. — *Podagra*
Lysias
Or. — *Orations*
Manetho
Aegyp. — *Aegyptiaca*
Marcus Aurelius
Med. — *Meditations*
Marinus
Proc. — *Life of Proclus*
Martial
Ep. — *Epigrams*
Maximus of Tyre
Or. — *Orations*
Nicolaus the Sophist
Prog. — *Progymnasmata*
Pachomius
Reg. — *Regula*
Philitas of Cos
Eleg. et Gramm. Frag. — *Elegiac and Grammatical Fragments*

Philodemus	
De poem.	*De poematis*
Photius	
Epit. Hist.	Epitome of the Ecclesiastical History of Philostorgius
Proclus	
in Parm.	Commentary on Parmenides
in Resp.	Commentary on Plato's "Republic"
in Tim.	Commentary on Plato's "Timaeus"
Pseudo-Callisthenes	
Alex. rom.	*Alexander Romance*
Pseudo-Cicero	
Rhet. Her.	*Rhetorica ad Herennium*
Pseudo-Justin	
Cohort. ad Graec.	*Cohortatio ad Graecos*
Quintus Smyrnaeus	
Posth.	*Posthomerica*
Sextus	
Sent.	*Sentences*
Simplicius	
in Cat.	*In Aristotelis Categorias*
Theon	
Prog.	*Progymnasmata*
Thucydides	
Hist.	*History of the Peloponnesian War*
Tibullus	
Eleg.	*Elegies*
Vellius Paterculus	
Hist.	*Historiae Romanae*

1

Introduction

Studies on individual Jewish authors in the Second Temple Period abound, but few studies have sought to take a holistic perspective by tracing the development of Jewish-Greek literature in the Hellenistic and Roman eras.[1] This work fills this gap by investigating how Jewish authors writing in Greek engaged with and participated in Greek genres.[2] Detailed investigations into the genre of individual works will be undertaken throughout this study, but the main contribution will be the synthesis of these data to provide a macro-perspective on the ways that Jewish authors participated in the composition of Greek works and the evolution of Greek genres. Almost all of our evidence falls between 330 BCE and circa 117 CE. The initial date corresponds (roughly) to the conquests of Alexander and the establishment of Greek as the dominant language for government, trade, and correspondence, and the end date corresponds to the conclusion of the Trajanic revolt.[3] The

1 Throughout this book I consciously adopt the adjective "Jewish," not because I do not recognize the arguments by Mason and others on the ways that Judeans were perceived in antiquity, but in order to avoid confusion. I employ "Judean" specifically to reference people or literary works that are geographically located and "Jewish" or "Jew" to refer broadly to all elements and authors of that ethnicity. On this topic, see S. Mason, "Jews, Judaeans, Judaizing, Judaism: Problems of Categorization in Ancient History," *JSJ* 38 (2007): 457–512; C. Baker, "A 'Jew' by Any Other Name?" *JAJ* 2 (2011): 152–80; S. Schwartz, "How Many Judaisms Were There? A Critique of Neusner and Smith on Definition and Mason and Boyarin on Categorization," *JAJ* 2 (2011): 208–38.

2 For methodological discussions of genres in Jewish works of the Second Temple Period, see J. L. Kugel, *The Idea of Biblical Poetry: Parallelism and Its History* (New Haven: Yale University Press, 1981); H. Najman, "The Idea of Biblical Genre: From Discourse to Constellation," in J. Penner, K. M. Penner, and C. Wassen, eds., *Prayer and Poetry in the Dead Sea Scrolls and Related Literature: Essays in Honor of Eileen Schuller on the Occasion of Her 65th Birthday* (STDJ 98; Leiden: Brill, 2012), 307–22.

3 M. P. Ben Zeev, *Diaspora Judaism in Turmoil, 116/117 CE: Ancient Sources and Modern Insights* (Leuven: Peeters, 2005); W. Horbury, *Jewish War under Trajan and Hadrian*

limited evidence from the rest of the second century CE could be interpreted as marking the end of Greek literary composition by Jewish authors. Conversely, it could be an accident of history. I am not beholden to the former view, and part of the contribution of this study is to challenge the firm temporal boundedness assumed by scholars.[4]

This study of genre is an historical investigation of the ways that Jewish authors engaged literary culture and constructed texts.[5] Although I will express positions on how a text participates within specific ancient genres, the goal of this project is not to constrain various interpretations or claim that there is only a single way to read a text (i.e., through one particular genre). Indeed, changing the lens by which a text is read can be enlightening, allowing for new interpretations. Such scholarly investigations have their place and should be encouraged. Nevertheless, for this study, the author and the task of writing in history will be the chief focus.[6]

(Cambridge: Cambridge University Press, 2014), especially 166–79; M. Mor, *The Second Jewish Revolt: The Bar Kokhba War, 132–136 CE* (BRLJ 50; Leiden: Brill, 2016); D. C. Allison Jr., *Testament of Abraham* (Berlin: De Gruyter, 2003), 34–40; K. Berger, "Hellenistische Gattungen im Neuen Testament," *ANRW* 2.25.2 (1984): 1031–432. For evidence of prohibition of Greek literary education by Jews at the time of Trajan, see m. Soṭah 9:14 (cf. the statement by R. Joshua in t. ʿAbod. Zar 1:20).

4 For the continued use of Greek by Jews, although with substantially fewer surviving literary works, see J. G. Krivoruchko, "Judeo-Greek," in L. Kahn and A. D. Rubin, eds., *Handbook of Jewish Languages* (BHL; Leiden: Brill, 2016), 194–225; J. C. Paget, *Jews, Christians, and Jewish Christians in Antiquity* (WUNT 1.251; Tübingen: Mohr Siebeck, 2010), 383–425. See also chapter 4 (Ps.-Clementine, *Hom.* 4.7–6.25).

Although I adopt roughly the same time period, I disagree with Wacholder that the term "Graeco-Jewish literature" should not be applied to any text prior to the appearance of the Septuagint. Although monumental, the Septuagint is likely not the first Jewish work composed in Greek, nor is it a fixed entity. Accordingly, limiting Jewish-Greek works to after its emergence is methodologically problematic. Cf. B. Z. Wacholder, *Eupolemus: A Study of Judaeo-Greek Literature* (HUMC 3; Cincinnati: Hebrew Union College Press, 1974), 262.

Determining Greek literacy rate of Jews or speculating on the quantity of Greek-speaking Jews in Palestine or in the diaspora is also outwith the purview of this study. For such investigations, see M. Bar-Ilan, "Illiteracy in the Land of Israel in the First Centuries C.E.," in S. Fishbane and S. Schoenfeld, with A. Goldschläger, eds., *Essays in the Social Scientific Study of Judaism and Jewish Society*, vol. 2 (Hoboken, N.J.: Ktav, 1992), 46–61; C. Hezser, *Jewish Literacy in Roman Palestine* (TSAJ 81; Tübingen: Mohr Siebeck, 2001), 496–504; J. Baines and C. Eyre, "Four Notes on Literacy," in J. Baines, ed., *Visual and Written Culture in Ancient Egypt* (Oxford: Oxford University Press, 2007), 64–73.

5 Although it might go without saying, all genre references within this work (unless otherwise noted) are to ancient genres and not to their modern counterparts (e.g., modern biography, history, novel, etc.). Mental defamiliarization is an important practice for scholars of antiquity, especially in the study of genre, as the same terms are used. To facilitate differentiation, I will use Greek and Latin terms when possible.

6 Reader perspectives and reception, although helpful and important to study, are not the focus of this work, but I will engage such discussions where appropriate. For theoretical discussions on terms such as "author" (real, implied), "narrator/narratee," "reader" (real, implied),

This chapter will provide the methodological framework for this monograph. I will begin with an outline of the focus of the study, what will and will not be discussed, as well as define key terms employed. A theoretical examination of genre follows this, providing an introduction to the theories that will underpin the remaining chapters. Finally, following the identification of specific limitations of the study of genre in antiquity, I will provide an overview of the work and its main contributions.

Definitions and Focus of the Study

Because of the large number of Jewish authors writing in Greek, constraints need to be established to ensure focus. First, I am limiting my study to works composed in Greek and so will not be evaluating translated texts, most notably the Septuagint. This is partly due to space limitations, but also due to the fact that Greek genres are the focus of this study and translated texts have their genre origins in a different language/literary culture.[7] More importantly, my lack of engagement with Septuagint books is not an indication of their inherent want of Greek culture or that their authors/translators did not look to Greek literature for inspiration or models. Although these "literal" translations have traditionally been thought to encode an inferior form of Greek, recent studies have shown that many Jewish translators were well versed in Greek poetry and literary culture and were able to adapt elements of the Hebrew text to please a Greek readership (both Jewish and non-Jewish).[8] Such investigations provide insight into the educational and reading practices of ancient Jewish translators, and these findings need to be included in wider studies of Greek-speaking and Greek-writing Judaism.

Second, I limit my study to literary works, and so do not engage with non-literary compositions, such as legal documents, magical texts, inscriptions, and amulets.[9] These artifacts provide insight into Jewish culture and history,

---

etc., see H. Link, *Rezeptionsforschung: Eine Einführung in Methoden und Probleme* (2nd ed.; Stuttgart: Kohlhammer, 1980), 16–38; W. Nelles, "Historical and Implied Authors and Readers," *Comparative Literature* 45 (1993): 22–46; I. J. F. de Jong, "Narratological Theory on Narrators, Narratees, and Narrative," in I. J. F. de Jong, R. Nünlist, and A. M. Bowie, eds., *Studies in Ancient Greek Narrative*, vol. 1, *Narrators, Narratees, and Narratives in Ancient Greek Literature* (MneSup 257; Leiden: Brill, 2004), 1–10.

7 The adoption of dominant genres into native language is an interesting topic and one that is worthy of investigation for Jewish and other ethnic groups in antiquity. Although these texts fall outside the scope of this work, we find examples in Demotic literature (e.g., *Egyptians and Amazons*, which echoes the story of Achilles and Penthesilea).

8 See, most recently, J. A. L. Lee, *The Greek of the Pentateuch: Grinfield Lectures on the Septuagint, 2011–2012* (Oxford: Oxford University Press, 2018).

9 These are important fields and have substantial bibliographies. See P. W. van der Horst, "Greek in Jewish Palestine in the Light of Jewish Epigraphy," in *Japheth in the Tents of Shem: Studies on Jewish Hellenism in Antiquity* (BET 32; Leuven: Peeters, 2002), 9–26; G. Bohak,

but they are beyond the scope of this work. Similarly, I also exclude documentary or personal letters from this study. However, many of the letters found in the New Testament—such as Hebrews and those composed by and/or attributed to Paul, Peter, and John—go beyond the traditional confines of the letter form and so could be considered a literary genre. This is especially the case for the larger letters of Paul, as their deep theological content could be argued to parallel philosophical treatises. These "literary letters," as well as the co-called Letter of Aristeas, will be discussed in chapter 5.

Third, I limit the texts studied to Jewish works that participate in Greek genres.[10] This claim has two potentially problematic phrases: "Jewish works" and "Greek genre." I have employed the term "Jewish" above, and many readers would have some intuitive idea of what I meant by this term. However, the understanding of a Judaism or Jewishness that is unified, homogenous, and fully distinct from other ethnicities has been rightly challenged in scholarship.[11] Three cultural relationships are important for this study: Greek, Samaritan, and Christian.[12]

Scholars have discussed Jewish-Greek relationships with varying levels of sophistication. Poor examples need not distract us at this moment, except to reassert that during the Hellenistic and Roman eras "Judaism" and "Hellenism" were not isolated entities, completely disassociated from each other,

---

Ancient Jewish Magic: A History (Cambridge: Cambridge University Press, 2008); D. Noy, H. Bloedhorn, and W. Ameling, eds., *Inscriptiones Judaicae Orientis* (3 vols.; TSAJ 99, 101, 102; Tübingen: Mohr Siebeck, 2004); W. Horbury and D. Noy, eds., *Jewish Inscriptions of Graeco-Roman Egypt* (Cambridge: Cambridge University Press, 1992); M. H. Williams, *Jews in a Graeco-Roman Environment* (WUNT 1.312; Tübingen: Mohr Siebeck, 2013); H. M. Cotton et al., eds., *Corpus Inscriptionum Iudaeae/Palaestinae* (Berlin: De Gruyter, 2010–).

10 Accordingly, I will not be discussing Jewish works written in Greek that adopt non-Greek genres, such as Revelation and apocalyptic-like works. For a discussion of the genre of Revelation that includes a range of examples, see G. L. Linton, "Reading the Apocalypse as Apocalypse: The Limits of Genre," in D. L. Barr, ed., *The Reality of Apocalypse: Rhetoric and Politics in the Book of Revelation* (SymS 39; Atlanta: SBL, 2006), 9–41; J. J. Collins, *The Apocalyptic Imagination: An Introduction to Jewish Apocalyptic Literature* (3rd ed.; Grand Rapids: Eerdmans, 2016), 3–16. For a reading of Revelation through the lens of pastiche, see M. Fletcher, *Reading Revelation as Pastiche: Imitating the Past* (LNTS 571; London: Bloomsbury, 2017), 182–213.

11 The uniformity of any culture, modern or ancient, has been rightfully challenged. Cf. C. Ulf, "Rethinking Cultural Contacts," *Ancient West and East* 8 (2009): 81–132; A. Wallace-Hadrill, *Rome's Cultural Revolution* (Cambridge: Cambridge University Press, 2008), 17; K. Ehrensperger, *Paul at the Crossroads of Cultures: Theologizing in the Space Between* (LNTS 456; London: Bloomsbury, 2013), 17–62.

12 These terms are not self-contained, discrete, or immutable entities, but possess considerable temporal, spatial, and ideological fluidity. These groups further overlap with other groups (e.g., Roman, Syrian, African, Egyptian, etc.), creating a complex web of connections that require sensitivity by the scholar.

and that one can no longer posit a "pure" Judaism, one "uncontaminated" or "uninfected" by the plague of Hellenism: Jews were integrated members of the ancient world.[13] Disparities of power, prestige, and influence also need to be recognized. Greek culture in the Hellenistic time period was the dominant culture, one that was associated with political and military conquest. Greek literary culture was presented and viewed as being sophisticated, highly refined, and associated with the elite. This culturally dominant position was not only held by the Greeks through the Hellenistic era, but was also adopted and reinforced by their Roman conquerors. Jewish culture, on the other hand, was viewed as culturally subordinate in comparison.[14] This does not mean that its adherents thought of it in that way—in fact, a number did not, which is part of the thesis of this work—or to claim that Jewish culture was somehow lacking, needing the more "complete" Greek culture to fill a cultural void.[15] Rather, the relationship between Greeks and Jews in the sphere of literature was always one of imbalance and inequality, with culturally perceived superiority favoring the Greeks.[16]

Second, the exact relationship between Jews and Samaritans is much more difficult to determine. The origins of the Samaritan people, along with when and how the divide between them and the Jews took place, are prominent topics in scholarship. Indeed, the previous view of a clear divide between the

13 Cf. M. Hengel, *Judaism and Hellenism: Studies in Their Encounter in Palestine during the Early Hellenistic Period* (trans. J. Bowden; 2 vols.; Philadelphia: Fortress, 1974); F. Millar, "The Background to the Maccabean Revolution: Reflections on Martin Hengel's 'Judaism and Hellenism,'" *JJS* 29 (1978): 1–21; J. A. Goldstein, "Jewish Acceptance and Rejection of Hellenism," in E. P. Sanders, A. I. Baumgarten, and A. Mendelson, eds., *Jewish and Christian Self-Definition* (2 vols.; Philadelphia: Fortress, 1981), 2.64–87; J. M. G. Barclay, *Jews in the Mediterranean Diaspora: From Alexander to Trajan (323 BCE–117 CE)* (Edinburgh: T&T Clark, 1996), 92–98; E. S. Gruen, *Heritage and Hellenism: The Reinvention of Jewish Tradition* (Berkeley: University of California Press, 1998), xiv–xvii; M. Niehoff, *Philo on Jewish Identity and Culture* (TSAJ 86; Tübingen: Mohr Siebeck, 2001). For an insightful critique of the concept of "Hellenism" and other related categories, see Wallace-Hadrill, *Rome's Cultural Revolution*, 9–14; Ehrensperger, *Paul at the Crossroads*, 20–29.

14 "The Jews knew perfectly well that the Greek culture of the day was the culture of the ruling power." T. Rajak, "Judaism and Hellenism Revisited," in *The Jewish Dialogue with Greece and Rome: Studies in Cultural and Social Interaction* (Leiden: Brill, 2002), 3.

15 For a critique of this perspective, see C. Dougherty and L. Kurke, "Introduction," in C. Dougherty and L. Kurke, eds., *The Cultures within Ancient Greek Culture: Contact, Conflict, Collaboration* (Cambridge: Cambridge University Press, 2003), 1–19. Even in antiquity there was an awareness that learning Greek or becoming a Roman citizen did not erase one's original identity (e.g., Ennius' "three hearts": Roman, Greek, and Oscan; cf. Aulus Gellius, *Noct. att.* 17.17.1).

16 On the complex relationship between power and culture, though in a different epoch, see T. Whitmarsh, *Greek Literature and the Roman Empire: The Politics of Imitation* (Oxford: Oxford University Press, 2001), 17–20. See also the discussion of hierarchy and royal genres below.

two groups is being (rightfully) challenged.[17] By the Hellenistic era, when authors from both groups lived and wrote, tensions between Jews and Samaritans were escalating, culminating in the destruction of the Temple at Mount Gerizim by John Hyrcanus in 111/110 BCE.[18] This relationship is important for a few authors (e.g., Theodotus, Pseudo-Eupolemus) as their ethnic identity (i.e., whether they are Jewish *or* Samarian) is questioned. The impact that Samaritan authorship would have on the overall contribution of this study is minimal, except that it would reinforce the view that engagement with Greek literary culture was not limited to Jewish writers, but was also practiced by related neighbors.

Third, beginning in the first century CE, Christians started to compose works using characters from Jewish Scripture. Previously, the adoption of biblical subject matter was thought to be a sure indication of Jewish (or Samaritan) authorship. James Davila, however, rightly argues that both Jewish and Christian authors drew from Jewish Scripture in the composition of texts and that biblical content does not necessitate Jewish authorship.[19] Christian, however, is not to imply non-Jewish, as Jewish-Christian authors also produced literary works at this time.[20] In light of the difficulty in determining the Jewish origins of certain texts, I have erred on the side of inclusion for select debated authors (e.g., Luke, Pseudo-Phocylides, Sibylline Oracles). Despite their origin, the preservation of Jewish works written in Greek is due primarily to Christian, non-Jewish scribes. As a result, their tastes, perspectives, motivations, and requirements determined which texts were preserved and which were not. Most of our fragmentary texts come to us through Eusebius and Clement and their use of Alexander Polyhistor, and so it is worth remembering that the sample of surviving texts is a direct result of Greek and Christian selection.

The phrase "Greek genre" is potentially problematic. It presupposes not only that genre is something recognizable (see below), but also that genre expressions can be associated with a specific culture. Although I would not argue that certain cultures have a claim to particular genres or that genres could

17 For important critiques of this rigid division, see E. J. Bickerman, *The Jews in the Greek Age* (Cambridge, Mass.: Harvard University Press, 1988), 190; R. Doran, "The Jewish Hellenistic Historians before Josephus," *ANRW* 2.20.1 (1987): 270–74; R. Doran, "Ps.-Eupolemus," in *OTP* 2.873–76; Gruen, *Heritage and Hellenism*, 146–48; D. A. Creech, "The Lawless Pride: Jewish Identity in the Fragments of Eupolemus," *ASE* 29 (2012): 39 n. 70. See most recently, R. Pummer, *The Samaritans: A Profile* (Grand Rapids: Eerdmans, 2016), especially 15–25.

18 Josephus, *Ant.* 13.254–258; cf. *Ant.* 20.118–136; *BJ* 3.307–315.

19 The now-standard work on this topic is J. R. Davila, *The Provenance of the Pseudepigrapha: Jewish, Christian, or Other?* (JSJSup 105; Leiden: Brill, 2005).

20 See J. C. Paget, "Jewish Christianity," in W. Horbury et al., eds., *Cambridge History of Judaism*, vol. 3, *The Early Roman Period* (Cambridge: Cambridge University Press, 1999), 731–75; Paget, *Jews*.

ever be owned, I would suggest that at specific points in history certain genres were associated primarily, if not exclusively, with individual cultures and that certain formal features signaled to the reader specific influences.[21] Language choice and metrical selection are initial indicators of a work's literary alignment, but they are not fully determinative of an author's literary engagement. For this study, which looks at Jewish literature written in Greek, we can clearly see that Jewish engagement with Hellenistic culture resulted in the composition of literary works participating in genres that had hitherto not been adopted by Jewish authors (e.g., epics and tragedies). Less clear is the writing of commentary or history, genres that were established in both literary cultures. Differences in content, practices, and forms could be conceptualized in terms of distinct genre expressions, but we will see that, when authors adopt these genres, literary features are regularly blended.[22]

The premise of this study is that Jewish authors, once exposed to Greek literary culture, especially through Greek education, began to compose works in genres that they had hitherto not participated in.[23] I argue that in the minds of these Jewish authors certain genres would be considered Greek. This association would be clearest at the beginning of the Hellenistic era, but would become muddied when other cultures (e.g., Jewish, Egyptian, Babylonian) engage with

21 Unfortunately, there are few explicit discussions of genre in antiquity with a view towards comparing cultures. Quintilian (*Inst.* 10.1.37–131) compares Greek and Latin literature as represented by authors who write in specific genres. He begins with Greek hexameter (i.e., epic, 46–57), elegy (58–59), iambic (59–60), and lyric (61–64). Following this, Quintilian examines old comedy (65–66), tragedy (66–68), new comedy (69–72), history (73–75), oratory (76–80), and philosophy (81–84). In his discussion of Latin literature, Quintilian includes most of the Greek genre categories, but with some differences: hexameter (i.e., epic, 85–92), elegy (93–94), satire (95), iambic (96), tragedy (97–98), comedy (99–100), history (101–104), oratory (105–122), and philosophy (123–131). The omission of certain categories in his discussion of Greek and Latin literature suggests that Quintilian did not see a comparable expression of that genre (e.g., satire for Greek and iambic for Latin; prose fiction for both languages). Cf. Cicero, *Opt. gen.* 2 and 6; *De or.* 2.51–64; Horace, *Sat.* 1.10.65–67. Interestingly, when one genre was composed in multiple languages (e.g., both Greek and Latin), Quintilian did not divide the genre culturally, but presented history, oratory, and philosophy as essentially/functionally the same genre despite the fact that they were written in different languages.

22 For discussions of "genre agnation," which address both similarities and differences between genres, see J. R. Martin, "Analysing Genre: Functional Parameters," in F. Christie and J. R. Martin, eds., *Genre and Institutions: Social Processes in the Workplace and School* (London: Cassell, 1997), 13; J. R. Martin and D. Rose, *Genre Relations: Mapping Culture* (London: Equinox, 2008), 130.

23 This raises the question: what exposure to Greek literary culture did Jews have prior to the conquests of Alexander? Unfortunately, there is little firm evidence with which to answer this question. It is not impossible that some Jews, especially those living in Greece or Asia Minor or near areas of Greek influence, would have been educated in Greek. Although historically improbable, Philo (*Mos.* 1.23) claims that Moses was educated in Greek, suggesting that in the minds of some Jews the beginning of Greek literary influence did not begin with Alexander.

Greek genres and add different, sometimes originally foreign elements.[24] The production of a text automatically places that work in a complex network of relationships with other compositions and in turn becomes a node of comparison for subsequent texts, possibly even becoming a prototypical example.[25] Because genres are not fixed, they continued to develop over the Hellenistic and Roman eras through interaction with other cultures, and so it is unclear when, if ever, cultural association of a genre would have stopped. This study provides evidence of Jewish engagement with and participation in genres associated with Greek literary culture (or maybe more correctly, a Greek version of a genre). Such an understanding is also not static and would change over time based on the individual's perspective and understanding of Greek genres.

The focus of this study on Greek genres is not to imply that foreign-language works will be excluded when discussing authorial influences. Jewish authors writing in Greek were not isolated from other literary outputs, especially those composed by other Jews. For example, Hebrew or Aramaic works transmitted in the Apocrypha and Pseudepigrapha, as well as those found at Qumran, are potentially part of the literary worldview of each author and so could contribute or influence his/her composition. The extent of this influence differs among authors, but should not be ignored or excluded from discussions of genre. As we will see, certain nonprototypical features in Greek genres are more prominent in Jewish texts, and so non-Greek texts should be considered as a possible source for innovation.

Genre Perspectives Adopted in This Study

The concept of genre is complex, requiring clear theoretical frameworks in order for it to become a serviceable analytical tool.[26] In this section I outline

24 A parallel example can be drawn from recent studies of colonial languages (i.e., "lingua francas"), in which scholars have argued that the nature of the dominant language can and does change in response to its use by other communities. J. E. Joseph, *Language and Identity: National, Ethnic, Religious* (New York: Palgrave Macmillan, 2004), 167; F. Sharifian, *Cultural Conceptualisations of Language: Theoretical Framework and Applications* (Philadelphia: John Benjamins, 2011), 34. Similarly, models of acculturation and assimilation also need to incorporate a diachronic measure, as a society or culture's relationship with another is also not static, especially when they mutually influence each other. *Pace* Barclay, *Jews*. For the use of different languages of Jews in Egypt (i.e., Aramaic in Upper Egypt), see N. Hacham, "The Third Century BCE: New Light on Egyptian Jewish History from the Papyri," in M. M. Piotrkowski, G. Herman, and S. Dönitz, eds., *Sources and Interpretation in Ancient Judaism: Studies for Tal Ilan at Sixty* (AJEC 104; Leiden: Brill, 2018), 135–36.

25 Cf. M. Corti, *An Introduction to Literary Semiotics* (trans. M. Bogat and A. Mandelbaum; Bloomington: Indiana University Press, 1978), 115; T. Todorov, *The Fantastic: A Structural Approach to a Literary Genre* (trans. R. Howard; Ithaca: Cornell University Press, 1975), 8.

26 The theory outlined below, especially the perspectives of genre by the ancients, is more fully developed in S. A. Adams, *The Genre of Acts and Collected Biography* (SNTSMS 156; Cambridge: Cambridge University Press, 2013), 26–67. See also J. Farrell, "Classical Genre in Theory

the ways that genre is understood and expressed in this study. This is not an exhaustive discussion, as specific genre theories will be incorporated in the chapters where appropriate, and in these discussions I look to make a contribution to genre theory. In this chapter I provide the key theoretical principles to which this study will adhere.

Genres are frameworks that establish expectations for the reader and signal appropriate ways of reading and/or distinguishing texts (sometimes referred to as "codes" or "contracts" between reader and author).[27] A literary work does not belong to a genre, but participates in it, being historically, geographically, and rhetorically situated.[28] This situatedness provides constraints, not only for the author, but also for subsequent reconstructions of the authorial world, affecting the scholar's understanding of the author's purpose and intention as well as the plausibility of their reconstruction.[29] Genre categories are a means of classification, but one should not make the mistake of thinking that they are well-defined, stable, or exhaustive.[30] Scholars widely agree that both the idea of genre and the employment of genre labels are social constructs employed in communities as communicative shorthand.[31]

One of the challenges when discussing genre, both now and in antiquity, is that a genre is never static or permanently fixed, but is constantly changing.[32]

---

and Practice," *New Literary History* 34 (2003): 383–408. For definitions of important terms (e.g., form, genre, mode, subgenre, etc.), see H. Dubrow, *Genre* (Critical Idiom 42; London: Methuen, 1982), 4–5.

27 E.g., Dubrow, *Genre*, 31: "Genre is a conceptual orienting device that suggests to the hearer the sort of receptorial conditions in which a fictive discourse might have been delivered." M. Depew and D. Obbink, "Introduction," in M. Depew and D. Obbink, eds., *Matrices of Genre: Authors, Canons, and Societies* (CHSC 4; Cambridge, Mass.: Harvard University Press, 2000), 6. T. Todorov, *Genres in Discourse* (trans. C. Porter; Cambridge: Cambridge University Press, 1990), 18–19.

28 R. Cohen, "History and Genre," *New Literary History* 17 (1986): 201–18; R. Cohen, "Genre Theory, Literary History, and Historical Change," in D. Perkins, ed., *Theoretical Issues in Literary History* (Cambridge, Mass.: Harvard University Press, 1991), 85–113; K. M. Jamieson, "Antecedent Genre as Rhetorical Constraint," *Quarterly Journal of Speech* 61 (1975): 405–15. *Pace* Derrida, who uses the language of "law" and "transgression." J. Derrida, "The Law of Genre," *Critical Inquiry* 7 (1980): 55–81, reprinted with revisions in D. Attridge, ed., *Acts of Literature* (London: Routledge, 1992), 221–52.

29 Cf. A. J. Devitt, *Writing Genres* (Carbondale: Southern Illinois University Press, 2004), 12–32; A. S. Bwarshi and M. J. Reiff, *Genre: An Introduction to History, Theory, Research, and Pedagogy* (West Lafayette, Ind.: Parlor Press, 2010), 69; J. Frow, *Genre* (2nd ed.; London: Routledge, 2015), 6–31.

30 A. Fowler, *Kinds of Literature: An Introduction to the Theory of Genres and Modes* (Oxford: Oxford University Press, 1982), 70–72.

31 Ancients also had this perspective. For example, Philodemus claims that genres exist not by nature (φύσει), but by convention (νόμωι, *De poem.* 1.117.13–16).

32 See J. Marincola, *Authority and Tradition in Ancient Historiography* (Cambridge: Cambridge University Press, 1997), 12–19; J. Marincola, "Genre, Convention, and Innovation in Greco-Roman Historiography," in C. S. Kraus, ed., *The Limits of Historiography: Genre and Narrative in*

Authorial experimentation and multiple participation across genres disrupt the idea of clear reader expectations or authorial norms, making it difficult to speak of *the* purpose of a genre and how a work must look in order to be classified properly in one specific category.[33] This inherent flexibility should not be considered a detriment, a flaw preventing scholars from creating perfectly neat and discrete categories. Rather, compositional plasticity is one of the remarkable features of literature, allowing for fresh and novel works, new literary expressions, and the inclusion of previously foreign material and formal features. Indeed, authors, both modern and ancient, took delight in transgressing boundaries, bending genres, and experimenting with different compositional arrangements.[34] The fact that there are boundaries to be crossed and reader expectations to exploit and/or fulfill implies that an understanding of genre existed in antiquity and that authors were aware of the blurry edges of specific literary forms. The expression of genre embodied in a work is shaped by the situation of its composition and at the same time shapes both the actions that are performed in response to it and subsequent texts that participate in the same genre and respond to this expression.[35]

Both ancient and modern literary theorists agree that evaluating the formal features of a text is necessary for understanding how a text participates in a genre.[36] For the ancients, certain features were thought to be core or determi-

Ancient Historical Texts (Leiden: Brill, 1999), 281–324; M. Fantuzzi and R. L. Hunter, *Tradition and Innovation in Hellenistic Poetry* (Cambridge: Cambridge University Press, 2004).

33 Reader expectations also influence how a text is received and what elements are deemed important or relevant. Cf. P. Hernadi, *Beyond Genre: New Directions in Literary Classifications* (Ithaca: Cornell University Press, 1972), 5–7; D. Sperber and D. Wilson, *Relevance: Communication and Cognition* (Oxford: Blackwell, 1986).

34 E.g., Lucretius' writing of philosophy in poetic verse in *De rerum natura* (1.945–946; 4.18–22, with the recognition that he did something that was not previously accomplished, 4.1–2); Satyrus' narrative *Life of Euripides* (P.Oxy. IX 1176); Rhianos of Bene (*FGrH* 265), who wrote a local history in verse (ἐν τοῖς ἔπεσιν, Pausanias, *Descr.* 4.6.1–3); Speusippus, who wrote memoirs (ὑπομνηματικοί) in dialogue (Diogenes Laertius, *Vit.* 4.5).

35 Contra B. Croce and his denial of genre's importance in antiquity. B. Croce, *Ultimi saggi* (Bari: Laterza & Figli, 1963), 22; B. Croce, *Cultura e vita morale* (2nd ed.; Bari: Laterza & Figli, 1936), 193. See more recently T. G. Rosenmeyer, "Ancient Literary Genres: A Mirage?" *Yearbook of Comparative and General Literature* 34 (1985): 74–84. On the playing of genres against each other in the creation of new genres, see M. Bakhtin, "Discourse in the Novel," in M. Holquist, ed., *The Dialogic Imagination: Four Essays by M. M. Bakhtin* (trans. C. Emerson and M. Holquist; Austin: University of Texas Press, 1981), 259–422.

36 E.g., R. Wellek and A. Warren, *Theory of Literature* (3rd ed.; Harmondsworth: Penguin, 1982), 231. For a helpful database of Jewish pseudepigraphal texts, see the Manchester literary typology project (TAPJLA): http://literarydatabase.humanities.manchester.ac.uk/Default.aspx. This project, under the leadership of Alexander Samely, adopts a different theoretical perspective on the construction of genre labels for ancient Jewish texts than the one applied in this study. Choosing to compile a near-exhaustive list of "structurally important features," Samely et al. distance their project from traditional genre labels in order to focus on independently verifiable literary elements. This project is valuable, but asks different ques-

native, especially in poetic texts (e.g., meter, length, subject, structure, style, etc.). A detailed catalogue of formal features can be an effective way to investigate the text. However, these data require interpretation. It is insufficient simply to count the number of formal features a work shares with different genres and claim that the genre with the most "hits" is the one that the author was evoking. One common finding, especially with prose composition, is that certain formal features are common among two or more genres. These points of contact reinforce the idea that genres are not discrete constructions, but share compositional features. Certain features are more determinative than others and so must be weighed appropriately.[37]

The relationship between the general (genre) and the specific (text) is complex, and there is no "perfect fit" or Platonic ideal to which a text must conform in order to participate in a genre; as no two works are exactly alike, works that share genre labels are not going to have exactly the same traits.[38] Distinctive elements in a work can often be a result of genre borrowing, in which an author incorporates one or more elements from a different genre, or the same genre expressed differently by another culture, into his composition. The "crossing of genres" (*Kreuzung der Gattungen*), famously identified by Wilhelm Kroll in Latin poetry, has repeatedly been shown to be a creative force in poetic and prose compositions throughout the Hellenistic period.[39] The principle of incorporating elements from a different, "guest" genre, while retaining the overall framework of the primary, "host" genre, was an important means of literary diversity and genre adaptation, resulting in works that share literary affiliations.[40]

Foundational to the theory of genre fluidity, and to this study, is a systemic understanding that views genres as forming a multinodal network.[41] This network outlines the meaningful choice selections that are available to the author

---

tions than those undertaken in this study. Cf. A. Samely et al., *Profiling Jewish Literature in Antiquity: An Inventory, from Second Temple Texts to the Talmuds* (Oxford: Oxford University Press, 2013).

37 For ancient discussions, see Farrell, "Classical Genre," 383–91; S. Hinds, "Epic Essentialism from Macer to Statius," in M. Depew and D. Obbink, eds., *Matrices of Genre: Authors, Canons, and Societies* (CHSC 4; Cambridge, Mass.: Harvard University Press, 2000), 221–44.

38 See the concept of games in Wittgenstein's theory of family resemblance and shared features. L. Wittgenstein, *Philosophical Investigations* (trans. G. E. M. Anscombe; Oxford: Basil Blackwell, 1967), §§65–71. This idea was fruitfully adapted by Fowler, *Kinds of Literature*, 40–42.

39 W. Kroll, *Studien zum Verständnis der römischen Literatur* (Stuttgart: Metzler, 1924), 202–24; Fantuzzi and Hunter, *Tradition and Innovation*, 17–41.

40 S. J. Harrison, *Generic Enrichment in Virgil and Horace* (Oxford: Oxford University Press, 2007), 6.

41 Cf. Y. Tynyanov, "On Literary Evolution," in L. Metejka and K. Pomorska, eds., *Readings in Russian Poetics: Formalist and Structuralist Views* (Cambridge, Mass.: MIT Press, 1971), 66–78; Dubrow, *Genre*, 90; D. Duff, "Introduction," in D. Duff, ed., *Modern Genre Theory* (LCR; London: Longman, 2000), 7–8; Fowler, *Kinds of Literature*, 250; P. Steiner, *Russian Formalism: A Metapoetics* (Ithaca: Cornell University Press, 1984), 99–137; R. Colie, *The Resources of Kind:*

and those that are dependent and restricted by the author's historical situation, geographic location, education, writing ability, personal experience, status, and so on.[42] By viewing genre as a system, and not solely in light of their component parts, one can organize genres into hierarchies and see them as existing in relationships with other genres. For example, Ireneusz Opacki discusses the concept of "royal genre," in which a genre acquires the greatest importance/prestige and becomes the dominant literary form.[43] This royal genre is composed of a characteristic set of literary features that distinguish it from other genres. Having acquired the dominant literary position (whether gradually or suddenly), the royal genre begins exerting downward pressure on subordinate or secondary genres, encouraging literary evolution.[44] This development occurs when specific generic features that characterize the royal genre are adopted by subordinate genres, sometimes subconsciously, but often as a conscious effort by an author to elevate the status of a particular literary work.[45] Mixing can lead to a blurring of genre distinctiveness, as characteristic features of the dominant genre are incorporated into other literary forms,[46] but it also can have the opposite effect of developing new, unique literary expressions. Each

---

Genre Theory in the Renaissance (ed. B. K. Lewalski; Berkeley: University of California Press, 1973), 2–31.

42 For parallel systemic approaches in linguistics, see M. A. K. Halliday, *An Introduction to Functional Grammar* (3rd ed.; rev. Christian M. I. M. Matthiessen; London: Edward Arnold, 2004); M. A. K. Halliday and R. Hasan, *Language, Context and Text: Aspects of Language in a Social-Semiotic Perspective* (Geelong, Australia: Deakin University, 1985), 44–47, 86.

43 I. Opacki, "Royal Genres," in D. Duff, ed., *Modern Genre Theory* (LCR; London: Longman, 2000), 118–26. Cf. R. Jakobson, "The Dominant," in L. Metejka and K. Pomorska, eds., *Readings in Russian Poetics: Formalist and Structuralist Views* (Cambridge, Mass.: MIT Press, 1971), 82–87.

44 Opacki, "Royal Genres," 120. Downward influence is not limited to the pinnacular genre, although that genre has the most influence. Rather, any "inferior" genre can potentially be influenced by those thought to be superior to it. The term "inferior" is used to describe less prestigious genres, but does not embody qualitative subjectivity in evaluating the genre's ability to communicate or function. It only implies that it is not as highly respected as other, "superior" genres.

45 A similar concept can be found in the study of language, in which the dominant or "prestige" language of the day exerts influence on the subordinate forms of language or dialect. In this case, society members who utilize a lower-status dialect attempt to imitate the more prestigious language style in order to raise their social position. Conversely, those with the prestigious language resist the adoption of subordinate features due to their inferior social implications. Not all "subordinate" language users imitate or adopt the dominant, choosing to enact and associate with a particular language expression for social or ideological reasons. For a discussion of this concept, see R. A. Hudson, *Sociolinguistics* (CTL; Cambridge: Cambridge University Press, 1980), 32–34; R. M. W. Dixon, *The Rise and Fall of Languages* (Cambridge: Cambridge University Press, 1997), 9–10.

46 Opacki, "Royal Genres," 123–24. Genres cannot discard all their characteristic features or else they risk leaving one genre classification without incorporating themselves in another genre that will provide adequate communicational cues to the reader.

genre is relative to the other genres within the synchronic system and changes as that system evolves.

This understanding of genre interaction and power relations is evident in ancient literature and comes to the fore during periods of transition, such as the Greek and Roman conquests. These newly dominant cultures have different literary emphases and preferences than those they conquered, as is evident in the Hellenistic era, in which Greek authors asserted literary superiority. The same cultural dominance was not fully enacted in the Latin conquests of the Mediterranean East. Latin authors admired the literary quality of Greek literature and were not hesitant to adopt a Greek literary form and imbue it with Latin characteristics, resulting in fields such as history and oratory becoming more practical and legally focused.[47] These shifts in the dominant culture to Greek-based and then to Latin-based genres and reading preferences precipitated a blending of literary forms. That there were similar, though not identical, genres in each culture, and that the importance of these genres was culturally derived, set the stage for shifts in genre hierarchy and a reconfiguration of genre features. The idea of royal genres and genre hierarchy provides us with a framework for investigating Jewish adoption, adaptation, subversion, emulation of, and participation in Greek genres. Jewish use of Greek genres represents the existence of cultural attraction, as these authors were not compelled to write in these genres. Associations of political power with specific cultural outputs may have influenced Jewish authors, but this is not the whole picture. Throughout this study we will attempt to be sensitive to cultural power dynamics and the perceived importance of various genres for each author based on the author's willingness to incorporate nonprototypical features from multiple sources.

Prototype genre theory, which is based on a cognitive psychology approach to genre, highlights the functionality and flexibility of genres and provides a theoretical underpinning for literary blending.[48] Within the mind of an author a genre is understood through core literary examples that provide

47 W. H. Atkins, *Literary Criticism in Antiquity: A Sketch of Its Development*, vol. 1, *Greek* (Cambridge: Cambridge University Press, 1934), 8; F. Cairns, *Generic Composition in Greek and Roman Poetry* (Edinburgh: Edinburgh University Press, 1972), 92–97. For Latin conquest of Greek literature through translation, see S. A. Adams, "Translating Texts: Contrasting Roman and Jewish Translation Practices," in S. A. Adams, ed., *Scholastic Culture in the Hellenistic and Roman Eras: Greek, Latin, and Jewish* (Transmissions 2; Berlin: De Gruyter, 2019), 147–67.

48 G. Lakoff, *Women, Fire, and Dangerous Things: What Categories Reveal about the Mind* (Chicago: University of Chicago Press, 1987); J. Swales, *Genre Analysis: English in Academic and Research Settings* (Cambridge: Cambridge University Press, 1991), 86; M. Sinding, "After Definitions: Genre, Categories, and Cognitive Science," *Genre* 35 (2002): 181–219; G. C. Bowker and S. L. Star, *Sorting Things Out: Classification and Its Consequences* (Cambridge, Mass.: MIT Press, 1999), 54. For application to Jewish texts, see B. G. Wright III, "Joining the Club: A Suggestion about Genre in Early Jewish Texts," *DSD* 17 (2010): 289–314; R. Williamson Jr., "Pesher: A Cognitive Model of the Genre," *DSD* 17 (2010): 336–60.

representative models of what constitutes that literary form, including default (i.e., core) and optional components (as identified by gestalt and schemata models).[49] Cognitive theory allows us to generate categories of genre that radiate outward from ideal, prototypical members. Other, less deterministic literary examples are placed in relationship to core models and create peripheral texts that partake of the genre, but are not central to the author's definition. One advantage of working from the prototype model is that complete fidelity to formal criteria is not required. Rather, one can debate how close one text is with its quintessential model(s), but no hard line can be drawn to differentiate participants from nonparticipants. The idea that the boundaries of literary forms overlap is equally important, allowing a text to be viewed in relationship to and a participant of multiple genres based on their realization of certain features.[50] The combination of elemental and relational aspects of prototype genre theory represents an advance over the traditional classification methods because it allows for variations among constituent texts and recognizes how authors are empowered to select their own repertoire of features.

The practice of borrowing also fits with the view that an author could have multiple literary models; a text could participate in multiple genres simultaneously, even if that participation is not equally balanced. This plurality of participation underpins much of this study, not only because it recognizes the ways that ancient authors innovated, but also because it provides a framework by which to speak of a work whose author might have drawn from multiple understandings of genre. Each author has their own prototypical models that relate to societal understandings embedded in the education system but are individualized and, therefore, unique. For example, a Jewish author who was educated in both Greek and Hebrew (or Aramaic, Demotic, etc.) would have knowledge of two different genre schemas. This individual would also have expertise in multiple genres, the names and concepts of which might be shared between cultures (e.g., history) or could be distinct.[51] This author would also have prototypical models from both languages that are organized in different hierarchies. As we will see, especially in chapters 4 ("Didactic Works") and 7 ("Jewish Historians"), Jewish authors blended features from both Hebrew and Greek models. I do not think it is accidental that some of the most nonprototypical examples of Jewish-Greek composition occur when both Greek and Jewish cultures have comparable genres. Prototype theory, when employed in

49 See the discussion in Sinding, "After Definitions," 194–98. This also fits with the practice by ancient authors, who define their work in comparison and relationship to others. E.g., Polybius, *Hist.* 1.4.2–3; 5.33.2–8; Jerome, *Vir. ill. praef.*

50 J. Frow, "'Reproducibles, Rubrics, and Everything You Need': Genre Theory Today," *PMLA* 122 (2007): 1626–34. For use of topology language to map genre relationships, see Martin and Rose, *Genre Relations*, 131–39.

51 Cf. Dubrow, *Genre*, 6–7. Even if genres from different cultures share the same name, it is highly unlikely that they will be the same, although there could be a number of similarities.

a multicultural, multilingual, and multieducational setting, has the potential to provide needed theoretical support to explore complex data.

Scholars have identified patterns in the evolution of genres. Alistair Fowler proposes that the majority of single-genre transformations occur through a change involving: topical invention (in which a new topic is developed often through specialization), combination (a pairing of two preexisting genres), aggregation (in which several short works are grouped together in an ordered collection), change of scale (in which the author enlarges, *macrologia*, or compacts, *brachylogia*, an existing genre), and/or change in function ("antigenre" or "inversion").[52] Fowler also recognizes transformations that involve multiple genres, such as inclusion (a literary work enclosed within another work), generic mixture (the inclusion of select literary features in another genre), and hybridization (where two or more complete repertoires are present in such proportions that no one of them dominates).[53] Fowler's discussion provides a vocabulary for discussing the ways that Jewish authors adapted Greek genres and will be incorporated into my application of prototype theory.

This project is diachronic, evaluating authors and texts over a period of five hundred years. The principle stated above—that genres are not static but evolve and change over time—adds an additional level of complexity to the discussion of Jewish Hellenistic writing; the literary world in which Philo Epicus wrote is not the same as that of Philo of Alexandria.[54] As a result, a genre—even though genre labels might be consistent (e.g., biography, history)—will not be the same throughout the centuries. Equally important for our study is the fact that favored literary models and reading preferences also change. Although Opacki, in his discussion of royal genres, presents a view of genre hierarchy at a societal level, the reality of antiquity (and today) is not so neat. Genre hierarchy is never fixed and each new work subtly, or sometimes radically, alters the existing ranking. The formation of genre rankings was also

52 Fowler, *Kinds of Literature*, 170–83; Todorov, *Genres in Discourse*, 13–26; T. Todorov, "The Origin of Genres," in D. Duff, ed., *Modern Genre Theory* (LCR; London: Longman, 2000), 197; G. Genette, *Palimpsests: Literature in the Second Degree* (trans. C. Newman and C. Doubinsky; Lincoln: University of Nebraska Press, 1997), 5–10. For an ancient perspective on genre development and change (covering the original use of *topoi*, inversion, reaction, inclusion, speaker-variation, and addressee-variation), see Cairns, *Generic Composition*, chaps. 4–9. For localized expansion or abridgment, see Theon, *Prog.* 107–108; Quintilian, *Inst.* 1.9.2–3.

53 Fowler, *Kinds of Literature*, 179–90; M. Hartner, "Hybrid Genres and Cultural Change: A Cognitive Approach," in M. Basseler, A. Nünning, and C. Schwanecke, eds., *The Cultural Dynamics of Generic Change in Contemporary Fiction: Theoretical Frameworks, Genres and Model Interpretations* (ELCH 56; Trier: Wissenschaftlicher Verlag Trier, 2013), 163–82.

54 For the challenges of discussing genre through a diachronic lens, see Colie, *Resources of Kind*, 30; Y. Tynyanov and R. Jakobson, "Problems in the Study of Literature and Language," in L. Metejka and K. Pomorska, eds., *Readings in Russian Poetics: Formalist and Structuralist Views* (Cambridge, Mass.: MIT Press, 1971), 79–81.

personal, with each author having his or her own preferences.[55] One suspects that personal genre hierarchies of prominent individuals influenced the larger societal genre hierarchy.[56] A society's genre hierarchy may be shaped and even fabricated by dominant individuals and literary groups. Within the Roman Empire no person had more power to influence than the Caesar, and the schools and writers he financially supported directly shaped literary culture, increasing the likeliness that a genre supported by him (or one of the Hellenistic kings) would become dominant or at least increase in popularity.[57] The selection of a genre, therefore, is not a benign act, but carries ideological freight related to that genre's status in its literary culture. An author's adoption of a genre that is not favored or in vogue with the literary elites is an intentional act and may be a way for the author to align him/herself with a specific subgroup or actively challenge the dominant perspective.[58]

Just as genre hierarchies differed between individuals, they also differed between cultures. Evidence for this is provided by Latin authors and their evaluation and comparison of Greek and Latin genres. These cultural preferences found their ideal expression in particular genres, which in turn came to be prized and incorporated into the national identity.[59] Unfortunately, Jewish authors, so far as we know, did not explicitly discuss genre preferences and hierarchies, but this does not mean that we lack the ability to gain insight. The types of texts found at Qumran indicate the literary preferences of the community.[60] Similarly, later compositions, such as the Mishnah and Talmud, and their preservation through oral tradition prior to being encoded in writing, indicate that collections of sayings and teachings were important.[61] One of the contributions of this work will be to provide an idea of Jewish-Greek genre preferences at different times during the Hellenistic and Roman eras.

55 Fowler, *Kinds of Literature*, 227. E.g., Aristotle, *Poet.* 26 (1461b25–1462b15); Horace, *Sat.* 1.4.24 and *Ep.* 2.2.58–60; Lucilius, fr. 608.

56 Jakobson, "Dominant," 83.

57 "The selective canons with most institutional force are formal curricula." Fowler, *Kinds of Literature*, 215. On the other hand, there might be reasons why some genres might be more appealing to a political leader than others and so increase the likeliness of their selection.

58 Dubrow, *Genre*, 13, 115.

59 Cf. Cicero, *Opt. gen.* 1–2, 6; Horace, *Sat.* 1.10.65–67; Quintilian, *Inst.* 10.1.96, 99, 123.

60 E.g., wisdom literature, scriptural texts, pesharim, etc. For a discussion on genre distinctions in Qumran literature, see M. Goff, "Qumran Wisdom Literature and the Problem of Genre," *DSD* 17 (2010): 286–306.

61 Cf. C. Hezser, "Rabbis as Intellectuals in the Context of Graeco-Roman and Byzantine Christian Scholasticism," in S. A. Adams, ed., *Scholastic Culture in the Hellenistic and Roman Eras: Greek, Latin, and Jewish* (Transmissions 2; Berlin: De Gruyter, 2019), 169–85. A similar example of this can be seen in Philo's *Questions*.

Project Overview and Contributions

I have attempted to be comprehensive in this study, discussing the full range of Jewish authors who composed literary works in Greek and participated in Greek genres. Certain texts receive more space and discussion than others. Sometimes this is because the work is larger or the author is prominent or prolific (e.g., Philo of Alexandria). At other times more space is dedicated to a work because I think that I have something new to contribute to the debate and/or a corrective to provide. At other times, texts are discussed more briefly. One reason might be that the work is highly fragmentary and so discussions of its genre are limited. For other texts, substantial scholarly works have been produced that, in my opinion, adequately cover the topic and so make it unnecessary for me to retread worn paths. Indeed, this work would have been substantially longer if that were the case. The chapters in this study are organized according to genre for ease of discussion, although I would resist the implication that texts mentioned therein only participate in one genre.

One of the inherent weaknesses of any study of Hellenistic literature is that surviving works are often fragmentary.[62] This is the case for many Jewish authors writing in Greek, whose works are compiled from quotations from Eusebius of Caesarea and Clement of Alexandria, who in turn were dependent on Cornelius Alexander (surnamed Polyhistor) and his work *On the Jews*. Despite scholarly confidence in the transmission of the fragments,[63] the fact that certain discussions are based on selected quotations twice removed and excised from their cover-texts is a reason for caution. Furthermore, making statements about a work's genre based on truncated evidence is undesirable. Indeed, we must also remember that Alexander Polyhistor (as well as Clement and Eusebius) was selective in the material that he adopted. Nevertheless, the nature of the sources and their transmission force us to use what evidence we have available.

62 On this issue see S. A. Stephens, "Commenting on Fragments," in R. K. Gibson and C. S. Kraus, eds., *The Classical Commentary: Histories, Practices, Theory* (Mnemosyne 232; Leiden: Brill, 2002), 67–88; S. Braune, "How to Analyze Texts That Were Burned, Lost, Fragmented, or Never Written," *Symploke* 21 (2013): 239–55; L. M. Yarrow, "How to Read a Diodoros Fragment," in L. I. Hau, A. Meeus, and B. Sheridan, eds., *Diodoros of Sicily: Historiographical Theory and Practice in the "Bibliotheke"* (SH 58; Leuven: Peeters, 2018), 247–74.

63 This confidence is based on Alexander Polyhistor's preservation of "poor" Greek as well as his inclusion of material that appears contrary to his position. For a larger discussion, see S. Inowlocki, *Eusebius and the Jewish Authors: His Citation Technique in an Apologetic Context* (AJEC 64; Leiden: Brill, 2006). For a good introduction, see W. Adler, "Alexander Polyhistor's *Peri Ioudaiôn* and Literary Culture in Republican Rome," in S. Inowlocki and C. Zamagni, eds., *Reconsidering Eusebius: Collected Papers on Literary, Historical, and Theological Issues* (VCS 107; Leiden: Brill, 2011), 225–40.

I have sought to make a scholarly contribution to each text discussed. However, the main contribution of this work is its macro perspective and the discussion of observations and patterns in chapter 9. By taking a holistic and diachronical approach to the question, we can see how Jewish writers as a whole approached Greek literary culture. Or, to put it differently, we can see how one minority group participated in the dominant culture's literary forms to address specific community needs.

In particular, I argue that: (1) Jewish authors writing in Greek were strongly influenced by Greek genres and that established literary practices regularly acted as constraints for composition; (2) there is a temporal element when considering genre use. By this I mean that most genres were not consistently adopted by Jewish authors throughout this time period, but that practices and preferences changed over time; (3) Jewish authors showed preferences for certain types of genres (especially history). I will argue that the selection of a genre and/or the avoidance of others (e.g., comedy) is directly tied to the purpose of text and the wider preferences of the reading community; (4) the employment of a specific genre implies a level of Greek education, the active selection of a literary model (i.e., prototype), and access to texts. I will argue that the authors discussed give strong evidence for diverse forms of Greek education (both Jewish and Greek literary models, including the use of the Septuagint) and that they must have had access to specific texts in order to compose their work; (5) education practices changed over time and differed based on geographic locale;[64] and (6) the choice of genre and the style of composition speak to the nature of ancient Jewish readers and their literary preferences.

64 Each of the authors studied in this monograph has knowledge of and ability in Greek composition. However, it would be problematic to claim that all were equal in their abilities or that every author understood each element of Greek culture equally well. Accordingly, it is not enough to say that an author had knowledge of Greek literature. Rather, we must construct each author's education in Greek culture as well as his/her social position and knowledge of Jewish culture. Unfortunately, this type of study is beyond the purview of this work. However, determining a work's genre and its literary influences provides important data for deepening our understanding of Jewish education in Greek. As a result, some comments about Greek education will be offered in the concluding chapter. For a similar perspective, but for Latin authors, see E. Fantham, *Roman Literary Culture: From Cicero to Apuleius* (Baltimore: Johns Hopkins University Press, 1996), 6.

2

Jewish Epic Poetry

Jewish epic poetry displays the highest levels of Greek literary knowledge and the clearest evidence of Jewish participation in Greek genres. The role and importance of epic in Greek literature were unrivaled in antiquity. Not only was Homer used as a model for later Greek epic writers (e.g., Apollonius' *Argonautica*), but the idea of the national epic was taken up by neighboring cultures (e.g., Virgil's *Aeneid*, Arctinus' *Aethiopis*).[1] In these periods the epic became a place for cultural negotiation, a flexible system for organizing, ranking, and contesting the relationships among different peoples.[2] In this chapter I will investigate the ways that Jewish writers—Philo Epicus, Theodotus, and Sosates—participated in the construction of epics with a Jewish subject. These authors provide strong examples of Jewish knowledge and adaptation of Greek literature through their use of hexameter, Homeric vocabulary, and sublime language, supporting the argument that they received a Greek education that focused on standard Greek literary models. In contrast, there is little evidence of Septuagint use despite the fact that the subjects of Philo and Theodotus' poems are taken from Genesis. These hexameter poems indicate the willingness by some Jews to engage in high-level cultural debates and to employ the quintessential genre of the dominant culture.

1 Cf. K. Ziegler, *Das Hellenistische Epos: Ein Vergessenes Kapitel Griechischer Dichtung* (2nd ed.; Leipzig: Teubner, 1966).
2 T. Whitmarsh, *Beyond the Second Sophistic: Adventures in Greek Postclassicism* (Berkeley: University of California Press, 2013), 228–29.

The Poets and Their Texts

Philo Epicus

Little is known about Philo the epic poet. He may be the Philo whom Josephus calls "the Elder" (*C. Ap.* 1.218). Clement of Alexandria (*Strom.* 1.21.141) mentions a Philo in his discussion of chronographers, placing him between Demetrius and Eupolemus, which suggests that Clement viewed this Philo as a historian. These statements from Josephus and Clement have been used to support a third/second-century BCE date for Philo Epicus.[3] Although valuable, these two literary references are insufficient in providing secure dates for Philo's life and work. First, in Judaea and the diaspora, Philo was not an uncommon name, and so it is not possible to forge secure links between the Philos.[4] Second, both Josephus and Clement appear to be discussing an author who wrote chronography, but this is far from the literary genre of epic poetry exhibited in Philo's fragments and so does not provide good evidence for equating the two writers.[5] Rather, the firm *terminus ante quem* for Philo Epicus is the citation of him by Alexander Polyhistor, who flourished in the last half of the first century BCE.[6]

The provenance of Philo's work is also unknown. Some have suggested (likely based on the poem's given title and his tentative association with Eupolemus) that Philo wrote his work in Jerusalem.[7] James Charlesworth, for example, is so confident about a Jerusalem provenance that he is surprised to find any disagreement.[8] Conversely, Martin Hengel claims that this assumption is "pure speculation" and opts for an Egyptian origin,[9] while Emil Schürer suggests that Philo could have written from anywhere in the diaspora.[10] All suggestions lack strong supporting evidence, and so the provenance question cannot be answered conclusively.

3 E. Schürer, *The History of the Jewish People in the Age of Jesus Christ (175 BC–AD 135)* (rev. and ed. G. Vermes et al.; 3 vols.; Edinburgh: T&T Clark, 1973–1987), 3.555–56.

4 T. Ilan, *Lexicon of Jewish Names in Late Antiquity* (4 vols.; TSAJ; Tübingen: Mohr Siebeck, 2002–2012), 1.311; 3.392–94. For the use of Philo as a name in history, see D. T. Runia, "Philonic Nomenclature," *SPhiloA* 6 (1994): 1–3.

5 Cf. A.-M. Denis, *Introduction à la Littérature Religieuse Judéo-Hellénistique* (Turnhout, Belgium: Brepols, 2000), 1192.

6 Cf. *Suda* A 1129.

7 J. Freudenthal, *Alexander Polyhistor und die von ihm erhaltenen Reste jüdischer und samaritanischer Geschichtswerke*, books 1 and 2 of *Hellenistische Studien* (Breslau: Skutsch, 1874–1875), 1.129; B. Z. Wacholder, "Philo (the Elder)," in M. Berenbaum and F. Skolnik, eds., *Encyclopedia Judaica* (2nd ed.; Detroit: Macmillan Reference, 2007), 16.58.

8 J. H. Charlesworth, *The Pseudepigrapha and Modern Research with a Supplement* (SCS 75; Atlanta: Scholars Press, 1981), 169.

9 Hengel, *Judaism and Hellenism*, 2.71.

10 Schürer, *History*, 3.1.560.

Twenty-four lines are all that remain of Philo's literary legacy. These lines, initially excerpted by Alexander Polyhistor, have come down to us through Eusebius' use of Polyhistor in his *Praeparatio evangelica* (9.20.1; 9.24.1; 9.37.1–3). Divided into six fragments, the lines, Eusebius informs us, are taken from books 1 and 14 of Philo's *On Jerusalem* and discuss Abraham (frs. 1–2), Joseph (fr. 6), and Jerusalem (frs. 3–5).[11] The text as it has been received in surviving manuscripts is stable; however, a number of scholars have posited emendations to the text due to the difficult nature of the verses.[12]

Philo's choice of hexameter—a form of poetry with metrical lines containing six feet, with each foot consisting of either two long syllables (a spondee), or a long and two short syllables (a dactyl)—is informative for signaling the nature of the work, as this was the prescribed meter for epic (e.g., Hesiod and Homer).[13] This meter's association with Homeric literature should not be underestimated, for any ancient reader of Greek would have recognized that Philo was signaling participation in the epic genre.[14]

Further confirmation of Philo's Greek education is seen in his vocabulary.[15] Certain words in Philo's poem are only extant in Homer or other school-

11 Freudenthal and others have argued that an error has crept into Eusebius' quotation of Alexander Polyhistor and that instead of Φίλων ἐν τῆι ιδ´ τῶν περὶ Ἱεροσόλυμα it ought to read ἐν τῆι δ´ and so indicate the fourth, not the fourteenth book. Freudenthal, *Alexander Polyhistor*, 1.100. See further discussion below. Some issues obscure the exact title of the work. First, there are two different spellings of Jerusalem, with fragments 1 and 3 giving Ἱεροσόλυμα and fragment 4 Ἱεροσολύμων. Second, there is inconsistency over the use of the article; manuscripts B, O, and N read περὶ, whereas manuscript I reads περὶ τὰ. Most English translations label the Joseph fragment as number 3 (following the citation order of Eusebius); whereas the Greek editions by Jacoby and Lloyd-Jones and Parsons label the Joseph fragment number 6 (following the order according to the books assigned by Eusebius). For this work I have followed the Greek numbering system.

12 The text adopted is H. Lloyd-Jones and P. Parsons, eds., *Supplementum Hellenisticum* (Berlin: De Gruyter, 1983), 328–30, with reference to K. Mras, ed. *Eusebius' Werke*, vol. 8, *Die Praeparatio evangelica*, Die griechischen christlichen Schriftsteller 43.1 and 43.2 (2nd ed.; Berlin: Akademie Verlag, 1982), 506–508, 517–518, 546; FHG 3.213–214; *FGrH* 729; and E. H. Gifford, ed. and trans., *Eusebius of Caesarea: Praeparatio Evangelica* (Oxford: Clarendon, 1903). A new edition was attempted by T. Kuhn, though he appears to be overly dependent on previous scholars. T. Kuhn, ed. and trans., *Die jüdisch-hellenistischen Epiker Theodot und Philon: Literarische Untersuchungen, kritische Edition und Übersetzung der Fragmente* (Vertumnus 9; Göttingen: Vandenhoeck & Ruprecht, 2012).

13 Hexameter was not limited to epic literature (e.g., Ovid, *Metamorphoses*; Horace, *Satires*), but was identified with that genre (e.g., Apollonius, *Argonautica*). Cf. Adams, *Genre*, 46–47. For Jewish epigrams in hexameter that have Homeric elements, see Horbury and Noy, *Jewish Inscriptions*, nos. 23 (Schedia), 29–39 (Leontopolis).

14 The role of Homer in the Greek curriculum was foundational, and so, accordingly, would have been the discussion of his metrical selection.

15 Using vocabulary as a criterion of literary relatedness is problematic: not only do we lack the majority of ancient literary works, we cannot know with certainty the location from which the author in question first learned or gleaned any specific term(s); a word in Philo's poem may

taught authors. In fragment 2.2, Philo uses σφαράγοιο; the only other prior occurrence of this word is Homer, *Od.* 9.390 and 440 in his well-known story of Odysseus and the Cyclops Polyphemus. In fragment 6.1, Philo employs the term ἄκτωρ as a reference for the "great leader" (whose identity in Philo's text is disputed: God, Joseph, Pharaoh).[16] This term is absent from all other classical writers with the exception of Aeschylus, who employs it twice, once in reference to Darius (*Pers.* 557) and the other time when describing the leaders of the Achaeans (*Eum.* 399). Similarly, in fragment 1.3 Philo employs the rare term μεγαυχήτοισι, whose only literary comparator is μεγαυχεῖ in Aeschylus, *Pers.* 642.[17]

One of the more striking aspects of the first fragment of Philo's work is his use of pagan epithets when describing God and Abraham. In fragment 1.5, Philo describes the God of Abraham as the "thunderer" (βριήπυος), an adjective not used to describe God in any other Jewish work and that is, in fact, only found in one other context, Homer's description of Ares in *Il.* 13.521. Philo describes the descendants of Abraham as πολύμνιον in fragment 1.7. In Hesiod's *Theog.* 78 the Muses are called "she of the many hymns [Πολύμνιά]," while the alternative spelling, πολύυμνος, is an appellation for Dionysius in Euripides' *Ion* 1074 and an adjective of "the many-hymned grove of Nemean Zeus' in Pindar's *Nem.* 2.5. In fragment 6.4, Joseph is called a θεσπιστής, a term which in this form is previously unattested, but whose root, θέσπις, "inspired," is regularly used to describe pagan oracles (Aeschylus, *Eum.* 922; Euripides, *Suppl.* 141; Sophocles, *Oed. tyr.* 971). A related example is the hapax κλυτοηχές, the root of which, κλυτός, "glorious, or renowned," frequently occurs in Homer, Hesiod, Pindar, and the tragedians as an epitaph

---

appear to have been taken from Homer, but may have been mediated through other authors. The benefit of being able to trace a word or phrase back to Homer (or Hesiod, Euripides, Aesop, etc.) is that we know that Homer was the primary text in Greek education. This does not mean that any instance of a Homeric term indicates participation in epic genre (other features are also needed); nevertheless, the use of such vocabulary is important in this regard. Cf. Fantuzzi and Hunter, *Tradition and Innovation*, 246–49.

16 For discussion, see C. R. Holladay, *Fragments from Hellenistic Jewish Authors*, vol. 2, *Poets* (SBLTT 40; SBLPS 14; Atlanta: Scholars Press, 1989), 267.

17 There are two examples of μεγαύχητος in inscriptions: one at Acarnania (E. Preuner, "Inschriften aus Akarnanien," *MDAI* 27 [1902]: 339) and one at Cnossos (*I.Cret.* 33). Both are from the second century BCE and are written in epic style. On each tombstone of these young men, who distinguished themselves in war, the term μεγαύχητος is applied to the fathers of the heroes to indicate their proud reputation in society.

Philo's knowledge of Homeric and classical Greek is also evident is his use of literary morphology. For example, instances of the -οιο genitive singular ending (αἰνογόνοιο, fr. 1.7; θνητοῖο, fr. 2.1; σφαράγοιο, fr. 2.2; μεγιστούχοιο, fr. 3.2; Ἀβραάμοιο, fr. 6.2; Αἰγύπτοιο, fr. 6.4), the -οισι dative plural ending (ἀρχεγόνοισι, fr. 1.1; μεγαυχήτοισι, fr. 1.3; ὑδροχόοισι, fr. 5.1; τοῖσιν, fr. 6.1; θρόνοισιν, fr. 6.4) as well as the -εσσι dative plural ending (χείρεσσι, fr. 2.3). Furthermore, there is the distinctive use of the adverbial suffix -θεν (πρόσθεν, fr. 6.2; τόθεν, fr. 6.3).

for gods and heroes, but is used by Philo as an adjective to describe Abraham (fr. 1.2).[18] These examples provide strong evidence that Philo knew standard Greek conventions for praising characters. The application of pantheonic attributes to the Jewish deity, as well as to Abraham and Joseph, challenges preconceived notions regarding the desire by Jews to differentiate their God from the Greek pantheon through a scrupulous use of distinctive lexical terms. This shows a willingness on the part of Philo Epicus to bring Greek and Jewish theological ideas into contact with each other and use established literary language to depict Jewish history.

Philo adopts a high literary register. Gutman describes the text as "high-flown and sometimes pompous,"[19] based on Philo's tendency to use extreme imagery that obscures the text from even the most dedicated reader. In fact, the difficulties in the Greek of Philo's fragments (especially fr. 1) have resulted in a number of excellent Greek scholars (e.g., Fr. Vigerus, E. H. Gifford) refraining from providing a translation, claiming that it is "untranslatable." However, it is very unlikely that Philo wrote in this challenging mode of expression with no intended purpose or with the belief that it could not be read by (some of) his contemporaries. I argue for an alternative hypothesis: Philo's work embodies a sublimity that seeks to express in words the matchless grandeur of his subject matter.[20] Or, to put it differently, Philo represents an ineffable concept through the materiality of language: its grammar, structure, and literary form.[21] Rather than being poorly written, Philo's epic models the purposeful obscurity witnessed in other Hellenistic epics.

Proper selection of lexical items is central to sublime writing, particularly terms that embody an esoteric or grand concept. For example, in fragment 1, Philo employs many terms within a specific semantic range: κλυτοηχές, "most famous" (fr. 1.2), παμφαές, "radiant" (fr. 1.3), μεγαυχήτοισι, "glorious" (fr. 1.3), λιπόντι, "radiant" (fr. 1.4), ἀγλαόν, "splendid, shining" (fr. 1.4), κῦδος, "glory" (fr. 1.7).[22] These words are linguistic representations of abstract concepts.

18 E.g., Homer, *Il.* 2.742; 9.362; 14.361; 20.320; *Od.* 5.422; 10.526; 24.409. Although not a term unique to Philo and Homer, ἕδος (fr. 6.1) is a word regularly used by Homer for the dwelling place of the gods (*Il.* 5.360, 367, 868; 8.456; 24.144) and also of men (*Il.* 4.406; 24.544; *Od.* 13.344). These lexical items are absent in the Septuagint, which suggests that the later Greek translators may have recognized their associations with Greek deities and avoided using them.

19 Y. Gutman, "Philo the Epic Poet," *ScrHier* 1 (1954): 37.

20 Whitmarsh, *Beyond*, 240–41. Contra Collins, who claims that Philo "did not in fact have a great command of the Greek language." J. J. Collins, *Between Athens and Jerusalem: Jewish Identity in the Hellenistic Diaspora* (2nd ed.; Grand Rapids: Eerdmans, 2000), 54. Kuhn (*Epiker*, 67–71) plausibly links Philo's obscure mode of expression to oracular poetics, comparing texts such as Lycophron's *Alexandra* and the Sibylline Oracles.

21 Cf. J. I. Porter, *The Origins of Aesthetic Thought in Ancient Greece: Matter, Sensation and Experience* (Cambridge: Cambridge University Press, 2010).

22 The abundance of water and light imagery is noted by Kuhn, *Epiker*, 65.

A similar view is possible for βριήπυος ("heavy-shouting," fr. 1.5; the first part derives from βρῖθος, "weight"), which imbues the text with a richness of metaphor. For the sublime writer, ideas need to be properly embodied in language.[23] Moreover, language needs to reflect and capture adequately the subject it is describing; heavy ideas require heavy, deep language that moves its listeners.[24] Ineffable, obscure ideas can only themselves be expressed in obscure language.[25] Accordingly, in order to bring extra "weight" or grandeur to a subject, the author needs to write in a grand manner and imbue the text with density.[26] Philo's poem supports the thesis that sublimity in ancient discourse is rooted in ideas about the materiality of language.[27]

The concept of sublimity as an influence on Philo's work is compelling for a few reasons. First, it provides a reasonable answer to the question of why Philo wrote in such a manner; grand ideas require grand language, and the grandest ideas, which resist being put into words, demand obscure morphology and opaque syntax. Second, it attributes a strong sense of authorial creativity to Philo's work. Rather than arguing that Philo merely adopted common literary practice, or that his text has been thoroughly corrupted, the attribution of sublime creativity indicates a high level of intentionality. This fits with the evidence above that Philo adopted lexical, morphological, and stylistic features of Homer and other classical writers in order to make explicit literary connections and to present his subject as worthy of consideration. Third, it reinforces the relationship among lexical selection, meter, and genre. This will be discussed further below, but it is well known that epic and epic-like poems take the grandest style of language; great ideas need to be properly encased in bold language.[28]

The above examples of Homeric vocabulary, inflected forms, and sublime style argue strongly that Philo was well acquainted with Greek literary culture and could adopt Greek authors as models for his composition. As Homer and the tragedians feature prominently in the school curriculum, an author who

23 See the recent, detailed study by J. I. Porter, *The Sublime in Antiquity* (Cambridge: Cambridge University Press, 2016), 51–53.

24 Ps.-Longinus, *Subl.* 8.1–2; 44.12. Although emotion is not always required for sublimity, its (supposed) absence in Caecilius' discussion was cause for critique. On emotion and sublimity in Pseudo-Longinus, see Porter, *Sublime*, 124–30.

25 Aristotle, *Rhet.* 3.2.3, 1404b; Ps.-Longinus, *Subl.* 9.3; Lucian, *Jupp. trag.* 6.

26 E.g., Hesiod, *Theog.* 687–710; Aristophanes, *Ran.* 814; Callimachus, *Aet.* 1.20.

27 Visualizations (i.e., φαντασίαι), including ἐνάργεια, are also part of sublime writing (Ps.-Longinus, *Subl.* 15.1–12; cf. Porter, *Sublime*, 155–60), and the rich depictions in Philo (frs. 4–5) and Theodotus (fr. 1) could be viewed as attempts to help the reader/hearer "see" through emotive language.

28 E.g., Ps.-Longinus, *Subl.* 7.2; 14.1; Aristotle, *Eth. nic.* 2.7, 1107b23; 4.2, 1122a18–b18; 4.3, 1125a17.

displays substantial awareness and skillful adaptation of them is one who likely had a full Greek education.[29] Philo's ability to structure a work on hexameter and embody the virtues of sublimity evidences his deep knowledge of Greek literary culture. The concept of sublimity was certainly not taught at the lower levels of education in which the student learned the key elements of literature and gained a familiarity with ancient authors (Ps.-Longinus, *Subl.* 1.1). If this is the case for Philo, it provides an early example of the willingness of at least one Jew to embrace Greek education and literary forms and pursue such education to its highest levels.[30]

The question of intended audience is surprisingly absent in the discussion of Philo Epicus. Although determining the provenance of the work would influence this decision, the ambiguity surrounding its derivation precludes its consideration. In light of the strong Homeric influence and the cultural convergence exhibited, I would suggest that Philo did not write solely for his coreligionists, but also for a non-Jewish audience. It would be difficult to argue, moreover, that the obscure language and syntax would have been readily understandable to anyone but the most highly educated.

Philo was not only knowledgeable about Greek literature, but was clearly familiar with the patriarchal narratives. What is noteworthy is *On Jerusalem*'s minimal lexical overlap with the Septuagint, but even in these instances the words are common and so would be shared with nearly all Greek literature. Rather, Philo's word selection, sentence construction, and style show no specific septuagintal influence. A good example of the difference between Philo and the LXX is the description of Abraham in fragment 2, in which little overlap or specific correlation exists between the texts. By this I do not mean that there are narratival differences; rather, there are few points of contact in vocabulary and phrasing that would suggest a literary relationship between these works.

Philo fr. 2: ἄρτι χερὸς θνητοῖο ξιφηφόρον ἐντύνοντος
λήμματι καὶ σφαράγοιο παρακλιδὸν ἀθροισθέντος·
ἀλλ” ὁ μὲν ἐν χείρεσσι κερασφόρον ὤπασε κριόν.

Gen 22:13: καὶ ἀναβλέψας Ἀβραὰμ τοῖς ὀφθαλμοῖς αὐτοῦ εἶδεν, καὶ ἰδοὺ κριὸς εἷς κατεχόμενος ἐν φυτῷ σαβὲκ τῶν κεράτων· καὶ ἐπορεύθη Ἀβραὰμ

29 A similar example is Rhianus of Crete in his *On Messenia* (third century BCE), who used Homeric language and imagery for his national/regional epic. Cf. *Suda* P 158; *FGrH* 265; Pausanias, *Descr.* 4.22.7; Suetonius, *Tib.* 70; Athenaeus, *Deipn.* 11.499d.

30 In light of the above discussion, I disagree with that the efforts of Philo and Ezekiel would have been "laughed at" as "feeble attempts." V. Tcherikover, "Jewish Apologetic Literature Reconsidered," *Eos* 48 (1956): 179.

> καὶ ἔλαβεν τὸν κριὸν καὶ ἀνήνεγκεν αὐτὸν εἰς ὁλοκάρπωσιν ἀντὶ Ἰσαὰκ τοῦ υἱοῦ αὐτοῦ.[31]

Between these two passages almost no vocabulary is shared (excluding conjunctions, articles, etc.). The two exceptions are κριός, "ram"—a word that is very common both in classical literature and in the Septuagint—and the root κέρας, "animal horn," which is given on its own in the Genesis narrative, but in the compound form, κερασφόρος, in Philo. This lack of lexical overlap argues strongly in favor of literary independence, a view that is only strengthened when one acknowledges the completely different phrasing and structure between the two passages. Philo's hexameter Greek is difficult and is not easily translated. Conversely, the Septuagint passage is easy to read, written in prose, and readily interpreted. These differences not only speak to the intended readership of each work, but indicate that Philo did not seek to include LXX resonances or borrow from the authority of that work (assuming that he had access to it). Indeed, some of the distinctively LXX features (such as the specification of the sabek plant) are absent in Philo's narrative.[32]

Overall, the use of the Abraham narrative reinforces Philo's connection with his Jewish heritage, and even from these small fragments it is clear that Philo had a strong knowledge of Scripture. It is not clear, however, which sources Philo used to gain this knowledge. Did Philo hear these stories in the synagogue? Was he formally taught them? Or, did he read them for himself? If the latter, did he use the LXX (or an older translation) or the Hebrew text (and could he read Hebrew)? The minimal overlap between Philo and the LXX in terms of literary structuring, vocabulary, and phrasing implies that the LXX did not exert much (if any) literary influence on Philo's composition.

Theodotus

Theodotus' Περὶ Ἰουδαίων, which is preserved in fragments excerpted by Eusebius' use of Alexander Polyhistor (*Praep. ev.* 9.22.1–11), also shows similar engagement with Greek literature. The eight preserved fragments (ranging from two to fifteen lines long) begin with a description of the city of Shechem (frs. 1–2, including Jacob's arrival), followed by a discussion of Jacob and his family (frs. 3–4), and ends with the rape of Dinah and the resulting slaughter of the

31 J. W. Wevers, ed., *Genesis*, vol. 1 (Vetus Testamentum Graecum. Auctoritate Academiae Scientiarum Gottingensis editum; Göttingen: Vandenhoeck & Ruprecht, 1974).

32 The lack of overlap between the two passages makes it difficult to understand why Holladay (*Fragments: Poets*, 265) posited the connection between LXX Gen 22:13 and fr. 2.3, except for the fact that both recount the Abraham narrative.

Shechemites by Simeon and Levi (frs. 4, 6–8).[33] Fragment 5 recalls the circumcision of Abraham's family and is loosely tied to Jacob's request for Hamar to be circumcised (fr. 4). In Eusebius' chapter, these fragments are held together by short summaries, which are written in prose and contrast the poetic form of Theodotus' poem. Fallon asserts that the content between Theodotus' fragments is Polyhistor's synopsis of the omitted parts of the poem and that Eusebius adopted his summaries.[34] Another possibility is that the summaries are Eusebius' own words or his synopsis of Polyhistor's work. Either way, the summaries are part of the larger cover text and provide an important frame for reading the fragments and so must be considered in any interpretation of Theodotus.

Although Theodotus' poem is titled *On the Jews* (Περὶ Ἰουδαίων) by Eusebius (who presumably took the title provided by Polyhistor), Holladay and others note that Polyhistor uses this phrase for the works of Eupolemus, Artapanus, and Aristeas, suggesting that it might be a description rather than a title.[35] Polyhistor, however, is neither careless nor indiscriminate with his title attributions; when identifying other poetic works, he regularly uses their specific titles (e.g., Philo, Περὶ Ἱεροσόλυμα; Ezekiel, Ἐξαγωγή).

Theodotus' ethnicity is a recurring question in scholarship; is he a Jew or a Samaritan?[36] The traditional opinion was established by Freudenthal, who argued that Theodotus was a Samaritan because of the centrality of Shechem and its description as a "holy city."[37] The argument, according to Freudenthal, is that Alexander Polyhistor (as a Greek) would not have been able to differentiate between Jews and Samaritans and so accidentally included Theodotus in his *On the Jews*.[38] In light of this theory, Jacoby and others have suggested renaming the poem ΣΙΚΙΜΩΝ ΚΤΙΣΙΣ, arguing that Theodotus adopted the Hellenistic poetic tradition of founding narratives.[39]

33 The Greek text used for Theodotus is Lloyd-Jones and Parsons, *Supplementum Hellenisticum*, 359–63, with reference to Mras, GCS 43.1, 512–16; FHG 3.217–19; *FGrH* 3C 732; Gifford, *Eusebius*; and Kuhn, *Epiker*.

34 F. Fallon, "Theodotus," in *OTP* 2.785. So also Holladay, *Fragments: Poets*, 52.

35 Holladay, *Fragments: Poets*, 128–29. Regarding Eusebius' use of Περὶ Ἰουδαίων, see *Praep. ev.* 9.17.2 (Eupolemus); 9.23.1 (Artapanus); 9.25.1 (Aristeas).

36 For a list of supporters and opponents, see R. Pummer, "Genesis 34 in Jewish Writings of the Hellenistic and Roman Periods," *HTR* 75 (1982): 177 nn. 2–3. See most recently, J. Bourgel, "Brethren or Strangers? Samaritans in the Eyes of Second-Century B.C.E. Jews," *Bib* 98 (2017): 402–4.

37 Freudenthal, *Alexander Polyhistor*, 1.99–100.

38 Freudenthal, *Alexander Polyhistor*, 1.99–100; P. M. Fraser, *Ptolemaic Alexandria* (3 vols.; Oxford: Clarendon, 1972), 2.986; Goodman in Schürer, *History*, 3.1.562.

39 Jacoby, *FGrH* 3.692; N. Walter, "Fragmente jüdisch-hellenistischer Epik: Philon, Theodotos," in *JSHRZ* 4.3, 155. Wacholder proposes either *On the Foundation of Shechem* or *On Jacob*. Wacholder, *Eupolemus*, 285.

This perspective has been challenged by Collins, who highlights a number of weaknesses to the Samaritan argument. First, we cannot be certain that our fragments are representative of the work. Second, the inhabitants of Shechem are represented in a negative light.[40] Third, there is no mention of Mount Gerizim, which, it is assumed, would be a requisite feature for a Samaritan.[41] Although these arguments undermine the strength of the Samaritan hypothesis, they are insufficient to argue for Jewish ethnicity. More recently, Mendels, van der Horst, and Daise have proposed a revised Samaritan perspective.[42] Daise proposes that Theodotus' poem should be read as the expressed desire on behalf of the Samaritans to recapture Shechem from their political rivals, the Seleucids.[43] Although intriguing and internally plausible within his reconstruction, Daise's argument implicitly depends on a reading of the poem in which the main ethnic groups are, in some way, symbolic: the author's Samaritan community view themselves as the Jewish characters (Jacob, Simeon, Levi) and Shechem as a hostile entity, a city occupied by their Seleucid enemies. Although it is possible for Samaritans to present themselves as Jewish descendants, the reading of the whole poem as a couched metaphor depicting the desire of the Samaritans is not compelling. Overall, the ethnicity of Theodotus is still open.

Associated with the discussion of Theodotus' ethnicity is the dating of the poem. Key to this discussion, for some, is the mention of "smooth walls" (τεῖχος λισσόν) in fragment 1. From the excavations at Tel Balatah (Shechem), Bull has determined that a wall enclosed the city between the dates of circa 331–circa 150 BCE. After this time the wall fell into disrepair and its stones were cannibalized for other building projects. As the poem implies that the wall is standing and in good repair, the dates offered by Bull would appear to be the time period in which the poem was penned.[44] This, however, is a rigid understanding of dating. The neglect of the wall was likely gradual and so cannot be dated precisely. More importantly, poetic language should not be expected to correlate perfectly with historical or physical reality and so does

40 This perspective has been nuanced by Pummer ("Genesis 34," 180), who argues that Theodotus is not "anti-Samaritan" per se, but recasts the Genesis narrative in order to portray the patriarchs in a positive light.

41 Collins, *Athens*, 57–60.

42 D. Mendels, *The Land of Israel as a Political Concept in Hasmonean Literature: Recourse to History in Second Century B.C. Claims to the Holy Land* (Tübingen: Mohr Siebeck, 1987), 109–16; P. W. van der Horst, "The Interpretation of the Bible by the Minor Hellenistic Jewish Authors," in M. J. Mulder, ed., *Mikra: Text, Translation, Reading and Interpretation of the Hebrew Bible in Ancient Judaism and Early Christianity* (CRINT 2.1; Philadelphia: Fortress, 1988), 527; M. Daise, "Samaritans, Seleucids, and the Epic of Theodotus," *JSP* 17 (1998): 25–51.

43 Daise, "Samaritans," 50–51.

44 R. J. Bull, "A Note on Theodotus's Description of Shechem," *HTR* 60 (1967): 227.

not provide a firm temporal boundary.[45] We lack sufficient evidence to offer a restricted dating range, but we can say with confidence that it was written prior to the work of Alexander Polyhistor.

One of the more discussed features of Theodotus' poem is his alleged syncretism, reported by Eusebius (*Praep. ev.* 9.22.1), in which Theodotus' claims that Shechem received its name from "Sikimius, son of Hermes." Such a reference to a Greek god, it is argued, could not have come from a Jewish writer (who presumably would never have indulged in such an act), but rather is characteristic of "Samaritan Hellenism."[46] This differentiation, however, is false, as other Jewish writers incorporated Greek religious ideas into their works (e.g., Pseudo-Eupolemus, Artapanus, Sibylline Oracles).[47] Theodotus exhibits knowledge of the Greco-Roman practice of attributing the founding of a city to a particular deity, reframing elements of his own people's history in light of the values of the dominant culture.[48]

Theodotus' poem reads much more straightforwardly than Philo's work, but this should not disguise the fact that Theodotus' text is far from clear, as is evidenced by the number of emendations and different translations.[49] Theodotus writes in hexameter and shows deep knowledge of Homer's poems, which is expressed in specific phrases, vocabulary, and imagery.[50] Many of the terms used in the first fragment of Theodotus are not well attested in Hellenistic literature, including the Septuagint.[51] Theodotus makes use of Homeric verb forms and syntax, such as using the locative suffix -θεν with a greater frequency than other nonepic works, and employs epic morphology in lieu of those preferred in Hellenistic prose.[52] One purported use of Homeric/epic

45 J. J. Collins, "The Epic of Theodotus and the Hellenism of the Hasmoneans," *HTR* 73 (1980): 101–2. Collins proposes a late second-century BCE date corresponding with the conquests of John Hyrcanus.

46 Freudenthal, *Alexander Polyhistor*, 1.100.

47 In LXX Job 42:14, Job's daughter receives the name "Horn of Amaltheia" (Ἀμαλθείας κέρας). Thanks to Marieke Dhont for this reference. Interestingly, Eusebius does not appear to find it problematic. For an excellent discussion of the various options, see Holladay, *Fragments: Poets*, 131–35.

48 Fraser, *Ptolemaic Alexandria*, 1.513–14, 632, 775–76.

49 Cf. Denis, *Introduction*, 1198; Gutman, "Philo," 37.

50 R. Pummer and M. Roussel, "A Note on Theodotus and Homer," *JSJ* 13 (1982): 177; Holladay, *Fragments: Poets*, 72; Kuhn, *Epiker*, 53. "Theodotus' style is generally that of the classical epic. His vocabulary is largely dependent on Homer, and his form of presentation also excels in the clarity, limpidity, and simplicity peculiar to the classical epic." Gutman, "Philo," 37.

51 E.g., ὑδρηλή (*Od.* 9.133); ὁδὸς δολιχὴ (*Od.* 4.393, 483; 17.426; Apollonius, *Argon.* 3.602); πόλιν εἰσαφικέσθαι (*Il.* 22.17); ἀγρόθεν (*Od.* 13.286; 15.428); δρίος (*Od.* 14.353); λαχνήεις (*Il.* 24.451). This list is not exhaustive.

52 E.g., ἀγρόθεν (fr. 1.3); ἔνερθεν (fr. 1.6, according to Grotius); αἴποθεν (fr. 1.9); ἄλλοθεν (fr. 4.2). For example, ἔτιον (fr. 7.1), from τίω, is the epic form of τιμάω. Likewise, ὠρώρει, the pluperfect form of ὄρνυμι, is used in fr. 7.4 and in other epics for ἦν (Apollonius, *Argon.* 2.473;

vocabulary and custom that is regularly discussed is the reference to the "holy city" (ἱερὸν ἄστυ) in fragment 1.7.[53] This argument is typically employed when challenging the Jewish ethnicity of Theodotus, but it is useful for our discussion of Homeric influence. The argument usually runs thus: if Theodotus is a Samaritan, then his calling it a "holy city" does not bear witness to Greek influence, but is his own personal view. Conversely, if Theodotus is not a Samaritan, but a Jew, then he could not have meant it literally, and so must have employed it as a literary trope. I would argue, however, that Theodotus' ethnicity and his use of literary modeling to discuss Shechem are not mutually exclusive; Theodotus could both mean what he says *and* be employing a standard poetic motif.

In light of verbal and morphological connections, some scholars have compared passages in Theodotus to specific stanzas in Homer. Holladay suggests that ἀγαθή τε καὶ αἰγινόμος (fr. 1.1) shows affinity to ἀλλ' ἀγαθὴ μέν, εὔβοος εὔμηλος in Homer, *Od.* 15.405–406.[54] This association, however, is tenuous at best as there is only one word of overlap and only a loose thematic connection. Similarly, Nickelsburg asserts that "the lush description of the landscape is paralleled by similar passages in Homer, which introduce such unhappy events as Odysseus' sojourn with Calypso (*Od.* 5.55–75) and his encounter with the Cyclops (*Od.* 9.105–142)."[55] Again, a specific connection between the selected passages in Theodotus and Homer is unsupportable. Rather, Theodotus adopted a literary pattern for epic poems in which the author paints a representative picture of the city and countryside in focus.

A stronger example of Theodotus' use of Homer is the study by Pummer and Roussel on fragment 7 (Eusebius, *Praep. ev.* 9.22.9). In this passage, Pummer and Roussel identify the opening βλάπτε, not as a direct imperative,[56] but as an "epic imperfective" lacking the initial epsilon augment.[57] Although

---

3.457); a use that is never witnessed in standard Hellenistic prose and has only four other occurrences: *Il.* 18.489; Aeschylus, *Ag.* 653; Sophocles, *Oed. col.* 1622; Apollonius, *Argon.* 4.1698.

53 The term ἄστυ is used 109 times in Homer and is unattested in the LXX. Scholars note that many cities in Homer's epics (as well as cities in epics modeled on Homer, i.e., Apollonius' *Argonautica*) are described as "holy." E.g., Troy: *Il.* 16.100; *Od.* 1.2; Athens: *Od.* 11.323; Pergamus: *Il.* 5.446. For other examples see Callimachus, *Hymn.* 4.285; Apollonius, *Argon.* 4.505, 1758; Philitas, *Eleg. et Gramm. Frag.* 23.1; 674.1; Quintus Smyrnaeus, *Posth.* 13.338. I question Holladay's suggested parallel of Apollonius, *Argon.* 4.1139, as it refers to the cave, rather than the city.

54 Holladay, *Fragments: Poets*, 136.

55 G. W. E. Nickelsburg, "The Bible Rewritten and Expanded," in M. E. Stone, ed., *Jewish Writings of the Second Temple Period: Apocrypha, Pseudepigrapha, Qumran Sectarian Writings, Philo, Josephus* (CRINT 2.2; Philadelphia: Fortress, 1984), 123.

56 So Collins, "Epic," 95.

57 Pummer and Roussel, "Note," 179. See also the epic aorist of βλάψε with omitted augment in Homer, *Il.* 23.774.

morphologically the imperative is signaled, the exclusion of syllabic augments is allowed in epic writings, particularly if required for metrical accuracy. Such flexibility is a requisite component of poetic writing and needs to be taken into account when translating a text. In this case, interpretational ambiguity may have been deliberate in order to provide multiple readings and a fuller range of possible interpretations for later readers to debate.

Continuing their discussion of fragment 7, Pummer and Roussel argue that Homer, *Od.* 22.414–15, is "so similar to the [passage] in our poem that it must have been Theodotus' model."[58] The framework of this passage is Odysseus' travel to the underworld and his discussion of the slain suitors, of whom he declares:

τούσδε δὲ μοῖρ' ἐδάμασσε θεῶν καὶ σχέτλια ἔργα·
οὔ τινα γὰρ τίεσκον ἐπιχθονίων ἀνθρώπων,
οὐ κακὸν οὐδὲ μὲν ἐσθλόν, ὅτίς σφεας εἰσαφίκοιτο·
τῷ καὶ ἀτασθαλίῃσιν ἀεικέα πότμον ἐπέσπον.

> These men here has the fate of the gods destroyed and their own reckless deeds, for they honored no one of men upon the earth, were he evil or good, whosoever came among them; wherefore by their wanton folly they brought on themselves a shameful death. (Homer, *Od.* 22.413–416, Murray)

Of note is the near verbal agreement with fragment 7.2, κακὸς οὐδὲ μὲν ἐσθλός, which differs only in the inflected endings. Although not noted by Pummer and Roussel, this phrase appears three other times in Homer's work (*Il.* 9.319; *Od.* 8.553; 23.66), making it a recognizable Homeric phrase. The strength of this connection is limited, as it is only four words and there is a reasonably strong collocation between κακός and ἐσθλός in Greek literature.[59] More importantly, the narrative context of *Od.* 22 provides a strong parallel to the Shechem massacre, namely the god-justified destruction of a group of people because they failed to honor people on earth. This aligns well with the perspective offered by Theodotus, that God sanctioned the destruction of the Shechemites because of their impious attitude.[60]

Theodotus uses classical Greek literary practices, but draws on Genesis for the topic of his epic. The extant fragments focus on Jacob's life and family

58 Pummer and Roussel, "Note," 181.

59 On the other hand, according to a TLG search, prior to Theodotus, only Homer used this particular construction.

60 For the pairing of Homer, *Od.* 9.215, with Theodotus, fr. 7.3, see Y. Gutman, *The Beginnings of Jewish-Hellenistic Literature* (in Hebrew) (Jerusalem: Mosad Byaliķ, 1958), 258.

(Gen 29–30) and the rape of Dinah by Shechem (Gen 34), and although the main story arc is consistent, the account in Theodotus differs from Genesis in significant aspects. First, the summary of Theodotus' narrative (*Praep. ev.* 9.22.9b) claims that God prompted the actions of Simeon and Levi (cf. T. Levi 5.3–5), whereas the biblical text is silent on this point (though their actions are condemned later; cf. Gen 49:5–7). This dissimilarity is associated with the second divergence, namely the allegation that the Shechemites were "ungodly" (ἀσεβεῖς) and so were deserving of punishment (*Praep. ev.* 9.22.9b; cf. Philo, *Mut.* 200; Jdt 9:2–4).[61] As a result, Jacob does not castigate Simeon and Levi in Theodotus' narrative, nor could he have if the action was sanctioned and inspired by God (cf. Jub. 30:17; Josephus, *Ant.* 1.341). Overall, the destruction of Shechem and its inhabitants is presented in a far more positive light than that depicted in the biblical account.

The second deviation from Gen 34 is the omission of Shechemite circumcision. Although the text describes Jacob and his sons urging the people of Shechem to be circumcised, there is no explicit recounting of this event in the surviving narrative. It is possible that it was simply omitted by Polyhistor or Eusebius (rather than by Theodotus); however, the acceptance of circumcision might also have been problematic in light of the subsequent massacre, and its omission might be due to the author's desire to present the patriarchs positively.[62] This tension is witnessed in other Jewish texts (cf. Josephus, *Ant.* 1.340–41; Philo, *Migr.* 224; Ps.-Philo, LAB 8.7), suggesting that Theodotus was not alone in making these changes, but that he constructed his narrative with sensitivity to his potential readers and an awareness of wider Jewish interpretive practices.

Regarding the similarities to the Genesis story, it is difficult to produce evidence that Theodotus made use of the LXX. As mentioned above, a majority of Theodotus' distinctive vocabulary is not found in the LXX, which implies that it was not a literary model, but does not prove that the Septuagint was not a narrative source. Theodotus' use of different orthographic representations to distinguish Shechem (the person) from Shechem (the place) parallels a similar practice in the LXX.[63] Whether this shows septuagintal influence, rather than a wider Jewish method of writing, is unclear.

That Theodotus used a Jewish story for his epic is important, not only because it is the primary reason for positing a Jewish/Samaritan writer, but also

61 Certain texts express that Levi saw (prophetically) that God had condemned the city and so acted accordingly. Cf. T. Levi 6.8; JA 23.2, 8, 14.

62 Pummer, "Genesis 34," 180.

63 Holladay, *Fragments: Poets*, 129–30. This differentiation is not inherent to the Hebrew (שכם).

because it models the joining of Jewish cultural perspective with Greek literary practice. This amalgamation has led Collins to claim, "The work is a striking instance of the fusion of a Greek form with an exclusive view of the Hebraic tradition. The epic form here could scarcely be intended to appeal to Gentiles."[64] Although I agree with Collins' first sentence, the last sentence is puzzling. First, the selection of Homeric meter and vocabulary indicates that Theodotus wrote for an educated audience, a majority of which at the time of writing would have been non-Jews. Second, and most importantly, we know that the poem was appealing to at least one gentile, Alexander Polyhistor.

Overall, Theodotus provides a strong example of a Jewish writer who was well versed in Greek literature and was able to write in hexameter, employ Homeric vocabulary and syntax, and enrobe a Jewish narrative in Greek literary garb.[65] It appears that there was no tension for Theodotus in his joint knowledge of Greek and Jewish culture and his uniting of them in the creation of his epic poem. Rather, the poem displays a willingness to present Jewish ideas in Greek form as well as to accommodate Greek literary practice and thought. The poem is also strongly rooted in Judaism and presents that culture in a way that was sensitive to Greek literary preferences in a genre that was respected in the Hellenistic era.

Sosates

A third Hellenistic Jewish epic writer, Sosates—said to have been known as the "Jewish Homer"—is attested in *Excerpta Latina Barbari* (or *Chronographia Scaligeriana*), an early medieval source:

> *Post hunc autem regnauit in Aegypto nouus Dionisus annos XXVIIII. Fiunt simul anni V milia CCCCVIIII. Fuit autem in Hierusalem princeps sacerdotum Simon annos VIII et Iohannis annos XX. Hisdem temporibus Sosates cognoscebatur ille Ebraicus Omirus in Alexandria* (ll. 24–29).

> After him [Ptolemy IX Soter II Lathyros] Neos Dionysos [i.e., Ptolemy XII Auletes] reigned over Egypt for twenty-nine years [80–51 BCE]. Together [from the creation] there are 5,409 years. In Jerusalem, Simon was high priest for eight years and John for twenty years. At this same time Sosates, the Jewish Homer, flourished in Alexandria.[66]

64 Collins, *Athens*, 60.

65 For Jewish themes, see, e.g., the importance of purity in the Hebrew race, fr. 4; the role of God in dispensing judgment, fr. 7.

66 Translation and text from C. Frick, ed., *Chronica Minora: Collegit et Emendavit* (Leipzig: Teubner, 1892), 278; S. J. D. Cohen, "Sosates, the Jewish Homer," *HTR* 74 (1981): 391.

Nothing of Sosates' work survives; however, the brief reference to him above provides important insights. In addition to his name, Sosates, we are told that he was well known (*cognoscebatur*) during the reign of Ptolemy Neos Dionysus (80–51 BCE) and/or the high priesthood of Simon and John (142–104 BCE), he resided in Alexandria, and he wrote a literary work that allowed for a comparison between him and Homer.

The main problem with the discussion of Sosates is the incompatibility of the dates.[67] The best attempt to reconcile this problem is by Shaye Cohen, who identifies the likely reasons for this confusion and proposes three possible ways that the reference to Sosates gained access to the *Excerpta Latina Barbari* narrative portion. According to Cohen, the most probable scenario is that the list of high priests included Sosates under the reign of Simon and John Hyrcanus, rather than with the Ptolemaic king list, and the chronological discrepancy arose when the two lists were combined. If this is the case, Sosates was a (near) contemporary to the litterateurs discussed above.[68] Recently, this theory has been challenged by R. W. Burgess, who argues that the Sosates was originally dated according to the list of Ptolemaic kings and so he must have lived in Alexander between roughly 80 and 51 BCE. [69] This date also provides a reasonable answer to why Sosates was not included in the writings of Alexander Polyhistor, as he lived and wrote in a later era. Both options are plausible, with little to commend one over the other.

Cohen tentatively speculates that Sosates is associated with Homer because he wrote "a Homeric epic celebrating the Maccabean conquest."[70] Other scholars have proposed that Sosates wrote a Homeric summary of biblical history or that he may have been the writer behind Pseudo-Phocylides (see chapter 4).[71] Although intriguing, all discussion of Sosates' work is speculative. Of importance for this study is the meaning behind the reference to Homer: is this name meant to symbolize the type of work Sosates wrote (i.e., epic), the meter of the work (i.e., hexameter), the quality/importance of the work (i.e., he was the pinnacular example), or his chronological priority (i.e., he was the first Jewish writer to adopt the epic/epyllion form)? These questions are not mutually exclusive, and all have the potential to be invoked when comparing someone to Homer. Assigning a Homeric epithet to a Jewish writer provides insight

67 Schürer, *History*, 3.1.559 n. 74; Fraser, *Ptolemaic Alexandria*, 1.986–87; R. W. Burgess, "Another Look at Sosates, the 'Jewish Homer,'" *JSJ* 44 (2013): 195–217.

68 Cohen, "Sosates," 395–96.

69 Burgess, "Another Look at Sosates," 207–8.

70 Cohen, "Sosates," 396.

71 For the former suggestion, see Wachsmuth *apud* Frick, *Chronica Minora*, 278. For the latter, see A. Schoene, "Eusebi Chronicorum libri duo," in *Göttingische gelehrte Anzeigen* (Göttingen: Dieterichschen, 1875), 1501–2.

into how the work was received by later readers (though not into how Sosates viewed himself). Not only does it speak to the wide knowledge of Homer and his importance in Greek literature, but it also suggests that at least some Jewish writers were being compared to Greek writers. I would argue that it is a favorable comparison; someone thought Sosates' work was of a similar genre and of sufficient quality in order to be worthy of comparison with Homer.[72] Regardless, the comparison between Jewish and Greek writers reinforces the idea that these literary groups were not isolated, but that Jews were actively engaged in writing Greek literature in ways that encouraged reading a Jewish work in light of Greek predecessors and prototypes.

Reevaluation of Genre Participation: Epic or Epyllion?

The majority of scholars classify Philo and Theodotus poems as epics. One of the major challenges to this classification is the fact that we only have a few lines of text and therefore do not know the original size and scope of each work. As a result, we are dependent on Eusebius, who, in his introduction to the different fragments of Philo, identifies which book the passage came from (*Praep. ev.* 9.20.1; 9.37.1). Of these statements, the most interesting is the claim that fragment 3 comes from book 14 of *On Jerusalem* (*Praep. ev.* 9.24.1). Many scholars think it unlikely that Philo's work was this large and so amend "fourteen" to read either "one" or "four."[73] Epics, almost by definition, are large works and so would occupy multiple books. By having to state that certain material came from a specific book (e.g., book 1), Eusebius implies that the work consisted of multiple books and so likely fit the typical range of Hellenistic epic.[74]

Half of our extant fragments (frs. 3–5) provide a description of Jerusalem, specifically its pools.[75] If, as the title suggests, the city of Jerusalem is the focus of the work and not the establishment of the Jewish people, this signals another important difference between Philo and ancient epics, which often recounted the deeds of a person or group of people. Even in Virgil's *Aeneid*, in which the founding of Rome is an important theme, there is no extended description of the future city with established waterworks or buildings. The description of the (presumably) contemporary city by Philo deviates from the established

72 See also the favorable comparison of Jewish writers and the Greek models by Jerome (*Epist.* 22.35.2): "Philo, Plato's imitator and also by Josephus, the Greek Livy." See also the Halicarnassus inscription that identifies Herodotus as the "prose Homer"; H. Lloyd-Jones, "The Pride of Halicarnassus," *ZPE* 124 (1999): 1–14.

73 Freudenthal, *Alexander Polyhistor*, 1.100; Gutman, "Philo," 38. For scholars who affirm the reading of fourteen, see Walter, "Epik," 140–41, 150; Mras, GCS 43.1, 517.

74 For example, Apollonius' *Argonautica* is divided into four (large) books.

75 Exactly what Philo is referring to is debated. For a detailed description of the options and their proponents, see Holladay, *Fragments: Poets*, 272–78.

pattern of focusing on the ancient past. Scenes such as the depiction of Aeneas' shield (*Aen.* 8.626–731) provide glimpses into the narrative's future (i.e., the author's present), but this is a small portion of the work and focuses on people and events rather than buildings and infrastructure. The emphasis on a city might be a Jewish adaptation of the Greek epic model. The city of Jerusalem, especially the Temple, was at the heart of Jewish cultural identity and the center of their religious traditions. Philo also included aspects of the Abraham and Joseph narratives, which indicates that Jerusalem was not the sole focus, though it may have been the climax of the poem and the ultimate topic to which all other people and narratives were subordinated. Overall, Philo's epic fits the broad contours of the Hellenistic genre (size, meter, grandness, etc.), but may indicate a Jewish adaptation of the genre by having a city as the prominent focus.

Philo's participation in the genre of epic indicates his active involvement in cultural negotiation. In the Hellenistic era, epic writing had a new, self-conscious purpose. Rather than seeking primarily to reinvent myth/history, the author positioned himself and his narrative in relation to Homer's and Hesiod's constructs.[76] Most often these authors wrote their country into the epic narratives or co-opted a Homeric character for a founding figure. The most famous example is Virgil's *Aeneid*, but other's works, such as Stasinus' *Cypria* and Arctinus' *Aethiopis*, promote specific people groups by composing epics that incorporate foreign races and individuals into Homer's narrative world.[77] In constructing the Abraham narrative in hexameter, Philo is placing his work among the epics constructed by other minority cultures that seek to carve out space for themselves and their ethnic group within the sphere of Greek literary culture. Philo, however, constructs his epic from Jewish narratives and avoids reference to Homer's world. This is an essential point of deviation from the contested space of mythology, in which foreign cultures were included into the wider Greek (i.e., Homeric) worldview. Philo's avoidance of Greek mythology likely indicates an implicit rejection of this foundational narrative and the attempt to establish a new one on Jewish terms. This selection makes a powerful statement, signaling the author's commitment to his heritage and the importance of his ethnic group in comparison to those of the Greeks and other peoples.

76 Whitmarsh, *Beyond*, 229.

77 There is only one example of a Jewish character being written into the epic narrative: "Letters were brought from Priam to Tautanes, King of the Assyrians, and to David, King of Jerusalem, asking for help [in resisting the Greek force]. David refused, but Tautanes sent Tithonus and Memnon with a large force" (Dictus of Crete, *FGrH* 49 F6). The exact purpose of this fragment is uncertain, though it is telling that the Jews are said to have declined Priam's petition, thus removing any potential claim to the narratives of Greek mythology.

In contrast to Philo, Eusebius does not reference which book Theodotus' fragments came from, but introduces each new snippet by stating, "further down" (ὑποβάς) or "later" (ὕστερον). In light of Eusebius' practice of mentioning book locations, the omission of any reference to books when discussing Theodotus' poem is notable and may indicate that the work was only one volume long. As a one-volume work does not align with the length expectations of epic works, I suggest that Theodotus' *On the Jews* may be fruitfully understood through the lens of epyllion.[78]

As far as we know, Alexandrian epics did not reach the lengths of their Homeric predecessors.[79] In addition to longer works (e.g., Apollonius, *Argonautica*), there emerged a trend of writing shorter poems (*brachylogia*), which scholars (with some support from later Greek writers) have labeled epyllia.[80] These works are typically signaled by two formal features: meter (hexameter) and small size. While the former criterion is widely agreed upon, there is continuing debate among scholars regarding the definition of "small" or "short"; a work might be small when compared to a multivolume history, but that does not mean it is short.[81] The aesthetic of miniature and the compression of ideas into smaller works was a growing practice in Alexandria (e.g., Posidippus), signaling a recognized literary movement.[82] In addition to these

78 Kuhn, *Epiker*, 72.

79 The creation of short hexameter poems indicates a development in poetic genre (cf. Callimachus, *Aet.* 1.1–38). For the view that this was a Hellenistic development, see (most recently) A. M. Wasyl, *Genres Rediscovered: Studies in Latin Miniature Epic, Love Elegy, and Epigram of the Roman-Barbaric Age* (Kraków: Jagiellonian University Press, 2011), 11. For perspective on older origins, see J. S. Burgess, *The Tradition of the Trojan Women and the Epic Cycle* (Baltimore: Johns Hopkins University Press, 2001), 143–48.

80 Athenaeus, *Deipn.* 2.65b; Clement, *Strom.* 3.3.24.2; Aristophanes, *Ach.* 398; *Pax* 532. Cf. E. Wolff, "Quelques précisions sur le mot 'Epyllion,'" *RevPhil* 62 (1988): 299–303. There is substantial debate over the texts that should be considered epyllia. Fantuzzi, for example, has a broad (though not exclusive) list of Greek epyllia: Moiro, *Mnemosyne*; Philitas, *Hermes*, *Telephos*, and *Demeter*; Alexander Aetolus, *Halieus* and *Kirka*; Hedyle, *Skulla*; Simias, *Apollon*; Callimachus, *Hecale*, *Galateia*, and *Gloukus*; Theocritus, *Id.* 13, 18, 22, 24, [25], 26; Nicaenetus, *Lyrkos*; Eratosthenes, *Hermes*, *Anterinys*, and *Erigone*; Moschus, *Europa*; Parthenius, *Anthippe* and *Heracles*. Cf. M. Fantuzzi, "Epyllion," in *BNP* 4.1170–71. To this list some would add select Homeric Hymns.

For this term's developmental history within scholarship, see S. Tilg, "On the Origins of the Modern Term 'Epyllion': Some Revisions to a Chapter in This History of Classical Scholarship," in M. Baumbach and S. Bär, eds., *Brill's Companion to Greek and Latin Epyllion and Its Reception* (Leiden: Brill, 2012), 29–54.

81 E.g., C. U. Merriam, *The Development of the Epyllion Genre through the Hellenistic and Roman Periods* (Studies in Classics 14; Lewiston, N.Y.: Edwin Mellen Press, 2001), 2; A. S. Hollis, "The Hellenistic Epyllion and Its Descendants," in S. F. Johnson, ed., *Greek Literature in Late Antiquity: Dynamism, Didactism, Classicism* (Aldershot: Ashgate, 2006), 142; Fantuzzi and Hunter, *Tradition and Innovation*, 191–96.

82 K. Gutzwiller, "Introduction," in K. Gutzwiller, ed., *The New Posidippus: A Hellenistic Poetry Book* (Oxford: Oxford University Press, 2005), 1–16.

formal features, scholars generally agree that epyllia are typically presented in third-person narration and progress linearly. Topic, in which a specific theme or episode in the life of a mythical figure was recounted, has been proposed as another core feature,[83] but this does not adequately describe the extant texts and so continues to be debated.[84]

One of the major problems scholars face when discussing this genre and with determining prototypical models is the limited number of surviving epyllia. Although some are (at least partially) extant, a number of possible epyllia are little more than titles.[85] The most famous extant epyllion is Callimachus' *Hecale*, a poem that recounts Theseus' stay with Hecale prior to his encounter with the Marathonian bull. Callimachus did not focus on Theseus' heroic deeds (frs. 67–69), but on the humbler scene of his desire to take shelter from the storm and the posthumous honoring of Hecale (frs. 79–83). The conversation between Theseus and Hecale afforded Callimachus the opportunity to introduce stories of Hecale's life (frs. 28–34) and Theseus' birth, childhood, and deeds (frs. 3–10), some of which were not traditionally part of the bull narrative. Compared to Greek epic, Callimachus adopts nonprototypical features, specifically his title and nontraditional focus that highlights the role of a secondary, female character.[86] Although Callimachus employs Homeric meter, vocabulary, and characters, he does not develop the epic in its entirety. Rather, he narrows its scope and highlights the deeds of a minor character. Most important for our discussion is Callimachus' clear awareness of his deviation from epic genre constraints and reader expectations.[87] In *Aet.* 1.1–28, Callimachus laments that ignorant readers (i.e., Telchines) have chastised him for writing short tales rather than one large poem on kings and heroes with many thousands of lines. In rebutting his detractors, Callimachus signals his practice of deviating from preferred, prototypical forms to provide a work that is short in length and on an "ignoble" topic.

83 M. M. Crump, *The Epyllion from Theocritus to Ovid* (Oxford: Blackwell, 1931), 22–23; M. Baumbach and S. Bär, "A Short Introduction to the Ancient Epyllion," in M. Baumbach and S. Bär, eds., *Brill's Companion to Greek and Latin Epyllion and Its Reception* (Leiden: Brill, 2012), ix.

84 For example, Ps.-Homer's *Batrachomyomachia* or Ps.-Virgil's *Culex*, draw on epic motifs and scenes, but undermine them through the use of parody.

85 E.g., Alexander Aetolus, *Fisherman* (Athenaeus, *Deipn.* 7.296e); *Crica* (Athenaeus, *Deipn.* 7.283a); Eratosthenes, *Hermes*; Philitas, *Hermes*. Cf. Fantuzzi, "Epyllion," 4.1170–71; K. Spanoudakis, *Philitas of Cos* (MneSup 229; Leiden: Brill, 2002).

86 A. S. Hollis, ed., *Callimachus, "Hecale": Edited with Introduction and Commentary* (2nd ed.; Oxford: Clarendon, 2009), 6; cf. Merriam, *Epyllion Genre*.

87 This practice of Callimachus is highlighted in the Diegesis to *Ia.* 13 (P.Med. 18 IX 32–38).

One of the most notable aspects of epyllia is their focus on women (i.e., a minor character from the tradition's perspective), thus challenging the traditional (i.e., male) worldview of epic poetry.[88] To be clear, these works are still written almost exclusively by men (although see Moiro, *Mnemosyne*), but by men who are willing to focus on lesser-discussed characters. The content of this new focus, however, does not always revitalize the role of women, as one of the dominant topics of epyllia is the rape/seduction of a virgin or a beautiful woman.[89] For example, Moschus' *Europa* recounts the capture of Europa by Zeus, beginning with a divinely given dream and concluding with her arrival at Crete in Zeus' possession.[90] Related to this theme is the seduction of Aphrodite by Anchises (according to the plan of Zeus) in the *Hymn to Aphrodite*.[91] In this work the author inverts the typical character roles of the male divine seducing/raping the female mortal. The female goddess is the pursuer, and the mortal male, despite being conquered (and in contrast to the typical fate of the human females), retains his autonomy and is rewarded with a son who will carry on his name and bring renown to his family.

Not all epyllia focus on minor characters, as is evidenced in Theocritus' *Id.* 13, 24, and 25, which recount the famous deeds of Heracles.[92] Once again a mythical topic is expanded, although the focus remains on the traditionally dominant character. This selection of Heracles by Theocritus is understandable, as Heracles is a figure of both Greek and Egyptian mythology and so would have been an ideal character for a bicultural audience.[93] The limitation of epyllia to a mythological topic is challenged by Theocritus' *Id.* 17, which is an encomium for King Ptolemy II.[94] However, despite the overarching focus on Ptolemy, there is substantial discussion of divine characters and invocation

88 Cf. Merriam, *Epyllion Genre*; M. Depew, "ἰαμβεῖον καλεῖται νῦν: Genre, Occasion, and Imitation in Callimachus, frr. 191 and 203Pf," *TAPA* 122 (1992): 313–30.

89 Cf. Theocritus, *Id.* 22.137–223. This topic is especially prominent in late antiquity. Cf. Dracontius, *Rape of Helen* (*Rom.* 8); Claudianus, *Rape of Persephone*; Colluthus, *Rape of Helen*.

90 Compare also the five fragments of Philitas' *Demeter*. Prior to Moschus, the author of the Homeric *Hymn to Demeter* (sixth to seventh century BCE) narrated the response of Demeter to the kidnapping and rape of Persephone by Hades in hexameter.

91 On this work's placement on the boundary of genres, see M. Baumbach, "Borderline Experiences with Genre: The Homeric *Hymn to Aphrodite* between Epic, Hymn and Epyllic Poetry," in M. Baumbach and S. Bär, eds., *Brill's Companion to Greek and Latin Epyllion and Its Reception* (Leiden: Brill, 2012), 135–48.

92 Cf. Moschus' *Megara*, a poem on Heracles' wife. Regarding the authorship of *Id.* 25, see A. S. F. Gow, ed. and trans., *Theocritus* (2 vols.; Cambridge: Cambridge University Press, 1950), 2.439–41. Hylas holds an equally prominent place with Heracles in *Id.* 13.

93 S. A. Stephens, *Seeing Double: Intercultural Poetics in Ptolemaic Alexandria* (HCS 37; Berkeley: University of California Press, 2003), 26–27, 131–32.

94 Pancrates' *Hadrian* is on a (living) contemporary figure.

of mythical themes and events. *Id.* 22 challenges the constraint to a singular focus, as it explicitly focuses on two characters: Castor and Polydeuces. This twin focus is understandable in light of the regular literary pairing of these brothers. Variation from the pattern of centering on one minor character indicates genre diversity, suggesting that topic is not the defining formal feature, that rigid divisions do not exist in this genre classification, and that non-prototypical expressions could be produced. Indeed, as discussed in chapter 1, genres rarely (if ever) have fixed features, and compositional flexibility is necessary in a genre, especially when it is emerging.

An important aspect of the epyllion genre is the assumption the author makes about the reader; these works are written for people who are already familiar with the narrative or myth from which they come (e.g., Theodotus, *Id.* 22.27, begins the narrative proper in midstory). One way this is evidenced is that a majority of epyllia do not introduce characters, but assume the reader is already familiar with them. This assumed knowledge allows the author to jump from scene to scene without transitions, placing the burden of knowledge on the reader (e.g., Theocritus, *Id.* 25, 26; Ps.-Virgil, *Ciris*). These practices indicate that the authors were writing for insiders and not outsiders who lacked Greek education or knowledge of cultural history. This is not to say that all epyllia are like this, as some (e.g., Moschus, *Europa*) have minimal narrative gaps. Rather, this practice indicates that cohesion of narrative is not a dominant feature of this genre. The brevity of the poem, which is often taken from a wider narrative, blurs the boundaries between closure and continuation, further encouraging the knowledgeable reader to go beyond the confines of the text.[95] What is common in nearly all extant epyllia is the addition of new material into known narratives. Space for this narrative expansion is provided though the adoption of a new perspective or focus (e.g., the focus on a minor character) and is often supplied by the characters' reported speech. This novel material is often in dialogue with the established perspective of Homer and traditional myths. As a result, we find that the function of epyllia is typically in tension with that of epic. The rejection of the size and scope of epic allows for the focus on a specific scene, which, once taken from its original context, can be adapted to say something new, different, or even contrary to the original epic. This recontextualization can then be used to promote a particular person, voice, or perspective, depending on the author's literary aim.

Overall, few core genre features distinguish epyllia: epyllia needed to have been composed in hexameter and be small in size.[96] Beyond these require-

95 For examples see Fantuzzi and Hunter, *Tradition and Innovation*, 215–24.

96 For a discussion of size range and possible differences arising over time, see Hollis, "Hellenistic Epyllion," 143–44; Fantuzzi and Hunter, *Tradition and Innovation*, 193–95.

ments there are recurring topics and emphases, although none of these are constitutive or essential for the genre.[97] First, the epyllion's topic and characters are heroic and typically drawn from the mythological past (often that described by Homer), but brought into contact with the everyday and the intimate. Second, the focus of the work is frequently on secondary, female characters within the tradition. Third, epyllia are structured on a single episode within a larger narrative, although the cohesion of this episode is variable and sometimes includes portions from other narratives. Some of these formal features overlap with epic, but overall epic and epyllia have distinguishable characteristics (e.g., size, scope, function, etc.).

We have focused on Greek epyllia written in the Hellenistic era. As is evidenced in both later Greek and Latin epyllia, this genre was flexible and allowed for authorial adaptation, likely facilitated by the limited number of requisite formal features needed to define the genre.[98] This in turn becomes one of the core features of the genre; epyllia are flexible and have the ability to incorporate and accommodate a range of formal features. This is not to imply that there are no boundaries, as meter appears to be fixed and size is relatively consistent. Rather, this loose framework afforded Hellenistic authors the opportunity to adapt the genre to their particular need and is a great example of genre fluidity.

Theodotus' poem has strong parallels with epyllia. First, *On the Jews* is written in hexameter and, so far as we can tell, is short. Second, the characters of the work are drawn from the distant past and are part of the Jewish people's founding narrative. Third, one of the central events in the narrative is the rape of a virgin (i.e., Dinah, frs. 4, 6–8), a common theme in Hellenistic and Roman epyllia. Similarly, the opening lines of fragment 1, which discuss the city of Shechem and the land around it (e.g., goats, fertile land, etc.), are also regularly found in Hellenistic epyllia modeled on Homer's epics.[99] Finally, the narrative cohesion of the work appears to be fairly stable, though there is at least one aside to indicate the Abrahamic origin of the practice of circumcision (fr. 5).

The interpretive payoff of viewing Theodotus' work as participating in epyllion is threefold. First, there is a difference in function between epics and epyllia. Epics seek to establish a narrative, whereas an epyllion provides a reinterpretation of an established narrative. In Theodotus' poem, Simeon and Levi's actions are said to be God-sanctioned, an affirmation that was lacking in the

97 Cf. I. Petrovic, "Rhapsodic Hymns and Epyllia," in M. Baumbach and S. Bär, eds., *Brill's Companion to Greek and Latin Epyllion and Its Reception* (Leiden: Brill, 2012), 169–70.

98 Hollis, "Hellenistic Epyllion," 141; cf. Wasyl, *Genres Rediscovered*, 20–22.

99 E.g., Theocritus' *Id.* 17.77–85 (which discusses the land of Egypt and the number of cities within it); *Id.* 25.85–152 (which discusses the plentiful livestock of King Augeas). Cf. Kuhn, *Epiker*, 56; Whitmarsh, *Beyond*, 244.

Genesis narrative. Second, this reading would reinforce the theory that Theodotus was writing for an audience who was already familiar with the Jacob account. This further implies that Theodotus was sufficiently knowledgeable of Jewish Scripture and its theological interpretations so as to provide a new rendering of the story. Third, if Theodotus was writing for insiders, his use of hexameter indicates that a sufficient number of Jewish people were highly educated to justify the creation of this text.

Conclusion

Each author in this chapter displays a high level of education and knowledge of Greek epic poetry. For Sosates, this is implied by his association with Homer, whereas for Philo and Theodotus it is seen in their use of hexameter and Homeric vocabulary and morphology. Reopening the question of genre provides a new interpretive framework by which to read these Jewish poems, reinforcing our understanding of Jewish authors' interaction with Greek literary culture. As both epic and epyllion are high-level literary forms, both genre options affirm the view that Jewish authors participated in dominant literary models in service of specific ethnic goals.[100] The use of hexameter to recount the Genesis narrative and bring renown to the Jewish capital provides an opportunity for cultural negotiation in which a "subordinate" culture could employ the dominant culture's literary models for its own culture's benefit. What we see in Philo's *On Jerusalem* is the melding of Greek and Jewish elements so that Jewish culture is presented in a way that is both palatable to Greek literary tastes and expressive of Jewish cultural sophistication. Such endeavors were not limited to Philo, but are exhibited by contemporary authors in surrounding cultures, suggesting that Philo was partaking of a widely accepted literary enterprise. Theodotus' participation in epyllion also affirms Jewish engagement with Greek literary models, specifically one that was becoming more popular.

In addition to their clear knowledge of Homer, both Philo and Theodotus made use of narratives found in Genesis, but there is no firm evidence that either used the LXX as a source. Verbal overlap between the LXX and Philo and Theodotus is lacking, and no distinctive LXX content is found in these authors' poems. As a result, claims that they used the LXX overstate the evidence. Because both Philo and Theodotus write in Greek, it is likely that they would

100 Gutman ("Philo," 43–53) argues that the language used by the epic Philo indicates his desire to influence "the Orphic world and its kindred currents" (p. 53). His argument, however, is unconvincing in that it places too much interpretive weight on a few lexical items and interprets these terms in light of their use by other later philosophical writers (Philo of Alexandria, Proclus).

have used a Greek source for their compositions. However, the claim of LXX use is based on this assumption and lacks firm evidence.

Overall, Philo and Theodotus are examples of Jewish authors who present ethnic narratives in Greek literary garb. In actively engaging Greek literary culture, they indicate that some Jews willingly participated in the literary forms of the dominant culture. It is worth mentioning here (although a fuller discussion will be reserved for chapter 9) that the few instances of Jewish authors adopting the genre of epic/epyllion occur earlier in the Hellenistic era. This may indicate that these genres lost favor among Jewish authors and/or readers, or it may be a result of changes in Jewish educational practices, in which texts other than Homer's epics became the primary didactic model.

3

Other Jewish-Greek Poets

In the previous chapter, we looked at Hellenistic-era Jewish poets who crafted epics and epyllia from biblical material. These authors exhibited high attainment of Greek literary culture through their familiarity with Homer and other Greek writers, which they used to reinterpret Jewish narrative. In this chapter we will continue to look at Jewish poets writing in Greek, focusing on Ezekiel the Tragedian, Pseudo-Orpheus, the Sibylline Oracles, and the fragments of pseudo-Greek poets. These authors display substantial knowledge of Greek composition practice through their ability to mimic the style and vocabulary of specific writers. Regarding their participation in Greek genres, some authors appear to pursue nonprototypical examples, whereas others adhere closely to established models, especially when adopting the persona of an established Greek author.

Ezekiel the Tragedian

Tragedy was an important genre in Hellenistic times. However, despite this popularity, Ezekiel's *Exagoge* is the only substantially extant representative of the genre between the last plays attributed to Euripides and Lucian's paratragedy *Podagra*.[1] Many tragedians are known to us from this time, including a pleiad of tragic poets operating in Alexandria, although only fragments of their works survive.[2] The 269 preserved lines of *Exagoge* retell the narrative

1 Lycophron's *Alexandra* is another potential candidate, although it is a monologue in iambic trimeter. See also the fragment of a historical tragedy on Gyges and Candaules in P.Oxy. XXIII 2382. Ezekiel likely wrote more than one tragedy, as is evidenced by Clement of Alexandria (*Strom.* 1.23.155–156, ὁ τῶν Ἰουδαϊκῶν τραγῳδιῶν ποιητής) and Eusebius (*Praep. ev.* 9.28.1, ὁ τῶν τραγῳδιῶν ποιητής).

2 Cf. Strabo, *Geogr.* 14.5.15. There are five different lists of "pleiads," not all of which are exclusively tragic. See the discussion in Fraser, *Ptolemaic Alexandria*, 1.619–20, 2.871–73; S. A. Stephens, *The Poets of Alexandria* (London: I. B. Tauris, 2018), 18–23. For another list of

of Exod 1–15, including the birth and early life of Moses, his vision and marriage to Sepphora, the plagues, the deliverance of Hebrew people from Egypt, the destruction of Pharaoh's army in the Red Sea, the arrival of the Hebrews at Elim, and the appearance of the phoenix.[3]

The exact dating of the play is difficult to determine, although a range of dates is possible to identify. The author's use of an LXX version indicates a date after the initial translation, while his inclusion in Alexander Polyhistor's *Concerning the Jews* provides the work's *terminus ante quem*. Within this range almost every possible date has been proposed by scholars, although a second century BCE date is most likely.[4] Less divisive is the discussion of provenance. Although there is little firm evidence, most scholars suggest that Ezekiel resided in Alexandria.[5] A recently published fragment of *Exagoge* from Oxyrhynchus containing an extract from Clement's version (P.Oxy. LXXXIII 5348) does not assist in determining provenance, but shows that this text was being read and used in Egypt around the third to fourth centuries CE.[6]

---

tragedians, some of whom were previously unknown, see P. Teb. III 695. For the most recent discussion of the fragments and translation into English, see A. Kotlińska-Toma, *Hellenistic Tragedy: Texts, Translations and a Critical Survey* (BCSM; London: Bloomsbury, 2015).

3 We are indebted to Eusebius and Clement of Alexandria (along with Pseudo-Eustathius) and their dependence on Alexander Polyhistor for our 269 lines of text. I side with Jacobson and others that the fragments come from a single play rather than a tetralogy (so Kohn). T. D. Kohn, "The Tragedies of Ezekiel," *GRBS* 43 (2002/3): 5–12; H. Jacobson, "Ezekiel's *Exagoge*, One Play or Four?" *GRBS* 43 (2002/3): 391–96. For a thorough discussion of the manuscript and transmission history, see P. Lanfranchi, *L'Exagoge d'Ezéchiel le Tragique: Introduction, texte, traduction et commentaire* (SVTP 21; Leiden: Brill, 2006), 73–99.

The "additions" to the Exodus narrative have been discussed in many articles and do not need to be rehearsed here. Cf. J. Heath, "Ezekiel Tragicus and Hellenistic Visuality: The Phoenix at Elim," *JTS* 57 (2006): 23–41; P. Lanfranchi, "Il sogno di Mose nell'exagoge di Ezechiele il Tragico," *Materia giudaica* 8 (2003): 105–12; P. W. van der Horst, "Moses' Throne Vision in Ezekiel the Dramatist," *JJS* 34 (1983): 21–29; Collins, *Athens*, 226–29; M. R. Niehoff, "The Phoenix in Rabbinic Literature," *HTR* 89 (1996): 245–65. For the view of recounting important offstage events onstage, especially horrific incidences, see Horace, *Ars* 179–188.

4 For a helpful discussion with references and critiques, see H. Jacobson, *The Exagoge of Ezekiel* (Cambridge: Cambridge University Press, 1983), 5–13; Holladay, *Fragments: Poets*, 311; Lanfranchi, *L'Exagoge*, 10. For a more thorough history of research, see Lanfranchi, *L'Exagoge*, 299–337.

5 E.g., J. Wieneke, ed., *Ezechielis Iudaei poetae Alexandrini fabulae quae inscribitur Ἐξαγωγή fragmenta* (Münster: Aschendorff, 1931). For a larger discussion, see Jacobson, *Exagoge*, 13–17; N. L. Collins, "Ezekiel, the Author of the *Exagoge*: His Calendar and Home," *JSJ* 22 (1991): 201–11. Some have challenged this geographic attribution, although again with little additional support. For example, Kuiper asserts a Samarian origin, whereas Gutman suggests Cyrene. K. Kuiper, "Le poète juif Ezéchiel," *REJ* 46 (1903): 174; Gutman, *Beginnings*, 66–69.

6 D. Colomo and D. Obbink, eds., "P.Oxy. 5348, Ezekiel Ἐξαγωγή," in P. J. Parsons and N. Gonis, eds., *The Oxyrhynchus Papyri LXXXIII* (London: Egypt Exploration Society, 2018), 14–19. For Philo's knowledge of the *Exagoge*, see G. E. Sterling, "From the Thick Marshes of the Nile to the Throne of God: Moses in Ezekiel the Tragedian and Philo of Alexandria," *SPhiloA* 26 (2014): 115–33.

Ezekiel, having written in trimeter, was strongly influenced by the pinnacular models of Greek tragedy: Aeschylus, Sophocles, and Euripides.[7] This recognition has been affirmed through numerous studies, with some scholars identifying specific plays that may have been prototypical models for Ezekiel.[8] For instance, a number of similarities in characterization, themes, motifs, grammar, and vocabulary exist between Ezekiel's *Exagoge* and Sophocles' *Oedipus coloneus*.[9] Although the number of parallels is suggestive, identifying the *Oedipus coloneus* as a specific model or template for Ezekiel goes beyond the evidence, nor is such a relationship necessary for recognizing Ezekiel's close relationship with classical tragedy.[10]

Unlike the works of the Jewish epic poets in chapter 2, in which we found little evidence of LXX influence, Ezekiel's *Exagoge* displays many linguistic and syntactic parallels, implying that Ezekiel recast an LXX translation of Exodus for his poetic work.[11] Of importance are the places where Ezekiel appears to follow the LXX over our extant Hebrew text. One example is *Exag.* 232 in which the wheels of the chariot refuse to turn (τροχοί οὐκ

7 Scholars differ on the quality of Ezekiel's poetry. Schürer (*History*, 3.1.565) asserts, "The Author's poetry is quite prosaic" and "the diction and versification are tolerably fluent." In recent studies there has been a greater acceptance of Ezekiel's poetic skill. Cf. Fraser, *Ptolemaic Alexandria*, 1.708.

8 Kuiper and Wieneke argue that Ezekiel drew heavily on Euripides for his vocabulary and phrasing (Kuiper, "Ezéchiel," 48–73, 161–77; Wieneke, *Ezechielis, passim*), and Jacobson offers Aeschylus' *Persae* and lost *Danaides* trilogy as well as Sophocles' *Oedipus coloneus* as thematic comparators. H. Jacobson, "Two Studies on Ezekiel the Tragedian," *GRBS* 22 (1981): 175–78; Jacobson, *Exagoge*, 23–28; B. Snell, *Szenen aus griechischen Dramen* (Berlin: De Gruyter, 1971), 176, also adduces Ezekiel's use of *Persae*.

9 E.g., both Moses and Oedipus are presented as murderers and wanderers (*Exag.* 45, 58; *Oed. col.* 124), and both bring help to specific nations (Jews: *Exag.* 107; Athenians: *Oed. col.* 1533). Also evident are potential similarities in religious rituals (Passover: *Exag.* 175–192; purification: *Oed. col.* 469–492) and the presentation of idyllic locations (Elim: *Exag.* 243–253; Coloneus: *Oed. col.* 668–693). There are also grammatical similarities: infinitive functioning as an imperative (*Exag.* 186; *Oed. col.* 477, 481, 484) and abundance of participles to delineate the actions of the performers (e.g., *Exag.* 172, 175, 179, 180, 182, 185, *Oed. col.* 470, 475, 477, 484). For a collection of studies on the how performance influences composition and the concept of genre, see L. Edmunds and R. W. Wallace, eds., *Poet, Public, and Performance in Ancient Greece* (Baltimore: Johns Hopkins University Press, 1997). See also W. Rösler, *Dichter und Gruppe: Eine Untersuchung zu den Bedingungen und zur historischen Funktion früher griechischer Lyrik am Beispiel Alkaios* (Theorie und Geschichte der Literatur und der schönen Künste 50; Munich: Fink, 1980).

10 Cf. R. B. Davies, "Reading Ezekiel's *Exagoge*: Tragedy, Sacrificial Ritual, and the Midrashic Tradition," *GRBS* 48 (2008): 394; E. J. Stewart, "Ezekiel's *Exagoge*: A Typical Hellenistic Tragedy?" *GRBS* 58 (2018): 223–52.

11 The foundational study is L. M. Philippson, *Ezechiel des jüdischen Trauerspieldichters Auszug aus Egypten und Philo des aelteren Jerusalem* (Berlin, 1830), 50–52. More examples are offered by Wieneke (*Ezechielis*, 2–26), Holladay (*Fragments: Poets*, 406–529), and E. Vogt ("Tragiker Ezechiel," in *JSHRZ* 4.3, 121–33).

ἐστρέφοντο), paralleling the Greek text of Exod 14:25 (συνέδησεν) as opposed to the Hebrew (ויסר). Similarly, both Ezekiel and LXX Exodus omit the reference to leprosy in Exod 4:6 and *Exag.* 130. Ezekiel differs from the LXX on occasion, most notably in his claim that seventy people came with Jacob to Egypt (*Exag.* 2, also found in the MT) rather than the seventy-five of LXX Exod 1:5.[12] Few would argue that Ezekiel knew Hebrew or was dependent on a Hebrew text, which implies that Ezekiel used a Greek translation of the Torah that is no longer extant.[13]

In light of Ezekiel's imitation of Greek tragic verse and his use of Exodus, some scholars have proposed that the *Exagoge* is midrash or "midrashic drama."[14] Neither of these labels, however, is sufficiently developed to describe adequately the *Exagoge* and the restructuring of a Jewish narrative through participation in a Greek genre. Davies and Jacobson are likely implying a less formal type of midrash (e.g., "implicit midrash") that naturally occurs when the Jewish Scriptures are reworked, but such a definition loses its interpretive power, as almost all poetic works that are based on Jewish narratives could be classified as midrash.[15] Important for this study is the movement beyond a strict comparison of the *Exagoge* with Greek tragedy and Jewish Scripture in order to understand how the mutual participation of these two elements influenced the creation of Ezekiel's poem. Ezekiel does not simply appropriate Greek tragedy whole cloth, but adapts it. Likewise, Ezekiel does not simply retell the Exodus story, but shapes the material to his selected genre and audience.[16] As a result, Ezekiel's participation in tragedy—a literary form as-

12 Gutman, *Beginnings*, 32; Snell, *Szenen*, 185. Cf. van der Horst, "Interpretation of the Bible," 521–25.

13 Jacobson, *Exagoge*, 40–47.

14 Jacobson, *Exagoge*, 26; Davies, "Reading," 411–14. Davies defines midrash as "exegetic storytelling," while Jacobson fails to explain his phrase.

15 E. E. Ellis, "Biblical Interpretation in the New Testament Church," in M. J. Mulder, ed., *Mikra: Text, Translation, Reading and Interpretation of the Hebrew Bible in Ancient Judaism and Early Christianity* (CRINT 2.1; Philadelphia: Fortress, 1988), 702–6. The *Exagoge* does not exhibit "rigorous study and painstaking, searching inquiry into the verses of the Bible," as is one definition of midrash, nor does it demonstrate the exegetical techniques exhibited by Greek scholars. Cf. M. D. Herr, "Midrash," in M. Berenbaum and F. Skolnik, eds., *Encyclopaedia Judaica* (2nd ed.; Detroit: Macmillan Reference, 2007), 14.182–85. Although scholars agree that Ezekiel drew his material from the book of Exodus, they disagree on his faithfulness to the text. Faithful: Gutman, *Beginnings*, 16; Fraser, *Ptolemaic Alexandria*, 1.708. Unfaithful: K. Ziegler, "Tragoedia," *PW* 6A.2 (1937): 1979–80; C. Kraus, "Ezechiele Poeta Tragico," *RFIC* 96 (1968): 173.

16 Scholars debate the intended audience. Jewish: Schürer, *History*, 3.1.565; M. Hadas, *Hellenistic Culture: Fusion and Diffusion* (New York: Columbia University Press, 1959), 100; Vogt, "Tragiker Ezechiel," 117; Lanfranchi, *L'Exagoge*, 58; Davies, "Reading," 399. Non-Jewish: Philippson, *Ezechiel*, 14–16; Holladay, *Fragments: Poets*, 303; Ziegler, "Tragoedia," 1981. Both: Gutman, *Beginnings*, 69; K. Kuiper, "De Ezechiele poeta Judaeo," *Mnemosyne* 28 (1900): 280; Jacobson, *Exagoge*, 17–18; Jacobson, "Two Studies," 171; Kraus, "Ezechiele," 175.

sociated with the dominant culture—becomes a powerful way of negotiating contemporary Jewish concerns.

The play as a whole, although adopting the form of Greek tragedy, does not adhere to all of the genre's characteristic features, but subordinates some of them to accommodate the subject matter.[17] Ezekiel follows prototypical examples by employing iambic trimeter (the meter commonly used in classical Greek tragedies),[18] using dialogue,[19] emphasizing travel and exile,[20] and appearing to create different "acts" (although specific divisions are not mentioned).[21] Two elements of his work are thought to differ from prescribed, although not always followed, features of classical tragedy: (1) the action is to be situated in one (general) locale, and (2) the work is not to exceed a twenty-four-hour time period (or close to it).[22] Ezekiel's variations do not stem from ignorance, but are intentional incorporations. Ezekiel is not the first to incorporate nonprototypical features in tragedy, as the tragic genre underwent substantial changes in the Hellenistic era; the change of scale, in this case *macrologia*, is a common means of genre adaptation and evolution.[23] That Ezekiel's atypical features align with distinctive source material supports the intentionality of the change

17 Lanfranchi, *L'Exagoge*, 15–21.

18 J. Strugnell, "Notes on the Text and Metre of Ezekiel the Tragedian's 'Exagoge,'" *HTR* 60 (1967): 449–57; B. Snell, "Die Iamben in Ezechiels Moses-Drama," *Glotta* 44 (1966): 25–32; Snell, *Szenen*, 172. The meter used for tragedy changed throughout the Hellenistic era; iambic trimeter, although adopted by Ezekiel, appears not to have been the dominant metrical form, as the Pleiad poets preferred the archaic iambic form popularized by Hipponax. Cf. M. L. West, *Studies in Greek Elegy and Iambus* (Berlin: De Gruyter, 1974), 22–39.

19 E.g., Plato, *Resp.* 3.394b–c.

20 E. J. Stewart, *Greek Tragedy on the Move: The Birth of a Panhellenic Art Form, c. 500–300 BC* (Oxford: Oxford University Press, 2017), 22–31.

21 Many parallels exist between Ezekiel's *Exagoge* and classical tragedies (cf. Stewart, "Ezekiel's *Exagoge*," 229–32). For ancient tragedies having five acts, see Horace, *Ars* 189–90. Whether Ezekiel's play was to be performed is a continuing debate; some poets' works were only meant for reading (Aristotle, *Rhet.* 1413b). For some of the positions, see A. Fountoulakis, "Greek Dramatic Conventions in Ezekiel's *Exagoge*," *Platon* 48 (1996): 88–112; Jacobson, *Exagoge*, 28–36; Lanfranchi, *L'Exagoge*, 25–32; Kotlińska-Toma, *Hellenistic Tragedy*, 225–26. For an argument that Jews in Palestine and in the diaspora attended and were familiar with the theater, see J. Jay, "The Problem of the Theater in Early Judaism," *JSJ* 44 (2013): 218–53; G. A. Keddie and J. MacLellan, "Ezekiel's *Exagoge* and the Politics of Hellenistic Theatre: Mosaic Hegemony on a Ptolemaic Model," *JAJ* 8 (2017): 170–87. The inclusion of a chorus is also debated. None of the fragments supports or refutes its existence, although the daughters of Raguel have been thought to play this role. E.g., Jacobson, *Exagoge*, 88; Lanfranchi, *L'Exagoge*, 29; Kotlińska-Toma, *Hellenistic Tragedy* 226–27; contra Wieneke, *Ezechielis*, 30.

22 These "unity principles" were outlined by Aristotle, *Poet.* 5, 1449b. Aeschylus' *Eumenides* and *Agamemnon*, Euripides' *Andromache*, and Sophocles' *Trachiniae*, however, did not always adhere to these "rules," although none have as wide a scope as the *Exagoge*. Theophrastus is reported to have emphasized the heroic fortune of the protagonist as a key, tragic component (Diomedes, *Ars Poetica*, 3, in Keil, *Grammatici Latini*, 1.487).

23 Fowler, *Kinds of Literature*, 172–73. Cf. Fantuzzi and Hunter, *Tradition and Innovation*, 432–43. Aristotle (*Poet.* 5, 1449b) claims that early tragedies (like epics) did not have time

and is not an indication of Ezekiel's lack of knowledge or mastery of the tragic genre. Individual features (e.g., staging and structure) can be read so as to allow the *Exagoge* to participate in the genre of tragedy in nonprototypical, but importantly not fully unprecedented, ways.[24] Because the models available to Ezekiel are not extant, we cannot be sure that he did not adhere to accepted practices or if he had different prototypical models upon which he based his composition.[25]

Ezekiel's selection of a historical, non-Greek (i.e., Jewish) subject is another distinctive feature of the *Exagoge*. Although a few Hellenistic poets composed tragedies based on tales from the exotic East,[26] Ezekiel is the first known author to write a tragedy on a story from Scripture. In classical tragedies, Greek mythology was often, though not always (e.g., Dionysius the Elder, *TrGF* 76), the subject (Aristotle, *Poet.* 13, 1453a16–22). In the Hellenistic era, mythological subjects still dominated, but tragedies started to address historical and contemporary life more frequently (e.g., Lycophron, *Cassandreians* and *Menedemus*; Python, *Agen*).[27] An important source of tragic material was the Trojan cycle, which could be used to explain or mythologize the origins of a people group. The expansion of a foundation narrative is also exhibited in the *Exagoge* (e.g., the inclusion of Moses' dream, *Exag.* 68–82, and the phoenix, *Exag.* 254–269). However, a majority of the work follows the Exodus narrative, retelling an established story and allowing the original account to direct, but not fully dictate, the dramatic representation.[28]

Recently, scholars have challenged the label of "tragedy," asking: "What is tragic about the story of Exodus?"[29] This is an important question. Ezekiel's unique participation in the tragedy genre is exemplified in his use of the Greek

---

limits, but that this was no longer the case. This is a good example of *brachylogia* being adopted in a genre. Perhaps Hellenistic-era tragic poets resurrected this lost feature.

24 For a good example, see Stewart, "Ezekiel's *Exagoge*," 241–51, who suggests that the extreme scene changes could be reduced by having Moses speak to Aaron (175–192) and the Egyptian survivor speak to Raguel (193–242).

25 Cf. M. Wright, *The Lost Plays of Greek Tragedy*, vol. 1, *Neglected Authors* (London: Bloomsbury, 2016), 117–75, for fragmentary or lost works from the fourth century BCE.

26 E.g., Ptolemy IV Philopater, *Adonis* (*TrGF* 119); Philiscus of Corcyra, *Adonis* (*Suda* Φ 357); and anon., *Gyges* (*TrGF* adespota F664).

27 Kotlińska-Toma, *Hellenistic Tragedy*, 23–32.

28 Kotlińska-Toma, *Hellenistic Tragedy*, 29–31. The wealth of predecessors for Greek Hellenistic tragedians, and the wide knowledge of Homer's epics, allowed Greek tragedians the freedom to choose diverse topics; although many followed the topics established by their classical forerunners.

29 Davies, "Reading," 400; P. Lanfranchi, "The Exagoge of Ezekiel the Tragedian," in V. Liapis and A. K. Petrides, eds., *Greek Tragedy after the Fifth Century: A Survey from ca. 400 BC to ca. AD 400* (Cambridge: Cambridge University Press, 2018), 132–34.

tragic form, but (apparently) emptying it of its definitional nature.[30] Contrary to ancient tragedies, which regularly recount a calamitous event in the life of a person or community, Ezekiel's *Exagoge* presents a narrative in which complete success is achieved not only for the main protagonist (Moses), but for the entire Hebrew people.[31] Ezekiel's presentation of Moses as confidently leading the Hebrew people and acting as God's agent during the charging of the Egyptian army near the Red Sea (*Exag.* 224–229) resonates with heroic depictions in other Hellenistic tragedies in which the lone hero single-handedly fights a host of enemies.[32] Pharaoh and the Egyptians are the ones who suffer loss; however, within the play, they are presented as the antagonists/opponents of God and of the Hebrew people, so there is no pathos at their destruction, nor is pity or fear employed to bring catharsis.[33] Throughout the whole play there is no reversal or recognition (περιπέτειαι καὶ ἀναγνωρίσεις), features that Aristotle claims are the most important for emotional effect (*Poet.* 6, 1450a). If this is the case, then we witness an adaptation of Greek tragedy by a non-Greek author, subordinating established literary features to portray a specific narrative.

The work's presumed lack of a tragic element, however, is predicated on two important assumptions. First, and less controversial, the play was intended to be viewed from a Jewish perspective. Although this is most likely the case, an Egyptian or Greek audience in Alexandria might react differently, aligning themselves with the dominant Egyptians who are led by Pharaoh.[34] The suffering of the Egyptians could satisfy the tragic component, but again this depends on the individual viewer.[35] The second assumption is that the arrival of the Jewish people at Elim acts as the conclusion of the *Exagoge*. This might

30 Cf. Epictetus, *Disc.* 1.4.26, who in context mentions Priam and Oedipus: "For what are tragedies but the portrayal in tragic verse of the sufferings of men who have admired things external."

31 Kotlińska-Toma (*Hellenistic Tragedy*, 229) concludes that *Exagoge* had a happy ending similar to Euripides' *Alcestis*. "The *Exagoge* is a drama about the Jewish people and as such it does not have a 'tragic hero' in the familiar sense" (Jacobson, *Exagoge*, 4). Although I agree with Jacobson's statement regarding the atypical "tragic hero," the construction of the poem clearly indicates that Moses is the protagonist and the Hebrew people are a secondary character. Furthermore, I am not convinced by the suggestion (so Barclay, *Jews*, 137) that Moses' fleeing of Egypt because of his murder constitutes a sufficient tragic event. Moreover, the possible parallel with Oedipus is unconvincing as there is no twist in Moses' murder, nor is it the cause of his downfall. Rather, it leads to his call and the redemption of the Jewish people.

32 E.g., Sositheus, *Aethlius* (*TrGF* 99 F3) and Moschion, *Themistocles* (*TrGF* 97 F1).

33 Aristotle, *Poet.* 6, 1449b: δι' ἐλέου καὶ φόβου περαίνουσα τὴν τῶν τοιούτων παθημάτων κάθαρσιν.

34 Klęczar interestingly proposes that the Egyptian princess who rescued Moses from the Nile, if brought back into focus at the end of the play, could be the tragic figure. Cf. A. Klęczar, *Ezechiel Tragik i jego dramat Exagoge Wyprowadzenie z Egiptu* (AST 1; Kraków-Mogilany: Enigma Press, 2006), 101, *apud* Kotlińska-Toma, *Hellenistic Tragedy*, 228–29.

35 So Whitmarsh, *Beyond*, 219–20.

be the case, but, as this is not explicitly stated by Eusebius, another alternative is possible, namely, that the play contained one or more additional scenes. Two elements are important for our discussion of tragedy here. The first is that, according to the biblical texts, only a few of the people delivered from Egypt make it to the promised land. This is due to their disobedience and their lack of faith, a theme not found in Exodus or the extant portions of the *Exagoge*, but prominent in the Pentateuch (e.g., Num 14:32–35; 32:11–13; Deut 1:34–40; cf. Heb 3:7–19). Second, Moses' acting out in anger, which could be seen as a fatal flaw, results in his exclusion from joining the nation on the other side of the Jordan (Num 20:11–12). The inability of both characters (Moses and the delivered generation) to reach their ultimate destination could evoke a sense of pathos in the reader/listener and, if depicted, could provide the type of reversal expected in a tragedy. Even if these elements were not explicitly included, the knowledge held by the Jewish auditor regarding these events may have produced a similar effect.

If the *Exagoge* does not follow prototypical examples of the tragedy genre, as far as we are able to discern, why did Ezekiel choose to compose a tragedy? What benefit was there to selecting this genre to retell the Exodus story? As one of the most popular forms of entertainment, a drama had a greater chance at reaching a wider audience. A Moses play, which would include props and nonverbal communication, would be an ideal way of educating an audience about a foundational Jewish character and would importantly allow for identity construction within the wider society. Revelatory experiences often form the bedrock of communal identity, and these afford the opportunity to explore the themes of foreigners and otherness, topics that are at the heart of Ezekiel's play.[36]

The theme of suffering is also an important component of tragedies. Typically, the protagonist would be the primary object of suffering, although his/her suffering might also lead to the suffering of others.[37] The *Exagoge*, in contrast, opens with a declaration of the suffering of the Hebrew people:

> When Jacob left Canaan he came to Egypt with seventy souls and fathered a great people that has suffered and been oppressed. Till this day (ἐσάχρι τούτων τῶν χρόνων) we have been ill-treated by evil men and a powerful regime. For king Pharaoh, when he saw our people increasing in number, devised many plans against us. He afflicted us with brickwork and the hard labor of construction and he had turreted cities built by our ill-fated men. (*Exag.* 1–11, Jacobson)

36 E.g., Euripides, *Bacchae*; Aeschylus, *Suppliants* and *Persae*.

37 E.g., the plague which attacks Thebes, the city in which Oedipus was residing (Sophocles, *Oed. tyr.*, *passim*), or Agave, the mother of slain Pentheus (Euripides, *Bacch.* 1216–1387).

This theme of suffering is applied, not to a specific individual, but to the Hebrew people as a collective. By the end of the play this suffering had transferred to the Egyptian people through the plagues and their loss in the Red Sea.

Although the narrative world of the *Exagoge* is situated in Pharaonic Egypt, the phrase "until this time" (ἐσάχρι τούτων τῶν χρόνων), spoken by Moses in the play's opening monologue, has the potential to function on multiple levels and encourages the insightful reader/listener to interpret the play as a discussion of contemporary events and cultural interactions.[38] The political nature of tragedies in antiquity, especially at festivals, such as the *Ptolemaieia* in Alexandria, encourages modern scholars to recognize the ways that specific elements of the *Exagoge* might have been received.[39] Activating multiple layers of meaning not only reinforces the historical nature of the text, but also makes the play relevant to those listening and watching by blurring temporal horizons. By chronologically linking the viewer with the characters in the narrative, Ezekiel lays a foundation for constructing an identity in which the present audience participates in the narrative of the past.[40] It is worth asking, therefore, how a Jew living in Egypt (the land from which the Hebrew people were led out of in both Exodus and the *Exagoge*) might have responded to this play. Might the recalling of God's mighty acts of deliverance and the establishment of his temple in a now-distant land have invoked pathos or longing in the Jewish watcher/listener? Of importance for Davies in determining the impact and function of the play is the fact that the *Exagoge* does not expand what the biblical text elides. This restraint signals Ezekiel's resistance to what she argues is one of the primary functions of tragedy, namely to exploit the silence of epic narratives in order to provide a new interpretation of events. Davies argues that this fidelity to the biblical text is a result of the deep significance that this text had for Jews. In this she is likely correct. Less certain is her claim that Ezekiel "adopts dramatic structure as a way of negotiating the problem of sacrifice in exile."[41] True, Ezekiel discusses the Passover (πάσχα) and the events surrounding it on two occasions (*Exag.* 156–160, 175–192), but nowhere does this suggest that the play is a "liturgical replacement" for the Passover sacrifice.[42] An important critique of this position is that the sacrifice is only described and not reenacted in the play (so far as we know). Ezekiel reinforces the aetiological origins of the Passover, but this does not necessarily

38 Contra Lanfranchi (*L'Exagoge*, 133), who, though rightly identifying the speaker as Moses, does not bring the implications of the phrase to Ezekiel's day.

39 See the insightful work by Keddie and MacLellan, "Ezekiel's *Exagoge*." For reconstructions of possible historical/political situations, see S. Gambetti, "Some Considerations on Ezekiel's *Exagoge*," *JAJ* 8 (2017): 188–207.

40 This is reinforced by the use of the first-person plural in the opening (*Exag.* 5, 7–8).

41 Davies, "Reading," 398.

42 Davies, "Reading," 399.

lead to the undermining of the physical institution. It is plausible that Ezekiel's emphasis on the feast's Egyptian origin would undermine the centrality of Jerusalem, but it does not go so far as to abolish the practice.[43] Rather, the tenor of the work reinforces its continued practice despite the geographic distance between the hearers and Jerusalem.

Overall, the *Exagoge* is a work of literary sophistication that participates in the genre of Greek tragedy. This example of literary participation models the importance of Greek literary culture and the willingness of minority cultures to adopt a Greek genre to tell a native story of identity formation.[44] Lanfranchi is incorrect, therefore, when he claims that the *Exagoge* is an example of rewriting the Bible to conform to dominant cultural ideals enforced by secular *paideia*.[45] Rather, what we witness in the *Exagoge* is a unique composition in which a highly acculturated Jew participates in a genre from the dominant culture to meet his literary needs. The play is positively orientated to Greek and Jewish cultures, but is explicitly antagonistic to Egyptian culture.[46] Ezekiel did not adopt the prototypical tragic form (as far as we can determine), but adapted the flexible genre to fit the Exodus story. Multiple concerns influence the construction of the text, but the play is not limited to one outlook (e.g., Greek *or* Jewish); neither overpowers the other. Ezekiel engages with the genre of tragedy, but in a way that allows him to express Jewish ideas and values without being fully beholden to Greek literary expectations.

Excursus: Nicolaus of Damascus

Nicolaus of Damascus is not Jewish, but his poetic composition is worth considering due to his relationship with Herod and his court.[47] Eustathius of Thessalonica, in his *Commentarium in Dionysii periegetae orbis descriptionem* 976.62–64,[48] claims that Nicolas of Damascus composed a play about Susanna:

43 Philo (*QE* 1.12) provides an allegorical interpretation of the Passover, but this does not necessitate that all Jews living in Alexandria abandoned physical sacrifice. Davies' parallel between diaspora Jews and Jews living after the destruction of the Temple does not provide adequate evidence.

44 The blending of Greek literature with native elements was not exclusively Jewish, but appears to have a parallel in at least one Egyptian, anti-Semitic work: Manetho's rewriting of the Exodus (Josephus, *C. Ap.* 1.102, 231). According to Josephus, Manetho claims that it was not only the leprous Jews that were expelled by the Egyptians, but also Danaus, whose noble heritage and return to Greece is narrated in Aeschylus' *Suppliants*.

45 P. Lanfranchi, "Ezéchiel le Tragique et la question du théâtre juif ancien," *Cahiers du Judaïsme* 14 (2003): 18–24.

46 For the presentation of Moses and the law as a challenge to the Greek veneration of Apollo, see C. R. Holladay, "The Portrait of Moses in Ezekiel the Tragedian," in G. W. MacRae, ed., *SBLSP 1976* (Missoula, Mont.: Scholars Press, 1976), 447–52.

47 For an important introduction, see B. Z. Wacholder, *Nicolaus of Damascus* (UCPH 75; Berkeley: University of California Press, 1962).

48 In vol. 2 of K. Müller, ed., *Geographi Graeci Minores* (2 vols.; Paris: A. Firmin Didot, 1882).

> καθὰ καὶ ὁ γράψας τὸ δρᾶμα τῆς Σωσάννης, οἶμαι ὁ Δαμασκηνός, ὡς ἐκ τῆς ἐπιγραφῆς φαίνεται.
>
> The same is also said about the one who wrote the drama of Susanna, I think it was Damaskenos, as is shown by the inscription.

This statement aligns with a comment in the *Suda* in which Nicolaus is said to have written, among other works, "famous tragedies and comedies" (αὐτός τε τραγῳδίας ἐποίει καὶ κωμῳδίας εὐδοκίμους, *Suda* N 393), although the compiler did not specify any title or subject. No other evidence of this play survives. If accurate, however, this testimony provides insight into the composition of Jewish plays in the first century BCE, something otherwise unattested.[49] This would be a rare instance in which a non-Jewish author adopted a Jewish subject. Nicolaus' rationale for choosing Susanna as a subject is almost certainly tied to his patron, King Herod, who either commissioned the piece or was expected to appreciate it. That this was likely composed for Herod implies that Greek dramas were recited and performed at court. It is worth speculating whether Nicolaus' *Susanna* was the only Jewish play commissioned by and/or written for Herod. It is possible that other plays were composed by Jews (or non-Jews) for the king and so would give evidence for a creative literary community in and around Jerusalem (cf. Josephus, *Ant.* 15.268).[50]

Pseudo-Orpheus

The poem by Pseudo-Orpheus, often called *Testament of Orpheus*, is an example of Jewish literary imitation. This work, which has been preserved in (up to) four recensions, contains from twenty-one to forty-six lines, depending on the tradition.[51] The poem is ascribed to the original Orpheus by patristic writers,

49 The story of Susanna is not found in Hebrew Scripture, but is included in the so-called deuterocanonical material as an addition to Daniel. The dedication of a literary work to a minor and relatively obscure biblical character is distinctive among Jewish compositions. On Susanna, see D. A. deSilva, *Introducing the Apocrypha: Message, Context, and Significance* (2nd ed.; Grand Rapids: Baker Academic, 2018), 249–56. For more, see chapter 6.

50 LA 316 tells of a certain tragic poet, Theodectus, who was afflicted with cataracts because he was about to include a passage from Scripture in his play. Although the veracity of the story is suspect, it implies that some authors thought that Jewish writers were using Greek poetry to express Jewish ideas and cultural values throughout the Hellenistic era, even before the translation of the LXX (cf. chapter 2). Cf. S. Honigman, *The Septuagint and Homeric Scholarship in Alexandria: A Study in the Narrative of the "Letter of Aristeas"* (London: Routledge, 2003), 60–62. Some Jews were also said to be actors in plays (Josephus, *Vita* 16; Martial, *Ep.* 7.82; *CIJ* 1.283), thus widening Jewish involvement in the creative arts. Cf. R. Bloch, "Part of the Scene: Jewish Theater in Antiquity," *JAJ* 8 (2017): 150–69. For Talmudic references, see Lanfranchi, *L'Exagoge*, 43.

51 For our sources of Pseudo-Orpheus, see Holladay, *Fragments*, vol. 4, *Orphica*, 43–48. Eusebius (*Praep. ev.* 13.12.5) claims he took the poem from Aristobulus, which, if accurate, would

but scholars now widely regard it as a Jewish composition (or at minimum a hymn with substantial Jewish interpolations) and not part of the original *Orphic Hymns* corpus.[52]

Unraveling the recensions and their interrelationships is arguably the most challenging aspect of Pseudo-Orphic scholarship.[53] This is an important endeavor, but one that goes beyond the purview of this study. The different interpretations drawn from respective recensions highlights the fact that not only the original author, but all subsequent redactors/interpolators, sought to embed Jewish cultural ideas into a Greek literary framework by attributing their compositions/amendments to a Greek author famous for his religious and philosophical instruction. The accretion of Jewish features does not only support the view that this poem was being circulated and read in Jewish communities and that different perspectives existed regarding what the composition should say. It implies a community of Jews with the ability to read archaic poetry.[54]

The structure and the language of the poem evidence explicit engagement with and knowledge of Greek literature. The ability of the author(s) to imitate Orpheus by using hexameter and archaic Greek is immediately apparent and indicates an extensive Greek education and skill in *prosopopoeia*. The author writes using Greek vocabulary and syntax that would have been available to

---

indicate at least a second century BCE date. Cf. C. Riedweg, *Jüdisch-hellenistische Imitation eines orphischen Hieros Logos: Beobachtungen zu OF 245 und 247 (sog. Testament des Orpheus)* (CM 7; Tübingen: Gunter Narr, 1993) (two versions); F. Jourdan, *Poème judéo-hellénistique attribute à Orphée: Production juive et reception chrétienne* (Paris: Les Belles Lettres, 2010), 117–61 (*trois rédactions*).

52 For the text of Orpheus' works, see O. Kern, *Orphicorum fragmenta* (Berlin: Apud, 1922); A. Bernabé, ed., *Orphicorum et Orphicis similium testimonia et fragmenta: Poetae Epici Graeci*, pars II, fasc. 1 (Bibliotheca Teubneriana; Munich: K. G. Saur, 2004). For the complex nature of Orphism and its presence in the Hellenistic and Roman eras, see M. Herrero de Jáuregui, *Orphism and Christianity in Late Antiquity* (Sozomena 7; Berlin: De Gruyter, 2010).

53 For the recensions and their possible relationships, see Holladay, *Fragments: Orphica*, 48–67; C. R. Holladay, "The Textual Tradition of Pseudo-Orpheus: Walter or Riedweg?" in H. Cancik, H. Lichtenberger, and P. Schäfer, eds., *Geschichte—Tradition—Reflection: Festschrift für Martin Hengel zum 70. Geburtstag* (3 vols.; Tübingen: Mohr Siebeck, 1996), 1.159–80; N. Walter, *Der Thoraausleger Aristobulos* (Berlin: Akademie Verlag, 1964), 202–59; N. Walter, "Pseudepigraphische jüdisch-hellenistischer Dichtung: Pseudo-Phokylides, Pseudo-Orpheus, Gefälschte Verse auf Namen griechischer Dichter," in *JSHRZ* 4.3, 217–30; Denis, *Introduction*, 1086–96. For convenience I will use the recension letters and verse numbers employed by Walter and Holladay. For a contrary position, see Riedweg, *Imitation*, 73–101. Other Orphic poems also survive in different recensions of books (e.g., *Theogony*) or traditions (e.g., the rape of Persephone: *Orphic Hymn* 18, 41), cf. M. L. West, ed., *The Orphic Poems* (Oxford: Clarendon, 1983), 1–2.

54 On the question of audience, see M. Lafargue, "The Jewish Orpheus," in P. J. Achtemeier, ed., *SBLSP 1978* (2 vols.; Missoula, Mont.: Scholars Press, 1978), 2.141; Schürer, *History*, 3.1.617; West, *Orphic Poems*, 33.

Orpheus in the sixth century BCE, drawing heavily on Greek epic poets, particularly Homer and Hesiod.[55] Philosophical and religious imagery to depict the one God is prominent, crafting a literary atmosphere consistent with the revelation of mystery teachings found in Orpheus' *Hymns*.[56] The work opens with the speaker telling Musaeus and the uninitiated (βέβηλοι) to "close the door" and "listen" (vv. 1–3). The name Orpheus does not appear in the text, but the author signals the adoption of the Orpheus persona through the naming of Musaeus (v. 3), who was well known in antiquity as Orpheus' disciple.[57] The first lines parallel the descriptions of mystery cults as well as the opening of the *Orphic Hymns*: "Attend Musaeus to my sacred song, and learn what rites to sacrifice belong" (*praef.* 1–2) and "I will sing to those who understand, close the doors, unconsecrated" (ἀείσω ξυνετοῖσι, θύρας δ᾽ ἐπίθεσθε βεβήλοι, fr. 334).[58] The vocabulary, syntax, and substance all indicate the intentional adoption of a Greek literary model with Orpheus' *Hymns* functioning as the prototype. This is not the first pseudipigraphical attribution to Orpheus (e.g., *Orphic Argonautica*), suggesting that this Jewish author was engaging with a wider, possibly accepted, literary practice.[59]

The monotheistic content of the poem, rather than its style or structure, signals its Jewish origin: "He is one, self-generated; all things have been brought forth as the offspring of this one" (Εἷς ἔστ᾽, αὐτογενής, ἑνὸς ἔκγονα πάντα τέτυκται, v. 10 [recension A]).[60] This one God is transcendent, enthroned in the heavens (v. 34), and presides over all the cosmos (vv. 8 and 17), which he created (v. 9).[61] These monotheistic assertions provided fodder for patristic authors to argue for Greek philosophy's dependence on and compatibility with Jewish ideas. This, however, was not the historical reality, but a fiction retrospectively

55 Cf. Riedweg, *Imitation*; Holladay, *Fragments: Orphica, passim.*

56 Cf. Pausanias, *Descr.* 2.30.2. For parallels between vv. 1–3 and ancient mystery religions, see Holladay, *Fragments: Orphica*, 154–56.

57 Cf. *Orphica* T18, 97, 166–72 (Kern). Filial and disciple addresses are seen in many wisdom texts (e.g., *Instruction of Ankhsheshonq* [P.BM 10508]; Prov 1:8). The relationship is inverted in Artapanus, F3.4, in which Musaeus is equated to Moses.

58 For shutting the door, see Derveni Papyrus col. vii.9; for a parody, see Plato, *Symp.* 218a–c. Cf. Riedweg, *Imitation*, 50–51; C. R. Holladay, "Pseudo-Orpheus: Tracking a Tradition," in A. J. Malherbe, F. W. Norris, and J. W. Thompson, eds., *The Early Church in Its Context: Essays in Honor of Everett Ferguson* (NovTSup 90; Leiden: Brill, 1998), 193. For other parallels, see Holladay, *Fragments: Orphica*, 154–56.

59 Cf. Aristotle, *De an.* 1.5.410b28–29; Cicero, *Nat. d.* 1.107–108; Herodotus, *Hist.* 2.81.2.

60 Cf. Sib. Or. 3.11–12. Walter ("Dichtung," 236 n. f) wishes to differentiate this line from the more "exclusive monotheistic" claims of other Jewish pseudepigraphical writers (especially Pseudo-Socrates).

61 This is found predominantly in recensions C and D. The use of τυπόω may have resonances with the philosophical treatises' discussion of the demiurge's role in shaping the preexisting matter, though it also is close to Philo's discussion. Cf. Philo, *Migr.* 103; *Somn.* 1.15.

placed in the mouth of Orpheus. For Holladay, this poem represents a rectification of a faulty tradition, "What this anonymous Jewish author found irresistible was the notion that knowledge of the one God eluded even Orpheus, whose reputation as poetic theologian and religious reformer was well established by the mid-second century BCE."[62] The attribution of Jewish ideas to Orpheus changes the contemporary power dynamic, promoting distinctively Jewish beliefs at the potential expense of a Greek literary icon.[63] By claiming similar beliefs, the Jewish author not only minimizes the gap between these two cultures, but also creates a scenario in which Jewish (and later Christian) authors could claim support from an illustrious Greek author. This retroactive legitimization facilitates claims of Jewish primacy (if not supremacy) and is part of a larger Hellenistic practice of minority cultures recrafting history in order to position themselves better within the new, multicultural landscape.

Some verses appear to challenge "orthodox" Jewish views, such as verse 14, whose problematic content for subsequent Jewish readers led to several "corrections." The earliest recensions of this verse reads, "from good he gives evil to mortals" (Οὗτος δ' ἐξ ἀγαθοῖο κακὸν θνητοῖσι δίδωσι[A]/φυτεύει[B]), implying that the one God is the origin of the evil perpetuated on humankind.[64] This view is found in the Homeric tradition, where Zeus (or the gods) is presented as giving troubles or blessings (*Il.* 24.525–33) along with good and evil (*Od.* 4.236–37; 8.62–63; cf. Hesiod, *Theog.* 904–906).[65] Some Jewish writers felt compelled to distance God from such actions and to identify him as a source only of good.[66] This position was held by the author/editor of recension C, who changed δίδωσι to οὐκ ἐπιτέλλει, disassociating God from negative actions. His modifications were thought to be insufficient by the redactor of recension D, however, who further clarified verses 15–16 to ensure that God was not responsible for bringing hated and war by changing recension C's "grace and hatred accompany him [i.e., God], as well as war, plague, and tearful sufferings" to "strife and hatred accompany them [i.e., humans], as well as war, plague,

62 Holladay, "Pseudo-Orpheus," 194.

63 Note the contrast of Pseudo-Orpheus' monotheistic presentation as compared to the looser monotheistic discussion by Pseudo-Phocylides (see chapter 4).

64 For other translations, see Walter, "Dichtung," 236 n. i; Riedweg, *Imitation*, 27–29.

65 Supporting this view are Hesiod, *Op.* 667–669; *Theog.* 218–220; Pindar, *Isthm.* 5.52; Menander, *Epitr.* 1085–1086. Challenging this view are Plato, *Resp.* 379a–e; *Tim.* 29e–30a; and Sextus, *Sent.* 114. In a different location, Hesiod (*Theog.* 633, 664) claims that the gods are "givers of good things" (θεοί δωτῆρες ἐάων).

66 Philo, *Opif.* 75; *Sacr.* 63; *Fug.* 79–80; *Conf.* 180; *Prob.* 84. Holladay (*Fragments: Orphica*, 164) cites two other passages as evidence: LA 205 and 1 En. 98:4. However, the first only identifies God as the giver of good things, but is silent regarding God's involvement in dispensing evil. Similarly, 1 En. 98:4 claims that humans are the originators of sin and so they are under a curse. It does not say that God does not give evil.

and tearful sufferings." That verse 14 in recensions A and B was difficult for subsequent readers is clear; however, this does not discount its Jewish origin. Even in antiquity Clement (*Strom.* 5.14.126) could cite Deut 32:29 as evidence of how verse 14 adheres to biblical tradition.[67]

Changes to the text did not stop at theological clarification, but included challenging the superiority of Orpheus, the adopted persona. Verses 27–28, which are found in recensions B through D and absent in A, claim that only one person has been able to see God, a certain person from the Chaldean race. This assertion stands in stark contrast with the statement by Orpheus in verse 21, "Even I do not see him," implying that no one is able to do so.[68] The allusion to Abraham here is strong, particularly in light of the description of his knowledge and abilities; he knew the procession of the sun, the movement of the spheres, and the turning of the earth on its axis (vv. 28–29).[69] Although such knowledge is attributed to wise men by many ancient authors, the Jewish author here forges a combative dichotomy: it is this person from Chaldea, and not Orpheus (cf. vv. 21, 25), who has the ability to see God. This claim undermines the authority of a respected Greek seer and asserts the superiority of a Jewish patriarch by stressing not only the priority but also the superiority of Jewish cultural tradition over that of a recognized Greek philosopher.[70] These changes emphasize the desire by some Jews to realign Jewish and Greek relationships, which does not appear to be the purpose of the author of recension A.

Allusions to biblical characters are further developed in the longer recensions of C and D, specifically with respect to Moses (vv. 41–42) and the Mosaic law (vv. 2, 9).[71] The absence of explicit mention of Torah and Moses allows for interpretive ambiguity; it is specific enough for Jewish readers to recognize their lawgiver, but ambiguous enough to be taken by non-Jewish readers in a philosophical sense to refer to the divine cosmic law.[72] The introduction of these new features, however, reinforces the poem's Jewish perspective and prompts alternative readings in certain passages. Specifically, the introduction

67 See also Isa 45:7; Amos 3:6b; Job 2:10; 5:17–18; 9:17; 12:13–25.

68 In recensions C and D the cloud obstructing humanity's vision is said to be tenfold (δεκάπτυχον) thicker for the regular person than for Orpheus.

69 Josephus (*Ant.* 1.158), Philo (*Virt.* 212; *Abr.* 69–71), and Pseudo-Eupolemus (fr. 1.2) speak of Abraham similarly. Philo, however, also calls Moses a Chaldean (*Mos.* 1.5). Cf. J. E. Taylor and D. M. Hay, "Astrology in Philo of Alexandria's *De Vita Contemplativa*," *ARAM Periodical* 24 (2012): 56–74. The probable identification changes depending on the recension and the inclusion or exclusion of Mosaic material. Clement (*Strom.* 5.14.123.1) identifies this individual as either Abraham *or* his son (Isaac). For a claim of Chaldean dependence on Egyptian practices, see Diodorus Siculus, *Bibl.* 1.50.1; 1.81.6.

70 Cf. the more extreme example in Artapanus fr. 3.4.

71 Holladay also suggests vv. 6 and 25. Holladay, "Pseudo-Orpheus," 196. Like Abraham, Moses is not explicitly named.

72 Holladay, *Fragments: Orphica*, 197; Riedweg, *Imitation*, 81–82.

of the Moses motif may undermine the allusion to Abraham, thereby making Moses the focal Jewish character of the poem, as he too is said to have cosmological knowledge and is reported to have seen God.[73]

For early Jewish readers, another problematic feature of recension A was the reference to Zeus (Ἀσθενέες δ' ἰδέειν Δία τὸν πάντων μεδέοντα, v. 24).[74] The main argument provided by scholars against the originality of this reading is the assumption that a Jewish author would avoid the name of Zeus in this discussion.[75] This use of Δία, however, is not unique (cf. LA 16) and fits the work's literary context. Moreover, it is unlikely to have been inserted by later Christian writers/scribes. In contrast, verse 24 is replaced in B and C with a completely new verse and redacted in D to read ἰδέειν τὸν δὴ πάντα μεδέοντα. These changes imply that the editors of the other recensions did not feel compelled to employ the name of Zeus to support the work's pseudepigraphic claim and that their theological concerns outweighed the perceived literary benefit. The use of Δία in recension A, conversely, indicates a willingness on behalf of the author to employ the name of Zeus—the head god of the Greek pantheon—to reference the one God. This choice is appropriate for the adoption of the Orpheus persona, but also supports the convergence of Jewish and Greek intellectual thought.[76] This convergence is strengthened when one remembers that the culturally antagonistic verses (vv. 27–28), which discuss the superseding of Orpheus by Abraham, are absent in recension A.

All of the recensions and their respective additions exhibit deep knowledge of Greek literary culture through their authors' ability to mimic archaic Greek verse and employ Homeric and Hesiodic vocabulary and phrasing. The additional lines in recensions B–D are consistent in style and construction, indicating that the later authors/redactors were sufficiently knowledgeable of classical Greek to pen suitable Orphean additions. Specific septuagintal influences are harder to identify. Holladay is likely correct in identifying biblical influence in verse 34, "He stands with the earth at his feet." However, it is far from "doubtless" that ὑπὸ ποσ(σ)ί draws from LXX Isa 66:1 (ὑποπόδιον τῶν

73 Philo, *Mos.* 1.23; Num 12:8.

74 This reading is adopted by a majority of modern scholars, though there are manuscript issues. For the particulars, see Holladay, *Fragments: Orphica*, 167.

75 Cf. Riedweg, *Imitation*, 30.

76 Related to this view is the possible capitalization of Ὠκεανοῖο in v. 35 by editors, which would indicate a reference to Oceanus, god of the primeval waters. This interpretation is less certain, but if accepted would support the reading of Zeus in v. 24. This reading is changed in recension B, though retained in C and D. The retention of ὠκεανοῖο by C and D in v. 35 might suggest that this was not how this verse was read by the authors of these two recensions.

ποδῶν) or that the author necessarily took this image from the LXX.[77] It is very likely that the author of this hymn was familiar with Jewish Scripture and theology, and this understanding no doubt "influenced" his writing (this becomes much more apparent in recensions C and D).[78] However, the poem lacks any overt use of biblical narrative, nor does the author draw from Jewish Scripture for his vocabulary and phrasing. Similarities in imagery, theology, and themes exist between the poem and biblical passages, but this does not provide firm evidence of LXX use.

Scholars acknowledge Pseudo-Orpheus' Greek literary parallels, but there is little discussion of how Pseudo-Orpheus might participate in Jewish genres. This omission is problematic, as Pseudo-Orpheus' poem has substantial resonances with scholarly definitions of wisdom literature, such as John Collins' four prototypical criteria: worldview, function, social setting, and literary form.[79] Pseudo-Orpheus presupposes an orderly nature to the cosmos and presents his teaching as insight into that structure (vv. 6, 8). The instruction is placed in a pedagogical social setting (vv. 1, 3–4) and takes the form of admonition and initiation, in which the student is to hear and learn from the teacher and then seek for him/herself.[80] Pseudo-Orpheus' lack of engagement with traditional concepts of biblical wisdom does not disqualify it from consideration, as certain wisdom texts from Qumran (e.g., 4QMysteries [4Q299–301]) also lack this feature. Indeed, the diversity of Early Jewish wisdom literature prohibits scholars from establishing firm boundaries.[81]

What, therefore, precludes a text like Pseudo-Orpheus from being considered a wisdom text? Two possible reasons for its exclusion are prominent: its composition in (classical) Greek and the pseudonymous nature of the work, specifically its attribution to a non-Jewish, Greek author. Neither feature is

77 Contra Holladay, *Fragments: Orphica*, 169–70; Schürer, *History*, 3.1.662; Denis, *Introduction*, 1097. The author's use of the Greek text over the Hebrew is much more likely, though not guaranteed.

78 For example, v. 36, which in A is similar to Homer, *Il.* 13.18–19, in the other recensions moves away from this strong Homeric resonance towards biblical imagery. However, a single lexical overlap does not constitute a sufficient "resonance" to claim LXX influence. See Holladay, *Fragment: Orphica*, 188.

79 J. J. Collins, "Wisdom Reconsidered, in Light of the Scrolls," *DSD* 4 (1997): 265. Cf. M. Kister, "Wisdom Literature and Its Relation to Other Genres: From Ben Sira to Mysteries," in J. J. Collins, G. E. Sterling, and R. A. Clements, eds., *Sapiential Perspectives: Wisdom Literature in Light of the Dead Sea Scrolls* (STDJ 51; Leiden: Brill, 2004), 13–47; J. L. Crenshaw, *Old Testament Wisdom: An Introduction* (rev. ed.; Louisville: Westminster John Knox, 1998), 11.

80 This fulfills the "noetic striving" criteria proposed by Goff, "Qumran Wisdom Literature," 298–301.

81 On the diversity of wisdom text, both at Qumran and in Jewish literature, see R. E. Murphy, *The Tree of Life: An Exploration of Biblical Wisdom Literature* (3rd ed.; Grand Rapids: Eerdmans, 2002), 7–12; Goff, "Qumran Wisdom Literature," 289–96.

explicitly mentioned in any definition of wisdom literature, implying that they are not determinative or prototypical elements. Even if one posits that wisdom literature is limited primarily (if not exclusively) to Eastern cultures (a position that I think is too restrictive), *Testament* is composed by Jews and so could presumably participate in the wisdom genre.[82] The inclusion of alternative, nonprototypical works in the discussion of wisdom literature would continue to broaden our understanding of their diversity. The example of Pseudo-Orpheus shows how didactic texts can be reconfigured in light of engagement with Greek culture.[83] The author(s) of *Testament* recognized the pliability of Greek mystical and educational texts and, exploring this opportunity, imbued a Greek teacher with Jewish ideology. The adoption of a Greek persona militated against substantial changes in the form, but did not restrict the author's enrobing of Jewish ideas and values in Greek literary garb. The revelatory language prominent in Greek mystic traditions fits with Jewish ruminations on the divine. The compatibility of these ideas was rightly identified by a Jewish author who skillfully combined them into a didactic hymn.

The different recensions of Pseudo-Orpheus provide a window into the ongoing debate among Jews about their relationship with their Greek neighbors. The redactive activity by subsequent Jewish authors indicates that this literary work held a liminal state of acceptability, although it was important enough that its place within Jewish literature continued to be negotiated. Pseudo-Orpheus evidences an array of Jewish authors with substantial knowledge and training in Greek, who differ in their expression of that relationship, but importantly, not in their participation in an Orphic hymn form.

Sibylline Oracles

The Sibylline Oracles are a collection of Jewish and Christian religious texts purporting to be utterances from a sibyl.[84] Their inclusion in this chapter is due in part to their adopting of a Greek persona and in part to the fact that they are composed in Greek hexameter. We will not be discussing all of the oracles, but only those that are widely thought to have been composed by Jews within our time period of interest, namely, oracles 1–5.[85] The compositional

82 The gnomic poem of Pseudo-Phocylides (chapter 4) is recognized by some as participating in wisdom. Cf. W. T. Wilson, *The Sentences of Pseudo-Phocylides* (CEJL; Berlin: De Gruyter, 2005), 69–71, 182.

83 Cf. H. Najman, *Seconding Sinai: The Development of Mosaic Discourse in Second Temple Judaism* (JSJSup 77; Leiden: Brill, 2003), 12–17.

84 For the Greek text, see J. Geffcken, ed., *Die Oracula Sibyllina* (GCS 8; Leipzig: Hinrichs, 1902).

85 *Oracle* 3 is thought to be the oldest, dating from the mid-second century BCE. Cf. J. Geffcken, *Komposition und Entstehungszeit der Oracula Sibyllina* (Leipzig: Hinrichs, 1902), 1–17; Fraser, *Ptolemaic Alexandria*, 1.711; J. J. Collins, *The Sibylline Oracles of Egyptian Judaism* (DS 13; Missoula, Mont.: Scholars Press, 1974), 28–33. Oracles 1 and 2 (which were originally one

histories of each of the Sibylline Oracles, as well as the corpus as a whole, are too complex to rehearse here; nor are they entirely relevant for our investigation.[86] Essentially, every oracle with Jewish underlay is thought to have elements of Christian interpolation; some, such as books 1–2, have more (e.g., 2.324–400), while others, such as book 5, have less (e.g., 5.256–269).[87] The amount of interpolation and the nature of each author's sources are highly debated and fall outwith the purview of this study, which will focus on the authors' participation in and potential adaptation of this literary form.

Scholars widely agree that the Sibylline Oracles are modeled on the literary form(s) of older oracles given by various sibyls, the number of whom was debated in antiquity.[88] Sibylline writings existed prior to their adoption by Jews in the Hellenistic era with established prototypical models and a tradition of literary composition.[89] This intentional participation is first signaled in the adoption of the sibyl persona at the openings, and sometimes closings, of Oracles 1–4 (1.1–4; 2.1–5, 339–347; 3.1–7, 809–829; 4.1–5).[90] The practice of first-person narration was particular to sibylline ecstatic utterances, as, unlike other ancient prophetesses, the sibyl was not fully submerged into the person of Apollo, but retained some autonomy to speak on her own behalf. Jewish authors maintained this distinctive tradition in their compositions, presenting the sibyl as speaking with her own voice, even if her will was subject to greater forces.

---

book) and oracles 4 and 5 were written after 70 CE, likely in the second century CE. Oracles 6–8 are thought to be Christian in origin, while oracles 9–14 are assigned dates outwith our purview. Cf. Schürer, *History*, 3.1.645–46.

86 Cf. J. J. Collins, "The Development of the Sibylline Tradition," *ANRW* 2.20.1 (1987): 421–59. For the discussion on book 3 alone, see Geffcken, *Komposition*, 1–17; Schürer, *History*, 3.1.632–33; Collins, *Sibylline Oracles*, 21–33; R. Buitenwerf, *Book III of the Sibylline Oracles and Its Social Setting* (SVTP 17; Leiden: Brill, 2003), 5–64.

87 For the nuanced discussion of authorship (Jewish or Christian) of certain oracles, see Davila, *Provenance*, 184–85; J. L. Lightfoot, *The Sibylline Oracles: With Introduction, Translation, and Commentary on the First and Second Books* (Oxford: Oxford University Press, 2007), 5–7, 77–93.

88 E.g., Pausanias, *Descr.* 10.12.1–11; Lactantius, *Inst.* 1.6. For a detailed discussion of pagan sibyl fragments, see I. Cervelli, "Questioni Sibilline," *Studi Storici* 4 (1993): 895–1001, especially 895–934. Goodenough, Momigliano, and others argue that in the Sibylline Oracles we have one of the most striking examples of Jewish authors adopting a non-Jewish, Hellenistic genre. Cf. E. R. Goodenough, *By Light, Light: The Mystic Gospel of Hellenistic Judaism* (Amsterdam: Philo Press, 1969), 282–89; A. Momigliano, "From the Pagan to the Christian Sibyl," in A. C. Dionisotti, A. Grafton, and J. Kraye, eds., *The Uses of Greek and Latin: Historical Essays* (London: Warburg Institute, 1988), 3–18.

89 For a learned discussion of this topic, see H. W. Parke, *Sibyls and Sibylline Prophecy in Classical Antiquity* (London: Routledge, 1988). To speak of a single, unified tradition clearly overlooks the diversity within sibylline works and ancient discussions. Cf. D. S. Potter, *Prophecy and History in the Crisis of the Roman Empire: A Historical Commentary on the Thirteenth Sibylline Oracle* (OCM; Oxford: Clarendon, 1990), 102.

90 The notable exception is the introduction of Oracle 5, in which 5.1 uses the first-person pronoun (μοι), but does not explicitly introduce the speaker (cf. 5.52, 111, 179, 333, 512).

The identity of the sybil as a pagan, female priestess, whose manic sayings are a manifestation of a Greek god (e.g., Apollo), has been viewed as a substantial accommodation of Greek culture. One way that a perceived tension between Jewish and Greek cultures was negotiated was by placing the sibylline tradition within the wider Jewish macro-narrative (flood and tower of Babel).[91] In Sib. Or. 3.823–827, followed by Prol. 34 and 1.287–290, we see Jewish authors identifying the sibyl as one of Noah's daughters-in-law. In doing so, the author can draw on her/Noah's knowledge of prediluvian history and speak forward in time to prophesy future events, being perfectly placed at the "midpoint of time" (1.292). At no point does the author align the sibyl with a specific ethnicity (Greek or Jewish). Rather, as the direct relative of the forefather of the human race, the sibyl embodies a universality that transcends ethnic affiliation, allowing her to speak "objectively" for the divine.[92]

The sibyl, although coming from different geographical regions, is undisputedly tied with Greek culture, and the authors of Oracles 1–5 follow this tradition.[93] First, all of the texts are written in Greek hexameter, with strong literary connections to the vocabulary and ideas of Homer and Hesiod.[94] Modeling the composition on Homer was likely part of sibylline tradition, although even he does not escape the negative assessment of the Jewish sibyl (3.419–432). Here, Homer is labeled a "false writer" (ψευδογράφος, 3.419) charged with two errors. First, even though war was classified as an immoral behavior earlier (3.204–205), he glorified and praised the heroes of war (3.426–428). Homer's second error was that he created gods to help humans (3.429), which stands in tension with the sibyl's monotheistic teaching (e.g., fr. iii.21–33; 3.108–158, 545–550). Despite these errors, the fame of Homer's work will have no end (3.418), and he will master the sibyl's words and meter, being the first person to open her books (3.424–425). This last idea reinforces the antiquity of the sibyl and her declared role in initiating hexameter; the sibyls did not model their

91 For a study of the author's attempt to align Jewish creation and flood narratives with Greek thought, see V. Nikiprowetzky, *La troisième Sibylle* (ÉB 9; Paris: Mouton, 1970), 112–94. For the discussion of the author's use of Pseudo-Eupolemus, see B. Z. Wacholder, "Pseudo-Eupolemus' Two Greek Fragments on the Life of Abraham," *HUCA* 34 (1963): 92–93.

92 Buitenwerf, *Sibylline Oracles*, 372–73.

93 For the importance and adoption of the sibyl in the Roman Empire, see Lactantius, *Inst.* 1.6.10–11; Virgil, *Aen.* 6.9–158.

94 E.g., hecatombs: Sib. Or. fr. i.21; 3.576; Homer, *Od.* 3.144; 4.478. Titans: Sib. Or. 3.110–155; Hesiod's *Theogony* and Euhermerus' *Sacred History* (cf. Diodorus Siculus, *Bibl.* 6.1.1–11; Lactantius, *Inst.* 1.11, 13–14, 17, 22). Cf. A. Kurfess, "Homer und Hesiod im 1 Buch der Oracula Sibyllina," *Phil* 100 (1956): 147–53; Whitmarsh, *Beyond*, 236–38; especially Lightfoot, *Sibylline Oracles*, 153–202. The sibyl did not speak in another poetic meter or in prose (cf. Tibullus, *Eleg.* 2.5.15–16; *Suda* H 541). However, the metrical quality was criticized, even in antiquity. Cf. Plutarch, *Mor.* 397a–b; Ps.-Justin, *Cohort. ad graec.* 36a; Sib. Or. Prol. 85–86.

speech on Homer, but he on them. This inversion of cultural origin resonates with similar Jewish claims, although here the argument is made more subtly.[95]

The type of prophetic utterances associated with the sibyls is also distinctive. Unlike the sayings attributed to other oracles of antiquity, which are given in response to specific questions asked by individuals or groups (e.g., Delphi), the Sibylline Oracles were written in discursive verse addressed to the world in general, rather than to any enquirer in particular.[96] This variation in audience implies that a key difference between sibylline and other oracles is length of utterance, with individuals often receiving short, enigmatic sayings, while the sibyls, followed by Jewish imitators, speak at length to the wider world.[97] As these sibylline works do not address individual questions, the oracles are free to foretell significant events that will impact groups of people (e.g., cities or nations): wars, famine, death, destruction, and natural disasters, especially earthquakes, floods, and volcanic eruptions.[98] This humanity-wide perspective, which resonates with the role and function of the biblical prophets, was ideal for facilitating Jewish international polemic and so could have been influential in the author's decision to adopt the sibylline persona over other Greek oracles/authors.

Another important difference is the medium of transmission. Most oracles are given verbally and are transmitted orally until encoded in writing (if ever). Although the oracles are presented as originating orally, they are fundamentally written prophecies, preserved and distributed through the use of physical artifacts, an idea that is reinforced by the recurring pairing of a sibyl in possession of a written document.[99] This shift to prioritize the written composition is fundamental for the recognition of a prototypical sibylline form and for allowing Jewish authors to participate in this literary practice. The tangibility and longevity of text allow for these works to be preserved and used as models by later authors.

The oracles are broadly in line with the literary conventions expected of a sibyl. However, this is not to imply that the Jewish authors did not adopt non-prototypical elements to better facilitate their purpose(s) in writing. Differences in purpose naturally result in specific innovations in literary practices.

95 Cf. Artapanus, F1; F3.4; Ps.-Eupolemus, F1.3–4.

96 Parke, *Sibyls and Sibylline Prophecy*, 6–7. Though, cf. Virgil, *Aen.* 6.42–155. Sibylline sayings could also be fabricated to apply to specific individuals, e.g., Lucian, *Alex.* 11; *Peregr.* 29–30.

97 E.g., Diogenes Laertius, *Vit.* 1.28; Dionysius of Halicarnassus, *Ant. rom.* 4.62.5–6; Diodorus Siculus, *Bibl.* 7.12.1–6; Pausanias, *Descr.* 10.24.1; Lucian, *Alex.* 47–54.

98 Cf. Plutarch, *Mor.* 398c–e.

99 Sib. Or. 3.425; cf. Dionysius of Halicarnassus, *Ant. rom.* 4.62.1–6; Tibullus, *Eleg.* 2.5.67–70; Lactantius, *Inst.* 1.6.

By far the most obvious difference is the sibyl's inclusion of Jewish ideas. In particular, the Jewish oracles have a strong emphasis on moral exhortation, such as critiquing idolatry (3.545–550; 4.6–11; 5.77–85, 353–356) and other corrupt practices, especially sexual misconduct.[100] Another difference is the strong monotheistic perspective advocated by the speaker. The sibyls exclusively use the singular noun to reference God and mention other gods only negatively (e.g., 4.4–5; 5.7), even challenging their existence (5.484–491).[101] In passages associated with the prohibition of idols or with the final judgment, the sibyls declare the oneness of God (e.g., fr. iii.21–33; 3.108–158, 545–550; 4.30; 5.173) and that he alone is immortal (e.g., 2.219–220; 5.66). In Sib. Or. 3.110–157, the Titans are presented as if they were just another kingdom (admittedly the first) to be judged and destroyed by God. Such declarations reinforce the Jewish perspective on the divine and emphasize the monotheistic stance of the authors.

Collins has argued that the oracles appear to be innovative in setting sibylline prophecies within a universal history, claiming that previous sibylline texts did not stretch their narrative to the ancient past.[102] This view is in tension with the claim by Parke that one of the great innovations of the original sibyl authors was to invest their speakers with antiquity so that they could accurately "prophesy" the future.[103] Situating *ex eventu* prophecies and writings in a wider historical frame is not only a Greek innovation, but is found in multiple ancient cultures, especially Jewish apocalyptic writings.[104] On the other hand, the use of *macrologia* to expand the scope of history within the oracles is an important development. Through this literary feature the author subsumed Greek history into a Jewish worldview.

These literary innovations are related to the novelty of new addressees. In the narrative world, the addressees of the oracles are the Greeks and other nations.[105] This perspective fits with the adoption of a Greek figure and her tradition of speaking to the Greek people. However, it is clear from the text that the primary intended readers are Jews, for whom these oracles reinforce their identity and distinct practices (e.g., 3.295–504; 5.238–285). The Jewish people are depicted as having religiously appropriate behavior and as the sole nation

100 E.g., 1.150–170, 174–198; 3.8–45, 218–264, 545–600, 715–731, 762–766; 4.31–34; 5.165–167, 386–393.

101 There are some passages in Sib. Or. 5 that do not appear to speak of the gods in totally negative terms, but recall elements of their narratives (e.g., 5.131, 140).

102 J. J. Collins, "The Jewish Transformation of Sibylline Oracles," in *Seers, Sibyls, and Sages in Hellenistic-Roman Judaism* (Leiden: Brill, 1997), 190–92.

103 Parke, *Sibyls and Sibylline Prophecy*, 7. So also Buitenwerf, *Sibylline Oracles*, 373.

104 J. J. Collins, *The Apocalyptic Imagination: An Introduction to Jewish Apocalyptic Literature* (2nd ed.; Grand Rapids: Eerdmans, 1998), 6.

105 E.g., fr. i.1, 25; fr. iii.38–45; 3.217, 624; 5.179, 204, 214, 287.

to acknowledge and worship the one and only God (3.218–247, 573–600). The change of intended audience and the addition of Jewish content are important differences to the oracular genre and highlight the plasticity of the genre.

The Sibylline Oracles have significant implications for our understanding of Jewish engagement with Greek literary culture. We witness in oracles the willingness to adopt a specific, non-Jewish narrator identity, indicating a strong engagement with Greek literary culture and the possibility that some Jewish authors thought positively about the sibyl (3.809–829). The incorporating of the sibyl into the Jewish metanarrative, even if tangentially, might have mitigated some perceived tensions. At the very least, subsequent Jewish (and Christian) readers must have appreciated and valued the contribution of the first Jewish sibylline work enough in order to create additional oracular texts. This first work, having been accepted within Jewish literary circles, became a prototype for subsequent compositions, establishing through adaptation a new nexus and constellation of literary features upon which later authors would model their work.

The Sibylline Oracles also provide a window into Jewish education practices, revealing that a number of Jewish (and later Christian) authors had sufficient competency in Greek hexameter and knowledge of sibylline traditions to compose these works.[106] We may also presume that, as these texts are intended for a Jewish readership, a number of Jews would have had prior knowledge of sibylline traditions and related literature, as well as the educational sophistication to read and appreciate these works. That these texts were written over multiple centuries and likely in different geographic locales (e.g., Asia Minor, Egypt) speaks to the prevalence of this level of education over time and geographic location, suggesting that throughout the Hellenistic and Roman eras Jews in certain communities continued to be educated in classical Greek literature.

Overall, the Sibylline Oracles provide a concrete example of a number of Jewish authors engaging with a specific type of Greek religious composition. As far as we are able to determine, Jewish authors followed their pagan predecessors in a majority of literary features (e.g., narrator, length, meter, general subject). However, Jewish authors also felt free to adapt a recognized Greek genre to accommodate Jewish ideas. In doing so, these authors imbued a Greek religious literary form with Jewish theological perspectives (e.g., specific elements of morality, monotheism, etc.) and so changed the nature of

106 The metrical irregularities might indicate a lack of mastery with regard to Greek poetry. At the same time, they might also be an intentional stylistic element, highlighting the scribe's inability to keep up with the sibyl's ecstatic utterance. Some corruption would surely have entered through the transmission of the texts, but it is likely that some ametrical verses stem back to the author(s).

this genre to something that would be viewed as prototypical by later Christian authors.

Fragments of Pseudo-Greek Poets

Related to the idea of adopting a Greek persona for the construction of an entire work is the practice of composing specific pseudonymous sayings. Although this does not directly address our primary interest of Jewish participation in Greek genres, this practice provides strong evidence of how some Jews attempted to negotiate space in the Hellenistic era.[107] These fragments of pseudo-Greek writers have come down to us in the works of Clement of Alexandria (*Protrepticus*, *Stromata*), Pseudo-Justin (*De monarchia*, *Cohortatio ad Gentiles*), and subsequently Eusebius (*Praeparatio evangelica*). These Christian authors employed Greek poetic quotes apologetically, in defense of the Jewish tradition of the oneness of God, and antagonistically, highlighting the problems with "pagan" worship practices.

These "excerpts" range from a single line (Homer, Hesiod) to a sixteen-line stanza (Philemon/Menander), all of which appear to have two features in common. First, every author to whom a quotation is attributed is famous and an icon of Greek culture (e.g., Homer, Hesiod, Pythagoras, Aeschylus, Sophocles, Euripides, Philemon, Diphilus, and Menander).[108] This criterion is understandable, as "inferior" Greek authors would not meet the presumed needs of those citing them. Second, the author in question needed to have said something (or at least reported to have) that could be used to support Jewish/Christian monotheistic theology.

Identifying the likely date(s) of composition for each fragment is not possible, nor is it necessary for this project, although there are some indications that these verses were composed and assembled prior to their use by Christian authors.[109] The two most extensive collections of fragments come from Clement's *Stromata* and Pseudo-Justin's *De monarchia*.[110] Both the order of the fragments and their individual lengths vary by author and do not provide a holistic organizing principle. Nevertheless, the similarities between these grouped ci-

107 This practice was not limited to Jewish authors, but was also part of Hellenistic literary practice. Cf. Wilson, *Sentences*, 5.

108 There is some confusion between Clement and Pseudo-Justin over the authorship of certain verses. This further undermines some of our confidence in the texts' authenticity.

109 Clement (*Strom.* 5.14.113) cites Hecataeus' *On Abraham and the Egyptians* as the source for his quotation of Sophocles, and Eusebius (*Praep. ev.* 8.11.3) claims took his citations from Aristobulus. The attribution by Clement is most likely wrong, but does not take away from its antiquity. Cf. Wacholder, *Eupolemus*, 264–66. For Christian collections of excerpts, see M. C. Albl, *"And Scripture Cannot Be Broken": The Form and Function of the Early Christian Testimonia Collections* (NovTSup 96; Leiden: Brill, 1999).

110 Where there is a difference in length, Pseudo-Justin's text is typically longer.

tations have led scholars to argue that many, if not all, of the fragments (especially tragic and comic passages) were collected in a single gnomologion or anthology seeking to show that Jewish monotheism was foreshadowed in classical literature.[111]

One of the struggles with discussing this collection is our uncertainty that any of these fragments in fact go back to their putative author. Many verses contain themes that are traditionally recognized as Jewish, such as the singularity and transcendence of God and the inferiority of idols and pagan worship, suggesting a Jewish origin. However, some stanzas contain themes that were discussed by non-Jewish authors (e.g., the number seven) and so could be authentic compositions by those to whom the passages are attributed. The argument of this section, however, does not rest on a singular instance, but on the collection as a whole and what this practice implies: certain Jewish writers used the appellation of notable Greek authors and their literary practices as a means to spread personal and cultural ideologies. This practice is not purely apologetic, as has been proposed, but is also oppositional in that it twists the writings of non-Jewish authors or attributes words to them that are then used to undermine the ascribed author's cultural values in favor of Jewish ones.[112] More broadly, these compositions situate specific ideas within the wider Greek worldview, which may or may not be in tension with the viewpoints of those to whom the texts are attributed.

The practice of composing verses under a Greek poet's name indicates the type and level of education received by these Jewish authors. Not only do these fragments display an awareness and knowledge of Greek literati, they also evidence an education in which Greek authors and works were taught. Success in the practice of *imitatio* takes skill and substantial knowledge of its model in order to be persuasive, and these quotations appear to have survived due in part to their convincing nature.[113] As a result, we can say with confidence that these passages indicate that their authors attained a high level of Greek literary culture, were familiar with the pillars of Greek literature, and viewed themselves as participating in the wider Hellenistic practice of cultural debate.[114]

111 H. W. Attridge, "Fragments of Pseudo-Greek Poets," in *OTP* 2.821.

112 D. Dawson, *Allegorical Readers and Cultural Revision in Ancient Alexandria* (Berkeley: University of California Press, 1992), 109.

113 We do not know how convincing these excerpts were, nor do we have non-Christian sources that cite them (as Stobaeus did for Pseudo-Phocylides). This suggests that they might have been seen as spurious. Cf. Walter, "Dichtung," 251–52. Nevertheless, their inclusion in Clement, Eusebius, and Pseudo-Justin suggests that they were at least convincing to some.

114 See most recently, J. P. J. Schedtler, "Perplexing Pseudepigraphy: The Pseudonymous Greek Poets," *JAJ* 8 (2017): 69–89.

Conclusion

Each author discussed above displays strong familiarity with Greek literature. Pseudo-Orpheus and the sibylline authors show skill in adopting the persona and writing style of their namesakes, Ezekiel exhibits knowledge of pinnacular Greek tragedians, and the poetic forgers display an awareness of literary tendencies specific to the author they are imitating. Each author indicates through their work that they are conversant with specific ancient authors and that they have the skills to tailor their writing styles to fit their literary agenda. Like Philo Epicus and Theodotus in chapter 2, these authors are very well educated, and their Greek education influenced their writing through their selection of Greek genres. The range of Greek authors used differs for each writer, influenced by their selected genre and temporally constrained by the adopted model author.

Knowledge of Jewish Scripture is seen in the works of Ezekiel and Pseudo-Orpheus and is understandably absent in the Greek poetic forgeries. The use of the LXX by these authors, as opposed to the Hebrew text, is less certain. Pseudo-Orpheus provides almost no evidence for or against LXX use. Conversely, there are a couple of instances in Ezekiel that suggest he was using a version of the LXX as a source. The LXX did not constrict or influence the author's Greek style; rather, it appears primarily to have been a source of information that the author used to construct his work.

All of the authors show clear participation in Greek genres. The lack of substantial adaptation by some writers is likely a result of the authors' adoption of a Greek persona, which requires closer affiliation to specific Greek literary forms, syntax, and language. However, even in these cases we witness Jewish authors including nonprototypical elements. Adherence to the scriptural narrative is less restricted, but is followed most prominently in Ezekiel's *Exagoge*, which remains (mostly) faithful to the biblical text, resulting in the inclusion of nonprototypical features within the Greek tragic genre to fit his material. Overall, these texts show that Jewish authors engaged with Greek poetic forms throughout the Hellenistic era and were able to make strategic genre choices and to adapt their chosen genre to align with their worldview and intended purpose.

4

Didactic Literature

A primary function of text creation in antiquity was to educate readers. For some genres this purpose was not prominent, but for others it was explicit. In this chapter we will evaluate the works of Aristobulus, Pseudo-Phocylides, Gospel of Thomas, and Philo of Alexandria, a range of authors whose texts engage the reader in acts of teaching and explanation.[1] These works participate in the wider Hellenistic practice of scholarship and source amalgamation, but also show evidence of nonprototypical elements, some of which parallel wider Jewish practices.

Aristobulus

Aristobulus was a Jewish writer whose perceived philosophical knowledge earned him the epitaph "the Peripatetic" (Clement, *Strom.* 1.72.4; Eusebius, *Praep. ev.* 13.12.*praef.*).[2] Of his *Explanations of the Book of Moses* only five fragments remain, having been preserved by Eusebius and Clement via Alexander Polyhistor.[3] The debate over the dating of Aristobulus' work arises from conflicting reports by Eusebius, who, in his discussion of the Passover (*Hist. eccl.* 7.32.14–18), states while excerpting a writing of Ana-

1 Some texts in chapters 3 and 5 also participate in didactic genres. The placement of texts in other chapters is not to imply that they do not overlap in formal features or in purpose.

2 For a critique of Christian authorship, see Walter, *Thoraausleger*, 35–123. For the history of discussion, see Holladay, *Fragments*, vol. 3, *Aristobulus*, 49–72; D. Winston, "Aristobulus from Walter to Holladay," *SPhiloA* 8 (1996): 155–66. For the most recent study of Aristobulus, see M. Mülke, *Aristobulos in Alexandria: Jüdische Bibelexegese zwischen Griechen und Ägyptern unter Ptolemaios VI. Philometor* (ULG 126; Berlin: De Gruyter, 2018). Unfortunately, I did not have sufficient time to fully engage with this work.

3 The edition used is that of Mras, GCS 43.1, 451–54; 43.2, 190–97. The passages are Eusebius, *Hist. eccl.* 7.32.6–8; *Praep. ev.* 8.9.38–8.10.17; 13.12.1–2; 13.12.3–8; 13.12.9–16. Although there are parallels in Clement, Eusebius' excerpts are thought to be superior. Clement implies that the work has multiple books (*Strom.* 1.22.150.1; 5.14.97.7).

tolius that Aristobulus dedicated exegetical books on the law of Moses to Ptolemy II Philadelphus (r. 283–246 BCE) and his father, Ptolemy I Soter (r. 305/4–282),[4] and that he was one of the seventy who translated the Torah into Greek.[5] This is in tension with the dating assumed by Clement and Eusebius in other passages, both of whom envision Ptolemy VI Philometor (r. 181–145 BCE) as the king to whom the work is dedicated. Based on Aristobulus' use of προγόνου ("ancestor") in his reference to "Philadelphus" (fr. 3.2) and his familiarity with the legend of the Septuagint's translation, the scholarly community holds that a date not prior to Ptolemy VI's reign in the middle of the second century BCE is most likely.[6]

Aristobulus' address to a Greek monarch fits with the rise of royal patronage and the growing practice of dedications during the Hellenistic period.[7] This dedication establishes a "dialogue" between two parties in which Aristobulus provides answers to questions purportedly asked by the king. Aristobulus uses language to delineate two parties, indicating his association with the Jewish people through the use of the first-person plural ("us," "our") and the phrases "our philosophical school [αἵρεσις]" and "our law" (fr. 4.8). Ptolemy is differentiated from this group through the use of the second-person singular ("you"), particularly in fragment 2, indicating that the addressee is an outsider. The historical reality of the address to Ptolemy is debated (was the composition actually dedicated and sent to the king, and, if it did reach Ptolemy, how was it received?).[8] More significant for this study is the literary value of the dedication and what its existence indicates about the work's function and the author's engagement with Greek literary expectations. The narrative construction of the addressee as an outsider suggests that Aristobulus' work has an apologetic aspect or, at minimum, he wished to frame his narrative in such a way.[9] Despite the explicit royal address, the internal narrative does not

4 For a discussion of regnal dates, see G. Hölbl, *A History of the Ptolemaic Empire* (trans. T. Saavedra; London: Routledge, 2001), 20–46.

5 Cf. Eusebius, *Praep. ev.* 7.13.7; Clement, *Strom.* 1.22.150.1.

6 Walter, *Thoraausleger*, 13–26; N. Walter, "Fragmente jüdisch-hellenisticher Exegeten: Aristobulos, Demetrios, Aristeas," in *JSHRZ* 3.2, 262; Hengel (*Judaism and Hellenism*, 1.163–69) argues for a date early in Ptolemy VI's reign.

7 For Hellenistic examples, see Callimachus, *Hymn.* 1.84; Manetho, *Aegyp.* fr. 3 (*FGrH* 609 T11b); Berossus, *FGrH* 680 T2; Apollodorus, *Chronology*, *FGrH* 244 T2; cf. Nicolaus, *FGrH* 90 F135; Josephus, *Ant.* 1.8–9; *CIJ* 2.1440–42; 2.1449.

8 Some scholars have argued that an address to the king by Aristobulus is not outwith the realm of possibility. E.g., Tcherikover, "Jewish Apologetic Literature," 178 n. 20; Hengel, *Judaism and Hellenism*, 2.106–7 n. 378. For a discussion of the reference to the king as a literary convention, see Bickerman, *Jews in the Greek Age*, 228.

9 Hengel, *Judaism and Hellenism*, 1.164; cf. M. Friedländer, *Geschichte der jüdischen Apologetik als Vorgeschichte des Christentums* (Zürich: Schmidt, 1903), 209; Mülke, *Aristobulos*, 203–8.

necessarily imply that the work was written only for outsiders. Rather, the use of the king as the interlocutor provides structure for the work, but does not constrain the intended audience to a single individual. Aristobulus' text looks beyond the person of the king and speaks to the enduring relation of Jewish and Greek cultures.[10]

Aristobulus' cultural positioning has implications for his presentation of philosophical schools. Aristobulus was called a Peripatetic and was viewed by later authors as someone who embodied both Jewish and Greek ideas.[11] Aristobulus displays knowledge of many philosophical schools, but is only beholden to one: the Jewish αἵρεσις.[12] By presenting Aristobulus as a bridge philosopher, one who is knowledgeable about two worlds of thought and competent to bring them into dialogue, he is recognized as one who could successfully develop dialogue between Jews and Greeks.[13]

The apologetic nature of Aristobulus' work has been well documented by scholars and does not need rehearsing.[14] Aristobulus, however, is not entirely

10 Tcherikover, in his classic article, argues that biblical commentaries could not have been written for Greek readers, as no gentile writer expressed interest in Greek Scriptures. Tcherikover, "Jewish Apologetic Literature," 177–78. Tcherikover's claim is not entirely accurate. Cf. Ps.-Longinus, *Subl.* 9.9; Alexander Polyhistor; Numenius of Apamea (Origen, *Cels.* 4.51); Agatharchides of Cnidus, *On the Red Sea* (cf. Josephus, *Ant.* 12.5–6); Nicolaus of Damascus, *Susanna.*

11 Eusebius, *Praep. ev.* 8.9.38, ὁ δὲ Ἀριστόβουλος καὶ τῆς κατ' Ἀριστοτέλην φιλοσοφίας πρὸς τῇ πατρίῳ μετειληχώς. Radice (among others) argues that Aristobulus was familiar with the work *De Mundo* attributed to Aristotle, especially the differentiation between God's "being" (οὐσία) and "power" (δύναμις, cf. *Mundo* 6, 397b9–27), and so could be considered a Peripatetic. Cf. R. Radice, *La filosofia di Aristobulo e i suoi nessi con il "De mundo" attribuito ad Aristotele* (Temi metafisici e problemi del pensiero antico, Studi e Testi 33; Milan: Vita e pensiero, 1994).

12 For instance, Aristobulus shows Stoic influence in his employment of a stock Stoic wisdom metaphor (fr. 5.12), his citation of Aratus (fr. 4.6), his insistence on the pervasive power of God (fr. 4.7), and his use of allegory. Pythagorean thought is seen in the relationship between the Sabbath and the number seven (fr. 5), and Cynic traditions in how he connects the nature of cosmic being with the unity of the Deity. Walter, *Thoraausleger*, 12–13; Schürer, *History*, 3.1.583. More recently, Maren Niehoff has challenged the claim of multiple philosophical influences, identifying a number of parallels between Aristobulus' approach to Scripture and the approaches of his Aristotelian contemporaries. Cf. M. R. Niehoff, *Jewish Exegesis and Homeric Scholarship in Alexandria* (Cambridge: Cambridge University Press, 2011), 58–74.

For Jewish use of αἵρεσις, see Josephus, *Vita* 10, 12, 191, 197; *BJ* 2.119; Acts 5:17. For the Jews as a race of philosophers, see Theophrastus in Porphyry, *Abst.* 2.26; Aristotle in Josephus, *C. Ap.* 1.179. Cf. LA 235.

13 See also 2 Macc 1:10, which presents Aristobulus as a leader of the Jewish community in Alexandria, as a relative of the anointed priests (ὄντι δὲ ἀπὸ τοῦ τῶν χριστῶν ἱερέων γένους), and as the teacher of King Ptolemy and of the Jews in Egypt (διδασκάλῳ Πτολεμαίου τοῦ βασιλέως . . . καὶ τοῖς ἐν Αἰγύπτῳ 'Ιουδαίοις).

14 Walter, *Thoraausleger*, 27–28; A. Y. Collins, "Aristobulus," in *OTP* 2.834; L. L. Grabbe, "Jewish Identity and Hellenism in the Fragmentary Jewish Writings in Greek," in P. Gray and G. R. O'Day, eds., *Scripture and Traditions: Essays on Early Judaism and Christianity in Honor of Carl R. Holladay* (NovTSup 129; Leiden: Brill, 2008), 28.

reconciliatory, challenging his readers to recognize the veracity and antiquity of Jewish thought. The originality of Greek philosophy is undermined by Aristobulus' claim that specific Greek authors were dependent on Moses and his writings. Aristobulus alleges that "philosophers . . . and many others, including poets, took significant material from him [Moses] and are admired accordingly,"[15] that "Plato imitated our legislator,"[16] and that Pythagoras "transferred many of our doctrines and integrated them into his own system of beliefs."[17] These claims are rearticulated in fragment 4.4 when Aristobulus states, "It seems to me that Pythagoras, Socrates, and Plato with great care follow him [Moses] in all respects."[18] Aristobulus also asserts that the preclassical writers Homer and Hesiod, as well as the legendary Linus, derived their knowledge of the seven-day week and its holy day from the law (fr. 5.13–16),[19] going so far as to claim that it is only due to their imitation of Moses that they have garnered their own reputation (fr. 2.4).

Fundamental to this relationship is the claim that the law of Moses was translated into Greek prior to the Septuagint and so was available to classical Greek authors (fr. 3.1). Aristobulus claims that, although the full translation of the law occurred during the reign of Ptolemy II Philadelphus (fr. 3.2), portions of the law had been translated prior to the conquests of Alexander and the Persians (fr. 3.1). Despite skepticism by modern scholars about the historical veracity of this assertion, this chronology is necessary if one is to claim that classical Greek authors made use of Moses' writings. Aristobulus' claim fabricates an extended historical interaction between these two cultures, asserting that Greek knowledge of Jewish philosophy is not limited to the time after the conquests of Alexander. The influence of this interaction, however, is (primarily) unidirectional in that it is the Jewish philosopher Moses who influenced Greek thought and not the inverse.[20] This claim overturns the current cultural relationship between Jews and Greeks at a time in which the latter culture was recognized as the dominant. As a result, Aristobulus' presentation of Jewish antiquity and Greek dependence cannot solely be understood as benign apol-

15 Fr. 2.4, ὧν εἰσιν οἱ προειρημένοι φιλόσοφοι καὶ πλείονες ἕτεροι καὶ ποιηταὶ παρ' αὐτοῦ μεγάλας ἀφορμὰς εἰληφότες, καθὸ καὶ θαυμάζονται.

16 Fr. 3.1, φανερὸν ὅτι κατηκολούθησεν ὁ Πλάτων τῇ καθ' ἡμᾶς νομοθεσίᾳ.

17 Fr. 3.1, καθὼς καὶ Πυθαγόρας πολλὰ τῶν παρ' ἡμῖν μετενέγκας εἰς τὴν ἑαυτοῦ δογματοποιίαν κατεχώρισεν.

18 Fr. 4.4, δοκοῦσι δέ μοι περιειργασμένοι πάντα κατηκολουθηκέναι τούτῳ Πυθαγόρας τε καὶ Σωκράτης καὶ Πλάτων.

19 For a thorough discussion of the citation of Greek authors, see Walter, *Thoraausleger*, 150–66.

20 Greeks have taken "hints" from Moses (παρ' αὐτοῦ μεγάλας ἀφορμὰς εἰληφότες, fr. 2.4). For the importance of the Jewish sage in engaging with Greek philosophers, see Clearchus of Soli, cited by Josephus, *C. Ap.* 1.175–182.

ogetics, as it challenges and even seeks to reframe the current relationship between these two cultures, arguing that Greek poets and philosophers advocate a specific type of wisdom derived from Moses.

This claim of philosophical and literary priority is not limited to Aristobulus, but was an important aspect of minority culture's engagement with Hellenism. The ambiguity surrounding Homer's origins, debated even in antiquity, allowed for disparate cultures to claim him for their own: Heliodorus (*Aeth.* 3.14) asserted that Homer was an Egyptian, while Meleager of Gadara claimed in *The Graces* that Homer was a Syrian.[21] These claims of alternative origins were not limited to Homer, but were asserted about individuals whose origins were secure (e.g., Alexander the Great in Ps.-Callisthenes, *Alex. rom.* 1.4).[22]

The fragmentary nature of the *Explanations of the Book of Moses* hinders our ability to determine fully which genre(s) Aristobulus' work participated in. Eusebius, citing Anatolius, describes Aristobulus' text as "exegetical books" (βίβλους ἐξηγητικάς) on Moses (*Hist. eccl.* 7.32.16). Aristobulus regularly cites and expounds the pentateuchal text for his reader, although no fragment provides a close exegesis of any particular passage.[23] Instead, Aristobulus adopts the hermeneutical practice of atomization in order to allow him to say something that the source text did not originally say. Aristobulus asserts that a surface reading of Moses (κατὰ τὴν ἐπιφάνειαν) fails to elucidate the prophetic insight recognized by those who can think properly (τὸ καλῶς νοεῖν, fr. 2.3–4). In these instances, Aristobulus does not defend the text solely on ethnic lines, but according to interpretive strategy, chastising both Jewish and Greek readers who, by clinging to the letter only (fr. 2.5), miss the many layers (πολλαχῶς) of the text, its ordered structure (μεγάλων πραγμάτων κατασκευάς), and its detailed arrangements of nature (φυσικὰς διαθέσεις, fr. 2.3).[24] If one took an overly literal approach to the text, one would miss the "real" meaning and so would "fall victim to mythological and human conceptions" (fr. 2.2).

21 Athenaeus, *Deipn.* 5.157b; cf. Dio Chrysostom, *Or.* 47.5; 55.7; Pausanias, *Descr.* 10.24.3.

22 Cf. Hadas, *Hellenistic Culture*, 72–82; T. Whitmarsh, "The Birth of a Prodigy: Heliodorus and the Genealogy of Hellenism," in R. L. Hunter, ed., *Studies in Heliodorus* (Cambridge: Cambridge Philological Society, 1998), 93–124.

23 The major exception to this statement would be the claim by Walter that fr. 5 is a "Spekulativen Erklärung" of Gen 2:1–4. Walter, *Thoraausleger*, 28. Six explicit citations of the law of Moses are found in the fragments: four are from Exodus (three in fr. 2.8 and one in fr. 5.12), one is from Genesis (fr. 4.3), and one is from Deuteronomy (fr. 2.13). For a discussion of this issue, see S. A. Adams, "Did Aristobulus Use the LXX for His Citations?" *JSJ* 45 (2014): 1–14. The conclusions of the article call into question the assertion by Walter ("Exegeten," 264) and Collins ("Aristobulus," 2.832) that Aristobulus used the LXX and opens the possibility that Aristobulus knew Hebrew or a Greek version different than that of the LXX.

24 Although there are some similarities between Aristobulus' interpretational method and that of the Stoics, Niehoff (*Jewish Exegesis*, 66–71) rightfully notes that they are not identical, highlighting significant differences in themes and perspectives.

This textual focus supports the view that *Explanations* participates in the genre of ζητήματα literature. This term is used once by Eusebius in describing Aristobulus' writings (*Hist. eccl.* 7.32.17, τὰ ζητούμενα) and once by Aristobulus (fr. 2.1) to refer to the query given by the king. Both statements recognize that one of the intended functions of the treatise is to provide answers for perceived interpretive difficulties. The genre of questions and answers was commonly used in philosophical discussions between two philosophical schools and was often part of a larger debate (e.g., Porphyry, *Vit. Plot.* 15).[25] As Aristobulus appears to provide a full explanation of the texts of Moses, looking at each instance (καθ' ἕκαστον) in which an interpretive issue might arise (fr. 2.6), his work aligns well with prototypical examples of this genre.[26]

One challenge to viewing Aristobulus' work as a zetematic composition is the lack of a recognizable question-and-answer structure and the sequential movement through the text that is regularly found in prototypical models (see below). Aristobulus also does not provide the presumed questions asked by the king. These dissimilarities could imply that Aristobulus' work is not a core participant of *quaestiones* literature, but also participates in general philosophical treatise in which questions are addressed and challenging theological ideas are unpacked.[27] This multiple participation finds support in Aristobulus' interest in and discussion of the divine being, who, although manifesting visually in the text, breaks the laws of nature, but fulfills the more fundamental order of the universe (e.g., fr. 2.15–17). Similarly, Aristobulus' argument that the power of God permeates all things (fr. 4.7) does not follow a typical question-and-answer format, but is a sustained argument complete with block quotations attributed to Greek authors in support of his position.[28]

25 For a more thorough discussion of the *quaestiones* literature, especially how it was used for and by insiders, see the section on Philo's *QG* and *QE* below.

26 Cf. fr. 2.8 (God's "hand"); 4.3 (God's "voice"); 5.9–16 (the explanation of the seven-day week and the Sabbath). Cf. Mülke, *Aristobulos*, 53–59. For a discussion of Aristobulus' transpositional hermeneutic, see A. Lange and Z. Pleše, "Derveni—Alexandria—Qumran: Transpositional Hermeneutics in Greek Culture," in S. H. Aufrère, P. S. Alexander, and Z. Pleše, eds., *On the Fringes of Commentary: Metatextuality in Ancient Near Eastern and Ancient Mediterranean Cultures* (OLA 232; Leuven: Peeters, 2014), 89–160, especially 115–29.

27 The fragmentary nature of the work and its selected extractions could also provide a rationale for this apparent lack. Similarly, the diversity of *quaestiones* literature is not fully known, and so one would not want to be too prescriptive.

28 Quotes: Orpheus, fr. 4.5; Aratus, fr. 4.6; Hesiod, fr. 5.13; Homer, fr. 5.14; Linus, fr. 5.16. References: Plato and Pythagoras, fr. 3.1; Pythagoras, Socrates, and Plato, fr. 4.4. Many scholars think it unlikely that Aristobulus was the person who originally compiled the citations, seeing him as dependent on a florilegium. Cf. Schürer, *History*, 3.1.583–84; Walter, *Thoraausleger*, 166; Collins, *Athens*, 178; Holladay, *Fragments: Aristobulus*, 70–71. This argument assumes that there were other Jewish authors prior to Aristobulus who penned and compiled the pseudepigraphical verses and that this collection was sufficiently available for Aristobulus to find, read, and

Another challenge is determining how the chronological discussions in fragment 1 relate to the rest of the work. Eusebius, drawing on Anatolius, claims that Aristobulus provides a detailed discussion of the astrological location of the sun at the time of year when Passover occurs (fr. 1.17–18). This section in Eusebius seeks to clarify the timing of Passover and so might indicate the discussion of an interpretive issue within Aristobulus' text. Aristobulus' other fragments do not provide detailed scientific answers to questions, but are primarily philosophical. The inclusion of scientific explanations (if representative of Aristobulus' work) increases the diversity of the text's contents, supporting the view that Aristobulus' *Explanations* does not fit neatly within one genre. Rather, the work participates broadly in philosophical literary forms in which elements of *quaestiones* literature are incorporated into a larger discussion of cultural debate.

Overall, we witness in Aristobulus a strong connection between Greek and Jewish approaches to texts. For Aristobulus this relationship began with the intellectual borrowing of Moses by the Greeks and ultimately resulted in a fundamental agreement between Jews and Greeks in certain topics. This text displays Aristobulus' knowledge of Greek and Jewish thought and his role in increasing dialogue between these two groups. At the same time, Aristobulus uses his knowledge of Greek literature to bolster the claims of Judaism, presenting it to Greek intellectuals and the Egyptian monarch as worthy of respect. Citing passages purported to be from respected Greek authors, Aristobulus draws upon Greece's literary heritage to support a correct interpretation of Jewish Scripture. His participation in Greek genres is an act of cultural engagement, as he presents Jewish ideas in a way that his Greek readers would have found familiar. That Aristobulus' text does not neatly fit within a specific genre does not undermine its impact. Rather, his work shows that there was a wide range of literature in which certain formal elements of other literary forms could be included (e.g., explicit answering of questions). Aristobulus' *Explanations* provides a distinctive example of combining academic and philosophical composition, supporting the view that Jewish authors contributed to its literary development.

Pseudo-Phocylides

Purporting to be a collection of γνῶμαι by Phocylides (v. 2), a sixth-century BCE poet, *Sentences* is widely thought to be a Jewish-Hellenistic pseudepigraphon written in the first-centuries BCE/CE.[29] *Sentences* consists of approximately 230

use. This assumption has important implications for our understanding of the Jewish literary community in Alexandria and the resources available to these writers.

29 Cf. Wilson, *Sentences*, 7. Greek texts used: D. Young, "Ps.-Phocylides," in A.-M. Denis, ed., *Fragmenta Pseudepigraphorum quae supersunt graeca* (Leiden: Brill, 1970), 149–56; P. Derron,

lines of monostichic sayings in rough dactylic hexameter (the form associated with epic and didactic poetry) and employs Ionic dialectic morphology, as befits the Phocylides persona.[30] The author's ability to employ Phocylides-era style, meter, and vocabulary indicates that he was well versed in preclassical Greek literature (e.g., Homer, Hesiod, Theognis).[31]

In antiquity, Phocylides was recognized as an important poet (e.g., Isocrates, *Ad Nic.* 43–44), and preeminent among the ancients for giving wise advice for daily life. The author presents Phocylides in a favorable light, identifying him as the "wisest of men" (ἀνδρῶν ὁ σοφώτατος, vv. 1–2), blessed with dispensing divine counsel (θεοῦ βουλεύματα) and the "mysteries of righteousness" (δικαιοσύνης μυστήρια, v. 229). Phocylides' renown is insufficient for indicating why a Jewish writer would employ a Greek pseudonym when a Jewish one (e.g., Solomon) was readily available and commonly used by other Jewish authors. What will be argued in this section is that Phocylides (rather than a Jewish author) offered a unique opportunity for the blending of Greek and Jewish ideas and the potential to engage both groups of readers.

Although the author's choice of Phocylides signals a close relationship with Greek literary culture, the gnomic format, content, and purpose of *Sentences* have parallels throughout the ancient world and represent a near-universal lit-

---

trans., *Pseudo-Phocylide: Sentences* (Collection des Universités de France [Budé]; Paris: Les Belles Lettres, 1986), lxvi–lxxxii.

Jewish authorship was first argued by J. Bernays, *Ueber das phokylideische Gedicht: Ein Beittrag zur hellenistischen Literatur* (Berlin, 1856), 250. For a succinct discussion, see P. W. van der Horst, *The Sentences of Pseudo-Phocylides* (SVTP; Leiden: Brill, 1978), 55–58; J. J. Collins, *Jewish Wisdom in the Hellenistic Age* (Edinburgh: T&T Clark, 1997), 158–77. The Jewish ethnicity of the author is debated with some positing a possible Christian or proselyte origin (e.g., Davila, *Provenance*, 35–37, 64–68). Most recently, after having drafted this book, I read Klawans' article, which makes a compelling case for Christian, although not necessarily non-Jewish, authorship. Because of the likely Christian origin of Pseudo-Phocylides, the evidence from this author will necessarily be held more loosely in our overall conclusion. Cf. J. Klawans, "The Pseudo-Jewishness of Pseudo-Phocylides," *JSP* 26 (2017): 201–33.

On the relationship between pseudepigraphy and forgery, especially with the intention to deceive, see B. D. Ehrman, *Forgery and Counterforgery: The Use of Literary Deceit in Early Christian Polemics* (New York: Oxford University Press, 2013), 29–32; cf. M. E. Stone, *Ancient Judaism: New Visions and Views* (Grand Rapids: Eerdmans, 2011), 90–121. The irony of using a pseudonym with the warnings about perjury (vv. 16–17) and the need for honesty (vv. 48–50) is amusing.

30 For charts of the thematic divisions offered by different scholars, see J. Thomas, *Der jüdische Phokylides: Formgeschichtliche Zugänge zu Pseudo-Phokylides und Vergleich mit der neutestamentlichen Paränese* (NTOA 23; Göttingen: Vandenhoeck & Ruprecht, 1992), 320–22.

31 Wilson, *Sentences*, 14–17; Denis, *Introduction*, 1053. One of the best demonstrations of the work's nonclassical origins is the discussion of anachronistic intrusions of meter, language, and style by Derron, *Sentences*, lxvi–lxxxii. The author's imitation of Phocylides was sophisticated enough that Stobaeus (*Anth.* 3.3.7; 3.3.28) and the compiler of the second *Sibylline Oracle* (2.56–148; *Suda* Φ 643) cite parts of the *Sentences* claiming it was by Phocylides.

erary phenomenon. Portions of Proverbs, Ben Sira, Wisdom of Solomon, and even some sapiential psalms all provide didactic instruction in the form of pithy sayings.[32] Yet even in this grouping the form, scope, and level of expansion are diverse. For example, Prov 10 and following provides sayings with little macro-structure or larger argument, although the pairing of antithetical sayings imply localized arrangement.[33] The gnomai in *Instruction of Ankhsheshonq*, a Demotic wisdom text, have some structure, but are diverse, encouraging utilitarian over idealistic actions.[34] The work of Ben Sira displays a larger structure, but breaks down at places.[35] At the far end of the spectrum, certain wisdom texts from Egypt and the Near East (e.g., *Instruction of Amenemope*, *Papyrus Insinger*) are highly structured and show a clear progression of thought.[36]

The range of gnomatic compositions complicates genre discussions.[37] Differentiating gnomic works based on specific features (e.g., purpose, structure, audience, etc.) allows for the identification of literary clusters, but does not provide firm boundaries. Of importance for the discussion of *Sentences* is the difference between gnomologia and gnomic poetry. Although both have gnomai as a defining feature, the latter is characterized by a greater emphasis on the author's involvement in shaping the sayings, often evidenced by a clearer sense of structure and overarching argument.[38] A majority of Pseudo-Phocylides scholars have,

32 For the discussion of the *Gospel of Thomas*, see below.

33 The Greek version of Proverbs has substantial changes, including the incorporation of Greek proverbs and occasional metrical verses. Cf. J. Cook, *The Septuagint of Proverbs: Jewish and/or Hellenistic Proverbs? Concerning the Hellenistic Colouring of LXX Proverbs* (VTSup 69; Leiden: Brill, 1997); J. K. Aitken and L. Cuppi, "Proverbs," in J. K. Aitken, ed., *The T&T Clark Companion to the Septuagint* (London: Bloomsbury, 2015), 341–55. The *Sayings* of Ahiqar show even less structure. Lack of structure often results in a more porous text, in which material can be added or omitted for a new context.

34 *Instruction of Ankhsheshonq* represents a unique blend of narrative and wisdom. The work opens with a narrative about a plot to assassinate the pharaoh (1.9–4.21), but the heart of the composition is a wisdom text that Ankhsheshonq writes to his son from prison (5.1–28.11). To our knowledge, the narrative frame is not taken up at the close of the work.

35 J. Corley, "Searching for Structure and Redaction in Ben Sira," in A. Passaro and G. Bella, eds., *The Wisdom of Ben Sira: Studies on Tradition, Redaction, and Theology* (DCLS 1; Berlin: De Gruyter, 2008), 21–48. So too the *Sentences of Sextus*.

36 M. Lichtheim, *Late Egyptian Wisdom in the International Context: A Study of Demotic Instructions* (OBO 52; Göttingen: Vandenhoeck & Ruprecht, 1983), 109–16. Jewish and other Near Eastern wisdom texts are often written in prose and have a more elaborate opening and closing in which the named sage addresses his specific listener (cf. W. T. Wilson, *The Mysteries of Righteousness: The Literary Composition and Genre of the Sentences of Pseudo-Phocylides* [TSAJ 40; Tübingen: Mohr Siebeck, 1993], 33–41).

37 For recent attempts by classicists to define didactic literature, see P. Toohey, *Epic Lessons: An Introduction to Didactic Poetry* (London: Routledge, 1996), 4; K. Volk, *The Poetics of Latin Didactic: Lucretius, Vergil, Ovid, Manilius* (Oxford: Oxford University Press, 2002), 36–41.

38 Wilson, *Mysteries*, 18–33. There is no firm division between these two groups. Rather, they form a spectrum of authorial structure.

either explicitly or implicitly, understood *Sentences* to be a gnomologion, a work with loose structure and limited formal design.[39] This perspective results in localized studies with little consideration of the work's macro-level organization or the author's overall argument. Recently, Wilson has emphasized coherence, arguing that its sophisticated and systematic organization implies a cohesive work.[40] Although the specifics of Wilson's proposal can be challenged, his imputing of intent to the author is correct; *Sentences* is most fully understood when viewed as an intentional gnomic composition.[41]

A version of the LXX, specifically the Pentateuch (Exod 20–23, Lev 18–20, and Deut 5 and 27) and wisdom literature, was the primary source for Pseudo-Phocylides' *Sentences*.[42] The author of the poem selected his content from the LXX passages that expressed broad ethical perspectives, rather than those emphasizing specific Jewish concerns (e.g., Sabbath, circumcision, idolatry). A good example of this is verses 3–8, a selected paraphrase of the ethical commands of the Decalogue, which omits the Jewish introductory formula "I am the Lord, your God . . ." and the commandments on idolatry prohibition and Sabbath observance.[43] The following section (vv. 9–41) consists of themes found primarily in Leviticus 19, although the author is careful to select ordi-

39 E.g., van der Horst, *Sentences*, 77–80; Walter, "Dichtung," 188–90; Derron, *Sentences*, xxvi–xxvii.

40 Wilson, *Mysteries*, 178–99; Wilson, *Sentences*, 9–13; cf. M. Hengel, "Anonymität, Pseudepigraphie und 'Literarische Fälschung' in der jüdisch-hellenistischen Literatur," in K. von Fritz, ed., *Pseudepigraphie*, vol. 1 (Entretiens sur l'antiquité classique 18; Geneva: Hardt, 1972), 297; Collins, *Athens*, 171.

41 Wilson (*Mysteries*, 184–99) also proposes that the genre of epitome functions as a "guest" genre in *Sentences*. Wilson provides parallels to Greco-Roman and Jewish authors, although I wonder how much summarization is already embedded into gnomic poetry in order to need to draw on another genre category. Rather, epitomization could be a recognized element of gnomic literature, a formal feature shared with other genres.

42 For a helpful chart of possible parallels, see K.-W. Niebuhr, *Gesetz und Paränese: Katechismusartige Weisungsreihen in der frühjüdischen Literatur* (WUNT 2.28; Tübingen: Mohr Siebeck, 1987), 10; Wilson, *Sentences*, 17–18. I (and most scholars) disagree with Lincke's claim that the Greek scriptural text (especially Lev 19 and the Decalogue) is dependent on Pseudo-Phocylides. K. F. A. Lincke, *Samaria und seine Propheten: Ein religionsgeschichtlicher Versuch; Mit einer Textbeilage, die Weisheitslehre des Phokylides* (Tübingen: Mohr Siebeck, 1903), 75; K. F. A. Lincke, "Phokylides und die Essener," *Die Grenzboten* 68 (1909): 136; cf. Wilson, *Sentences*, 17–22.

One passage that supports Pseudo-Phocylides' use of an LXX translation over a Hebrew text is the discussion of the industry of ants and bees in vv. 164–174, which parallels LXX Prov 6:6–8c; a passage that is not found in any extant Hebrew text. Other examples of LXX parallels include vv. 84–85 (Deut 22:6); v. 140 (Exod 23:5; Deut 22:4); vv. 147–148 (Exod 22:30; Lev 22:8). Cf. J. Cook, "The Dating of Septuagint Proverbs," *ETL* 69 (1993): 383–99. Cf. van der Horst, *Sentences*, 222–25; Thomas, *Phokylides*, 464. For an extended list, see Derron, *Sentences*, 35–54.

43 Alternative orderings of commandments six and seven in vv. 3–4 have parallels in LXX Exod 20:13, 14; Deut 5:17, 18; and Philo, *Spec.* 3.8, 83; *Decal.* 36, 51. Cf. van der Horst, *Sentences*, 110–12; Niebuhr, *Gesetz und Paränese*, 15–16; Derron, *Sentences*, xxvi. Derron also finds

nances that are applicable to both Jews and non-Jews.[44] This appropriation of Torah is part of a larger discussion on Pseudo-Phocylides' use of sources. The difference in meter and dialect between *Sentences* and other identified Jewish sources, at minimum, resists the assumption of rote paraphrasing and suggests intentional appropriation and refining of material.[45] Indeed, the differences in meter (dactylic hexameter), language, and structuring principles are the primary reasons for reading *Sentences* as participating in a Greek genre.[46]

The possible relationship between *Sentences* and Greek authors is also important.[47] No significant overlap in content exists between the preserved Phocylides fragments and *Sentences*, although this does not imply that Phocylides' compositions were not prototypical for Pseudo-Phocylides.[48] The author likely paraphrases Homer, *Od.* 6.182–184, in verses 195–197, which encourage strong mutual affection between a husband and wife. These Homeric verses, which achieved proverbial status in the Hellenistic era, also resonate with attitudes found in other Jewish texts.[49] A majority of the poem espouses a universal ethic that would not be out of place in either Jewish or Greek communities. However, certain verses lack strong parallels with Greek literature.[50] One example is the work's monotheistic perspective, expressed through the use of the singular for God (vv. 8, 11, 17, 29, etc.). More explicitly, the author claims in verse 54 that there is only one God ("[the] one God is wise and mighty," εἷς θεός ἐστι σοφὸς δυνατός), the phrasing of which is similar to other Jewish monotheistic statements.[51] The attribution of wisdom and might to God (or

---

specific Greek parallels in the Delphic precepts. A similar distillation of Jewish ethics is found in Josephus, *C. Ap.* 2.190–219; Philo, *Hypothetica*.

44 Niebuhr, *Gesetz und Paränese*, 5–72. The strong adoption of pentateuchal material distances the work from those typically associated with Solomon. The selection of a Jewish author might have made omission of Jewish practices and identity markers problematic.

45 For the view of a common source for Pseudo-Phocylides, Philo, *Hypoth.* 8.7.1–20, and Josephus, *C. Ap.* 2.190–219, see P. W. van der Horst, "Pseudo-Phocylides and the New Testament," *ZNW* 69 (1978): 197. This implies that there was another Greek ethical composition that has since been lost.

46 *Sentences* is also a member of an expanding Jewish literary corpus in Greek and so should not be read solely through a Greek lens.

47 Denis, *Introduction*, 1043–44. For a list of (nearly) all possible parallels with Greek literature, see Derron, *Sentences*, 35–54. Unfortunately, Derron does not provide any rationale for his parallels, nor does he identify which are significant and which are of marginal importance.

48 T. Bergk, ed., *Poetae Lyrici Graeci*, vol. 2 (4th ed.; Leipzig: Teubner, 1883), 68–73; E. Diehl, ed., *Anthologia Lyrica Graeca* (3 vols.; Leipzig: Teubner, 1949–1952), 2.58–62; M. L. West, ed., *Theognidis et Phocylidis Fragmenta et Adespota quaedam Gnomica* (Berlin: De Gruyter, 1978).

49 E.g., Prov 31:10–12; Sir 26:1–4, 13–18; Philo, *Spec.* 1.138; 1 Cor 7:3.

50 E.g., concern for the stranger (v. 39), bodily resurrection (vv. 103–104), forbidding of eating meat from a torn animal (vv. 147–148). The positive attitude to work presented in v. 153 parallels the views of Hesiod (*Op.* 311) and Phocylides (fr. 7), and aligns with scriptural admonition.

51 E.g., Deut 6:4; Sir 1:8; LA 132; Philo, *Opif.* 171; Sib. Or. 3.11.

the gods) is not contrary to Greek authors. The undermining of the pantheon by asserting a singular God would be viewed as suspect by some, though importantly not all.[52] In contrast, scholars have struggled to accept that verse 104, which identifies the resurrected as "gods" (ὀπίσω δὲ θεοὶ τελέθονται), was written by a Jew.[53] This verse is part of a wider discussion of the afterlife (vv. 97–115) and summarizes the (primarily) Jewish concept of physical resurrection (vv. 103–104).[54] It is now widely understood as a variation of a Jewish theme of using divine epitaphs for angels and stars, calling them "gods."[55] Overall, enforcing a strict dichotomy between Jewish and Greek thought in Pseudo-Phocylides is difficult and ultimately damages the text, as this runs counter to the entire thrust of the narrative. The author fundamentally integrates Jewish and Greek ideas so that they blur together into one universal, ethical outlook.

The ambiguity of the evidence resists proposals for one specific audience for the poem and a single reason for its composition.[56] Gedaliah Alon has suggested that Pseudo-Phocylides wrote to Jews to provide a synthesis of Torah teaching. Specifically, this set of ethical principles was composed in the guise of a non-Jewish writer in order to strengthen Jewish resolve and check their decline into a non-Jewish way of life. According to Alon, *Sentences* accomplishes this by showing that Jews are not missing out by holding fast to scrip-

52 E.g., Diogenes Laertius, *Vit.* 1.12; Maximus of Tyre, *Or.* 11.5. This perspective is paralleled in v. 194, in which the author subtly challenges Greek mythology by employing a potential double referent for Eros, "For ἔρος is not a God, but a passion destructive of all" (οὐ γὰρ ἔρος θεός ἐστι, πάθος δ' ἀΐδηλον ἁπάντων). Cf. Thomas, *Phokylides*, 203; Wilson, *Sentences*, 198–99. Cf. Plutarch, *Mor.* 23a–24c. On "pagan" use of monotheistic language, see P. Athanassiadi and M. Frede, *Pagan Monotheism in Late Antiquity* (Oxford: Oxford University Press, 1999), 3.

53 E.g., Bernays, *Phokylideische*, 204.

54 Cf. Aeschylus, *Eum.* 648, οὔτις ἔστι ἀνάστασις. Some Jewish examples include 2 Macc 7:9–14; 1 En. 22:13; 51:1–5; 2 Bar. 50:2; T. Jud. 25:1; Sib. Or. 4.181–182. D. B. Martin, *The Corinthian Body* (New Haven: Yale University Press, 1995), 110–14. Martin rightly highlights the oversimplification perpetuated by scholars regarding the Jewish and Greek views on resurrection; whereas Collins emphasizes the diversity of Jewish perspectives on physical resurrection. J. J. Collins, "Life after Death in Pseudo-Phocylides," in F. García Martínez and G. P. Luttikhuizen, eds., *Jerusalem, Alexandria, Rome: Studies in Ancient Cultural Interaction in Honour of A. Hilhorst* (JSJSup 82; Leiden: Brill, 2003), 77–78. For a response to Collins, see P. W. van der Horst, "Pseudo-Phocylides on the Afterlife: A Rejoinder to John J. Collins," *JSJ* 35 (2004): 70–75.

55 Ps 8:5[6]; 1 Kgdms 28:13; 1QM XIV,15; XV,14; 2 Bar. 51:10; 1 En. 51:1–4; Philo, *Opif.* 27. Cf. van der Horst, *Sentences*, 186–88; Hengel, "Anonymität," 297; J. J. Collins, "Powers in Heaven: God, Gods, and Angels in the Dead Sea Scrolls," in J. J. Collins and R. A. Kugler, eds., *Religion in the Dead Sea Scrolls* (Grand Rapids: Eerdmans, 2000), 1–28. This practice finds parallels in vv. 75 and 163, in which the heavenly bodies are called μάκαρες, and in v. 71, which mentions the Οὐρανίδαι.

56 van der Horst, *Sentences*, 54. For a good discussion of the purpose options, see 70–76. For a critique of the Jewish apologetic view, see Schürer, *History*, 3.1.690; P. W. van der Horst, "Pseudo-Phocylides Revisited," *JSP* 3 (1988): 16. For the claim that there is no clear Jewish purpose, see Klawans, "Pseudo-Jewishness," 214.

tural ideals because a highly respected Greek author already endorses them.[57] The omission of specifically Jewish cultural elements is necessitated by his Greek alias, but would naturally have been an assumed cultural component. This thesis accounts for the use of a pseudonym as well as the nonproselytizing nature of the poem. Following Alon, Niebuhr has argued that the Pseudo-Phocylides poem is not propagandistic, apologetic, or missionary focused, but is written solely for a Jewish audience.[58] In particular, the purpose of the work is to edify the Jewish community by providing concrete ethical parameters for daily life in a Greek environ. This epitome incorporated select nonbiblical material which was considered to be consistent with Scripture and of value for Hellenized Jews negotiating Greek culture.[59]

An element of critique may also be embedded in the author's adoption of a pseudonym. A Jewish reader, recognizing the purported author's extensive reliance on Torah through the activation of multiple layers of meaning by the actual author, could understand Phocylides' moral directives and concepts to be derivative.[60] This is not to deny the unifying tendencies of the work or the work's implicit claim of Jew/Greek compatibility, but means that the presentation of a Greek author dependent on Jewish thought might undermine, in the eyes of some Jews, the lofty podium on which Phocylides was placed by Greek readers. By recasting the relationship between Greeks and Jews in the classical past, the author of *Sentences* changes the nature of Jewish-Greek relations in the Hellenistic present. This reconfiguration not only allows for an increasing parity between these two parties, but also facilitates the current integration of Jewish and Greek ideas.[61]

An integration of Jewish and Greek cultures underlies both audience perspectives. Accordingly, although the work's likely intended audience is primarily Jewish, it is possible for there to be wider agreement on the effect of the work, namely that Pseudo-Phocylides' *Sentences* appears to promote greater connections between Jewish and Greek cultures by providing a universal ethic applicable to all people groups.[62] Neither culture is presented negatively, nor do the cultural values of one group dominate

57 G. Alon, "The Halakah in the Teaching of the Twelve Apostles (Hebrew)," in *Studies in Jewish History in the Times of the Second Temple, the Mishnah and the Talmud* (2nd ed.; Tel Aviv: Hakibbutz Hameuchad, 1967), 278, *apud* Niebuhr.

58 Niebuhr, *Gesetz und Paränese*, 67–69, 72; van der Horst, "Pseudo-Phocylides Revisited," 16.

59 Wilson, *Mysteries*, 13.

60 Wilson (*Mysteries*, 196) is not wrong when he suggests that this would imply that Greek wisdom could be "improved," though I think this critique speaks more to the claimed source of Greek knowledge.

61 Klawans ("Pseudo-Jewishness") also identifies a critique in the adoption of Phocylides, but an inverse: Jewish ideas were prefigured by Greeks.

62 Collins, *Athens*, 144; Wilson, *Mysteries*, 5.

the other. We can identify Jewish themes and values, but the ones that are expressed are not at odds with wider Greco-Roman culture. Rather, Pseudo-Phocylides aligns Greek virtues with Jewish moral precepts, situating the ethical teachings of Torah within the moral context of its Hellenistic environment.

This understanding suggests that Alon and Niebuhr's claim—that the *Sentences* assisted Jews in resisting greater adoption of Greek culture—requires further refinement. The author of *Sentences* has "Phocylides" present Jewish ideas in a positive manner, which covertly reinforces Jewish identity and values. These values, moreover, are presented in classical Greek literary garb and represent the work of a highly acculturated Jew. Rather than being undermined by Jewish values, Greek morals are presented as compatible with (certain) Jewish ideals (and vice versa), and so the text presents, not a resisting of Greek culture, but a way for Jews to accommodate certain aspects of Hellenism and to integrate their lives within a multicultural framework. The argument that the omitted cultural markers (e.g., circumcision, Sabbath, avoidance of idolatry, etc.) should be assumed or "self-evident" for Hellenistic Jews may be accurate for specific communities, but cannot be imported into the discussion of the text. The text purposefully does not engage in this debate, not only because of the persona adopted, but also because such topics would not have allowed for the neat accommodation between the two cultures. We cannot assume that the author adhered to every form of distinguishing Jewish practice (although he may have done so) and so imposed these views on the text. Rather, we must deal explicitly with the text at hand, which positively summarizes Jewish ethical thought by participation in a Greek genre. In identifying places of commonality and overlap, *Sentences* does not form a manual of resistance or necessarily vaccinate Jews from further investigating Greek culture.[63] Moreover, its silence on idolatry and other Jewish customs minimizes the gulf between Jews participating in Hellenistic life and/or God-fearers straddling the religious and cultural divide.[64]

63 The use of part of this work (vv. 5–79) in Sib. Or. 2.55–149 (with additional interpolations) suggests that this author also found it conducive for assimilating Jewish and Greek culture. Pseudo-Phocylides is included in the Ψ manuscript group by the time of Sudias (*Suda* Φ 643), but is absent from the oldest manuscripts. For a discussion of Pseudo-Phocylides in Sib. Or., see O. Wassmuth, *Sibyllinische Orakel 1–2: Studien und Kommentar* (AJEC 76; Leiden: Brill, 2011), 305–39.

64 Barclay (*Jews*, 342–43) correctly notes that it was not problematic for Jews to insert anti-idol sayings in works attributed to Greek writers. E.g., LA 128–138; Sib. Or. 2.59, 96.

The most likely purpose of *Sentences* is educational. The use of gnomologies and similar collections of aphorisms was common in Greek philosophical and literary education and so would have been known to the author.[65] van der Horst posits that Pseudo-Phocylides, recognizing the importance of γνῶμαι in Greek literary education, wrote for Jewish schoolboys to provide them with γνῶμαι compatible with Jewish values from which they could practice their Greek.[66] The thought behind this proposal is that Jewish teachers would not have found the Greek ethical teachings in Homer, Hesiod, Theognis, and Phocylides profitable for Jewish boys to assimilate. Embedding Jewish ideals into the Greek education system allows pupils to learn Greek in the traditional manner (from a "real" Greek writer), but not be "compromised" by Greek worldviews.[67] This perspective gains some support from the manuscript tradition (*Sentences* is consistently found in collections of school texts), from the adoption of the persona of Phocylides, whose texts had some didactic structure (e.g., fr. 13, which is addressed to a boy), and from the condensing and summarizing nature, the practice of which is well known in school contexts (e.g., Theon, *Prog.* 107; Quintilian, *Inst.* 1.9.2).[68]

Because gnomic literature was closely associated with philosophical schools in the Hellenistic era, the creation of a gnomic poem could indicate the author's engagement with philosophical discourse or higher-level education.[69] The wide coverage of Jewish ethical thought, both in terms of virtue and personal relationships, suggests that *Sentences* could be viewed as a distillation of the author's philosophical perspective. This understanding, however, stands in tension with van der Horst's proposal, as the synthesis of philosophical systems was not regularly undertaken at lower levels. The fundamental structure of the virtue section (vv. 9–131) would not be fully recognizable to those who had not received an education that included a Greek worldview. Both issues militate against the proposal of van der Horst that *Sentences* was composed for lower-level education and/or for pupils who did not want to engage with Greek literature and ideas.

65 R. Cribiore, *Gymnastics of the Mind: Greek Education in Hellenistic and Roman Egypt* (Princeton: Princeton University Press, 2005), 179, 202; T. Morgan, *Literate Education in the Hellenistic and Roman Worlds* (CCS; Cambridge: Cambridge University Press, 1999), 120–25.

66 van der Horst, *Sentences*, 72–73; cf. Derron, *Sentences*, xlvii–li; Collins, *Jewish Wisdom*, 175–77; Cribiore, *Gymnastics*, 162, 200; Morgan, *Literate Education*, 125–44; M. L. West, "Phocylides," *JHS* 98 (1978): 164–67. For an excellent survey of gnomologies, though slightly dated, see M. Küchler, *Frühjüdische Weisheitstraditionen: Zum Fortgang weisheitlichen Denkens im Bereich des frühjüdischen Jahweglaubens* (OBO 26; Freiburg: Universitätsverlag, 1979), 236–302.

67 van der Horst, "Pseudo-Phocylides Revisited," 16.

68 On the manuscripts, see Derron, *Sentences*, lxxxiii.

69 E.g., Seneca, *Ep.* 33.1–5; Diogenes Laertius, *Vit.* 10.35–83, 84–116, 122–135.

What we witness in *Sentences* is a strong example of classical imitation and fusing of past and present through the invoking of Phocylides.[70] Imitation is not, however, a passive action: it acknowledges literary forebears and seeks to follow in their footsteps, while at the same time it repurposes literary forms, phrases, and motifs to speak into a new context. Often the imitation of an author or work is in positive dialogue with its predecessors, advancing their ideas by espousing them afresh. However, imitators do not always uphold the values of their literary models, but challenge them, using their own voice as a means of undermining the original message. This memetic practice allows for a renegotiation of values and ideas, especially when the literary model is co-opted or employed by those outwith the original community. In *Sentences*, the literary voice and model of Phocylides is adopted, but imbued with foreign elements. These foreign elements are not simply inserted, but woven into the fabric of the poem to create a text that is both Jewish and Greek; one that maintains the essence of the original voice, but with added, unfamiliar material with which the new author speaks to a different group. In contrast to Ezekiel in chapter 3, Pseudo-Phocylides does not reformulate a Greek genre, but participates in an established one and imbues it with Jewish material to create a cross-cultural work that reframes Jewish and Greek relationships.

Gospel of Thomas

Gospel of Thomas is a collection of 114 sayings attributed to Jesus that were said to have been compiled by [Judas] Thomas (Didymus Judas Thomas, in Coptic).[71] The dating of the Greek composition is debated, with a broad range of dates argued, most often in line with the scholar's understanding of Thomas' relationship to the Synoptic Gospels (ca. mid-first to late second centuries CE).[72] The differences between the highly fragmented Greek texts and the Coptic manuscript raise the difficult question of which text we are attempting to interpret and the stability of that text over time. The interplay between orality and written composition, as well as the fluidity of texts in antiquity (e.g., augmentation, accretion, etc.), highlights the challenges of interpretation and claims to the fixity of a work's genre.[73]

70 Whitmarsh, *Greek Literature*, 26–29, 41–89.

71 For critical editions, see B. Layton, ed., *Nag Hammadi Codex II* (Leiden: Brill, 1989) (Coptic) and P.Oxy. I 1; IV 654; IV 655 (Greek).

72 M. Bockmuehl, *Ancient Apocryphal Gospels* (Interpretation; Louisville: Westminster John Knox, 2017), 170–76; S. Gathercole, *The Gospel of Thomas: Introduction and Commentary* (TENTS 11; Leiden: Brill, 2014), 110–27. For a recent argument for a Greek original, see S. Gathercole, *The Composition of the Gospel of Thomas: Original Language and Influences* (SNTSMS 151; Cambridge: Cambridge University Press, 2012), 105–25.

73 A compositional approach is modeled prominently by A. D. DeConick, *Recovering the Original Gospel of Thomas: A History of the Gospel and Its Growth* (LNTS 286; London: T&T

Thomas opens by identifying its contents as "secret sayings" (οἱ λόγοι οἱ [ἀπόκρυφοι . . . , Gos. Thom. *praef.*), signaling alignment with gnomic traditions.[74] As discussed above, gnomatic compositions are diverse, affording the author a range of prototypical models. These prototypes are not limited to Greek sapiential traditions, but are found in Jewish and Near Eastern wisdom literature.[75] Scholars of Thomas have struggled to find specific ancient models used by the author or to discern a strong, cohesive structure, although many argue for authorial intentionality and compositional coherence, especially in light of the prologue.[76]

A number of Greek sources and the postscript of the fourth-century Coptic manuscript identify the work as a "Gospel."[77] However, Thomas differs substantially from the Synoptics and John, challenging a simple genre or literary equation (see chapter 8). Thomas is not the same type of composition as the texts that later became the canonical Gospels, but it is clear from its ascribed title that subsequent readers and copyists viewed them in a similar light, with

---

Clark, 2005); A. D. DeConick, *The Original Gospel of Thomas in Translation: With a Commentary and New English Translation of the Complete Gospel* (LNTS 287; London: T&T Clark, 2006). For a critique of the confidence of scholars on identifying oral elements and for the polarization of orality and literary, see Gathercole, *Composition of the Gospel of Thomas*, 3–16.

74 E.g., J. M. Robinson and H. Koester, *Trajectories through Early Christianity* (Philadelphia: Fortress, 1971), 71–113, who were instrumental in labeling Thomas as a *logoi sophon* and who have been followed by many others. Cf. M. Lelyveld, *Les Logia de la vie dans l'Évangile selon Thomas: À la recherche d'une tradition et d'une redaction* (NHMS; Leiden: Brill, 1987), 3–10. For an overview of genre theories, see N. Perrin and C. W. Skinner, "Recent Trends in *Gospel of Thomas* Research (1989–2011), Part II: Genre, Theology and Relationship to the Gospel of John," *CBR* 11 (2012): 66–70.

75 Cf. H. Chadwick, "Florilegium," *RAC* 7 (1960): 1131–59. Rightly highlighted for Thomas by S. J. Patterson, *The Gospel of Thomas and Jesus* (FFRS; Sonoma: Polebridge Press, 1993); S. J. Patterson, "Wisdom in Q and Thomas," in L. G. Perdue, B. Brandon, and W. J. Wiseman, eds., *In Search of Wisdom: Essays in Memory of John G. Gammie* (Louisville: Westminster John Knox, 1993), 187–221.

For the difference between Thomas and Q, and the need to interpret Thomas through a historical-critical lens, see J. Schröter, *Erinnerung an Jesu Worte: Studien zur Rezeption der Logienüberlieferung in Markus, Q und Thomas* (WMANT 76; Neukirchen-Vluyn: Neukirchener, 1997), 478–81. The rhetorical approach and literary environment advocated by Robbins provide one way of interpreting the text, although his discussions of genre implications are minimal. V. K. Robbins, "Progymnastic Rhetorical Composition and Pre-Gospel Traditions: A New Approach," in C. Focant, ed., *Synoptic Gospels: Source Criticism and the New Literary Criticism* (BETL 110; Leuven: Leuven University Press, 1993), 111–47.

76 E.g., J.-M. Sevrin, "Remarques sur le genre litteraire de *l'Évangile selon Thomas* (II,2)," in L. Painchaud and A. Pasquier, eds., *Les textes de Nag Hammadi et le problème de leur classification: Actes du colloque tenu à Québec du 15 au 19 septembre 1993* (BCNH 3; Leuven: Peeters, 1995), 263–78. Sevrin is followed by others. Sevrin's gnostic approach informs his developmental view of Thomas.

77 For a flexible definition of "Gospel," see A. F. Gregory and C. M. Tuckett, "New Editions of Non-canonical Gospels," *Theology* 111 (2008): 178–84. For ancient references to Thomas as Gospel, see Gathercole, *Gospel of Thomas*, 35–61.

the latter functioning prototypically for the former.[78] Thomas' focus on the sayings of a single individual, who is mentioned at the opening of most logia, implies a biographical focus and so participation in *bios*. However, Thomas is not orientated in the same ways as most *bioi*; its minimal overarching narrative and exclusive use of sayings do not align with prototypical examples of this genre.[79] In contrast, Thomas has affinities with Pseudo-Phocylides and other gnomic works that focus, sometimes exclusively, on the pithy statements and instructions of a teacher. The importance of the canonical Gospels and their influence on subsequent compositions are clear, and Thomas provides a strong example of how the label of "Gospel" came to encompass a diverse range of texts. Thomas, however, can be profitably viewed as participating in multiple genres (e.g., *bios* and gnomologia) and not limited strictly to one.[80]

Philo of Alexandria

By far the best-known Jewish philosopher is Philo of Alexandria, for whom we have a substantial extant corpus but little knowledge of the individual.[81] Writing in Roman Alexandria, Philo models how a highly educated Jew engaged with Greek literature and philosophic thought. In this section, we will be limiting our investigation to Philo's *Allegorical Commentary* and *Quaestiones*, reserving our discussion of *Contemplativa* to chapter 5 and his biographies until chapter 8.[82] Space does not permit us the opportunity for a thorough investigation of Philo's philosophical thought or to cover all of the

78 The theme of salvation (Gos. Thom. 1) and freedom from the world (Gos. Thom. 42) and its contents (Gos. Thom. 63–65) provide important points of contact between Thomas and other identified Gospels.

79 Some logia have narrative elements and additional characters (especially the disciples: Gos. Thom. 6, 12, 13, 18, 20, etc.; Mary: 21, 114; Salome: 62; Peter: 13, 114), but there is essentially no narrative connection between logia.

80 The label "Gospel" might not signal genre participation by the author, but a shared topical understanding with the canonical Gospels from the perspective of later readers. Cf. Gathercole, *Gospel of Thomas*, 617–18.

81 See P. Borgen, *Philo of Alexandria: An Exegete for His Time* (NovTSup 86; Leiden: Brill, 1997), 14–19; D. R. Schwartz, "Philo, His Family, and His Times," in A. Kamesar, ed., *The Cambridge Companion to Philo* (Cambridge: Cambridge University Press, 2009), 9–31; M. R. Niehoff, *Philo of Alexandria: An Intellectual Biography* (AYBRL; New Haven: Yale University Press, 2018); A. Appelbaum, "A Fresh Look at Philo's Family," *SPhiloA* 30 (2018): 93–113. For a proposed time line of his compositions, see Niehoff, *Philo of Alexandria*, 245–46. For the Greek texts used, see L. Cohn, I. Heinemann, and W. Theiler, eds., *Philo von Alexandria: Die Werke in deutscher Überstzung* (7 vols.; Berlin: De Gruyter, 1909–1964).

82 I recognize that this division, particularly when considering *Abraham* and *Joseph*, is somewhat arbitrary if one considers the overarching unity of Philo's corpus, but this is discussed in chapter 8. Cf. D. T. Runia, ed. and trans., *Philo of Alexandria: On the Creation of the Cosmos According to Moses; Introduction, Translation, and Commentary* (PACS 1; Leiden: Brill, 2001), 6.

many contours of his works. Rather, we will focus on Philo's discussion and participation in genre.

Scholar have identified parallels between Philo and Aristobulus; however, their engagement with Greek philosophers has important distinctions that affect any claims of dependency.[83] This has been insightfully argued by Niehoff, who has identified specific differences between these two authors by placing each within his specific temporal and cultural setting.[84] Aristobulus, writing in the middle of the Hellenistic era, was (as far as we can tell) primarily concerned with subordinating Greek ideas and authors to their Jewish predecessors. Although there is an element of this practice in Philo's works, that is not his ultimate end.[85] In Philo's compositions, we witness an early example of a Jewish writer who claims the priority of Jewish Scripture and undertakes an explicit comparison and integration of cultures.[86] Such comparison was characteristic of Roman intellectuals, who assumed a contrary view towards Greek culture, seeing it as a separate and foreign entity that was often at odds with traditional Roman values.[87] Philo, despite his occasional chastising of Greek culture (e.g., *Contempl.* 40–58), still employs Greek genres for this endeavor.

We will begin this section with a discussion of Philo's genre consciousness, identifying and unpacking elements of his works that indicate how he thought about the role, shape, form, and function of genres. Following this, we will turn our attention to three works, *Quaestiones et solutiones in Genesin*, *Quaestiones et solutiones in Exodum*, and the *Allegorical Commentary*. All three of these works participate in Greek genres, but, as we will see, Philo adapts them in specific ways. These adaptations and differences are important for understanding Philo's purpose(s) and provide examples of the diverse ways Jewish authors engaged with Greek literary culture.

83 Philo notes his debt to earlier allegorical exegetes in such places as *Spec.* 2.159; *Mut.* 141; *Prob.* 82; *Contempl.* 28–29.

84 Niehoff, *Philo on Jewish Identity*, 137–58.

85 Despite claiming that Plato was ἱερώτατος ("most holy," *Prob.* 13), a true philosopher (*Contempl.* 57), and "great" (*Aet.* 52), Philo still subordinates him to Moses, crediting Moses with his idea of the dipartite nature of the universe (causal and passive, *Opif.* 8). Although Philo resists claiming (as did Aristobulus) that Plato got his ideas from Moses, Moses is still presented as the initiator of the idea, with Plato later coming to the same idea. Both Zeno (*Prob.* 57) and Socrates (*QG* 2.6) derived their ideas from Scripture. Cf. D. Winston, "Philo and the Hellenistic Jewish Encounter," *SPhiloA* 7 (1995): 124–42; D. T. Runia, *Philo of Alexandria and the "Timaeus" of Plato* (Leiden: Brill, 1986), 528–29; G. E. Sterling, "Platonizing Moses: Philo and Middle Platonism," *SPhiloA* 5 (1993): 96–111.

86 Niehoff, *Philo on Jewish Identity*, 142.

87 Examples can be taken from Cato, Cicero, and Seneca, all of whom made favorable and unfavorable comparisons with Greek culture, depicting Greek thought in ways that worked with their literary agenda. Cf. Cicero, *Fin.* 1.1; 2.2; *Flac.* 62–64; Seneca, *Ep.* 44.3–4; 58.30; 64.10; Plutarch, *Cato mai.* 8.8; 12.5; 23.1.

Philo's Genre Consciousness

Unlike most other Jewish authors investigated in this work, Philo explicitly discusses ancient education (e.g., *Agr.* 18; *Congr.* 74; *Cher.* 105). Preliminary studies and subsequent philosophical training are important concepts for Philo, not only when engaging in allegorical interpretation (*Congr.* 11–12), but also when discussing the nature of texts and what specific texts are doing (e.g., the books of Moses, *Praem.* 1–2). It is in these discussions that Philo comments on the function and genre of specific texts, offering a glimpse of his genre awareness. Philo never provides a comprehensive discussion of his understanding of genre. Nevertheless, individual comments allow us to recognize some of his organizing principles.

At the most fundamental level, Philo divides texts into poetry and prose. This is consistent with the literary divisions of his contemporaries, and is indicated by the explicit pairing of ποιητής and λογογράφος four times (*Opif.* 4; *Plant.* 159; *Contempl.* 1; *Spec.* 4.230) and ποιητής and συγγραφεύς five times (*Det.* 99; *Congr.* 15, 148; *Prob.* 98; *Legat.* 165).[88] In these passages ποιητής and λογογράφος/συγγραφεύς indicate the full range of authors and encompass the entirety of literature (e.g., *Opif.* 4, οὐδεὶς οὔτε ποιητὴς οὔτε λογογράγος ἀξίως ἂν ὑμνῆσαι δύναιτο). Although λογογράφος is regularly glossed "historian," it is unlikely that Philo understood history as the antithesis to poetry (though there are differences in how they relate to "truth").[89] Rather, as history was the dominant prose genre at that time, it is more likely that he is using λογογράφος to represent the broader literary category of prose writing.[90] At the same time, history was a standard component of higher Greek education, and when Philo says he became acquainted with the works of the poets and historians, he is certainly referencing actual poems and histories (e.g., *Cher.* 105; *Congr.* 74).

Philo comments on genre throughout his corpus, primarily concerning poets and poetry, though often in dialogue with historians and history. First, Philo sees poets as potential witnesses to the state of humanity, claiming that

88 E.g., Isocrates, *Antid.* 45; Dionysius of Halicarnassus, *Comp.* 3; Quintilian, *Inst.* 10.1.46–84. Philo does not use the term ἄμετρος to describe prose (so Dionysius), but employs it when describing something (i.e., vice, flocks) that is done in excess or without limits. The exception is *Fug.* 42, which critiques specific poems as being unmetrical, though this is not meant to imply prose text. For the pairing of ποίημα and συγγραμμα, see *Abr.* 23; *Mos.* 1.3. On the difference between σύνταξις and λόγος in Philo's description of his own works, see A. Terian, "The Priority of the *Quaestiones* among Philo's Exegetical Commentaries," in D. M. Hay, ed., *Both Literal and Allegorical: Studies in Philo of Alexandria's "Questions and Answers on Genesis and Exodus"* (BJS 232; Atlanta: Scholars Press, 1991), 32–33.

89 For Philo's presentation of myth, poetry, tragedy, and comedy as without substance, see *Congr.* 61.

90 Adams, *Genre*, 49–53.

they (along with historians) bear abundant testimony to the fact that unrestrained passions are responsible for the destruction of cities, countries, and nations (*Det.* 99). Poetry and history are not limited to tragic events, but are recognized for their ability to record the glorious actions of men (*Sacr.* 78). Despite this witness, Philo has reservations about the historical veracity of poetic works, as they regularly propagate myths and are not exclusively beholden to truth (*Gig.* 58). Conversely, histories contain records of ancient transactions for future ages (*Congr.* 15), but if these are just written or read for pleasure, they are not advantageous for the reader (*Mos.* 2.48).[91] Philo references other genres and aspects of literary education, noting the strong association between comedy and tragedy (*Congr.* 61) and their differences in rhythm, meter (*Cher.* 105), and theatrical imagery (*Flacc.* 20, 34).[92]

Second, Philo ranks authors and their works hierarchically. Homer, who is the Greek author most cited in Philo, is the greatest and most esteemed of poets (ὁ μέγιστος καὶ δοκιμώτατος τῶν ποιητῶν Ὅμηρος, *Conf.* 4, cf. *Mut.* 179), receiving the appellation "the poet" to distinguish him from innumerable others (*Abr.* 10).[93] Comparing authors was so well established in antiquity that it formed a central part of the educational curriculum.[94] For Philo, the best grammatical education is the study of the high works (ἀνάπτυξις) of poets and historians (*Congr.* 148), implying that there are works not of a soaring nature that would not be worthy of the pupil's attention.

Philo evaluates genres in terms of their utility and their ability to represent the world and God's creation accurately. When describing Esau in *Congr.* 61, Philo employs the terms μῦθος, τραῳδία, and κωμικός as examples of

91 This is in contrast to tragedies and comedies, which are almost entirely designed for giving pleasure. Cf. *Leg.* 2.75; *Prob.* 141. For a noteworthy example by Philo that the comic poet speaks some truth, see *Her.* 5.

92 Although Philo discusses the nature of poetry and history, these are not the genres that he employs. Rather, he describes his works as βίος (*Mos.* 1.1) and σύνταξις, which Philo uses twenty times in his corpus, eleven of which are internal references to specific works of his (*Her.* 1; *Mut.* 53; *Abr.* 1, 13; *Mos.* 2.1; *Decal.* 1; *Spec.* 1.1; 2.1; *Virt.* 52, 101; *Praem.* 3). The term σύνταξις is regularly glossed "treatise" or "orderly composition" and is a general term for a didactic or systematic prose work. The use of σύνταξις in *Mos.* 2.1 is revealing, as this was not the term that described the work at its opening (βίος, 1.1). This suggests that σύνταξις does not necessarily correspond to a specific genre, but could be a general term for a work, a view supported by *Virt.* 52, in which Philo states, ἐν δυσὶ συντάξεσιν, ἃς ἀνέγραψα περὶ τοῦ βίου Μωυσέως (in the two treatises, which I set forth concerning the life of Moses). Nikiprowetzky correctly notes that Philo is distinct in using σύνταξις for a treatise and not a book in several parts. V. Nikiprowetzky, *Le commentaire de l'Écriture chez Philon d'Alexandrie: Son caractère et sa portée; Observations philologiques* (ALGHJ 11; Leiden: Brill, 1977), 221 n. 179.

93 Cf. D. Lincicum, "A Preliminary Index to Philo's Non-biblical Citations and Allusions," *SPhiloA* 25 (2013): 139–67.

94 Hierarchy is also embedded in art. See *The Apotheosis of Homer* in the British Museum, in which representations of the genres of myth, history, poetry, tragedy, and comedy (among others) come to pay Homer and his epics tribute.

something created that has no truthful value.[95] In *Post.* 165, Philo compares the creation of tragedies and their focus on stories of love and arrogance to the Egyptian practice of deifying created objects (e.g., bulls, rams, goats) and creating fictitious and false gods to worship. In contrast, the writings of Moses are not mythic (μῦθος) or the creation of the author (e.g., *Opif.* 157; *Gig.* 7, 60; *Abr.* 243), but factual repositories of divine truth. As a result, Philo creates an explicit personal genre hierarchy with poetry and works of fiction subordinate to history and those that impart truth (i.e., philosophical treatises, as will be seen below; cf. *Congr.* 15).[96]

Third, Philo discusses genre at the beginning of *De praemiis et poenis*, asserting that the Pentateuch (i.e., "the oracles of the prophet Moses") is made up of three ἰδέαι: τήν μὲν περὶ κοσμοποιίας, τὴν δὲ ἱστορικήν, τὴν δὲ τρίτην νομοθετικήν ("the creation of the world, that concerning history, and the third with legislation," *Praem.* 1; cf. *Mos.* 2.45–48; Josephus, *Ant.* 1.18). Although Philo's discussion of the divisions of the Pentateuch is important for understanding Moses,[97] we are focused here on Philo's claim that a unified work might be composed of multiple literary forms. This will be of importance for our discussion of *De vita contemplativa* in chapter 5 and of Philo's biographies in chapter 8.

Fourth, Philo recognizes that genres, such as poetry and history, are not fixed, but are being developed by contemporary writers. Ancient poets and historians, according to Philo, sought to improve their works and perfect their literary forms through the inclusion of philosophy and discussions of virtue. In contrast, contemporary writers (using the metaphor of cooks and confectioners, ὀψαρτυταὶ καὶ σιτοπόνοι) improvise and develop new colors, scents, or flavors in order to tantalize the observer, but neglect the development of the mind (*Plant.* 159). Philo recognizes that authors from different times do different things with literary forms and that genres adapt and develop, both for the better and for the worse (in his opinion).

Allegorical Commentary

The commentary became an increasingly important genre in the Hellenistic and Roman eras. It was characterized by the commentator's conscious need to

95 Philo applies this language to the staged hearing of the Jewish embassy from Alexandria (e.g., *Legat.* 351).

96 For a discussion of fables in Philo, see S. A. Adams, "Fables in Philo of Alexandria: λόγος, μῦθος, and παραβολή," in A. Oegema, J. Pater, and M. Stoutjesdijk, eds., *Parables and Fables in the Graeco-Roman World* (WUNT 1; Tübingen: Mohr Siebeck, forthcoming 2020).

97 For a discussion of this passage with the goal of situating Philo in his wider literary environment, see A. Kamesar, "The Literary Genres of the Pentateuch as Seen from the Greek Perspective: The Testimony of Philo of Alexandria," *SPhiloA* 9 (1997): 143–89.

position his/her work, as the author wrote not only about the source text, but also to wider scholarly debates, both traditional and contemporary. The presumed purpose of this genre was to help the then-contemporary user bridge the epistemological gap that arises when reading a text written in a different location (historical, social, cultural, geographic, linguistic, etc.).[98] The need for this interpretation, especially for culturally or communally significant texts written years earlier, was felt in many (if not all) societies.

The nature and form of metatextual composition changed over time, especially in light of cultural interaction.[99] The similarities in form, primarily due to parallel functions, as well as the fragmentary nature of early commentaries, prohibit definitive claims of origin. The development of this genre was not unidirectional, and extant commentaries allow for some discussion of distinctive features. In what follows, we will evaluate the extant commentaries and their fragments, outlining the broad contours of what this genre might have looked like in antiquity, especially during Philo's career. Following this, we will

98 See I. Sluiter, "The Dialectics of Genre: Some Aspects of Secondary Literature and Genre in Antiquity," in M. Depew and D. Obbink, eds., *Matrices of Genre: Authors, Canons, and Society* (Cambridge, Mass.: Harvard University Press, 2000), 183–203, especially 187–89; S. H. Aufrère, "About Strategies and Objectives of Metatextuality," in S. H. Aufrère, P. S. Alexander, and Z. Pleše, eds., *On the Fringes of Commentary: Metatextuality in Ancient Near Eastern and Ancient Mediterranean Cultures* (OLA 232; Leuven: Peeters, 2014), 3–85. Aufrère provides an excellent introduction to the challenges of investigating the commentary genre, employing the phrase from Genette "metatextual literature" (pp. 6–9) to avoid unduly restricting participation. For a more focused definition, see M. Bockmuehl, "The Dead Sea Scrolls and the Origin of Biblical Commentary," in R. A. Clements and D. R. Schwartz, eds., *Text, Thought, and Practice in Qumran and Early Christianity: Proceedings of the Ninth International Symposium of the Orion Center for the Study of the Dead Sea Scrolls and Associated Literature, Jointly Sponsored by the Hebrew University Center for the Study of Christianity, 11–13 January, 2004* (STDJ 84; Leiden: Brill, 2009), 1–29, especially 4–6. The definition of "commentary" as "works consisting primarily of sequential, expository annotation of the identified texts that are themselves distinguished from the comments and reproduce them intact, whether partially or continuously" (p. 4), allows us to differentiate this form of interpretation from related texts (e.g., paraphrase, citation, scholion, etc.). See also P. B. Hartog, *Pesher and Hypomnema: A Comparison of Two Commentary Traditions from the Hellenistic-Roman World* (STDJ 121; Leiden: Brill, 2017), 28–38.

Scholars typically divide commentaries into two types based on their engagement with the source text: continuous and selected. This division is not discussed in our time periods and so might not be emic to the ancients. Nevertheless, it is a helpful rubric for differentiating texts, especially as there is a relationship between structure and purpose. Cf. M. Del Fabbro, "Il commentario nella tradizione papiracea," *SPap* 18 (1979): 69–132, especially 70–81. For Galen's understanding of the function of a commentary, see *in Hipp. Epid. III Comm. I* 17.1.516; cf. Jerome, *Ruf.* 1.16.

99 In antiquity, authors ascribed the origin of ὑπομνήματα to the Egyptian Thoth-Hermes (i.e., Sanchuniathon) (Diodorus Siculus, *Bibl.* 1.16.2; Philo of Byblos, *History of the Phoenicians*, in Eusebius, *Praep. ev.* 1.9.24; cf. Diogenes Laertius, *Vit.* 9.15 for Antisthenes). For an argument claiming Babylonian origins, see E. Frahm, *Babylonian and Assyrian Text Commentaries: Origins of Interpretation* (GMTR 5; Münster: Ugarit-Verlag, 2011).

evaluate Philo's *Allegorical Commentary*, identifying similarities and differences and what they might tell us about Philo's participation in this genre and his prototypical models.

Insufficient ancient commentaries have survived to understand the full extent of this genre.[100] Firmly differentiating between commentaries (ὑπομνήματα/*commentari[i]*) and other scholarly products (such as *syngrammata*, scholia, encyclopaedias, sermons, etc.) is problematic and undesirable, as there was substantial functional overlap among these texts.[101] More often, scholars have identified structural features to help differentiate these works on formal grounds, and here papyrological texts provide important evidence.[102]

Almost all papyri commentaries are anonymous, although a few can be ascribed to particular writers based on their overlap with extant scholia.[103] These works comment primarily on well-known poetic texts (e.g., Homer, Alcman, Hipponax, Alcaeus, Sappho, Pindar), with fewer engaging with prose (Thucydides, Herodotus).[104] There are limited examples of philosophical commentar-

100 For the definition of "commentary" (ὑπόμνημα), see F. Montanari, "Hypomnema," in *BNP* 6.642–43; F. Schironi, "Greek Commentaries," *DSD* 19 (2012): 399–400. For the writing of commentaries in the Greco-Roman world, see F. Bömer, "Der Commentarius: Zur Vorgeschichte und literarischen Form der Schriften Caesars," *Hermes* 81 (1953): 210–50; and Del Fabbro, "Il commentario."

101 Cf. G. Arrighetti, "Hypomnemata e scholia: Alcuni problemi," *MPL* 2 (1977): 49–67. Additional overlap occurs with the scholia; cf. E. Dickey, "The Sources of Our Knowledge of Ancient Scholarship," in F. Montanari, S. Matthaios, and A. Rengakos, eds., *Brill's Companion to Ancient Greek Scholarship*, vol. 1, *History, Disciplinary Profiles* (Leiden: Brill, 2015), 459–514. For example, cf. P.Oxy. XV 1808, a philosophical text with shorthand marginalia on Plato's *Resp.* 8.546b–c. For an example of a shorthand commentary, see P.Oxy. XXXVI 2752.

102 For example, fifty-two commentary fragments from Oxyrhynchus have been published, ranging in date from the first century BCE to the fourth century CE. P.Oxy. VI 853; XVIII 2176; XIX 2221; XX 2262; XXI 2292–2293, 2306–2307; XXIII 2367–2368; XXIV 2389–2392, 2397; XXV 2429; XXV 2434; XXVI 2449, 2451; XXVII 2463; XXIX 2506; XXX 2527–2528; XXXII 2636–2637; XXXV 2733, 2737–2738, 2740 (addendum), 2741, 2744; XXXVI 2752; XXXVII 2811–2813, 2819; XXXIX 2886–2888; XLV 3210; LIII 3710–3711; LIV 3722; LXIV 4426, 4432; LXV 4451–4456; LXXVI 5095; LXXIX 5201. Cf. T. Dorandi, "Le commentaire dans la tradition papyrologique: Quelques cas Controversés," in M.-O. Goulet-Cazé, ed., *Le commentaire entre tradition et innovation, Actes du Colloque international de l'Institut des Traditions textuelles (Paris et Villejuif, 22–25 septembre 1999)* (Paris: Vrin, 2000), 15–28; F. Montanari, "Gli *Homerica* su papiro: Per una distinzione di generi," in *Studi di filologia omerica antica*, vol. 2 (Pisa: Giardini, 1995), 69–85; Schironi, "Greek Commentaries," 409–11.

103 E.g., P.Oxy. XIX 2221 is thought to have been written by Theon. Some later commentaries include citations that are found in scholia (e.g., P.Oxy. XXXV 2737), suggesting a relationship between these two groups of texts.

104 Cf. J. Lundon, "Homeric Commentaries on Papyrus: A Survey," in S. Matthaios, F. Montanari, and A. Rengakos, eds., *Ancient Scholarship and Grammar: Archetypes, Concepts and Contexts* (TCSup 8; Berlin: De Gruyter, 2011), 159–79. For the most recent study of commentaries on comedies, see S. Trojahn, *Die auf Papyri erhaltenen Kommentare zur Alten Komödie: Ein Beitrag zur Geschichte der antiken Philologie* (BzA 175; Munich: Saur, 2002). For the genres that

ies. This might be due to chance, but it also might indicate that commentaries on philosophical treatises were less common in the early Principate, flourishing later in antiquity.[105]

Most commentaries adopt the format of lemma + comment, making it a core, prototypical feature.[106] Authors offer interpretations to challenging features in the text, drawing from a range of sources to do so, most commonly

---

Hellenistic scholars commented on, see M. Broggiato, "Beyond the Canon: Hellenistic Scholars and Their Texts," in G. Colesanti and M. Giorgano, eds., *Submerged Literature in Ancient Greek Culture: An Introduction* (Berlin: De Gruyter, 2014), 46–60.

105 In late antiquity, we witness a wider range of commentaries (especially by Proclus, 412–485 CE). The most important of Proclus' commentaries is his *Commentary on Plato's Timaeus*, which appears to have begun as lecture notes, as indicated by some of his introductory remarks (H. Tarrant, ed. and trans., *Proclus: Commentary on Plato's "Timaeus,"* vol. 1, *Book 1: Proclus on the Socratic State and Atlantis* [Cambridge: Cambridge University Press, 2007], 13–14). In his sentence-by-sentence progression through the *Timaeus*, Proclus interprets the lemma by drawing on other Platonic works for clarification, thus showing internal consistency in Plato's works and allowing Plato to interpret himself. His reading of Plato, however, is strongly influenced by his predecessors/teachers, especially Porphyry and Iamblichus (*in Parm.* 4.1053.38–1055.25; 1089.30–1090.23; 1106.31–1108.19; 1114.1–35; 1118.19–33; book 5: 1140.26–1142.10; 1150.2–1151.7; 1173.7–1174.12; 1216.15–1217.13; 1226.6–26). Proclus occasionally quotes other writers, particularly Homer and Orpheus, in order to show that Plato was part of the chain of teaching on the truth of divine matters (e.g., Homer: *in Tim.* 1.163.18; 1.167.16–21; 1.168.4, 13, 20–21; Orpheus: *in Tim.* 1.161.25; 1.166.24; 1.169.3, 19; 1.170.9; 1.175.13; 1.187.9–10; Hesiod: 1.173.8–9).

A nonprototypical example is Proclus' *Commentary on Plato's Republic*, which consists of sixteen essays. Although most essays are short and noncontinuous, Essay 16 is substantial and provides a sentence-by-sentence commentary on Plato's "Myth of Er" (*Resp.* 10.614b–621d). See A. Sheppard, "Proclus' Place in the Reception of Plato's *Republic*," in A. Sheppard, ed., *Ancient Approaches to Plato's Republic* (London: University College London, 2013), 107–16. Of interest is Essay 5, in which Proclus attempts to answer ten perceived problems in the text (e.g., *in Resp.* 5.K43–49, "why did Plato prescribe both honour and exile to the poets?" cf. *Resp.* 3.398a) by drawing from Plato's other works (e.g., *Timaeus, Laws, Republic*). These essays appear to be part of a school curriculum, blending question and answer with commentary. The heading for the first essay opens with the term συνανάγνωσις "reading in class," and Proclus identifies his addressees as τοῖς συσχολάζουσιν (*in Resp.* 1.K5r.20), "those who are studying together." Cf. Marinus, *Proc.* 12, 13, 22; Porphyry, *Plot.* 14. Cf. P. Hoffmann, "What Was Commentary in Late Antiquity? The Example of Neoplatonic Commentators," in M. L. Gill and P. Pellegrin, eds., *A Companion to Ancient Philosophy* (Oxford: Blackwell, 2006), 600–601.

106 E.g., P.Oxy. VI 853 (Thucydides); XIX 2221 (Nicander); XX 2262 (Callimachus); XXV 2429 (Epicharmus); XXVI 2449, 2451 (Pindar); XXX 2528 (Euphorion?); LIII 3710 (Homer); LXIV 4426 (Aratus); LXXIX 5201 (Pindar). Cf. P.Köln IV 176; IX 400v, 401r; P.Berl.inv. 11749; P.Berl.inv. 13282; PSI X 1173; P.Yale II 106; P.Ryl. I 24r; P.GraecMon 21; P.Amh. II 12. At least one commentary paraphrases, as opposed to quotes, the lemma. E.g., P.Oxy. XIX 2221 (Homer); XXI 2292–93 (Sappho), where the author Atticizes the little text provided. For Homeric paraphrases, see J. A. Fernández Delgado, "Paráfrasis homéricas en papiros, tablillas y óstraka," *EC* 15 (2011): 3–45.

For an example of a commentary that does not appear to be structured on the typical lemma-and-comment model, but rather gives large portions of Plato prior to giving comment, see *Cod. Taur.* VI,1 (commentary on Plato's *Parmenides*).

from the corpus of the author in focus.[107] Not every commentary cites supporting passages or outside authorities, asserting with confidence their explanations of the text (mostly grammatical and historical; rarely allegorical).[108] Some commentaries adopt an alternative form, providing nonprototypical examples of this genre. In P.Oxy. XXIX 2506, a commentary on lyric poetry, the author provides quotations from four ancient authors (Alcman, Stesichorus, Sappho, and Alcaeus), which are followed by lengthy discussions. The exact relationship among these passages is not clear, as the fragments lack a strong unifying theme and overall sense of cohesion. Nevertheless, the way that the author provides explanations to the lemmata follows the practice found in other commentaries, namely that the author regularly draws on different works, some by the author in focus and some from other authors, to interpret the passage. His engagement with multiple authors is distinctive and shows the range of ways commentaries were written in antiquity.

The fragmentary text of P.Oxy. LIII 3711 is another atypical commentary. This second-century CE work begins with a quotation of Alcaeus (fr. 1 II.31–33) and would appear to be a commentary. However, as the text progresses, it moves away from Alcaeus to discuss the history of Lesbos and various historical issues. The text reads like a προβλήματα, but without the typical questions that are characteristic of this genre (see below). In order to answer specific issues, the commentator quotes other ancient authors in support of his position (e.g., fr. 1 I.5, 9, 17, 27), but the focus on Alcaeus that one would expect in a commentary is not consistent. A similar example is found in a commentary on Homer (P.Oxy. LXV 4453), in which certain aspects of the *Odyssey* are discussed in ways similar to other "Homeric problems."[109] These

107 The commentator of P.Oxy. XXIII 2368 does not quote other poets, but cites another critic (Aristarchus) in support of his position (I.9). Cf. P.Oxy. XXIV 2390 fr. 2 II.4, for references to two other grammarians, Theon and Tyrannio. The author of P.Oxy. XXVII 2463 quotes at least two other writers in a small surviving fragment. P.Oxy. LXV 4452 fr. 1.18–23 cites three Homeric scholars. Cf. P.Oxy. XX 2262, in which the author quotes Bacchylides (fr. 2(a) I.25–27); P.Oxy. XXV 2429 frs. 7, 12, 15, in which the writer quotes from the *Odyssey*. The author of P.Oxy. XXXII 2637 shows knowledge of a wide range of ancient poets, citing Ibycus, Pindar, Akesander, Timaeus, and Theodorus, and the commentator in P.Oxy. XXXVII 2812 quotes Dionysius, Nicander, and possibly Alcman. The author of the commentary on Nicander's *Theriaca* (P.Oxy. XIX 2221) quotes many other authors (e.g., Hesiod, Callimachus, Sophocles, and possibly Nicander, II.18–19).

108 A great example is Didymus' commentary on Demosthenes' *Orations* 9–11, and 13, in which lemmata and quotations from other sources were typically marked by *ekthesis* and *paragraphoi*. The only other commentary at Oxyrhynchus with a clear practice of referencing other passages of the author in support of his interpretation is P.Oxy. LIV 3722 (Anacreon, e.g., fr. 1.19; 27.7; 39.4; 73.10).

109 For an overview of Homeric commentaries, see Lundon, "Homeric Commentaries on Papyrus," 159–79.

texts, although adopting structural elements of commentaries, employ them for different, if related, purposes. Accordingly, they provide examples of the diversity of didactic literature, implying that a literary relationship existed between the genres of *quaestiones* literature and ancient commentary.

The need for philosophical commentaries appears to have increased during the late Hellenistic and early Roman eras, a development resulting from the increased temporal distance between the reader and the text and the growth of new or rejuvenated philosophical schools.[110] One of the most important is *Anonymous Theaetetus Commentary* (P.Berol.inv. 9782), which begins with a brief introduction to Plato's treatise, outlining its general contents and what Plato was hoping to accomplish (II.1–III.28).[111] The commentator employs the standard lemma + comment construction, although he regularly provides a paraphrase immediately following the lemma to unpack more fully what the characters in *Theaetetus* were saying.[112] This additional interpretive step provides a clear understanding of how the commentator read Plato's text and often prepares the reader for what the author wishes to discuss in the commentary section (e.g., XXII.24–30; XLVII.24–30; XLVIII.35–44; LIV.14–30).[113] The commentator progresses systematically through the text, although occasionally he will skip a few lines or a small section from *Theaetetus* that, presumably, was not worthy of comment or thought to be self-explanatory or not of interest

110 Aristotle's *Categories* was regularly studied. One of the most important philosophical commentators is Boethus (75–10 BCE), whose "word-by-word exegesis" was thought to be superior to the commentary of Andronicus (fl. ca. 60 BCE), who is said to have "paraphrased the *Categories*" (Simplicius, *in Cat.* 29.28–30.5). In the first and second centuries CE, Alexander, Adrastus, and Aspasius also established themselves as respected interpreters of Aristotle, and they became the common dialogue partners for later commentators (Porphyry, *Plot.* 14; Galen, *Lib. prop.* 19.42–43). We also have a first-century BCE commentary on Aristotle's *Topica*, P.Fay. 3.

111 G. Bastianini and D. N. Sedley, eds. and trans., "Commentarium in Platonis *Theaetetum*: PBerol.inv. 9782," in *Corpus dei Papiri Filosofici greci e latini*, pt. 3, *Commentary* (Florence: Olschki, 1995), 227–562. For the discussion of dating, see 251–56.

112 Demetrius the Chronographer also paraphrased lemma in his discussion of Exod 5:3 (fr. 5).

113 The use of *diplai* to visually mark quoted text is important. For a more detailed discussion of this paratextual feature, see R. Pfeiffer, *History of Classical Scholarship: From the Beginnings to the End of the Hellenistic Age* (Oxford: Clarendon, 1968), especially 210–33; L. D. Reynolds and N. G. Wilson, *Scribes and Scholars: A Guide to the Transmission of Greek and Latin Literature* (4th ed.; Oxford: Oxford University Press, 2013), 11; E. M. Thompson, *An Introduction to Greek and Latin Palaeography* (Oxford: Clarendon, 1912), 63; E. G. Turner, *Greek Manuscripts of the Ancient World* (Princeton: Princeton University Press, 1971), 12 (see 117–18 for a list of manuscripts with *diplai*); R. Clemens and T. Graham, *Introduction to Manuscript Studies* (Ithaca: Cornell University Press, 2007), 86–87; S. A. Adams and S. M. Ehorn, "Composite Citations in Early Christian Manuscripts," in S. E. Porter, D. I. Yoon, and C. S. Stevens, eds., *Paratextual Features of New Testament Papyrology and Early Christian Manuscripts* (TENTS; Leiden: Brill, forthcoming 2020).

or relevance.[114] As most of the lemmata are of Socrates' words, it is best to understand the commentator as prioritizing this doctrine over those espoused by the other characters. In the commentary section, the author occasionally mentions (XI.23; XXII.39; XXIV.32) and quotes (XV.16–29; XXIV.30–XXV. 29) other authors (once referencing another of his commentaries, XLVIII.10–11), although it is more common for him to invoke Socrates' statements in Plato's other works in order to provide the best interpretation of the lemma, implying a unified "Socrates" across the treatises.[115]

Galen (129–ca. 200/216 CE, cf. *Suda* Γ 32) devoted a good portion of his literary activities to the writing of commentaries, especially on Hippocrates' treatises.[116] In *On My Own Books*, Galen recognizes his dependence on his predecessors when writing commentaries, claiming that some had produced word-by-word commentaries on Hippocrates' works (ἐξηγήσεις δὲ καθ' ἑκάστην αὐτοῦ λέξιν ἤδη πολλοῖς τῶν πρὸ ἐμοῦ γεγραμμένας οὐ φαύλως εἰδώς, *Lib. prop.* 19.34). In light of this commentary tradition, Galen felt obliged to explain why he did not regularly cite them in his works; his books were still in Asia and were not available to him in Rome (*Lib. prop.* 19.34–35).[117] This suggests that the acknowledgment of sources and other commentators might have been expected in a commentary, especially for such a well-known figure as Hippocrates.[118] An important aspect of Galen's early commentaries was that he wrote them for himself and did not expect them to be made public. Later he shared them with his friends (*Lib. prop.* 19.33), a decision that directly influenced the material included and how it was presented.[119]

114 Most comments are not long, but the section on *Theaet.* 147d3–5 consists of ten columns (XXV.30–XXXIV.9), and the comment on *Theaet.* 148b2 runs for four (XLI.17–XLIV.40). Passages that require the most commentary are paired with drawings to help explain the mathematical discussion, col. XXXI, XXXIII, and XLIII. Visuals are also found in Apollonius of Citium's commentary on Hippocrates' *On Joints*.

115 E.g., *Republic*: XIII.8; LIX.9; *Meno*: XV.20; XXVIII.43; LVI.27; *Timaeus*: XXXV.11; *Symposium*: LVII.15.

116 *Lib. prop.* 19.33–37; C. G. Kühn, ed., *Claudii Galeni Opera Omnia* (Leipzig: C. Cnobloch, 1821–1833). Cf. D. Manetti and A. Roselli, "Galeno commentatore di Ippocrate," *ANRW* 2.37.2 (1994): 1529–635.

117 Galen rarely references other Hippocratic works, authors, or commentators (e.g., Hippocrates: G. 5; G. 8; G. 10; G. 50n; Aristotle: G. 36; Euclid: G. 50h; Hesiod: G. 50j; G. 50l; G. 50n). Cf. A. Wasserstein, ed. and trans., *Galen's Commentary on the Hippocratic Treatise Airs, Waters, Places: In the Hebrew Translation of Solomon ha-Me'ati* (Jerusalem: Israel Academy of Science and Humanities, 1982).

118 In his extant commentary on Plato's *Timaeus* (cod. Paris Gr. 2838, cf. *Lib. prop.* 19.41–48) Galen occasionally provides specific comments by ancient authors (e.g., fr. 2.70–71; fr. 5.25–27). Galen does not make regular, explicit recourse to Plato when interpreting Plato, although he does do so when he considers it necessary (e.g., fr. 15.14–23). Nevertheless, allowing an author to interpret himself is one of Galen's stated methods of exegesis (*Dig. puls.* iv 8.958.6, Kühn).

119 Galen's school notes were secretly published due to the demand for his work (*Lib. prop.* 19.42–43), which led to greater intentionally about what he released to the public. Galen wrote

Some commentaries participate in the commentary genre atypically, implying a wider diversity of expressions and multiple prototypical forms. One example is our earliest extant Greek commentary, the Derveni Papyrus (ca. 340–320 BCE), which defends Orpheus, addressing issues of Orphic cosmogony, and offers an interpretation to noninitiates of Orpheus' purposefully obscure poetic riddles (VII.6–7).[120] Following a discussion of sacrificial practices and the underworld (cols. III–VI), the commentator structures the work on lemmata from a poem attributed to Orpheus (e.g., VIII.2, 4–5; XI.10; XII.2; XIII.1, 4; XIV.6, etc.).[121] In addition to quoting specific lemmata, the author also paraphrases Orpheus (VIII.7–8; XIV.3), sometimes immediately after a quotation and sometimes as an explanation of what was said.[122]

Because Orpheus' work is a riddling discourse "from the very first word to the last" and was intended for those who are pure of hearing (VII.4–11), the commentator makes recourse to allegorical interpretation in order to tease out the true meaning of Orpheus' intentionally vague poem (XXV.12–13). In doing so, the author atomizes the text, breaking it into smaller portions in order to explain the text's true meaning.[123] In particular, odd semantic choices and difficult grammatical combinations are viewed as signals of deeper meaning.[124] Accordingly, etymology is strategically employed to reinforce specific interpretations; Zeus is interpreted as "Mind" (XVI.8–14) and "Air" (XVII.3–6; XIX.3), thus making him the first principle of the cosmos. The commentator equates the sun with a phallus (XVI.1) and claims that certain words invoke specific ideas (e.g., "wide" for heavens and "long" for Olympus, XII.7–10). Importantly for the commentator, "each verse" (καθ' ἔπος ἕκαστον, XIII.5–6) contains hidden elements that can only be discerned through allegorical interpretation.

---

different types of commentaries, tailoring them to what he perceived was the intended audience (e.g., beginner or advanced reader), although all with the general public and not a specific individual in mind (*Lib. prop.* 19.35).

120 For the Greek text, see G. Betegh, *The Derveni Papyrus: Cosmology, Theology, and Interpretation* (Cambridge: Cambridge University Press, 2004). Cf. T. Kouremenos, K. Tsantsanoglou, and G. Parássoglou, eds., *The Derveni Papyrus* (STCPF 13; Florence: Olschki, 2006); A. Lamedica, "Il Papiro di Derveni come commentario: Problemi formali," in A. H. S. El-Mosalamy, ed., *Proceedings of the XIXth International Congress of Papyrology, Cairo 2–9 September 1989* (2 vols.; Cairo: Ain Shams University, 1992), 1.325–33. Cf. Clement, *Strom.* 5.8.124–126, for references to other Hellenistic interpreters of Orpheus.

121 These lemmata are indicated by *paragraphoi* and followed by corresponding interpretations. For a reconstruction of the Orphic text from the lemmata, see Betegh, *Derveni Papyrus*, 92–97.

122 The commentator draws almost exclusively on Orpheus, although he cites Heraclitus once (IV.5).

123 For a discussion of atomization as a key element of transpositional hermeneutics, see Lange and Pleše, "Derveni—Alexandria—Qumran," 89–160.

124 E.g., XIX.4–5; XXIII.1–10. The use of diction as a means of interpretation has a long history. It has been traced back to Theagenes of Rhegium (sixth century BCE); cf. schol. B *Il.* 20.67.

This allegorical reading appropriates a philological approach to the text, allowing the commentator to discuss the text on multiple levels and to draw upon particular features where beneficial. It is this revelation that the author, as an insider member (V.4–5), is offering to the reader as a corrective to those who employ the craft of holy rites but do not, or cannot, explain the rituals, leaving in ignorance those who are in attendance (XX.2–12).[125]

Another nonprototypical commentary from the Hellenistic era is the work of Hipparchus of Nicaea on Aratus' *Phaenomena* (second century BCE).[126] Unlike the majority of commentaries discussed—as well as the commentary by Attalus of Rhodes, which Hipparchus cites (1.2.1–1.3.12)—Hipparchus' work is a polemical commentary in which he did not seek to explain Aratus' text to interested readers, but to demonstrate its author's errors.[127] Hipparchus regularly cites passages from Aratus' *Phaenomena* (approx. 250 lines are given) and Eudoxus of Cnidus (whom Aratus used as a source), but he does not proceed sequentially through either text. Rather, he cites specific passages (some of which more than once) when they are appropriate for the immediate discussion. This lack of sequential progression is a result of the author's purpose, which was not to provide an explanation of Aratus' *Phaenomena*, but to expose its technical flaws and present the commentator's own astronomical theories, suggesting that the genres of commentary and polemical treatise could be fruitfully combined.[128]

Participation in the genre of commentary is also undertaken by Jewish authors.[129] Many examples of Jewish commentary writing come from the Qum-

125 For the importance of divining oracles in order to acquire understanding, see Betegh, *Derveni Papyrus*, 364–70.

126 K. Manitius, *In Arati et Eudoxi Phaenomena commentariorum libri tres* (Leipzig: Teubner, 1894).

127 Another example of a polemical commentary is Origen's *Contra Celsum*. Hipparchus also asserts that if Aratus had written in prose, his work would have been ignored (1.1.7). Hipparchus introduces this focus at the beginning of his work, which begins with a prefixed letter to his friend Aeschrion (Ἵππαρχος Αἰσχρίωνι χαίρειν, 1.1. *praef.*). This greeting is interesting for our discussion, as it signals the author's engagement with other genres. See also the discussion of epistolary greetings prefixed to literary works in chapter 5 (Letter of Aristeas).

128 Cf. E. Dickey, *Ancient Greek Scholarship: A Guide to Finding, Reading, and Understanding Scholia, Commentaries, Lexica, and Grammatical Treatises, from Their Beginnings to the Byzantine Period* (Oxford: Oxford University Press, 2007), 56–60.

129 Above we discussed Aristobulus (second century BCE), who provided an allegorical interpretation for specific passages of the Books of Moses and dedicated the work to King Ptolemy. In his composition, Aristobulus provides explanatory readings that challenge surface readings of the text in favor of a "proper," allegorical one (fr. 2.1–6; e.g., fr. 2.8 [God's "hand"]; 4.3 [God's "voice"]; 5.9–16 [seven-day week and Sabbath]). The work, as far as we know, was not systematic in its coverage, but atomistic, seeking to address specific interpretive issues raised by readers of the text through allegorical interpretation. Philo mentions Jewish interpreters in *Leg.* 1.59, *Sacr.* 131, and *Plant.* 52, and it is likely that these, if written, are undertaken in Greek. Justus of

ran community, and scholars have identified different types of *pesharim*: "thematic *pesharim*" (e.g., 4QFlor; 4QCatena; 4Q180) interpret collected scriptural quotation on a specific theme or topic; "isolated *pesharim*" (e.g., CD IV,14; XIX,5–13; 1QS VIII,3–15) represent individual passages where פשר or *pesher*-like interpretation is employed; and "continuous *pesharim*" move, lemma by lemma, through a source text (i.e., scriptural book).[130] Similar to the form of Greek commentaries discussed above, continuous *pesharim* are structured on lemma + commentary units, with the biblical lemma often, but not always, followed by a phrase that includes פשר "interpretation" (e.g., פשר הדבר or פשרו על) and/or a blank space (*vacat*) to introduce the comment.[131] Although direct

---

Tiberias is also reported to have written commentaries (cf. Jerome, *Vir. ill.* 14; *Suda* I 450). For the "commentary turn" in Judaism, see S. D. Fraade, *From Tradition to Commentary: Torah and Its Interpretation in the Midrash Sifre to Deuteronomy* (Albany: State University of New York Press, 1991), 1–23.

130 Fifteen examples of continuous *pesher* on biblical books are extant from Qumran: Isaiah (4QpIsa[a–e] [4Q161–165]), Hosea (4QpHos[a–b] [4Q166–167]), Micah (1QpMic [1Q14]), Nahum (4QpNah [4Q169]), Habakkuk (1QpHab), Zephaniah (1QpZeph [1Q15], 4QpZeph [4Q170]), and Psalms (1QpPs [1Q16], 4QpPs[a,b] [4Q171, 173]). A two-part division (continuous or thematic) was proposed by J. Carmignac, "Le document de Qumrân sur Melkisédek," *RevQ* 7 (1969): 342–78. On thematic, see G. J. Brooke, "Thematic Commentaries on Prophetic Scripture," in M. Henze, ed., *Biblical Interpretation at Qumran* (Grand Rapids: Eerdmans, 2005), 134–57. A three-part division was proposed by D. Dimant, "Qumran Sectarian Literature," in M. E. Stone, ed., *Jewish Writings of the Second Temple Period: Apocrypha, Pseudepigrapha, Qumran Sectarian Writings, Philo, Josephus* (CRINT 2.2; Philadelphia: Fortress, 1984), 504–8; Williamson, "Pesher." Most recently, a four-part categorization has been offered by B. Brown-deVost, *Commentary and Authority in Mesopotamia and Qumran* (JAJSup 29; Göttingen: Vandenhoeck & Ruprecht, 2019). For the foundational study of *pesharim*, see M. P. Horgan, *Pesharim: Qumran Interpretations of Biblical Books* (CBQMS 8; Washington, D.C.: Catholic Biblical Association of America, 1979), especially 229–59. M. J. Bernstein, "Introductory Formulas for the Citation and Re-citation of Biblical Verses in the Qumran Pesharim: Observations on a Pesher Technique," *DSD* 1 (1994): 30–70, rightly judges these categories to be too simplistic; however, they remain useful shorthands. S. L. Berrin, *Pesher Nahum Scroll from Qumran: An Exegetical Study of 4Q169* (STDJ 53; Leiden: Brill, 2004), 9–12.

For an introduction to the scrolls and the archaeology of Qumran, see J. Magness, *The Archeology of Qumran and the Dead Sea Scrolls* (Grand Rapids: Eerdmans, 2002). Unless stated, all Hebrew and English quotes are from D. W. Parry and E. Tov, with G. I. Clements, eds., *The Dead Sea Scrolls Reader* (2nd ed., rev. and expanded; 2 vols.; Leiden: Brill, 2014).

On the relationship between commentaries at Qumran and those of the ancient Near East, see M. Fishbane, "The Qumran Pesher and Traits of Ancient Hermeneutics," in A. Shinan, ed., *Proceedings of the Sixth World Congress of Jewish Studies* (4 vols.; Jerusalem: World Union of Jewish Studies, 1977), 1.97–114; U. Gabbay, "Akkadian Commentaries from Ancient Mesopotamia and Their Relation to Early Hebrew Exegesis," *DSD* 19 (2012): 267–312; B. Brown-deVost, "The Compositional Development of Qumran Pesharim in Light of Mesopotamian Commentaries," *JBL* 135 (2016): 525–41. For a detailed discussion of Mesopotamian commentaries, see Frahm, *Babylonian and Assyrian Text Commentaries*. For the argument that *pesharim* are related to ANE dream and omen literature, see A. P. Jassen, "The Pesharim and the Rise of Commentary in Early Jewish Scriptural Interpretation," *DSD* 19 (2012): 363–98.

131 On parallels between the Qumran *pesharim* and Greek *hypomnemata*, see M. R. Niehoff, "Commentary Culture in the Land of Israel from an Alexandrian Perspective," *DSD* 19 (2012):

quotation of the scriptural text was most common, some authors felt comfortable adding to or subtracting from authoritative texts, thus blurring the line between author and commentator.[132] This practice could be viewed as a parallel to paraphrasing identified above, in which the commentator (re)articulates the source text in his own words, and in so doing subtly alters the original to align better with his interpretation.

The continuous commentaries interpret prophetic books whose content was thought to contain hidden messages that the interpreter could apply to the present, eschatological situation of his community.[133] Pesherists did not focus on historical or grammatical issues, but sought to actualize the meaning of the text for their current time period.[134] The primary hermeneutical approach of pesherists was to interpret prophetic texts as aligning with the broader narrative that viewed the community as living in the "last days." Adopting this interpretive lens allowed the the prophetic texts to be viewed as speaking to and reinforcing the views of the community, importantly not bifurcating interpretations into historical and figurative readings.

442–63; R. G. Kratz, "Text and Commentary: The *Pesharim* of Qumran in the Context of Hellenistic Scholarship," in T. L. Thompson and P. Wajdenbaum, eds., *The Bible and Hellenism: Greek Influence on Jewish and Early Christian Literature* (Durham: Acumen, 2014), 212–29; especially Hartog, *Pesher and Hypomnema*.

4QpIsa[a] and 4QpIsa[b] employ פשר inconsistently, lacking the formula at 4QpIsa[a] 8–10, 7, 9, 10, 12; 4QpIsa[b] II,6–7, 10. The quotations in 1QpHab are short, whereas lemma in 4QpIsa[a] (4Q163) are comparably long, with shorter and less elaborate interpretations. Cf. Bernstein, "Introductory Formulas." Brown-deVost (*Commentary and Authority*, 30) identifies sequential order as one of the key criteria for genre participation. I would agree that it is most common, but not required. Lim argues that formal features shared by continuous *pesharim* are not particularly numerous, identifying *pesher* with a "scholarly construct." T. H. Lim, *Pesharim* (CQS 3; London: Sheffield, 2002), 40, 53. For a detailed discussion of the layout of the *pesharim*, see Hartog, *Pesher and Hypomnema*, 136–82.

132 Cf. Horgan, *Pesharim*, 245. For a nuanced discussion taking into account textual pluriformity, see T. H. Lim, *Holy Scripture in the Qumran Commentaries and Pauline Letters* (Oxford: Clarendon, 1997), 69–109, 179; T. H. Lim, "Biblical Quotations in the Pesharim and the Text of the Bible—Methodological Considerations," in E. D. Herbert and E. Tov, eds., *The Bible as Book: The Hebrew Bible and the Judaean Desert Discoveries* (London: British Library, 2002), 71–79.

133 Passages from the Psalms, the Pentateuch, and the Former Prophets that were either poetic/prophetic (e.g., the "Blessings of Jacob" in Gen 49; 4Q252 IV–V) or were considered eschatologically laden (e.g., Lev 25; 11QMelch II) also attracted interpreters. Both Moses (Deut 34:10) and David (11QPs[a] XXVII,11; Acts 2:30) were considered prophets. Cf. P. W. Flint, "The Prophet David at Qumran," in M. Henze, ed., *Biblical Interpretation at Qumran* (Grand Rapids: Eerdmans, 2005), 158–67. Within the prophetic books, the commentators appear to prioritize poetic texts (e.g., 4QpIsa[b], which omits the prose text of Isa 6:1–8). However, 3QpIsa (3Q4) comments on prose text (Isa 1:1).

134 The pesherist employed allegorical interpretation on occasion (e.g., 1QpHab II,12–13; XII,4; 4Q169 III,8–9). Cf. E. Matusova, "Allegorical Interpretation of the Pentateuch in Alexandria: Inscribing Aristobulos and Philo in a Wider Literary Context," *SPhiloA* 22 (2010): 2–10.

The Qumran commentators did not cite any text outside the scriptural corpus, and only quoted texts from different books on rare occasions (e.g., 4QpIsa[a] X,8; XXIII,14), reinforcing the importance of these texts and their authoritative position within their community.[135] The ability to interpret these sacred texts through the community's narrative is limited and principally located in the Teacher of Righteousness (מורה הצדק).[136] "When it says, 'so that with ease someone can read it,' this refers to the Teacher of Righteousness, to whom God made known all the mysterious revelations of his servants the prophets. 'For a prophecy testifies of a specific period; it speaks of that time and does not deceive.' This means that the Last Days will be long, much longer than the prophets had said; for God's revelations are truly mysterious" (1QpHab VII,3–8, Parry and Tov). Here the author claims that the true meaning of the prophet's words regarding the final generation (דור האחרון) and the divine "mysteries" (רזים) were hidden from the prophet and only later revealed to the Teacher of Righteousness.[137]

Some have argued that *pesharim* are a special literary genre particular to the Qumran community.[138] In some ways, these scholars are correct, as the communal eschatological approach to the text is atypical and integral to the communally. The pesherist's view of authorship is also distinctive, for unlike Alexandrian scholars, who highlighted the human author responsible for the text, the author of lQpHab downplays human composition and the person of Habakkuk, never studying him as an author with particular writing habits or literary style. Rather, the prophet and his text acted as a means of communication between God and the Teacher of Righteousness.[139] Many features of the *pesharim* (e.g., lemmatic focus, need for an interpretive approach, application to authoritative texts, regular formatting to introduce interpretations, etc.) are shared across authors and cultures, which suggests that the *pesharim* can be viewed as participating in the wider genre of commentary writing.

Commentaries at Qumran are not identical, and some texts appear to be nonprototypical examples of *pesher* or could be viewed as participating in

135 Cf. A. Lange, "From Literature to Scripture: The Unity and Plurality of the Hebrew Scriptures in Light of the Qumran Library," in C. Helmer and C. Landmesser, eds., *One Scripture or Many? Canon from Biblical, Theological, and Philosophical Perspectives* (Oxford: Oxford University Press, 2004), 51–107.

136 E.g., CD I,11; 1QpHab I,13; II,2.

137 Cf. 1QpHab II,1–10. On the use and importance of רז in the Scrolls, see S. I. Thomas, *The "Mysteries" of Qumran: Mystery, Secrecy, and Esotericism in the Dead Sea Scrolls* (Atlanta: SBL, 2009), especially 241–44.

138 Cf. W. H. Brownlee, *The Midrash-Pesher Habakkuk* (Missoula, Mont.: Scholars Press, 1977), 23–36; G. J. Brooke, "Qumran Pesher: Towards the Redefinition of a Genre," *RevQ* 10 (1981): 483–503, "Qumran midrash."

139 Niehoff, "Commentary Culture," 454–57.

multiple genres.[140] The most prominent example is 4Q252 (4QCommGen A), in which the author interprets select issues from Genesis 6–49, but with no overt governing principle. The pesherist employs a heading once, "The Blessing of Jacob" (ברכות יעקוב, IV,3) to signal a new interpretive section, the lemma of which is followed by the only use of פשר (פשרו אשר, with *vacat*, IV,5), evidencing a knowledge of Qumran commentary practices.[141] Column V,1–7 continues the author's exegesis of Genesis (here Gen 49:10), offering a partial ideological understanding found in other Qumran texts (V,3–5).[142] Importantly, the author does not reflect upon or apply the Genesis text to contemporary events. In other sections, such as II,8–10, the author does not provide a biblical lemma, but rewrites the Genesis narrative to clarify a chronological issue. The discussion of the binding of Isaac in III,6–9, to our knowledge, does not address a specific interpretive issue, but is an abridged retelling of the narrative. These practices represent a substantial departure from the commentary format and offer a unique witness to an author's willingness to unite typically discrete methods of interpretation: one that distinguishes the source text from interpretation (*pesharim*) and one that blurs that distinction (rewritten Scripture).[143]

Overall, similarities in structure (lemma + comment, use of *vacats*), purpose (explanation of a text), and relationship (priority/authority of base text over interpretation) suggest that *pesharim* can be viewed as participating in the genre of commentary. Specific particularities of *pesharim* (e.g., use of פשר, eschatological interpretation, "inspired" interpreter [מורה הצדק], etc.) imply that the Qumran community had a different prototypical model from Greek authors, but not one that would necessitate the construction of a new genre. Although the *pesharim* do not show an explicit connection between the Qumran community and the wider literary world, the shared used of this interpretive literary form supports the view that both Jewish and Greek scholars

140 For the argument to distinguish direct and indirect forms of commentary, see S. D. Fraade, "Rewritten Bible and Rabbinic Midrash as Commentary," in C. Bakhos, ed., *Current Trends in the Study of Midrash* (Leiden: Brill, 2006), 59–78.

141 The use of the lemma + comment form is found in other sections (II,5–8), despite the absence of פשר. Other interpretations include: explanation of biblical actions (Noah exited the ark at the "appointed time" [למועד, II,4–5] and why Noah cursed Canaan and not Ham, who had sinned [II,5–7]); explanatory glosses (IV,1–2; V,2–3); and explicit chronological determinations (I,1, 6–10).

142 Not all of the exegesis in this column is sectarian, as rightly noted by M. J. Bernstein, "4Q252: From Re-written Bible to Biblical Commentary," in *Reading and Re-reading Scripture at Qumran* (2 vols.; STDJ 107; Leiden: Brill, 2013), 1.115–16.

143 For the possible writing of an explanation in poetic form (II,7–8), see G. J. Brooke, "The Genre of 4Q252: From Poetry to Pesher," *DSD* 1 (1994): 167–68. For the blurring of commentary and rewritten Scripture categories, see S. W. Crawford, *Rewriting Scripture in Second Temple Times* (Grand Rapids: Eerdmans, 2008), 130–43.

partook in Hellenistic-era intellectual culture and jointly saw the value of this genre.[144]

From the above investigation we can identify core aspects of commentaries in antiquity. First, all commentaries commented on something, specifically a text that was already in circulation. Second, almost all commentaries focused on important works, of both prose and poetry. For Greeks, these were compositions by well-known authors; whereas at Qumran interpreters commentated primarily on authoritative prophetic texts. These texts held cultural value for their respective communities and so warranted the investment of resources by both the author and the intended readers. Third, a majority of commentaries were similarly structured with a lemma followed by commentary. There was no consistency in the length of the comment section, which varied with the perceived importance of the passage, its difficulty, and the intention of the author. Fourth, most continuous commentaries worked sequentially through a work and did not omit large portions of the text. Some commentaries, however, were thematically based, and the evidence from Qumran shows that multiple approaches to interpreting a text could be employed within a community. Fifth, commentators regularly, though not consistently, mentioned other interpreters and authors. They also cited other works/passages from the author under consideration in order to assist in providing a "consistent" or internal interpretation of the passage. Sixth, most commentators had some interest in the philological, text-critical, logical, lexical, and historical aspects of the text.[145] Allegory was rarely the dominant method of explanation, although some texts (especially Derveni Papyrus) and authors (e.g., Crates) regularly employed it. For those in the Qumran community, the inspired interpretation of the Teacher of Righteousness rendered the cryptic prophetic text intelligible and relevant, fitting it within the community's eschatological worldview. Seventh, and finally, all but one of the commentaries (Hipparchus of Nicaea's on Aratus' *Phaenomena*) were complementary to the text being evaluated and were (presumably) written for readers who were interested in bridging the hermeneutical gap in order to read the text better.[146]

144 Cf. Hartog, *Pesher and Hypomnema*, 51–62, who argues, not unduly, for Jewish adoption of Greek practices, and not vice versa.

145 A good example of this is the scholia on Homer and the work by Aristarchus. Cf. H. Erbse, ed., *Scholia Graeca in Homeri Iliadem: Scholia vetera* (7 vols.; Berlin: De Gruyter, 1969–1988); H. Erbse, "Über Aristarchs Iliasausgaben," *Hermes* 87 (1959): 279.

146 Although I agree with Bonazzi that commentating on a text is not a neutral practice, the extent to which all are "polemic tools" is debatable. M. Bonazzi, "The Commentary as Polemical Tool: The Anonymous Commentator on the *Theaetetus* against the Stoics," *Laval Théologique et Philosophique* 64 (2008): 597–605.

Philo's *Allegorical Commentary* is a collection of (at least) nineteen treatises that interpret of a substantial portion of the Greek text of Genesis.[147] The works within the *Allegorical Commentary* have a similar structure to those mentioned above; Philo provides a quotation of a biblical lemma, which is then interpreted. This format is complicated by Philo's tendency to quote additional passages from the Pentateuch (secondary or tertiary lemmata) as part of the comment section, which occasionally overshadow the original quotation.[148] Philo's philosophical interpretations can take him some distance from the text, which ultimately results in commentary sections that are substantially larger than those discussed above.[149] Extreme examples would be Philo's *De agricultura* and *De plantatione*, two whole books which are dedicated to commenting on one verse (Gen 9:20), and *De ebrietate*, which only covers one verse (Gen 9:21). Although Philo is grounded in the text, the fact that he breaks away from commenting on a particular lemma so frequently and for so long suggests that he is adopting a fringe genre position.[150]

Despite Philo's tendency to provide large commentary on short passages of text, he does not seek to outline a philosophical system, but rather takes the scriptural text as his point of departure. Philo is a commentator on Scripture, and for him the text has layers of meaning and does not always allow for literal, simplistic, or straightforward interpretations. In this way Philo is similar to other commentators in that all of them understand their job as necessary because of the complexity of the base text. Philo does not always aim to give the definitive explanation of the hidden meanings behind Moses' text, but offers an interpretation that is consistent with his hermeneutical framework.[151] As a result, his exegesis remains provisional, allowing for the possibility that other readers might also express the truth of the text through their exegesis.[152] This

147 The full extent of the commentary is unclear, though there is little reason to think that it went beyond Genesis. At the very minimum it ranged from Gen 2:1 (*Leg.* 1.1) to Gen 17:22 (*Mut.* 270). Cf. Eusebius, *Hist. eccl.* 2.18.1.

Surviving commentaries in Greek are almost entirely limited to works penned by Greek authors and originally written in Greek. Philo's practice is distinctive, as he is writing a commentary on a translated text. Other examples of this practice are few, such as the reported commentary by Hermippus, the student of Callimachus, on the works of Zoroaster (Pliny the Elder, *Nat. hist.* 30.4).

148 D. T. Runia, "Further Observations on the Structure of Philo's Allegorical Treatises," *VC* 41 (1987): 105–38.

149 For the accusation of Philo as "rambling," see C. H. Colson, trans., *Philo* (10 vols., 2 supps.; LCL; Cambridge, Mass.: Harvard University Press; London: William Heinemann, 1929), 1:x–xi.

150 The closest parallels are Proclus' *Commentary on Plato's Republic* 16 on Plato's "Myth of Er" (*Resp.* 10.614b–621d) and portions of *Anonymous Theaetetus Commentary*, but Philo is substantially longer.

151 Runia, "Structure," 237–38.

152 Nikiprowetzky, *Le commentaire*, 183–92.

perspective helps explain the phenomenon of multiple, and sometimes contradictory, explanations, especially when one recognizes that much of Philo's exegesis is context dependent.[153] At the same time, every commentary author has his/her own interests and purposes, which result in the commentator shifting the reader's focus away from the original import of the hypotext, imbuing it with new meaning.[154] Philo is conspicuous in this regard, but the development of new interpretations is a reality of every form of explanation.

Philo does not read his text in isolation, but brings in other texts to assist in his interpretation. These additional, presumably linked texts are predominantly taken from the Pentateuch, which results in the forging of parallel readings; Moses interpreting and illuminating Moses. In doing so, Philo adopts a similar approach attributed to Aristarchus: "Homer to clarify Homer."[155] However, Philo does not limit his use of additional texts to the Pentateuch, but draws from other authoritative works to support his explanation. Scriptural texts are most prominent, but Philo also employs Greek philosophers, especially Plato, adopting his terminology and conceptual categories to illuminate the deep meaning of the text.[156] These Greek philosophical ideas, according to Philo, are not foreign impositions to the text, but are compatible with and have their ultimate source in divine thought and so are a logically consistent way of reading the Pentateuch. Philo, therefore, is distinct among his predecessors and contemporaries in his overt amalgamation of Jewish and Greek thought.[157]

One feature of Philo's commentary stands out as atypical in comparison to the other commentaries mentioned above, namely, the use of allegory. Philo

153 Runia, "Structure," 238. For example, the exegesis of Gen 1:2 in *Opif.* 32 and *Gig.* 22. Cf. *QG* 4.5. For a discussion of Philo's commentaries as performances with similarities to sermons, although formally structured as commentaries, see D. T. Runia, "The Theme of Flight and Exile in the Allegorical Thought-World of Philo of Alexandria," *SPhiloA* 21 (2009): 8.

154 C. S. Kraus, "Introduction: Reading Commentaries/Commentaries as Reading," in R. K. Gibson and C. S. Kraus, eds., *The Classical Commentary: Histories, Practices, Theory* (Mnemosyne 232; Leiden: Brill, 2002), 1–27.

155 Cf. Porphyry, *Quaes. hom.* 2.297.16–17, "Considering it right to explain Homer with Homer, I have shown that Homer interprets himself sometimes in passages which are nearby, sometimes in other passages." Cf. Galen, *Dig. puls.* iv 8.958.6 (Kühn); Plutarch, *Adol. poet. aud.* 4 [*Mor.* 20d–e]. On different approaches to commentated texts, see Sluiter, "Dialectics of Genre," 187–92.

156 Despite the clear influence of Greco-Roman authors, Philo does not regularly cite Greek authors at length, nor are their perspectives determinative. Cf. Lincicum, "Preliminary Index"; D. Lincicum, "Philo's Library," *SPhiloA* 26 (2014): 99–114; E. Koskenniemi, *Greek Writers and Philosophers in Philo and Josephus: A Study of Their Secular Education and Educational Ideals* (Philo 9; Leiden: Brill, 2019).

157 Philo also provides explanatory glosses to Hebrew terms, especially names, a practice with strong parallels in Egyptian (e.g., *Papyrus of Tanis, Papyrus of Tebtynis, Edwin Smith Surgical Papyrus*) and Mesopotamian commentaries. Cf. L. L. Grabbe, *Etymology in Early Jewish Interpretation: The Hebrew Names in Philo* (BJS 115; Atlanta: Scholars Press, 1988).

argues that allegorical interpretation is necessary for a full and complete understanding of the Mosaic text.[158] A similar reading approach is adopted by other authors: Proclus argues in *Essays* 5 and 6 that, when Homer is read symbolically, he aligns with Plato's philosophy, and Heraclitus (*Quaes. hom.* 1.1; 53.2) asserts that Homer must have used allegory, because if he did not, he would have committed many types of blasphemy. These occasional and localized uses of allegory differ from Philo, who applies allegorical interpretation to the whole text, not just when a literal interpretation is problematic (e.g., *Ios.* 28), but because deep-level meaning was intentionally embedded in the text by its original author (cf. *Prob.* 29; *Det.* 15; *Fug.* 194; *Deus* 23, 94–95, 128).[159] This perspective aligns Philo with the interpretative approach of the pesherists, in which the text, properly interpreted, speaks to deeper truths that are relevant to the contemporary reader/community. The texts' prophetic nature and origin with God allow for both interpretive communities to view the text polyvalently. An important differentiation is that Philo would argue that Moses was fully aware of the deeper truth of his composition, whereas the pesherists imply that the original prophet was not fully cognizant of the pluriform meaning of his utterance.

Philo's *Allegorical Commentary* could also be viewed as a blend of continuous and thematic exegesis. Each treatise from Philo's *Commentary* interprets a passage from Genesis in a continuous manner. However, the scope of the passage in question is narrow compared to the size of the treatise. Philo's focus on a small group of verses allows him to tailor the discussion within each work to a specific topic. The inclusion of secondary and tertiary lemmata facilitates a topical discussion and allows Philo to broaden his discussion beyond the primary lemma. This practice parallels some Greek commentaries above (e.g., Nicaea) as well as later rabbinic interpretation in which a treatise addresses a specific topic (e.g., the orders of the Mishnah: *Zeraim*, *Moed*, *Nashim*, *Nezikin*, *Kodashim*, and *Tohorot*).

Philo's prevalent use of allegory parallels the major difference found in his *Quaestiones et solutiones* (below). This and other features have led Victor Nikiprowetzky to argue that the *Allegorical Commentary* might be an expanded form of *quaestiones* literature.[160] This position has found support from Runia

158 For a fuller discussion, see J. Pépin, *La tradition de l'allégorie de Philon d'Alexandrie à Dante: Études historiques* (Paris: Études Augustiniennes, 1987), 34–40.

159 Porphyry, *Christ.* fr. 39 (Eusebius, *Hist. eccl.* 6.19.8) identifies a handful of Pythagorean and two Stoic commentators who used allegory in their interpretations of ancient texts, particularly those about Greek mysteries. The Derveni Papyrus also regularly employs figurative reading.

160 V. Nikiprowetzky, "L'exégèse de Philon d'Alexandrie dans le *De Gigantibus* et le *Quod Deus*," in D. Winston and J. Dillon, eds., *Two Treatises of Philo of Alexandria: A Commentary*

and Borgen and Skarsten and is not surprising given that both types of literature were didactic in purpose and used in ancient classrooms.[161] Although later a similar combination of questions and commentary is found in the final version of Proclus' *Commentary on Plato's Republic*, the major difference is that in Proclus' work certain treatises focus on addressing problems in the texts (e.g., *in Resp.* 5), whereas other essays provide a detailed commentary that follows the text (e.g., *in Resp.* 16); he does not seek the integration that Philo does.

The relationship between *quaestiones* literature and commentary blurs conceptual boundaries and reinforces the idea that texts could participate in multiple genres.[162] Although structural differences between *quaestiones* and commentaries are identified, Philo adopts a similar approach to the text in both genres, namely the use of lemma followed by commentary/answer.[163] Both works by Philo, however, look and read differently and so are differentiated by their readers. Despite formal differences, the function of the works is not totally distinguishable; both seek to address issues in the text and assist the reader in gaining a fuller understanding of the text's contents and what its author (Moses) meant. Both genres are regularly found in school settings and so have related, though not identical, intended audiences.[164] Both texts are thought to

---

on De Gigantibus and Quod Deus Sit Immutabilis (BJS 25; Chico: Scholars Press, 1983), 54. Cf. Nikiprowetzky, *Le commentaire*, 170–80.

161 P. Borgen and R. Skarsten, "*Questiones et solutiones*: Some Observations on the Form of Philo's Exegesis," *SPhilo* 4 (1976–1977): 1–16; P. Borgen, "Philo of Alexandria: A Critical and Synthetical Survey of Research since World War II," *ANRW* 2.21.1 (1984): 134; Runia, "Structure," 227, 230. For a more nuanced position, see D. T. Runia, "The Structure of Philo's Allegorical Treatise *De Agricultura*," *SPhiloA* 22 (2010): 87–109, especially 94. G. E. Sterling, "'The School of Sacred Laws': The Social Setting of Philo's Treatises," *VC* 53 (1999): 148–64; G. E. Sterling, "Philo's School: The Social Setting of Ancient Commentaries," in B. Wyss, R. Hirsch-Luipold, and S.-J. Hirschi, eds., *Sophisten im Hellenismus und Kaiserzeit: Orte, Methoden und Personen der Bildungsvermittlung* (STAC 101; Tübingen: Mohr Siebeck, 2017), 121–42; G. E. Sterling, "The School of Moses in Alexandria: An Attempt to Reconstruct the School of Philo," in J. Zurawski and G. Boccaccini, eds., *Second Temple Jewish "Paideia" in Context* (BZNW 228; Berlin: De Gruyter, 2017), 141–66. Cf. *Anim.* 6. References to commentaries are also found in the *Hermenumata* (e.g., ME 2o; cf. E. Dickey, *The Colloquia of the Hermeneumata Pseudodositheana* [2 vols.; CCTC; Cambridge: Cambridge University Press, 2012–2015], 1.107).

162 Cf. Schironi, "Greek Commentaries," 400.

163 An important variation occurs in *De agricultura*, *De plantatione*, and *De ebrietate*, which are much more thematic in the way the texts are structured. Adler argued that this indicated a development in Philo's commentary writing, but his view is unsustainable, as subsequent commentaries do not continue this practice. Cf. M. Adler, *Studien zu Philon von Alexandreia* (Breslau: Marcus, 1929), 48–53. For the view that *De sacrificiis* is a moral sermon, see A. Le Boulluec, "La place des concepts philosophiques dans la réflexion de Philon sur le plaisir," in C. Lévy, ed., *Philon d'Alexandrie et le langage de la philosophie* (Monothéismes et philosophie; Turnhout: Brepols, 1998), 129–52.

164 P. W. van der Horst, "Philo and the Rabbis on Genesis: Similar Questions, Different Answers," in A. Volgers and C. Zamagni, eds., *Erotapokriseis: Early Christian Question-and-Answer Literature in Context* (CBET 37; Leuven: Peeters, 2004), 57.

be directed to insiders, although the *Allegorical Commentary* is considered by scholars to be for initiated members with a substantial knowledge of the Pentateuch and allegorical exegesis.[165] These differences are important for understanding how Philo differentiated his works and how certain genres were thought to be better suited to certain readers.

Philo's *Allegorical Commentary* actively participates in the genre of commentary, as is signaled by similarities with contemporary works, especially Philo's use of lemma + commentary and his focus on explaining an important text. We have seen above that the commentary genre allowed for a range of expressions, although certain features (systematic progression, use of lemmata with comment, positive intended purpose) are typical and so suggest that they could be viewed as core or possibly requisite elements of the genre. Philo's commentary does not undermine these central elements, but differs with regard to how certain elements are used (length of comment, use of allegory to the near exclusion of the literal interpretation, commentary on secondary lemma). These differences place Philo's *Allegorical Commentary* at the periphery of the genre (so far as we can reconstruct it), but do not exclude its inclusion. Rather, what we witness is an exploitation of a malleable genre in order to employ it as the commentator desired. The size of Philo's comment sections, his use of secondary Scripture quotations, the presence of homiletic content, and the explicit use of an interpretive, allegorical hermeneutic to tease out the deeper meaning of the text all have notable, although not exclusive, parallels in Hebrew and Aramaic sources. This suggests that Philo did not look exclusively to Greek literary models and that his prototypical commentary was comparable to that adopted by Jewish authors (e.g., Qumran, rabbinic). As a result, Philo's *Allegorical Commentary* provides a unique example of how one author can participate in a similar genre shared by two cultures and craft a work that would be coherent and recognizable to both.

The inclusion of so-called "homiletic material" in Philo's text further complicates the discussion, as this material suggests an alternative social setting from the academic sphere in which the commentaries were typically found as well as the close genre relationship between sermon and commentary. Cf. Cohn et al., *Philo von Alexandria*, 3.5. On the possible relationship between Philo's *quaestiones* and synogogal practice, see Nikiprowetzky, *Le commentaire*; Nikiprowetzky, "L'exégèse de Philon," 5–9, 53–54; and Borgen and Skarsten, "*Quaestiones et solutiones*." A major issue here is that we know very little about synagogal practices from this time, although *Contempl.* 29 and 78 provide some support to this view.

165 Contra Friedländer, *Geschichte der jüdischen Apologetik*, 209; E. R. Goodenough, *The Politics of Philo Judaeus: Practice and Theory* (New Haven: Yale University Press, 1938), 21. Not all commentaries were written by or for insiders: for example, Aristobulus, fr. 2.1; Poseidonius on Plato's *Timaeus* (Sextus Empiricus, *Math.* 7.93).

Philo's *Quaestiones et solutiones*

Philo's *Quaestiones et solutiones in Genesin* and *Quaestiones et solutiones in Exodum*, as is suggested by the titles, belong to a genre of literature known as ζητήματα or questions and answers (cf. Eusebius, *Hist. eccl.* 2.8.1), and represent another form of commentary employed by Philo.[166] Ζητήματα καὶ λύσεις is a type of literature that dates back to the classical era, when dedicated readers found "problems" in the works of Homer (and other authors).[167] Other readers defended Homer by providing "solutions" to proposed questions. In his now-classic encyclopaedia article "Λύσεις," Gudeman argues that there are two types of *quaestiones* literature: one that provides an exposition of a text and another that, independent of a text, addressed philosophical questions.[168] It is the former branch that we will be focusing on in this study, although the latter division is helpful for understanding the full range of this genre.

There has not been substantial discussion of the question-and-answer literary form. This is not because scholars are uninterested in the topic, but because the genre seems to be readily understandable—two items are required: questions on a specific literary work and answers that seek to justify in some way the perceived "problem." *Quaestiones* literature is written in prose, often composed by literary critics and philosophers who inquire about minute points in sacred and popular texts. Outsiders regularly use this genre to undermine the position of a rival group, while those questioned respond in order to defend the veracity of their position or the coherence of important texts.[169] One issue for understanding the full diversity

166 Philo's *Quaestiones* are only extant in Armenian, which could affect our recognition of its genre and our understanding of it (e.g., use of terminology, syntax of questions as questions). The Greek fragments support the view that we can use the Armenian text as a fair representation of Philo's original, although some change is likely. For the texts, see J. B. Aucher, trans., *Philonis Judaei: Paralipomena Armena* (Venice, 1826); F. Petit, ed., *Quaestiones in Genesim et in Exodum, Fragmenta Graeca: Introduction, texte critique et notes* (PAPM 33; Paris: Éditions du Cerf, 1978); J. R. Royse, "Further Greek Fragments of Philo's *Quaestiones*," in F. E. Greenspan, E. Hilgert, and B. L. Mack, eds., *Nourished with Peace: Studies in Hellenistic Judaism in Memory of Samuel Sandmel* (SPHS; Chico: Scholars Press, 1984), 143–53.

For the claim that *Quaestiones* is the prolegomena to the *Allegorical Commentary*, see G. E. Sterling, "Philo's *Quaestiones*: Prolegomena or Afterthought," in D. M. Hay, ed., *Both Literal and Allegorical: Studies in Philo of Alexandria's "Questions and Answers on Genesis and Exodus"* (BJS 232; Atlanta: Scholars Press, 1991), 99–123. For an argument for a less formal connection (which I would espouse), see Borgen, *Philo of Alexandria*, 80–101.

167 A similar type of format (i.e., ἐρωτήσεις καὶ ἀποκρίσεις) is found in select educational texts (e.g., Stephani version of the *Hermenumata*). See Dickey, *Colloquia*, 1.26–27.

168 A. Gudeman, "Λύσεις," *PW* 13 (1927): 2511–29. See also more recent investigations, though all have strong ties to Gudeman: H. A. Gartner, "Zetema," *DNP* 12 (2002): 778–79; O. Dreyer, "Luseis," *KP* (1975): 832–33.

169 H. Dörrie and H. Dörries, "Erotapokriseis," *RAC* 6 (1966): 342–70. A. Kamesar, *Jerome, Greek Scholarship, and the Hebrew Bible: A Study of the "Quaestiones Hebraicae in Genesim"* (Oxford: Oxford University Press, 1993), 84–86.

of this literary form is the fragmentary nature of extant texts.[170] Few examples have survived in their entirety; rather, a majority have come to us through quotations, whether in literary works, scholia, or classroom exercises.[171]

The earliest extant and likely best-known example of this genre is Aristotle's *Poet.* 25. This chapter, embedded in a larger work on poetics, does not neatly conform to the standard format of questions and answers, but provides a discussion of possible types of faults a poet might make (1460b14–16; 1461b22–25) and what should and should not be considered a mistake (ἁμαρτία) in poetry. This chapter, although focusing more on the theoretical rationale of fault-finding, is related to Aristotle's six-volume work Ἀπορήματα Ὁμηρικά (Diogenes Laertius, *Vit.* 5.26), which addresses perceived issues in Homer and seeks to defend him without recourse to allegorical interpretation.[172] Aristotle's Ἀπορήματα Ὁμηρικά has not survived, but it is possible to argue that the structure of Ἀπορήματα Ὁμηρικά became the model for later Hellenistic scholars.[173]

Greeks were not the only reading community that developed *quaestiones* literature. Questions and answers shape the Demotic *Book of Thoth*, a Ptolemaic-era composition of multiple recensions in which a master addresses questions posed to him by a disciple.[174] This Egyptian work, although scrutinizing not an existing text but broader cultural knowledge, enriches our understanding

170 For a list of many such works, see Gudeman, "Λύσεις," 2511–22. See also the various sayings in Homeric scholia.

171 The question-and-answer format was used in elementary school settings, as is evidenced by *PSI* I 19, which reads, "Who were the gods on the side of Troy? Who was the king of the Trojans? [Who was] their general?" These questions, however, differ from Philo's, as they are basic and seek to determine the knowledge of the pupil. Philo's questions, and those of other *quaestiones* literature, presupposed a substantial amount of knowledge and address perceived challenges in the text's coherence.

172 E.g., *Poet.* 1461a2–4, the weapons used by Illyrians (*Il.* 10.152); 1461a16–20, whether "all" the gods and men were asleep (*Il.* 10.1–2); 1461a29–31, why Homer said Ganymede poured wine for Zeus (*Il.* 20.234, when the gods do not drink wine). Aristotle also speaks of other poets (e.g., Sophocles, Euripides, Xenophanes: 1460b32–36), but his primary focus is clearly Homer. Cf. R. Mayhew, *Aristotle's Lost "Homeric Problems": Textual Studies* (Oxford: Oxford University Press, 2019).

173 For instance, within the Peripatetic school there is substantial continuity between the questions posed by Aristotle and those by Heraclides, with some identical examples found in the surviving fragments (e.g., Heraclides, fr. 171 [Wehrli] = Aristotle, fr. 146 [V. Rose]; Heraclides, fr. 172 [Wehrli] = Aristotle, fr. 147 [V. Rose]). Cf. *P. Herc.* 1012 (Demetrius Lacon's *Questions* on Epictetus). Cf. Simplicius, *in Cat.* 1.12–14; C. Jacob, "Questions sur les questions: Archéologie d'une pratique intellectuelle et d'une forme discursive," in A. Volgers and C. Zamagni, eds., *Erotapokriseis: Early Christian Question-and-Answer Literature in Context* (CBET 37; Leuven: Peeters, 2004), 25–54.

174 E.g., *Thoth* 1, 339, 351, 373, these lines are written in red ink, signaling a new section within the work.

of the literary world in which Philo composed his *Quaestiones*.[175] Rabbinic use of the question-and-answer format further supports the view that this literary form was not limited to Greek authors.[176] One parallel example arises in an attempt to explain the order of creation and why humans were created last. Philo draws on the image of a host preparing a banquet prior to the arrival of the guests and to an event organizer securing competitors and entertainment prior to the coming of the spectators (*Opif.* 77–88). The text of *t. Sanh.* 8:9, employing the language of "parable," also uses the image of the banquet (although not the games or dramatic contests) in order to answer this same question.[177] As discussed above, some *pesharim* from Qumran evidence the author's attempt to explain interpretive "issues" or clarify the text, often progressing sequentially through the work.

Philo's *Quaestiones* has similarities with other extant ζητήματα works.[178] The most prominent example is Philo's preference for "why" (διὰ τί) to introduce his question. Philo and others initiate questions through lexical variety (e.g., τί, πῶς, τίς, πόθεν, ἀπὸ τίνος), but διὰ τί is the most common, and Philo follows other authors in this preference.[179] Philo differs in the way that he constructs his questions. Typically, in the question section the author would identify the problem that was to be discussed.[180] Philo, in contrast, regularly provides a quotation of the biblical lemma without identifying the problem,

175 R. Jasnow and K.-T. Zauzich, eds. and trans., *The Ancient Egyptian Book of Thoth: A Demotic Discourse on Knowledge and Pendant to Classical Hermetica* (2 vols.; Wiesbaden: Harrassowitz, 2005), 1.72–73; J. F. Quack, *Einführung in die altägyptische Literaturgeschichte*, vol. 3, *Die demotische und gräko-ägyptische Literatur* (2nd ed.; Münster: LIT Verlag, 2009), 140–42. Another Egyptian example of questions and answers is the famous spell 125 of the *Book of the Dead.*

176 Cf. Borgen, *Philo*, 80–101, and especially S. D. Fraade, "Early Rabbinic Midrash between Philo and Qumran," in M. L. Satlow, ed., *Strength to Strength: Essays in Appreciation of Shaye J. D. Cohen* (Providence: Brown Judaic Studies, 2018), 281–93. See also the discussion of questions and answers in relationship to Demetrius and Aristobulus. For differences based on location and time period, see M. R. Niehoff, "Questions and Answers in Philo and Genesis Rabbah," *JSJ* 39 (2008): 337–66.

177 For other rabbinic parallels, see P. Borgen, "Man's Sovereignty over Animals and Nature According to Philo of Alexandria," in T. Fornberg and D. Hellholm, eds., *Texts and Contexts: Biblical Texts in Their Textual and Situational Contexts: Essays in Honor of Lars Hartman* (Oslo: Scandinavian University Press, 1995), 369–89.

178 Although the treatises of *Quaestiones* are the focus of this section, questions and answers (πεύσεως καὶ ἀποκρίσεως) are also found in other texts (e.g., *Mos.* 2.188, 192, 221, 233; *Decal.* 2–17, 36–43).

179 E.g., Aristotle's *Problems*; Plutarch's *Roman Questions* and *Greek Questions*. Some exceptions would be Ps.-Aristotle, *Probl.* 1.55–57, which does not begin with a question at all, but with a statement regarding the nature of fevers.

180 E.g., Plutarch, *Quaest. rom.* 12: "Why do they consider Saturn father of Truth?"; *Quaest. rom.* 26: "Why do women in mourning wear white robes and white head-dresses?"; *Quaest. rom.* 54: "Why do they call the meat-markets *macella* and *macellae*?"

forcing the reader to search the answer to determine what issue Philo was seeking to address.[181] According to Wan, this type of ambiguous question accounts for 53.4 percent of all questions asked by Philo.[182] This is not to claim that other authors (e.g., Aristotle) did not cite passages of Homer or others in their questions, but these quotations were short and the issues were sufficiently signaled to the reader. Philo explicitly introduces issues in many of his questions (46.6 percent), but his tendency of not signaling to the reader what will be discussed is atypical, although not unique, suggesting that diversity in question type might be a recognized feature of this genre.[183]

Regarding Philo's answers, he is similar to every other writer of *quaestiones* literature in that he provides an answer for every question that is raised.[184] Oftentimes Philo provides multiple answers to a question, and although this is not witnessed in every author, it is not unique.[185] More distinctive is the fact that Philo's answers are typically much longer than the responses found in the fragments of Aristotle's Ἀπορήματα Ὁμηρικά, in which the question, rather than the answer, appears to be more important,[186] but are closer to Plutarch's

181 E.g., *QG* 1.36: "What is the meaning of the words, 'You will be as gods, knowing good and evil'?" which is followed by the question "Whence did the serpent know this plural noun 'gods'?" in the *solutio*. Cf. *QG* 1.3, 93; 2.30, 31, 54, 61, 67, etc. S.-K. Wan, "Philo's *Quaestiones et solutiones in Genesim*: A Synoptic Approach," in E. H. Lovering, ed., *SBLSP 1993* (Atlanta: Scholars Press, 1993), 33–34. On the inclusion of a secondary lemma (approx. 10 percent of the time), see D. T. Runia, "Secondary Texts in Philo's *Quaestiones*," in D. M. Hay, ed., *Both Literal and Allegorical: Studies in Philo of Alexandria's "Questions and Answers on Genesis and Exodus"* (BJS 232; Atlanta: Scholars Press, 1991), 47–79.

182 This number is arrived at by combining "rhetorical" questions and "periphrastic" questions, both of which are built on the citation or paraphrase of scriptural lemma for the question. Wan, "Philo's *Quaestiones et solutiones in Genesim*," 34.

183 E.g., Porphyry's *Homeric Questions*, in which no direct question exists in all of book 1. J. A. MacPhail Jr., ed. and trans., *Porphyry's "Homeric Questions" on the "Iliad"* (TUK 36; Berlin: De Gruyter, 2011), 3–6.

184 Plutarch regularly answers a question with another question ("Is it because . . . or rather, is it . . ."), without providing any further explanation or evaluation of the "answers." Cf. *Quaest. rom.* 1, 2, 7, 8, 9, 11, 12, 13, 15, 17, 18, 36, 48, 66, 88, 89, 94, 95, 100, 104, 106, 108; *Quaest. graec.* 31, 36, 39, 46, 50, 52, 53. The practice of giving questions to questions is not unique to Plutarch and is a regular feature of the answers in Ps.-Aristotle's *Problems*. E.g., 26.25, 43, 53; cf. Athenaeus, *Deipn.* 15.669f–670e.

185 E.g., Plutarch, *Quaest. plat.* 5.1 (1003c); 9.1 (1008b); Porphyry, *Quaes. hom.* 19.221–224.2.

186 Out of the thirty-seven fragments of Ἀπορήματα Ὁμηρικά edited by V. Rose, there are twenty-nine examples of questions and answers (fr. 174 has two questions). Fragments 144, 154, 162, 165, 167–169, 175, 177 either do not have both parts or are paraphrases and so do not give good data for how long Aristotle's questions would have been. The total word count for the twenty-nine questions and answers is 2,281 (Greek), with examples ranging from 37 words (fr. 172) to 252 words (fr. 161), and a total average of 78.6 words per question-and-answer pairing. For the importance of questions, see Aristotle, fr. 144, 146, 148, 153. Perrone also claims that Philo does not adhere entirely to the classical model of ζητήματα καὶ λύσεις and the classical problem categories. L. Perrone, "Sulla preistoria delle 'quaestiones' nella letteratura patristica:

Platonic Questions.[187] The longer length might be a result of the answer's content, which often provides detailed textual commentary in addition to philosophical insights and is not simply explanatory. The *quaestiones* genre was not static, but evolved over the Hellenistic era. It could be that longer answers were becoming more prototypical, either because of the number of different interpretive options available or because of the growing complexity of the questions being asked.

The major difference in Philo's answers, however, is his incorporation of both allegorical and literal explanations. Out of the 636 answers provided in *QG* and *QE*, 226 (35.5 percent) contain only literal interpretations, 188 (29.6 percent) contain only allegorical interpretations, and 211 (33.2 percent) have both literal and allegorical answers.[188] Both allegorical and literal interpretations are important for Philo, although it is clear at certain points that preference is given to allegorical interpretations, with Philo chastising those who do not go beyond the plain reading of the text.[189] The use of allegory as an interpretive technique is not evidenced by any pre-Philonic *quaestiones* author. This could suggest that the application of allegorical interpretations is an original adaptation by Philo, although the integration of allegory in Heraclitus's *Homeric Problems* (ca. 100 CE) suggests that Philo was not the first.[190] By prioritizing allegory, however, Philo distances himself from his contemporaries and predecessors, who were committed primarily to the literal sense of the text.[191]

Another nonprototypical feature in Philo's *Quaestiones* is the lack of a textual problem in many of Philo's question-and-answer pairings. Many questions in *QG* and *QE* do not identify a specific issue, forcing the reader to look to the answer portion to determine what was problematic with the biblical lemma. However, at times the answer portion does not explicitly outline a problem either, accepting the literal meaning while also providing a deeper, allegorical

---

presupposti e sviluppi del genere letterario fino al IV sec.," *Annali di storia dell'exegesi* 8 (1991): 492–500.

187 Plutarch's *Platonic Questions* has ten questions and is 6,320 words long (Greek), giving an average of 632 words per question-and-answer pairing. Question six is the shortest, with 100 words, and question 10 is the longest with 1,281 words. In contrast, Plutarch's *Roman and Greek Questions* has 19,550 words (Greek) and 172 questions, giving an average of 113.7 words per question-and-answer pairing.

188 Wan, "Philo's *Quaestiones et solutiones in Genesim*," 35. The remaining examples are somewhat ambiguous in that they reject the literal meaning and only support the allegorical. In these cases both interpretations are offered, though it is clear that one is to be preferred.

189 E.g., *QG* 1.58; 2.79; 4.60; *QE* 2.45.

190 Cf. D. A. Russell and D. Konstan, eds. and trans., *Heraclitus: Homeric Problems* (WGRW 14; Atlanta: SBL, 2005), xvi–xxvii.

191 Niehoff, *Jewish Exegesis*, 156.

interpretation.[192] The lack of interpretive issues in many questions suggests a nonprototypical use of this genre and implies that for Philo the explanation of problems was not the primary concern. Rather, the use of the question-and-answer structure provided a platform from which he could interpret the text.

Finally, the organizational principle of Philo's *Quaestiones* is unlike that of other extant texts; Philo provides systematic comments for the majority of Genesis and Exodus, whereas other ancient writers (e.g., Aristotle, Plutarch) do not exhaustively cover the text, but provide notes to isolated, sometimes nonsequential problems.[193] We cannot be sure that Philo is the first to have adapted *quaestiones* literature in such a manner, although we know with certainty that he was not the first to apply the question-and-answer method to Jewish Scripture.[194] Philo's changes indicate that he thought that the texts of Genesis and Exodus required greater and more comprehensive coverage.[195] As a result, Philo's *Quaestiones* represents the first time this genre served as a framework for organizing and transmitting a coherent body of teaching.[196]

David Runia, recognizing a number of unique features in the format of Philo's commentaries, has concluded that Philo was a *sui generis* writer.[197] Although Runia is no doubt correct when he highlights the unique aspects of Philo's writings, he goes too far. Not only do we lack a majority of ancient literary works in order to make such a claim accurately, but this claim downplays the points of contact between Philo and other writers. At the very least, Philo's distinctive features indicate the diversity of this genre and a range of possible prototypical texts.[198] They arise from Philo's tailoring of his work to

192 E.g., *QG* 2.34; 3.32; 4.176, 241. Philo rarely rejects the literal reading in favor of the allegorical (e.g., *QG* 1.39; 2.79; 3.33; 4.88, 168, 175; *QE* 1.16).

193 Dörrie and Dörries, "Erotapokriseis," 344. Although there are gaps in our texts, it is generally thought that Philo's original text covered the whole of Genesis and Exodus, but not the other pentateuchal books. Cf. J. R. Royse, "The Original Structure of Philo's *Quaestiones*," *SPhiloA* 4 (1976–1977): 41–78.

194 Philo was preceded by Aristobulus, whose *Commentaries* attempted to clarify for King Ptolemy potentially confusing aspects of Jewish Scripture (fr. 2). Prior to Aristobulus, Demetrius also engaged in addressing textual issues (fr. 2.13–14), though again his text was not specifically created for that purpose. Although neither text was addressed to insiders, it shows that there was a history of Jews using the question-and-answer format to engage in explanatory practices. Cf. Freudenthal, *Alexander Polyhistor*, 1.44–46.

195 The closest comparison would be the *Anonymous Theatetus Commentary*, which provides a running commentary on Plato's *Theatetus*, but much less thoroughly. Cf. H. Diels and W. Schubart, eds., *Anonymer Kommentar zu Platons Theatet (Papyrus 9782)* (Berlin: Weidmann, 1905).

196 Niehoff, *Jewish Exegesis*, 160.

197 D. T. Runia, "The Structure of Philo's Allegorical Treatises: A Review of Two Recent Studies and Some Additional Comments," *VC* 38 (1984) 209–56; Runia, "Further Observations," 120.

198 In the case of the philosophical *haireseis* there was considerable variation in the commentaries written. D. T. Runia, "Philo of Alexandria and the Greek *Hairesis* Model," *VC* 53 (1999): 130.

his personal situation and his practice of combining exegesis with exhortation.[199] These unique features provide insight into the purpose of the text and allow us to posit what Philo was trying to accomplish by its composition. Philo was not content to limit his work to solely addressing "problems" in the text, but was interested in providing a thorough interpretation of Jewish Scripture. A comprehensive and detailed level of interpretation would not be applicable in every environment, but would be more relevant to those who sought to acquire a deep knowledge of Scripture, a population most likely found in an educational setting.[200]

That the text was likely written for insiders assists us in understanding why certain changes might have been made. Although *quaestiones* literature had a relationship with philosophical schools,[201] it was regularly used to address concerns or problems raised by outsiders and not solely or necessarily an educational text for pupils (e.g., Porphyry, *Plot.* 15).[202] Philo's work addresses issues, but this does not appear to be the primary function of the composition, which is to provide a deep and wide-ranging set of interpretations of Genesis and Exodus. This marked change from the prototypical purpose of the genre indicates that Philo was using a literary form for related but atypical reasons.

Summary

Philo's didactic works participate in and provide nonprototypical examples of their respective genres. Philo's most common adaptation was the application of allegorical methodology (*QG*, *QE*, and *Allegorical Commentary*), but this is not the only distinctive feature. We witness Philo employing recognized genres in ways that are distinct from other extant examples. These changes help us understand the range of genre expressions in antiquity and one of the ways Jewish authors engaged with Greek literary culture. Philo's choice of nonprototypical compositions is valuable for our discussion because

199 Runia, "Philo of Alexandria," 130.

200 The confidence with which Philo speaks of his position in *Quaestiones*, as opposed to his discussions of the same topics in the *Allegorical Commentary* (e.g., *QG* 3.11 and *Her.* 280–281; *QG* 1.18 and *Leg.* 2.9–10; *QG* 1.69 and *Det.* 57–60), suggests a greater level of authority. Cf. S. A. Adams, "Philo's *Questions* and the Adaptation of Greek Literary Curriculum," in J. Zurawski and G. Boccaccini, eds., *Second Temple Jewish "Paideia" in Context* (BZNW 228; Berlin: De Gruyter, 2017), 167–84; Niehoff, *Jewish Exegesis*, 155–58.

201 Cf. Adams, "Philo's *Questions*," 170–78.

202 Porphyry presented his *Homeric Questions* as "preliminary studies," choosing to defer "greater studies on Homer to the appropriate time" (τὰς μὲν μείζους εἰς Ὅμηρον πραγματείας ὑπερτιθέμενος εἰς καιρὸν σκέψεως τὸν προσήκοντα, ταυτὶ δὲ οἷον προγύμνασμα τῶν εἰς αὐτὸν ἀγώνων, *Quaes. hom.* 1.24–27, recension V); A. R. Sodano, ed., *Porphyrii quaestionum Homericarum liber i* (Naples: Giannini, 1970).

of his familiarity with Greek literature and his clear awareness of the role and function of genres.

We also witness in Philo the selection of related but differentiated genres. Both the *Allegorical Commentary* and *Quaestiones* have overlapping formal similarities (e.g., quotation of a lemma followed by an explanation) and could be considered varieties of ancient commentaries. That Philo used two types of didactic genres for interpreting the same texts implies that each had a particular function and intended audience. This differentiation reinforces our understanding of Philo as one who was highly knowledgeable on Greek genres and was able to adapt them to meet his literary needs.

Conclusion

Unlike in chapters 2 and 3, in which Jewish authors participated in Greek genres for which there was no Jewish analogue, many ancient Near Eastern cultures (e.g., Jewish, Babylonian, Egyptian) produced didactic works and in wide variety. The availability of other options reinforces the meaningfulness of choosing to participate in Greek genres. These Greek genres are not hermetically sealed from evolution or adaptation, and the texts studied in this chapter provide support for the theory that some of the nonprototypical features found in Greek-language compositions stemmed from Jewish authors' literary borrowing from similar genres developed in other cultures, especially their own. The decision to participate in and employ features from multiple genres highlights the fluidity of genres in antiquity and ancient authors' ability to create bespoke texts that optimize the utility of their composition.

5

Jewish Philosophical Treatises

In this chapter we will continue the argument developed in the previous chapters—that Jewish authors explored the fluidity and flexibility of genres and adapted them to fit their intended purpose. We will evaluate Letter of Aristeas, 4 Maccabees, Philo's *Vita Contemplativa*, Josephus' *Against Apion*, Pseudo-Clementine's *Homilies* 4.7–6.25, and Jewish letters (including those in the New Testament), works that participate in Greek philosophical genres but also engage with other related genres, including didactic literature.[1] These authors model the different uses of Greek philosophical learning, seeking to negotiate ideas developed by Greek intellectuals and apply theoretical frameworks to Jewish Scriptures.

Letter of Aristeas

The Letter of Aristeas[2] (henceforth LA) is a second-century BCE prose work composed in Alexandria in which the narrator, Aristeas, purporting to be a non-Jew, writes to Philocrates to inform him about the Jewish people.[3] The

1 Although their texts are lost, we have testimonial evidence of Jews engaging in Greek philosophy and composing anti-Christian works in the second and third centuries CE: the anonymous Jew mentioned by Origen (*Cels.* 2.28) and Philosabbatius (Epiphanius, *Pan.* 51.8.1). Cf. P. W. van der Horst, "Philosabbatius, a Forgotten Early Jewish Philosopher," *JJS* 69 (2018): 256–61; M. R. Niehoff, "A Jewish Critique of Christianity from Second-Century Alexandria: Revisiting the Jew Mentioned in *Contra Celsum*," *JECS* 21 (2013): 151–75. For a discussion on Caecilius of Calacte, a possible Jewish rhetorician, see Schürer, *History*, 3.1.701–3; G. Kennedy, *The Art of Rhetoric in the Roman World, 300 B.C.–A.D. 300* (Princeton: Princeton University Press, 1972), 364–69.

2 A version of this section was presented at the conference "Being Jewish, Writing Greek" in Cambridge in September 2017. I would like to thank Max Kramer and Max Leventhal for their invitation and the participants for their comments.

3 On the scholarly proposals for the date of Aristeas, see B. G. Wright III, *The Letter of Aristeas: "Aristeas to Philocrates" or "On the Translation of the Law of the Jews"* (CEJL; Berlin: De Gruyter, 2015), 21–30.

work is framed by the discussion of the translation of the Jewish law into Greek, with the majority of the work describing aspects of Jewish culture, religious practices, and philosophy.

There are a few passages that provide insight into Pseudo-Aristeas' genre awareness. For instance, §31 appears to divide literature into three categories: writers, poets, and historians (οἵ τε συγγραφεῖς καὶ ποιηταὶ καὶ τὸ τῶν ἱστορικῶν πλῆθος τῆς ἐπιμνήσεως τῶν προειρημένων βιβλίων). This is an atypical division of literary works, not only because this combination is otherwise unattested, but also because Josephus felt the need to change it in *Ant.* 12.38 to a more regular expression (διὸ καὶ τοὺς ποιητὰς αὐτῆς καὶ τοὺς συγγραφεῖς τῶν ἱστοριῶν). The pairing of writers and poets (οἵ τε συγγραφεῖς καὶ ποιηταί) is consistent with other authors, but the specific addition of the multitude of historians (τὸ τῶν ἱστορικῶν πλῆθος) implies that they are in a different category from the former two groups.[4]

Scholars have recently revisited the topic of LA's genre.[5] Although its modern title implies participation in the genre of letter, a number of scholars do not adopt this position.[6] Moses Hadas argued that a number of LA's formal features (e.g., use of vocatives, internal addresses, διήγησις) disqualified it from being classified as a letter and that the inclusion of rhetorical forms (e.g., *ekphrasis*, *chreia*, *synkrisis*) aligned the work with rhetorical composition.[7] As a result, Hadas labels LA a πλάσμα and places it in the sphere of historiography, specifically the third category of Asclepiades of Myrlea's subdivisions of history, "as if it were true" (ὡς ἀληθῆ, Sextus Empiricus, *Math.* 1.252).[8] Although reading LA through this lens is appealing, Hadas is mistaken when his assigns πλάσμα to Asclepiades' third category. According to Sextus Empiricus, Asclepiades places both πλάσματα and μύθους in the second subdivision of history, that of "the false" (ψευδῆ δέ), reserving his third category for com-

4 For some idea of the genre awareness of later ancients, see Photius, *Bibl.* 94.73b.

5 For a survey of genre suggestions, see W. Schmidt, *Untersuchungen zur Fälschung historischer Dokumente bei Pseudo-Aristaios* (Bonn: Habelt Verlag, 1986), 11–13; L. Doering, *Ancient Jewish Letters and the Beginnings of Christian Epistolography* (WUNT 1.298; Tübingen: Mohr Siebeck, 2012), 217–20. For the edition used, see A. Pelletier, ed. and trans., *Lettre d'Aristée à Philocrate: Texte critique, traduction et notes* (SC 89; Paris: Éditions du Cerf, 1962), 100–240.

6 "Letter" was not the appellation adopted by ancient writers who cited LA (e.g., Josephus, *Ant.* 12.100; Eusebius, *Praep. ev.* 9.38.1, ὁ Ἀριστέας ἐν τῷ γραφέντι αὐτῷ βιβλίῳ Περὶ τῆς ἑρμηνείας τοῦ τῶν Ἰουδαίων νόμου ταῦτα ἱστορεῖ). The "Letter" superscription does not appear on manuscripts until the fourteenth century. Cf. Wright, *Letter of Aristeas*, 15–16.

7 M. Hadas, *Aristeas to Philocrates (Letter of Aristeas)* (New York: Harper and Brothers, 1951), 56–57.

8 Hadas, *Aristeas to Philocrates*, 57–58.

edy and mimes.[9] Sextus Empiricus later appears to associate πλάσμα with fictitious events, but those that are similar to real events in the telling, such as the hypothetical situations in comedies and mimes (*Math.* 1.263; cf. *Rhet. Her.* 1.12–13). This association with comedies and mimes does not imply that πλάσμα supersedes categorical boundaries (cf. *Math.* 1.265), but that comedies and mimes might be classified differently depending on their perceived relationship to history. This misclassification by Hadas does not completely undermine his proposal—that LA should be understood in light of ancient historiography (as we will see below)—but it does mean that LA does not conform to Hadas' view of the classifications outlined by Asclepiades.

Following Hadas, some scholars have also argued that LA is not a letter, but a type of narrative (διήγησις). Sylvia Honigman has made a strong case for viewing LA as "a kind of historical monograph."[10] Honigman begins by evaluating the work's opening and its supposed self-designation as a διήγησις, linking this claim to the rhetorical handbooks, specifically that of Aphthonius.[11] Honigman attempts to connect the perceived subject of the work, "political deeds," with the way that historians typically introduce their subjects in their prefaces. According to Honigman, the subject of the work is the Jewish embassy and the translation of the Hebrew Scriptures, with a secondary subject being the release of the Jews from slavery (cf. *C. Ord. Ptol.* 22). All other material is labeled "digression." To justify this point, Honigman claims, "Logically, the definition of the subject must refer to the central narrative of the work, not the digressions."[12] I appreciate this position and think that there is merit to her claim. However, I struggle with the view that a majority of the work (nearly 75 percent of LA) is described as a "digression." I propose that the central section of the work should play a greater role in understanding the subject and genre of the work.[13]

9 Sextus Empiricus, *Math.* 1.252–53: τῆς γὰρ ἱστορίας τὴν μέν τινα ἀληθῆ εἶναί φησι τὴν δὲ ψευδῆ τὴν δὲ ὡς ἀληθῆ, καὶ ἀληθῆ μὲν τὴν πρακτικήν, ψευδῆ δὲ τὴν περὶ πλάσματα καὶ μύθους, ὡς ἀληθῆ δὲ οἷά ἐστιν ἡ κωμῳδία καὶ οἱ μῖμοι. Cf. *Math.* 1.92; scholia D.T. 173.3–4; 475.8–25.

10 Honigman, *Septuagint*, 29–35, especially 30. See also R. L. Hunter, "The Letter of Aristeas," in A. Erskine and L. Llewellyn-Jones, eds., *Creating a Hellenistic World* (Swansea: Classical Press of Wales, 2011), 47–60.

11 On the nature of διήγησις in the *progymnasmata*, see S. A. Adams, "Luke and *Progymnasmata*: Rhetorical Handbooks, Rhetorical Sophistication, and Genre Selection," in M. R. Hauge and A. W. Pitts, eds., *Ancient Education and Early Christianity* (LNTS 533; London: Bloomsbury, 2016), 144–46.

12 Honigman, *Septuagint*, 29–30, 149–50.

13 Some ancient authors thought digression was the point (e.g., Herodotus, *Hist.* 4.30). Alternatively, the focus professed by the author is not always the true object of the treatise. For example, Plato's *Ep.* 7 implies that purpose of the work is to offer counsel (323e–324a; 352a),

One of the strengths of Honigman's work is her awareness of genre variability at this time.[14] Recognizing that literary hybridization was common and widespread is essential for understanding LA and many other compositions that do not neatly fit rigid genre boxes. However, I am not convinced that LA represents an integration of philosophy into historiography, with history being the dominant, primary genre. Rather, I would argue that LA participates in multiple genres, with the author setting his philosophical discussions within a wider narrative framework, possibly through participation with history. This perspective stands in some tension with Honigman's claim that LA "is not a philosophical allegory, but a 'true' *diegesis*."[15] The blurring of fact and fiction was common in antiquity, so, despite the claim by Pseudo-Aristeas in §322, the contents of the narrative might not be "true" in the way that we would classify it.[16]

More recently, the view that LA is a letter has been revived by Lutz Doering, who argues that LA is best understood as an epistolary treatise of Langslow's "Type B," in which texts have a dedicatory preface and epilogue as well as sustained second-person contact throughout the work.[17] According to Doering, this classification allows for the best accounting of the evidence, especially the regular addressing of Philocrates at strategic points in the work. Doering recognizes the malleability of genres and so allows for the inclusion of certain features that are more common in nonepistolary forms, such as providing

---

but this discussion only occurs in select sections (331d; 334c; 336e–337e). Rather, the autobiographical letter is more akin to an apology for Plato's involvement in Syracuse (e.g., 330b–c).

14 Honigman (*Septuagint*, 32) is correct in her claim that Hellenistic historians began to blend history and philosophy in their narratives (e.g., Diodorus Siculus, *Bibl.* 1.1–6). See also the excellent work by Marincola, "Genre, Convention, and Innovation."

15 Honigman, *Septuagint*, 35.

16 Honigman's chapter on genres embedded in LA (e.g., *ekphrasis*, travelogue, *politeia*, *synkrisis*) highlights the author's localized knowledge of literary trends in Alexandria and how these rhetorical and narrative pieces were brought together into a literary whole. Her argument for demotic literary influences on LA, in addition to Greek, is insightful and highlights the geographic situatedness of the text. S. Honigman, "Literary Genres and Identity in the *Letter of Aristeas*: Courtly and Demotic Models," in C. R. Katz, N. Hacham, G. Herman, and L. Sagiv, eds., *A Question of Identity: Formation, Transition, Negotiation* (Berlin: De Gruyter Oldenbourg, 2019), 223–44. For LA as a *poikilia*, see E. Matusova, *The Meaning of the Letter of Aristeas: In Light of Biblical Interpretation and Grammatical Tradition, and with Reference to Its Historical Context* (FRLANT 260; Göttingen: Vandenhoeck & Ruprecht, 2015), 7.

17 Doering, *Ancient Jewish Letters*, 217–32; D. R. Langslow, "The *Epistula* in Ancient Scientific and Technical Literature, with Special Reference to Medicine," in R. Morello and A. D. Morrison, eds., *Ancient Letters: Classical and Late Antique Epistolography* (Oxford: Oxford University Press, 2007), 211–34. Cf. T. Rajak, *Translation and Survival: The Greek Bible of the Ancient Jewish Diaspora* (Oxford: Oxford University Press, 2009), 31.

full transcripts of letters. Doering acknowledges Honigman's perspective, although Doering adapts it to prioritize the genre of letter.[18]

I agree with the perspective that LA does not participate solely in one genre. Authors in the Hellenistic era regularly pushed the boundaries of literary forms and experimented with different ways to construct texts and narratives. The focus in the above discussions has been on the genres of history and epistolography, and while I think LA participates in both genres to a greater or lesser extent, one literary form is regularly overlooked in discussions: philosophical treatises.[19] This is surprising given that references to philosophy occur frequently and about one-third of the work is dedicated to symposia (§§187–294).[20] In what follows, I identify parallels between LA and philosophical (especially sympotic) literature, arguing that this genre lens assists us in gaining a richer perspective on the text. I am not arguing that LA is a *symposium* in the form of Plato or Xenophon, although I think that these texts were prototypical examples of this genre and influenced Pseudo-Aristeas. Nor am I interested in determining the historicity of the depicted events.[21] Rather, I propose that LA participates in the genres of *symposia* and other philosophical texts through the blurring of narrator and participant, the use of questions, the theme of learning, and the importance of piety.

One of the challenges in this discussion is how we differentiate a philosophical treatise that is presented as written and sent to someone from ancient letters. The latter can be strictly defined in a way that essentially eliminates overlap;[22] whereas the former does not necessarily have features that would allow for an epistolary classification. Creating a rigid divide between the two groups artificially separates works that have a similar function, namely, communicating in writing with someone who is geographically removed.[23] Philosophical writings often are substantially different from their epistolary counterparts. LA lacks "standard" epistolary opening and closing

18 This hybridization of genres is followed most recently by Ben Wright, who claims that LA is "related to Hellenistic historiography, *and* it is related to the technical treatises with which Doering compares *Aristeas*." Wright, *Letter of Aristeas*, 51 (italics original). For LA as a rewriting of the Exodus narrative, see Wright, *Letter of Aristeas*, 56; N. Hacham, "The *Letter of Aristeas*: A New Exodus Story?" *JSJ* 36 (2005): 2–20.

19 Cf. G. Zuntz, "Aristeas Studies I: 'The Seven Banquets,'" *JSS* 4 (1959): 21–36.

20 For references to συμποσία, see LA 181, 203, 220, 236, 286, 294, 297.

21 For a detailed discussion of symposia in the Hellenistic era, see O. Murray, "Hellenistic Royal Symposia," in P. Bilde, T. Engberg-Pedersen, L. Hannestad, and J. Zahle, eds., *Aspects of Hellenistic Kingship* (Aarhus: Aarhus University Press, 1996), 16–27.

22 E.g., M. B. Trapp, ed., *Greek and Latin Letters: An Anthology with Translation* (Cambridge: Cambridge University Press, 2003), 1–3, 34–38.

23 For more on this topic, see the discussion of "literary letters" below.

features,[24] although it is clear that Pseudo-Aristeas was familiar with them, as he includes them in the letters recorded in his narrative (e.g., §§34, 41). The adoption of epistolary features, however, is a literary construct, and so represents an authorial fiction rather than the historical reality.[25]

Doering, following Langslow, argues that the repeated use of the vocative to address Philocrates (§§1, 120, 171, 295) supports the view that LA is a letter. However, Langslow acknowledges that, "in prose at least, on some definitions, a text of type B would not count as a letter."[26] When we look at ancient philosophical works, we see a tendency for the narrator to address his reader throughout the work, often by invoking the internal narratee. At practically every major break in his *Symposium*, Plato has his narrator intrude into the narrative with first-person references to move the plot along and to highlight what he was told from Aristodemus.[27] This is similar to the way that LA is constructed (§§34, 51, 83, 112, 120, 131, 295), although this practice tapers off in the last third of the work, in which there is only one invocation (§§295–300).[28] Although the relationship between the narrator and the narrative is different in LA and Plato's *Symposium*, both authors develop internal narrators, thus blurring the line between narrator and character (e.g., *Symp*. 173b–d).[29]

Plutarch's two sympotic works also provide important comparators for LA's narration. In Plutarch's *Dinner of the Seven Wise Men*, the narrator addresses his recipient (Nicarchus) at key points in the text (beginning, middle, and end, *Mor*. 146b; 160c; 164d) through the use of the vocative. Plutarch's *Table Talk* displays substantial literary adaptability and Plutarch's willingness to play with

24 Cf. S. A. Adams, "Paul's Letter Opening and Its Relationship to Ancient Greek Letters: A Study in Epistolary Presence," in S. E. Porter and S. A. Adams, eds., *Paul and the Ancient Letter Form* (PAST 6; Leiden: Brill, 2010), 33–55.

25 On the difference between author and narrator, see I. J. F. de Jong, *Narratology and Classics: A Practical Guide* (Oxford: Oxford University Press, 2014), 17–42.

26 Langslow, "*Epistula*," 216.

27 Plato, *Symp*. 172a; 173b–c; 178a; 180c; 185d; 198a. On the internal, embedded narrator of Plato's works, see K. A. Morgan, "Plato," in I. J. F. de Jong, R. Nünlist, and A. M. Bowie, eds., *Studies in Ancient Greek Narrative*, vol. 1, *Narrators, Narratees, and Narratives in Ancient Greek Literature* (MneSup 257; Leiden: Brill, 2004), 357–76.

28 Doering, *Ancient Jewish Letters*, 222. Cf. Wright, *Letter of Aristeas*, 430.

29 In contrast, Xenophon's *Symposium* uses the first person only at the opening (1.1); the rest is exclusively in the third-person narrative. Plato's complex layering of reported speech within his text results in an increased engagement with the reader by the secondary narrator. This model is also followed by Athenaeus, *Deipn*. 1.1f. For a nuanced discussion of narrator persona (although in historiography), see L. I. Hau, "Narrator and Narratorial Persona in Diodoros' *Bibliotheke* (and Their Implications for the Tradition of Greek Historiography)," in L. I. Hau, A. Meeus, and B. Sheridan, eds., *Diodoros of Sicily: Historiographical Theory and Practice in the Bibliotheke* (SH 58; Leuven: Peeters, 2018), 277–301.

established genres.[30] Plutarch was not the first to adapt the *symposium*,[31] but he highlights his ingenuity by placing his work within the genre's larger history: Plato, Xenophon, Aristotle, Speusippus, Epicurus, Prytanis, Hieronymus, Dio of the Academy (*Mor.* 612d–e).[32] This list, arranged in chronological order, shows Plutarch's genre awareness by identifying whom he views as prototypical authors and signaling his intention to follow a literary practice, one with which he assumes his reader is familiar.[33] One of the main variations developed by Plutarch is the move away from a larger, singular narrative to focusing on the questions raised in a composite of events. Plutarch divides his work into nine parts, with each part having ten questions, providing a rough parallel to LA's seven dinners of ten questions.[34] Because Plutarch's books were written and sent in installments, the opening of every volume includes an introductory prologue to his friend and patron, Sossius Senecio.[35] Despite the fact that we are told that multiple books were sent at one time (*Mor.* 612e), Plutarch includes a preface for each book, which not only acts as a way to tie the volumes together into a cohesive whole, but functions as an interlude when reading multiple books at a time. In this way, first-person narration structures the text, allowing the primary narrator to maintain close contact with the reader throughout the work.

The narrator–narratee relationship is further complicated because both Plutarch and Sossius are included in certain *Table Talk* narratives.[36] Plutarch does not blur the distinction between first-person speech in the narrative preface and third-person speech in the main body of the text. Conversely, in *Dinner* the narrator is internal, using the first person in both narration and speech (e.g., *Mor.* 146c, f; 152a; 158f). In LA, Aristeas is presented as both the narrator and as an actor, regularly using the first person to report speech and events

30 Plutarch played with literary features established by Plato and Xenophon (e.g., description of inappropriate dance by guests, *Mor.* 704d–e). Cf. F. Klotz and K. Oikonomopoulou, "Introduction," in F. Klotz and K. Oikonomopoulou, eds., *The Philosopher's Banquet: Plutarch's Table Talk in the Intellectual Culture of the Roman Empire* (Oxford: Oxford University Press, 2011), 1–31.

31 The *Sympotic Dialogues* by the Stoic Persaeus of Citium were reported to have strong satirical aspects (Athenaeus, *Deipn.* 4.162b–e). Similarly, Lucian's *Symposium* explicitly played with the major features of the *Symposia* written by Plato and Xenophon (*Symp.* 37).

32 On this point, see Klotz and Oikonomopoulou, "Introduction," 13–18. These are not the only symposia in antiquity (e.g., Athenaeus, *Deipn.* 2.64a; 2.67e; 3.79e–80a).

33 Later, Macrobius (*Sat.* 7.3.23) identifies Plutarch as part of this tradition.

34 Both works add additional questions to the last dinner scene (Plutarch, *Mor.* 741c–748d; LA 273–274, 291–292).

35 *Mor.* 612c; 629c; 644f; 659e; 672d; 686a; 697c; 716d; 736c; 748d. Cf. F. E. Brenk, "'In Learned Conversation': Plutarch's Symposiac Literature and the Elusive Authorial Voice," in J. R. Ferreira et al., eds., *Symposion and Philanthropia in Plutarch* (Coimbra, Portugal: Classica Digitalia, 2009), 51–61.

36 For Sossius, see *Mor.* 613d; 622c; 623a; 635e; 636f; 666d–e.

in which he was a participant (cf. §12, 15, 167). This use of an internal (i.e., first-person) narrator, although part of historiography (e.g., Herodotus), is not exclusively employed by historians in the Hellenistic era, but is also found in a range of genres to increase the appearance of veracity.[37] The claims of personal involvement made by the character of Aristeas (§§10, 83, 91, 96, 100, 297), as well as his care to indicate reliable sources when reporting other events (e.g., §§28, 112, 300), resonate with the practices found in ancient works of history.[38] As a result, we could argue that the use of the first-person voice functions on multiple levels—giving structure to the narrative and assurance of historical accuracy. This is an example of how a literary feature could be formally similar but functionally different across genres and how a skilled author could activate multiple aspects of a feature in order to engage the reader in layered ways.

Embedding texts is atypical for letters and philosophical treatises.[39] The inclusion of πρόσταγμα (§§22–25), reports (εἴσδοσις, §§29–32), and letters (ἐπιστολή, §§35–40, 41–46) in LA is unusual, although not uncommon in antiquity, especially in works that are larger in size (e.g., histories, biographies, novels, etc.).[40] The author of LA also includes a short *politeia* (§§83–120), an ethnographic narrative about the political and social organization of Jerusalem and the Jewish people.[41] Important for our inquiry is the inclusion of a multi-day symposium in LA. Sympotic scenes are included in many Greek literary works,[42] suggesting that embedding or recounting symposia was a wider literary practice.[43] Their inclusion is rare, however, in works as short as LA,

37 Honigman, *Septuagint*, 67–71. First-person speech is also common in ancient letters, but does not have the same narrative function.

38 E.g., L. Alexander, *The Preface to Luke's Gospel: Literary Convention and Social Context in Luke 1.1–4 and Acts 1.1* (SNTSMS 78; Cambridge: Cambridge University Press, 1993), 34–41.

39 Cf. Lucian, *Symp.* 22–27; Diogenes Laertius, *Vit.* 9.13–14. Even Athenaeus' *Deipnosophists*, which has extracts of literary works that would be longer than many letters found in LA, does not include letters or decrees in his work. This is most likely because they were not relevant to the narrative that the author was creating.

40 So Honigman, *Septuagint*, 71–72. For a double embedded letter, see Philo, *Legat.* 314–315; Josephus, *Ant.* 13.126–128.

41 Cf. S. Honigman, *Tales of High Priests and Taxes: The Books of the Maccabees and the Judean Rebellion against Antiochos IV* (Berkeley: University of California Press, 2014), 115–17; Honigman, "Literary Genres," 223–44.

42 E.g., Homer, *Od.* 3.29–336; 4.65–598; 14.462–506. Cf. Athenaeus, *Deipn.* 1.5a–b; 5.186d–193c. See also M. Węcowski, "Homer and the Origins of the Symposion," in F. Montanari and P. Ascheri, eds., *Omero tremila anni dopo* (Rome: Edizione di Storia e Letteratura, 2002), 625–37. Josephus (*Ant.* 12.99–100), when writing his history, did not think that the inclusion of the symposia was relevant.

43 E.g., Aristophanes, *Vesp.* 1208–1264; Achilles Tatius, *Leuc. Clit.* 1.5.1–7; Petronius, *Sat.* 26–78.

except for works that would be associated with the *symposia* genre.[44] One major difference is that the dinner party in *symposia* is presented as a primary narrative element, whereas in LA the dinner parties are minimized. This difference militates against the view that LA is a *symposium*. The proportion of the text the symposia encompass in LA also challenges its strict classification as a history or letter, as there is no comparable example in antiquity of either genre including a proportionally large symposium.

The force of Aristeas' symposia has been underappreciated in light of the narrative apology that follows it (§§295–300).[45] In this section, the narrator, Aristeas, asks Philocrates to forgive him if he overindulged when describing the dinner parties (ἐγὼ δὲ εἰ πεπλεόνακα τούτοις, ὦ Φιλόκρατες, συγγνώμην ἔχειν). Parallels have been drawn between this passage and a similar narrative aside by Diodorus Siculus (e.g., *Bibl.* 1.90.4), in which the author apologizes for being overly descriptive of Egyptian customs and sacred animals. Both authors foreground the marvelous nature of their subject and justify its inclusion with the excuse of providing a thorough account. For Pseudo-Aristeas this is further supported with another reference to Philocrates' φιλομάθεια, implying that, as a person who loves knowledge, Philocrates would have been interested in its content (see more below).[46] Not only does the symposium show that Jewish thinkers can excel at Greek cultural events, a fact emphasized in the narrative by Aristeas and the reaction of Greek philosophers (e.g., §§201, 235), it also reinforces major themes of the work, such as Jewish knowledge, cultural sophistication, and training.[47] The lack of disagreement, conflict, or contest within the symposia is notable, as these were common motifs

44 Another Jewish example is found in Philo, *Contempl.* 40–89, although the symposium occupies the majority of the work.

45 The notable exception being Zuntz, "Aristeas Studies I."

46 Philo links φιλομαθής and testimony (*Congr.* 73), suggesting that he and Pseudo-Aristeas might have a similar perspective on their natures.

47 During the Hellenistic era, the *symposia* genre became increasingly used as a way to display cultural knowledge and acumen. This was primarily achieved though discussing intellectual ideas and learning and by structuring the work on the asking and answering of questions. Although collections of questions are recognised as a literary type at this time (see chapter 4), questions and answers are not limited to Ζητημάτων literature, but are a prominent element of philosophical treatises, including *symposia*. For example, Plutarch explicitly references Ζητημάτων in his *Table Talks*, highlighting their appropriateness for dinner conversation. E.g., Plutarch, *Mor.* 645c; 660d; 736c; cf. Athenaeus, *Deipn.* 5.186e; Philo, *Contempl.* 75–76. See J. Goeken, "Orateurs et sophists au banquet," in B. Wyss, R. Hirsch-Luipold, and S.-J. Hirschi, eds., *Sophisten im Hellenismus und Kaiserzeit: Orte, Methoden und Personen der Bildungsvermittlung* (STAC 101; Tübingen: Mohr Siebeck, 2017), 83–97; S. A. Adams, "Sympotic Learning: Symposia Literature and Cultural Education," in J. Norton, L. Askin, and G. Allen, eds., *Bookish Circles: Varieties of Adult Learning and Literacy in the Greco-Roman Mediterranean and the Early Church* (WUNT 1; Tübingen: Mohr Siebeck, forthcoming 2020).

in Greek *symposia*.[48] The unity exhibited by the Jewish symposiasts not only speaks to the peaceful nature of the translators, but also mirrors the nature of the translation, which, due to divine inspiration, is without contradiction (§§307–311). We must not confuse narrative apology with secondary material. Rather, §§295–300 and its inversion of typical Greek elements highlight the importance of the symposia for our understanding of the Jewish translators, the value of Jewish wisdom, and why translating their Scriptures is necessary.[49]

LA is also full of questions, and it would be a mistake to overlook the way that questions function throughout the text to advance the narrative and provide opportunities for the author to educate his reader. The highest concentration of questions is located in §§187–294, in which King Ptolemy queries each of the seventy-two Jewish translators over the course of seven evenings. About half of these questions are on the nature of kingship (so §294) and could have been taken from a *Königsspiegel*.[50] The other questions range from domestic life (§§241, 250) to grief (§§232, 268) to dreams (§213) and show broad similarities to popular Greek philosophical thought.[51] These questions occupy almost the entirety of the symposia section; little attention is paid to the meal itself, except for a minor introduction confirming that the food would be in line with Jewish eating practices (§§181–182).[52] The dinner scene, although pivotal for the justification of the questions, is in actuality a narrative shell that the author fills with material that he believes to be important. This way of constructing narratives—namely, by crafting an account that creates an opportunity for a question to be asked and an answer to be given—is foundational to a range of philosophical treatises (including ancient *symposia*). Indeed, the dinner party itself is almost immaterial; it is the questions and conversations that matter.[53]

48 E.g., Plato, *Symp*. 177c–178a; 180e; Lucian, *Symp*. 19, 30, 33; Aulus Gellius, *Noct. att*. 18.1.2. In contrast, see Philo, *Contempl*. 77. Cf. Y. L. Too, "The Walking Library: The Performance of Cultural Memories," in D. Braund and J. Wilkins, eds., *Athenaeus and His World: Reading Greek Culture in the Roman Empire* (Exeter: University of Exeter Press, 2001), 111–23.

49 O. Murray, "Aristeas and Ptolemaic Kingship," *JTS* 18 (1967): 361. Cf. Wright, *Letter of Aristeas*, 427–29.

50 Zuntz, "Aristeas Studies I," 24–30. This view is challenged, rightly, by Murray, "Aristeas and Ptolemaic Kingship"; O. Murray, "Philosophy and Monarchy in the Hellenistic World," in R. Rajak et al., eds., *Jewish Perspectives on Hellenistic Rulers* (HCS 50; Berkeley: University of California Press, 2007), 13–28. For a Latin example of one question per person at a symposion, see Aulus Gellius, *Noct. att*. 18.2.3.

51 Zuntz, "Aristeas Studies I," 31; Wright, *Letter of Aristeas*, 425.

52 The king wishes to avoid the ἡδονή of Alexandria (§108) and of kinship (§§223, 245, 277) and so seeks wisdom from his guests. This parallels Athenaeus, *Deipn*. 10.421f, which advocates intellectual learning through conversation over the ἡδονή of food. Cf. Plutarch, *Mor*. 645e–f.

53 Answers given at the symposia are akin to the collection of sayings found in Latin (Aulus Gellius) and Hebrew (Mishnah) works. Cf. Hezser, "Rabbis as Intellectuals," 169–85.

The structure of LA is based on the asking and answering of questions, but the questions do not all function on the same level. The narrative proper opens with questions about the size of the library (§10) and the issues obstructing Demetrius from procuring the Jewish law books (§11). This is followed by a rhetorical question from Aristeas (§15) and a direct question from the king regarding the number of Jews in captivity in Egypt (§19). These questions initiate the narrative arc and lay the foundation on which the wider story is built. Subsequent questions are less plot-driven, but didactic, providing an opportunity for the narrator to educate the reader about specific Jewish objects or practices. The use of gentile "ignorance" in the form of a question is the standard trigger for an extended discussion on a specific topic in LA, a structural feature that is strongly associated with philosophical texts. The king, indirectly, asks a question about the size of the table in the temple (§§52–53), which opens a lengthy *ekphrasis* of the artisanal work (§§51–82). In a subsequent scene, Andreas and Aristeas ask Eleazar why (διὰ τί) Jews legislate against eating certain food (§129), which results in a substantial apology on dietary practices (§§128–171), with the practical effect that Pharaoh conforms his eating patterns to those of the Jews (§184).[54] In §176, the king asks the Jews questions about their books, and, following the symposium, Aristeas asks why Jews need to wash their hands in the sea before praying (§306). The final question, found in §312, returns to the opening questions by having the king ask why historians have not engaged with Jewish Scriptures before. This is a major issue within LA's narrative, and the author uses a question from the mouth of a respected outsider to explicitly address this concern: it is not because the Jewish texts are unimportant, but because divine intervention and the lack of piety by previous authors have prevented their translation (§§313–317).[55] All of the questions are asked by non-Jews and answers are provided by the Jewish characters; there is no reciprocity. In LA, it is the Greeks who ask the questions and who are shown to be in need of tutelage. In contrast, the Jewish people do not show interest in Greek or Egyptian practices, either because they are beneath them or because they are already knowledgeable about them. This imbalance reinforces the focus of the narrative and the perceived asymmetrical relationship between members of both cultures.

In the symposium section of LA the focus is on the questions asked by the king to the Jewish interpreters. Giving advice to the king of Egypt at sympotic events was a central feature of Plutarch's *Dinner of the Seven Wise Men*, in which the symposiasts solve riddles and provide answers to questions asked

54 This scene exemplifies the description of the translators; namely that they are said to be able to answer every question appropriately (§122).

55 Cf. Diodorus Siculus, *Bibl.* 1.27.6; Iamblichus, *Vit. Pyth.* 88–89, 246–47.

by the Egyptian monarch. Like LA, and the works by Plato and Xenophon, a version of Plutarch's dinner party is reported to have taken place in the historical past, but the author presents the story in the narrative present. The Egyptian messenger Neiloxenus provides the impetus for the discussion as he was sent to gain answers from Bias regarding how to solve a riddle presented to the Egyptian king by the Ethiopian king (*Mor.* 151b–c). Unsatisfied with answering the (easy) riddle, Bias and the other dinner guests take the liberty of instructing the Egyptian king about the nature of government, fortune, and "what is best" through pithy sayings, expressing that kings, like despots, require taming that can only come from frank speech (*Mor.* 147b).

The role of questions and answers, learning and teaching, is the essence of sympotic philosophical texts. The quintessential example is Socrates, who models how to adopt a posture of humility in the pursuit of knowledge. Although Socrates is teaching in the text, he is the ideal learner in that he is willing to express ignorance and his need for instruction (e.g., Plato, *Symp.* 207c). As a result, as Socrates learns so also does the reader. Characters in *symposia* often express a desire to learn (e.g., Plato, *Symp.* 206b; Xenophon, *Symp.* 2.16; Athenaeus, *Deipn.* 3.97d), which allows for someone in the narrative to educate him/her. In LA, this position is adopted by King Ptolemy, who, though being described as a powerful and successful king, asks those who are not kings about the nature of rule and life. In doing so, Pseudo-Aristeas creates a delicate balance as the king both judges and learns from his guests. Ptolemy does not adopt the humility of Socrates; however, he does model how a person in a superior position should recognize Jewish wisdom and the intellectual worth of his guests. Unlike in histories and epistles, the presentation of a philosopher-king (or at least a king interested and open to philosophy) is an important theme in philosophical writings,[56] emphasizing the central position that a philosophical perspective holds throughout LA, both in the symposia and in the larger macro narrative.

These dinner events, and indeed the whole of LA, fulfill an earlier declaration by Eleazar that the authority of the text could only be fully understood through oral instruction (ἀκρόασις): "The good life, [Eleazar] said, consisted in obeying the laws, and this aim was achieved by hearing much more than by reading" (§127).[57] This passage, near the middle of the work, fits well with

56 The respected king is one who consults philosophers (e.g., Darius I's petition of Heraclitus; Diogenes Laertius, *Vit.* 9.13–14). Cf. Plato, *Ep.* 7.326a–b; *Resp.* 5.473c–d; Philo, *Mos.* 2.2; Aulus Gellius, *Noct. att.* 20.5.7–13.

57 The preference for a living voice was present throughout antiquity. For example, "Of course, the living voice . . . will help you more than the written word" (Seneca, *Ep.* 6.5). Cf. Papias in Eusebius, *Hist. eccl.* 3.39.4. On books being secondary to oral teaching and to be used under guidance, see L. Alexander, "The Living Voice: Scepticism towards the Written Word in

both the structure of LA and the symposia, as here the king will see and hear deep wisdom in action; a model that he would not gain from reading alone (cf. §§286, 294). The symposia and other didactic sections, therefore, reinforce a central theme of LA, namely the value of learning and the importance of applying that learning to life by engaging with those who embody wisdom.[58] The questions by Ptolemy and the presence of Eleazar and the Jewish translators are not secondary to the narrative, but integral to it. The translation of the law is important, but for Pseudo-Aristeas it is not to be separated from oral instruction (§15). For Pseudo-Aristeas both are required for the establishment of the Greek translation as a sacred text and to educate adequately those who would seek to learn.[59] This perspective resonates with the view of Plato (*Ep.* 7.341c–e), who claims that the deepest doctrines do not allow for written expression, but must be acquired through models and extensive study. "Serious ideas" (τῶν ὄντων σπουδαίων), moreover, should not be made freely available to the public in writing, but need to be provided through a mediator (344c–345c), emphasizing the need for personal tutelage in order to provide a space to ask questions, receive explanations, and control ideas.[60]

The role of asking questions is essential for advancing the plot in LA. In many philosophical works, including *symposia*, questions form the backbone of the text and facilitate the progression of the narrative.[61] Unlike these *symposia*, LA does not have a strong narrative thread in the symposia proper, nor are the pithy answers given by the Jewish sages akin to the lengthy and learned debates in the *symposia*.[62] The absence of narrative structure in LA's symposia, however, does not stretch to the remainder of the text, which clearly shows that the intention of the author is to educate his reader through the presentation of a series of questions. The asking and answering of questions,

---

Early Christian and Greco-Roman Texts," in D. J. A. Clines, S. E. Fowl, and S. E. Porter, eds., *The Bible in Three Dimensions: Essays in Celebration of Forty Years of Biblical Studies in the University of Sheffield* (JSOTSup 87; Sheffield: JSOT Press, 1990), 221–47, especially 231–32; J. Dillon, *The Middle Platonists* (London: Duckworth, 1977), 338.

58 For example, the translators are said to be mature in experience and to have lived exemplary lives (§32). Cf. §§43, 122–125, and especially 171–172.

59 D. de Crom, "The *Letter of Aristeas* and the Authority of the Septuagint," *JSP* 17 (2008): 150–54.

60 M. Finkelberg, "Elitist Orality and the Triviality of Writing," in C. Cooper, ed., *Politics of Orality* (MneSup 280; OLAC 6; Leiden: Brill, 2007), 293–305.

61 Plato, *Symp.* 172b; 174a–b, e; 176a; 177a; 180d; 199d; 203a; 207c; 213a; Xenophon, *Symp.* 1.15; 2.3–5, 15, 17; 3.2, 4; 4.52; 5.1; 6.1; 7.1; 8.1–3. Athenaeus also uses questions and "problems" to discuss issues, e.g., *Deipn.* 1.19d; 1.23b; 1.24e. Additionally, every section of Plutarch's *Table Talk* begins with an explicit question.

62 The need for all of the sages to speak naturally precludes lengthy speeches and discussions in LA. Pseudo-Aristeas' focus on the philosophical ideas of kingship and piety differs from the grammatical and literary discussions of later *symposia*.

therefore, is a significant structuring element of LA and one that is not seen to be a literary component of either ancient historiography or epistolography.

Recognizing the importance of questions highlights one of the issues with current interpretations of LA, namely that some (although not all) scholars have been overly fixated on what they claim is the main theme (i.e., the creation of the LXX) and have relegated the rest of the text to the background.[63] Although the narrative frame of LA is said to describe the origins of the LXX, there is little description of it within the text.[64] Rather, the LXX finds its value in the quality of the translators, who support the higher theme of sharing and acquiring knowledge.[65] The proposed narrative rationale in LA is that Philocrates has a deep love of learning (κατειληφὼς ἣν ἔχεις φιλομαθῆ διάθεσιν, §1), and so would be interested in hearing about Aristeas' experiences. This concept of φιλομάθεια becomes a repeated declaration from Aristeas about the nature and character of Philocrates (§§7, 171, 300) and so shapes the way that the reader understands the nature and purpose of the text; the implied reader is to be like Philocrates and share his love of learning.[66]

Knowledge of Greek culture is attributed to all of the characters in LA. Of the Greek individuals, King Ptolemy and Demetrius are intimately connected with the Alexandrian library (§§9, 124), while Aristeas and Andreas are described by Eleazar as καλοὶ καὶ ἀγαθοί and outstanding in education (παιδείᾳ διαφέροντες, §43). The Jewish translators are similarly depicted as having excellent education (παιδείᾳ διαφέροντας) and as masters of both Jewish and Greek literature (§121). According to the text, the pursuit of culture (παιδεία) is thought to be the highest good (§8; cf. §§43, 121, 290), and is regularly recognized as an essential attribute for dinner guests by ancient authors.[67] Equally important, the author of LA displays substantial learning, a necessary ability for the successful adoption of a Greek literary persona.[68]

63 E.g., R. J. H. Shutt, "Letter of Aristeas," in *OTP* 2.7; Honigman, *Septuagint*, 149–50.

64 Rightly highlighted by E. J. Bickerman, "Zur Datierung des Pseudo-Aristeas," *ZNW* 29 (1930): 280–98.

65 Cf. §151 (righteousness and holy living). Furthermore, law is about character and understanding its embodiment in history (e.g., §§153–161, especially 163).

66 The implied reader is also thought to share Philocrates' interest in the Jewish people, religious topics, as well as the ultimate importance of piety (§§2, 5). In LA's symposia scene we find resonances with other *symposia* and philosophical texts, with the themes of φιλομάθεια, παιδεία, and εὐσέβεια found throughout the work (especially §§1–8). These topics regularly feature in philosophical works, but are not common in histories or ancient letters. Cf. Alexander, *Preface*, 100, who identifies examples of φιλομάθεια in technical prose works.

67 Cf. Athenaeus, *Deipn.* 1.1a, c; 1.2b. Athenaeus' understanding and expression of παιδεία differs from Pseudo-Aristeas', as the latter is more focused on philosophical learning while the former prioritizes literary prowess.

68 E. S. Gruen, *Diaspora: Jews amidst Greeks and Romans* (Cambridge, Mass.: Harvard University Press, 2002), 124–25; Matusova, *Meaning of the Letter*, 44–90.

Associated with learning is the concept of piety (εὐσέβεια), a central theme in LA (§§24, 42, 131, 210, 239) that is described as "the most important thing of all" (§2). The ideas of learning and piety in LA are connected from the outset of the work, especially as Philocrates and Aristeas have made a special study of the things of God (τὴν προαίρεσιν ἔχοντες ἡμεῖς πρὸς τὸ περιέργως τὰ θεῖα κατανοεῖν, §3).[69] No place is this emphasis more apparent than in the symposia, in which almost every response by the Jewish sages includes a reference to proper actions towards God and the need for his help.[70] The importance of piety is also found in Greek *symposia*. In Plato's *Symposium*, both Eryximachus (*Symp.* 188c) and Aristophanes (*Symp.* 193d) conclude their speeches on love with overtures to the importance of piety. Similarly, piety is identified by Plutarch as an appropriate topic at dinner parties (*Mor.* 614b).[71] The intricate pairing of learning and piety is not prominent within LXX Pentateuch. However, it is widespread in other Jewish texts (e.g., Proverbs, 4QInstruction) and in Hellenistic philosophy, particularly within the *Corpus Hermeticum*.[72]

The focus on piety in LA challenges the view that LA is specifically about political deeds, which are prominent in historiography. Honigman acknowledges that the subject of piety is atypical for historiography and was borrowed from the "philosophical epistle." Unfortunately Honigman does not provide substantial examples of why she determined this motif came from philosophical *epistles*, specifically, rather than philosophical literature more broadly. Furthermore, there are insufficient examples of the genre to make such strong claims, and Honigman is aware of this.[73] I agree with Honigman that the lack of surviving texts likely indicates that LA is not as "unusual" in its time as it now looks today. However, her focus on "philosophical allegory," and her view that "moral benefit can be derived only from a reliable account," in my opinion, does not adequately represent the range and ethos of philosophical works

---

The theme of φιλομάθεια is also prominent in philosophical texts, as it not only characterizes the ideal practitioner, but in some cases is equated with philosophy (e.g., Plato, *Resp.* 2.376b; 5.475c; *Phaed.* 67b; 82c; 82d–83a; *Phaedr.* 230d; Plutarch, *Mor.* 612d; 618e; 628b; 778a; Macrobius, *Sat.* 7.3.23). The term φιλομαθής is not limited to philosophical discourse, but can be found in other contexts (e.g., Galen, *Ars med.* 1.355), although in the case of Galen he would also claim that the best doctor is also a philosopher (cf. *Opt. Med.* 1.53–63).

69 Cf. G. Boccaccini, "La sapienza dello Pseudo-Aristea," in A. Vivian, ed., *Biblische und judaistische Studien. Festschrift für Paolo Sacchi* (Frankfurt am Main: Peter Lang, 1990), 166.

70 Zuntz, "Aristeas Studies I," 22.

71 This is located in Plutarch's positive answer to the work's opening question: is philosophy a fitting topic for conversation at a drinking party? (*Mor.* 612e–615c). Cf. Athenaeus, *Deipn.* 1.1a–b.

72 E.g., ἡ μετὰ γνώσεως εὐσέβεια (*Corp. Herm.* 6.5); εὐσέβεια δέ ἐστι θεοῦ γνῶσις (9.4), cf. 1.27; 10.19; 18.15. A similar pairing of instruction and piety is found in *Thoth* 13.

73 Honigman points to Euhermerus' *Sacred History* in Diodorus Siculus, *Bibl.* 6.1.1–11, as a possible comparison for the inclusion of religious thought into Greek historiography.

and so leads her to underplay the author's primary participation in philosophical treatise.[74]

Our study has focused on underexplored elements of LA, but it is important to recognize features that do not align with prototypical philosophic genres, such as the larger narrative arc of translation, the role of an eyewitness as a claim for veracity, the travelogue, as well as the embedding of genres (e.g., letters, decrees).[75] These features overlap with historiography and suggest that Pseudo-Aristeas participated in multiple genres in the composition of LA.

4 Maccabees

Fourth Maccabees is an anonymous work with an unknown provenance, likely written in the first or early second century CE. [76] The work is a treatise on the ability of reason to subdue the passions, with Jewish and Greek characters representing virtue and vice, respectively. The work's content fits with the title used by Eusebius (*Hist. eccl.* 3.10.6): "On the absolute power of reason" (Περὶ αὐτοκράτορος λογισμοῦ).[77] The work is well written, incorporating many rhetorical elements, and displays a fair understanding of Hellenistic philosophy, all of which indicate that its author had significant education in Greek.[78] These features have led to a diversity of genre designations, ranging from sermon to diatribe, encomium to development of a thesis, or some combination of the above, with scholars highlighting specific elements as determinative for genre

74 Honigman, *Septuagint*, 33, 35.

75 Lucian also includes a letter in his *Symposium* (22–27), suggesting that the inclusion of other texts is not limited to larger works (although they are much more common in them) and that genres in antiquity allowed for variation.

76 Eusebius (*Hist. eccl.* 3.10.6) and Jerome (*Vir. ill.* 13; *Pelag.* 2.6) attributed the work to Josephus, though this position is not held by modern scholars. Cf. H. Anderson, "4 Maccabees: A New Translation and Introduction," in *OTP* 2.533; D. S. Williams, "Josephus and the Authorship of IV Maccabees: A Critical Investigation" (PhD diss., Hebrew Union College, 1987). For discussions of dating, see A. Dupont-Sommer, *Le quatrième livre des Machabées: Introduction, traduction et notes* (Paris: H. Champion, 1939), 78–81; J. W. van Henten, "Datierung und Herkunft des Vierten Makkabäerbuches," in J. W. van Henten et al., eds., *Tradition and Re-interpretation in Jewish and Early Christian Literature* (Leiden: Brill, 1986), 136–49; J. W. van Henten, *The Maccabean Martyrs as Saviours of the Jewish People: A Study of 2 and 4 Maccabees* (JSJSup 57; Leiden: Brill, 1997), 73–81; D. A. deSilva, *4 Maccabees: Introduction and Commentary on the Greek Text of Codex Sinaiticus* (SEPT; Leiden: Brill, 2006), xiv–xvii. For a recent discussion of Antioch as the provenance, see T. Rajak, "*Paideia* in the Fourth Book of Maccabees," in G. J. Brooke and R. Smithuis, eds., *Jewish Education from Antiquity to the Middle Ages: Studies in Honour of Philip S. Alexander* (AJEC 100; Leiden: Brill, 2017), 75–80.

77 Cf. Jerome (*Vir. ill.* 13). Gregory Nazianzen follows this tradition when he refers to this book as "the book which philosophizes about reason being supreme over the passions" (*Or. Bas.* 15; *PG* 35.913). Cf. Dupont-Sommer, *Quatrième Livre des Machabées*, 2.

78 H.-J. Klauck, *4 Makkabäerbuch*, *JSHRZ* 3.6, 665. For recent, detailed investigations, see D. A. deSilva, "The Author of 4 Maccabees and Greek *Paideia*: Facets of the Formation of a Hellenistic Jewish Rhetor," in J. Zurawski and G. Boccaccini, eds., *Second Temple Jewish "Paideia" in Context* (BZNW 228; Berlin: De Gruyter, 2017), 205–38; Rajak, "*Paideia*."

designations.[79] In this investigation, we will see how the author of 4 Maccabees adeptly brings together philosophical, rhetorical, and narrative elements to create a work that is not beholden to one literary form, but fruitfully participates in multiple genres.[80]

Fourth Maccabees begins by declaring that the work addresses a most philosophical topic (φιλοσοφώτατον λόγον, 1:1) and that his subject is essential for all who are seeking knowledge (ἐπιστήμη) and the highest virtue: rational judgment (φρόνησις, 1:2).[81] Specifically, the author seeks to prove to his reader that devout reason (εὐσεβὴς λογισμός) is sovereign over the emotions.[82] The author identifies the virtue of σωφροσύνη as the main topic of his inquiry, claiming that he will be able to show through select examples that its adoption grants its holder the ability to overcome base passions, desires, and emotions (1:3–4). This well-structured opening (1:1–12) resonates with classical *exordia* (e.g., Aristotle, *Rhet.* 1414b–1415a), which prepares the reader for what follows, arguing that the work's thesis is worthy of consideration and of value to the reader.[83]

The subject of the work, namely reason's ability to overcome passion, was a central idea among ancient philosophers, including some Jewish authors.[84]

79 Sermon: J. Freudenthal, *Die Flavius Josephus beigelegte Schrift über die Herrschaft der Vernunft (IV Makkabäerbuch), eine Predigt aus dem ersten nachchristlichen Jahrhundert* (Breslau: Skutsch, 1869), 105; H. Thyen, *Der Stil der jüdische-hellenistischen Homilie* (Göttingen: Vandenhoeck & Ruprecht, 1955), 13. Diatribe: E. Norden, *Die antike Kunstprosa vom VI. Jahrhundert v. Chr. bis in die Zeit der Renaissance* (Leipzig: Teubner, 1923), 1.303–4; A. Deissmann, "Das vierte Makkabäerbuch," in E. Kautzsch, ed., *Die Apokryphen und Pseudepigraphen des Alten Testaments* (2 vols.; Hildesheim: Georg Olms, 1900), 2.151. Encomium: Dupont-Sommer, *Quatrième Livre des Machabées*, 20–25; M. Hadas, *The Third and Fourth Books of Maccabees* (New York: Harper, 1953), 101–2. Development of a thesis: S. K. Stowers, "4 Maccabees," in J. L. Mays, ed., *The HarperCollins Bible Commentary* (San Francisco: HarperSanFrancisco, 2000), 844–45. Combination: Van Henten, *Maccabean Martyrs*, 60–67.

80 Philostorgius, according to Photius, says, "The Fourth Book [of Maccabees] he asserts to have been the work of Josephus, and to be regarded rather as an encomium (ἐγκώμιον) of Eleazar and the seven Maccabean boys, than as a regular history of events (ἱστορία)" (*Epit. Hist.* 1). This quotation hints that debate over the genre of 4 Maccabees might have existed even in antiquity.

81 The cardinal virtue of σωφροσύνη is also highlighted (1:18; 3:1) and is seen to be instrumental in subduing passion (e.g., 1:31–32, 36; 2:1, 18, 23; 3:17, 19). A critical edition of 4 Maccabees has yet to be produced; accordingly, the text is taken from Rahlfs-Hanhart, *Septuaginta*.

82 Cf. S. Lauer, "*Eusebes Logismos* in IV Macc," *JJS* 6 (1955): 170–71. Fourth Macc 1:1, 13; 6:31; 7:16; 8:1; 13:1; 18:2, though in 1:13 the modifier εὐσεβής is missing in a number of manuscripts.

83 For a detailed rhetorical analysis of 4 Macc 1:1–12 as exordium, see H.-J. Klauck, "Hellenistiche Rhetorik im Diasporajudentum: Das Exordium des vierten Makkabäerbuchs (4 Makk 1.1–12)," *NTS* 35 (1989): 451–65.

84 On the contest between reason and passion, see Plutarch, *Mor.* 441c–d; Marcus Aurelius, *Med.* 2.5. For the soul's need to discipline and control passions, see Plato, *Phaed.* 94d. LA claims that the highest achievement was "to rule oneself and not be carried away by the passions"

In 4 Maccabees, reason is embedded within Torah and so is an integral part of Jewish life and religious practice. At the same time, the author of 4 Maccabees incorporates elements from Greek philosophical thought (e.g., Stoic, Peripatetic, Platonic) and presents his position as fully compatible with both groups. This is best seen in the author's definition of wisdom and how he identifies wisdom's virtues: "Wisdom is the knowledge of divine and human matters and the causes of these" (1:16).[85] However, unlike his non-Jewish interlocutors, the writer of 4 Maccabees claims that such matters are to be found primarily in the law (1:7; 5:22–24).[86]

Fourth Maccabees' author did not limit his work solely to philosophical argument, but included narrative exempla as proofs. The transition from philosophical argument to narrative first occurs at 3:19. Having already given a number of scriptural examples of important figures who had overcome emotions (e.g., Joseph, 2:2–4; Moses, 2:17; Jacob, 2:19–20; David, 3:6–15), the author moves to his primary examples that he introduced earlier: those who overcame extreme torture though rational thought (1:8). Eleazar is presented as sage-like, knowing Scripture, having priestly connections, and having achieved old age (5:4). In contrast, Antiochus IV is presented as the quintessential tyrant, brutally retaliating and plundering the people for a perceived slight and draconianly enforcing cultural prohibitions (4:23–26). This type of confrontation (sage-tyrant) is well documented in Greek literature, but this commonality does not undermine the emotional and argumentative impact of this engagement.[87] As the stereotypical tyrant, Antiochus IV would have been immediately recognized as a negative character and naturally antagonistic to the virtues and values held by the citizenry and, more prominently here, the sage. Antiochus' arrogance (4:15; 9:30; 12:11–14) and the overt use of force naturally place him in opposition to the use of reason and virtue, becoming the foil for Eleazar, the seven sons, and their mother. As the narrative progresses, the author alternates between vivid depictions of torture and his argument regarding virtue. The pairing becomes the primary structure of the work, with the author returning to his thesis statement at each juncture in

(221–222), and that a good ruler should be able to perform his duties properly by moderating the emotions and impulses through careful and intentional deliberation (256).

85 This is a common understanding of Sophia (e.g., Philo, *Congr.* 79; Cicero, *Off.* 2.5; Seneca, *Ep.* 89.4; Sextus Empiricus, *Math.* 9.13). On the four kinds of wisdom (i.e., φρόνησις, δικαιοσύνη, ἀνδρεία, and σωφροσύνη, 1:18, cf. 1:6), see Wis 8:7; Philo, *Cher.* 5; *Det.* 143; *Congr.* 2; *Abr.* 219; Plato, *Resp.* 4.427e; *Phaed.* 69b–c; Diogenes Laertius, *Vit.* 3.80, 90–91; Arius Didymus, *Epit.* 5b2; Aristotle, *Pol.* 1323b34; *Rhet.* 1366b1–2.

86 For a thorough discussion of the philosophical content and contribution of 4 Maccabees, see D. A. deSilva, *4 Maccabees* (Sheffield: Sheffield Academic Press, 1998), 51–75.

87 See, for example, Philo, *Prob.* 106–109; Diogenes Laertius, *Vit.* 9.26–27, 58–59; Cicero, *Tusc.* 2.52; Iamblichus, *Vit. Pyth.* 215–222. Cf. Lucian, *Phal.* 1–2.

the narrative (6:31–35; 7:16–23; 13:1–5; 16:1–4; 18:1–2). The use of narrative, therefore, does not detract from the philosophical argument, but rather is an integral component to the work's composition.

The self-conscious use of progymnasmatic components in the text emphasizes the work's participation in rhetorical composition.[88] In keeping with the practice of placing appropriate speeches on the lips of individuals (i.e., *prosopopoeia*; e.g., Thucydides, *Hist.* 1.22.1–4; Quintilian, *Inst.* 6.1.25–26; 9.2.29–30), the author seeks to embody his philosophical discussion in the words and actions of his characters. The philosophical debate is established through the opening speech of Antiochus IV (5:5–13) and Eleazar's rebuttals (5:14–38; 6:16–23), with each martyr contributing a pithy predeath declaration (e.g., 6:27–30; 9:23–25, 29–32; 10:10–11, 18–21; 11:12, 20–27; 12:16–19). Theoretical interchange is at the center of each encounter, but the viability of each person's philosophical position is displayed through their actions (7:9); Antiochus is easily enraged and resorts to violence to coerce his opponent (6:1; 9:10), while Eleazar, despite being naked, is adorned with piety (6:1–2).[89] In other parts of the narrative, the author of 4 Maccabees adopts the persona of a coward and provides a speech that would have been made by a mother who had lost her children (16:5–11) or one of the sons if he had succumbed to tyrannical pressure (8:16–26). These prosopopoeic speeches not only indicate the author's awareness of Greek rhetorical practice, but also allow the author to explore counterarguments more fully.

The substantial linguistic and rhetorical unity of 4 Maccabees challenges the understanding of 4 Maccabees as formed of two discrete sections.[90] Some have argued that 3:19–18:24 should be viewed separately and interpreted as an epideictic speech (λόγος ἐπιδεικτικός), which is typically associated with praise, encomia, and funeral orations (ἐπιτάφιος λόγος).[91] Although praise of those who have died is prominent in 4 Maccabees (7:1–23; 13:1–14:10; cf. 14:11–17:1 and 17:2–18:24) and reference is made to a memorial (17:7–8),

88 For a recent discussion, see deSilva, "Author of 4 Maccabees," 206–25; Rajak, "*Paideia*," 72–73.

89 On the pairing of words and actions for true and false philosophers, see Lucian, *Alex.*; *Demon.*; *Nigr.*; *Peregr.*

90 For stylistic but not philosophical unity, see U. Breitenstein, *Beobachtungen zu Sprache, Stil und Gedankengut des Vierten Makkabäerbuchs* (Stuttgart: Schwabe, 1978), 91–130. On the integration of the work as a whole, see deSilva, *4 Maccabees*, xxvi–xxix.

91 Klauck, "Hellenistische Rhetorik," 104. This understanding led Lebram to hypothesize that 4 Maccabees was modeled on a specific epideictic speech, namely the Athenian funeral oration. J. C. H. Lebram, "Die literarische Form des vierten Makkabäerbuches," *VC* 28 (1974): 81–96; J. W. van Henten and F. Avemarie, *Martyrdom and Noble Death: Selected Texts from Graeco-Roman, Jewish and Christian Antiquity* (London: Routledge, 2002), 18. E.g., Thucydides, *Hist.* 2.34–46; Lysias, *Or.* 2; Demosthenes, *Or.* 60; Hyperides, *Or.* 6. Cf. Ps.-Dionysius of Halicarnassus, *Ars rhet.* 6; *Dem.* 23, 44; Aristotle, *Rhet.* 1415b; Lucian, *Alex.* 60.

notable differences are also found, especially the inclusion of gruesome torture and death scenes and the interwoven philosophical dialogue. The intent of this structure is reinforced by the author's statement in 3:19, "this moment now invites us to a narrative demonstration (ἀπόδειξιν) of temperate reason." The use of ἀπόδειξις, and other related terms (e.g., ἐπιδείκνυσθαι, 1:1; ἀπέδειξα, 16:4) indicates an underlying structure that aligns well with Aristotle's prescription concerning necessary speech components: the subject of the work is to be followed by a demonstration or proof that supports the original claim (*Rhet.* 1414a31–37). The cohesion of the two parts, thesis and description, is reinforced regularly by the recapitulation of the thesis following each martyrdom account. Prominent themes in the second half, such as the use of praise, are prefigured in the introduction (1:2, 10; 2:2), creating strong links between the sections. This does not undermine the potential connections with ἐπιτάφιος λόγος literature, but it does require that they be subsumed within a larger whole.

Fourth Maccabees' participation in multiple genres is distinct, and the author does not signal an immediate literary prototype. One verse in the introduction has the potential to speak to this blending of philosophical discourse and dramatic narrative. Right before the opening of the main text, the author speaks of the necessity to begin his work by stating his main principles prior to turning to his narrative (δὴ λέγειν ἐξέσται ἀρξαμένῳ τῆς ὑποθέσεως ὅπερ εἴωθα ποιεῖν καὶ οὕτως εἰς τὸν περὶ αὐτῶν τρέψομαι λόγον, 1:12). Within a rhetorical context, moving from hypothesis to proof is expected, although διήγησις, rather than λόγος, is the standard term employed.[92] In Theon's discussion of διήγησις (*Prog.* 78–96) we witness the pairing of depiction and speeches, with the student encouraged to draw upon famous or important people as examples for their argument. This reference to custom suggests that the author of 4 Maccabees was participating in a wider literary practice, either within his corpora or within ancient literature as a whole. Although there are differences, ancient readers would have recognized 4 Maccabees as an epideictic composition, specifically a *logos protreptikos*, which uses the martyrs as pinnacular examples of philosophic virtue attained through uncompromising adherence to Jewish philosophy.[93] Such unreserved praise challenges the reader to pursue similar composure in the face of external challenges.

The presentation of a philosophical topos in a rhetorical structure is distinct among extant Jewish authors in antiquity. Fourth Maccabees has sub-

92 Aristotle, *Rhet.* 1415b; Theon, *Prog.* 78. Cf. Ps.-Cicero, *Rhet. Her.* 1.12–13.

93 Aristotle, *Rhet.* 1417b; Quintilian, *Inst.* 5.11.6. Epideictic style is most suitable for reading: Aristotle, *Rhet.* 1414a. There are a few aspects of the text that suggest that is was in fact given as a speech. Cf. κατὰ τοῦτον τον καιρόν, 1:10; ὁ καιρος ἡμᾶς καλεῖ, 3:19, and the effect of the audience in 14:9. These could also be literary inventions to give the impression of a speech.

stantial points of contact with 2 Maccabees, indicating that martyrdom and oppression under tyranny was a common topos.[94] Although both authors used the same examples, they presented them in different ways by employing different genres (see chapter 7). Fourth Maccabees, therefore, provides a strong example of the way that literary types and elements can be brought together to create one unified text, challenging the way that some scholars create discrete genre categories.

Philo of Alexandria, *De Vita Contemplativa*

Philo's *De vita contemplativa* depicts a Jewish philosophical sect, the adherents of which, called Therapeutae and Therapeutrides, pursue the contemplative life. Our investigation does not seek to engage in the question of who the members of this sect were; rather, we will investigate the literary method Philo employed in his composition and what this might indicate about the genre and purpose of the work.

Through the practice of architextuality, the author can signal to the reader by the title how the work is generically positioned.[95] For this text, the manuscripts indicate a conflation of traditions, creating uncertainty which title, if any, originated from Philo: Περὶ βίου θεωρητικοῦ ἢ ἱκετῶν ἀρετῶν τὸ δ' (On the Contemplative Life or On the Suppliants, On Virtues [book] 4).[96] Although the title(s) may not have originated from Philo, they are still useful for understanding the genre of a work, because each indicates how the work was interpreted and categorized by later readers through paratextuality.[97] For example, both the manuscript tradition and Eusebius identify *Contemplativa* as a philosophical work, though there are some differences. For example, Cod. Paris. 435(c) has only the title ἱκετῶν ἀρετῶν τὸ δ' and lacks Περὶ βίου θεωρητικοῦ, which suggests that the scribe (or his exemplar) only considered or knew *Contemplativa* to be part of a larger work on virtues and not a freestanding composition.[98]

Philo begins his work by indicating that he had discussed the "active life" (πρακτικὸν . . . βίον, *Contempl.* 1) in a previous work and will now proceed to address the topic of the life of contemplation (περὶ τῶν θεωρίαν ἀσπασαμένων). Philo presents his study of the contemplative life as something "required by the

94 On the relationship between 2 and 4 Maccabees, including a helpful chart, see Klauck, *4 Makkabäerbuch*, 654.

95 Adams, *Genre*, 117–20. For architextuality, see Genette, *Palimpsests*, 1–10.

96 So too Eusebius, *Hist. eccl.* 2.17.3; 2.18.7, though without indicating that it was the fourth part of a larger work.

97 For a more thorough discussion of the titles and *Contemplativa*'s possible relationship to *On Virtues*, see J. E. Taylor, *Jewish Women Philosophers of First-Century Alexandria: Philo's "Therapeutae" Reconsidered* (Oxford: Oxford University Press, 2003), 34–39.

98 F. C. Conybeare, ed., *Philo: About the Contemplative Life* (Oxford: Clarendon, 1895), 25.

subject/treatise" (ἀκολουθίᾳ τῆς πραγματείας), signaling his awareness of and adherence to established compositional practices. Stating that he is going to be investigating the highest model of life, that of contemplation (θεωρίαν), Philo presents his work as a scientific treatise in the tradition originally developed by Aristotle (*Eth. nic.* 1.5; 10.7–8), although he does not claim to follow any specific individual or prototype.[99] Having stated his literary aims, Philo identifies what he will not be doing in this work; he will not add anything to improve the facts, but will only provide the truth (ἀλλ' ἀτεχνῶς αὐτῆς περιεχόμενος τῆς ἀληθείας, §1). Philo contrasts his practice with the practices of the poets and historians (ποιηταῖς καὶ λογογράφοις), who need to embellish the details of their subjects to make them worthy of remembering. By making this differentiation, Philo not only employs a common motif (cf. *Opif.* 4–5), but actively places himself in a different literary tradition (i.e., not poetry or history).

The claims of the opening paragraph are worked out in the remainder of the composition. Philo begins his investigation by introducing the Therapeutae and Therapeutrides (*Contempl.* 2, 16–39) and compares (συγκρίνειν) the content, activities, and perceived function of dinner gatherings, explicitly contrasting Jewish sympotic practices with those of the other nations (ἀντιτάξας τὰ τῶν ἄλλων συμπόσια, *Contempl.* 40). Although Philo begins by discussing "typical" events at dinner parties (*Contempl.* 40–56), he focuses on the symposia of Plato and Xenophon, chastising the drunken frivolity and the base topics of discussion found in these pinnacular examples (*Contempl.* 57–58; cf. Athenaeus, *Deipn.* 11.508d). In contrast, Philo sets out the type of dinner gathering that true seekers of the contemplative life should emulate (*Contempl.* 64–90).[100] This strong critique of Greek culture is not unique to Philo, but parallels Roman rhetoric in identifying Greek flaws.[101] This joint practice is, understandably, absent from previous generations of Jewish writers and so marks an important shift in Jewish engagement with Greek culture. No longer is Hellenism the solely dominant culture; rather, Roman culture is seen as a potential rival along with Jewish practices. The presentation of a sophisticated and highly philosophic community lends support to the dominant assessment that Philo's *Contemplativa* participates in moral philosophy.[102]

99 Cf. A. Grilli, *Il problema della vita contemplativa nel mondo greco-romano* (Rome: Fratelli Bocca, 1953), 125–29. On Philo's pairing of active and contemplative lives, see *Decal.* 101. A similar pairing is found in the discussions of philosophers, e.g., Cicero, *Fin.* 5.57; Diogenes Laertius, *Vit.* 7.92, 130. On Aristotle's topos, see J. M. Cooper, *Pursuits of Wisdom: Six Ways of Life in Ancient Philosophy from Socrates to Plotinus* (Princeton: Princeton University Press, 2012), 70–143.
100 On the role of learning and teaching within literary symposia, see Adams, "Sympotic Learning." Cf. Arius Didymus, *Epit.* 5b9.
101 Niehoff, *Philo on Jewish Identity*, 142; Niehoff, *Philo of Alexandria*, 86–88.
102 J. Riaud, "Les Thérapeutes d'Alexandrie dans la tradition et dans la recherche critique jusqu'aux découvertes de Qumran," *ANRW* 2.20.2 (1987): 1189–295; F. Dumas, ed., and P.

This perspective has been challenged by Engberg-Pedersen, who rightfully highlights the importance of genre for interpreting a work, arguing that Philo's work should be read as participating in the genre of "philosopher's dream," "invented fiction," or "utopian fantasy done for a serious purpose."[103] Drawing on Plato's dichotomy of πλασθέντα μῦθον and ἀληθινὸν λόγον in *Timaeus* 26e4–5, Engberg-Pedersen proposes that the *Contemplativa* adopts an (x) + (y) + (z) form found in similar works modeled on Plato.[104] Of importance for Engberg-Pedersen is Philo's intentional avoidance of any acknowledgment (explicitly or implicitly) of the content's fictional nature. For Engberg-Pedersen these four literary features provide the core, requisite components of this genre and are found in a few representative texts in antiquity, specifically Plato and Zeno's *Republics* and Plato's *Timaeus*.[105] According to Engberg-Pedersen, these works were identified by Aristotle as a specific literary genre, the "*pragmateia* or 'systematic or scientific treaty,'" and this genre label should be applied to *Contemplativa*.[106] I am not convinced, however, that there is sufficient evidence for the argument that πραγματεία was a recognized genre in antiquity or that Philo uses πραγματεία in a technical manner.[107] Philo uses πραγματεία twenty-three times in his corpus, but rarely are literary forms being discussed. The possible exception is *Congr.* 147, in which Philo uses the term to describe the works of philosophers (ἡ περὶ ὅρων πραγματεία πᾶσα τῷ φιλοσόφῳ), although the strength of this example is undermined in *Congr.* 149, in which πραγματεία has a clear non-genre application.

One of the central tenets of Engberg-Pedersen's argument is the role of historicity in genre determination and, importantly for him, how scholars should approach the text.[108] For example, the likeliness that Philo did not have

Miquel, trans., *De Vita Contemplativa* (PAPM 29; Paris: Éditions du Cerf, 1963).

103 T. Engberg-Pedersen, "Philo's *De vita contemplativa* as Philosopher's Dream," *JSJ* 30 (1999): 43. Cf. M. A. Beavis, "Philo's Therapeutai: Philosopher's Dream or Utopian Construction?" *JSP* 14 (2004): 30–42.

104 Engberg-Pedersen ("Philo's *De vita contemplativa*," 44) defines these components as: "(x) a story, (y) designed for the purpose of describing an ideal state and its citizens as acting, that is, as 'engaging in some of the activities for which they appear to be formed,' (z) claimed (falsely) for that purpose to be historically true, (v) *but* also implicitly acknowledged as a piece of fiction, a *plastheis mythos* of the kind that Plato notoriously delighted in creating."

105 Cf. Plutarch, *Alex. fort.* 6 (*Mor.* 329a–b); the discussion in Josephus, *C. Ap.* 2.220–224; Lucian, *Ver. hist.* 1.2–4.

106 Engberg-Pedersen, "Philo's *De vita contemplativa*," 41, citing Aristotle, *Eth. nic.* 2.2.

107 Bömer and Manetti have shown that πραγματεία did not have generic weight, but signaled "work" or "treatise." Bömer, "Der Commentarius," especially section II; D. Manetti, "Heliodorus, *Chirurgumena*," in A. Carlini and M. G. Calvini, eds., *Papiri letterari greci della Bayerische Staatsbibliothek di Monaco di Baviera* (Stuttgart: Teubner, 1986), 19–25, especially 25.

108 Engberg-Pedersen ("Philo's *De vita contemplativa*," 45) separates the fictitious tales of *Timaeus* and the two *Republics* from the "marvellous tales" (*paradoxologoumenon*) of travel narratives, though rightly highlights that Josephus saw them as related.

a previous work in which he discussed the Essenes is, for Engberg-Pedersen, puzzling and one reason for not assigning the *Contemplativa* to the genre of philosophical treatise.[109] For him, a "straightforward" reading would, at best, force scholars to realize that *Contemplativa* is only a fragment. If the work is simply incomplete, then Engberg-Pedersen's proposal becomes less necessary (which he acknowledges). However, if Philo's *Contemplativa* is complete, in that there was no narrative either leading up to or following from the work, does that necessitate a new genre designation? Engberg-Pedersen thinks so, but this perspective rests on the argument that no such Therapeutae community existed. Such a fabrication would require understanding *Contemplativa* as πλασθέντα μῦθον, which would fall outside of the realm of ἀληθινὸν λόγον.

Although the question of historicity in genre determination is identified by Plato and others (e.g., Quintilian, *Inst.* 2.4.2; Lucian, *Hist.* 7–9), it is not clear how this criterion works in philosophical discussions. Both Plato (*Tim.* 26e) and Josephus (*C. Ap.* 2.220–224) identify historicity as important, but in both cases the rigid division between "truth" and "fiction" is blurred; any society that appears too good to be true will inevitably be thought of as fictional, and Plato's construction of utopian societies was regularly criticized in antiquity.[110] Even more important is the role of "truth" in philosophic discourse. In the discussions of philosophical or utopian societies, it is understandable (and possibly expected) that one needs to construct and present something that does not (yet) exist. The description of such a community does not rest on historicity, but on the logical outworking of the philosopher's ideals. Here Engberg-Pedersen makes an important observation: Philo does not present his community as a future possibility, but as a current reality. For Engberg-Pedersen, this claim is a literary fiction, and as a result would undermine *Contemplativa*'s classification as a *true* work.[111]

If one accepts Engberg-Pedersen's dichotomy between πλασθέντα μῦθον and ἀληθινὸν λόγον, with the determining component being historicity, then his theory of *Contemplativa* as "invented fiction" could be plausible, although this rests heavily on his reading of the internal and external coherence of the

109 Engberg-Pedersen, "Philo's *De vita contemplativa*," 42.

110 Cf. Aristotle, *Pol.* 1260a–1266a; Polybius, *Hist.* 6.47.7–10; Cicero, *Rep.* 2.21–22, 52; Plutarch, *Lyc.* 31; Lucian, *Ver. hist.* 1.1–4; Athenaeus, *Deipn.* 11.508a–c. See also Homer's depiction of Scheria (*Od.* 6) as a utopia. M. I. Finlay, *The World of Odysseus* (New York: Viking Press, 1965), 100–102. On the blurring of truth and fiction, see E. Gabba, "True History and False History in Classical Antiquity," *JRS* 71 (1981): 50–62.

111 There have been a number of studies that would contest the view that the *Contemplativa* is entirely or mostly fictional. E.g., J. E. Taylor and P. R. Davies, "The So-Called Therapeutai of *De vita contemplativa*: Identity and Character," *HTR* 91 (1998): 3–24; Beavis, "Philo's Therapeutai." For a nuanced understanding of the relationship between "truth" and rhetoric, see Taylor, *Jewish Women Philosophers*, 11–12.

work.[112] I am not convinced, however, that Plato's discussion of πλασθέντα μῦθον and ἀληθινὸν λόγον, firmly based on the criterion of historicity, speaks to actual genre divisions adopted by Plato and other authors. Plato argues that literary kinds must remain discrete, unmixed (ἀκρᾶτος), following the ideal (*Resp.* 3.397d).[113] Although this division works in theory, it is far from the practice that is found in antiquity.[114] Even in the *Timeaus* Plato does not rigidly keep truth and fiction apart, but reassigns labels—"And the city with its citizens which you described to us yesterday, as it were in a fable (μύθῳ), we will now transport into the realm of fact (τἀληθές)" (*Tim.* 26c–d)—based on what would furnish a satisfactory discourse, which in all cases is the greatest task (ὅπερ ἐν ἅπασι τοῖς τοιοῖσδε μέγιστον ἔργον, *Tim.* 26a).[115]

Nor do I think that the traditional genre assessment of *Contemplativa* as a moral philosophic treatise in the tradition of Aristotle crumbles if the historical Therapeutae community is not exactly as Philo depicted it to be.[116] This is not to dismiss the idea of historical veracity, but rather to claim that employing a rigid dichotomy of true or false does not allow for a nuanced discussion of how "truth," rhetoric, and argument worked in antiquity.

More important than either of the genre discussions by Plato or Aristotle is how genre was employed during the time of Philo. Although the works of Plato and Aristotle influenced authors and literary critics throughout the Hellenistic era, it is clear that the literary world in which Philo worked was different from classical Athens. Unfortunately, we have insufficient examples with which to compare Philo's *Contemplativa*. What we witness in the Hellenistic and early Roman eras is the blending of cultures and the willingness by authors to adapt established genres to accommodate present needs. Aristotle's ideas were perpetuated and developed by Theophrastus and other Peripatetics, which resulted in unique expressions and substantial debate over which was the best type of life (practical or theoretical).[117] These discussions are of a philosophical nature and do not address the issue of genre presentation.[118] Nevertheless, they are important, as discussions of philosophical ideals regularly

112 Engberg-Pedersen, "Philo's *De vita contemplativa*," 48–49.

113 Cf. *Resp.* 3.392d–394d, in which Plato identifies three divisions of literature (διήγησις οὖσα τυγχάνει ἢ γεγονόντων ἢ ὄντων ἢ μελλόντων).

114 For a more thorough discussion of genre mixing in antiquity, see Adams, *Genre*, 53–57.

115 Cf. Epictetus, *Disc.* 1.7.1–33; Horace, *Ars* 151.

116 I am not claiming that truth and history are unimportant to Aristotle or his followers; they are (e.g., *Eth. nic.* 1.6; 10.1, 7–8; contra poets, *Poet.* 9, 1451a38–1451b5), but this is not the sole criterion for determining genre participation. Cf. Adams, *Genre*, 27–31.

117 Cf. Cicero, *Att.* 2.16.3; *Leg.* 3.14. For discussion, see S. McConnell, *Philosophical Life in Cicero's Letters* (CCS; Cambridge: Cambridge University Press, 2014), 115–60. Moses is said to have practiced both, *Mos.* 1.48.

118 For Philo's perspective on the different types of lives, see V. Laurand, "La Contemplation chez Philon d'Alexandrie," in T. Bénatouïl and M. Bonazzi, eds., *Theoria, Praxis, and the Contemplative Life after Plato and Aristotle* (Leiden: Brill, 2012), 121–38.

draw upon historical examples; individuals that have embodied the different types of lives.

The closest example to Philo of a text depicting a specific, local people pursuing the contemplative life is Chaeremon of Alexandria's *On the Egyptian Priests*, which is preserved in an epitomized form by Porphyry (*Abst.* 4.6–8).[119] In this work, Chaeremon, a first-century CE stoic philosopher and *hierogrammateus*, is reported to have described the habits and practices of certain Egyptian priests who cloistered themselves away from society in order to pursue a life of contemplation. Due to its abridged nature we are not able to determine the extent to which Chaeremon's work parallels Philo's in terms of form and structure. However, it is clear that Philo was not alone in his desire to present members from his ethnic community as having attained the highest type of philosophical life.[120] That both a Jew and an Egyptian from Alexandria pursued the same goals suggests that the creation of philosophical works was a recognized way of engaging Greek readers in order to present one's ethnic group in the best possible light.

The similarities between Philo and Chaeremon bring us back to the question of subject matter and the presentation of groups. Both authors present their main examples in complementary terms and as possessing peak philosophical virtue. Both example communities are drawn from the local vicinity and are presented as actual groups of people. The major difference between Philo and Chaeremon, as far as we are able to determine, is that Chaeremon's *On the Egyptian Priests* is an independent essay, whereas Philo's *Contemplativa* presents itself as part of a larger work. This difference is important and suggests that, despite the clear similarities, they are not identical and should be viewed as two different ways of participating in this genre.[121]

This discussion highlights the fact that, regardless of one's perspective on the form of Philo's *Contemplativa*, it does not fit neatly into one literary category. If Engberg-Pedersen's proposal is accurate, then we witness two types of adaptation by Philo. First, Philo excludes a reference to the fictional nature of the group, the inclusion of which Engberg-Pedersen identified as a key component of πλασθέντα μῦθον. Second, if Philo is basing his work

119 Cf. also Jerome, *Jov.* 2.13. For the text and translation, see P. W. van der Horst, ed. and trans., *Chaeremon: Egyptian Priest and Stoic Philosopher; The Fragments, Collected and Translated with Explanatory Notes* (Leiden: Brill, 1984).

120 Drawing on common tropes in order to present an idealized group is not limited to Philo and Chaeremon, and is likely behind their presentation of their respected communities. For further discussion and examples, see I. Heinemann, "Therapeutae," *PW* 5a (1934): 2337–38.

121 Porphyry's pairing of Charemon with Josephus' discussion of the Essenes (4.11–14), as well as the Syrians (4.15), Persians (4.16), and the Indian gymnosophists (4.17–20), suggests that he also viewed these foreign sects similarly.

on "utopian fantasy," he omits a key feature of the genre: the distant nature of the community in discussion. The primary reason for this distance is the inability of the readers to discern whether what was said was true. It would not be difficult to determine if the "children of the sun" actually had split tongues, bendable bones, and amazing longevity if they were situated near Alexandria and not on a "very far-off island" (Diodorus Siculus, *Bibl.* 2.55–60, citing Iambulus). This genre depends on the framework of a distant voyage that takes the narrator beyond recognized civilization (cf. Herodotus, *Hist.* 3.116; Hist. Rech. 6.1–18.2). If Philo used this genre, then it is clear that he deviated from standard expectations. Philo's localized placement of the group (*Contempl.* 22–23) makes the Therapeutae accessible and, more importantly, verifiable.[122] This decision lends some credence to the view that the Therapeutae were a historical community, though it does not mean that every aspect of the work perfectly reflects the group's activities. Philo's *Contemplativa* is a highly rhetorical text in which he develops his arguments through a subtle blend of truth and selectivity.[123]

On the other hand, if *Contemplativa* participates in the genre of "moral philosophical treatise," then one has to explain the (possibly) fragmentary nature of the entire work. Engberg-Pedersen claims that "Philo only presented his work in the way suggested in the straightforward answer, whereas in fact it neither originated in a larger work nor belonged to the genre ostensibly suggested by Philo."[124] If the opening and closing paragraphs are literary fictions to frame Philo's discussion, then we see a specific adaptation of a literary form, in that his framing implies that Philo knew the accepted literary format and that he actively modeled his work to match it. As a result, Philo's potential innovation is that he did not fulfill this requirement of the genre, but adapted it by adopting deictic markers with no substance in order to accommodate his desire to write only one treatise on a particular type of life.

If, as the manuscript tradition informs us, *Contemplativa* was book 4 of the larger work *On Virtues* (to be distinguished from *De virtutibus*), then the question of Philo's framing in terms of βίοι become more prominent. We are told by Eusebius (*Hist. eccl.* 2.6.2) that book 1 of *On Virtues* was *Legatio ad Gaium* and that book 2 recounted the other atrocities in the reign of Gaius (*Hist. eccl.* 2.6.3), referred to as a παλινῳδία by Philo (*Legat.* 373).[125] We do not know

122 R. Kraemer, "Monastic Jewish Women in Greco-Roman Egypt: Philo Judaeus on the Therapeutrides," *Signs* 14 (1989): 347. The definition of a nome in *Contempl.* 21 implies that Philo's recipients are not living in Egypt.
123 Taylor, *Jewish Women Philosophers*, 8–11.
124 Engberg-Pedersen, "Philo's *De vita contemplativa*," 42.
125 This content overlaps with part of *In Flaccum*, though there is debate over the relatedness of these works. Cf. J. Morris, "The Jewish Philosopher Philo," in E. Schürer, *The History of the*

what the supposed content of book 3 was, but if the opening of *Contemplativa* is any indication, then it was a treatise on the Essenes and the "practical life" (πρακτικὸν . . . βίον).[126] This progression would make sense, as the practical life comes before the contemplative life (*Fug.* 36; *Praem.* 11). Similarly, book 5 is also a mystery, but it is thought to be an unknown conclusion.[127]

If this five-part configuration is the best way to understand Philo's *Contemplativa*, then we witness Philo incorporating a specific philosophical genre into a larger construction. This practice was not uncommon in antiquity, as certain smaller literary forms (e.g., letters, inscriptions) were regularly included in larger genres (e.g., history, biography). However, in so far as I am able to determine, we have no comparable example of this configuration of works extant from antiquity. The absence of comparators does not necessarily mean that Philo was unique in incorporating a treatise-sized example into a larger body of work. However, it does mean that *Contemplativa* represents a nonprototypical example of this genre. Moreover, if *Contemplativa* is to be formally associated with *Legatio ad Gaium*, as it appears that it was for a number of ancient readers, then it challenges the way that Engberg-Pedersen and others wish to define the historical genre in antiquity.[128] That a work could be composed of multiple genres is suggested by Philo in his description of the Pentateuch (*Praem.* 1; *Mos.* 2.45–48) and allows for the possibility of one of his works to be formed through participation in multiple literary forms.

It could be argued that Philo also adapts the traditional purpose of the text away from a theoretical discussion of an ideal life, to a defense of the Jewish people by presenting them in the best possible light to their Roman readers. In this case, the Therapeutae (and presumably the Essenes of the previous work) as a whole become a single, composite life that provides the biographical exemplar for its readers in their pursuit of virtue (cf. *Leg.* 1.57–58).[129] Philo clearly works within a tradition, one that he also acknowledges, but this does not hinder him from adapting this genre to meet his literary needs.[130] If one considers

---

Jewish People in the Age of Jesus Christ (175 BC–AD 135) (rev. and ed. G. Vermes et al.; 3 vols.; Edinburgh: T&T Clark, 1973–1987), 3.2.859–64.

126 Cf. Jerome (*Jov.* 2.14), who also claims that Philo wrote a treatise on the Essenes.

127 Taylor, *Jewish Women Philosophers*, 36–38.

128 For a good example of one who resists this possibility, see J. R. Royse, "The Works of Philo," in A. Kamesar, ed., *The Cambridge Companion to Philo* (Cambridge: Cambridge University Press, 2009), 52–53.

129 This idea arose in discussion with Joan Taylor at the First UK Philo Colloquium in Glasgow in July 2016. The idea of *Contemplativa* as *bios* has been developed recently by Elisa Uusimäki, who rightly highlights the biographical elements of *Contemplativa*, although does not argue that it participates in *bios*. Cf. E. Uusimäki, "Local and Global: Philo of Alexandria on the Philosophical Life of the Therapeutae," *Henoch* 40 (2018): 305–8.

130 For an ancient parallel of explicitly praising one's own sect, see Galen, *Lib. prop.* 19.51.

this work in light of Philo's lament in *Plant.* 159—that poets and historians of old tailored their works for the development of virtue while those of today only produce works of indulgence—this could account for the inclusion of one of Philo's so-called historical works (e.g., *Legatio ad Gaium*) into a larger work titled *On Virtues*.[131] More accurately, it might indicate that for Philo the traditional philosophical classification of *Virtues* is best understood when it is embodied by current exemplars who model how virtuous lives could be a present reality.

Josephus, *Against Apion*

Josephus is primarily known as a historian (see chapter 7), but his work *Against Apion*—a two-volume treatise defending the Jewish people from outsider accusations—participates in a different genre. This work, likely written in the mid- to late nineties CE, was not, to our knowledge, given a title by Josephus, but acquired one through the copying and reading of his text.[132] To date, some work has been done on the genre of *Apion*, and scholars recognize that the work is highly rhetorical and seeks to make a persuasive argument for the antiquity of the Jewish people and the value of their culture.

An early discussion of the genre of *Apion* was provided by Mason, who identifies shared formal features between *Against Apion* and *logos protreptikos*: the demonstration of the value of Jewish philosophy and the refutation of its detractors.[133] Mason suggests that the function of *Apion*, namely to encourage "conversion" to Jewish philosophy, is important for how the text is read. Mason rightly differentiates the function of a work from its genre, although these two concepts are related. Similarly, genre classifications at a macro level differ from the way that elements of the genre are employed or instantiated locally. In the case of *Apion*, both refutation and demonstration are at work, and

131 *Legatio* also contains a preface with philosophical ideas (1–7) as well as a number of pithy, proverbial sayings that either open or close a discussion (e.g., *Legat.* 14, 29, 39, 61, 67, 68, 69, etc.).

132 For a discussion with references, see J. M. G. Barclay, trans., *Flavius Josephus: Against Apion, Translation and Commentary* (Leiden: Brill, 2007), xxvi–xxx.

133 S. Mason, "The *Contra Apionem* in Social and Literary Context: An Invitation to Judean Philosophy," in L. H. Feldman and J. R. Levison, eds., *Josephus' "Contra Apionem": Studies in Its Character and Contexts with a Latin Concordance to the Portion Missing in Greek* (AGJU 34; Leiden: Brill, 1996), 187–228. This genre division is taken from D. E. Aune, "Romans as a *Logos Protreptikos*," in K. P. Donfried, ed., *The Romans Debate*, rev. and expanded ed. (Peabody, Mass.: Hendrickson, 1991), 278–96. Regarding the difficulty of creating a genre definition for *logoi protreptikoi*, see M. D. Jordan, "Ancient Philosophic Protreptic and the Problem of Persuasive Genres," *Rhetorica* 4 (1986): 330. For another rhetorical genre proposal, from which he has now moved away, see J. M. G. Barclay, "Josephus v. Apion: Analysis of an Argument," in S. Mason, ed., *Understanding Josephus: Seven Perspectives* (LSTS 32; Sheffield: Sheffield Academic Press, 1998), 194–221.

Mason highlights commonalities between *Apion* and other identified *protreptikoi*. Mason's claim, that *Apion* is "a streamlined, methodical essay" that uses historical material in service of positive and negative appeals, is accurate,[134] but he stops short of offering a specific genre classification.[135]

Josephus does not signal the genre of the work to the reader in the opening section (1.1–5), but asserts that he writes in response to those who doubt the antiquity of the Jewish people (1.2) and who spread lies because of malice (1.3; cf. 2.287–96).[136] Our best insight into the genre of *Apion* is *C. Ap.* 2.147, in which Josephus claims that he is not writing an encomium, but an apology (οὐ γὰρ ἐγκώμιον ἡμῶν αὐτῶν προειλόμην συγγράφειν, ἀλλὰ πολλὰ καὶ ψευδῆ κατηγορουμένοις ἡμῖν ταύτην ἀπολογίαν δικαιοτάτην). This literary distinction is common among ancient authors, who recognize the generic overlap of the two literary forms.[137] The language of apology is supplemented by regular use of κατηγορία language (e.g., 1.53; 2.4, 147–148, 258, 288), other legal terms (e.g., witness, slander, insult, etc.), and descriptions by Josephus of various charges leveled against the Jews.[138] This terminology is also present at the conclusion, in which Josephus claims that he has refuted (ἐξελέγχω) his detractors (2.296).[139] Such linguistic consistency creates a literary unity in which, despite the different parts of the work, a common theme and purpose can be identified.

134 For a detailed investigation of Josephus' refutation strategies, read primarily through the lens of Aristotle's *Rhetoric*, see J. W. van Henten and R. Abusch, "The Jews as Typhonians and Josephus' Strategy of Refutation in *Contra Apionem*," in L. H. Feldman and J. R. Levison, eds., *Josephus' "Contra Apionem": Studies in Its Character and Contexts with a Latin Concordance to the Portion Missing in Greek* (AGJU 34; Leiden: Brill, 1996), 295–308; Mason, "*Contra Apionem*," 209. Although stating that *Apion* is an apology, Shaye Cohen had earlier argued that *Apion* was also "an essay in historiography and historical criticism." Cf. S. J. D. Cohen, "History and Historiography in the *Against Apion* of Josephus," *History and Theory* 27 (1988): 1.

135 Mason, in personal correspondence (16–18 February 2018), nuanced his position in light of recent scholarship and developments in his own thinking, making it clear that it was not his intention to claim a specific genre for *Apion*, but to evaluate *Apion*'s relationship to later, Christian *protreptikoi* in light of the similarities in language, purpose, tone, and content. He concludes that his inability to differentiate Josephus and Christian authors suggests a literary relationship, but recognizes that other differences (e.g., structure, length, and occasion) make a genre claim less tenable.

136 When describing *Apion*, Josephus often uses general, non-genre-specifying terms: γραφή (2.147, 288), βιβλία (1.320; 2.1, 196), or λόγος (1.219; 2.144), although the latter is potentially useful (see below).

137 E.g., Josephus, *Ant.* 16.185; Demosthenes, *Cor.* 3–4; Isocrates, *Hel. end.* 14; Ps.-Dionysius of Halicarnassus, *Ars rhet.* 9.11; Theon, *Prog.* 112.

138 Examples of legal terms include μάρτυς/μαρτυρία (1.4, 59, 217, 219; 2.1, 288), βλασφημία (1.4, 59; 2.5, 32), and λοιδορία (1.3, 219; 2.4), with cognates. On the pairing of ἀπολογλια and κατηγορία, see Theon, *Prog.* 61; Nicolaus the Sophist, *Prog.* 4, 78.

139 Josephus' use of ἀντίρρησις at the opening of the second book (2.1–2) also supports the theme of refutation.

Scholars argue that the genre of *Against Apion* is that of apology, but what "apology" means with regard to genre has been disputed.[140] Some scholars have a loose definition that allows a broad range of texts to fall under the label of "apologetic."[141] Although this breadth may be useful for expressing one of the purposes of the work, it lacks genre efficacy; in essence, scholars move from using apology as a noun to employing it as an adjective. In contrast, the definition proposed by John Barclay has merit: an apology is "a) directly formulated against explicit accusations (legal charges or non-legal slurs), and b) directed towards observers (rather than 'insiders'), at least at the rhetorical level (the actual or intended audience is another matter)."[142] This definition, in light of the internal evidence above, strongly suggests that *Apion* participates in the genre of apology, although diversity of apologies in antiquity cautions against firm genre delimitations and the identification of Josephus' prototypical model(s).[143]

Pseudo-Clementine *Homilies* 4.7–6.25

The Pseudo-Clementine corpus consists of two works/versions, *Homilies* and *Recognitions*, which were originally written in Greek and whose final forms are dated to the fourth century CE.[144] These are Christian compositions, but some have argued that the fourth-century authors may have embedded earlier,

140 E.g., C. Gerber, *Ein Bild des Judentums für Nichtjuden von Flavius Josephus: Untersuchungen ze seiner Schrift Contra Apionum* (Leiden: Brill, 1997), 78–88; C. Gerber, "Des Josephus Apologie für das Judentum: Prolegomena zu einer Interpretation von C 2:145ff.," in J. U. Kalms and F. Siegert, eds., *Internationales Josephus-Kolloquium Brüssel 1998* (Münster: LIT Verlag, 1999), 251–69; Barclay, *Against Apion*, xxxiii–xxxvi. For a critique of a specific Alexandrian Jewish apology, see M. Goodman, "Josephus' Treatise *Against Apion*," in M. J. Edwards, M. Goodman, and S. Price, with C. Rowland, eds., *Apologetics in the Roman Empire: Pagans, Jews, and Christians* (Oxford: Oxford University Press, 1999), 47–50. For the range of apologetic works, see the other contributions in that volume.

141 For a challenge to the wide view of Jewish apologetics, see Tcherikover, "Jewish Apologetic Literature."

142 Barclay, *Against Apion*, xxxv. Cf. R. M. Grant, *Greek Apologists of the Second Century* (London: SCM Press, 1988), 9, who specifically associates apology with minority cultures.

143 J. M. G. Barclay, "Josephus' *Contra Apionem* as Jewish Apologetics," in A.-C. Jacobsen, J. Ulrich, and D. Brakke, eds., *Critique and Apologetics: Jews, Christians and Pagans in Antiquity* (ECCA; Frankfurt am Main: Peter Lang, 2009), 265–82.

144 The overlap between these two texts is best explained by the sharing of a common source ("Grundschrift" [G]), which is thought to be a composite work written in the third century. Cf. F. S. Jones, "The Pseudo-Clementines: A History of Research," *Second Century* 2 (1982): 1–33, 63–95; F. S. Jones, "The Pseudo-Clementines," in M. Jackson-McCabe, ed., *Jewish Christianity Reconsidered: Rethinking Ancient Groups and Texts* (Minneapolis: Fortress, 2007), 285–304; G. N. Stanton, "Evidence in the Pseudo-Clementic Writings for Jewish Believers in Jesus," in O. Skarsaune and R. Hvalvik, eds., *Jewish Believers in Jesus* (Peabody, Mass.: Hendrickson, 2008), 305–24. For the Greek text, see B. Rehm, ed., *Die Pseudoklementinen*, vol. 1, *Homilien* (3rd ed., updated by G. Strecker; GCS 42; Berlin: Akademie Verlag, 1992).

Jewish works. The most important for our discussion is *Hom.* 4.7–6.25.[145] In this section, Clement arrives in Tyre, having been sent by Peter, and learns from Berenice of the activities of Simon the Magician (4.1–5). Simon, however, leaves (4.6) and Clement meets Apion, a highly educated individual and follower of Simon, who challenges him to explain why he has abandoned his ancestral practices and adopted the faith of the "barbarians" (i.e., Jews, 4.7). In the remainder of the section, Clement uses his *paideia* (cf. *Hom.* 1.3) to show the folly of Greek education. He defends Jewish thought through a critique of Greek depictions of the "gods" and chastises the anti-Semite Apion and Greek intellectuals who justify acts of impiety as imitations of the gods and who exonerate the gods through allegorical interpretation (e.g., *Hom.* 4.16; "Encomium of Adultery," 5.9–19).[146]

The original independence of this passage is supported by specific differences from *Recognitions* and the rest of the *Homilies*, namely, the abrupt introduction and conclusion, the lack of narrative connections between the characters here and in the rest of the work, the autonomy of Clement, who acts apart from Peter (cf. *Hom.* 12.5; *Rec.* 7.5), the superior writing style, the larger number of *hapax legomena*, its deep engagement with Greek learning (although see *Rec.* 10.17–52), its pro-Jewish stance, and the lack of references to Christianity aligned with a preference for terms, such as God, law, piety, and monotheism (e.g., *Hom.* 4.7–8, 22, 24; 5.28).[147] These last features are important for the argument that *Hom.* 4.7–6.25 was originally a Jewish composition, although full confidence is not possible. The dating of the presumed original narrative has also generated discussion, with a majority of scholars dating it to the early second century, prior to 117 or 135 BCE (depending on the argued provenance), assuming that,

145 H. Waitz, *Die Pseudoklementinen: Homilien und Rekognitionen; Eine quellenkritische Untersuchung* (Leipzig: Hinrichs, 1904), 251–56 (a source, but not Jewish); G. Strecker, *Das Judenchristentum in den Pseudoklementinen* (2nd ed.; Berlin: Akademie Verlag, 1981); W. Adler, "Apion's 'Encomium of Adultery': A Jewish Satire of Greek Paideia in the Pseudo-Clementine *Homilies*," *HUCA* 64 (1993): 15–49 (from Alexandria); Paget, *Jews*, 427–92, who suggests a Syrian provenance.

146 For the argument that Apion in *Homilies* is the same Apion in Josephus' work, see J. Dillery, "Putting Him Back Together Again: Apion Historian, Apion Grammatikos," *CPhil* 98 (2003): 383–90.

147 Cf. Waitz, *Pseudoklementinen*, 252–54; Paget, *Jews*, 430–36. For parallels between *Hom.* 4.7–6.25 and 20.11–23, see Strecker, *Judenchristentum*, 80; Waitz, *Pseudoklementinen*, 31–32. For recent arguments for greater integration of *Hom.* 4–6 and for reading *Homilies* as a unity, see D. Côté, "Rhetoric and Jewish-Christianity: The Case of the Grammarian Apion in the Pseudo-Clementine *Homilies*," in P. Piovanelli and T. Burke, eds., *Rediscovering the Apocryphal Continent: New Perspectives on Early Christian and Late Antique Apocryphal Texts and Traditions* (WUNT 1.349; Tübingen: Mohr Siebeck, 2015), 369–90; B. De Vos, "The Role of the *Homilistic* Disputes with Appion," *VC* 73 (2019): 54–88. For a discussion of the issue of determining provenance, see Davila, *Provenance*, 44–45.

in the wake of the Trajanic and Hadrianic revolts, Jewish authors withdrew from engagement with Greek and Roman culture and stopped composing works in Greek.[148] The former view is now thoroughly undermined, as the rabbis and other Jewish intellectuals continued to engage in cultural dialogue.[149] The latter view is harder to evaluate, as little remains of Jewish compositions in the second century. This dearth could support the view of the cession of Jewish composition, but the argument from silence is deceptive, as it also allows us to reconstruct the period and interpret possible counterevidence in a way that aligns with established scholarly narratives. Although I agree with the arguments for a second-century dating of the Apion narrative, the lack of clear temporal indicators allows for the possibility of a mid- to late second-century date, with this text providing counterevidence to the cession argument.[150]

The author of *Hom.* 4.7–6.25 is clearly well educated, displaying substantial knowledge of Greek myths and philosophy.[151] The negative reaction to Greek education within the narrative, such as Clement's decrying it as a "dreadful fabrication of a wicked demon" (4.12.1), should not detract from the Greekness of the work. The topic of *paideia* is prominent in this narrative and signals to the reader an intentional engagement with Greek literary culture, both in the content of the work and in its genre participation. Regarding the genre of *Hom.* 4.7–6.25, or the Jewish source that gave rise to it, there have been few propositions. One of the most recent is by Bernard Pouderon, who argued that the Apion narrative and other passages (e.g., *Hom.* 2.20–21; 13.7; 20.22 and *Recognitions* parallels) were taken from a Jewish romance.[152] The difficulty is that, barring the "flashback" in *Hom.* 5, where Clement and Apion's past interaction is recounted, there are few novelistic elements in the Apion narrative. Furthermore, the novelistic features included in the *Homilies* and *Recognitions* more broadly could be a result of the Christian author adapting the Jewish source to its new literary setting.[153] This claim does not exclude the Clement-Apion work from participating in novel, but suggests that it was a secondary genre.

148 E.g., B. Pouderon, "Aux origines du Roman pseudo clémentin: Prototype païen, refonte judéo-héllénistique, remaniement chrétien," in F. S. Jones and S. C. Mimouni, eds., *Le judéo-christianisme dans tous ses états: Actes du Colloque de Jérusalem 6–10 juillet 1998* (Paris: Éditions du Cerf, 2001), 248–49.

149 E.g., R. Hildary, *Rabbis and Classical Rhetoric: Sophistic Education and Oratory in the Talmud and Midrash* (Cambridge: Cambridge University Press, 2018); Hezser, "Rabbis as Intellectuals."

150 See most recently, Paget, *Jews*, 383–425, 477–80.

151 E.g., *Hom.* 5.12–17, 22–24 (gods); 5.18 (philosophers).

152 B. Pouderon, "Flavius Clemens et le Proto-Clément juif du Roman pseudo-clémentin," *Apocrypha* 7 (1996): 63–97; Pouderon, "Aux origines du Roman pseudo clémentin." His position regarding the number of Jewish texts changes from two or more (1996) to one (2001).

153 Also recognized by Paget, *Jews*, 454–55.

Engagement with and reference to specific mythological tales, philosophical discussions, and rhetorical topics all evidence that the author of this section possessed a substantial knowledge of Greek literary culture. This view is deepened if one adopts the argument of William Adler, who posited that *Hom.* 4.7–6.25 draws from the tale of Antiochus, the prince of Stratonice, who fell madly in love with his stepmother and whose physician, Erasistratus, through deception, successfully persuaded Antiochus' father to give his wife to his son.[154] The twist in *Hom.* 4.7–6.25 is that Clement succeeds in getting Apion to undermine his own position by failing to see though the deception. The appropriation of this story, as well as its adaptation to undermine Greek education, represents a sophisticated use of humor and supports the view that the author drew on the genre of satire. The use of rhetorical theses in the debate reinforces our understanding of the author's education and fits with his participation in the genres of novel and philosophy, as both ancient novelists and philosophers regularly incorporated rhetorical elements in their compositions.[155] In *Hom.* 4.7–6.25 we see the author actively engage with multiple genres. By far the most prominent is that of philosophy, but it could be argued that the Apion narrative also participates in the genres of novel and satire. If the latter is correct, then we have a rare example of a Jewish author engaging with this genre. The likely second-century date places this work firmly in the Roman era and evidences Jewish engagement with a literary form that grew in prominence during the Roman era.

"Literary" Letters

Letters were prolific in antiquity, and scholars both ancient and modern have proposed interpretive criteria in order to classify them.[156] In this section we are not concerned with private letters that are everyday communications (e.g., Elephantine, Bar Kokhba).[157] Nor do we evaluate official letters, such as those sent by Jewish leaders to sections of the population, both in Judaea and in the diaspora (e.g., 2 Macc 1:1–10a; 1:10b–2:18; 4QMMT). Rather, we will focus on

154 Adler, "Apion's 'Encomium,'" 21–28. For the story see Appian, *Syrian Wars*, in *Appian: Greek Texts with Facing English Translation* (trans. H. White; LCL 4; Cambridge, Mass.: Harvard University Press, 1912–1913), 59–61; Valerius Maximus 5.7, ext. 1.

155 Cf. Theon, *Prog.* 120–128 (Spengel); Hermogenes, *Prog.* 24–26; Nicolaus the Sophist, *Prog.* 71–76; Aulus Gellius, *Noct. att.* 2.7.1; R. F. Hock, "The Rhetoric of Romance," in S. E. Porter, ed., *Handbook of Classical Rhetoric in the Hellenistic Period (330 B.C.–A.D. 400)* (Leiden: Brill, 2001), 445–65.

156 E.g., Ps.-Demetrius, Τύποι Ἐποστολικοί; Ps.-Libanius, Ἐπιστολιμαῖοι Χαρακτῆρες; Cicero, *Flac.* 37 (public and private letters); S. K. Stowers, *Letter Writing in Greco-Roman Antiquity* (LEC 5; Philadelphia: Westminster Press, 1986), 51–57; A. J. Malherbe, *Ancient Epistolary Theorists* (SBLSBS 19; Atlanta: Scholars Press, 1988); D. E. Aune, *The New Testament in Its Literary Environment* (LEC 8; Philadelphia: Westminster, 1987), 158–82.

157 For an excellent and comprehensive study on all types of Jewish letters, see Doering, *Ancient Jewish Letters*. For the Bar Kokhba letters, see M. O. Wise, *Language and Literacy in Roman Judaea: A Study of the Bar Kokhba Documents* (AYBRL; New Haven: Yale University Press, 2015).

compositions that, although adopting epistolary features, appear to go beyond the typical constraints of private or official letters.[158] The difference between a literary letter and other correspondence is not clear, and no firm division is possible or, more importantly, desirable.[159] As we will see, the letters found in the New Testament share formal features with private and official correspondence, but also have marked differences, raising the question of whether or not they are literary compositions.

Before turning to specific letters, we must address the issue of whether or not a letter can be viewed as a genre. Some scholars have argued that the letter is not a recognized genre (*Gattung*), literary form, or text type, but a more basic phenomenon of communication; because means of communication (e.g., book) cannot be associated with only one genre, nor does the letter function at that register, it is outwith the theoretical parameters of genre evaluation.[160] I see merit to this understanding of the letter and would broadly agree. Where the boundary between mode and genre blurs is in the category of literary letters. I am not arguing that every text that has come to be viewed as literature participates in the genre of literary letter. Mode of transmission, apart from other criteria (e.g., authorial intention), is not a sufficient criterion by which to establish a genre category or to adjudicate participants. However, some texts, although adopting certain features of the letter form, show an aspiration by the author for the wide dissemination of the work and an intentionality of seeing the composition go beyond the identified recipient(s). I would argue that these

158 The term "literary" is problematic, as it implies a certain elevation of writing style that a writer might not claim for him/herself and/or actively deny. Nevertheless, I will adopt this term in lieu of using a negative descriptor (i.e., nondocumentary, etc.). Stirewalt's "letter-essay" is a reasonable option, but it limits the type of work to nonnarrative. Cf. M. L. Stirewalt Jr., "The Form and Function of the Greek Letter-Essay," in K. P. Donfried, ed., *The Romans Debate* (rev. and expanded ed.; Edinburgh: T&T Clark, 1991), 147–48. By literary letters, I do not mean private or official letters embedded in a larger work (e.g., Josephus, *Ant.* 20.11–14; Acts 15:23–29) or those composed to expand a literary work (e.g., 1 Macc 10:3–8, 17–20, 25–45; Additions B and E to Esther), although the latter could be fruitfully discussed with respect to genre. Cf. Aune, *New Testament*, 169; P. A. Rosenmeyer, *Ancient Epistolary Fictions: The Letter in Greek Literature* (Cambridge: Cambridge University Press, 2004), 45–60, 133–68.

159 I am not looking to reproduce Deissmann's distinction between the letter (i.e., real correspondence between actual people in history) and epistle (i.e., a product of literary art). A. Deissmann, *Bible Studies* (trans. A. Grieve; Edinburgh: T&T Clark, 1901); A. Deissmann, *Light from the Ancient East: The New Testament Illustrated by Recently Discovered Texts of the Graeco-Roman World* (4th ed.; trans. L. R. M. Strachan; London: Hodder and Stoughton, 1927). For divisions of letters into broad categories (e.g., nonliterary/documentary, diplomatic/royal/imperial, and literary), see Aune, *New Testament*, 162–69; J. White, *Light from Ancient Letters* (Philadelphia: Fortress, 1986), 3–5; H.-J. Klauck, *Ancient Letters and the New Testament: A Guide to Context and Exegesis* (Waco: Baylor University Press, 2006), 68–71. Doty helpfully places letters on a spectrum of "more private" to "less private." W. G. Doty, *Letters in Primitive Christianity* (Philadelphia: Fortress, 1973), 5–8.

160 Doering, *Ancient Jewish Letters*, 18–25 (with references). For an attempt to define the letter, see Trapp, *Greek and Latin Letters*, 1.

texts could be viewed as participating in genre, especially when formal features found in other genres (e.g., narrative, dialogue, etc.) are activated within the text.

Ancient authors, most famously Artemon, who is cited by Demetrius, appear to support the view that the private letter was not a genre, likening it to speech and conversation: "Artemon, the one who edited Aristotle's letters, says that one ought to write letters the same way as dialogues; for a letter is similar to one side of a dialogue. He speaks the truth in this, but not all of it. For a letter ought to be slightly more formal than a dialogue, because a dialogue imitates speaking extemporaneously while a letter is written and sent as a gift in some way" (*Eloc.* 223–224).[161] Demetrius does not accept Artemon's perspective, challenging the direct equating of speech and letters; letters fall between speech and literary writing, rising above the former but not attaining the latter (so too Quintilian, *Inst.* 9.4.20). Their omission from literary classifications and genre discussions by Greek and Latin theorists suggests that, at best, they were not recognized as an important or suitable genre for comment.[162] However, the ancients recognized when a composition went beyond the expectations of a letter. In particular, ancient authors identified a few reasons for arguing that a letter had become a literary work: expansion of length (*macrologia*), crafting prosopopoeic speech, and the adoption of specific topics, such as philosophy and politics.[163] The most famous example is Plato's *Ep.* 7, which is not a philosophical treatise, but an autobiographical narrative of his trips to Sicily and a defense of his engagement with Dionysius, the tyrant of Syracuse.[164] The guise of giving counsel to Dion's friends, the addressees (351e–352a), pales in

161 See also Demetrius, *Eloc.* 223–24; Seneca, *Ep.* 38.1; 75.1; Quintilian, *Inst.* 9.4.19–20.

162 For instance, in outlining his reading program (*Inst.* 1.8.1–21; 10.1), Quintilian does not identify the letter as a literary category. However, Quintilian recognizes that both Demosthenes and Cicero wrote letters (*Inst.* 10.1.107) and cites Cicero's letters when their contents suit his argument (e.g., *Inst.* 3.8.41; 8.3.6; 8.6.20). The quality of Cicero's letters was admired in antiquity (e.g., Pliny the Younger, *Ep.* 9.2.2). This absence in Quintilian's discussion is not firm evidence that the letter was not considered a genre, as genres of lesser prestige (e.g., epigram, fable, novel, mime, etc.) are also omitted. For a discussion of the usefulness of Quintilian, and his limitations for genre discussions, see M. Citroni, "Quintilian and the Perception of the System of Poetic Genres in the Flavian Age," in R. R. Nauta, H. van Dam, and H. Smolenaars, eds., *Flavian Poetry* (MneSup 270; Leiden: Brill, 2005), 1–19.

163 Quintilian, *Inst.* 9.4.19; Demetrius, *Eloc.* 230, citing a lost treatise of Aristotle (fr. 670, V. Rose). E.g., Diogenes Laertius, *Vit.* 10.35–83, 84–116, 122–135. Diogenes Laertius, *Vit.* 6.101, identifies Menippus of Gadara as writing letters "artificially composed as if by a god" (Ἐπιστολαὶ κεκομψευμέναι ἀπὸ τῶν θεῶν προσώπου). These changes are identified by Fowler as means by which genres develop (*Kinds of Literature*, 170–78). In the third century CE, Philostratus (*De epistolis*) argues that letters have specific forms and styles, and he ranks those who have written letters, suggesting a change in perspective on letters.

164 See also the *Martyrdom of Polycarp*, which is a narrative of the bishop's death encased in epistolary opening and closing.

comparison to Plato's need to defend himself against false narratives (352a). Letters written in verse (e.g., Pindar, *Pyth.* 2, 3; *Isth.* 2; Theocritus, *Id.* 11, 13, 28) also challenge firm literary boundaries, creatively adapting aspects of the epistle (e.g., distance) for the exposition of a specific topic.[165]

Demetrius (*Eloc.* 228, 231) distinguishes literary letters, such as those by Thucydides, Plato, and Aristotle, from "true" letters, as he claims the former are more like treatises with initial letter openings and the latter are shorter and grounded in details of friendship.[166] In particular, Demetrius argues that philosophical discussions (proverbs excepted) are out of place in letters, implying that works that employed epistolary features but treated philosophical topics were not viewed only as letters, but as possibly participating in multiple genres, and should be classified differently.[167] In Egypt, the tradition of writing letters that engage in satire and have narrative elements, including fables, has a long history.[168] These examples and discussions reinforce the idea that certain compositions transcended the letter as mode of communication and were viewed as participating in genre.

New Testament Letters

By ancient criteria the New Testament letters were certainly viewed as correspondence, but would they have been considered "literary"? In what follows, we will look at Jewish letters, including those collected in the New Testament, and discuss two topics: (1) if the letters are "literary," and so fit within our discussion of genre, and (2) identify possible Jewish and Greek influences.

Paul's Letters

Thirteen letters are attributed to Paul in the New Testament, representing the oldest surviving Christian texts.[169] Paul was a Jew from Tarsus (Acts 9:11), who was initially hostile to Jesus' followers prior to his revelatory experience

165 A similar practice of narratival distance creation is seen in LA 1–8. Open letters, such as Ovid's *Epistulae ex Ponto* and *Tristia*, also stretch the form and function of letters. For a thought experiment on how Cicero's *De officiis* could be viewed as a letter, see R. K. Gibson and A. D. Morrison, "Introduction: What Is a Letter?" in R. Morello and A. D. Morrison, eds., *Ancient Letters: Classical and Late Antique Epistolography* (Oxford: Oxford University Press, 2007), 9–13.

166 Cf. Eusebius, *Hist. eccl.* 7.26.3. Gregory Nazianzen (*Ep.* 51.2) states that length of letters is determined by need (ἔστι δὲ μέτρον τῶν ἐπιστολῶν, ἡ χρεία).

167 Demetrius, *Eloc.* 232; cf. Julius Victor, *Rhet.* 27; Cicero, *Fam.* 2.4.1; Quintilian, *Inst.* 9.4.20.

168 E. Wente, *Letters from Ancient Egypt* (Atlanta: SBL, 1990), 66. See also the votive letter, Berlin Museum 12845, which includes the fable of the swallow and the sea within a letter.

169 Romans, 1 and 2 Corinthians, Galatians, Ephesians, Philippians, Colossians, 1 and 2 Thessalonians, 1 and 2 Timothy, Titus, and Philemon. For the discussion of authorship, see J. D. G. Dunn, ed., *The Cambridge Companion to St. Paul* (Cambridge: Cambridge University Press, 2003), *passim*. For the time line of Paul's letter compositions, with comparisons, see C. Roetzel,

(Acts 9:1–20; Gal 1:13–17).[170] His letters, which are written in koine Greek, evidence a Greek education, although his level of attainment is debated.[171] Paul was clearly aware of Greek epistolary practice, as all of his letters open and close with standard epistolary features.[172] Nevertheless, the way he opens his letters, χάρις ὑμῖν καὶ εἰρήνη (with expansions), is distinctive.[173] Although this has been viewed as a combination of the standard Greek opening of χαίρειν and the Hebrew greeting of *shalom* (שלום), it is more likely an adaptation (perhaps originally) by Paul of established Jewish epistolary greetings, framed by a specific christological understanding (i.e., coming from God the Father *and* the Lord Jesus Christ).[174] Certain letters have expanded openings in which Paul identifies specific themes that will be subsequently unpacked (e.g., Rom 1:1–7; Gal 1:1–5; Titus 1:1–5). The use of expanded introductions that foreshadow themes and topics indicates the work's unity and cohesion, both of which are important components of literary letters.[175]

The view that these letters are from Paul is not entirely accurate, as almost all of them (with the notable exceptions of Romans and Ephesians) identify multiple coaddressors (e.g., Timothy, Silas, Sosthenes).[176] Having multiple senders is uncommon in private letters, but is found more commonly in official letters.[177] The communal address of the letters—written to a group of

Paul: The Man and the Myth (Minneapolis: Fortress, 1999), 178–83. For earlier dates, see D. A. Campbell, *Framing Paul: An Epistolary Biography* (Grand Rapids: Eerdmans, 2014), 404–11.

170 On the relationship between Paul and Acts, see S. A. Adams, "How Should We Reconstruct the Historical Paul? Review Essay of Thomas Phillips' *Paul, His Letters, and Acts*," *Journal for the Study of Paul and His Letters* 1 (2011): 93–100.

171 Paul's Greek is more sophisticated than that found in private letters, yet his syntax still lacks the hypotactic or periodic style expected from a polished literary work. Paul's statement that he did manual labor (Acts 20:34; 1 Cor 4:12) and had a trade (Acts 18:3) potentially challenges the view that he received a full rhetorical education. Paul's Jewish/Hebrew education is suggested in Acts 22:3 and 26:4, but is not widely held by scholars. For more discussion, see Stowers, *Letter Writing*, 25; R. S. Schellenberg, *Rethinking Paul's Rhetorical Education: Comparative Rhetoric and 2 Corinthians 10–13* (ECL 10; Atlanta: SBL, 2013).

172 See S. E. Porter and S. A. Adams, eds., *Paul and the Ancient Letter Form* (PAST 6; Leiden: Brill, 2010); J. A. D. Weima, *Paul the Letter Writer: An Introduction to Epistolary Analysis* (Grand Rapids: Baker Academic, 2016).

173 Rom 1:7; 1 Cor 1:3; 2 Cor 1:2; Gal 1:3; Eph 1:2; Col 1:2; 1 Thess 1:1; 2 Thess 1:2; Phlm 3.

174 E.g., 2 Bar. 78:2. Cf. Doering, *Ancient Jewish Letters*, 406–15. The phrase "grace and peace" was recognized in antiquity as being Jewish (Tertullian, *Marc.* 5.5.1). For claims of Jewish epistolary influence on Paul, see I. Taatz, *Frühjüdische Briefe: Die paulinischen Briefe im Rahmen der offiziellen religiösen Briefe des Frühjudentums* (NTOA 16; Göttingen: Vandenhoeck & Ruprecht, 1991), 111–14.

175 E.g., Stirewalt, "Greek Letter-Essay," 156–59.

176 This does not address the issue of Paul's use of amanuenses (e.g., Rom 16:22). Cf. E. R. Richards, *Paul and First-Century Letter Writing: Secretaries, Composition and Collection* (Downers Grove: IVP, 2004), 59–93.

177 Adams, "Letter Opening," 40–44. Cf. M. L. Stirewalt Jr., *Paul, the Letter Writer* (Grand Rapids: Eerdmans, 2003), 25–55; Klauck, *Ancient Letters*, 78.

believers (τοῖς ἁγίοις or ἐκκλησία) in a particular city or region—also distinguishes Paul's letters from private correspondence, aligning them more closely with public documents.[178] In his address Paul does not employ diaspora or "exile" terminology, which is a prominent feature of official Jewish letters in the Hellenistic and Roman eras.[179] This absence limits the explicit connection with certain Jewish letters and suggests that Paul did not view these letters as fully prototypical. On the other hand, the use of a thanksgiving formula at the beginning of the letter, in which the addressor gives thanks (εὐχαριστῶ) to God for the addressees, is not often found in Greek correspondence but could be understood as being related to Jewish epistolary eulogies.[180] Neither letter practice provides a clear model for Paul's thanksgiving, which differs syntactically, semantically, and in christological outlook. Both traditions appear to be important for Paul and were likely creatively used by him in his compositions.

The size and topics of Paul's letters are relevant for our discussion of literariness. First Corinthians and Romans are about seven thousand words each, and even Paul's modestly sized letters (e.g., Philippians, 1 Thessalonians) are well above the average size of ancient letters.[181] The letters also have extended theological discussions and so could be viewed in light of philosophical letters.[182] Paul's letters, however, are not timeless compositions, but are grounded in specific temporal, geographical, religious, and political contexts. This historical rootedness is found in all of Paul's letters, as he often has a close relationship with his addressees (signaled through the greetings) and is writing to address specific theological, communal, or pastoral issues that he heard about through other people (1 Cor 1:11; 2 Cor 7:6–7; 1 Thess 3:6) or from letters that he received (1 Cor 7:1).[183] This combination is best seen in the transition from the

178 The notable exception is 2 Timothy (and possibly 1 Timothy and Titus), which is private correspondence. At this point they are not fully public, having been sent to a specific community, but the larger readership no doubt facilitated their later dissemination with the wider Christian social network.

179 Doering, *Ancient Jewish Letters*, 405.

180 See P. Schubert, *Form and Function of the Pauline Thanksgiving* (BZNW 20; Berlin: Töpelmann, 1939), 10–39; Doering, *Ancient Jewish Letters*, 417–21, citing 2 Macc 1:2–5, 11, Eupolemus (Eusebius, *Praep. ev.* 9.34.1), and 2 Bar. 78:3–7.

181 E. R. Richards, *The Secretary in the Letters of St. Paul* (WUNT 2.42; Tübingen: Mohr Siebeck, 1991), 213.

182 In particular, the letter body of Romans dedicates substantial space to theological discussions: God's righteousness and the world's sinfulness (1:18–4:25), how they relate to the life of faith (5:1–8:39), and the destiny of the people of Israel (9:1–11:36).

183 Paul's use of remembrance language is not hypothetical or a trope, but draws on historical events experienced with his addressees (e.g., 1 Cor 12:1–3; 1 Thess 2:1–2).

discussion of theological issues to practical, paraenetic material in which Paul informs his readers how the Christian life is to be outworked.[184]

Another consideration for determining literary classification is discerning the intended audience. That Paul's letters were subsequently viewed as literature, and so brought together into a collection, does not specifically address the question of authorial intention.[185] Occasionally Paul specifies what the community should do with the letter once they had received it. In 1 Thess 5:27, Paul commands a rereading of the letter "to all the brothers," a feature not prominent in private correspondence and indicating an expanded readership.[186] The sending of a letter "to all God's beloved in Rome" (Rom 1:7; in Rome there were multiple house churches, cf. Rom 16:5), the extension of the letter "to all Achaia" (2 Cor 1:1), and the address in Gal 1:2 to an entire region (Galatia) would have resulted in the publication of the text through readings in multiple locations and likely would have necessitated making several copies.[187] The sharing of letters is also encouraged in Col 4:16 (cf. Mart. Pol. 20:1), thus minimizing (to some extent) the work's temporal and geographic boundedness.[188] This prescribed action suggests that Paul thought that his letters were broadly applicable and so should be widely read throughout Christian communities, implying a level of intention that approaches that of literary publication.

In sum, Paul appears to be influenced by both Jewish and Greek epistolary practices and is able to combine features of each of them into a unified work that became a prototype for subsequent Christian epistolographers. Paul's letters are distinct in antiquity, not only for their size, but also for the way that theological content is paired with situationally grounded, paraenetic material. Paul's formulaic expressions have parallels with both Jewish

184 This shift is reinforced by the switch from predominantly third-person indicatives to second-person imperatives (e.g., Rom 12:1; 1 Thess 4:1; Eph 4:1). The pairing of teaching and behavioral response also happens at the localized level (e.g., Rom 13:11–14; 1 Cor 5:1–13).

185 This statement is based on the assumption that Paul did not collect his letters for publication. Cf. D. Trobisch, *Die Entstehung der Paulusbriefsammlung: Studien zu den Anfängen christlicher Publizistik* (NTOA 10; Göttingen: Vandenhoeck & Ruprecht, 1989), 89–104. The reception of the letters, especially their early collection, as is evidenced by codex P^{46} and 2 Pet 3:15–16, supports the view that rereading Paul's letters was practiced in the early church and that they were viewed as valuable. Cf. H. Y. Gamble, *Books and Readers in the Early Church: A History of Early Christian Texts* (New Haven: Yale University Press, 1995), 96–100.

186 It is ambiguous how encompassing "all the brothers" is meant to be; is it only the brothers in Thessalonica or those more broadly? Cf. Eusebius, *Hist. eccl.* 4.23.11.

187 The possible circular letter of Ephesus would also support the wide dissemination of Pauline letters.

188 The debate over the authorship of Colossians undermines the force of this evidence. Even if Colossians is not written by Paul, this passage implies that the author thought that this practice would be recognized as Pauline. For discussion of authorship, see Ehrman, *Forgery and Counterforgery*, 172–77.

and Greek practices, but are regularly adapted and expanded to facilitate his purpose.

Because Paul's letters are clearly grounded in a historical context, there is a case for them not to be considered "literary."[189] This view is tempered by Paul's extended theological discussions and apparent desire for wide distribution. These features stand in tension and could be profitably understood through prototype genre theory, which allows a work to participate in multiple genres, in this case letter and treatise, embodying elements of each. The unique aspect in this discussion is the debate over whether a letter is a genre or a mode of communication, and, if the latter, whether or not it disqualifies the adoption of prototype theory. If letters were strictly modal, then prototype theory, which focuses on genre, may be inappropriate. The challenge is that, although a means of communication, the letter form was sufficiently established to allow for authorial appropriation and creative expansion and adaptation. Accordingly, the form of the letter appears to function at the level of genre in the mind of some ancients and so would not be limited to communicative mode. The inability of scholars to classify Paul's letters and the examples of other literary letters in antiquity suggests that a strict dichotomy between mode and genre should not be rigidly adopted for the letter and that in antiquity the letter could be both a mode of communication and a recognized literary form.

Other New Testament Letters

The so-called Catholic Epistles (i.e., Hebrews, James, 1 and 2 Peter, 1, 2, and 3 John, and Jude) are similar to Paul's letters in that they are written to Christ followers, but are generally shorter and adopt slightly different forms. These texts lack many of the personal elements prevalent in Paul's letters, although most have a specific addressee. For example, both 1 Peter (1:1) and James (1:1) are addressed to communities in the diaspora.[190] In addition to the theological significance of appropriating a Jewish category as a metaphor for Christ followers, the use of διασπορά language is significant for this study because it signals participation in what scholars have labeled the "diaspora letter" form.[191] This letter type is characterized by authoritative address by Jews living in Jerusalem (e.g., Jeremiah, Baruch, Jewish leaders) to Jews living abroad, emphasizing both the unity of the Jewish people (regardless of location) and

189 Within the Pauline corpus different letters would have a greater or lesser claim to literary status. In particular, Romans would be the best candidate to be viewed as literary, whereas Philemon is closest to private correspondence.

190 For James, it is the twelve tribes, and for 1 Peter it is the chosen exiles of the diaspora in Pontus, Galatia, Cappadocia, Asia, and Bithynia.

191 Doering, *Ancient Jewish Letters*, 430–34 (with references).

the need of those in the diaspora to adhere to the rules and customs outlined in the correspondence.[192]

The anonymous book of Hebrews differs strongly from the above New Testament letters because it does not have a typical epistolary opening, thus lacking an explicit sender and addressee.[193] Rather, the text begins with a statement about the way that God had spoken to his people through the person of Jesus (Heb 1:1–5). Of importance is the way that the author uses first-person plural pronouns (e.g., ἡμῖν, 1:2; ἡμᾶς, 2:1; ἡμεῖς, 2:3) to signal his connection with his readers. This is reinforced at the end of the work when the author closes by stating that he has written a letter in few words (γὰρ διὰ βραχέων ἐπέστειλα ὑμῖν, Heb 13:22). The sermonic nature of the work has led scholars to question whether or not Hebrews was originally a letter, or if an epistolary closing was appended at a later point.[194] This dichotomous approach to Hebrews typifies the inherent problems of previous approaches to genre by attempting to force a work into one category. A prototype approach allows for both epistolary and sermonic features, recognizing that the author could have been participating in both genres and possibly even more (e.g., deliberative speech of Greco-Roman rhetoric). As a result, Hebrews represents a distinct literary expression and displays the relationship and flexibility of literary forms that have strong communicative elements.

Jewish Expanded Letters (Baruch, Epistle of Jeremiah, 1 Enoch, 2 Baruch)

The expansion of the letter is also witnessed in two Jewish literary compositions from the Hellenistic era: Baruch and the Epistle of Jeremiah.[195] The opening of Baruch (1:1–13) provides the narrative setting and identifies specific

192 For the paraenetic view of James, see L. L. Cheung, *The Genre, Composition and Hermeneutics of the Epistle of James* (PBM; Milton Keynes: Paternoster, 2003), 15–52.

193 Cf. also 1 John. The closing implies that the letter is sent from Italy (Heb 13:24). On the issues of dating and authorship, see P. Ellingworth, *The Epistle to the Hebrews: A Commentary on the Greek Text* (NIGTC; Grand Rapids: Eerdmans, 1993), 3–33; H. W. Attridge, *The Epistle to the Hebrews: A Commentary on the Epistle to the Hebrews* (Hermeneia; Philadelphia: Fortress, 1989), 1–9.

194 Cf. Ellingworth, *Hebrews*, 61. Viewing Hebrews as deliberative speech raises the text's possible relation to the rhetorical handbooks; cf. M. W. Martin and J. A. Whitlark, *Inventing Hebrews: Design and Purpose in Ancient Rhetoric* (SNTSMS 171; Cambridge: Cambridge University Press, 2018). For Hebrews as Jewish homily and midrash, see D. Boyarin, "Midrash in Hebrews / Hebrews as Midrash," in G. Gelardini and H. W. Attridge, eds., *Hebrews in Context* (AJEC 91; Leiden: Brill, 2016), 15–30.

195 On the debate over the original language of both works, see S. A. Adams, *Baruch and The Epistle of Jeremiah: A Commentary on the Greek Text of Codex Vaticanus* (SEPT; Leiden: Brill, 2014), 11–12, 150–51. For dating see 4–6 and 148–49, respectively. Cf. C. A. Moore, "Towards the Dating of the Book of Baruch," *CBQ* 36 (1974): 312–20. Very few letters are preserved in rabbinic literature. See D. Pardee, *Handbook of Ancient Hebrew Letters* (SBLSBS 15; Chico: Scholars Press, 1982), 183–211; P. S. Alexander, "Epistolary Literature," in M. E. Stone, ed., *Jewish Writings of the Second Temple Period: Apocrypha, Pseudepigrapha, Qumran Sectarian Writings, Philo, Josephus* (CRINT 2.2; Philadelphia: Fortress, 1984), 579–96.

elements that are being sent from Babylon to those living in Jerusalem (i.e., silver, a book written by Baruch, temple vessels). However, the body of the work (1:14–5:9) is presented as the content of the book (cf. 1:1), and the author does not return to the narrative frame. The introductory section, therefore, creates a loose epistolary macro-narrative, but does not fully participate in the letter genre. In contrast, the Epistle of Jeremiah has as much more explicit epistolary opening—"A copy of the epistle which Jeremiah sent to those . . ." (*praef.*)—but likewise lacks any subsequent letter elements in its polemic against and satirical depiction of idolatry. Both texts use formal features to signal a letter at the opening of their text, but quickly drop the facade in the main body of work. These examples could indicate the erosion of firm epistolary traditions for Jewish authors and the freedom for authors to engage in literary creativity.

More developed is the so-called "Epistle of Enoch" (1 En. 92:1–105:2), a second-century BCE Aramaic composition that begins with a superscription in which Enoch is said to have written to all his sons (92:1; cf. 4Q212 1.ii.22).[196] The content of this missive is diverse (woes, exhortations, apocalypse of weeks, etc.), but minimally conforms to epistolary structures through the opening and closing sections.[197] Specific epistolary terms are lacking, and the author employs the language of "saying" (93:1).[198] However, the sending of a written text over a distance (both geographical and temporal) allows for the use of letter terminology when describing this section and functions as the narrative frame for Enoch to communicate his visions to his descendants.[199] As a result, the Epistle of Enoch provides an example of the ways that the letter could be creatively employed within a larger narrative frame and evidence the expansion of the letter within Jewish literature.

Another example of Jewish literary letters is the Epistle of Baruch (2 Bar. 78:1–87:1), which was written by a Jewish author, possibly in Greek (2 Bar. 1:1), in the early second century CE. [200] Similar to 1 Enoch, the letter is integrated into a larger work and has an important role in disseminating revelatory

196 L. Stuckenbruck, *1 Enoch 91–108* (CEJL; Berlin: De Gruyter, 2008), 60–62; Doering, *Ancient Jewish Letters*, 174–83.

197 For example, the peace-wish and command to rejoice in 105:2 function as the letter closing. Cf. G. W. E. Nickelsburg, *1 Enoch 1: A Commentary on the Book of 1 Enoch, Chapters 1–36; 81–108* (Hermeneia; Minneapolis: Fortress, 2001), 431, 535.

198 Certain manuscripts use book language in lieu of "saying," providing a parallel with Baruch. Cf. Nickelsburg, *1 Enoch 1*, 435.

199 The use of stone tablets (93:2) also allows the text to transcend the letter form by participating in a wider Jewish literary motif. Cf. Stuckenbruck, *1 Enoch*, 83. However, Paul in 2 Cor 3:2–3 mentions stone tablets in the context of letter sending.

200 Davila, *Provenance*, 128–30. P.-M. Bogaert, *Apocalypse de Baruch: Introduction, tradition du Syriaque et commentaire* (SC 144 and 145; Paris: Éditions du Cerf, 1969), 1.353–80; Taatz, *Frühjüdische Briefe*, 59–76. For the preserved Syriac text, see D. M. Gurtner, ed. and trans., *Second Baruch: A Critical Edition of the Syriac Text, with Greek and Latin Fragments, English Translation, Introduction, and Concordances* (JCTCRS; London: T&T Clark, 2009).

material to the intended recipients, specified as the lost nine and one-half tribes (77:19).[201] This letter opens with a blessing, "mercy/grace and peace be with you" (2 Bar. 78:2), which is thought to be Jewish in origin.[202] The double-wish form, its address to a larger community, and the adoption of fictive kinship language ("brothers," 78:3) parallel Pauline and other New Testament letters, suggesting that these authors were participating in recognized epistolary practices.[203] The letter body begins by recounting the destruction of Jerusalem and the Temple (2 Bar. 79–80), and is followed by words of comfort (81–83), Baruch's testimony (84), and the role of the law in the final judgment (85).[204] The communal nature of the letter is reinforced in the closing, in which the addressees are told to read the letter in their assemblies, especially on fast days (86:1–3; cf. Bar 1:14).[205] This repeated reading practice signals that the content of the letter is not limited to the addressees' immediate situation, but has enduring value. The mention of Baruch's death in 78:5, along with his testimony in 84:1–11, also represent the blending of testimony with epistolography and the willingness of the author to expand the letter form and incorporate elements that advanced the narrative thrust.[206] The author also participates in the development of Jeremianic epistolography and the close association between specific characters (especially Baruch and Jeremiah) and letter writing.[207]

That the two longest embedded letters are found within Jewish apocalyptic literature supports the view that the letter was adaptable, easily incorporated within literary works, and of specific use for authors writing apocalypses.[208] However, even within these works there is an expansion of the form and function of the letter to fit the wider narrative. Accordingly, these texts provide

201 For an argument for the unity of the letter (2 Bar. 78–87) and the apocalypse (2 Bar. 1–77), see Bogaert, *Apocalypse de Baruch*, 1.77–78; M. F. Whitters, *The Epistle of Second Baruch: A Study in Form and Message* (JSPSup 42; Sheffield: Sheffield Academic Press, 2003), 64.

202 ἔλεος καὶ εἰρήνη: 1 Tim 1:2; 2 John 3; Jude 2; χάρις ὑμῖν καὶ εἰρήνη: Rom 1:7; 1 Cor 1:3; 2 Cor 1:2.

203 The possible thanksgiving at 78:3 (although here the one remembering is God, not the sender) and the extended introduction in which major themes of the letter are introduced (78:3–7) also parallel the certain proems in Pauline letters (Rom 1:8–17; 1 Cor 1:4–9). Klauck, *Ancient Letters*, 277. Cf. Jer 29:1–5.

204 Doering, *Ancient Jewish Letters*, 249–51.

205 The unity of the nine and one-half tribes with the other tribes is reinforced, not only by their common suffering (1:2–5; 78:4), but also by Baruch's sending both communities letters with similar content (77:19; 85:6). Cf. Col 4:16.

206 Klauck (*Ancient Letters*, 279) notes parallels with 2 Timothy and its blending of hortatory, instruction, consolation, and testimony.

207 Cf. 4QapocrJer C[d] (= 4Q389).

208 See also Rev 2:1–3:22, in which the seer sends letters to the angels of the seven churches to reveal to them a divine message.

good examples of how Jewish authors (writing in Greek, Hebrew, and Aramaic) adapted the letter to fit their compositional needs.

Summary

The lack of determinative features (beyond epistolary openings) results in a high degree of flexibility, allowing authors to write with freedom and creativity. The diversity of letter types in the New Testament is a result of the high variability within the letter form, but a consistent element is authorial expansion (i.e., *macrologia*). The letter form is highly adaptable, and, as is shown by its appropriation by the ancients, is not strictly limited to a mode of communication, but was recognized as a literary form that could be adopted and adapted for specific purposes. The question of whether or not the New Testament letters transcend mode and participate in genre is still open. No letter in the New Testament fully presents itself as literary, and there is good reason to see them as participating in both categories.

A different view could be held for the other Jewish letters discussed. In the cases of 2 Baruch and 1 Enoch, the embedding of an extended letter within a larger literary work (apocalypse) allowed the letter to take on a new dimension, specifically advancing the larger narrative of the work. As a result, the letter becomes an additional literary element, creating explicit ties between disparate literary forms, and goes beyond the restrictions typically imposed on it.

Conclusion

The texts studied in this chapter evidence a conscious participation in philosophy genres by Jewish authors. Many of these authors use philosophic topics to speak to the enduring relation of Jewish and Greek cultures, promoting Jewish antiquity and intellectual sophistication. This goal is accomplished by composing works that participate not only in philosophical genres, but also in other compatible literary forms, such as narrative and letters. As a result, the texts discussed in this chapter resist being defined by one genre. Rather, viewing these compositions as interacting with and being modeled on multiple literary prototypes coming from multiple cultures highlights their unique features and allows for a multilayered reading.

6

Jewish Novelists

Scholars have struggled to determine the genre of novel in the Hellenistic and early Roman eras.[1] Few novels from antiquity are extant, and traditionally the study of Greek novels has focused primarily on the "big five."[2] However, over the past century, engagement with fragmentary and marginal texts has undermined the neat categories and chronology advanced earlier, and scholars now agree that a greater diversity and number of novels existed and that they were read by a wide range of people.[3]

Ancient novels have come to be regarded as fruitful media for the study of race, class, gender, and the processes of "identity-building" at the fringes

1 A number of scholars have posited that the novel was not a recognized genre in antiquity, primarily based on the lack of explicit discussion. This omission is problematic, but it does not *a priori* mean its absence in antiquity. Cf. D. Selden, "Genre of Genre," in J. Tatum, ed., *The Search for the Ancient Novel* (Baltimore: Johns Hopkins University Press, 1994), 39–64, especially 57 n. 81; Farrell, "Classical Genre," 391–92. Cf. S. A. Nimis, "The Novel," in G. Boys-Stones, B. Graziosi, and P. Vasunia, eds., *Oxford Handbook of Hellenic Studies* (Oxford: Oxford University Press, 2009), 617–27: "Heterogeneity may be the only common thread" (p. 617).

2 Chariton, *Chaereas and Callirhoe*; Xenophon of Ephesus, *An Ephesian Tale*; Achilles Tatius, *Leucippe and Clitophon*; Longus, *Daphnis and Chloe*; Heliodorus, *An Ethiopian Tale*. Other extant Greek novels include *Alexander Romance* and Lucian, *True Story*. Two Latin novels are also extant (Petronius, *Satyricon*; Apuleius, *Metamorphoses*), and the similarities they have with their Greek counterparts blur any clear differentiation between the two groups.

3 E.g., E. Rohde, *Der griechische Roman und seine Vorläufer* (4th ed.; Hildesheim: Olms, 1876). For a collection of Greek novel fragments, see S. A. Stephens and J. J. Winkler, eds. and trans., *Ancient Greek Novels: The Fragments; Introduction, Text, Translations, and Commentary* (Princeton: Princeton University Press, 1995). Cf. R. L. Hunter, "Ancient Readers," in T. Whitmarsh, ed., *The Cambridge Companion to the Greek and Roman Novel* (Cambridge: Cambridge University Press, 2008), 261–71. For an argument on the use of the term "novel" despite its lack of antiquity, see S. Goldhill, "Genre," in T. Whitmarsh, ed., *The Cambridge Companion to the Greek and Roman Novel* (Cambridge: Cambridge University Press, 2008), 191.

of the Hellenistic and Roman worlds.[4] One of the problems when discussing this genre is that ancient novels are not a unified corpus with a common perspective, purpose, or set of principles. Some scholars have identified dominant themes, especially travel and romance;[5] however, such mechanical means of identification are now recognized as too simplistic. Rather, the novel is a genre that lacks clear boundary determinants, making use of a broad range of formal features.[6] The varied examples of ancient novels challenge rigid genre boundaries and the corresponding practice of collecting them into a unified group.[7] From this perspective the novel might be determined, not as having a coherent set of features that defines it as a separate genre, but as a genre that is identified by its interaction with other genres and as having many prototypical models from which to choose.[8] The literary quality of some novels is high, with authors fully exploring the range of rhetorical conventions and tropes. The plasticity of the genre, with authors fusing and amalgamating literary components, gives the impression of a high level of education and implies that the authors' intended audiences were equally equipped to appreciate them.[9]

The lack of explicit engagement with this genre in critical literary discussions in the Hellenistic and early Roman eras compounds our discussion.[10] This dearth, which could be a result of lower literary prestige and the genre's later development, prohibits an understanding of the novel that exists for oth-

4 L. M. Wills, "Jewish Novellas in a Greek and Roman Age: Fiction and Identity," *JSJ* 42 (2011): 141–65; T. Whitmarsh, *Narrative and Identity in the Ancient Greek Novel: Returning Romance* (Cambridge: Cambridge University Press, 2011).

5 E.g., Achilles Tatius, *Leuc. Clit.* 1.6, 9, etc., especially 4.9; Longus, *Daphn.* 1.13.5; 1.17.1–2; 1.22.3–4, *passim*; Chariton, *Chaer.* 1.1; 2.8, etc., especially 8.1.

6 R. I. Pervo, *Profit with Delight: The Literary Genre of the Acts of the Apostles* (Minneapolis: Fortress, 1987), 101; R. I. Pervo, "Joseph and Asenath and the Greek Novel," in G. W. MacRae, ed., *SBLSP 1976* (Missoula, Mont.: Scholars Press, 1976), 172. Pervo describes the novel as "undefined, open, syncretistic, and somewhat unrestrained."

7 Selden, "Genre of Genre," 43, 51.

8 For the novel as an "anti-genre," see S. Nimis, "The Prosaics of the Ancient Novel," *Arethusa* 27 (1994): 398. One of the central elements of ancient novels and related literary forms is that they retell stories with adaptations and new elements. For example, Ovid's *Heroides* retell older stories with some major changes and the addition of psychological insight, and Apuleius' *Metamorphoses* contains a number of older legends repackaged. Stephens and Winkler, *Ancient Greek Novels*, 9. Cf. M. Bakhtin, *The Dialogic Imagination: Four Essays by M. M. Bakhtin* (ed. M. Holquist; trans. C. Emerson and M. Holquist; Austin: University of Texas Press, 1981), 89.

9 For example, *Alexander Romance* includes speeches as well as documentary material (i.e., letters), which gives the novel the varnish of history. Cf. S. A. Stephens, "Who Read Ancient Novels?" in J. Tatum, ed., *The Search for the Ancient Novel* (Baltimore: Johns Hopkins University Press, 1994), 405–18; E. L. Bowie, "The Readership of Greek Novels in the Ancient World," in J. Tatum, ed., *The Search for the Ancient Novel* (Baltimore: Johns Hopkins University Press, 1994), 435–59.

10 See, however, the reference to *Callirhoe* in Persius, *Sat.* 1.134; Philostratus of Lemnos, *Ep.* 66.

er (mostly poetic) genres.[11] Scholars debate where, when, and by whom this genre was created, with the quest for the origins of the genre following three (not mutually exclusive) paths.[12] The first theory was that the novel naturally developed from Greek literary ancestors, such as New Comedy, history, and rhetoric.[13] Other scholars have posited that some ancient novels were intended to be read as religious texts, deriving their basic structure and many of their details from mystery religions and popular myths.[14] Although both views have adherents, they have been challenged,[15] and the dominant view today is that the Greek novel developed through engagement with foreign cultures and texts.[16] How exactly this might have happened is unknown, and the problems of chronology have precluded positive answers. Indeed, the novel is too complex a phenomenon to be reduced to a single impetus.

Chronology and influence are important issues for our investigation as we seek to tease out the relationships between Jewish and Greek literary works. In previous chapters there has been a clear case for presupposing that the genre adopted by Jewish authors had already been established by their Greek predecessors (e.g., epic, tragedy, etc.) or existed in a different form (e.g., letters and historiography). In this chapter that position cannot be assumed, as one of the earliest proposed examples of the genre is a Jewish work, Joseph and Aseneth. There are few known novelistic texts that have been dated to the early or middle Hellenistic period (e.g., prototype[s] of *Alexander Romance*, *Nectanebo's Dream*).[17] The earliest surviving Greek novel is a fragment of *Ninus* (P.Berol. 6926), which dates to the first century CE but could have been originally

11 For ancient discussion of genre hierarchy, see Aristotle, *Poet.* 5, 1449a38; 9, 1451b5–8; 26, 1461b25–6; Philodemus, *De poem.* 4.112.34–113.3; Horace, *Ep.* 2.2.58–60; Quintilian, *Inst. or.* 10.1.73–5; cf. Adams, *Genre*, 49–53. The antiquity of a genre was an important influence on its ranking. Accordingly, the novel, as a comparatively young genre, lacked history of interpretation/ranking. One might also speculate that its lack of prestige also hindered its integration into the education curriculum. If the novel is an example of Greek adoption and adaptation of a foreign literary genre (cf. Diogenes Laertius, *Vit.* 1.3), as some have argued, then this lack of prestige might be a result of introducing "inferior" elements into the Greek literary corpus.

12 For an overview, see B. P. Reardon, *Courants littéraires grecs des IIe et IIIe siècles après J.-C.* (Paris: Les Belles Lettres, 1971), 311–33; B. E. Perry, *The Ancient Romances: A Literary-Historical Account of Their Origins* (Berkeley: University of California Press, 1967), 3–43.

13 Rohde, *Der griechische Roman*, 33–37.

14 E.g., K. Kerenyi, *Die griechische-orientalische Romanliteratur in religionsgeschichtlicher Beleuchtung* (Tübingen: Mohr, 1927); R. Merkelbach, *Roman und Mysterium in der Antike* (Munich: C. H. Beck, 1962); A. Henrichs, *Die "Phoinikika" des Lollianos* (PTA 14; Bonn: R. Habelt, 1972), 78.

15 E.g., Perry, *Ancient Romances*, 8–17; Reardon, *Courants*, 325–28.

16 Reardon, *Courants*, 312–33; G. Anderson, *Ancient Fiction: The Novel in the Graeco-Roman World* (London: Croom Helm, 1984), 1–24.

17 Depending on how one defines novel, one could also include Xenophon's *Cyropaedia*. Recently, Nawotka has classified *Alexander Romance* as "pagan hagiography," although I am unsure that the religious element is fully satisfied. K. Nawotka, *The Alexander Romance by Ps.-Callisthenes: A Historical Commentary* (MneSup 399; Leiden: Brill, 2017), 18.

composed in the first century BCE.[18] As a result, it is difficult to argue that Jewish authors adopted or participated in a Greek genre when one does not have a contemporary Greek comparator.

This chapter will discuss the nature and features of Jewish novels in light of Greek novels in order to determine how these Jewish works might relate to their Greco-Roman counterparts. We will focus on four Jewish works that have been associated with ancient novels: Joseph and Aseneth, the work by Artapanus, 3 Maccabees, and Danielic additions (Bel and the Dragon and Susanna). These texts do not represent the full range of what have been considered Jewish novels. However, they do represent those that are thought to be closest in nature to Greek literature.

Joseph and Aseneth

Scholars disagree over the exact genre category to which Joseph and Aseneth (henceforth JA) should be assigned and whether or not its author was influenced by the Greek novel genre (whatever that might have been at the time). JA is the Jewish work that has the greatest number of similarities with Greek novels, although its exact relationship is debated and requires further inquiry.[19] In this section we will begin by evaluating the current arguments regarding JA's relationship with the novel and then turn our attention to another genre proposed for JA, rewritten Scripture.

Two interrelated issues complicate this discussion. First, scholars disagree when JA was originally written, and second, some scholars question whether JA is a Jewish composition. Regarding the former question, JA is held by many scholars to have been composed between the first century BCE and the early second century CE.[20] Some, such as Bohak and Braginskaya, have argued for a second-century BCE date, while Kraemer has argued that a third/fourth-century CE date best accounts for the evidence.[21] The dating of JA has

18 E. L. Bowie, "The Greek Novel," in S. Swain, ed., *Oxford Readings in the Greek Novel* (Oxford: Oxford University Press, 1999), 39–59.

19 E.g., L. M. Wills, *The Jewish Novel in the Ancient World* (Ithaca: Cornell University Press, 1995), 176; C. Hezser, "'Joseph and Aseneth' in the Context of Ancient Greek Erotic Novels," *FJB* 24 (1997): 1–40.

20 E.g., A. Standhartinger, *Das Frauenbild im Judentum der hellenistischen Zeit: Ein Beitrag anhand von "Joseph und Aseneth"* (AGJU 26; Leiden: Brill, 1995); R. D. Chesnutt, *From Death to Life: Conversion in Joseph and Aseneth* (JSPSup 16; Sheffield: Sheffield Academic Press, 1995), 80–85.

21 G. Bohak, "Asenath's Honeycomb and Onias' Temple: The Key to 'Joseph and Asenath,'" in D. Assaf, ed., *Proceedings of the Eleventh World Congress of Jewish Studies, Division A: The Bible and Its World* (Jerusalem: Magnes Press, 1994), 163–70; G. Bohak, *"Joseph and Aseneth" and the Jewish Temple in Heliopolis* (EJL 10; Atlanta: Scholars Press, 1996); N. V. Braginskaya, "'Joseph and Aseneth' in Greek Literary History: The Case of the 'First Novel,'" in M. P. F. Pinheiro, J. Perkins, and R. I. Pervo, eds., *The Ancient Novel and Early Christian and Jewish Narrative: Fictional Intersections* (ANS 16; Groningen: Barkhuis, 2012), 79–105.

strong implications for this study, as the latter date would all but ensure that the author of JA drew from the Greek novel tradition in the creation of their work. In contrast, if one adopts the widely held date of first century BCE to second century CE, then more ambiguity regarding this relationship arises.[22] I am persuaded that JA is a Jewish text, particularly because of the issues it addresses and the way that it appears to speak to historical tensions among Jews and Egyptians.[23] This is not to deny that JA could have been penned by a Christian author, as even in the second century CE these categories are not mutually exclusive. The issue of dating is further problematized by the number of text forms surviving for JA, which prevents the reconstruction of a singular autograph. This pluriformity complicates any discussion as the range of texts points to a multiplicity of inputs and authorial perspectives and away from the attempted reconstruction of a singular author with a now-corrupted original manuscript.[24]

Most scholarship on ancient novels has focused on the major Greek and Latin works and has not adequately explored fringe texts, including JA, despite calls for its inclusion.[25] Some scholars have found significant similarities in details, motifs, and themes between JA and Greek novels, which have

---

R. S. Kraemer, *When Aseneth Met Joseph: A Late Antique Tale of the Biblical Patriarch and His Egyptian Wife, Reconsidered* (Oxford: Oxford University Press, 1998), 224–44. For her earlier position, see R. S. Kraemer, "Women's Authorship of Jewish and Christian Literature in the Greco-Roman Period," in A.-J. Levine, ed., *"Women Like This": New Perspectives on Jewish Women in the Greco-Roman World* (EJL 1; Atlanta: Scholars Press, 1991), 221–42.

22 Those holding to an early date often assign a Jewish provenance to the text, while those advocating a later date identify greater Christian influence and possible authorship. E. M. Humphrey, *Joseph and Aseneth* (GAP; Sheffield: Sheffield Academic Press, 2000), 55–57; J. J. Collins, "Joseph and Aseneth: Jewish or Christian?" in J. J. Collins, ed., *Jewish Cult and Hellenistic Culture: Essays on the Jewish Encounter with Hellenism and Roman Rule* (JSJSup 100; Leiden: Brill, 2005), 125–26; Kraemer, *When Aseneth Met Joseph*, 238.

23 Cf. S. R. Johnson, *Historical Fictions and Hellenistic Jewish Identity: Third Maccabees in Its Cultural Context* (HCS 43; Berkeley: University of California Press, 2004), 117–20. I consider an Egyptian provenance most likely.

24 There are two major editions of JA. Shorter (which is to be preferred): M. Philonenko, ed. and trans., *Joseph et Aséneth: Introduction, texte critique, traduction et notes* (StPB 13; Leiden: Brill, 1968). Longer: C. Burchard, ed., *Joseph und Aseneth: Kritisch herausgegeben von Christoph Burchard mit Unterstützung von Carsten Burfeind und Uta Barbara Fink* (PVTG 5; Leiden: Brill, 2003), with revisions by P.-R. Tragan, ed., *Josep i Asenet: Introduccio, text grec revisat i notes* (Literatura Intertestamenaria Supplementa 4; Barcelona: Ed. Alpha, 2005), and U. B. Fink, ed., *Joseph und Aseneth: Revision des griechischen Textes und Edition der zweiten lateinischen Übersetzung* (FSBP 5; Berlin: De Gruyter, 2008). Both editions are eclectic and therefore do not fully represent the manuscript tradition. For a detailed overview, see A. Standhartinger, "Recent Scholarship on *Joseph and Aseneth* (1988–2013)," *CBR* 12 (2014): 354–63. For a wider discussion, including the issue of translation, see D. Selden, "Text Networks," *Ancient Narrative* 8 (2010): 1–23.

25 E.g., S. West, "*Joseph and Asenath*: A Neglected Greek Romance," *CQ* 24 (1974): 70–81. Most recently by R. Bloch, *Jüdische Drehbühnen: Biblische Variationen im antiken Judentum* (TrC 7; Tübingen: Mohr Siebeck, 2013), 1–28.

been used to show genre participation and relatedness.[26] These studies laid the groundwork for subsequent scholars to view JA through a novelistic lens and its author as being influenced by this Greek literary practice.[27]

Some scholars have argued at length that Jewish novels in general, and JA in particular, influenced the development of Greek romances.[28] Braginskaya, who holds to a second-century BCE date, has recently argued that JA was "neither conceived as a novel nor was subject to the novel's influence," but was "a source of inspiration for the Alexandrian authors of novels."[29] Braginskaya argues that the parallels with Apuleius' *Metamorphoses* and Chariton's *Callirhoe* proposed by Burchard do not indicate dependence by JA on Greek or Latin novels (so recently Ahearne-Kroll), but the inverse.[30] Rather, the author of JA drew from Jewish Scripture. In highlighting possible alternative sources, Braginskaya rightfully problematizes the confidence of scholars that the author of JA adapted standard motifs found in Greco-Roman novels. Her case for supposing that JA was a source of influence for subsequent novelists is less convincing. Overlapping features and motifs exist, but these are not sufficiently robust to support direct or even indirect influence. Rather, one could argue that the images adopted by Greek and Latin authors could have come from surrounding literary motifs, folklore, or projections of life events in Greek literature and so did not necessarily arise because "ancient novels borrowed the plot based on obstacles to marriage" from JA.[31]

Equally problematic is Braginskaya's overarching assumption of how literature develops. Braginskaya presents literature as moving from serious to hu-

26 Cf. Philonenko, *Joseph et Aséneth*, 43–48; C. Burchard, *Untersuchungen zu Joseph und Aseneth: Überlieferung—Ortsbestimmung* (WUNT 1.8; Tübingen: Mohr Siebeck, 1965). C. Burchard, "Joseph et Aseneth: Questions actuelles," in *Gesammelte Studien zu Joseph & Aseneth* (SVTP 39; Leiden: Brill, 1996), 223–61. C. Burchard, "Joseph and Aseneth," in *OTP* 2.177–247; Braginskaya, "'Joseph and Aseneth'"; P. Ahearne-Kroll, "Joseph and Aseneth and Jewish Identity in Greco-Roman Egypt" (PhD diss., University of Chicago, 2005), 88–142.

27 For example, Pervo (*Profit*, 121) claims that "Jewish novels came under the influence and tended to evolve in the direction favored by Greek novels," whereas Johnson (*Historical Fictions*, 120) asserts, "The author of *Joseph and Aseneth* drew deliberately on the conventions of the ancient novel in order to explore proselytism in the diaspora both from the perspective of the individual convert and from the perspective of the Jewish community." Cf. Hezser, "'Joseph and Aseneth,'" 4; Pervo, "Joseph and Asenath," 177. For an overview see Standhartinger, "Recent Scholarship," 375–80.

28 T. Whitmarsh, "Joseph et Aseneth: Erotisme et Religion," in C. Bost Pouderon and B. Pouderon, eds., *Les hommes et les dieux dans l'ancien roman: Actes du colloque des Tours, 22–24 octobre 2009* (Lyon: Maison de l'Orient et de la Méditerranée, 2012), 237–52. West expresses the conundrum well: "It is clearly debatable whether JA is a crude imitation of a genre already established as respectable, or typical of a class of popular narrative which stimulated Chariton and other literary men to more polished productions" ("*Joseph and Asenath*," 81).

29 Braginskaya, "'Joseph and Aseneth,'" 81 and 85, respectively.

30 Cf. Ahearne-Kroll, "Joseph and Aseneth," 142.

31 Braginskaya, "'Joseph and Aseneth,'" 102.

morous, real to artificial/artistic, and ritualistic to psychological, with the first stage implied as being a prerequisite to the second.[32] Not only does this model impose a rigid development of literature in general, and the novel genre in particular, but it does not adequately match well with surviving novel examples, almost all of which would fall into Braginskaya's latter division. In fact, there is little evidence for understanding the genre of novels to have a "serious" beginning if one removes the Jewish examples from the data set. This then becomes a circular argument, with Braginskaya's theory of genre development shaping her structuring of how the novel evolved. Although Braginskaya recognizes the lacunae in the surviving literary record, her thesis does not sufficiently allow for what must have been a much more diverse evolutionary process. The Greek and Roman novels we current possess are large, intricate works that display well-developed, though not universal, literary conventions (e.g., motifs, such as romance and travel, characterization, narrative suspense, etc.). It is possible that early Greek works took their cues from Jewish novels, but it is difficult to claim that JA would have directly (or even indirectly) inspired a majority of the novels that have survived, especially in light of the paucity of early Greek novels that have survived and the limited evidence of Greeks and Romans reading Jewish texts.

Braginskaya's argument, although somewhat problematic, rightly focuses on important questions of purpose, audience, and literary structure, highlighting the importance of Greek Scripture for the author of JA and challenging unsupported claims that JA made use of Greek novels in a "distinct way." Braginskaya does not come to a conclusion regarding the genre of JA. If JA was not conceived of as a novel, but was a forerunner to Greek novels, in which literary form (if any) did the author of JA think s/he was participating? If JA was not originally composed as a novel, is it to be considered as participating in the genre of novel based on our understanding of contemporary works, or is there a different, more appropriate, genre category?

The argument to take the Jewish nature of the text seriously was prefigured by Richard Pervo, who contends that JA participates in the genre of "sapiential novel." The imbuing of wisdom into a narrative frame, according to Pervo, has strong parallels with other Jewish narratives on important biblical themes and personnel (e.g., *Ahiqar*, Tobit, Dan 1–6), but is distinct from Jewish "historical novels" that lack the wisdom element (e.g., Judith, Esther, 3 Maccabees). Pervo does not deny the influence of Greek novels on JA, but claims that the author of JA adopted a Jewish literary form having "taken as a base one or more traditional popular stories . . . and enriched this core with rather substantial doses of contemporary wisdom material."[33]

32 Braginskaya, "'Joseph and Aseneth,'" 102.
33 Pervo, "Joseph and Asenath," 174.

Few have considered the possible influence of Egyptian literature on the formation of Jewish novels despite JA's narrative setting and the proposal of Egyptian provenance.[34] This geographic perspective and the integration of an additional corpus have important ramifications for our study of Jewish literature.[35] *Prophecy of Petesis* (or *Nectanebo's Dream*), a prophecy concerning the demise of Nectanebo II, and *The Myth of the Sun's Eye* (*Leiden Dem. Pap.* I 384), a tale depicting Tefnut's departure and return to Egypt, were popular in Egypt.[36] These texts, which were translated into Greek, show substantial parallels with Greek literary traditions, including the embedding of moralistic fables.[37] Although texts are fragmentary, they evidence a range of narrative types and sizes,[38] thus providing relevant comparators for Jewish narratives composed in Egypt and broadening our understanding of prototypes available to Jewish authors writing in Egypt. Participation in multiple genres is also evident in the blending of narrative and wisdom literature and/or oracular sayings (e.g., *Instruction of Ankhsheshonq*, *Demotic Chronicle*, *Oracle of the Lamb*).

Females are prominent in some Egyptian novels. The first part of the *Setne I* is narrated by a female character, Ahwere, who recounts the tale of how her

34 Cf. I. Rutherford, "Greek Fiction and Egyptian Fiction: Are They Related and, if So, How?" in T. Whitmarsh and S. Thompson, eds., *The Romance between Greece and the East* (Cambridge: Cambridge University Press, 2013), 23–37. Chyutin has argued that JA was influenced by Egyptian stories, such as "The Doomed Prince" and "The Two Brothers." M. Chyutin, *Tendentious Hagiographies: Jewish Propagandist Fiction BCE* (LSTS; London: T&T Clark, 2011), 211–15. For texts, see F. Hoffmann and J. F. Quack, *Anthologie der demotischen Literatur: Einführungen und Quellentexte zur Ägyptologie* (Berlin: LIT Verlag, 2018).

35 For Egyptian prose influence on Greek novels, see I. Rutherford, "Kalasiris and Setne Khamwas: How Greek Literature Appropriated an Egyptian Narrative-Motif," *JHS* 117 (1997): 203–9; S. Vinson, "Good and Bad Women in Egyptian and Greek Fiction," in I. Rutherford, ed., *Greco-Egyptian Interactions: Literature, Translation, and Culture, 500 BCE–300 CE* (Oxford: Oxford University Press, 2016), 245–66.

36 R. Jasnow, "Between Two Waters: The Book of Thoth and the Problem of Greco-Egyptian Interaction," in I. Rutherford, ed., *Greco-Egyptian Interactions: Literature, Translation, and Culture, 500 BCE–300 CE* (Oxford: Oxford University Press, 2016), 317–56; Jasnow and Zauzich, *Ancient Egyptian Book of Thoth*, vol. 1, *Texts*; F. Feder, "The Legend of the Sun's Eye: The Translation of an Egyptian Novel into Greek," in S. T. Tovar and J. P. Monferrer-Sala, eds., *Cultures in Contact: Transfer of Knowledge in the Mediterranean Context; Selected Papers* (Cordoba: Oriens Academic, 2013), 3–12. For the text of *Myth*, see F. de Cenival, trans., *Le Mythe de l'Oeil du Soleil: Translittération et Traduction avec Commentaire Philologique* (DS 9; Sommerhausen: Zauzich Verlag, 1988). For the text and translation of *Prophecy*, see K. Ryholt, "Nectanebo's Dream or The Prophecy of Petesis," in A. Blasius and B. U. Schipper, eds., *Apokalyptik und Ägypten: Eine kritische Analyse der relevanten Texte aus dem griechisch-römischen Ägypten* (OLA 107; Leuven: Peeters, 2002), 221–41. For an important study of translation techniques evidenced in *Myth*, which could have bearing on Septuagint translation approaches, see H.-J. Thissen, "Lost in Translation? Von Übersetzungen und Übersetzern," in H.-W. Fischer-Elfert and T. S. Richter, eds., *Literatur und Religion im Alten Ägypten—Ein Symposium zu Ehren von Elke Blumenthal* (Stuttgart: Hirzel, 2011), 125–63. Cf. the depiction of a dream in P. Mich. 3378.

37 E.g., the Mouse and the Lion (*Myth* 17.9–18.31; Babrius, *Fab.* 107).

38 E.g., manuscript evidence implies that *Myth* is 124 columns long. Cf. Feder, "Legend," 7.

brother and husband, Naneferkaptah, found the *Book of Thoth* (3.1–4.27). The sexual power of Egyptian beauty, associated with the trappings of wealth (i.e., clothing, jewelry, servants) and social prominence (i.e., priestly rank), is a prominent theme in the vignette of Setne Khamwas and Tabubu (*Setne I* 4.38–5.35). In JA, a number of these themes are inverted. Joseph is not moved by traditional elegance, nor is he interested in seducing her (7.1–8.7), but is amazed at her transformed beauty, which came from repentance (18.10; 19.4–7). Aseneth, in contrast to Tabubu, humbles herself through the degradation of her body (10.1–3, 14–17) and by disposing of her jewelry, clothing, and rich food (10.9–13). The topos of "conversion" and the rejection of Egyptian idols and deities (e.g., 8.9; 10.12; 11.7–14; 15.7–8) challenge the worldview of Egyptian works and clearly differentiate Jews from Egyptians (e.g., 7.1; 8.5–7).

The short length of JA aligns more with Jewish novels or novellas than with extant Greek works. Both Greek and Jewish novels are concerned with defining and maintaining boundaries (social, political, religious).[39] Each narrative prioritizes different values based on the ethnicity and social allegiance of the author and his/her goals, but fundamentally, the purpose of an ancient novel was to use narrative to address broader social topics and issues. In the case of JA, the question of a patriarch's marriage to an Egyptian needed to be answered, which is accomplished in part through the conversion of Aseneth.[40] At the macro level of the text, the author, like other Greco-Roman novelists, combined entertainment and moral education to communicate important ideas.[41] For example, both Tobit and Judith have engaging and entertaining stories with a strong religious/moral component to them.[42] The authors of these works are clearly influenced by scriptural texts and have modeled their compositions on biblical narratives, although both do so in different ways.[43] Tobit, as a non-Greek-language composition, shows a fidelity to Jewish Scripture that has minimal engagement with Greek literature.[44] Judith, which is increasingly recognized as a Greek composition, also displays substantial engagement with

39 Hezser, "'Joseph and Aseneth,'" 2.

40 Cf. M. Thiessen, "Aseneth's Eight-Day Transformation as Scriptural Justification for Conversion," *JSJ* 45 (2014): 229–49.

41 Pervo, "Joseph and Asenath," 173; H. Kuch, "Funktionswandlungen des antiken Romans," in H. Kuch, ed., *Der antike Roman: Untersuchungen zur literarischen Kommunikation und Gattungsgeschichte* (Berlin: Akademie Verlag, 1989), 65–66.

42 The additions to Daniel and Esther would also fit this rubric; see below. Cf. L. M. Wills, "The Jewish Novellas Daniel, Esther, Tobit, Judith, Joseph and Aseneth," in J. R. Morgan and R. Stoneman, eds., *Greek Fiction: The Greek Novel in Context* (London: Routledge, 1994), 231–33.

43 Cf. D. L. Gera, *Judith* (CEJL; Berlin: De Gruyter, 2014), 45–56; for use of LXX in quotations, see pp. 89–91. For a recent overview of the genre of Judith, see L. M. Wills, *Judith: A Commentary on the Book of Judith* (Hermeneia; Minneapolis: Fortress, 2019), 78–106. Unfortunately, this work came out too late for me to engage with thoroughly.

44 On the debate over the original language of Tobit (i.e., Hebrew or Aramaic), see J. A. Fitzmyer, *Tobit* (CEJL; Berlin: De Gruyter, 2002), 18–28.

Scripture, but incorporates elements of Greek literature more broadly.[45] These texts show part of the range of Jewish literary composition in the Hellenistic era and reinforce the view that, like JA, a text could have a variety of literary influences and participate in multiple genres. In the cases of Judith and JA, the authors did not solely participate in Greek literary practices, but followed Jewish authors who composed narrative works with topics that reinforced Jewish beliefs and worldviews.

JA is a narrative that has sufficient parallels with Greek novels so as to allow for it to be viewed as participating in that genre.[46] This is not to say that JA was influenced by currently extant Greek or Latin novels, but that the work incorporates elements that are not typically associated with Jewish composition (so far as we know) and so suggests the author's adoption of alternative literary practices and prototypical models. For some elements, Greek literary influence is probable, although one should also consider the possible influence from Egyptian texts. Most importantly, JA shows clear connections with Jewish narrative works that take their starting point from scriptural texts (e.g., Tobit, Judith, Additions to Esther and Daniel). The author's clear use of the LXX and scriptural characters helps associate JA with similar Jewish authors who expounded upon sacred texts.[47] The multitude of ties to both Greek and Jewish literature exhibited by JA cautions associating it with one genre category (i.e., Greek novel *or* Jewish novel). JA is a unique blend of literary inputs that represents the cultural and textual blending found in Hellenistic literature and in the genre of novel in particular.

Joseph and Aseneth as Rewritten Scripture?

Susan Docherty has recently argued that JA is best understood in light of the genre of rewritten Scripture, claiming that it matches eight of the nine char-

45 Wills, "Jewish Novellas in a Greek and Roman Age," 159–60. Gera (*Judith*, 79–97) rightly argues that, despite the original language of composition (which in her mind is indeterminable), one must conclude that the author of Judith had knowledge of Greek literature (p. 94) (e.g., Jud 5:3–4; 7:30; 10:6–10; 13:8). Cf. J. Joosten, "The Original Language and Historical Milieu of the Book of Judith," in *Collected Studies on the Septuagint* (FAT 83; Tübingen: Mohr Siebeck, 2012), 195–209.

46 E.g., the opening of the text and its parallels in other novels (JA 1:3–6; Chariton, *Chaer.* 1.1–2; Xenophon of Ephesus, *Eph.* 1.1.1–3). For an incestual twist on the theme of a beautiful daughter needing a suitor, see anon., *Apollonius, King of Tyre* 1. For an argument that JA is a Christianized allegory of Greek novels, see R. M. Price, "Implied Reader Response and the Evolution of Genres: Transitional Stages between the Ancient Novels and the Apocryphal Act," *HTS* 53 (1997): 909–38.

47 For the author's engagement with Septuagintal language, see G. Delling, "Einwirkungen der Sprache der Septuaginta in 'Joseph and Aseneth,'" *JSJ* 9 (1978): 29–56.

acteristics of rewritten Bible as formulated by Philip Alexander.[48] Docherty shows that the author of JA drew widely from the Joseph narrative and other scriptural texts, integrating these elements into a cohesive narrative.[49] The author of JA presupposes that his readers know the biblical stories and was selective in what was included, omitted, and expanded.[50] In light of these strong connections with Jewish Scripture, Docherty claims that JA is best aligned with the Jewish literary tradition of rewritten Scripture.[51]

Few scholars have seriously considered Docherty's argument. Braginskaya dismisses Docherty's position, claiming that rewritten Bible is "a meta-generic definition."[52] In some sense, Braginskaya is correct; reformulations of biblical passages can be found in many genres. However, I am not sure that Braginskaya understands Docherty on her own terms, but rather has imposed her view of rewritten Scripture as process and so devoid of genre associations. In contrast, Docherty not only argues that JA incorporates a range of scriptural passages, but also challenges Alexander's criterion that rewritten Bible needs to cover large sections of Jewish Scripture to be considered as participating in that genre.[53]

Rewritten Scripture is a complex topic, and a number of scholars are now arguing that it should best be understood as an exegetical process rather than

48 S. Docherty, "*Joseph and Aseneth*: Rewritten Bible or Narrative Expansion?" *JSJ* 35 (2004): 27–48; cf. P. S. Alexander, "Retelling the Old Testament," in D. A. Carson and H. G. M. Williamson, eds., *It Is Written: Scripture Citing Scripture* (Cambridge: Cambridge University Press, 1988), 99–120; Rajak, *Translation and Survival*, 224; J. L. Kugel, *In Potiphar's House: The Interpretive Life of Biblical Texts* (San Francisco: HarperSanFrancisco, 1990), 264, labels JA "Retold Bible." I will be using "rewritten Scripture" throughout. For discussions of the issues with the phrases "rewritten Bible" and "rewritten Scripture," see J. G. Campbell, "Rewritten Bible: A Terminological Reassessment," in J. Zsengellér, ed., *"Rewritten Bible" after Fifty Years: Texts, Terms, or Techniques? A Last Dialogue with Geza Vermes* (JSJSup 166; Leiden: Brill, 2014), 58–64.

49 Docherty, "*Joseph and Aseneth*," 34–43.

50 Both Alexander and Docherty say that rewritten Bible involves the use of the Hebrew Bible. However, it the case of JA at least, it is likely that a Greek text of Genesis is the author's source. This is especially evident in the use of names: Pentephres (LXX; MT Potiphera), the priest of Heliopolis (LXX; MT On), and Aseneth (LXX; MT Asenath).

51 In her more recent work, Docherty has moved away from this position, classifying JA under "parabiblical" literature. Cf. S. Docherty, *The Jewish Pseudepigrapha: An Introduction to the Literature of the Second Temple Period* (London: SPCK, 2014), 38–50.

52 There is some confusion with Braginskaya's description of rewritten Scripture, as the process of rewriting individual verses that is found widely in Jewish literature does not function at the level above the genre as the labels of "Apocrypha" and "Pseudepigrapha" do. The literary practice of rewriting individual verses, as described by Braginskaya, in my opinion, functions at the localized level below the genre. Braginskaya, "'Joseph and Aseneth,'" 80–81. Cf. D. J. Harrington, "Palestinian Adaptations of Biblical Narratives and Prophecies," in R. A. Kraft and G. W. E. Nickelsburg, eds., *Early Judaism and Its Modern Interpreters* (Philadelphia: Fortress, 1986), 239–58, especially 243.

53 Docherty ("*Joseph and Aseneth*," 46–47), challenging Alexander, "Retelling the Old Testament."

a genre.[54] Under the former rubric, JA could still be understood as a rewriting of Genesis 41–49 that adheres to aspects of its *Vorlage*, but would be stripped of its generic implications. If rewritten Scripture is viewed solely through the lens of process, JA could be understood as both rewritten Scripture and novel, as they function on different classification levels. In this case, the activity of the author (rewriting an existing work) as well as his/her source element (i.e., Scripture) is recognized, but the work's genre classification is still undetermined.[55]

A key element of this debate is the often-unspoken assumption that rewritten Scripture does not, or maybe more properly cannot, apply to *both* genre and interpretive process. The main challenge to understanding rewritten Scripture as a discrete genre, according to Daniel Harrington and others, is the diversity of texts that it currently encompasses.[56] These range from Jubilees to 4QReworked Pentateuch[a] to *Temple Scroll* and include both narrative and legal texts. According to Harrington, member texts of a genre category need to have specific, identifiable features that allow for genre identification by the reader. Developments in genre theory, however, allow for alternative perspectives on this topic.

Molly Zahn, drawing from modern genre theorists, provides a fresh understanding of this topic that bypasses simplistic categorizations and highlights the functionality and flexibility of genres.[57] Reconfiguring the discussion of rewritten Scripture as genre by framing it in light of prototype genre theory, Zahn proposes that the texts typically categorized as participating in rewritten Scripture have a sufficiently distinct profile for them to be classified together generically.[58] According to Zahn, the contours of this genre are based on three

54 Engagement with scriptural texts is now viewed along a continuum, with scribal copying at one pole and complete rewriting of a text at the other. For work on rewritten Scripture, see M. J. Bernstein, "'Rewritten Bible': A Generic Category Which Has Outlived Its Usefulness?" *Textus* 22 (2005): 169–96; G. J. Brooke, "Genre Theory, Rewritten Bible, and Pesher," *DSD* 17 (2010): 332–57; D. A. Machiela, "Once More, with Feeling: Rewritten Scripture in Ancient Judaism—A Review of Recent Developments," *JJS* 61 (2010): 308–20; M. M. Zahn, "Talking about Rewritten Texts: Some Reflections on Terminology," in H. von Weissenberg, J. Pakkala, and M. Marttila, eds., *Changes in Scripture: Rewriting and Interpreting Authoritative Traditions in the Second Temple Period* (BZAW 419; Berlin: De Gruyter, 2011), 93–119; M. M. Zahn, "Genre and Rewritten Scripture: A Reassessment," *JBL* 131 (2012): 271–88; Campbell, "Rewritten Bible," 64–65.

55 Unlike Jubilees, JA does not obviously present itself as Scripture, nor, like Josephus' *Ant.* 1–11, is it presented as a translation.

56 E.g., Harrington, "Palestinian Adaptations"; Zahn, "Talking about Rewritten Texts"; G. J. Brooke, "Rewritten Bible," in L. H. Schiffman and J. C. VanderKam, eds., *Encyclopedia of the Dead Sea Scrolls* (2 vols.; Oxford: Oxford University Press, 2000), 2:780.

57 Zahn, "Genre and Rewritten Scripture."

58 Sinding, "After Definitions." For application to Jewish texts, see Wright, "Joining the Club"; Williamson, "Pesher." Petersen has suggested a different position, suggesting that rewritten Scripture would not have been a meaningful generic category to ancient Jewish authors

elements: "first, status as a new work (as opposed to a copy of a biblical book); second, a concern with interpretation of specific scriptural passages; and, third, the situating of the new work as part of the same 'discourse' or 'stream of tradition' as the original work that formed the basis of the rewriting."[59] These features have similarities with those advanced by Alexander, including replicating the form of biblical books in a new, distinct work.[60] Zahn's criteria, however, differ in important ways: she removes the narrative requirement, minimizes the focus on sequential use of scriptural sources, and does not necessitate all characteristics to be satisfied in order to qualify as participating in the genre.[61] Zahn does not address the nature of JA, providing an opportunity to test her theory on a noncore example of the genre. As we will see, applying these criteria to nonprototypical members highlights a number of interpretive difficulties and some of the additional assumptions embedded in Zahn's work.

There is no doubt that JA satisfies the first criterion, "status as a new work." No modern or ancient reader has confused or conflated JA with the Genesis narrative, nor has there been any risk of seeing JA as a poorly copied text. Zahn's second category, "interpretation of specific scriptural passages," provides some challenge to classifying JA as rewritten Scripture, because she defines this to mean "the sustained interpretation of a succession of specific scriptural texts."[62] One of the inherent issues in this definition is the lack of clarity regarding the term "sustained." At what point does a text reach sustained engagement? A flexible view of genre, especially one that adheres to a prototype model, resists rigid definitions or benchmarks and so allows for greater interpretative freedom. The definition of sustained will be different among scholars and ancient writers and so will inevitably lead to debate and different views.

Docherty has shown that the author of JA had a strong concern to interpret a scriptural narrative (i.e., part of the Joseph story, Gen 41–49), even if his/her engagement with Scripture is nonlinear and is more focused on filling gaps than recasting existing passages.[63] The author of JA structures the narrative according to the events outlined in Genesis and reconnects with the Genesis narrative by having characters recall biblical stories (JA 4.7–10;

---

or readers, but that for modern scholars it can function as a viable category. A. K. Petersen, "Rewritten Bible as a Borderline Phenomenon—Genre, Textual Strategy, or Canonical Anachronism?" in A. Hilhorst, E. Puech, and E. Tigchelaar, eds., *Flores Florentino: Dead Sea Scrolls and Other Early Jewish Studies in Honour of Florentino García Martínez* (JSJSup 122; Leiden: Brill, 2007), 285–306, especially 303–5.

59 Zahn, "Genre and Rewritten Scripture," 282.

60 Alexander, "Retelling the Old Testament," 116–18.

61 This last element is not made explicitly by Zahn, but it is part of the prototype understanding of genre.

62 Zahn, "Genre and Rewritten Scripture," 283.

63 Docherty, "*Joseph and Aseneth*," 45–46.

23.2, 14).[64] Both works are written in prose with the same characters and similar narrative events.[65] In contrast, each text has a different protagonist: Joseph in Genesis and Aseneth in JA. JA has substantial additions to the Genesis text, such as the plot by Pharaoh's son and his recruitment of four of Joseph's brothers (23.1–29.9), the more pronounced theme of romance and physical attraction (e.g., JA 1.4–6; 5.5; 8.5; 18.9; cf. Gen 39:6–7), and the repentance narrative of Aseneth. Divine actions also play a much larger role in JA (e.g., rescues 27.10–11; angelic visitation 14.1–17.10; 19.9), whereas dreams and interpretations, although mentioned (4.9–10), are almost completely absent.[66]

Additions, alterations, and omissions to a biblical book are elements of rewritten Scripture. The issue, according to Zahn's criteria, is whether or not JA sustains an interpretive progression through the text. Again, the term "progression" is fluid and invites a range of interpretations, lacking clear upper and lower limits. JA fills an interpretive lacuna(e) in the Joseph narrative in Gen 41:45–52, and a majority of our text inhabits this narrative gap. This action is not rewriting as traditionally defined, but gap-filling. Alternatively, it could be argued that the author of JA took the Genesis narrative as his starting point, all the while bringing in other elements of the Joseph narrative to round out the story. In this case, JA would not be rewritten Scripture, but what Crawford and others call "parabiblical works."[67] However, unlike many parabiblical works, JA does not use a biblical character to create an entirely new narrative. Rather, much of JA fits within the scriptural Joseph story and its narrative gaps. The crux of the issue is whether or not the filling of a single gap within the source text, such as the meeting, conversion, and relationship between Joseph and Aseneth, qualifies as fulfilling this criterion of rewritten Scripture.[68] In my opinion, this aspect of JA could be classified as rewritten Scripture. The last section of JA (23.1–29.9), for which there is minimal scriptural precedent, falls more comfortably within the definition of "parabiblical work." The inclu-

64 E.g., time references (JA 1.1–2; 3.1; 22.2), the marriage of Joseph and Aseneth by Pharaoh (JA 20.9; 21.2–8), the birth of Manasseh and Ephraim (JA 21.9).

65 Almost all of the biblical characters are included in JA (e.g., Joseph, his father Jacob, his brothers, Pharaoh, Pentephres, Aseneth). The major exception is Pharaoh's son, although his inclusion could be inferred from the text.

66 For other themes and texts, see Docherty, *Jewish Pseudepigrapha*, 41–50.

67 S. W. Crawford, "The 'Rewritten Bible' at Qumran: A Look at Three Texts," *Eretz-Israel* 26 (1999): 1, followed by Bernstein, "'Rewritten Bible,'" 196; J. G. Campbell, "'Rewritten Bible' and 'Parabiblical Texts': A Terminological and Ideological Critique," in J. G. Campbell, W. J. Lyons, and L. K. Pietersen, eds., *New Directions in Qumran Studies: Proceedings of the Bristol Colloquium on the Dead Sea Scrolls, 8–10 September 2003* (LNTS 52; London: T&T Clark, 2005), 43–68. D. Dimant, "Use and Interpretation of Mikra in the Apocrypha and Pseudepigrapha," in M. J. Mulder, ed., *Mikra* (Assen: Van Gorcum, 1988), 401, who labels JA "Biblical Expansion."

68 JA 22.1–10 could be viewed as a narrative expansion of Gen 47:11–12, 27.

sion of both elements within a single work challenges the neat divide created by scholars between parabiblical and rewritten texts, blurring the boundaries of what must have been a very fluid understanding in antiquity. At best, we would have to conclude that JA would not easily satisfy Zahn's second criterion and would be peripheral rather than core.

One might also debate whether or not JA adequately satisfies Zahn's third criterion of situating the new work in the same discourse or stream as the original, which she defines as "the same kind of text" as the source.[69] The first challenge, therefore, is to determine the nature of the original discourse; are we to consider the genre of the Joseph narrative proper, or are we to look to the genre of the original whole (i.e., Genesis, or the Pentateuch)? In this case, it is clear that the author of JA had no intentions of reconfiguring the whole of Genesis or the Pentateuch, but limited his vision to Joseph's story. This criterion is problematic, as the composite whole of a text can regularly be classified differently than selected portions of the same text.[70] Extraction, furthermore, will be artificial in that the original author would have constructed the work differently, adding features to or omitting them from the text if it was composed discretely. Did the author of JA and other ancient writers view the Joseph narrative as a self-contained unit that could be extracted from Genesis without substantial issue? From the number of Joseph texts in antiquity, it is likely that multiple authors, in addition to that of JA, thought that it could be.

Considered on its own, the Joseph story (Gen 37:1–50:26) is a prose narrative that focuses on specific events in the life of Joseph. Although there are other characters, such as his brothers and father, and the reader is given insight into some of their thoughts and actions (e.g., Gen 38:1–30; 42:1–5; 42:26–43:15), Joseph is the clear protagonist. The Genesis narrative includes short stories of his birth, childhood, and death, but focuses on the catastrophes and triumphs of his life, paralleling ancient biographies. However, the focus on extreme rescues that are attributed to the divine and the monumental reversal of fortune from prisoner to second in command in Egypt resonate with ancient novels.[71] As a result, the Joseph narrative could be viewed in the Hellenistic and Roman eras as participating in both novel and biography.[72]

The narrative similarities suggest that the author of JA crafted his work with the Joseph narrative in mind. These similarities do not equate to genre

69 Zahn, "Genre and Rewritten Scripture," 284–85.

70 For example, taking a narrative of an individual out of a history would change how one would classify the excised text in comparison to the incorporated whole.

71 E.g., Chariton, *Chaer.* 5.6; Achilles Tatius, *Leuc. Clit.* 1.3; Xenophon of Ephesus, *Eph.* 5.9; *Ninus*, fr. C. 41; Heliodorus, *Aeth.* 8.17; Iamblichus, *Babyloniaca* 6. Cf. Stephens and Winkler, *Ancient Greek Novels*, 248.

72 Cf. Wills, *Jewish Novel*, 158.

sharing, but they do show that the Genesis text strongly influenced the creation of JA. Both texts have a moralizing purpose, although the specific intentions are different. In the Joseph narrative, the author highlights the importance of God's provenance and how trust in him will be rewarded (Gen 41:25, 39; 45:5). This is also found in the divine rescue of Aseneth (JA 27.10–11) and the reference to the preordination of Joseph and Aseneth's marriage (21.3; cf. 23.3), but this theme is clearly subordinate to the larger discussions of idolatry and repentance (10.13; 11.18; 13.13), ethics (21.1; 23.9; 29.3), and navigating Jew–Egyptian relationships (7.1; 8.5). If JA is compared solely with the Joseph narrative, it is possible to argue that it satisfies the third criterion, but not without reservation.

From the above investigation, JA could be viewed as participating in the genre of rewritten Scripture, as it arguably meets all three of the criteria proposed by Zahn, although criteria two and three are less secure. One advantage of working from the prototype model is that complete criteria fidelity is not required. Rather, one can debate the closeness that one text has with its quintessential model(s), but there is no hard line that can be drawn to differentiate members from nonmembers. For rewritten Scripture, texts such as Jubilees, Chronicles, and others form the center from which other examples radiate. Compared to these texts, JA would be a peripheral example of this genre, but there is a case to be made that JA should be viewed as a participant.

The above discussion and its application to JA have important methodological implications for our understanding of rewritten Scripture as a genre. First, it is easiest to identify prototypical members of a group, but harder to determine fringe members. Wrestling with peripheral examples helps provide clarity to the loose and fuzzy boundaries of the genre. As JA is a borderline case for criteria two and three, it becomes an important example for the potential diversity of this genre and provides fodder for future investigations. In criterion three, there could be greater clarity regarding what qualifies as "original discourse" when an author only engages with a portion of the original text. In the case of JA, the Joseph narrative, and not the whole of Genesis or the Pentateuch, was taken as a discrete unit for comparison. Similarly, criterion two—"sustained interpretation of a succession of specific scriptural texts"—could be further unpacked and nuanced, again with a focus on peripheral examples, but also with an eye towards determining key terms and ideas, such as "sustained" and "succession of scriptural texts." Claiming that JA participates in the genre of rewritten Scripture does not imply that the author thought that s/he was doing the same thing as Genesis, nor should we allow the canonical text to restrict interpretation or unduly constrain readings. Although the author appropriates characters from Genesis, s/he is doing something different. Thus, the work needs to be read on its own terms: not as a supplement to the "real" narrative but as a work that constructs cultural and theological ideas.[73]

Conclusion

A flexible view of genre encourages us to avoid thinking in binary terms (e.g., rewritten Scripture vs. novel), but to see JA as participating in both genre categories.[74] This approach to JA is attractive, as it militates against the need to identify a singular genre at the expense of another. The need to label works as belonging to one specific genre has led in the past to the proliferation of genre categories and an intentional downplaying of similarities that a given text might have with other genres. Such actions artificially divide genre categories and fail to acknowledge the inherent flexibility and fluidity of genres, particularly in the Hellenistic era. Viewing JA as engaging with both novel and rewritten Scripture allows us to make the best sense of the work and to appreciate its distinctive and peripheral status among the genre categories as they are currently understood.

Although in previous chapters we have seen strong evidence for Jewish authors adopting and adapting Greek literary forms, with regard to ancient novels the direction of influence is much less clear. Indeed, regarding the genre of novel, we have good evidence for arguing that literary and cultural influence is not unidirectional.[75] There are similarities between JA and Greco-Roman novels; however, there are also substantial differences that belie simplistic genre associations. JA has strong literary relationships with Jewish literature, but this does not mean that it is devoid of Greek influence. I do not think that the author of JA actively adopted a Greek literary form for his composition, but rather adapted preexisting Jewish literary forms, such as Jewish novellas and rewritten Scripture. This, however, does not negate the parallels with Greek novels, for which there is evidence. Rather, the author of JA appropriated both Jewish and Greek literary elements for the creation of his work and so represents a natural development of Jewish response to Greek literary influence.

73 For a recent example of this approach for JA, see J. Hicks-Keeton, *Arguing with Aseneth: Gentile Access to Israel's Living God in Jewish Antiquity* (Oxford: Oxford University Press, 2018). For a wider argument, see E. Mroczek, *The Literary Imagination in Jewish Antiquity* (Oxford: Oxford University Press, 2016), especially 3–18 and *passim*.

74 Derrida, "Law of Genre"; Fowler, *Kinds of Literature*, 37; Devitt, *Writing Genres*, 7.

75 Cf. H. Bhabha, *The Location of Culture* (London: Routledge, 1994), 85–92.

Artapanus

Artapanus is a Jewish author who wrote between 250 and 50 BCE.[76] Eusebius, making use of Alexander Polyhistor, has preserved three fragments and gives the impression that the excerpts from Artapanus are from one single work, despite referencing it by two names (Ἰουδαϊκά, fr. 1.1; Περὶ Ἰουδαίων, fr. 2.1; 3.1; cf. Clement, *Strom.* 1.23.154.2).[77] The fragments recount the history of the Jewish people in Egypt through the characters of Abraham, Joseph, and Moses, praising their deeds and accomplishments. Artapanus uses Jewish Scripture as his point of departure (i.e., Gen 12:10–20; Gen 37–50; Exod 1–16), and strong linguistic parallels suggest he was familiar with the LXX and likely not the Hebrew text.[78] Although Artapanus took his inspiration from Scripture, he was not constrained by its contents, but freely included additional material and adapted biblical accounts to fit his literary purpose.[79] Artapanus' willingness to pair Jewish religious ideas with those from Egyptian and Greek origins is distinct among his surviving contemporaries.[80]

Unlike Joseph and Aseneth, which has been readily classified as a novel, Artapanus' narrative has traditionally been viewed as participating in historiography.[81] More recently, scholars have identified novelistic elements, which have led some to classify Artapanus' work as a novel.[82] Wills asserts

76 Collins, *Athens*, 38. For the view that Artapanus, despite his Persian name, is a Jewish author, see Freudenthal, *Alexander Polyhistor*, 1.143–53. For a recent challenge to this position, see H. Jacobson, "Artapanus Judaeus," *JJS* 57 (2006): 210–21. While Jacobson makes some important points, I am not convinced by the certainty with which he claims that "no Jew would have used the tale of Moses as institutor of Egyptian animal worship" (pp. 219–20).

77 "Description" might be a more accurate term than "fragment." Cf. Eusebius, *Praep. ev.* 9.18.1; 9.23.1–4; 9.27.1–37, with the latter Moses passage partially paralleled by Clement, *Strom.* 1.23.154.2–3. For an edition of the text, see Mras, GCS 43.1, 504, 516, 519–24; *FGrH* 726.

78 Fruedenthal, *Alexander Polyhistor*, 1.216; G. E. Sterling, *Historiography and Self-Definition: Josephos, Luke-Acts, and Apologetic History* (NovTSup 64; Leiden: Brill, 1992), 173–75. Artapanus' description of the Jews as "Hebrews" (fr. 1.1), however, follows the Hebrew or a different Greek translation rather than the LXX text.

79 According to Artapanus (fr. 3.18), Moses kills an Egyptian (here named Chanethothes), but in self-defense. This is in contrast to the incident in Exod 2:12 in which Moses murders an unnamed Egyptian for striking a Hebrew slave. For a concise engagement with the additions and adaptations of Artapanus, see Jacobson, "Artapanus Judaeus."

80 Examples of aligning Jewish and Egyptian ideas include Moses being identified with Hermes and so being worthy of divine honors (fr. 3.6; cf. Diodorus Siculus, *Bibl.* 1.16.2) and Moses' founding of Egyptian animal worship (fr. 3.4). The Jewish God is still viewed as the "master of the universe" (fr. 3.22) and is never presented as subservient or equal to the extant text.

81 For a detailed history of interpretation, see D. Barbu, "Artapan: Introduction Historique et Historiographique," in P. Borgeaud, T. Römer, and Y. Volokhine, eds., *Interprétations de Moïse: Égypte, Judée, Grèce et Rome* (JSRC 10; Leiden: Brill, 2010), 3–23. Cf. Doran, "Jewish Hellenistic Historians," 257–63, who places Artapanus with historians.

82 E.g., Charlesworth, in *OTP* 2.889–903; L. M. Wills, ed. and trans., *Ancient Jewish Novels: An Anthology* (Oxford: Oxford University Press, 2002), 165–73.

that "among Jews, Artapanus' *Moses Romance* (and related fragments) fits the sub-genre of national hero romance."[83] We will return to the idea of national hero below, but first we must address Wills' label of "Moses Romance," which is a misleading name for Artapanus' work, as it implies that the text is focused solely on the character of Moses.[84] Although the Moses fragment in Eusebius is much larger than those of Abraham and Joseph, it is not necessarily representative of the original work. Rather, the inclusion of Abraham and Joseph is important for understanding the work as a whole, which is not limited to the life of a single individual (i.e., Moses), but includes other prominent figures from Jewish history. Of particular importance is the opening of the third fragment, which situates the Moses narrative within the larger confines of Abraham's narrative: "Artapanus says in his book *Concerning the Jews* that after Abraham and his son Mempsasthenoth died, the king of the Egyptians died as well" (fr. 3.1).[85] This narrative hook challenges the Moses-focused reading and forces the reader to associate this fragment with the characters that preceded it.

This understanding does not necessarily undermine the view that Artapanus' work is a national hero romance, although it would be better labeled as a national heroes romance. The inclusion of multiple characters, however, makes Artapanus' work substantially different from other prototypical novels from antiquity. In extant Jewish, Egyptian, Greek, and Latin novels, the narrative revolves around one main character or couple.[86] This focus results in a single (or parallel) story arc that is anchored in the life events of the main character(s) and concludes when the conflicting issue is resolved. This does not appear to be the case in Artapanus' narrative, in which elements of the lives of Abraham, Joseph, and Moses are recalled, presumably creating multiple, successive story arcs. The linking feature among these characters is their importance in the history of Jewish people, particularly in Egypt.[87]

83 Wills, "Jewish Novellas in a Greek and Roman Age," 143.

84 Similarly problematic is Fraser's use of "Moses biography" (*Ptolemaic Alexandria*, 1.704) and Walter's "Mose-Roman" (*Fragmente jüdisch-hellenistischer Historiker*, *JSHRZ* 1.2, 121).

85 There is substantial debate over the reading of this passage, namely the identity of Mempsasthenoth and whether or not Artapanus, a scribe, or Alexander Polyhistor mistakenly wrote Abraham when Joseph or Jacob was intended. Regardless of the decisions, it is clear that this passage (which clearly draws from Exod 1:8–14) and the Moses story are couched within the larger narrative. For a discussion of the issues, see Sterling, *Historiography*, 172–73.

86 The titles of ancient novels are regularly named after these characters, e.g., Judith, Joseph and Aseneth, *Daphnis and Chloe*, *Leucippe and Clitophon*, etc.

87 All of the elements preserved by Eusebius locate the narrative in Egypt. Additionally, most non-Egyptian stories have been removed, including the characters of Isaac and Jacob, who do not spend significant time in Egypt. On the close association between Jewish and Egyptians implied by the narratives, see Gruen, *Diaspora*, 210–11.

Genres function at the level of the literary whole, and so working with fragments has inherent pitfalls. In the case of Artapanus, a number of scholars have focused too closely on Moses and so have essentially ignored Abraham and Joseph.[88] This myopic approach skews one's vision of the whole and places emphasis on what is only part of the original text. Indeed, the focus on Moses does not necessarily represent the perspective of Artapanus, but what was thought to be useful by Eusebius, Clement, and/or Alexander Polyhistor. In light of the whole, which focuses on a specific ethnic group, it is best to understand Artapanus' work as participating principally, although not exclusively, in the genre of history, distinguished from more prototypical members, but well within the literary tradition of ethnic comparison through contrasting depictions of culturally important individuals. Scholars have labeled Artapanus' work a "competitive historiography" in relation to those by Manetho and Berossos, a "historical romance," or a "romantic national history" focused on the building of national heroes.[89] By identifying *Concerning the Jews* as participating in history, scholars are not arguing that Artapanus' narrative is historically accurate, although some have identified historical parallels.[90] Rather, the focus on a people group through individuals is a recognized feature of ancient historiography.[91] At the same time, scholars do not think that Artapanus' work is a prototypical example of history, as is indicated above by the colabeling of the work as history and romance, possibly signaling participation in multiple genres.

A good illustration of this struggle comes from Eve-Marie Becker, who describes Artapanus' work as "a novel-like, person-centred telling of history."[92] I sympathize with Becker, as it is clear that our typical labels of "history," "biography," and "novel" do not adequately capture the distinctive elements of an individual text. Artapanus has the greatest points of contact with ancient historiography, and the inclusion of multiple characters encourages readers to focus beyond the individual to the nation as a whole. The collection of individuals become more than the sum of their parts by depicting a nation with multiple idealized founders and leaders. This person-focused way of writing

88 E.g., Wills, *Ancient Jewish Novels*, 165–73.

89 Collins, *Athens*, 39–43; Schürer, *History*, 3.1.521; Sterling, *Historiography*, 173–86, respectively.

90 Freudenthal (*Alexander Polyhistor*, 1.155–56) argued that Moses' campaign to Ethiopia was based on an historical campaign by a person named "Messu."

91 E.g., Diodorus Siculus, *Bibl.* 1.44.1–1.68.6.

92 E.-M. Becker, "Artapanus: 'Judaica': A Contribution to Early Jewish Historiography," in N. Calduch-Benages and J. Liesen, eds., *History and Identity: How Israel's Later Authors Viewed Its Earlier History* (Berlin: De Gruyter, 2006), 297–320.

history has roots in both Jewish and Greek historiography and fits within a recognized methodological approach (see chapter 7).[93]

Artapanus' writing, although once maligned as provincial, is now being recognized for its literary creativity.[94] Similar to other Hellenistic historians, Artapanus presents his work as historiography (e.g., title, contents, use of native sources [fr. 3.8, 35–37], etc.).[95] Artapanus' narrative presents Jewish culture as superior to that of the Egyptians, describing the history of the Jewish people in Egypt in a way that highlights positive and omits or smooths over negative aspects of the biblical narrative. Not only are elements of the pentateuchal text addressed, but Artapanus appears to challenge counternarratives. Artapanus (implicitly) rebuts specific claims advanced by Manetho (as reported by Josephus), such as the view that Moses (fr. 3.37//*C. Ap.* 1.279) and the Jews (fr. 3.20//*C. Ap.* 1.229, 233) were lepers, and that Moses was an Egyptian (fr. 3.3//*C. Ap.* 1.250) who opposed Egyptian cults (fr. 3.4, 12//*C. Ap.* 1.239, 244, 249) and fled to Ethiopia (fr. 3.7–10//*C. Ap.* 1.246–247).[96]

The inclusion of the term "romance" by scholars when describing Artapanus highlights the fictitious and entertaining nature of the work's contents.[97] This label, however, is not necessary, as fact and fiction in ancient histories were not as rigidly divided as they are today.[98] Fiction or literary imagination does not equate to novel, just as fact is not the sole prerogative of history.[99] Indeed, there are many different types of "facts" that must be considered when making this type of judgment, and the inclusion of what we would label "fiction" does not transgress the bounds of ancient historiography, although at times it potentially stands in tension with truth claims made

93 Describing and recounting famous individuals was an important component of Greek historiography (e.g., Diodorus Siculus, *Bibl.* 1.1.2).

94 E.g., Gruen, *Heritage and Hellenism*, 156; Gruen, *Diaspora*, 201–11; Johnson, *Historical Fictions*, 95.

95 His presentation, which is at times playful, is not limited to humor, but has literary purpose. Gruen (*Heritage and Hellenism*, 155–60), although right to highlight Artapanus' desire to entertain, potentially undermines more serious elements through labels, such as "whimsical."

96 For the connections between Artapanus and Manetho, see Freudenthal, *Alexander Polyhistor*, 1.161–62; Fraser, *Ptolemaic Alexandria*, 1.705–6; Barclay, *Jews*, 129–30. Cf. Gruen, *Heritage and Hellenism*, 41–72, for the intriguing view that Manetho represents an alternative Jewish history. Artapanus would therefore not be engaging in a defense against outsiders, but in intra-Jewish debate.

97 "In no sense do the Artapanus fragments belong to the category of serious history in the way Herodotus and Thucydides do. . . . Because they provide a glorified treatment of Israel's heroes, they are now widely regarded as belonging to the genre of popular romance literature." Holladay, *Fragments*, vol. 1, *Historians*, 1.190.

98 Cf. Gabba, "True History and False History."

99 Implied by Pervo, *Profit*, 119. For a good example of an author playing with literary expectations of fiction and history, see Antonius Diogenes, *The Incredible Things beyond Thule*, in Photius, *Bibl.* 166.111a30–111b2.

by authors.[100] Nor does an engaging and entertaining narrative necessarily call for understanding a work as novelistic, as ancient historians also sought to produce a work that was enjoyable to read.[101] A better argument for the additional descriptors is that the text's nationalistic focus embodies cultural interaction, which is recognized as an important element in ancient novels.[102] This aspect of the novel has been highlighted in recent years and should be taken seriously when considering the work's genre.[103] Although I do not deny this aspect of ancient novels or Artapanus' work, ethnographic narratives are not limited to novels (e.g., Manetho, Berossos). Rather, the inclusion of nationalistic constructions and the focus on ethnic groups are shared literary elements, especially with ancient histories.

The focus on individuals also speaks to the overarching purpose of the work. Artapanus draws on the lives of (at least) three individuals (Abraham, Joseph, Moses), presenting them as culture bringers to the Egyptians: Abraham taught astrology to the king of Egypt (fr. 1.1);[104] Joseph taught the Egyptians land reform (fr. 2.2) and the use of weights and measures (fr. 2.3); and Moses, among other activities, invented ships and stone-cutting methods (fr. 3.4), organized Egyptian animal worship (fr. 3.4), and discovered philosophy (fr. 3.4). These achievements correlate well with "national hero" narratives and have parallels with the novelistic works of *Alexander Romance*, *Ninus*, *Sesonchosis*, and *Calligone*, as well as the expectations in antiquity of what makes a great civilization (cf. Josephus, *C. Ap.* 2.13).[105]

However, unlike the writers of other Greek novels, Artapanus does not limit his story to one individual, but includes at least three people, following the trajectory established in Genesis and Exodus.[106] The embedding of individual heroes within a larger historical work focused on an ethnic group also has literary precedents, and scholars have noted the parallels between Artapanus' Moses and the story of Sesostris, king of Egypt, in Diodorus Siculus' *Bibl.*

100 E.g., Thucydides, *Hist.* 1.22.1–4; Dionysius of Halicarnassus, *Rom. ant.* 1.1.2; Josephus, *BJ* 1.12; *Ant.* 1.17; Herodian, *Hist.* 1.1.1. Cf. Luke 1:4; Diogenes Laertius, *Vit.* 3.47.

101 The creation of a pleasing narrative became more important than the message for some ancient historians, and subsequent authors critiqued them for such actions. E.g., Josephus, *BJ* 1.1–2.

102 Cf. Stephens and Winkler, *Ancient Greek Novels*, 8.

103 Wills, "Jewish Novellas in a Greek and Roman Age"; Whitmarsh, *Narrative and Identity*.

104 Cf. Josephus, *Ant.* 1.166–168; Jub. 12:23.

105 E.g., M. Braun, *History and Romance in Graeco-Oriental Literature* (Oxford: Basil Blackwell, 1938), 4–5; Barclay, *Jews*, 129; Collins, *Athens*, 39–46; Johnson, *Historical Fictions*, 99–102.

106 Although the order of the fragments presented in Eusebius through Alexander Polyhistor does not necessarily represent the order of the passages in Artapanus' original work, the biblical order is most likely and should be considered definitive.

1.53.1–1.58.5.[107] Artapanus' implicit comparison with Sesostris has potential, as Diodorus describes him as surpassing all Egyptian kings preceding him (1.53.1) and as having conquered more territory than Alexander the Great (1.55.3), thus identifying him as one worthy of comparison and the champion of Egyptian history and culture.[108] Like Sesostris, Artapanus' Moses divided Egypt into thirty-six nomes (fr. 3.4//*Bibl.* 1.54.3), organized Egyptian animal worship (fr. 3.4//*Bibl.* 1.56.2), and invented ships (fr. 3.4//*Bibl.* 1.55.2). Both leaders also conquered Ethiopia (fr. 3.8//*Bibl.* 1.55.1), had influence over Arabia (fr. 3.17//*Bibl.* 1.53.5), and through their campaigns became very popular (fr. 3.6, 10//*Bibl.* 1.54.2). However, in addition to these similarities, Moses also surpasses Sesostris by subduing Egypt (fr. 3.27–33) and displaying power superior to that of Isis (fr. 3.32). This *synkrisis* of ethnic champions speaks to the overarching purpose of the work and falls outwith the traditional purview associated with ancient novels.

Although no Greek or Egyptian author/character is explicitly addressed in our fragments, there is good evidence to suggest that Artapanus consciously and purposefully engaged with non-Jewish literary works during the construction of his text and that these outside sources influenced Artapanus' method of composition and the work's contents, especially the Moses narrative.[109] At the same time, Artapanus drew heavily from Jewish Scripture, and his Greek text provided the basic content and macro structure of the narrative.[110] Artapanus' work exemplifies the inherent diversity of ancient genres and highlights the challenges modern scholars face when attempting to apply a genre label. Artapanus clearly engages with Hellenistic literary forms and conventions, particularly in the way that he attempts to configure Jewish literature and national identity vis-à-vis their Egyptian and Greek neighbors. Artapanus employs traditional historical practices when crafting his text, signaling his participation in this genre.[111] Concurrently, Artapanus' work could be viewed as also participating in novel, especially through the exploration of cultural identity,

107 Cf. D. L. Tiede, *The Charismatic Figure as Miracle Worker* (SBLDS 1; Missoula, Mont.: Scholars Press, 1972), 149–60.

108 A similar, elevated story is found in Herodotus, *Hist.* 2.102–110. Cf. P.Oxy. XXVII 2466; XLVII 3319.

109 For parallels between Moses' prison escape and that reported in Euripides' *Bacchae*, see C. J. P. Friesen, *Reading Dionysus: Euripides' "Bacchae" and the Cultural Contestations of Greeks, Jews, Romans, and Christians* (STAC 95; Tübingen: Mohr Siebeck, 2015), 136–48.

110 For the importance of Jewish models for Artapanus, see E. S. Gruen, "The Twisted Tales of Artapanus: Biblical Rewritings as Novelistic Narrative," in *The Construct of Identity in Hellenistic Judaism: Essays on Early Jewish Literature and History* (DCLS 29; Berlin: De Gruyter, 2016), 447–50.

111 The tone of the text, in this case potentially humorous (cf. Gruen, *Heritage and Hellenism*, 153–60), does not undermine or preclude genre participation, although it may be prototypically more common for novelistic works.

although the creation of national identities is something that participants of both genres engage in and so would be a shared feature.

3 Maccabees

Third Maccabees is an anonymous Jewish work likely composed in the first century BCE. Despite its name, it has nothing to do with the Maccabees.[112] Rather, 3 Maccabees details the oppression of the Jewish people in Egypt by Ptolemy IV Philopater and their supernatural protection and release. This work does not begin with an authorial preface but with the conflict between Ptolemy IV and Antiochus III *in medias res* leading up to the battle of Raphia (1:1–7), an opening that has strong parallels with Polybius.[113] Both 3 Macc 1:2–3 and Polybius, *Hist.* 5.81.1–7, tell the story of Theodotus, a would-be assassin entering into the tent of Ptolemy and killing the person sleeping therein, but not the king, who was in a different tent. The primary difference between the accounts is that 3 Maccabees attributes the assassin's failure to the foresight of Dositheus, an apostatized Jew (1:3), whereas according to Polybius, it was the assassin's lack of preparation that was his undoing (*Hist.* 5.81.7). Both texts report that at one point in the following battle Ptolemy's army was in disarray and being overrun by Antiochus' forces (3 Macc 1:4; *Hist.* 5.84.10), but they differ on the explanation of the reversal. Arsinoë, although mentioned as being present at the battle (*Hist.* 5.83.3), is not reported by Polybius to have played any role in securing the victory (so 3 Macc 1:4–5).[114] Rather, Polybius attributes the battle's success to Ptolemy and his ability to inspire his troops and surprise Antiochus (*Hist.* 5.85.8), whose inexperience did not allow him to picture the events accurately (*Hist.* 5.85.11–13). These parallels suggest that the author of

112 For a detailed discussion, see Johnson, *Historical Fictions*, 129–41. For a broad, recent overview, see S. R. Johnson, "3 Maccabees," in J. K. Aitken, ed., *T&T Clark Companion to the Septuagint* (London: Bloomsbury, 2015), 292–305. For a detailed discussion of the history of interpretation, see F. Parente, "The Third Book of Maccabees as Ideological Document and Historical Source," *Henoch* 10 (1988): 143–82. Edition used: R. Hanhart, ed., *Septuaginta: Vetus Testamentum Graecum*, vol. IX.3, *Maccabaeorum liber III* (2nd ed.; Göttingen: Vandenhoeck & Ruprecht, 1980).

113 Croy has argued that this abruptness is due to omission of the first part of the work; whereas other scholars have suggested that the text of 3 Maccabees has been truncated or excerpted. Although there are some awkward elements (e.g., 2:25), the opening as it has been transmitted is understandable, will be taken as original, and signals to the readers that they should expect to read Hellenistic historiography. N. C. Croy, *3 Maccabees* (SEPT; Leiden: Brill, 2006), xviii. H. Anderson, "3 Maccabees," in *OTP* 2.512–13; Hadas, *Third and Fourth Books*, 4–5; V. A. Tcherikover, "The Third Book of Maccabees as a Historical Source of Augustus' Time," *ScrHier* 7 (1961): 2.

114 The depiction of Arsinoë as passive is also found in the Raphia Decree (CM 31088), which has a picture of Arsinoë standing while Ptolemy attacks on horseback (cf. "It shall be so designed that he shall be in act to slay one kneeling, figured as a king, with the long spear in his hand, like the spear which the victorious king carried in the battle," ll. 36–37).

3 Maccabees had knowledge of the battle and/or access to a source that depicted it. As for the unique elements in 3 Maccabees, it is not possible to determine with certainty whether or not they were created by the author of 3 Maccabees or if he inherited them from his source(s).

Polybius' narrative does not fully detail the events following the battle, although he does say that Ptolemy toured Coele Syria (*Hist.* 5.86.7–11). The Raphia Decree (also known as the Pithom stele, CG 31088//SEG 8.467), a triscriptural, diglossic inscription found in Memphis, Egypt, in 1902, explicitly recounts Ptolemy's religious observance and his reverence for the gods of other temples: "He [Ptolemy] made a progress through the other places which were in his kingdom. He went into the temples which were there. He offered burnt offerings and libations, and all the inhabitants of the cities received him with gladness of heart" (ll. 15–16, trans. E. R. Bevan).[115] Ptolemy is said to have refurnished the temples, replaced their treasuries, and restored the gods desecrated by Antiochus (ll. 18–19, 27–29). These actions align closely with the narrative in 3 Maccabees, in which Ptolemy endowed sacred enclosures with gifts (1:7) and made sacrifices at the temple in Jerusalem (1:9). During his visit to the temple, Ptolemy expressed the desire to enter the sanctuary, claiming that the rules of its inviolability did not apply to him (1:10–15). The Raphia Decree further illuminates this representation, as it depicts Ptolemy as being welcomed and included in the divine space through the incorporation of his image in temple stelae (ll. 32–34). These similarities further support the idea that the author of 3 Maccabees was influenced by existing narratives in Egypt regarding the policies and actions of Ptolemy IV, providing a good example of how the author of 3 Maccabees exploited his sources, grafting in narrative branches to make a new, holistic story.

Battles and wars have long been recognized as motifs for ancient histories, and the author of 3 Maccabees begins his work by invoking this literary topos. However, unlike other histories, this earthly battle is not the central idea of his work, but sets the stage for the more important conflict, that between a powerful king and the Jewish God. Once again, the Raphia Decree provides important insight into the religious nature of Ptolemy's actions that shapes how the remainder of 3 Maccabees unfolds. In the decree, Ptolemy is not only praised for his piety, but is afforded divine honors: "Many caused a wreath of gold to be made for him, undertaking to set up a royal statue in his honour and to build temples. It came to pass that the king went on his ways as a man divine" (l. 17).

115 For editions, see R. S. Simpson, *Demotic Grammar in the Ptolemaic Sacerdotal Decrees* (Oxford: Griffith Institute, Ashmolean Museum, 1996), 3–4, 242–57; A. Bernard, trans., *La prose sur pierre dans l'Égypte hellénistique et romaine* (2 vols.; Paris: Éditions du CNRS, 1992), vol. 1 #14; D. Klotz, "Who Was with Antiochos III at Raphia? Revisiting the Hieroglyphic Versions of the Raphia Decree (CG 31008 and 50048)," *CdE* 87 (2013): 45–59.

This claim, which is also echoed by Polybius (*Hist.* 5.86.11), elevates the nature of the discussion from the earthly to the divine realm and provides a strong historical rationale for the use of Ptolemy IV by the author of 3 Maccabees.

The opening of a work is important for its ability to set the stage for the remaining narrative, as Polybius claims: "so we should think that beginnings do not only reach half way, but reach to the end, and both writers and readers of a general history should pay the greatest attention to them" (*Hist.* 5.32.5).[116] Although it is too much to claim that the author of 3 Maccabees directly knew the work of Polybius, the importance of a proper opening was not lost on him,[117] providing the necessary perspective on Ptolemy IV, who after his victory was the most powerful person in the eastern Mediterranean, which led him to become arrogant (ὑπερηφανής, 3 Macc 1:27; 2:5). By presenting Ptolemy at the peak of his power at the beginning of the work, the author of 3 Maccabees sets up his reversal and downfall through his conflict with the transcendent power of God and his total control over humanity.[118] Beginning at 1:16, the narrative contains more nonprototypical features for Greek historiography, such as the description of the Jewish people lamenting in unison at the imminent violation of the sanctuary[119] and God's supernatural intervention within the plot (e.g., 2:21–22; 4:21; 5:11–12, 28; 6:18).[120] These features are more common in Jewish texts and could suggest a Jewish prototype.[121]

Scholars identify parallels between 3 Maccabees and Esther.[122] In both works the king makes a declaration that threatens the Jewish people (Esth 3:13;

116 This statement by Polybius introduces the section on Ptolemy IV and his battle with Antiochus III at Raphia.

117 Cf. Philo, *Congr.* 11. On the importance of the opening to frame properly a history, see Dionysius of Halicarnassus, *Pomp.* 3; Cicero, *Fam.* 5.12.2–6.

118 The collocation of motifs of an arrogant foreign king who enters or robs the Temple and so must be punished by God has a number of scriptural parallels. E.g., LXX Ps 73:3, 22–23; 1 Macc 1:21–23; Pss. Sol. 2:1–2; cf. Dan 11:31.

119 We also find exaggerated numbers and descriptions throughout the text (e.g., 3 Macc 4:20; 5:2).

120 On the thematic relationship between 3 Maccabees and Esther, Daniel, Letter of Aristeas, and 2 Maccabees, see Johnson, *Historical Fictions*, 141–69.

121 One example is the attempted massacre of the Jews by drunken elephants, which is also recounted by Josephus (*C. Ap.* 2.51–55//3 Macc 5:2, 10, 45). Despite elephantine similarities, there are some important differences, such as Josephus' attributing this event to Ptolemy VIII Physcon (r. 146–117 BCE) and not to IV Philopater (r. 221–204 BCE) and a different rationale for its actions—that Physcon was angry with his general's rebellion, but did not want to attack Onias due to his fear of the general and his army. The strength of the parallels has led some scholars to posit that the Josephus and the author of 3 Maccabees had independently adopted a common source, which, according to Tromp, became the foundation for 3 Macc 3–7. J. Tromp, "The Formation of the Third Book of Maccabees," *Henoch* 17 (1995): 315–18.

122 On the relationship between 3 Maccabees and the Greek book of Esther, see R. B. Motzo, "Il rifacimento greco di 'Ester' e il 'III Macc,'" in *Saggi di storia e letteratura giudeo-ellenistica* (Florence: F. Le Monnier, 1924), 272–90; J. R. C. Cousland, "Reversal, Recidivism, and Reward

B 6–7; 3 Macc 2:27; 3:1, 25–26), which is eventually rescinded (Esth 8:10–11; E 15–18; 3 Macc 6:27–29; 7:8), and the Jewish people inaugurate a festival in celebration.[123] Both feature a Jew foiling an assassination plot (Esth 2:21–23; 3 Macc 1:2–3); a false accusation of Jewish disloyalty to the state (Esth 3:8; 3 Macc 3:2–7, 16–26); the sending of two royal letters, with the second canceling the edict of the first (Esth B 1–7; E 1–24; 3 Macc 3:12–29; 7:1–9); the same number of gentiles killed following the redemption of the Jewish people (i.e., 300; Esth 9:15; 3 Macc 7:14–15); the divine manipulation of sleep to preserve the Jewish people (Esth 6:1; 3 Macc 5:11–12); and a dramatic reversal of fortune from near death to full redemption and prominence. These thematic parallels, although many, lack the specificity that would allow for claims of direct literary dependence. More helpful have been some of the linguistic similarities identified, as they are concentrated in the royal letter additions to Esther (i.e., Additions B and E).[124] This clustering strongly implies a connection between the author of the royal correspondence in the Esther additions and 3 Maccabees, though this does not speak to the dependence in the rest of Esther.[125]

Even more prominent is the relationship between 2 Maccabees and 3 Maccabees. In both works a gentile leader threatens to violate the sanctuary (2 Macc 3:13–14, 23; 3 Macc 1:9–15), which leads to a panic among the population of Jerusalem (2 Macc 2:14–21; 3 Macc 1:16–29). The high priest offers an effectual prayer (2 Macc 3:31–34; 3 Macc 2:1–20), and God chastens the arrogant foreigner but does not kill him (2 Macc 3:22–30; 3 Macc 2:21–24). This results in a Hellenization crisis in which some Jews, out of fear of the actions of the gentile leader, apostasize to the cult of Dionysius (2 Macc 6:1–11, cf. 4:7–17; 3 Macc 2:25–33),[126] while faithful Jews are persecuted (2 Macc 6:12–7:42; 3 Macc 3:1–5:51). God ultimately intervenes through the prayers of Eleazar and other Jews (2 Macc 6:26–30; 7:37–38; 8:5; 3 Macc 6:1–21), granting the Jewish people victory through angelic intervention (2 Macc 8:5–9:29; 3 Macc 6:18–21) and the repentance of the gentile leader (2 Macc 3:35; 3 Macc 6:22). In response to their preservation, the Jews inaugurate a festival that is to be observed in perpetuity (2 Macc 10:1–8; 3 Macc 6:30–40). The substantial narrative overlap of both texts as well as specific linguistic similarities suggest

---

in 3 Maccabees: Structure and Purpose," *JSJ* 31 (2003): 39–51; N. Hacham, "3 Maccabees and Esther: Parallels, Intertextuality, and Diaspora Identity," *JBL* 126 (2007): 765–85.

123 For the many references to festivals and feasting in these works by both Jews and gentiles, see Esth 1:3–4, 5–12; 2:18; 5:4–8; 6:14–7:8; 8:17; 9:17–19, 22–23; 3 Macc 4:1, 16; 5:3, 15–17, 36–39; 6:30–31, 33, 35–36, 40; 7:15, 18–20.

124 E.g., Motzo, "Il rifacimento greco del 'Ester,'" 275–78, 280–82.

125 Hacham, "3 Maccabees and Esther," 778–79, supporting the previous work by C. A. Moore, "On the Origins of the LXX Additions to the Book of Esther," *JBL* 92 (1973): 384–85.

126 On this topic see A. Kasher, *The Jews in Hellenistic and Roman Egypt* (TSAJ 7; Tübingen: Mohr Siebeck, 1985), 214–26.

a direct literary connection between the two works, and scholars are broadly in agreement that the author of 3 Maccabees made use of 2 Maccabees, the nonabridged history by Jason of Cyrene, or a common source.[127]

The author of 3 Maccabees highlights the ethnic component of the narrative, regularly differentiating between Jewish and non-Jewish groups, defining the Jewish people as a nation (ἔθνος, 1.11; 2.27, 33) or race (γένος, 1:3; 3:2, 6; 6:4, 9, 13; φῦλον, 4:14; 5:5) and Jews as "fellow nationals" (ὁμοεθνεῖς, 4:12; 7:14). In contrast, non-Jews are called ἀλλοεθνεῖς (4:6) or ἀλλόφυλοι (3:6). In the non-Jewish category, importance is given to "the Greeks" as a composite character and their willingness to support the Jews in their time of need (e.g., 3:8–10). This excludes the person of Ptolemy, who in the ancient world would have been considered a Greek, but within the narrative world is a distinct character. This emphasis on national identity, along with the inherent vulnerability of the Jewish people, resonates with other Jewish works (e.g., Esther, Daniel, other Maccabaean literature), especially the genres of novel and history, as discussed above. The themes of divine election (2:2–20; 6:2–15) and the dangers of apostasy (2:31–33; 7:10–16) further reinforce religious distinctives, strengthening determined Jews to hold fast to their core identity.

The author of 3 Maccabees was aware of Greek historiography and attempted to employ certain literary practices. The primary issue for scholars is that the inclusion of fictitious events subsequent to the opening, especially divine acts of intervention, undermines their conceptions of the nature of Greek historiography. This apparent incompatibility of blending history with fiction challenges this preconceived idea, which results in the genre category of "historical romance" or "historical fiction."[128] The label "historical fiction" is not an emic category germane to ancient authors. Some (rightly) claim that the grammarian Asclepiades discusses false history when he subdivides the historical part of his grammar into three subsections: true, false, and one as if true (τῆς γὰρ ἱστορίας τὴν μέν τινα ἀληθῆ εἶναί φησι τὴν δὲ ψευδῆ τὴν δὲ ὡς ἀληθῆ, Sextus Empiricus, *Math.* 1.252). This reference to "false history," however, is limited in the following section to genealogies: "and of false histories (that is, the legendary) there is, he says, one kind only, the genealogical."[129] Discussions

127 Tromp, "The Formation of the Third Book of Maccabees," 318–24; deSilva, *Introducing the Apocrypha*, 342. For a list of words unique to 2 Macc and 3 Macc, see C. W. Emmet, "The Third Book of Maccabees," in *APOT* 1.156.

128 Anderson, "3 Maccabees," 2.510; Croy, *3 Maccabees*, xv; deSilva, *Introducing the Apocrypha*, 310; Hadas, *Third and Fourth Books*, 13–15; Wills, "Jewish Novellas in a Greek and Roman Age," 142. "Third Maccabees is, in short, in terms of its genre, too fabulous to be history and too much like history to be legend; and the label 'romance' that it has earned in consequence merely names the problem without solving it." Johnson, *Historical Fictions*, 192.

129 Sextus Empiricus, *Math.* 1.253, τῆς δὲ ψευδοῦς, τουτέστι τῆς μυθικῆς, ἓν εἶδος μόνον ὑπάρχειν λέγει τὸ γενεαλογικόν.

about persons (gods, heroes, and notable men), places/times, and actions are all, according to Asclepiades, located in the category of "true history" (*Math.* 1.253). The ancients did have a concept of "false history," although it is limited to a specific type of work. The content that we might identify as "false," namely stories of the gods or heroes, is categorized as "true history," thus creating a strong divide between modern and ancient understandings.

Historical fiction, as we understand it, is a modern construct that identifies a pattern of combining fictional elements with historically situated narratives. One of the key features of this defined genre is its narrative base, which is grounded in recognized historical characters, geographic locales, and select historical events. In the case of 3 Maccabees, the main protagonist is Ptolemy IV Philopater, who reigned over Egypt for seventeen years (r. 221–204 BCE; cf. 3 Macc 1:1). The narrative is set following the battle of Raphia (22 June 217 BCE) and records events both at the temple in Jerusalem (1:9–2:24) and at Alexandria, although there are few references to the city (2:30; 3:1, 21). These elements anchor the text within a particular time period of history and give the work the veneer of historicity. But all of this is for a purpose: the use of historical "fact" allows the author to communicate a particular message that transcends historical veracity and speaks to "truths" that are beyond historical events.

This leads to the central question, what did the author of 3 Maccabees think he was writing? Select elements in his work suggest that he was writing a history; however, the primary issue for modern scholars in accepting this genre designation is the inclusion of what they define as clearly fictional elements. The assumption of historicity as determinative for history and its perceived transgression by the author are foundational for the genre label assigned to 3 Maccabees (and other works). Rarely is the question asked, did the author of 3 Maccabees consider the events historical? If we say that the author of 3 Maccabees thought that the events described were historical, then we might consider him naïve or a poor historian who did not adequately research his topic. But would this perspective change our understanding of his work? Does our understanding of the author's belief in his narrative influence the genre label we apply to a text? These considerations are rarely discussed, although they are central to whether or not we identify a text as participating in the genre of history. I suggest that the author's perspective on the text not only influences how s/he thought about the work's genre, but should be considered when scholars identify genre participation. If it could be determined that the author of 3 Maccabees thought that the events actually happened as he reported, then it would be difficult to not see 3 Maccabees as participating in history.[130]

130 The evaluation of its quality (i.e., good or poor) is a different question. It might be evaluated poorly by Greek standards, but it was clearly appreciated by certain Jewish (and later Christian) communities in order to ensure its survival.

In the case of 3 Maccabees we see an author aligning his text with Jewish exemplars and adopting patterns found in Esther and 2 Maccabees. Scholars are often content to identify parallels and sources, but fail to ask the deeper question of whether or not these relationships influence our understanding of the genre of the work(s) in question. To put it more directly, does the fact that the author of 3 Maccabees appears to have modeled his work on 2 Maccabees (or a related source) influence our decision as to the genre of 3 Maccabees? The use of a source does not make the subsequent text part of the same genre category; however, using a work as a literary model suggests a similarity in genre. Genres are often defined in relationship and counterdistinction to other genres, with works defined as prototypical influencing how authors and readers determine participation, especially when a dependent relationship can be determined. In the case of 3 Maccabees, its relationship with 2 Maccabees should be taken into account when attempting to determine in which genre 3 Maccabees participated.

This perspective fits well with our prototypical understanding of genre, in which certain works are identified by modern scholars or by ancient authors/readers as being quintessential examples of a literary form. The use of common themes and motifs by the author of 3 Maccabees lends credence to the idea that our author identified elements of 2 Maccabees as key for the construction of his and viewed 2 Maccabees (or its predecessor) as prototypical for the type of literary work he was trying to compose.[131] When compared to prototypical Greek histories, such as the works of Diodorus Siculus or Polybius, 3 Maccabees would be viewed as a fringe participant of historiography.[132] However, if we were to adopt the viewpoint of the author, I would argue that we would see a different orientation, especially if one were to place 2 Maccabees and Esther as prototypical members of a literary form. Comparing 3 Maccabees with Greek historiography, therefore, misses the intention of the author, who, though aware of ancient practices, did not consider them as being foremost in importance for the creation of his work. This revised center accepts that each individual, both modern and ancient, has their own, unique understanding of

131 The similarities between 2 and 3 Maccabees, including the role of the divine in preserving the Jewish people and the strong theological themes, are widely discussed. DeSilva, *Introducing the Apocrypha*, 270–72; R. Doran, *2 Maccabees: A Critical Commentary* (Hermeneia; Minneapolis: Fortress, 2012), 6. For discussion, see chapter 7. Theomachic narratives are not outwith the purview of ancient historians (e.g., Pausanias, *Descr.* 10.23.1–14; Diodorus Siculus, *Bibl.* 24.9.1–3), and this appears to be an important element of both Jewish narratives (2 Macc 5:17, 21; 7:19; 9:8–10; 15:5–6; 3 Macc 1:9–15; 2:21–24; 3:17–19; 5:42–44). Cf. R. Doran, *Temple Propaganda: The Purpose and Character of 2 Maccabees* (CBQMS 12; Washington, D.C.: Catholic Biblical Association, 1981), 103–4.

132 For historical elements of 3 Maccabees, see J. M. Modrzejewski, *The Jews of Egypt from Ramses II to Emperor Hadrian* (trans. R. Cornman; Philadelphia: Jewish Publication Society, 1995), 147–52.

genres, with potentially different prototypical examples inhabiting the centers of their genre categories.[133] The author of 3 Maccabees aligns his narrative primarily with his Jewish exemplars but also engages with standard Greek literary forms, suggesting multiple participation and a unique example of blending Jewish and Greek historiography.

Septuagintal Additions: Susanna, Bel and the Dragon

The final texts evaluated in this chapter are Susanna and Bel and the Dragon, which scholars have labeled "septuagintal additions." These works and others like them have not come down to us as individual stories, but as appended (and sometimes embedded) narratives associate with specific biblical texts (e.g., Daniel).[134] The way that these stories have been preserved provides insight into how literature was collected and disseminated in written form and offers a small window on the popularity of short stories in the Hellenistic era. The general lack of discrete short stories is not due to their absence or unpopularity in antiquity, but to the problems of distribution and preservation arising from their brevity. As a result, when they do survive, they are usually found within a collection or incorporated into a larger work. Susanna and Bel and the Dragon are good examples of this phenomenon and could be fruitfully read as part of Greek Daniel.[135] However, their original compositions—which are inspired by scriptural Daniel, but may not have been written primarily for inclusion within Daniel—need to be considered independently.[136]

Both Susanna and Bel and the Dragon align themselves with the book of Daniel through the use of the Daniel character.[137] In Susanna the young Dan-

133 A parallel example would be the individual preference in genre hierarchies, which, though culturally influenced and situated, exhibit differences by person. Cf. Quintilian, *Inst.* 1.4.3; Adams, *Genre*, 49–53.

134 Integrated into the text, between the switch from Hebrew to Aramaic at Dan 3:23/24, are the Prayer of Azariah and the Song of the Three Young Men (OG 3:24–90). These are Danielic additions, but are not discrete, stand-alone narratives.

135 These additions influence the reading of the Greek version of Daniel. By adding features that are associated with specific genres, especially novel, there is a greater likeliness that readers will view Greek Daniel as participating in novel. The large apocalyptic section in Dan 7–12 makes Greek Daniel a nonprototypical member of this genre and would encourage the reader to view it as participating in multiple genres.

136 The practice of collecting short, generically related works into one volume becomes prominent during the Roman period, but was also practiced in earlier epochs (e.g., Horace, *Epodes*; *Odes*; *Letters*; *Satires*; Ovid, *Heroides*; *Amores*; Plutarch, *Moralia*). For the collection of Egyptian stories, see book 2 of Herodotus' *Histories*.

137 The textual history of these additions is complex, with substantial differences between OG/967 and Theodotian (θ′), not only in terms of their content, but also in their placement within the manuscripts. For recent discussions see L. DiTommaso, *The Book of Daniel and the Apocryphal Daniel Literature* (SVTP 20; Leiden: Brill, 2005), 1–20; F. Borchardt, "How Bel and the Serpent Went from Addition to Edition of Daniel," *CBQ* 80 (2018): 409–28. For the critical Greek edition of these texts, see J. Ziegler, O. Munnich, and D. Fraenkel, eds., *Susanna, Daniel,*

iel (Sus 45, θ′64) appears in the latter part of the work to reveal the treachery of the two judges through his insight and cross-examination, rescuing Susanna from death (Sus 47–62).[138] The adult Daniel is the main character in Bel and the Dragon and is depicted in scenes of conflict with the priests of Bel (Bel 1–22) and with members of the royal court (Bel 23–42). In both narratives Daniel's intelligence and resourcefulness are highlighted, often at the expense of the other characters, such as the Jewish crowd in Susanna and the Babylonian king in Bel (Sus 48; Bel θ′ 7, 19). Although divine actions are part of each story (Sus 45; Bel 33–37), they are minor and the focus is placed on the bright, if divinely gifted, human. The freedom with which the texts are crafted, along with the emphasis on the character of Daniel, erotic themes, humor, and so on, allow for Susanna and Bel to be profitably read as participating in novel.

Bel and the Dragon could also be viewed as engaging with the genre of satire. Certain features in Bel are not core to ancient novels, especially the parodic and religiously combative elements. Rather, the story of Bel narrativizes anti-idol polemics (e.g., Jer 10; Epistle of Jeremiah), and the dragon tale could be viewed as a parody of Babylonian texts (e.g., *Enuma Elish*).[139] The primary challenge to this proposal is that satire was widely viewed in antiquity as a Latin genre, and participation in it by Greek authors, or Greek versions of the genre during the Hellenistic era, is not well attested.[140] Delineating how the genre is bounded is also problematic, as variation among constituent texts appears to be widespread. The core feature of this genre is the critique of a person, group, practice, or institution primarily through the use of humor, but this is

Bel et Draco, vol. XVI.2 (2nd ed.; Göttingen: Vandenhoeck & Ruprecht, 1999). For the original independence of these texts (based on, for example, the superscription and the anonymous character of the king in Bel), see L. M. Wills, *The Jew in the Court of the Foreign King: Ancient Jewish Court Legends* (HDR 26; Minneapolis: Fortress, 1990), 130. For discussion of the original languages of these works, with bibliography, see C. A. Moore, trans., *Daniel, Esther, and Jeremiah: The Additions* (AYBC; New Haven: Yale University Press, 1995), 81–84 (Susanna) and 119–20 (Bel).

138 Susanna is presented as the main character and is introduced to the reader through the importance of her parents and her husband, Joakim (Sus θ′ 1–4).

139 For the former see Adams, *Baruch and The Epistle of Jeremiah*, 155–57. For the discussion of the latter, see R. H. Pfeiffer, *History of New Testament Times: With an Introduction to the Apocrypha* (New York: Harper and Brothers, 1949), 456.

140 Menippus of Gadara and his contemporary Meleager were said to have written works full of derision (καταγέλωτος γέμει, Diogenes Laertius, *Vit.* 6.99). For comparison of Latin and Greek satire, see Horace, *Sat.* 1.4, 10; 2.1; Quintilian, *Inst.* 10.1.93–95 (*satura tota nostra est*). Cf. C. J. Classen, "Satire—The Elusive Genre," *Symbolae Osloenses* 63 (1988): 95–121; G. B. Conte, *Latin Literature: A History* (trans. J. B. Solodow; rev. D. Fowler and G. W. Most; Baltimore: Johns Hopkins University Press, 1994), 298–99. For seeing satire as related to Old Comedy, see D. M. Hooley, *Roman Satire* (Oxford: Blackwell, 2007), 13–27.

not exclusive to satires.[141] Most satirical works in antiquity are not anonymous compositions, but by named authors, which would make the anonymous Bel and the Dragon atypical. This choice, as well as the adoption of the character of Daniel, distances the composition from a specific, later historical situation and affords its critique a wider universality. The fluid boundary of satire allows for easier participation by authors, and it is plausible to understand Bel and the Dragon as engaging with this literary expression.

The story of the three bodyguards in 1 Esd 3:1–5:6 provides an example of embedding a short story within a larger narrative.[142] Unlike most of 1 Esdras, which has clear parallels to other scriptural texts (e.g., 2 Chronicles, Ezra, and possibly Nehemiah) and could be read as rewritten Scripture, the story of Darius' bodyguards is previously unattested and so represents new material to the biblical texts.[143] Given the practice of the author of 1 Esdras to use sources, coupled with the likeliness that the story was not originally written in Greek, this embedded narrative was likely in circulation prior to its inclusion, possibly as a story with non-Jewish origins (e.g., Greek, Persian, or Egyptian).[144] The contest, however, clearly resonates with the Jewish motif of the wise Jewish advisor impressing the king and, in turn, receiving rewards that benefit both the individual and the nation.[145] Although much can be and has been said about this story, its importance for this chapter resides in its parallels with other septuagintal additions as evidence of a wider practice of Jewish composing and adapting short stories.

The writing of short stories was a wide literary phenomenon with extant examples from many ancient communities. A number of short stories survive from Egypt, originally written in Demotic with a few translated into Greek. Most were of modest length (much less than one scroll) and written in prose

141 Conte, *Latin Literature*, 298–99; Hooley, *Roman Satire*, 18.

142 See also the narratives on Tobiads (Josephus, *Ant.* 12.154–236) and the royal family of Adiabene (Josephus, *Ant.* 20.17–96).

143 For the use of Scripture in 1 Esdras, see Z. Talshir, *1 Esdras: From Origin to Translation* (SCS 47; Atlanta: SBL, 1999); Z. Talshir, *1 Esdras: A Text Critical Commentary* (SCS 50; Atlanta: SBL, 2001). For the (intentional?) omission of Nehemiah, see J. L. Wright, "Remember Nehemiah: 1 Esdras and the *Damnatio Memoriae Nehemiae*," in L. S. Fried, ed., *Was 1 Esdras First? An Investigation into the Priority and Nature of 1 Esdras* (AIL 7; Atlanta: SBL, 2011), 145–63. For the view of 1 Esdras as rewritten Scripture, see K. de Troyer, *Rewriting the Sacred Text: What the Old Greek Texts Tell Us about the Literary Growth of the Bible* (TCSt 4; Atlanta: SBL, 2003), 91–126.

144 Cf. Gruen, *Heritage and Hellenism*, 160–67. For a recent overview, see M. F. Bird, *1 Esdras: Introduction and Commentary on the Greek Text in Codex Vaticanus* (SEPT; Leiden: Brill, 2012), 141–89.

145 E.g., Esther, Daniel, Joseph. Cf. LA 12–27.

(unlike literature from the Middle Kingdom, which was metrical).[146] These stories, such as *Prophecy of Petesis* (or *Nectanebo's Dream*) and *Myth of the Sun's Eye*, typically have a third-person narrative framework which encompasses a substantial amount of first-person accounts with extensive direct speech.[147] The parallels between *Prophecy of Petesis* and *Alexander Romance*, for example, imply a practice of cultural interaction and literary appropriation and challenge the idea that Demotic or non-Greek compositions in Egypt were limited only to Egyptian readers.[148] These Egyptian-Greek texts militate against strict claims of Jewish literary originality and support the view that constructing short stories was a wider, if not universal, practice. The practice of *brachylogia* was witnessed in the Hellenistic era in the form of epyllia, short stories written in poetic meter that regularly focus on mythological narratives.[149] The surviving Egyptian short stories, as well as works of Susanna and Bel and the Dragon, have clear points of contact with epyllia (e.g., narrative and brevity), but have specific formal differences (especially difference in use of metered language), facilitating readers to see a conceptual relation while allowing for distinguished genre prototypes.

Conclusion

In this chapter we evaluated texts that participate to some degree in the ancient genre of novel. In every case we found that genre associations are complex and greater nuance is needed for teasing out inherent assumptions about ancient genres, whether that is the role of fiction in determining a work's genre or how a text's relationship with other works influences our genre labels. I have argued that the use of prototype genre theory can alleviate some of the inherent tensions and constraints found in previous discussions. Joseph and Aseneth, 3 Maccabees, and the work of Artapanus are not core examples of a genre, but are peripheral, participating in multiple genres. As such, they evidence the range of literature that could be produced in antiquity.

The works discussed here were not fully beholden to established Greek literary forms but drew from Jewish works, especially Scripture, and may have also been influenced by Egyptian narratives. This is not to claim that these authors were not influenced by Greek genres or that they were unaware of

146 Cf. J. Tait, "Egyptian Fiction in Demotic Greek," in J. R. Morgan and R. Stoneman, eds., *Ancient Fiction: The Greek Novel in Context* (London: Routledge, 1994), 206.

147 K. Ryholt, "A Demotic Version of Nectanebo's Dream (P. Carlsberg 562)," *ZPE* 122 (1998): 197–200. Cf. *P. Carl.* 424, 499, and 559, which are also from the Tebtunis temple. *Myth* also has a series of embedded fables which Thoth tells to Tefnut.

148 Cf. B. E. Perry, "The Egyptian Legend of Nectanebus," *TAPA* 97 (1996): 327–33; Rutherford, "Greek Fiction and Egyptian Fiction."

149 For a larger discussion, see chapter 2, pp. 35–42.

particular literary practices. All of the works evidence this engagement, with the work by Artapanus and 3 Maccabees showing strong awareness of Greek historiography. The joining of diverse features to embody one text shows the inherent complexity of literary composition in antiquity and reinforces the idea that rigid divisions between Greek and Jewish literature did not exist in the minds of at least some ancient Jewish authors.

7

Jewish Historians

In this chapter I evaluate Jewish authors who participate in the genre of Greek historiography. This task is difficult, as the practice of writing history was already well established among Jewish authors prior to the conquests of Alexander. The number and diversity of Jewish authors writing in Greek, however, suggest that engagement with Greek literary culture provided new impetuses for composition.[1] History writing was an important genre from the beginning of the Hellenistic era, and its prominence in Greek culture was a strong factor for why native authors actively took up this genre.[2] This prominence led to a diversity of historiographic approaches and styles available in the Hellenistic era, which belies simplistic categorizations. No systematic division of history by the grammarians was universally adopted (cf. Sextus Empiricus, *Math.* 1.266–69). The most prominent modern subdivision of Greek historiography is by Felix Jacoby, who identified five subgenres based on his reconstruction of genre development: mythography or genealogy, ethnography, chronography,

1 Momigliano suggests that the revival of Jewish historiography is "inseparable from Greek influence." A. Momigliano, "The Second Book of Maccabees," *CP* 70 (1975): 88. Holladay (*Fragments: Historians*, 1.1) claims that Jewish history writers "are the first clear examples of Jewish authors self-consciously writing in explicitly Greek literary modes." This is accurate in light of some of the authorial discussions (especially Josephus), but I would suggest that Holladay might have undervalued the poetic pieces (chapters 2 and 3) because of their fragmentary nature. For an introduction to historiography in the Hasmonean Period and the role of scriptural texts, see K. Berthelot, *In Search of the Promised Land? The Hasmonean Dynasty between Biblical Models and Hellenistic Diplomacy* (trans. M. Rigaud; JAJSup 24; Göttingen: Vandenhoeck & Ruprecht, 2018).

2 For a set of examples, see J. Dillery, *Clio's Other Sons: Berossus and Manetho* (Ann Arbor: University of Michigan Press, 2015), 4–32.

contemporary history (*Zeitgeschichte*), and local history or horography.[3] Although this classification system is useful, prototype theory challenges the boundedness of subgenres and neat scholarly categorization, highlighting Jewish diversity of participation.

The number of Jewish authors who are reported to have composed histories and the quantity of fragments that have survived make a full investigation difficult.[4] Space limitations do not permit me to discuss all of these authors in depth, and I have not been able to address a number of fragmentary works (e.g., the annals of John Hyrcanus I,[5] Philo the Elder,[6] Aristeas,[7] Cleodemus [or Malchus] the Prophet,[8] Thallus,[9]

3 F. Jacoby, "Über die Entwicklung der griechischen Historiographie und den Plan einer neuen Sammlung der griechischen Historikerfragmente," *Kilo* 9 (1909): 80–123, reprinted in H. Bloch, ed., *Abhandlungen der griechischen Geschichtsschreibung* (Leiden: Brill, 1956), 16–64. Cf. Marincola, "Genre, Convention, and Innovation." On the limitations of Jacoby's edition, see C. A. Baron, *Timaeus of Tauromenium and Hellenistic Historiography* (Cambridge: Cambridge University Press, 2012), 9–12.

4 For a recent discussion of the problems of use of source criticism to glean fragments of historians from their "cover text," see Baron, *Timaeus*, 12–14.

5 1 Macc 16:23–24 (= *FGrH* 736). See Schürer, *History*, 3.1.185–86, for a possible reference to this work in Sixtus Senensis's *Bibliotheca Sancta* (1566).

6 Clement (*Strom*. 1.21.141.3) claims that this Philo wrote on the Jewish kings in a way that differed from that adopted by Demetrius the Chronographer (Φίλων δὲ καὶ αὐτὸς ἀνέγραψε τοὺς βασιλεῖς τοὺς Ἰουδαίων διαφώνως τῷ Δημητρίῳ). Josephus (*C. Ap*. 1.218) identifies him as a non-Jewish author, but he is regularly associated with Philo Epicus (see chapter 2). None of his work has survived.

7 One fragment of Aristeas' Περὶ Ἰουδαίων has been preserved via Alexander Polyhistor (Eusebius, *Praep. ev*. 9.25.1–4 = *FGrH* 725; see possible references in LA 6; Eusebius, *Praep. ev*. 9.38.2–3). Recounting the story of Job by expanding Gen 36:33, the fragment shows close resemblance to the epilogue of Greek Job 42:17b–e. The ethnicity of the author, along with his relationship to Pseudo-Aristeas, is debated. See Walter, "Exegeten," 256–99; A. Reed, "Job as Jobab: The Interpretation of Job in LXX Job 42:19b–e," *JBL* 120 (2001): 38–40.

8 Κλεόδημος δέ φησιν ὁ προφήτης ὁ καὶ Μάλχος, *Ant*. 1.240 (cf. Eusebius, *Praep. ev*. 9.20.2–4; *FGrH* 727). Little is known about this work, and there is substantial debate over the author's ethnicity (cf. Holladay, *Fragments: Historians*, 245–46, 248). Josephus reports that Alexander Polyhistor preserved part of the work, describing it as a "History of the Jews" (ἱστορῶν τὰ περὶ Ἰουδαίων) just as it was narrated by Moses (καθὼς καὶ Μωυσῆς ἱστόρησεν ὁ νομοθέτης αὐτῶν). Most notable in this fragment is the blending of Greek and Jewish traditions. Cleodemus claims that two sons of Abraham (Japhras and Apheras) joined Heracles on his expedition against Antaeus in Libya and that Heracles married the daughter of Aphranes (*Ant*. 1.241). Such genealogical interest was common in antiquity, particularly for those individuals who founded cities or nations (e.g., Plutarch, *Sert*. 9). This is not the only attempt by a Jewish author to forge links between the Jewish community and neighboring peoples (e.g., 1 Macc 12:20–23).

9 Thallus (*BNJ* 256) is reported to have written a history with at least three books (ἐν τρίτῃ τῶν Ἱστοριῶν, *FGrH* 256 F1). Although T1 suggests that the work ranged from the Trojan War to the 167th Olympiad (i.e., 112–109 BCE), FF1–4 report events that both precede and follow this time period. The fragments imply that Thallus' history was a chronologically focused account (like that of Demetrius the Chronographer, see below) in which he attempted to integrate Jewish and Greek recordings of history in order to show Moses' antiquity. For discussion of the author's ethnicity and dates, see Holladay, *Fragments: Historians*, 343–69; B. Garstad, "Thallos (256)," in *BNJ*.

Herod the Great,[10] Caecilius of Calacte,[11] Theophilus,[12] Pseudo-Hystaspes,[13] Judas[14]). These fragments evidence the importance of historiography for Jews in antiquity, and no doubt many now-lost works would have expanded our understanding of Jewish compositional practices even further. We will focus our attention on Eupolemus, Pseudo-Eupolemus, Pseudo-Hecataeus, Demetrius the Chronographer, 2 Maccabees/Jason of Cyrene, Justus of Tiberias, and Josephus, all of whom are Jewish authors who present the history of the Jewish people.[15] Many draw on scriptural sources for their content, but all of them seek to situate the Jewish people within their wider Hellenistic and Roman contexts.[16] As a result, although Jewish historians participate in a range of literary forms, there is a common element that binds them together.

Eupolemus

Eupolemus is a Jewish author whose work has survived fragmentarily through excerpts from Clement of Alexandria and Eusebius of Caesarea through their use of Alexander Polyhistor.[17] Widely thought to be the same individual

10 Josephus (*Ant.* 15.164–68, 174) mentions the "memoirs" (ὑπομνήματα) of Herod the Great, although there is little information regarding their nature.

11 Caecilius (*FGrH* 183) was an influential author during his lifetime and composed many rhetorical works. Reported to be a Jewish author by the *Suda* (K 1165, "I am surprised by his being Jewish: a Jew clever in things Greek," πῶς δὲ Ἰουδαῖος τοῦτο θαυμάζω: Ἰουδαῖος σοφὸς τὰ Ἑλληνικά), he had extensive knowledge of literary criticism and was compared to Dionysius of Halicarnassus. He is also reported to have written two histories (*History of the Slave Wars* and *On History*, Athenaeus, *Deipn.* 6.272f; 11.466a), but there is practically nothing extant of these works. Caecilius' Jewish heritage is questioned. Cf. Kennedy, *Art of Rhetoric*, 364–69.

12 Possibly a non-Jewish author (so Josephus, *C. Ap.* 1.215–16), Theophilus wrote about Solomon and his relationship with the king of Tyre (Eusebius, *Praep. ev.* 9.34.19). Cf. Holladay, *Fragments: Historians*, 337–42.

13 A Greek apocalyptic work was attributed to Hystaspes, the father of Darius, and mentioned by Justin (*1 Apol.* 20.1), Clement (*Strom.* 6.5.43.1–2), and Lactantius (*Epit.* 7.15.19; 7.18.2–3). No fragments have survived, and it is debated if the author was Jewish or Christian (cf. Denis, *Introduction*, 268–69).

14 Eusebius (*Hist. eccl.* 6.6.7) claims that Judas (*FGrH* 261) wrote "a discourse on the seventy weeks in the book of Daniel, stopping his chronology in the tenth year of Severus" (εἰς τὰς παρὰ τῶι Δανιὴλ ἑβδομήκοντα ἑβδομάδας ἐγγράφως διαλεχθείς, ἐπὶ τὸ δέκατον τῆς Σευήρου βασιλείας ἵστησιν τὴν χρονογραφίαν). Cf. Jerome, *Vir. ill.* 52.

15 First Esdras, which is a mix of translation and compositional elements, also provides an important example of the development of Jewish historiography in Greek. Cf. K. de Troyer, "Zerubbabel and Ezra: A Revived and Revised Solomon and Josiah? A Survey of Current 1 Esdras Research," *CBR* 1 (2002): 30–60.

16 Beyond the purview of this investigation, but important to keep in mind, is the diversity of Jewish historiography practices composed in Hebrew or Aramaic. For this discussion, see G. J. Brooke, "Types of Historiography in the Qumran Scrolls," in G. J. Brooke and T. Römer, eds., *Ancient and Modern Scriptural Historiography* (BETL 207; Leuven: Leuven University Press, 2007), 211–30.

17 For the text of Eusebius, see Mras, *Eusebius' Werke*. For the text of Clement, see O. Stählin and L. Früchtel, eds., *Clemens Alexandrinus*, vol. 2, *Stromata Buch I–VI* (3rd ed.; GCS 52; Berlin: Akademie Verlag, 1960).

mentioned in 1 Macc 8:17, 2 Macc 4:11, and Josephus, *Ant.* 12.415 (cf. *C. Ap.* 1.218), Eupolemus lived in Judaea, likely Jerusalem, and wrote in the mid-second century BCE.[18] Support for a second-century date comes from fragment 5 (Clement, *Strom.* 1.21.141.4–5), in which the author places his writing in the fifth year of Demetrius and the twelfth year of Ptolemy.[19] Scholars have debated if the seven fragments attributed to Eupolemus are from a Jewish or non-Jewish author, a debate complicated by the claim that one passage attributed to Eupolemus by Eusebius (*Praep. ev.* 9.17.2–9) is the work of a second-century BCE Samarian author now known as Pseudo-Eupolemus (see discussion below).[20]

According to Clement (*Strom.* 1.23.153.4), the title of Eupolemus' work was *Concerning the Kings of Judaea* (περὶ τῶν ἐν τῇ Ἰουδαιᾳ βασιλέων); whereas Eusebius (*Praep. ev.* 9.30.1) provides the appellation *Concerning the Prophecy of Elijah* (περὶ τῆς Ἐλίου προφητείας).[21] Of these two titles, the first better represents the work's contents, as the fragments lack any mention of Elijah.[22] According to Ben Zion Wacholder, Eupolemus' title indicates a Jewish, rather than Hellenistic background, as "Concerning the Kings of . . ." was atypical for a Greek work.[23] Wacholder goes too far in saying that this is distinctly a

18 Cf. Freudenthal, *Alexander Polyhistor*, 1.127; Wacholder, *Eupolemus*, 1–26; S. L. Sørensen, "Identifying the Jewish Eupolemoi: An Onomastic Approach," *JJS* 66 (2015): 24–35. For the view that they are two individuals, see Gruen, *Heritage and Hellenism*, 139–40; F. Clancy, "Eupolemus the Chronographer and 141 BCE," *SJOT* 23 (2009): 274–81; G. A. Keddie, "Solomon to His Friends: The Role of Epistolarity in Eupolemus," *JSP* 22 (2013): 228–29.

19 Walter (*Historiker*, 97) considers Eupolemus to be the oldest of the Jewish historians; whereas Mendels pushes the date of composition to ca. 125 BCE. Mendels, *Land of Israel*, 57–88. For the identification of these monarchs as Demetrius I Soter and Ptolemy VIII Euergetes II Physcon, see Freudenthal, *Alexander Polyhistor*, 1.213–14, followed by Wacholder, *Eupolemus*, 41–44. For the argument that the reference is to Demetrius II Nicator and Ptolemy VIII (specifically 141 BCE), see Müller, FHG 3.208; Clancy, "Eupolemus the Chronographer," 274–81; Keddie, "Solomon to His Friends," 225–29.

20 This debate is ancient in origin (see Josephus, *C. Ap.* 1.218; Eusebius, *Hist. eccl.* 6.13.7; Jerome, *Vir. ill.* 38). For modern scholars who have posited a Christian author, see Wacholder, *Eupolemus*, 27 n. 1. I hold to a Jewish author. Cf. Freudenthal, *Alexander Polyhistor*, 1.99; Holladay, *Fragments: Historians*, 157.

21 A third title option, *On the Jews of Assyria*, is also provided by Eusebius (*Praep. ev.* 9.17.2); however, this fragment is corrupt and is now attributed to Pseudo-Eupolemus and so does not feature regularly in discussions.

22 The full extent of Eupolemus' work is unknown. The content of F5 has been used to suggest that Eupolemus wrote a continuous history up to the second century BCE (so Wacholder, *Eupolemus*, 25). However, this could also be part of the prologue or a summary, so Doran, "Jewish Hellenistic Historians," 264; cf. Freudenthal, *Alexander Polyhistor*, 1.82–92, 207–9; Wacholder, *Eupolemus*, 21–26. Wacholder (22–24) posits that Elijah might not have been the original reference, but Eli, the chief priest of Shiloh. Schürer (*History*, 3.1.517) suggests that *Concerning the Prophecy of Elijah* might be a chapter title, rather than that of the book.

23 Wacholder, *Eupolemus*, 24–25.

non-Greek title, as some Greek authors do employ a similar construction.[24] On the other hand, the close relationship between history and prophecy is not prominent in Greek literature, but is evidenced in some Egyptian texts, such as the *Demotic Chronicle* (P.Bib.Nat. 215).[25]

Many scholars have slated Eupolemus' perceived poor quality of Greek. Jacob Freudenthal asserts that Eupolemus is "den judäischen Schriftsteller, der nur oberflächlich vom Geiste der griechischen Litteratur angehaucht," while Jacoby laments, "sein Stil ist miserabel, der Wortschatz dürftig, der Satzbau plump."[26] Their comments, however, are based on evaluations of quality in which Eupolemus is compared with classical-era authors and not with contemporary Hellenistic authors. When this latter comparison is undertaken, a number of co-called "Hebraisms" or poor elements are witnessed in Greek authors, implying that they were accepted literary constructions.[27] Eupolemus' perceived lack of proficiency in Greek is also paired with the claim that he knew Hebrew and had access to a Hebrew version of Kings and Chronicles. This view is supported by the Hebrew spelling of certain names (e.g., Σούρον, *Praep. ev.* 9.33.1; 9.34.1), the following of the Hebrew text over the surviving Greek translation at places,[28] and the use of translational glosses where 4 Reigns has transliterations.[29] These elements, if they do not indicate a different

24 E.g., Clearchus, Περὶ τοῦ Περσῶν βασιλέως (Athenaeus, *Deipn.* 12.529d); Chrysippus, F692 l.4, Χρύσιππος περὶ τῶν τοῦ Βοσπόρου βασιλέων τῶν περὶ Λεύκωνα; Diodorus Siculus, *Bibl.* 2. *praef.* 21, Περὶ τῶν βασιλέων τῶν κατὰ τὴν Μηδίαν; Athenaeus (Athenaeus, *Deipn.* 5.211a) Περὶ τῶν ἐν Συρίαι βασιλευσάντων; Nicolaus of Damascus (*FGrH* 90) F66.1; Diogenes Laertius, *Vit.* 7.167.

25 W. Spiegelberg, ed., *Die sogenannte Demotische Chronik des Pap. 215 der Bibliothèque Nationale zu Paris nebst den auf der Rückseite des Papyrus stehenden Texten* (Leipzig: Hinrichs, 1914); H. Felber, "Die demotische Chronik," in A. Blasius and B. U. Schipper, eds., *Apokalyptik und Ägypten: Eine kritische Analyse der relevanten Texte aus dem griechisch-römischen Ägypten* (OLA 107; Leuven: Peeters, 2002), 65–111.

26 Freudenthal, *Alexander Polyhistor*, 1.109–10; F. Jacoby, "Eupolemos," *PW* 11 (1907): 1229.

27 Cf. M. Dhont, "The Appreciation of Jewish Literature in the Hellenistic Era: The Case of Eupolemus," presented at SBL Boston, November 2017.

28 E.g., the use of cedar wood (1 Kgs 6:15; F2 *Praep. ev.* 9.34.5) over pine (3 Kgdms 6:15) in the construction of the temple walls and specifying the material for the temple pillars (i.e., bronze, 1 Kgs 7:15, F2 *Praep. ev.* 9.34.6), which is omitted in 3 Kgdms 7:3.

29 Eupolemus' use of Greek versions of 1 Kings and 2 Chronicles is debated. Freudenthal (*Alexander Polyhistor*, 1.118–20), Walter (*Historiker*, 101), and Holladay (*Fragments*, 1.101) all assume that Eupolemus used and/or had access to Greek translations of 1 Kings and 2 Chronicles. Wacholder (*Eupolemus*, 250–54) denies this, claiming that Eupolemus made use of the Hebrew versions. Wacholder (*Eupolemus*, 243–46) has undertaken a detailed study of the scriptural sources used by Eupolemus, and I have drawn on his findings for this discussion. Cf. J. Giblet, "Eupolème et l'historiographie de Judaïsme hellénistique," *ETL* 39 (1963): 548; Sterling, *Historiography*, 214–15. An important assumption in this discussion is that an alternative, now-lost Greek translation with these characteristics did not exist and was not used by Eupolemus.

Greek translation, imply that Eupolemus was bilingual, leading scholars to question if Greek was his first language.[30]

This debate overlooks an important question: if Eupolemus was more confident with Hebrew, why did he write in Greek, especially as both were recognized languages for historiographical composition? Knowledge of alternative language options reinforces the intentionality of Eupolemus' choice to write in Greek, which in turn influences our understanding of the author's purpose and intended audience. The composition of history in a different linguistic register is an important adaptation of an established genre. Ancient authors, as well as modern theories, claim that the relationship between the style or language of composition can be strongly linked to a genre.[31] The evocation of a genre creates expectations about its style, and when a genre is presented in a new style, the change in expression is viewed as atypical and either is rejected as a violation or results in a new expression.[32] In the case of Eupolemus, the language of composition has been viewed by scholars as a violation (or at least a failed attempt) of historiography. This pejorative outlook fails to appreciate Eupolemus' literary intent and his attempt at renewing Jewish historiographical practices to more closely align with his scriptural model(s), which he viewed as prototypical.

Determining Eupolemus' sources and literary model(s) is another challenge, as (excluding the biblical narratives) no other Hellenistic Jewish account of the monarchical period has survived. Other Jewish authors likely composed works on this topic (e.g., Pseudo-Philo), but the lack of literary comparators limits our ability to determine possible narrative sources and influential works. All of Eupolemus' surviving fragments, however, appear to be dependent on scriptural narratives. At the most fundamental level, we can say that Eupolemus knew certain scriptural books, specifically the Greek Hexateuch and the Hebrew (and possibly Greek) texts of Jeremiah, Kings, and Chronicles.[33]

Far from being a straight retelling of Scripture, Eupolemus' history presents an adapted narrative, which provides insight into his authorial situation. In F2, Eupolemus claims that David was allied with Vaphres of Egypt and at war with Suron of Tyre. Such details are not part of the biblical narrative, but better match the time period of the author, in which the Phoenicians and the Syrians were associated with the Seleucid Empire and Egypt with the then-favorable Ptolemies.[34] Eupolemus also presents a much more positive narrative of how

30 "His syntax and sentence formation left more of the Hebraic literary structure intact than did that of any other Hellenistic writer." Wacholder, *Eupolemus*, 255.

31 E.g., Philodemus, *De poem.* 1.61.16–27; Dionysius of Halicarnassus, *Ant. rom.* 1.1.2.

32 M. M. Bakhtin, *Speech Genres and Other Late Essays* (trans. V. W. McGee; Austin: University of Texas Press, 1986), 60–67.

33 Bickerman, *Jews in the Greek Age*, 179.

34 Wacholder, *Eupolemus*, 135–39. However, Gruen (*Heritage and Hellenism*, 140–41) highlights some foundational weaknesses of this association.

the temple location was chosen, attributing the selected locale to an angelic messenger, "Dianathan," who was responding to David's prayers, and omitting any reference to David's census and the angel of death (2 Sam 24:1–25; 1 Chr 21:1–22:1; cf. 2 Chr 3:1). Eupolemus exaggerated many numbers taken from scriptural texts (e.g., Solomon's age [F2] and length of reign [F3]) and provided new numerical details that were not part of his biblical sources (e.g., total expenses, tribute offered, pay for workers, etc.). Some changes seek to reconcile differences in his source texts.[35] This rewriting of narratives is not atypical for Hellenistic historians, who regularly wrote with an eye towards current events. Nor is this practice foreign to certain Hebrew authors, who also crafted new literary works from existing narratives.

Eupolemus also has substantial material that is unique to his narrative, such as the claim that Moses, as the "first wise man" (πρῶτον σοφόν), invented writing and gave it to the Jewish people (F1; *Praep. ev.* 9.26.1). Here, Eupolemus actively subordinates Greek culture, making it twice derivative of other ethnicities in its adoption of writing and letters (e.g., Jews and Phoenicians).[36] Other nations are also in view when Eupolemus credits Moses with being the first person to make written laws (cf. Diodorus Siculus, *Bibl.* 1.94.1–2). Many details of Jerusalem (e.g., its walls, towers, and trenches) and the temple's construction (e.g., bells to scare away birds) are also only found in Eupolemus' account (F2). Similarly, the causal link between Jeremiah's prophecy against Jerusalem and Nebuchadnezzar's campaign is unique (F4).[37]

Scholars debate Eupolemus' engagement with nonscriptural sources, especially Greek literary works. Wacholder argues that Eupolemus "made use of the works of Herodotus, Hecataeus of Abdera, Ctesias of Cnidus . . . Manetho . . . and the Greek histories of Phoenicia," as well as a book that "fused the accounts of Herodotus and Ctesias with some native Babylonian and Jewish traditions."[38] These claims are based on the noted parallels between Eupolemus' description of the Egyptian king Vaphres' workers (F2, *Praep. ev.* 9.32.1) and the organization of Egyptian nomes in Herodotus, *Hist.* 2.161–71 (especially 2.164–66).[39] The claim of Herodotus as a source, however, need

35 For example, when Eupolemus is discussing the lampstands in F2 (*Praep. ev.* 9.34.7–8), he references Moses (Exod 25:31–40; 37:17–24; cf. Num 8:4), indicating his divergence from the descriptions in 1 Kings 7:49 and 2 Chron 4:7. Eupolemus reconciles the two by claiming that there were ten lampstands, each with seven lamps.

36 The discussion of heroic firsts was recognized as something that was highly pleasing for an audience (Quintilian, *Inst.* 3.7.16).

37 For a recent discussion of the development of Jeremianic narratives in this time period, see S. A. Adams, "Jeremiah in the Old Testament Apocrypha and Pseudepigrapha," in J. Lundbom, C. A. Evans, and B. Anderson, eds., *The Book of Jeremiah: Composition, Reception, and Interpretation* (VTSup 178; FIOTL; Leiden: Brill, 2018), 359–78.

38 Wacholder, *Eupolemus*, 13 (citing Freudenthal, *Alexander Polyhistor*, 1.110–12), 232.

39 Freudenthal, *Alexander Polyhistor*, 1.210; Wacholder, *Eupolemus*, 164.

not be the case. These deltic nomes were well known in antiquity and so are not necessarily derived from Herodotus.[40] More important for Wacholder's argument is that the nomic digression was embedded within the narrative of Apries (Ἀπρίης) and his (failed) attack on Tyre and Sidon (*Hist.* 2.161). This pairing lends additional support to his argument, but the exact connection is debatable. Less likely is the suggestion that Herodotus, *Hist.* 2.17 (although being from the same book), was the possible source for Eupolemus' knowledge that the Mendesian and Sebennytic nomes were prosperous and that ancient readers would attribute the additional troops provided by them as evidence of Eupolemus' knowledge of Herodotus. Most unlikely is Wacholder's claim that Eupolemus (F4, *Praep. ev.* 9.39.5) modeled his depiction of Nebuchadnezzar's military strategy of conquering weaker cities before taking Jerusalem on Herodotus' narrative of Darius and Xerxes' invasion of Greece (*Hist.* 6.94–102).[41] Not only is this a recognized military strategy (e.g., Vespasian and Titus in the Jewish War, cf. *BJ* 6.339), but Wacholder places too much emphasis on the conquest's order. Overall, Eupolemus' use of Herodotus is questionable, although not impossible.

Eupolemus' knowledge of Ctesias is inferred from the shared use of Astibares, a name that is thought to have been fabricated by Ctesias in his *Persica*.[42] Eupolemus' use of Hecataeus of Abdera follows a similar argument, namely, that Eupolemus modeled his claim that Moses was the first to create written laws on the assertion by Hecateaus that Mneves was "the first to persuade the masses of Egypt to adopt written laws" (ἐγγράπτοις νόμοις, cf. Diodorus Siculus, *Bibl.* 1.94.1).[43] Given the popularity of Ctesias and Hecataeus in antiquity, it is possible that they were used by Eupolemus, although this is far from certain.

More pressing for our discussion is the claim by a number of scholars that Eupolemus' *History* is written in the vein of Manetho and Berossus.[44] Although Wacholder finds that there is "no doubt" that Eupolemus used Manetho, he provides no examples.[45] Explicit evidence is also lacking in Freudenthal's work, although he is happy to hold up Manetho and Berossus as prototypical literary examples that other ethnic writers could emulate.[46] This absence does not nec-

40 E.g., Strabo, *Geogr.* 17.1.18–20 (within the larger discussion of 17.1.2–54); Pliny the Elder, *Nat. hist.* 5.9.49–50.

41 Wacholder, *Eupolemus*, 234–35.

42 *FGrH* 688 F5; cf. Diodorus Siculus, *Bibl.* 2.34.1–2, 6.

43 Wacholder, *Eupolemus*, 86.

44 A. Momigliano, *Alien Wisdom: The Limits of Hellenization* (Cambridge: Cambridge University Press, 1975), 92–93; Holladay, *Fragments: Historians*, 95; D. Mendels, "'Creative History' in the Hellenistic Near East in the Third and Second Centuries BCE: The Jewish Case," *JSP* 2 (1988): 17.

45 Wacholder, *Eupolemus*, 107.

46 Freudenthal, *Alexander Polyhistor*, *passim*, but especially 1.117.

essarily mean that Eupolemus did not know of these authors or did not view them as literary models. However, it does reduce the likeliness of this position and certainly undermines the confidence with which Wacholder and others speak. The speculative nature of this endeavor to identify influences is further exacerbated by the fragmentary nature of all three works.

Eupolemus does not highlight or mention any of his non-Jewish sources in his surviving fragments. As a result, the number of identified sources used by Eupolemus is too bold given our limited evidence. Also problematic is the assumption by scholars that Eupolemus would have had access to these sources, especially as access to large quantities of texts in antiquity was often limited to the social elite. Wacholder claims that a library of Greek historical works existed in Jerusalem at the turn of the second century BCE and that Eupolemus used it.[47] This explanation is not inconceivable and has some corroborating evidence to support it.[48] Nevertheless, Wacholder is unclear in his assertion of the breadth of texts that Eupolemus would have had access to: is Wacholder claiming that Eupolemus had access to *all* of Herodotus, Ctesias, Manetho, and so on, or is he limiting Eupolemus' access to one or more specific books or collected notes? What does this claim imply about Eupolemus' social standing and level of wealth? The fact that Eupolemus was educated in two languages

47 Wacholder, *Eupolemus*, 13. For Herod's library in the first century CE, see Wacholder, *Nicolaus*, 81–86.

48 There is evidence of translation work happening with the Jerusalem community (e.g., colophon of Greek Esther 10:31, F11) in the first century BCE. Also, 2 Macc 2:13–16 speaks of a library (βιβλιοθήκην) that housed material on Jewish kings and prophets, including the writings of David. The letter further states that access to this material could be obtained by the recipients if needed (2:16), but the historicity of the library has been questioned. Archives (ἀρχεῖα) in Jerusalem are mentioned by Josephus, but without any literary connection (*BJ* 2.426–427; 6.354; 7.61). An important question would be whether or not this library included works by Greek authors (as implied by LA 121). Similarly, if Jason, with permission from Antiochus IV, was responsible for building the first major gymnasium and ephebate (γυμνλασιον καὶ ἐφηβεῖον) in Jerusalem (2 Macc 4:9), does this imply that there was also a corresponding Greek library founded in the city? Cf. R. Doran, "Jason's Gymnasion," in H. W. Attridge, J. J. Collins, and T. H. Tobin, eds., *Of Scribes and Scrolls: Studies on the Hebrew Bible, Intertestamental Judaism and Christian Origins* (Lanham, Md.: University Press of America, 1990), 99–109; R. Doran, "The High Cost of a Good Education," in J. J. Collins and G. E. Sterling, eds., *Hellenism in the Land of Israel* (Notre Dame: University of Notre Dame Press, 2001), 94–115; K. Groß-Albenhausen, "Bedeutung und Function der Gymnasien für die Hellenisierung Ostens," in D. Kah and P. Scholz, eds., *Das hellenistische Gymnasion* (WGW 8; Berlin: Akademie Verlag, 2004), 317–19; A. S. Chankowski, "Les souverains hellénistiques et l'institution du gymnase: Politiques royales et modèles culturels," in O. Curty and M. Piérart, eds., *L'huile et l'argent: Gymnasiarchie et évergétisme dans la Grèce hellénistique. Actes du colloque tenu à Fribourg, du 13 au 15 octobre 2005, publiés en l'honneur du Prof. Marcel Piérart à l'occasion de son 60ème anniversaire* (Paris: De Boccard, 2009), 114. A gymnasium, however, does not necessarily imply a full education system. Cf. P. Scholz, "Elementarunterricht und intellektuelle Bildung im hellenistischen Gymnasion," in D. Kah and P. Scholz, eds., *Das hellenistische Gymnasion* (WGW 8; Berlin: Akademie Verlag, 2004), 103.

(Hebrew and Greek) and, if the same person, was a primary delegate to Rome (1 Macc 8:17; Josephus, *Ant.* 12.415) suggests a high level of social standing and likely access to wealth, which would increase the possibility that he had a personal library of Greek texts.[49]

More important than the sources used by Eupolemus for our discussion is the historiographic tradition(s) that influenced his composition. In this regard, Wacholder's argument that Eupolemus was indebted to "the histographic [*sic*] school as illustrated in the Books of Chronicles, Ezra and Nehemiah" is important and on much firmer ground.[50] According to Wacholder, Eupolemus' active reshaping of his material to correct and fill in the gaps left by previous authors indicates that he "must be regarded as a follower of the Chronicler's school."[51] Although I agree that Eupolemus shares the Chronicler's concern for crafting a "correct" historical narrative, the practice of writing corrective history was not limited to a Chronicler school; this is a fundamental component of rewritten Scripture as well as non-Jewish composition practices.

The discussions of a historiographic school and the quality of his Greek composition are linked to the question of Eupolemus' Greek education. Wacholder claims that Eupolemus had a "priestly education"; however, he does not specify exactly what this would entail.[52] Although one could assume that a priest would need to have knowledge of Scripture, it does not necessarily follow that their education included learning composition within a particular tradition (Jewish or Greek). On another occasion Wacholder labels Eupolemus "the Hellenistically half-educated priest of Jerusalem," but again there is no specification as to which educational "half" Eupolemus would have had.[53] Presumably, Wacholder is implying that he did not have a full Greek education and so did not complete the higher stages in which composition was emphasized.[54] However, the (supposed) lack of higher-level compositional skill in Greek and the clear modeling on Hebrew and translated texts might alternatively suggest that Eupolemus was educated using nontraditional Greek texts (i.e., Jewish ones, possibly the Septuagint).

49 On potential ways to access textual artifacts, see Hezser, *Literacy*, 145–68.

50 Wacholder, *Eupolemus*, 249.

51 Wacholder, *Eupolemus*, 250.

52 E.g., Wacholder, *Eupolemus*, 12. For the argument of Eupolemus' priestly background, see Giblet, "Eupolème," 553.

53 Wacholder, *Eupolemus*, 169. Eupolemus provides "a faulty replica of pagan Hellenistic book learning" (p. 259).

54 This position, however, sits in some tension with the claim by Wacholder above that Eupolemus made an intentional selection of an "inferior" type of Greek for his composition (cf. *Eupolemus*, 256–57). On composition in Greek education, particularly narrative (διήγημα), see Theon, *Prog.* 78–96.

Eupolemus' linguistic knowledge is not limited to "translational Greek."[55] The correspondence between Solomon and foreign kings (Vaphres and Souron) is likely an authorial composition, and his interpretation of 2 Chr 2:3–16 and 1 Kgs 5:1–12 provides evidence of Eupolemus' knowledge of Hellenistic culture.[56] Crafting bespoke documents and embedding them within a narrative was a practice of Hellenistic and Roman historians.[57] Josephus also expands the Solomonic narrative by including a letter from Solomon to Hiram (*Ant.* 8.50–55), filling in the voids of the biblical texts.[58] The tendency to add, rather than omit, documents is part of a larger trend by Greek translators of Hebrew Scripture and Jewish authors composing original works in Greek.[59] This practice of penning royal correspondence of foreign kings suggests participation in Greek historiography, but also aligns with Jewish practices of Greek composition.

Eupolemus' letters contain recognizable elements of Hellenistic epistolary convention, such as standard Greek openings, the theme of friendship, and the crafting of a realistic epistolary situation.[60] The sending of gifts, such as a golden statue to be housed in the temple of Zeus (F2, *Praep. ev.* 9.34.18), also fits with Hellenistic monarchical practices.[61] These literary features, however, are not limited to Greek composition. The author of 1 Maccabees also embeds letters in his work.[62] The likeliness that the letters are original to the Hebrew text of 1 Maccabees, and not additions to the

55 Note the differences in technical vocabulary between Eupolemus and 3 Kgdms 6–7 (Wacholder, *Eupolemus*, 251–52).

56 Cf. Keddie, "Solomon to His Friends." Contra Gutman, *Beginnings*, 84.

57 Thucydides, *Hist.* 1.128.7; 1.129.3; 1.137.4; 7.11.1–7.15.2; Herodotus, *Hist.* 1.124; 3.40; 8.22; Xenophon, *Hell.* 1.1.23. Such letters are lacking in Xenophon and Polybius.

58 Cf. Doering, *Ancient Jewish Letters*, 232–41, 275–78.

59 E.g., 2 Macc 1:1–9; 1:10–2:18; 11:16–21, 22–26, 27–33, 34–38; 3 Macc 3:12–30; 7:1–9; Add Esth B1–7; E1–24; LA 35–40, 41–46. See the helpful chart by Doering, *Ancient Jewish Letters*, 127–30.

60 See especially, Keddie, "Solomon to His Friends," 208–25. Cf. D. Mendels, "Hellenistic Writers of the Second Century BCE on the Hiram-Solomon Relationship," *Studia Phoenicia* 5 (1986): 445–55. For Greek letter openings, see Adams, "Letter Opening."

61 This narrative is challenged by a fragment of Theophilus also preserved by Alexander Polyhistor through Eusebius (*Praep. ev.* 9.34.19). No title is given for the fragment, and it is thought that this might be a non-Jewish historical composition (e.g., M. Stern, ed., *Greek and Latin Authors on Jews and Judaism* [3 vols.; Jerusalem: Israel Academy of Sciences and Humanities, 1974–1984], 1.126–27; cf. Josephus, *C. Ap.* 1.216). Cf. Doran, "Jewish Hellenistic Historians," 254–55 (Jewish author).

62 First Macc 5:10–13; 8:23–32; 10:17–20, 25–45; 11:29–37; 12:5–18, 19–23; 13:35–40; 14:20–23, 27–45; 15:1–9, 15–21. For similar reported communication (i.e., "message," λόγος), see 1 Macc 5:48; 7:27; 10:52–54, 55–56, 70–73; 11:42–43. Some letters are also mentioned and summarized, but not included (e.g., 1 Macc 1:41–50; 2:31; 3:27; 9:60; 10:3, 7; 12:2; 15:22; 16:18–19).

Greek translation,[63] suggests that Hebrew historiography was also developing during this time period, interacting with the practices of its Greek-speaking neighbors.

Eupolemus' work is presented as a history,[64] but the genre of history was diverse (and diversifying) in the Hellenistic era. This is true not only for subgenres of Greek historiography, but also for types of histories composed in different languages and from parallel literary traditions (e.g., Hebrew, Egyptian, Babylonian, Latin). Certain scholars emphasize the similarities between Eupolemus' work and Greek literary texts and identify *Concerning the Kings* as participating in "encomiastic history" or ethnography in the tradition of Manetho and Berossus.[65] Gregory Sterling has noted Eupolemus' use of chronology and has highlighted the parallels with Greek chronographic works.[66] All of these discussions recognize elements within Eupolemus' work that are not germane to traditional Jewish historiography and are likely a result of Eupolemus' participation in a Greek genre and his engagement with contemporary literary practices.

Some scholars argue for a more Jewish type of historiography: "Eupolemus, more often than not, tended to agree with the Chronicler, because both belonged to the same priestly school of biblical historiography."[67] The way that Eupolemus handled his sources has led some scholars to claim that his history

63 Doering, *Ancient Jewish Letters*, 138–45. Doering suggests that the royal correspondence was likely originally composed in Greek and translated into Hebrew by the author of 1 Maccabees (pp. 141–42). The possibility that the letters were added later was suggested by Gauger, but with little evidential support. Cf. J.-D. Gauger, *Authentizität und Methode: Untersuchungen zum historischen Wert des persich-griechischen Herrscherbriefs in literarischer Tradition* (SGA 6; Hamburg: Kovač, 2000), 309 n. 33. The awareness of Greek epistolary practice is most likely attributable to the translator.

64 E.g., H. W. Attridge, "Historiography," in M. E. Stone, ed., *Jewish Writings of the Second Temple Period: Apocrypha, Pseudepigrapha, Qumran Sectarian Writings, Philo, Josephus* (CRINT 2.2; Philadelphia: Fortress, 1984), 162–65.

65 Holladay, *Fragments: Historians*, 95; Momigliano, *Alien Wisdom*, 92–93.

66 Sterling, *Historiography*, 212. Eupolemus was not the only Jewish author to take an interest in calculating dates and epochs, although his interest is not as extreme as that of Demetrius (see below). Jewish elements are also found in Ps.-Apollodorus, *FGrH* 244 FF83–87. Walter (*Historiker*, 95) leaves open the possibility that Eupolemus might not have extended his chronological discussions throughout the work.

67 Sterling (*Historiography*, 216–17) speculates that the opening of Eupolemus' work was not as thorough or as detailed as the later sections on David and Solomon and that this mirrors the compositional program of Chronicles. This view matches with the fragments that have survived, especially the beginning of F2, but lacks additional supporting evidence. Alexander Polyhistor clearly had a variety of sources for the lives of Abraham and Moses, but appears to have been particularly dependent on Eupolemus for his discussion of the monarchy. The absence of Eupolemus' work for earlier narratives more likely indicates the nature of the sources available to Alexander and his (potential) lack of preference for Eupolemus, rather than being indicative of the work's contents. Wacholder, *Eupolemus*, 148. Unfortunately, Wacholder does not specify what he identifies as "biblical historiography."

is midrashic or haggadic,[68] with David Balch claiming that Eupolemus wrote in the "genre of haggadah."[69] Although Balch does not clearly define the nature of this genre, his comparisons with Jubilees, Genesis Apocryphon, and Pseudo-Philo's LAB suggest that he is speaking about "rewritten Scripture." Rewritten Scripture does not capture the whole of Eupolemus' work, but it is not unrepresentative, suggesting possible participation. Repurposing sources was a common literary practice in antiquity, especially by historians. This is true not only for Greek authors, but also for those writing in Hebrew as well.

Overall, Eupolemus consciously blends Jewish and Greek historiographic practices.[70] His work is close to his Jewish models, especially Chronicles, but there are distinct aspects of his work that show the adoption of Greek practices: the composition of regal correspondence, which includes Hellenistic epistolary conventions; the increased use of chronological references; and the explicit comparison of cultures. Eupolemus' decision to compose a work in Greek, when he could possibly have written in Hebrew or Aramaic, indicates his desire to engage with a specific, and possibly wider, readership. The use of a different linguistic style for writing history shows the flexibility of the genre and how a Jewish author could adopt a different register that he thought would be most appropriate for his subject matter and audience. Ultimately, Eupolemus' work shows a reinterpretation of Jewish history in light of current events, with an eye towards shaping the perception (both internal and external) of the Jewish people.[71]

Pseudo-Eupolemus

Scholars attribute two fragments to the writer known as Pseudo-Eupolemus. The first (*Praep. ev.* 9.17.2–9), mentioned above, is attributed to Eupolemus by Eusebius (hence the moniker), and the second is an anonymous quotation (ἐν δὲ ἀδεσπότοις, *Praep. ev.* 9.18.2). The similarities in content between the fragments have led scholars to posit that they come from the same work/author.[72] Since Freudenthal, many scholars argue that Pseudo-Eupolemus is

68 So Holladay, *Fragments: Historians*, 96–97; Bickerman, *Jews in the Greek Age*, 180.

69 D. L. Balch, "Attitudes towards Foreigners in 2 Maccabees, Eupolemus, Esther, Aristeas, and Luke-Acts," in A. J. Malherbe, F. W. Norris, and J. W. Thompson, eds., *The Early Church in Its Context: Essays in Honor of Everett Ferguson* (NovTSup 90; Leiden: Brill, 1998), 35.

70 I am not convinced by Wacholder's claim (*Eupolemus*, 257–58) that "it is the concern for the architectural minutiae that makes the fragments of Eupolemus a bridge between biblical and Greek literature." Although this is not particularly common in Greek texts, it is not entirely absent (e.g., Callixenes' *On Alexandria*; Athenaeus, *Deipn.* 5.196a–203b). Polybius (*Hist.* 12.25d–e) also speaks of the importance to a historian of acquiring a full understanding of the cities, places, rivers, lakes, etc. that he will be using in his history.

71 Mendels, "'Creative History,'" 17–18.

72 For a detailed discussion of the issues surrounding this relationship, see Sterling, *Historiography*, 191–94. For a challenge to this perspective and the view that F2 could not have come

a Samaritan who wrote in the second century BCE, prior to the Hasmonean era, citing as evidence the reference to Argarizin (ἱερὸν Ἀργαριζίν, ὃ εἶναι μεθερμηνευόμενον ὄρος ὑψίστου, F1.5) and Abraham's being hosted by, and receiving gifts from, the priest and king Melchizedek (F1.6).[73] Not all scholars are fully content with this distinction, especially the rigid division between Jewish and Samaritan peoples.[74]

Robert Doran has made a strong case that the supposed differences between Eupolemus and Pseudo-Eupolemus (specifically *Praep. ev.* 9.17.2–9) are overplayed and that there is no inherent contradiction in attributing this fragment to Eupolemus, as Eusebius and Polyhistor did.[75] Doran's arguments have merit and caution against accepting the majority position without critical evaluation. Less satisfying is his lack of an alternative theory to explain the content overlap between the two fragments attributed to Pseudo-Eupolemus.[76] Sterling identifies three options to explain the similarities: (1) they both stem from different readings of a common source; (2) F2 is an editorial synopsis of F1; or (3) they are from two different authors.[77] In my opinion, there is insufficient differentiation between options 1 and 3, as the similarities between the two fragments militate against complete fabrication by two separate authors, implying a shared source or tradition at some point in the past. Or, to put it another way, if an author, editor, or synthesizer made changes to their source text (however small), when does s/he start to be an independent writer? Sterling opts for option 2 and provides a possible (if specific) outline of how these two passages were included into Polyhistor's work.

The differing views of Doran, Sterling, and others ultimately rest on their interpretation(s) of what counts as "similarities" and "differences" in content. This is not an easy issue to navigate, as no criterion exists by which to determine the blurry edges of sameness and differentness. Overall, Doran is right to challenge the scholarly presupposition of seeing F1 as being incompatible with the rest of the work of Eupolemus and to claim that scholars have been

from a Jewish or Samaritan author because of its polytheistic outlook, see Walter, *Historiker*, 137 n. 4; N. Walter, "Zu Pseudo-Eupolemus," *Kilo* 43/45 (1965): 282–90; Doran, "Jewish Hellenistic Historians," 270–71.

73 E.g., Freudenthal, *Alexander Polyhistor*, 1.82–103, especially 82–91; Hengel, *Judaism and Hellenism*, 1.91.

74 For important critiques of the firmness of this position, see Bickerman, *Jews in the Greek Age*, 190; Doran, "Jewish Hellenistic Historians," 270–74; Doran, "Ps.-Eupolemus," 2.873–76; Gruen, *Heritage and Hellenism*, 146–48; Creech, "Lawless Pride," 39 n. 70. See most recently, Pummer, *Samaritans*, especially 15–25.

75 Doran, "Jewish Hellenistic Historians," 271–74.

76 Doran, "Jewish Hellenistic Historians," 271. Doran ("Ps.-Eupolemus," 2.878) later attributes the potpourri of F2 to Polyhistor, but this stands in tension with Polyhistor's typical method of text citation.

77 Sterling, *Historiography*, 192–93, but with minor changes.

too restrictive in determining what a Jewish author from antiquity would or would not think or write. As a result, attributing F1 to Eupolemus is plausible and should remain the default position. F2 is likely a synopsis of a larger narrative, but I am not certain as to its relationship with F1, except that there must be some shared tradition.

The argument made by Doran is based on the content of the fragments, but he did not engage with the larger question of literary structure and genre. If Freudenthal and other scholars are correct that the fragments attributed to Eupolemus by Eusebius (and Alexander Polyhistor) are derived from two authors, rather than one, then we have an additional example of authors in this region adopting historiographic practices that reframe scripture.[78] There is little difference in methodology or genre between the works of Eupolemus and Pseudo-Eupolemus (F1) as reconstructed from their fragments; both authors structure their work from scriptural texts and include additional material to enhance their narrative.[79] The primary change is F1's explicit engagement with non-Jewish/Samaritan sources, indicated by the phrases βαβυλονίους γὰρ λέγειν, ὑπὸ τῶν Ἑλλήνων λέγεσθαι, and Ἕλληνας δὲ λέγειν (F1.9).[80]

Although the brevity of the fragments precludes certainty, Pseudo-Eupolemus—if we want to apply this moniker to the unattributed F2—appears to participate in the genre of Hellenistic historiography in order to recast the Abrahamic narrative. Textual embellishment and the adoption of wider literary practices do not require the need to posit a "Greek school

78 Although one might default to saying that this is a Jewish practice, the fact that it might also be adopted by Samaritan authors undermines the restrictive nature inherent in this label. Given the fact that one or more Samaritan versions of the Books of Moses existed in antiquity, we might also need to refrain from labeling the text adapted by Pseudo-Eupolemus as "Jewish Scripture."

79 F1 shares the wider Jewish interpretation of God protecting Sarah from Pharaoh's advances (F1.7; 1Q20 XX,1–32; Josephus, *Ant.* 1.162–165), suggesting that the author drew on Jewish sources. See Sterling, *Historiography*, 196–99. Pseudo-Eupolemus' use of the Greek version of Genesis is based on the spelling of the names. His knowledge of Hebrew is debated. Hengel, *Judaism and Hellenism*, 1.89; Wacholder, "Pseudo-Eupolemus' Two Greek Fragments," 87 (poor use); Sterling, *Historiography*, 200. For critical comments, see Walter, *Historiker*, 139.

80 Contra Freudenthal (*Alexander Polyhistor*, 1.96), who claims that the integration of associating Enoch with Atlas (F1.9) was made carelessly or ignorantly. The difference is hardly determinative for authorial debates. On the use of Berossus as a source, see Freudenthal, *Alexander Polyhistor*, 1.94. Cf. the description of Bel as the founding deity (*FGrH* 680 F1.8; cf. Ctesias, *FGrH* 688 F1b); for the description of Abraham, see the Berossus quotation in Josephus, *Ant.* 1.158 (= F6). This position was argued against by P. Schnabel, *Berossos und die babylonisch-hellenistische Literatur* (Leipzig: Teubner, 1923), 246. For a discussion of other possible Greek sources, see Wacholder, "Pseudo-Eupolemus," 88, 90–93. Hellenistic elements are particularly evident in the historicizing of myths (F1.2–3) and depicting the spread and development of culture among civilizations (F1.4, 8). Schürer, *History*, 3.1.529. For the discussion of culture bringers, see A. J. Droge, *Homer or Moses? Early Christian Interpretation of the History of Culture* (Tübingen: Mohr Siebeck, 1989), especially 19–25.

of biblical historiography" at the time of Pseudo-Eupolemus.[81] Rather, we witness in the works of Pseudo-Eupolemus and others a growing awareness of Greek historiographical practices and a willingness to incorporate nonprototypical elements that were deemed to be beneficial for the author's argument.

Pseudo-Hecataeus

Hecataeus of Abdera (or Teos)[82] was a prominent author who lived during the reigns of Alexander the Great and Ptolemy I Soter.[83] He was known for his philosophical, scholastic, and historical writings, but his most important contribution, and one that is pertinent to our discussion, is his prototypical ethnography *On the Egyptians* (Αἰγυπτιακά), a treatise that praises the Egyptians for their antiquity and cultural superiority.[84] The importance of Hecataeus' work for our discussion is twofold: first, important digressions discuss the Jewish people; and second, *On the Egyptians* (and to a lesser extent *Concerning the Hyperboreans*, Περὶ Ὑπερβορέων) is assumed to be the model for subsequent ethnographies, including the Jewish forgery *On the Jews*. Scholars debate the authenticity, extent, and nature of the Hecataeus passages cited by ancient Jewish and Christian authors.[85] Widely accepted are the references to the Jewish people in Αἰγυπτιακά (e.g., Diodorus, *Bibl.* 1.28.2–3; 1.94.2; 40.3.1–8). These comments, which are mostly evenhanded, are likely the primary reason for subsequent pseudepigraphal compositions by Jews in Hecataeus' name; Hecataeus had already shown knowledge of and, to some extent, sympathy towards the Jewish people, and his reputation in ethnographic writing makes him an obvious choice.[86]

81 Rightly, Wacholder, "Pseudo-Eupolemus," 88.

82 For Abdera, see *Suda* E 359; Diogenes Laertius, *Vit.* 9.69. For Teos, see *FGrH* 264 F13; Strabo, *Geogr.* 14.1.30.

83 Cf. F. Jacoby, "Hekataios aus Abdera," *PW* 7 (1912): 2750–69. Fraser, *Ptolemaic Alexandria*, 1.496–505. For a discussion of dating, see M. Stern and O. Murray, "Hecataeus of Abdera and Theophrastus on Jews and Egyptians," *JEA* 59 (1973): 159–68.

84 This work has not survived, although large fragments have been preserved by Diodorus Siculus in *Bibl.* 1.10.1–1.98.10. For the debate over how much of this material is part of Hecataeus' work and how much should be attributed to Diodorus or another author, see A. Burton, *Diodorus Siculus, Book I: A Commentary* (Leiden: Brill, 1972): 1–34; O. Murray, "Hecataeus of Abdera and Pharaonic Kingship," *JEA* 56 (1970): 141–71; B. Bar-Kochva, *Pseudo-Hecataeus, "On the Jews": Legitimizing the Jewish Diaspora* (HCS 21; Berkeley: University of California Press, 1996), 289–90.

85 For an overview of the debate and a catalogue of scholarly opinion, see Holladay, *Fragments: Historians*, 278, 294 nn. 27–29; Sterling, *Historiography*, 81–83; A. Kasher, "Hecataeus of Abdera on Mosollamus the Jewish Mounted Archer (Contra Apionem 1.200–204)," in H. Cancik, H. Lichtenberger, and P. Schäfer, eds., *Geschichte—Tradition—Reflexion: Festschrift für Martin Hengel zum 70. Geburtstag* (3 vols.; Tübingen: Mohr Siebeck, 1996), 1.148–50.

86 Cf. Bar-Kochva, *Pseudo-Hecataeus*, 24; K. Berthelot, "Hecataeus of Abdera and Jewish 'Misanthropy,'" *BCRFJ* 19 (2008): n.p. LA 31 mentions Hecataeus as one who praised the Jewish people and their adherence to the holy laws. However, no individual work is mentioned.

Two Jewish-focused works are attributed to Hecataeus: *On Abraham (and the Egyptians)* and *On the Jews*. The former is mentioned by both Josephus (*Ant.* 1.159) and Clement (*Strom.* 5.14.113.1), but the only fragment from this (potentially) biographical work to survive is a quotation of Sophocles chastising the creation of idols (*Strom.* 5.14.113.1–2). This otherwise unattested passage from Sophocles (which is also not thought to be authentic), along with the wider context of the quotation in Clement's work, does not provide sufficient data with which to speculate on the possible nature of this composition or what form it might have taken.[87]

The major fragment of Pseudo-Hecataeus' *On the Jews* is found in Josephus, *C. Ap.* 1.183–204, which Josephus describes as ἀλλὰ περὶ αὐτῶν Ἰουδαίων συγγέγραφε βιβλίον (1.183) and later is called περὶ Ἰουδαίων βιβλίον by Origen (*Cels.* 1.15).[88] Scholars debate the authenticity of this work, with a majority viewing it as pseudepigraphal. There have been strong arguments in favor of its authenticity; however, Bar-Kochva has recently undermined this position in his detailed investigation.[89]

The selected elements of the work preserved by Josephus (ἐξ οὗ βούλομαι κεφαλαιωδῶς ἐπιδραμεῖν ἔνια τῶν εἰρημένων, *C. Ap.* 1.183) provide sufficient information to posit what *On the Jews* might have looked like. Josephus claims that Hecataeus' *On the Jews* was a comprehensive, one-book treatise that focused primarily on the Jewish people (βιβλίον; *C. Ap.* 1.205, 214). Based on the references to it by Origen (*Cels.* 1.15) and Josephus' encouragement for his readers to locate the book themselves (*C. Ap.* 1.205), the book was known by the title *On the Jews*, *Ioudaika*, or something similar.[90] As the

87 Walter (*Historiker*, 149–50) has argued (rightly) that the Sophocles passage could fit within a work on Abraham. However, his proposal that this work was a major source for Josephus' discussion of Abraham (along with his reconstruction of the work) goes beyond the evidence. For the forging of the Sophocles quote, see Freudenthal, *Alexander Polyhistor*, 1.166; Walter, *Aristobulos*, 195–201.

88 Whether or not Pseudo-Hecataeus should be regarded as "the first Graeco-Palestinian writer, an analogue of the Babylonian Berossos and the Egyptian Manetho" (so Wacholder, *Eupolemus*, 272), depends strongly on the assigned date (and location) of composition. In this regard, I would follow Bar-Kochva (*Pseudo-Hecataeus*, 122–42) and date Pseudo-Hecataeus to the latter half of the second or the beginning of the first century BCE. For discussion of the work's author and provenance, see Bar-Kochva, *Pseudo-Hecataeus*, 143–81; contra Wacholder, *Eupolemus*, 263–73.

89 Bar-Kochva, *Pseudo-Hecataeus*, 54–121. Now followed by Gruen, *Heritage and Hellenism*, 202–3; Collins, *Athens*, 53; Barclay, *Against Apion*, 338–40. For authenticity, see H. Lewy, "Hekataios von Abdera περὶ Ἰουδαίων," *ZNW* 31 (1932): 117–32; J. G. Gager, "Pseudo-Hecataeus Again," *ZNW* 60 (1969): 130–39; V. A. Tcherikover, *Hellenistic Civilization and the Jews* (trans. S. Applebaum; New York: Atheneum, 1977), 426–27; J. D. Gauger, "Zitate in der jüdischen Apologetik und die Authentizität der Hekataios-Passagen bei Flavius Josephus und im Ps. Aristeas-Brief," *JSJ* 13 (1982): 6–46; Sterling, *Historiography*, 88–91.

90 For *On the Jews* as the book's title, and so an indication of its genre, see Bar-Kochva, *Pseudo-Hecataeus*, 187–89.

nation or land area in focus was regularly named in Hellenistic ethnographies, the title Περὶ Ἰουδαίων would support the view of Pseudo-Hecataeus' work as an ethnography.[91] A title with reference to the Jews would further align the work with the practice modeled by the original Hecataeus.

Prototypical ethnographies, including Hecataeus' *On the Egyptians* and *Concerning the Hyperboreans*, had a recognized structured in order to give standard information about the people group in focus: (1) origins; (2) geography; (3) customs; and (4) history of rulers.[92] Looking at the excerpted section of Pseudo-Hecataeus by Josephus, we can see that the work covered a specific selection of topics: war and recent history (*C. Ap.* 1.184–186, 200–204); high priest as leader (1.187–188); customs (especially religious practices and beliefs) (1.188–193); population (1.194); and geography and cities (1.195–199).[93] Notably absent is the typical discussion of the *origo* of the Jewish people along with mention of their ancestors, exodus, and founders. Rather, Josephus opens his narrative with Hezekiah. The function of this divergence, along with the way that it is not consistent with Hecataeus' digression on the Jews in Diodorus (*Hist.* 40.3.1–3), indicates both a deep awareness of the prototypical genre and the willingness by a Jewish author to adapt this Greek genre to address specific concerns of his readers.[94] As a result, the fragments now attributed to Pseudo-Hecataeus provide evidence that at least one Jewish author participated in ethnography modeled on a Greek author.[95]

91 E.g., Alexander Polyhistor, Περὶ Ἰουδαίων (*FGrH* 273); Herennius Philo of Byblos, Περὶ Ἰουδαίων (*FGrH* 790); Damocritus, Περὶ Ἰουδαίων (*FGrH* 730; *Suda* Δ 49).

92 For example, Hecataeus' *On the Egyptians* follows the basic pattern of ethnographic works: religion (1.10.1–1.29.6); geography (1.30.1–1.41.10); history (1.42.1–1.68.6); customs (νόμοι) (1.69.1–1.95.6); Greek-Egyptian relations (1.96.1–1.98.10). Similarly, Diodorus' summary of *Hyperboreans* (*Hist.* 2.47.1–6) follows the basic pattern of ethnography: details of location (2.47.1); religion (2.47.2–3); language and relationship to Greece (2.47.4–5a); wondrous elements (2.47.5b–6a); and rulers (2.47.6b). Other surviving fragments of *Hyperboreans* (e.g., FF8–14) also fit within these categories. For *On the Egyptians* as an important model for subsequent ethnographies, see Bar-Kochva, *Pseudo-Hecataeus*, 9–18. A. Dihle, "Zur hellenistischen Ethnographie," in *Grecs et barbares* (Entretiens sur l'Antiquité classique 8; Geneva: Fondation Hardt, 1961), 207–39; Fraser, *Ptolemaic Alexandria*, 1.497; Bar-Kochva, *Pseudo-Hecataeus*, 192–219. This might also include native cosmology and theology; e.g., Strabo, *Geogr.* 16.2.35–36.

93 Philosophical terminology is absent in *On the Jews*. Not only does this stand in tension with Hecataeus' discussion and explanation of the Jews in his Αἰγυπτιακά (e.g., Diodorus, *Bibl.* 40.3.3, 5), but it does not align with approaches adopted by other Egyptian Jews (e.g., Philo, Pseudo-Aristeas, the author of Wisdom of Solomon, etc.). This suggests both a lack of Greek philosophical education by the author and a diversity of approach for presenting Jewish thought in Greek garb.

94 Bar-Kochva, *Pseudo-Hecataeus*, 226–31; Holladay, *Fragments: Historians*, 290.

95 For *On the Jews* as ethnography: Holladay, *Fragments: Historians*, 290; Sterling, *Historiography*, 87; Bar-Kochva, *Pseudo-Hecataeus*, 250–51.

Demetrius the Chronographer

Demetrius, often called "the chronographer," was a Jewish historian who likely wrote in Alexandria during the third century BCE.[96] Up to seven fragments are attributed to him, having been preserved by Eusebius and Clement's use of Alexander Polyhistor.[97] According to Clement (*Strom.* 1.21.141.1), the work is called *Concerning the Kings in Judaea* (Περὶ τῶν ἐν τῇ Ἰουδίᾳ βασιλέων), but this title does not fully reflect the content of the other fragments, which focus on events in the life of the patriarchs. This title might be a mistake or indicate that a second work was written by him, but there is a case to be made for accepting the title as covering all of the fragments and the lost material.[98]

Demetrius' work is almost universally categorized as chronography, a type of historiography that came to prominence through the interaction of Greek authors with Eastern literary practices.[99] Regnal lists were important compositions in many Eastern empires (e.g., Babylonians, Egyptians, etc.); however, they evolved during the Hellenistic era, when authors, primarily from subordinated cultures, engaged with Greek historiographical practices to compose chronological works in defense of their cultural heritage.[100] Berossus' *History of Babylonia* covers the full span of history, beginning with the creation of the world by Bel (FF1, 21) and continuing until the sole reign of Antiochus I Soter, when the work was published (278 BCE).[101] The creation narrative is followed by an account of how humans came to have culture (F1), descriptions of the

96 Schürer, *History*, 3.1.515; Holladay, *Fragments: Historians*, 51–52; cf. Freudenthal, *Alexander Polyhistor*, 1.59–62, for Ptolemy III. For an important challenge and alternative date (160–131 BCE), see Niehoff, *Jewish Exegesis*, 54–55. For a "Palestinian" origin, see Wacholder, *Eupolemus*, 280–82.

97 Fragment 1 is technically anonymous and is appended to a quotation of Apollonius Molon by Polyhistor. However, following Freudenthal (*Alexander Polyhistor*, 1.35–36), scholars attribute it to Demetrius. Although Freudenthal's identification of unadorned style and shared forms of Ἀβραάμ and Ἰσαάκ is valid, I am not fully convinced that this warrants attributing this fragment to Demetrius. Greek texts and fragment numbers are from *FGrH* 722.

98 Gruen, *Heritage and Hellenism*, 113 n. 12 (multiple works); Dillery, *Clio's Other Sons*, 362.

99 For a thorough overview of this literary form, see Wacholder, *Eupolemus*, 97–128.

100 E.g., *Sumerian King-List*; *Uruk King-List* (*ANET* 566); *Synchronistic King-List/Chronicle* (*ANET* 272–73); *King List A*; *Ptolemaic Canon*. For the *Babylonian Chronicle*, a fragmentary cuneiform account of third-century BCE events, see A. K. Grayson, ed. and trans., *Assyrian and Babylonian Chronicles* (TCS 5; Locust Valley, N.Y.: Augustin, 1975), nos. 11–13. King lists using traditional formulations continued to be produced in the Hellenistic era in native languages. For example, BM 35603, a cuneiform king list written in Babylon, begins with Alexander the Great and traces Seleucid kings into the early second century BCE. Cf. A. J. Sachs and D. J. Wiseman, "A Babylonian King List of the Hellenistic Period," *Iraq* 16 (1954): 202–11.

101 On Berossus' relationship to historiography and other similar works, see C. Tuplin, "Berossus and Greek Historiography," in J. Haubold et al., eds., *The World of Berossos: Proceedings of the 4th International Colloquium on "The Ancient Near East between Classical and Ancient Oriental Traditions," Hatfield College, Durham 7th–9th July 2010* (CO 5; Wiesbaden: Harrassowitz Verlag, 2013), 177–97.

heavens (FF16–19), and a depiction of some festivals (F2).[102] In his second book, Berossus reproduces a postdiluvian king list with minimal narrative on the lives of the rulers or major events (F3). Book 3 offers an account of kings and events from the Neo-Babylonian Empire (FF7–13). Similarly, Manetho's *History of Egypt* also begins with the demigods and continues until the time of Alexander's conquest (F2a).[103] Manetho's work, like Berossus', is structured chronologically through the use of royal genealogies and the division of time into dynasties (FF2a, 5–6, 10).[104] In addition to lists and dates, Manetho also includes narrative retellings of select events, which are preserved primarily by Josephus.[105]

Important chronologies were subsequently penned by Greek scholars. Eratosthenes of Cyrene, who lived in the third century BCE (cf. *Suda* E 2898), developed a chronology of the ancient world based on Olympiadic divisions.[106] His important and subsequently prototypical innovation was that he began his history with the fall of Troy (1184/3 BCE) in order to omit mythological events.[107] As far as the surviving fragments show, Eratosthenes' chronology was composed in the form of tables and was not a narrative history.[108] The most popular Greek chronological work in antiquity was Apollodorus of Athens' *Chronology* (ca. 180–ca. 120 BCE). Written in verse, this work covered

102 Cf. G. P. Verbrugghe and J. M. Wickersham, ed. and trans., *Berossos and Manetho, Introduced and Translated: Native Traditions in Ancient Mesopotamia and Egypt* (Ann Arbor: University of Michigan Press, 1996), 17.

103 Fraser, *Ptolemaic Alexandria*, 509–10.

104 Maintaining the "annals of the kings" is one of the tasks of a temple scribe (cf. *Thoth* 55–56). Cf. D. B. Redford, *Pharaonic King-Lists, Annals and Day-Books: A Contribution to the Study of Egyptian Sense of History* (SSEA 4; Mississauga: Benben, 1986), 65–96.

105 E.g., *C. Ap.* 1.74–92, 93–105, 223, 226–235, 287. For Manetho's use of Greek narrative schemes, see J. Dillery, "Manetho," in T. Whitmarsh and S. Thomson, eds., *The Romance between Greece and the East* (Cambridge: Cambridge University Press, 2013), 42–47; P. J. Kosmin, "Seleucid Ethnography and Indigenous Kingship: The Babylonian Education of Antiochus I," in J. Haubold, G. B. Lanfranchi, R. Rollinger, and J. M. Steele, eds., *The World of Berossos: Proceedings of the 4th International Colloquium on "The Ancient Near East between Classical and Ancient Oriental Traditions," Hatfield College, Durham 7th–9th July 2010* (CO 5; Wiesbaden: Harrassowitz Verlag, 2013), 199–212. Other examples of non-Greek chronographers include Fabius Pictor (Roman, *FGrH* 809) and Philo of Byblos (Phoenician, *FGrH* 790; cf. Eusebius, *Praep. ev.* 1.9.20–21).

106 Jacoby ("Entwicklung," 24–25) identifies Hellanicus of Lesbos as the first chronographer and also recognizes its close affinity to local history. Prior to Eratosthenes, a number of individuals (e.g., Hippias, Aristotle) had attempted to create and refine lists of Olympiad victors (e.g., P.Oxy. II 222; XVII 2082; and XXIII 2381). Some of these lists also included important events that occurred in those four years (e.g., P.Oxy. I 12). Similar chronological lists are also found in inscriptions (e.g., *IG* 14.1297; *Marmor Parium*). For more, see P. Christesen, *Olympic Victor Lists and Ancient Greek History* (Cambridge: Cambridge University Press, 2007).

107 Subsequently followed by Vellius Paterculus, *Hist.* 1.2.1.

108 *FGrH* 241 FF3 and 9 imply that some literary information was also included in Eratosthenes' work.

major events and the lives of famous individuals from the fall of Troy until at least 119 BCE.[109] Many fragments of the text have survived, but the extent of the work or its larger structure is unknown. All of our chronographies from this epoch are fragmentary, so it is difficult to make firm conclusions regarding their genre and how the works of Eratosthenes and Apollodorus functioned prototypically.[110] Scholars are content to group these authors together as representative of a particular type of Greek history writing in the Hellenistic era. A key determinant for participation within this group is a distinctive focus on dates and time periods, often at the expense of a holistic narrative.[111] This is not to say that these works lacked any sense of plot. Rather, inclusion of stories and recounting of events in detail often appear to be secondary to establishing chronological continuity.

Demetrius' fragments have a strong chronological focus, although with what looks to be a stronger narrative arc.[112] For Demetrius, understanding the ages and structure of the patriarchs' lives appears to be of primary concern, although tracing royal successions is also within his purview (cf. F6.1–2). Demetrius also details when major episodes occurred, using Jewish Scripture to divide history by Jewish events (e.g., flood, migration to Egypt: F1.18; exile: F6.1–2) and not those from Greek history (especially Troy).[113] Although

109 E.g., the lives of famous poets, see *FGrH* 244 FF43, 46, 49, 63.

110 For other examples, see Eratosthenes and Menander of Ephesus' *List of the Kings of Tyre* (Josephus, *C. Ap.* 1.18); Philistus of Naucratis, *FGrH* 615; Charon of Naucratis, *FGrH* 612; Timaeus of Tauromenium, *FGrH* 566. Cf. Fraser, *Ptolemaic Alexandria*, 1.713.

111 Though not always, cf. Lyceas of Naucratis, *FGrH* 613.

112 Although this investigation is focused primarily on the genre of the work, Mittmann-Richert rightly highlights the importance of theological interpretation for a fuller understanding of the work in its ancient context. Cf. U. Mittmann-Richert, "Demetrios the Exegete and Chronographer," in I. H. Henderson and G. S. Oegema, eds., *The Changing Face of Judaism, Christianity, and Other Greco-Roman Religions in Antiquity: Presented to James H. Charlesworth on the Occasion of His 65th Birthday* (SJSHRZ 2; Gütersloh: Gütersloher Verlagshaus, 2006), 186–209.

113 For example, Jubilees (*praef.*; 1.1, 29) divides Jewish history by weeks of years from creation until Sinai. First Enoch 83–90 uses important Jewish events to divide history and chronological terminology ("weeks") to divine the future (e.g., 1 En. 93:1–10; 91:11–17). In 1 En. 72–82, the author argues for the importance of a 364-day calendar. An important difference for these authors is that history is not divided by Greek constructs (i.e., Olympiads). For the importance of calendars and dates in Qumran, see S. Stern, "Qumran Calendars and Sectarianism," in T. H. Lim and J. J. Collins, eds., *The Oxford Handbook to the Dead Sea Scrolls* (Oxford: Oxford University Press, 2010), 232–53. Babylonian dates were astronomically established, even throughout the Hellenistic period (cf. the so-called *Astronomical Diaries*, BM 36761 + BM 36390; BM 45745).

Dillery (*Clio's Other Sons*, 357–61) rightly highlights important differences in Demetrius' work as compared to Berossus' and Manetho's. Specifically, Berossus and Manetho were writing at the beginning of the Hellenistic era and did not have an established narrative of their nations in Greek. In contrast, Demetrius was writing at least two generations later and was dependent on the LXX for his composition.

Demetrius parallels his fellow Jewish authors in composing a history using Scripture as his primary source, his work is different from other Jewish histories in a few notable ways. First, important biblical stories (as far as we can tell) are omitted, abbreviated, or mentioned only in passing. When discussing the life of Jacob in F1, Demetrius does not describe Jacob's conflict with Laban (F1.6), the issues surrounding the marriage to Leah (F1.3), his heavenly vision, his divine blessing, or his reconciliation with Esau (F1.8).[114] Important events in Joseph's life are missing, such as his time in Potiphar's house (F1.11) and his incarceration (F1.12). Demetrius does not embellish the lives of important biblical figures, nor does he portray them with Hellenistic values. Second, Demetrius primarily uses the biblical narrative to establish chronology and historical time lines, showing less interest in ethical or moral debates. Demetrius explicitly calculates the ages of the characters whenever he mentions a temporal reference (e.g., F1.2, 3–5, 8, 9–10, 11, 16, 17–19), even when this calculation is not necessary to the text or if he has just done so in the previous paragraph (e.g., F1.9). The strong focus on the dates of the biblical narratives is foundational for scholars' understanding Demetrius' work as participating in chronology, although these two points highlight the ways that Demetrius' work differs from surviving Greek contemporaries.

Also atypical is his inclusion of answers to potential interpretive issues within his scriptural source text. Many detailed explanations given by Demetrius imply that he is answering specific questions about the text of Genesis and Exodus: How could twelve children have been born to Jacob within seven years (F1.3–5)? Why is the thigh tendon of animals not eaten by Jews (F1.7)? Why did Joseph wait nine years to tell his father in Canaan that he was flourishing in Egypt (F1.13)? How could Moses have married Zipporah, as they are separated by three generations (F2.1–3)? Why is it said that Moses had an Ethiopian wife (F2.3)?[115] There are also two explicit questions posed by Demetrius: why (διαπορεῖσθαι διὰ τί) did Joseph show partiality to Benjamin and therefore slight his other brothers (F1.14–15)? How (ἐπιζητεῖν δέ τινα πῶς) did the Israelites, who left Egypt unarmed, manage to obtain weapons with which they fought after crossing the Red Sea (F5.1)?

Supplying answers to potential historical issues is part of the task of chronography, although the author often focuses on issues of dates and relative timing.[116] Chronographers make explicit what is often implicit in the texts, calculating ages and time periods based on references found in their source

114 The explicit introduction of Shechem in F1.8 suggests that this stop was omitted in Demetrius' telling of the Abraham narrative.

115 The issue of Moses' foreign wife is notably omitted in Jub. 47–48.

116 For example, see the discussions of where to place Homer in ancient chronologies (e.g., Eratosthenes, *FGrH* 241 F9a, 9b; Apollodorus *FGrH* 244 F63). Issues of chronology are not limited to histories, but are also found in other genres, such as commentaries (e.g., 4Q252 II,8–10).

material. This practice helps provide data to explain temporal elements and so can be used to answer interpretive issues. The care and effort expended by Demetrius suggest that eliminating chronological discrepancies was one purpose of writing. For example, the calculation in F1.16 shows that the patriarchs spent 215 years in Canaan (25 + 60 + 130) and the Jewish people spent the same number of years in exile (60 – 43 + 40 + 78 + 80, F1.19), allowing Demetrius to address the problem of determining the number of generations in Egypt.[117] The calculation of the years from Adam to the arrival of Jacob to Egypt (3,624 years) and from the flood to Jacob's arrival (1,360, F1.18)[118] aligns better with the biblical narrative than the time lines offered by surrounding nations.[119] Such arithmetic activity provides numerical support for specific interpretations of the text and the events they depict.

However, Demetrius clearly moves beyond this temporal focus to engage with additional interpretive questions that readers within his community found within the text.[120] As discussed in the chapter on Philo (chapter 4), the tradition of close textual readings in Alexandria led to the prominence of the questions and answers literary form. These works were regularly composed by and written to those who were familiar with the text, and were designed to clarify interpretive issues that were identified by close, detailed reading. This literary structure is found later in Aristobulus and Philo, but Demetrius might be the first extant Jewish example of this practice. Unfortunately, the passages from Genesis and Exodus that Demetrius identified as having potential interpretive issues are no longer extant in Philo's *Quaestiones*. However, they do have parallels in Josephus' work, indicating that Demetrius was part of a larger writing tradition that attempted to address textual difficulties.[121]

117 Wacholder, *Eupolemus*, 101–2; J. Hughes, *Secrets of the Times: Myth and History in Biblical Chronology* (JSOT 66; Sheffield: Sheffield Academic Press, 1990), 34–36.

118 On Demetrius' use of the LXX, see Holladay, *Fragments: Historians*, 56 n. 7. Contra Wacholder (*Eupolemus*, 103–4), who implies that Demetrius was involved in the divergence from the Hebrew dating by the LXX translators. A similar interest in determining temporal divisions in the Abraham narrative is found in 1Q20 (Genesis Apocryphon), although in a more muted fashion (e.g., 1Q20 XIX,23; XX,18; XXI,26–27; XXII,27–28) as well as Jubilees (e.g., 13:10–12, 17; 15:1).

119 E.g., Berossus and Manetho, who claim that early men lived much longer than those in the Genesis narrative. Cf. Manetho, *FGrH* 609 FF5–6; Ctesias, *FGrH* 688 F2; Berossus, *FGrH* 680 F3; F4a; Eusebius, *Chron.* 4.11–6.4. Cf. R. Bedrosian, trans., *Eusebius' Chronicle: Translated from the Original Aramaic* (SAT; Long Branch: self-pub., 2008).

120 Cf. Denis, *Introduction*, 251; Walter, "Exegeten," 282; Sterling, *Historiography*, 162–63; van der Horst, "Interpretation of the Bible," 529–32.

121 For example, Josephus explains how the Israelites had weapons (*Ant.* 2.349) and how Moses had an Ethiopian wife (*Ant.* 2.252–253; cf. Num 12:1), and fixes a problematic reading by having Benjamin receiving only a double portion of meat (*Ant.* 2.123), not five portions (F1.14). Josephus does not address the issue of cowherds (*Ant.* 2.186–188) or the potential age difference between Moses and Zipporah (*Ant.* 2.263). Another parallel to the question of how twelve children could have been born to Jacob within seven years (F1.3–5) is found in Jub.

The blending of chronography and nontemporal interpretive questions by Demetrius is distinctive and is not found in the chronographical works of his contemporaries.[122] In contrast, the use of διαπορεῖσθαι διὰ τί in F1.14, στοχάζεσθαι and ἀντιπίπτει in F2.1–3, and ἐπιζητεῖν δέ τινα, πῶς in F5.1 parallel Greek scholarship and are regularly found in Homeric scholia when possible narrative inconsistencies are addressed.[123] Both *quaestiones* and chronological histories were prominent in Alexandrian scholastic tradition and embody similar approaches to text that make them compatible for generic blending and joint participation.

2 Maccabees and Jason of Cyrene

The epitome that later became known as 2 Maccabees provides evidence of a substantial work of history written by Jason of Cyrene.[124] According to the anonymous epitomist,[125] the original work consisted of five books (2 Macc 2:23) and described (among other topics) the struggle of Judas Maccabeus and his brothers against Antiochus Epiphanes and Eupator, the recovery of the temple, the reestablishment of the laws, and the divine actions that allowed for all of these events to transpire (2:19–22).[126] Little more can be said of the original work by Jason, except that it was clearly recognized as a contemporary history by the epitomist, with a strong biographical focus on Judas

28:9–24. The author of Jubilees omits other potential issues, such as Joseph giving five portions to Benjamin and the reason why Joseph delayed in calling his father. A similar interest in the order of birth is found in 1Q33 III,14; V,1.

122 Cf. Niehoff, *Jewish Exegesis*, 53. It is uncertain (though unlikely) whether this work had any impact on the development of the Greek genre of chronography. Bickerman, however, makes his position clear: "Demetrius' influence on Greek historiography was nil." E. J. Bickerman, "The Jewish Historian Demetrios," in J. Neusner, ed., *Christianity, Judaism and Other Greco-Roman Cults: Studies for Morton Smith at Sixty; Part 3: Judaism before 70* (Leiden: Brill, 1975), 79.

123 For examples, see R. Nünlist, *The Ancient Critic at Work: Terms and Concepts of Literary Criticism in Greek Scholia* (Cambridge: Cambridge University Press, 2009), 11; Niehoff, *Jewish Exegesis*, 39–44; Dillery, *Clio's Other Sons*, 376–81.

124 For a discussion of the letters and their relationship to the history/epitome, see Doran, *Temple Propaganda*, 3–12; D. S. Williams, "Recent Research in 2 Maccabees," *CBR* 2 (2003): 71–73; Doering, *Ancient Jewish Letters*, 160–67. The text used for 2 Maccabees is from W. Kappler and R. Hanhart, eds., *Maccabaeorum liber II*, vol. IX.2 (3rd ed.; Göttingen: Vandenhoeck & Ruprecht, 2008).

125 Cf. D. R. Schwartz, *2 Maccabees* (CEJL; Berlin: De Gruyter, 2008), 28, who rejects the term "epitomator" in favor of "author" (37). So too Honigman, *Tales of High Priests*, 8. Although I agree that the epitomist of Jason's work is an author in his own right, I will use the terms "epitome" and "epitomist" for convenience to differentiate him from Jason and his history. Cf. V. Parker, "The Letters in II Maccabees: Reflections on the Book's Composition," *ZAW* 119 (2007): 401; G. Morrison, "The Composition of II Maccabees: Insights Provided by a Literary *Topos*," *Bib* 90 (2009): 571–72. Some authors in antiquity epitomized their own work (e.g., Agatharchides of Knidos, Photius, *Bibl.* 213.3).

126 Wacholder (*Eupolemus*, 28 n. 6) is too skeptical of the epitomist's claim. For an overview of the plot and points of contact with 3 Maccabees, see chapter 6.

Maccabaeus (possibly among others, 2:24, 30–32).[127] Similar challenges exist for our reconstruction of the author.[128] Jason lived and wrote in the middle of the second century BCE, making him a contemporary of Judas, and may have been a participant in and eyewitness to the events he narrated. Possible support for this position comes from equating Jason of Cyrene with Jason son of Eleazar in 1 Maccabees 8:17, although one must be cautious, as the name Jason was popular among Jews in antiquity.[129] Jason was almost certainly a Jew who likely grew up in a diasporan location (i.e., Cyrene). Although the latter is highly likely, it does not necessarily follow that his origin is diasporic, as the moniker "Cyrene" could indicate family origins. Indeed, there is a strong case for seeing Jason as hailing from Judaea, possibly even Jerusalem.[130]

The epitomist clearly differentiates Jason's history from his epitome.[131] In so doing, the epitomist provides insight into the presumed expectations of his readers and allows us to infer something of his reading and compositional environment.[132] According to the epitomist, there were two prominent issues with Jason's history that made an epitome necessary: length and substantial numerical detail (2:24).[133] These features are not problematic in that they are atypical or undesirable for historical treatises, and the epitomist agrees that a proper historian, just like a master builder, needs to have a comprehensive understanding of the subject's topology and to take concern with the full range of details (2:29–30). His position, therefore, is not that Jason's work is poor

127 Wills (*Jewish Novel*, 193–201) labels 2 Maccabees a "historical novel." Although recognizing some important features, this is a problematic categorization. Cf. Gruen, *Diaspora*, 176.

128 Cf. J. Sievers, *The Hasmoneans and Their Supporters: From Mattathias to the Death of John Hyrcanus I* (SFSHJ 6; Atlanta: Scholars Press, 1990), 4; cf. J. A. Goldstein, trans., *II Maccabees: A New Translation with Introduction and Commentary* (AB 41A; Garden City, N.Y.: Doubleday, 1983), 55–70.

129 For an overview of this discussion, see Tcherikover, *Hellenistic Civilization*, 384–86. Cf. Ilan, *Lexicon of Jewish Names*, 1.288–90; 3.309–12.

130 E.g., Honigman, *Tales of High Priests*, 8–9; Barclay, *Jews*, 12 (implicitly). Cf. Doran, *2 Maccabees*, 15–17. On his education, see Wacholder, *Eupolemus*, 38; Tcherikover, *Hellenistic Civilization*, 387; Schwartz, *2 Maccabees*, 45–51; A. Schlatter, *Jason von Kyrene: Ein Beitrag zu seiner Wiederherstellung* (Munich: C. H. Beck, 1891), 52; Hengel, *Judaism and Hellenism*, 1.95–100.

131 F. Borchardt, "Reading Aid: 2 Maccabees and the History of Jason of Cyrene Reconsidered," *JSJ* 47 (2016): 71–87; L. Neubert, "Inventing Jason of Cyrene? 2 Maccabees and the Epitome," in F. Avemarie et al., eds., *Die Makkabäer* (WUNT 1.382; Tübingen: Mohr Siebeck, 2017), 187–207.

132 See M. Dubischar, "Survival of the Most Condensed? Auxiliary Texts, Communications Theory, and Condensation of Knowledge," in M. Horster and C. Reitz, eds., *Condensing Texts—Condensed Texts* (Stuttgart: Steiner, 2010), 39–68, especially 44–47.

133 Schwartz (*2 Maccabees*, 176) is likely correct when he suggests that these numerical details (τὸ χύμα τῶν ἀριθμῶν) were regarding armies, distances, etc. Motives for abridgment (e.g., removal of excess, eliminating complex and redundant speech) are found in the so-called *Aretalogy of Imhotep-Asclepius*, a Greco-Egyptian translation, in which Nechautes recounts his "translation" of the work (P.Oxy. XI 1381 ll. 174–181).

history (although some criticism is possibly implied in τὸ χύμα τῶν ἀριθμῶν), but that it is not useful to a certain contingent, himself included. The proposed solution is to make a one-volume epitome, written with a strong command of Greek rhetoric, that would make the text more entertaining to read, easier to memorize, and beneficial for all subsequent readers (2:25). These changes result in a work distinct from Jason's original, resulting in two discrete, if related, data points for understanding Jewish historiography in the Hellenistic era.

Although points of comparison with history are rightly noted (see below), little discussion has been given to 2 Maccabees as part of the genus of epitome. This is understandable, as the recognition of epitome as a distinct literary form with its own criteria of design has only recently been undertaken.[134] This is not to say that there is a singular genre of epitome or that epitome could or should be understood as a genre. Rather, if we are to view the epitomist as an author in his/her own right, the natural progression is to view their literary output as adopting and in dialogue with established literary practices. In light of this, the phrase τὸ δὲ ἐπιπορεύεσθαι τοῖς ὑπογραμμοῖς τῆς ἐπιτομῆς διαπονοῦντες (2:28) is important. The collocation of ὑπογραμμός and ἐπιτομή is unique to 2 Maccabees and so potentially provides a new insight into the nature of epitomization in antiquity. The crux of the issue is how one understands and interprets ὑπογραμμός, which is often glossed as "pattern," "model," or "outline."[135] Doran renders this term "general description," relating it to the concept of appearance through comparisons with ὑπογρᾶφω.[136] This association is understandable given the lexical overlap between ὑπογρᾶφω and ὑπογραμμός. However, is it possible that the phrase in 2:28 implies a deeper structuring principle rather than speaking only to the outline of the work? The context of 2:28–29 invokes the image of a painter/decorator, who adorns the house after it has been constructed. Here the creation of outlines was an important first step for the painter in order to complete the job well. However, the metaphor of the painter and his craft implies previous training and an expertise that would ensure both a recognized final image (one adopting acceptable and known models) and quality execution. Even the concept of "tracing over" embedded within ὑπογρᾶφω implies that someone has gone before and that there is an acceptable form that a picture, or in this case an epitome, should take. Thus, in both 2:28 and the wider introductory preface, the epitomist presents

134 See J. Jarecsni, "The 'Epitome': An Original Work or a Copy? An Analysis of the First Eleven Chapters of the Epitome of Caesaribus," *ACD* 33 (1997): 203–14.

135 So LSJ and *Brill Dictionary of Ancient Greek*.

136 Doran, *2 Maccabees*, 72 (cf. Plato, *Prot.* 326d; *Resp.* 8.548d; Isocrates, *Phil.* 5.85; Strabo, *Geogr.* 13.1.25). Unfortunately, little attention is paid to this phrase by Goldstein (*II Maccabees*, 193) or Schwartz (*2 Maccabees*, 178).

his work as following a set of principles; ones that he expects his readers to recognize and accept.

Scholars have demonstrated that prior models and author/reader expectations constrain the production of epitomes and that at times there might only be a very tenuous relationship between the source work and its abridgment.[137] Although overlapping in content (but not in detail), the constructed epitome occupies a different functional space. This is explicitly highlighted by the epitomist, who, using the metaphor of mixing wine, produces a work to the taste of his readers (15:39).[138] As a result, the epitome has a new relationship with the genre of history, one that is different from the original text and fulfills a new purpose. The epitomist, by abbreviating the narrative (τὸ δὲ σύντομον τῆς λέξεως, 2:31), implies that the new work is also a history, but with different historiographical expectations.[139] Here, I differentiate the epitome of Jason's history from 2 Maccabees as it has been transmitted, as I do not find it convincing that the epitomist would append two letters prior to his preface. That 2 Maccabees was transmitted with introductory letters provides insight into how certain later readers viewed the relationship between letters and narrative, suggesting that they were viewed as compatible in content and that there was not a rigid genre discrepancy.

In light of the work's content, a number of scholars have labeled 2 Maccabees "pathetic history."[140] This association is not without merit, as 2 Maccabees is a prose narrative that depicts historical events using emotion and rhetoric.[141]

137 M. Horster and C. Reitz, "'Condensation' of Literature and the Pragmatics of Literary Production," in M. Horster and C. Reitz, eds., *Condensing Texts—Condensed Texts* (Stuttgart: Steiner, 2010), 3–14, especially 7–10; M. Mülke, "Die Epitome—das bessere Original?" in M. Horster and C. Reitz, eds., *Condensing Texts—Condensed Texts* (Stuttgart: Steiner, 2010), 69–89. Cf. Diogenes Laertius, *Vit.* 10.35, 84–85.

138 For change of taste as a wider phenomenon of condensed works, see G. Schepens and S. Schorn, "Verkürzungen in und von Historiographie in klassischer und hellenistischer Zeit," in M. Horster and C. Reitz, eds., *Condensing Texts—Condensed Texts* (Stuttgart: Steiner, 2010), 403–10.

139 2 Macc 2:32, ἐντεῦθεν οὖν ἀρξώμεθα τῆς διηγήσεως τοῖς προειρημένοις τοσοῦτον ἐπιζεύξαντες εὔηθες γὰρ τὸ μὲν πρὸ τῆς ἱστορίας πλεονάζειν, τὴν δὲ ἱστορίαν ἐπιτεμεῖν. It is possible to see the referent in this verse as Jason's history, but that is unlikely. A related understanding of ἱστορία through the use of epitome language (ἐπιτέμνω) is found in Plutarch, *Alex.* 1.1–2. For similar epitome language (καὶ αὐτὸ ὂν βραχὺ καὶ σύντομον τὴν λέξιν), see Simplicius on Aristotle's *Cat. proleg.* F8b (Ven. 1499).

140 Tcherikover, *Hellenistic Civilization*, 387; B. Bar-Kochva, *Judas Maccabaeus: The Jewish Struggle against the Seleucids* (Cambridge: Cambridge University Press, 1989), 172–78; Schwartz, *2 Maccabees*, 78–80, in discussion with Diodorus Siculus, *Bibl.* 17.35.4–17.36.4; Polybius, *Hist.* 2.56.7–11. For critique, see Doran, *Temple Propaganda*, 84–89; R. Doran, "2 Maccabees and 'Tragic History,'" *HUCA* 50 (1979): 107–14.

141 For examples, see Schwartz, *2 Maccabees*, 67–84; J. Jay, *The Tragic in Mark: A Literary-Historical Interpretation* (HUT 66; Tübingen: Mohr Siebeck, 2014), 118–28.

However, to claim that the use of rhetorical or emotional language is limited to or the special purview of pathetic histories is inaccurate, as all histories, especially those written in the Hellenistic and Roman eras, are rhetorical.[142] Other scholars have labeled 2 Maccabees "historical fiction," highlighting the author's use of novelistic elements.[143] Narrative composition in novels and histories have some functional overlap, and both employ similar features. More prominent, according to ancient authors, is their relationship to "truth." Some novels make claims to authenticity (Chariton, *Chaer.* 1.1). However, their relationship to truth is often complex; some are recognized as fictional, signaling to the reader that the events depicted lack credibility (Lucian, *Ver. hist.* 1.1–4), whereas others might not be historically true but depict other forms of truth (e.g., emotion).[144] In contrast, ancient historians regularly and strongly assert historical veracity and see that as a requisite feature of the genre.[145] The epitomist is more aligned with the latter, focusing on history and not hinting to the reader that the events depicted are fictitious or even exaggerated.[146] Accordingly, the subgenres of dynastic and local history have the most potential as proposed genres of participation, as they provide a reasonable description of the work, but do not overly specify the nature of the epitome.[147]

142 On the blending of history and tragedy, see Polybius, *Hist.* 2.56.1–2.63.6. See the critic of the term "tragic history" in F. W. Walbank, *Polybius* (SCL 42; Berkeley: University of California Press, 1972), 38; F. W. Walbank, "History and Tragedy," *Historia* 9 (1960): 216–34; Doran, "2 Maccabees"; J. Marincola, "Beyond Pity and Fear: The Emotions of History," *Ancient Society* 33 (2003): 285–315.

143 Wills, *Jewish Novel*, 193–201. For discussion of comedic elements, see Gruen, *Diaspora*, 176–80.

144 Cf. R. L. Hunter, "History and Historicity in the Romance of Chariton," *ANRW* 2.34.2 (1994): 1055–86.

145 E.g., Dionysius of Halicarnassus, *Ant. rom.* 1.1.2; Josephus, *BJ* 1.2; *Ant.* 1.1; Thucydides, *Hist.* 1.22.1–4; Polybius, *Hist.* 12.7.1–6.

146 I resist the idea of the work as "theological history," finding the category to be problematic. Clearly theological ideas are resonant in the text, but this subject does not necessarily result in a specific, formal genre. For a strong critique with references, see Honigman, *Tales of High Priests*, 9–11.

Classification of the work as festal legend (so Bunge and Momigliano) is problematic for understanding the epitome, as this view is strongly influenced by the two preceding letters and does not really address the nature of the epitomized text (although the explanation of the ending is insightful). Cf. J. G. Bunge, "Untersuchungen zum zweiten Makkabäerbuch: Quellenkritische, literarische, chronologische und historische Untersuchungen zum zweiten Makkabäerbuch als Quelle syrisch-palästinensischer Geschichte im 2. Jh. v. Chr." (PhD diss., University of Bonn, 1971), 184–90; Momigliano, "Maccabees," 81–88. For a recent discussion of holidays in 2 Maccabees, see M. Z. Simkovich, "Greek Influence on the Composition of 2 Maccabees," *JSJ* 42 (2011): 296–303.

147 Firmly differentiating these two subgroups is problematic. For dynastic history, see Honigman, *Tales of High Priests*, 35–41. For local history, see Doran, *2 Maccabees*, 6–7. Doran provides Eudemus (*FGrH* 524), Myron of Priene (*FGrH* 106 F5), Syriskos of Chersonesos (*FGrH* 807), and Timocritus (*FGrH* 522) as comparators, although other local historians writing about

Overall, determining in which genre 2 Maccabees participates has proven to be problematic. I suggest that this is because the abridged work of Jason is not a prototypical historical composition, but an epitome. The epitome is not removed from genre or reading expectations, but this difference might account for why it is harder to discern than other historical texts. One could also ask whether or not it is appropriate to expect an epitome to fit with specific genre expectations or if this imposition by modern scholarship misses an important element of ancient literary composition.

Josephus

Josephus is the most important Jewish-Greek historian whose works have survived. Writing in the latter part of the first century CE from Rome, Josephus composed four Greek-language works: *Jewish War*, *Antiquities of the Jews*, *Against Apion*, and *Life*.[148] There is a mountain of scholarly work dedicated to Josephus, and I am not able to engage thoroughly with the many issues in Josephan studies.[149] Rather, I will limit my focus to discussions of genre and literary forms, although even here, substantial work has been undertaken and I will not unduly retrace arguments that are well established. Before turning my attention to specific works, I will articulate Josephus' genre awareness and his discussion of ancient literary forms, an important topic that has not received sufficient scholarly attention.

Josephus' Genre Consciousness

At the basic level, Josephus appears to divide literature into prose and poetry (e.g., *Ant.* 20.263).[150] For example, in *Ant.* 12.38 and 110, Josephus uses "poets and historians" (διὸ καὶ τοὺς ποιητὰς . . . καὶ τοὺς συγγραφεῖς τῶν ἱστοριῶν

important events could have been offered (e.g., Rhianos of Bene, *FGrH* 265, who wrote in verse, and others cited in the *Lydian Chronicle* F4 ll. 47–59).

148 For the importance of Josephus as situated and writing in Rome, and the need to take that geographical placement seriously when identifying his elite audience(s) and interpreting his texts, see S. Mason, "Of Audience and Meaning: Reading Josephus' *Bellum Judaicum* in the Context of a Flavian Audience," in J. Sievers and G. Lembi, eds., *Jewish History in Flavian Rome and Beyond* (JSJSup 104; Leiden: Brill, 2005), 71–100. For a broad introduction to Josephus, see T. Rajak, *Josephus: The Historian and His Society* (2nd ed.; London: Duckworth, 2002); H. H. Chapman and Z. Rodgers, eds., *A Companion to Josephus* (Oxford: Wiley-Blackwell, 2016). For the Greek text, see B. Niese, ed., *Flavii Iosephi opera* (7 vols.; 1885; repr., Berlin: Weidmann, 1955).

149 For bibliography on Josephus, see H. Schreckenberg, *Bibliographie zu Flavius Josephus* (ALGHJ 1; Leiden: Brill, 1968); L. H. Feldman, *Josephus and Modern Scholarship (1937–1980)* (Berlin: De Gruyter, 1984); S. Mason, Project on Ancient Cultural Engagement (PACE), https://pace.webhosting.rug.nl/york/york/index.htm (http://etana.org/node/11168).

150 For a statement against the mixing of prose and poetry, see Lucian, *Hist.* 8. For history as "prose poem" without metered language, see Quintilian, *Inst.* 10.1.31.

and οὐδεὶς οὔτε τῶν ἱστορικῶν . . . οὔτε τῶν ποιητῶν) to represent the range of poetic and prose authors.[151] Explicit mention of this dichotomy is lacking in the rest of his corpus, and there is no other pairing of ποιητής with λογογράφος or συγγραφεύς, as was witnessed in Philo (chapter 4) and other ancient writers.[152] This lack of comparison might be due to the fact that there are very few references to poets and poetry in Josephus' corpus. He mentions only a few of them in his discussions and then only provides basic information about their person and writings (e.g., *Ant.* 1.16).[153] Homer is the poet most discussed by Josephus, but even here there is only limited explicit engagement. Josephus knows about textual debates due to oral transmission (*C. Ap.* 1.12) and the dispute over his birthplace (*C. Ap.* 2.14), and speaks about the content of Homer's poems twice, claiming that Homer calls Jerusalem "Hierosolyma" (*Ant.* 7.67) and that he does not employ the word νόμος (*C. Ap.* 2.155). Josephus criticizes poets (along with legislators, *Ant.* 1.22) for spreading poor notions of the gods (*C. Ap.* 2.239) and for attributing to the gods various passions (*C. Ap.* 2.251), rightly noting that Plato barred them from his ideal state (*C. Ap.* 2.256; cf. Plato, *Resp.* 3.398a).[154] However, beyond these few mentions, Josephus does not provide in-depth discussions of poets or poetry. Similarly, Josephus only mentions tragedies twice (*Ant.* 14.153; *C. Ap.* 2.97; cf. *BJ* 2.348) and does not speak about comedies. Nevertheless, parts of Josephus' works echo Greek poets, and there are a number of passages in his corpus that evoke Greek poetic works.[155] For example, in his discussion of the Essenes' view of

151 Not all references to historians encompass all other prose genres (see below). The former passage is said to be from Hecataeus of Abdera and is drawn from LA 312. Both of which imply that Hecataeus and Pseudo-Aristeas held this view and that Josephus willingly adopted it. On the relationship between Josephus and *Aristeas*, see A. Pelletier, *Flavius Josèphe, Adaptateur de la Lettre d'Aristée: Une réaction atticisante contre la koinè* (ÉC 45; Paris: Klincksieck, 1962); S. J. D. Cohen, *Josephus in Galilee and Rome* (Leiden: Brill, 1979), 34–35.

152 E.g., Plato, *Resp.* 3.392a, ποιηταὶ καὶ λογοποιοί; Dionysius of Halicarnassus, *Thuc.* 1. Cf. G. Avenarius, *Lukians Schrift zur Geschichtsschreibung* (Meisenheim: Hain, 1956), 16–22.

153 Hesiod: *Ant.* 1.108; *C. Ap.* 1.16; Choerilus: *C. Ap.* 1.172–75. Josephus also recognizes different poetic metres (e.g., hexameter: *Ant.* 2.346; 4.303; trimeter: *Ant.* 7.305; pentameter: *Ant.* 7.305) and types of poetry (e.g., Theodectes, the tragic poet, *Ant.* 12.113). Koskenniemi, *Greek Writers and Philosophers*, 158–71.

154 Josephus possibly had knowledge of the Platonic discussion of poetic genres that directly preceded his allusion (e.g., *Resp.* 3.392a–395a).

155 For references, see H. St. J. Thackeray, trans., *Josephus: Wars* (LCL; Cambridge, Mass.: Harvard University Press, 1956), xv–xix; S. Schwartz, *Josephus and Judean Politics* (CSCT 18; Leiden: Brill, 1990), 35–39, 227–32; L. H. Feldman, *Josephus's Interpretation of the Bible* (Berkeley: University of California Press, 1998), 218; L. H. Feldman, "The Influence of Greek Tragedians on Josephus," in A. Ovadiah, ed., *The Howard Gilman International Conferences I: Hellenic and Jewish Arts* (Tel Aviv: RAMOT, 1998), 51–80; H. H. Chapman, "'By the Waters of Babylon': Josephus and Greek Poetry," in J. Sievers and G. Lembi, eds., *Josephus and Jewish History in Flavian Rome and Beyond* (JSJSup 104; Leiden: Brill, 2005), 121–46. One complication to claims of authorial knowledge is the way that scholars evaluate the nature and veracity of allusions to

the afterlife (*BJ* 2.154–158), Josephus mentions Oceanus and the Islands of the Blessed and alludes to Hesiod's fourth age of man (*Op.* 159–170). This appropriation implies a deep understanding of Greek literature and signals his education in Greek literature.[156]

Mention of prose works is scattered throughout Josephus' texts, but, with such a substantial surviving corpus, it is surprising that Josephus provides so little discussion about other literary works.[157] Philosophers and the study of philosophy are discussed on occasion, particularly with regard to the nature of God and Jewish Scripture (e.g., *Ant.* 12.101). Josephus claims to have "studied the philosophy" of the sacred writings (μετεσχηκὼς τῆς φιλοσοφίας τῆς ἐν ἐκείνοις τοῖς γράμμασι, *C. Ap.* 1.54) and identifies both the law (*Ant.* 12.37; 16.398) and Solomon's compositions (*Ant.* 8.44) as being philosophic in nature.[158] Josephus shows awareness of major figures in Greek philosophy, but they are discussed primarily in clusters. For instance, in providing Greek evidence of Jewish antiquity, Josephus calls upon Pythagoras and Hermippus (*C. Ap.* 1.162–165), Theophrastus (*C. Ap.* 1.166–167), and Clearchus and Aristotle (*C. Ap.* 1.176–183), but these authors are essentially absent in the remainder of his works.[159] Other philosophers are mentioned, but often to have their positions summarily refuted (e.g., *Ant.* 10.277; *C. Ap.* 1.14). The primary exception to this is Plato, with whom Josephus shows more (though not substantial) knowledge of specific texts (*C. Ap.* 2.168, 223–225, 256–261). This lack of deep engagement suggests that Josephus did not have a strong grounding in Greek philosophy and that he undertook research on specific topics for a purpose (e.g., God's nature, *C. Ap.* 2.168; God's existence, *C. Ap.* 2.180; Athenian punishments for impiety, *C. Ap.* 2.262–268). The way Josephus cites non-Jewish philosophers further suggests that he may have acquired their names and positions through a source, rather than through his own reading of their texts (e.g., *Ant.* 1.107–108; *C. Ap.* 2.135). Josephus himself does not lay claim to broad reading of Greek works (οὐ γὰρ ἔγωγε πᾶσιν ἐντετύχηκα τοῖς βιβλίοις,

---

determine knowledge and imitation by Josephus. This is a difficult topic and deserves a careful investigation in its own right.

156 I am not convinced that Josephus knew much Latin literature. Some have also questioned our ability to attribute knowledge of Greek authors directly to Josephus. Most prominent is the question of how much of Josephus' material comes from him and how much comes from his "assistants" (συνεργοῖς, *C. Ap.* 1.50). Although either option is possible, I would attribute the knowledge showcased in his works to Josephus. On this issue, see Rajak, *Josephus*, 233–36; L. Ullmann and J. Price, "Drama and History in Josephus' *Bellum Judaicum*," *Scripta Classica Israelica* 21 (2002): 97–111; Chapman, "'Waters of Babylon,'" 122–24. For discussion of Josephus' Jewish (not Greek) education, see Rajak, *Josephus*, 26–32.

157 E.g., epitaphs (*Ant.* 7.42); prophecies (*Ant.* 10.93, 267); πράξεις (*Ant.* 12.5); μῦθος/μυθολογία (*Ant.* 1.15; *BJ* 2.156; 3.420; *C. Ap.* 1.25, 105; 2.256).

158 For the descriptions of Jewish sects as "philosophies," see *Ant.* 18.25; *Vita* 12.

159 Pythagoras is mentioned a few other times (e.g., *Ant.* 15.371; *C. Ap.* 1.14; 2.14, 168).

C. Ap. 1.216, although cf. *Ant.* 20.263), nor might we expect this of someone who came to the serious study of Greek literature later in life.[160] However, such self-deprecating comments are regularly paired with displays of learning (e.g., *C. Ap.* 1.220–22) and so should be investigated thoroughly before taking them at face value.[161] Josephus seems to be aware that philosophical discussion, especially of Stoicism, would be appreciated by his readers, and so he includes specific vocabulary into his discussion.[162]

History is by far the most discussed genre in Josephus' corpus, and from his comments we see that he has certain assumptions about this literary form: what content is and is not expected to be included in a history, how a history is supposed to be constructed, and its intended purpose.[163] Equally important is Josephus' expectation that his readers will both recognize these components and agree that they align with prototypical historiography. This assumption by Josephus provides insight into his perspective, suggesting that he believed he had internalized Greek literary expectations regarding history and was fully able to engage not only in the practice of composition, but also in the evaluation and critique of other historians.

Josephus shows a strong awareness of different Greek historians, regularly citing them throughout his works.[164] Josephus especially appears to be interested in historians writing in Greek who are not Roman or Greek by ethnicity, providing substantial quotations from a number of these authors (οἱ τὰς βαρβαρικὰς ἱστορίας ἀναγεγραφότες, e.g., Berossus, Hestiaeus, Hieronymus

160 On the inherent struggles and learning late in life, see *C. Ap.* 1.10; Lucian, *Merc. cond.* 23; Athenaeus, *Deipn.* 3.127b; Plutarch, *Mor.* 334c. For a positive example of late learning, see Plato, *Resp.* 409b; *Soph.* 251b. Aulus Gellius wrote his *Attic Nights* with the hope of inspiring the desire to learn in his readers, whether by books or by teachers (*praef.* 12, 17).

161 Rightly noted by Barclay, *Against Apion*, 128.

162 L. H. Feldman, "Use, Authority and Exegesis of Mikra in the Writings of Josephus," in M. J. Mulder, ed., *Mikra: Text, Translation, Reading and Interpretation of the Hebrew Bible in Ancient Judaism and Early Christianity* (CRINT 2.1; Philadelphia: Fortress, 1988), 488–94, 498–500.

163 Josephus primarily uses συγγραφ- when discussing prose composition in general (74 ×), and regularly collocates συγγραφ- words with ἱστορία (both the lexical term and the titles of historical works) (e.g., *Ant.* 1.6, 94, 107; 10.20; 12.38; 14.1–3, 68; *BJ* 1.13; *Vita* 359; *C. Ap.* 1.1, 13–15, 17–18, etc. [especially in book 1]; 2.1), suggesting that these words/concepts are semantically linked. However, συγγραφεύς is not limited to historiographical writing and can be used to represent prose narratives more broadly (*Ant.* 6.346, ἐν ταῖς ἱστορίαις καὶ τοῖς ἄλλοις συγγράμμασιν εἰρήκασιν; cf. Dionysius of Halicarnassus, *Thuc.* 1). Discussion of the specific genres of Josephus' works will be pursued below. Here, we will take this opportunity to look at his displayed understanding of historiography more holistically.

164 E.g., *Ant.* 1.108; 10.227–228; 14.68; *C. Ap.* 1.13–18, 216, 221; 2.84. In contrast, Josephus rarely mentions Latin historians (e.g., Livy: *Ant.* 14.68; cf. *BJ* 4.496), suggesting that he was not well versed in this corpus of literature. For Josephus' use of Nicolaus, see Wacholder, *Nicolaus*, 60–64.

the Egyptian, Justus, Manetho, Mnaseas, etc.; cf. *Ant.* 1.93–94, 107; 10.228).[165] This preference could indicate an acknowledged affiliation between the purpose of Josephus' work and those by non-Greek historians as well as examples of different prototypical models. Authors of Greek origin are thought to excel in eloquence and literary ability, but in terms of their accuracy when writing about other nations, they are inadequate (*C. Ap.* 1.27). Josephus' statement, although self-promoting and rhetorically loaded, implies a practice of comparing literary compositions through an ethnic lens (particularly when the subject matter is ethnographic) and distinguishing between Near Eastern and Western historiographical practices.

Regarding the nature of composition, histories are to be written on certain subjects. A history, as one might expect, is to recount deeds and events that have already happened and not report on things that are yet to come (οὐκ ἔδοξε τοῦτο ἱστορεῖν τὰ παρελθόντα καὶ τὰ γεγενημένα συγγράφειν οὐ τὰ μέλλοντα ὀφείλοντι, *Ant.* 10.210). Josephus' view on the relationship between prophecy and history, namely that prophets were authors of Jewish historiography (*BJ* 1.18; 6.109; *C. Ap.* 1.37), complicates this understanding. The positive association of seers and prophets with history writing is unparalleled in Greek and Latin circles, and is strongly criticized by Lucian (*Hist.* 31).[166] More typically, a history could focus on a war between cities or nations, chronicling the rise and fall of empires and peoples (*BJ* 1.1). Similarly, although with important differences, one could also write about the history of a nation, including its unexpected reversals, fortunes in war, brave commanders, and changes in government (καὶ παντοῖαι μέν εἰσι παράλογοι περιπέτειαι, πολλαὶ δὲ τύχαι πολέμων καὶ στρατηγῶν ἀνδραγαθίαι καὶ πολιτευμάτων μεταβολαί, *Ant.* 1.13). Origins, geography, and customs are typical topics of discussion, indicating a relationship between history and ethnography.

165 Manetho (*C. Ap.* 1.75–82, 85–90, 94–102, 232–250), Dius the Tyrian (*C. Ap.* 1.113–115), Menander of Ephesus (*C. Ap.* 1.116–125), Berossus (*C. Ap.* 1.134–141, 146–153), and Apion (*C. Ap.* 2.10–11, 92–96, 112–114).

Scholars debate whether Josephus read these texts or was dependent on another work whose author had already extracted the passages. For example, Verbrugghe and Wickersham (*Berossos and Manetho*, 28–29) assert that Josephus likely did not read Berossus' *History* directly, but took his information from Alexander Polyhistor's epitome of the work. Although this is possible, there is insufficient evidence for or against this position, and Verbrugghe and Wickersham do not provide a rationale for their claim. Identifying that the quotation comes from the "third book" (ἐν τῇ τρίτῃ βίβλῳ τῶν Χαλδαϊκῶν, *C. Ap.* 1.142) implies autopsy (although this does not need to be the case), and there is little evidence for *a priori* discounting Josephus' knowledge of historical works.

166 For the connection between Josephus' works and the Jewish canon, see P. Bilde, "*Contra Apionem* 1.28–56: An Essay on Josephus' View of His Own Work," in E.-M. Becker, M. H. Jensen, and J. Mortensen, eds., *Collected Studies on Philo and Josephus* (SANt 7; Göttingen: Vandenhoeck & Ruprecht, 2016), 105–20.

This differentiation suggests that Josephus recognized subgenres of histories. For example, he mentions and makes use of chronologies (e.g., *C. Ap.* 1.184; 2.84; *Ant.* 9.283), which differ in structure, content, and purpose to histories of wars and nations. *Atthides* (works of local Attic history) are also mentioned by Josephus in his critique of Greek historians (*C. Ap.* 1.17). Josephus knows about genealogical traditions (γενεαλογία, *C. Ap.* 1.15–17; cf. *Ant.* 11.71; *BJ* 1.476) and ὑπομνήματα, associating both with the composition of history.[167] Letters, although functioning independently in everyday life, are important pieces of evidence and so are incorporated into a history at strategic locations.[168]

Most importantly for Josephus, history has a fundamental relationship with truth and needs to be written with accuracy (μετ' ἀκριβείας, *BJ* 1.2, 9; 7.454; *Ant.* 14.3; 20.154–157; *C. Ap.* 1.19–43; *Vita* 40, 336–339).[169] Historians writing about current events are expected to rely on autopsy and use reliable sources of recent events, not depending on hearsay or unsubstantiated reports (ἀκοή, *BJ* 1.1).[170] Proper resources include accounts from other historians, but also decrees and inscriptions that are available to the public and open to scrutiny (e.g., *Ant.* 8.55; 14.188; 16.174–178).[171] Ultimately, a good historian should not add or omit anything pertinent to the history (οὐδὲν οὔτε ἀποκρυπτόμενος

167 Every mention of ὑπομνήματα as a written composition in Josephus' corpus is associated with royalty (e.g., Persian kings: *Ant.* 11.94, 98, 104, 208, 248; King Herod: *Ant.* 15.174; Caesars: *Vita* 342, 358; *C. Ap.* 1.56). This implies that Josephus had a specific idea of the nature and purpose of this type of literary work and challenges the rendering of ὑπομνήματα as "field notes" (so Barclay). On the polished nature of Julius Caesar's composition, see Marincola, *Authority*, 80–82.

168 For the discussion of Josephus' letters, see Doering, *Jewish Letters*, 270–342. In a similar fashion, decrees and inscriptions are also relevant for the historian and could be used as evidence to convince his readers (e.g., *Ant.* 16.174–178). On this section, see R. Laqueur, *Der jüdische Historiker Flavius Josephus: Ein biographischer Versuch auf neuer quellenkritischer Grundlage* (1920; repr., Darmstadt: Wissenschaftliche Buchgesellschaft, 1970), 221–23.

169 On the supposed dichotomy of simple truth versus artful speech in history writing, see Thucydides, *Hist.* 1.22.1–4; Polybius, *Hist.* 12.7.1–6; 12.12.1–7; Cicero, *Fam.* 5.12.3; Lucian, *Hist.* 7, 40; Josephus, *BJ* 1.13–16; *Ant.* 20.263–264; *C. Ap.* 1.27. Cf. Marincola, *Authority*, 115–16.

170 E.g., *C. Ap.* 1.46, 53–55; 2.37, 62; *Vita* 357–360; cf. Thucydides, *Hist.* 1.22.2–3; Polybius, *Hist.* 4.2.2–3; 12.4c.3–5; 12.25g.1–5; Lucian, *Hist.* 29, 47. Not all histories have this as a necessary feature. For example, Aulus Gellius (*Noct. att.* 5.18.1–6) differentiates between histories and annals by their author's level of participation in events, in addition to their respective uses of chronological structure, discussion of purpose, and time period in focus (cf. Polybius, *Hist.* 12.25e.1–7; Dionysius of Halicarnassus, *Ant. rom.* 1.7.3). Cf. Marincola, *Authority*, 63–86; Alexander, *Preface*, 34–41; S. A. Adams, "Luke's Preface (1.1–4) and Its Relationship to Greek Historical Prefaces: A Response to Loveday Alexander," *JGRChJ* 3 (2006): 187–90. Historians writing about distant history must rely on reports, which is viewed as a hindrance (e.g., Polybius, *Hist.* 4.1.1–4; Plutarch, *Per.* 13.12).

171 A good history is also internally consistent and in line with other authorities (*C. Ap.* 1.293; 2.22–24).

οὔτε προστιθεὶς τοῖς πεφωραμένοις, *BJ* 1.26).[172] In particular, Josephus speaks out against writing to deceive one's readers, molding (πλάσμα) a narrative to fit personal desire (*BJ* 1.6). The term πλάσμα has technical meaning and has been associated with "false history" (ψευδῆ) and "myths" (μύθους, Sextus Empiricus, *Math.* 1.252).[173] Such manipulations of facts undermine "true" history and so should not bear the title of history (*BJ* 1.7).

There are many reasons (αἰτία) why someone would choose to write a history (*Ant.* 1.1–3); however, not all motivations are noble or to be accepted as valid. Histories are not to be written out of spite (ἔχθρα) or partiality (χάρις, *Vita* 336), flattery (κολακεία) or hatred (μῖσος, *BJ* 1.2).[174] Rather, they are to depict noble and courageous actions (*Ant.* 6.346–349) and to provide a lesson for the careful reader (μάθοι τῆς ἱστορίας, *Ant.* 1.14), who will profitably pursue virtue more effectively (*Ant.* 6.343). To write a history that focuses on the reader's enjoyment through the depiction of plausible (but false) events (τέρψιν ἐπαγωγοῖς τὴν ἱστορίαν) and thus avoids the critical evaluation of truth (however painful) is to miss the fundamental purpose of the genre, debasing it so as to reduce or eliminate its value (*Ant.* 8.56).[175]

The history is directed to one or more specific audiences depending on the author's purpose. Generally, a history is written so that people who were not part of the selected events (and so do not have personal knowledge of them) might know and learn from those who were participants (*Ant.* 14.3; *BJ* 4.496).[176] For Josephus, this audience is not limited to a specific person (such as Nicolaus of Damascus' *History*, which was written for King Agrippa, *Ant.* 16.186), but has a wider purview, such as the "barbarians" (*BJ* 1.3), the Greek people (*Ant.* 16.174; 20.262), or the Greek and Roman members of the Roman Empire (*BJ* 1.3, 6, 16).[177] The purpose of the work shapes the nature of

172 E.g., *Ant.* 1.17; 14.1; cf. *Vita* 339; Dionysius of Halicarnassus, *Thuc.* 5, 8; Lucian, *Hist.* 47. Although this is declared to be a standing principle of historiography, it was not always adhered to, and sometimes it was blatantly disregarded.

173 For other pairings of πλάσμα and falsehoods, see *Ant.* 16.349; *C. Ap.* 2.122. For more on Asclepiades' divisions of history, see chapter 5 under Letter of Aristeas.

174 Cf. Polybius, *Hist.* 12.7.1. For parallel passages, see Avenarius, *Lukians Schrift*, 49–54.

175 Cf. Thucydides, *Hist.* 1.21.1; Polybius, *Hist.* 1.14.6; 12.12.1–7; Seneca, *Nat.* 7.16.1–2. On lying historians, see T. P. Wiseman, "Lying Historians: Seven Types of Mendacity," in C. Gill and T. P. Wiseman, eds., *Lies and Fiction in the Ancient World* (Austin: University of Texas Press, 1993), 122–46.

176 This, of course, does not exclude those who participated in or know about the events to read the history (cf. *Vita* 359–360; *C. Ap.* 1.51). For a wider discussion, see Polybius, *Hist.* 9.1.1–9.2.7.

177 Cf. S. A. Adams, "Luke, Josephus, and Self-Definition: The Genre of Luke-Acts and Its Relationship to Apologetic Historiography and Collected Biography," in S. E. Porter and A. W. Pitts, eds., *Christian Origins and Hellenistic Judaism: Social and Literary Contexts for the New Testament* (TENTS 10; Leiden: Brill, 2013), 447–48.

composition as well as the content that is included. In order to best communicate one's message, the work needs to be well arranged and follow an ordered structure (e.g., εὔτακτος, *Ant.* 8.224).[178] This requires that the historian know what is appropriate or inappropriate for his history or any historical work, and what would be outwith the "normal" or core parameters of the genre (at least in Josephus' mind).[179] This type of history, namely one that is both accurate and well composed, is not easily accomplished, but requires much research (*Vita* 338) and the expenditure of money and energy (*BJ* 1.16; Lucian, *Hist.* 47). Honesty in writing also creates enemies, resulting in slanderous comments by those who are jealous and resentful (*C. Ap.* 1.213; *Vita* 425; cf. Aulus Gellius, *Noct. att.* 4.15.2).

Occasionally, Josephus makes a comment that provides insight into how he distinguishes between different genres. In *Ant.* 1.18, Josephus describes the necessity of introducing Moses in order to ensure that the readers do not question why philosophical inquiry is included in his *Antiquities* (ὅπως μή τινες τῶν ἀναγνωσομένων διαπορῶσι, πόθεν ἡμῖν ὁ λόγος περὶ νόμων καὶ πράξεων ἔχων τὴν ἀναγραφὴν ἐπὶ τοσοῦτον φυσιολογίας κεκοινώνηκεν). This comment implies that Josephus did not expect his readers to view philosophical discussions as appropriate for inclusion within a work of history and that these genres would be differentiated by content.[180] Indeed, Josephus claims that he will reserve his discussion of the nature of God and Jewish customs for a separate work because of its strong philosophical content (λίαν φιλόσοφος, *Ant.* 1.25; 20.268).[181]

Josephus also differentiates encomium from history, a practice that became more prominent in the first few centuries CE, suggesting a growing overlap between these two genres that was not welcomed by all authors.[182] Encomia are not inherently bad (e.g., *Ant.* 2.195; *C. Ap.* 1.212), but they do have the

178 On the need for a history to be written in a good and appropriate style, see *Ant.* 14.2–3; *BJ* 7.455; *C. Ap.* 1.27; cf. Aulus Gellius, *Noct. att.* 11.8.1–3.

179 Cf. *Ant.* 7.244; 8.224; 10.218; 12.59; 15.372; 16.178; 18.127, 261. For example, providing certain biographical details regarding people mentioned in the narrative (e.g., parentage, origin, etc., *C. Ap.* 1.316). For the historian's practice of being obliged to recount the facts, but allowing the reader to think what s/he wants, see *Ant.* 1.108; 3.81; Lucian, *Hist.* 60; cf. Thucydides, *Hist.* 6.2.1; Herodotus, *Hist.* 3.122.

180 Pseudo-Longinus associates φυσιολογία and ἱστορία, suggesting that both genres allow for their authors to overwhelm their readers with a flood of rhetoric (δεῖ τὸν ἀκροατὴν τὸ σύνολον ἐκπλῆξαι) and diffuse style (ἐν χύσει, *Subl.* 12.5).

181 A similar concern is expressed by Philo (*Mos.* 2.47–48; cf. *Opif.* 1–2) regarding the inclusion of the creation of the world in a history/work of legislature. For support for a philosophical prelude to a law work, see Plato, *Leg.* 723e; Cicero, *Leg.* 2.14. In contrast, see the view of Posidonius in Seneca, *Ep.* 94.38.

182 Lucian distinguishes history from encomium (*Hist.* 7) and its poetic style of praising individuals (*Hist.* 8). Cf. Polybius, *Hist.* 8.8.6; Theon, *Prog.* 121; Eunapius, *Frag.* 205.19. L. Dindorf, ed., *Historici Graeci minores* (2 vols.; Leipzig: Teubner, 1870–1871), 1.205–74.

potential to be twisted by people to construct false praise and so stand in contrast to the truth of history (ἀλήθεια τῆς ἱστορίας, *Ant.* 14.68). Encomia are able to be embedded within history, but at the risk of a potential disjuncture between the respective purposes of each genre.[183] In order to defend his work from accusations of falsehood, Josephus explicitly calls upon "those who have written about the acts of Pompey, and, among them, to Strabo and Nicolaus [of Damascus], and to Titus Livy, the writer of the Roman history" to validate his story (οἱ τὰς κατὰ Πομπήιον πράξεις ἀναγράψαντες, ἐν οἷς καὶ Στράβων καὶ Νικόλαος καὶ πρὸς αὐτοῖς Τίτος Λίβιος ὁ τῆς Ῥωμαϊκῆς ἱστορίας συγγραφεύς, *Ant.* 14.68). By invoking historians as support for his claims of Jewish piety and to prove that he is not creating encomiastic boasts, Josephus differentiates encomia from history, placing the former on the side of unsubstantiated exaggeration and the latter on the side of truth and established fact.[184]

Encomion is also differentiated from *apologia* by Josephus (οὐ γὰρ ἐγκώμιον ἡμῶν αὐτῶν προειλόμην συγγράφειν, ἀλλὰ πολλὰ καὶ ψευδῆ κατηγορουμένοις ἡμῖν ταύτην ἀπολογίαν δικαιοτάτην εἶναι νομίζω τὴν ἀπὸ τῶν νόμων, *C. Ap.* 2.147).[185] The need to distinguish between these two genres suggests that their prototypical centers are close, with sufficient commonalities between them to possibly lead to the reader's confusion. Part of Josephus' defense is that the Jewish people are worthy of encomia (*C. Ap.* 1.212), but this should not distract the reader from the work's true purpose: to correct the misunderstandings and slanders of the Jewish people made by various individuals (*C. Ap.* 2.287) (see the discussion of *Against Apion* in chapter 5).

Insight into Josephus' understanding of the relationship between history and biography is important for our discussion of *Vita* below and can be gleaned from his identification of Hermippus as a historian (ἀνὴρ περὶ πᾶσαν ἱστορίαν ἐπιμελής, *C. Ap.* 1.163). In antiquity Hermippus was primarily known for his

183 Cf. Dionysius of Halicarnassus, *Thuc.* 8. For an example of including encomium in *War*, see Josephus' comments on Ananus (4.319–322).

Bakhtin divides texts into two categories, with "secondary" or "complex" genres being able to incorporate/embed "primary" or "simple" genres. Although I agree broadly with this division, I would suggest that there could possibly be three categories: (1) primary genres, which are simple and do not have the ability to embed other genres (e.g., maxim); (2) secondary genres, those that can embed other genres, but still in turn be embedded (e.g., encomium, biography); and (3) tertiary genres, those that can embed other genres and also resist being embedded (e.g., history, epic). M. Bakhtin, "Epic and Novel: Toward a Methodology for the Study of the Novel," in M. Holquist, ed., *The Dialogic Imagination: Four Essays by M. M. Bakhtin* (trans. C. Emerson and M. Holquist; Austin: University of Texas Press, 1981), 3–13, 18–21.

184 The contrasting of history and encomium with regard to accuracy (τὸ ἀκριβές) is also found in *BJ* 1.2 and *C. Ap.* 2.147. Encomia are also associated with songs of praise and hexameter verse (*Ant.* 2.346) as well as acting in tragedies (ἐγκώμια τραγῳδοῦσιν, *BJ* 2.348).

185 On the difference between encomium and apology, see the extended discussion by (Ps.-) Dionysius of Halicarnassus, *Ars rhet.* 9.11.43–64; cf. Aristotle, *Rhet.* 1.9.33; Theon, *Prog.* 109–112.

biographical works on philosophers and is not identified as a historian.[186] There are a few options for why Josephus identified Hermippus as a historian: (1) he might have known of other works by Hermippus that were histories (which are, as yet, unattested) and so viewed him through this lens;[187] (2) he knew his collected biographies, but viewed them as histories; (3) he knew that Hermippus was a biographer, but claimed that he was a historian for some reason, perhaps to bolster his claim of accuracy;[188] and (4) he was not fully aware of Hermippus' work and reputation, knowing him primarily through sources, and so mislabeled him. Of these possibilities, option 1 is the least likely as it lacks evidential support. Similarly, option 3, although possible, is less probable in that it would require us to postulate a specific rhetorical purpose for the change that does not appear to be warranted.[189] Option 4 has been proposed by Wehrli, but this view has been strongly challenged by Bollansée.[190]

As this is the only reference to Hermippus in Josephus' corpus, it is difficult to make a firm conclusion. However, Josephus' citation of the biography περὶ Πυθαγόρου is informative, suggesting that he might have viewed this work as a history.[191] Following option 2, it is possible that Josephus read Hermippus' philosophical succession narratives in light of (royal) succession narratives

186 E.g., ὁ τοὺς Ἰσοκράτους μαθητὰς ἀναγράψας Ἕρμιππος, Dionysius of Halicarnassus, *Is.* 1; Diogenes Laertius, *Vit.* 1.33; 2.13; 5.2; Athenaeus, *Deipn.* 8.342c; 10.451e; Jerome, *Vir. ill. praef.* On Hermippus as an author of collected biographies, see Adams, *Genre*, 95–96; S. A. Adams, "What Are Bioi/Vitae? Generic Self-Consciousness in Ancient Biography," in K. De Temmerman, ed., *Oxford Handbook of Ancient Biography* (Oxford: Oxford University Press, 2020), 21–35. For a current edition of his fragments, see J. Bollansée, ed., "Hermippos of Smyrna," in *FGrH* IVA.3 (Leiden: Brill, 1999) (i.e., *FGrH* 1026).

187 Cf. Hermippus, *On Legislators* (P.Oxy. XI 1367). J. Bollansée, *Hermippos of Smyrna and His Biographical Writings: A Reappraisal* (SH 35; Leuven: Peeters, 1999), 89–93. However, Photius, *Bibl.* 167, lists Hermippus among the regular sources used by historians and rhetoricians.

188 This, of course, presupposes that the word of a historian would be preferred over that of a biographer. Although accuracy is a regular motif in history writing, and less so in biographies (cf. Luke 1:1–4), there is little evidence that ancients held this distinction. Cf. Adams, "Luke's Preface," 185–87.

189 It is not that changes for rhetorical reasons did not take place, but that the detriment of mislabeling Hermippus would not be offset by the perceived gain. In the case of Apion, Josephus calls him a grammarian (Ἀπίωνα τὸν γραμματικόν, *C. Ap.* 2.2), but can still attribute a history to him (τῶν Αἰγυπτιακῶν, *C. Ap.* 2.10).

190 F. Wehrli, ed., *Hermippos der Kallimacher: Die Schule des Aristoteles*, supp. vol. 1 (Basel: Schwabe, 1974), 58–59; Bollansée, "Hermippos of Smyrna" (*FGrH* 1026 F21).

191 Josephus references the first book on Hermippus' work on Pythagoras (ἐν τῷ πρώτῳ τῶν περὶ Πυθαγόρου βιβλίων, *C. Ap.* 1.164; cf. Diogenes Laertius, *Vit.* 8.10). For other fragments, see Bollansée, *Hermippos of Smyrna* (*FGrH*), 32–37. For a discussion of the quotation by Josephus, see E. S. Gruen, "Jews and Greeks as Philosophers: A Challenge to Otherness," in *The Construct of Identity in Hellenistic Judaism: Essays on Early Jewish Literature and History* (DCLS 29; Berlin: De Gruyter, 2016), 147–52.

found in 1–2 Samuel, 1–2 Kings, and 1–2 Chronicles.[192] Such a view is found in Josephus' description of his *Antiquities*, which includes the succession of Jewish kings (ἀπλανῆ δὲ πεποίημαι καὶ τὴν περὶ τοὺς βασιλεῖς διαδοχὴν τὰς πράξεις αὐτῶν καὶ τὰς πολιτείας ἀπαγγέλλων μοναρχῶν τε δυναστείας, *Ant.* 20.261).[193] If this is the perspective that Josephus holds, then *C. Ap.* 1.163–65 is an example of a Jewish author interpreting Greek literature through the lens of his heritage, previous training, and native texts.[194]

Overall, this investigation allows us to make a few comments regarding Josephus' genre consciousness. First, he shares the standard division of literature into poetry and prose. Second, these broad categories can be further subdivided into specific genres that are differentiated through specific formal features (e.g., prose, topic, content, etc.). Third, Josephus has a clear understanding of what constitutes a history, which includes specific characteristics (i.e., truth, use of sources, etc.). Fourth, Josephus expresses a strong view of the purpose of history and its intention, especially vis-à-vis the recounting of truth. This is shown most forcefully in his polemical statements (e.g., *C. Ap.* 1.57; *Vita* 336–367). Fifth, Josephus believes that his readers share his expectations of history (and other genres) and that his perspective is not anomalous. Sixth, and finally, Josephus recognizes that certain genres are related to other genres and so require disambiguation to ensure effective communication with his reader (e.g., encomium and apology).

Jewish War

Jewish War, written at Rome late in the reign of Vespasian, was the first Greek work composed by Josephus, who described it as a Ἑλλάδι γλώσσῃ μεταβαλών from Aramaic (τῇ πατρίῳ, *BJ* 1.3). It is no longer widely accepted that *War* is a straight "translation" of the earlier version or that our understanding of *War* should be constricted by this previous work.[195] Rather, *War* is a rhetorically sophisticated work that is written for an elite, Greek-speaking audience.

192 The substantial overlap between the genres of biography and history in antiquity could account for this perspective (cf. Adams, *Genre*, 171). The association of ὁ τὰς τῶν διαδόχων πράξεις συγγραψάμενος and τὰς κατὰ πράξεις Πομπήιον with historians in *Ant.* 12.5 and 14.68, respectively, also supports the blurring of history and biography genres by Josephus.

193 A similar question is raised about Josephus' reading of Agathachides' τῶν κατὰ τὴν Εὐρώπην (*Ant.* 12.5). Cf. B. Bar-Kochva, *The Image of the Jews in Greek Literature: The Hellenistic Period* (Berkeley: University of California Press, 2010), 288–91.

194 For a detailed discussion of the Josephus fragment and its relationship to Pythagorean thought, see the comments by J. Bollansée on *FGrH* 1026 F21.

195 The Aramaic version of Josephus' *War* has not survived, and so we are not in a position to discuss its relationship with the Greek "translation." Pelletier (*Flavius Josèphe*, 22–24) reads too much meaning into μεταβάλλω regarding the physical process of script conversion (cf. *Ant.* 12.14). For a discussion of this issue and a critique of using the Aramaic as a key to understanding the Greek version, see G. Hata, "Is the Greek Version of Josephus' 'Jewish War' a Translation

There is substantial variation in the title of *Jewish War*, both in the manuscript tradition and in references to the work by ancient authors.[196] Many works in antiquity lacked authorial titles and were given one by subsequent readers.[197] In the case of *War*, Josephus' opening words, "The war of the Jews against the Romans" (Ἐπειδὴ τὸν Ἰουδαίων πρὸς Ῥωμαίους πόλεμον . . . , *BJ* 1.1), would have been sufficient for a reader to understand the content and nature of the work.[198] Similarly, references to this work by Josephus in his other texts also support this understanding.[199] Such internal references clearly indicate that Josephus thought of his work as participating in contemporary historiography (ἱστορία), one that focused on the war between the Judeans and Romans.[200]

Following Josephus' outlining of his credentials at the opening of *War*, specifically his family heritage, social position, and involvement in the events (*BJ* 1.3), he turns his attention to the content of the work: the events leading up to the war, its conclusion, and the suffering that it brought to the Jewish people (ὅθεν τε ἤρξατο καὶ δι' ὅσων ἐχώρησεν παθῶν ὁ πόλεμος καὶ ὅπως κατέστρεψεν, *BJ* 1.6; cf. *Ant.* 1.7).[201] Within these strictures, narrating the origins and development of the Jewish people is out of place. Rather, such an endeavor is a history in its own right, one that has been undertaken sufficiently well (μετ' ἀκριβείας) by others before him (*BJ* 1.17–18).[202] By assigning

---

or a Rewriting of the First Version?" *JQR* 66 (1975): 89–108; Rajak, *Josephus*, 176–81; S. Mason, *A History of the Jewish War, A.D. 66–74* (Cambridge: Cambridge University Press, 2016), 92. On Jewish literary translation, see Adams, "Translating Texts," 147–67. For a date during the reign of Titus and Domitian, see T. D. Barnes, "The Sack of the Temple in Josephus and Tacitus," in J. Edmondson, S. Mason, and J. Rives, eds., *Flavius Josephus and Flavian Rome* (Oxford: Oxford University Press, 2005), 129–44; Mason, *History*, 91–93.

196 Cf. Niese, *Flavii Iosephi*, 1.vi–ix.

197 D. Earl, "Prologue-Form in Ancient Historiography," *ANRW* 1.2 (1972): 842–56, 851–56; G. W. Houston, *Inside Roman Libraries: Book Collections and Their Management in Antiquity* (Chapel Hill: University of North Carolina Press, 2014), 8–10.

198 Adams, *Genre*, 117–25.

199 E.g., τοῦ δὲ πολέμου τὴν ἱστορίαν ἔγραψα (*C. Ap.* 1.55); τοῦ δὲ πολέμου πρὸς Ῥωμαίους Ἰουδαίοις (*Vita* 27); ταῖς περὶ τοῦ Ἰουδαϊκοῦ πολέμου βίβλοις (*Vita* 412); τὸν Ἰουδαϊκὸν ἀναφράφοντι πόλεμον (*Ant.* 1.203); ἐν τῇ δευτέρᾳ βίβλῳ τοῦ Ἰουδαϊκοῦ πολέμου (*Ant.* 18.11); περὶ τοῦ Ἰουδαϊκοῦ πολέμου (*Ant.* 20.258).

200 *Vita* 362, 367 (presented to King Agrippa); *C. Ap.* 1.53 (μου τὴν ἱστορίαν), 1.55 (τοῦ δὲ πολέμου τὴν ἱστορίαν). The reference to ταῖς ἱστορίαις in *Vita* 345 could refer to histories of Josephus, Justus, or both. For a discussion of "distance" (temporal and other) in historical writing, see M. S. Phillips, "Histories, Micro- and Literary: Problems of Genre and Distance," *NLH* 34 (2003): 216–18.

201 A summary of the work's contents is provided in *BJ* 1.19–29.

202 On Josephus' change of assessment, see D. R. Schwartz, "Josephus on His Jewish Forerunners (*Contra Apionem* 1.218)," in S. J. D. Cohen and J. J. Schwartz, eds., *Studies in Josephus and the Varieties of Ancient Judaism: Louis H. Feldman Jubilee Volume* (AJEC 67; Leiden: Brill, 2007), 195–206.

specific elements to different histories, Josephus provides insight into the different ways that he subdivides historiography, distinguishing history written on major contemporary events (i.e., wars) from history that traces the origins and development of a people group (cf. Polybius, *Hist.* 1.3.1–6). In contrast to other works of Jewish antiquity, Josephus claims that he will not retrace well-trodden paths (*BJ* 1.15; cf. *Ant.* 1.6), but will recount the events of his lifetime as a "memorial of great achievements" (τὴν μνήμην τῶν κατορθωμάτων) for future generations (*BJ* 1.16; 7.96).[203] There are times when Josephus must recount events that were covered by other historians and likely known to his intended readers. In these instances, it is his responsibility as a historian not to include unnecessary detail, but to provide sufficient material to avoid breaks in his narrative (*BJ* 4.496).

Josephus recognizes that his audience will expect the writer of history to be emotionally neutral and detached from passion (πάθος) in recounting his narrative, going so far as to describe this practice as a "law of history" (παρὰ τὸν τῆς ἱστορίας νόμον, *BJ* 1.11). Accordingly, he feels compelled to apologize in advance for the sentiment that will be included, begging for a concession (συγγνώμη) by claiming that he cannot help but be moved by the suffering and devastation of his country (*BJ* 1.9–12). This petition fits within his larger purview of claiming to be a participant in the events, but also requires him to claim that, even though he will defy a recognized practice, his emotion will not lead him to transgress the bounds of history writing (*BJ* 1.9) by compromising the truth or unduly maligning the opposing nation (something that he has criticized other historians for doing, *BJ* 1.2; cf. Polybius, *Hist.* 2.56.6–7).

A prominent element of Josephus' *War* and his other writings is their rhetorical nature; Josephus wrote like his Greek contemporaries, with a keen awareness of the prescriptions of rhetoric.[204] The polemical nature of ancient historiography and the explicit critique and comparison of previous works are fundamental elements of history writing, especially with regard to the author's self-presentation within his preface.[205] In light of this use of rhetoric, scholars have suggested that *War* is best understood as rhetorical historiography, but this implies that there are other histories that are not rhetorical. On the contrary, essentially all Greek history writing in antiquity was rhetorical at heart,

203 On this theme, see Lucian, *Hist.* 42, 61; cf. Thucydides, *Hist.* 1.22.4. For the theme of writing on a neglected but important topic, see Thucydides, *Hist.* 1.97.2; Dionysius of Halicarnassus, *Thuc.* 11; Josephus, *BJ* 6.199; Cicero, *Leg.* 1.8.

204 A. J. Woodman, *Rhetoric in Classical Historiography* (London: Croom Helm, 1988); Kennedy, *Art of Rhetoric*, 292–97; Mason, *History*, 73–80.

205 For the polemical nature of historiography, especially with regard to self-definition, see Marincola, *Authority*, 218–36.

and so the label "rhetorical history" creates a false distinction.[206] More helpful is the argument that Josephus viewed Thucydides' history as prototypical for his *War*, drawing on his method and approach in the construction of his own work.[207] The parallels between Josephus and Thucydides in the opening preface would overtly signal to the reader a literary affiliation and the need to read *War* through a particular lens (e.g., *BJ* 1.1 // Thucydides, *Hist.* 1.1.1–2; *BJ* 1.16, 26 // Thucydides, *Hist.* 1.22.2–3).

Concluding that Josephus' *War* participates in the genre of history, however, is not to claim that Josephus' work is identical in form or expression to his Greek models. Indeed, his use and shaping of polemic and apology as well as tragic themes are impressive and imbue his work with a distinctive expression.[208] Josephus interprets differences in Jewish eschatological religious thought in terms of political and psychological *stasis* categories found in Greek historiography, thus using a Greek category to frame Jewish religious debates.[209] At the same, Josephus' method of interpreting events is also distinctly Jewish, viewing history through the lens of a Jewish worldview and divine provenance, thus integrating a native method into a Greek literary form.[210]

Excursus: Justus (or Justin) of Tiberias

Justus of Tiberias was a Jewish historian who wrote contemporaneously with Josephus. Well educated and influential in Galilee (*Vita* 40), Justus had strong ties with Agrippa II and Bernice (*Vita* 178, 343, 354–356).[211] Almost none of

206 S. Mason, *Flavius Josephus on the Pharisees: A Composition-Critical Study* (Leiden: Brill, 1991), 376–83.

207 Marincola, *Authority*, 17; Rajak, *Josephus*, 9; Cohen, *Josephus*, 90; G. Mader, *Josephus and the Politics of Historiography: Apologetic and Impression-Management in the "Bellum Judaicum"* (MneSup 205; Leiden: Brill, 2000), 55–103, 148–50; Feldman, *Josephus's Interpretation*, 9 (cf. Cicero, *Fam.* 5.12.1–10). Cohen (*Josephus*, 53 n. 99) differentiates the historical genres of *War* and *Antiquities* based on their relationship to contemporary events. On the blending of different types of historiography, see F. Parente, "The Impotence of Titus, or Flavius Josephus's *Bellum Judaicum* as an Example of 'Pathetic' Historiography," in J. Sievers and G. Lembi, eds., *Josephus and Jewish History in Flavian Rome and Beyond* (JSJSup 104; Leiden: Brill, 2005), 45–69.

208 Mader, *Josephus*, ix, 147–57.

209 Mader, *Josephus*, 148; Feldman, *Josephus's Interpretation*, 197–204.

210 For example, in *BJ* 3.354 and 4.622, Josephus employs τύχη to describe divine control over human affairs, although his preferred term in *Antiquities* is πρόνοια (e.g., *Ant.* 2.174; 10.277–278; 20.18; cf. 8.314). On the typical practice of downplaying religion in Greek and Roman historiographical practices, see J. Davies, "Religion in Historiography," in A. Feldherr, ed., *The Cambridge Companion to Roman Historians* (Cambridge: Cambridge University Press, 2009), 170. However, for a more integrated view, see E.-M. Becker, *The Birth of Christian History: Memory and Time from Mark to Luke-Acts* (AYBRL; New Haven: Yale University Press, 2017), 51–59.

211 For an overview of Justus, see T. Rajak, "Justus of Tiberias," *CQ* 23 (1973): 345–68; A. Barzanò, "Giusto di Tiberiade," *ANRW* 2.20.1 (1987): 337–58.

his work survives, but the polemical attacks against him by Josephus (especially *Vita* 336–367) allow us to discern part of his literary contribution.[212] First, Justus' work is an account of the war between the Jews and Rome (*Vita* 336, 338), which includes, at least, a discussion of events in Galilee (including the rebellion of Tiberias and engagements with Sepphoris, *Vita* 340–354) and a narrative of the sieges of Jotapata (357) and Jerusalem (354, 358). Second, Josephus claims that Justus presented his work as a history, one that was superior to others (ἄμεινον, *Vita* 357, 359) and accurate (μετὰ ἀκριβείας, *Vita* 358, 360). Third, there were discrepancies between Josephus' and Justus' works, which led to Josephus developing both an *apologia* for his character and actions (e.g., *Vita* 80–84) and a polemical attack against Justus' person and claims (e.g., *Vita* 32–42).[213] No doubt Justus offered alternative explanations of what happened during the war and substantial criticisms of Josephus. What is not clear is the scope and length of the work, for such aspersions could be provided in a few pages or a full-length treatise with multiple volumes. That it was polemical does not imply that it could not have also been a history; these two concepts are not mutually exclusive. Ultimately, Josephus deemed Justus' work sufficiently important and problematic that a strong response was necessary.

Josephus is not the only ancient to discuss Justus' compositions, although, being the earliest, he influenced its reception by later authors. Both Jerome (*Vir. ill.* 14) and the author of the *Suda* (I 450) claim that Justus "attempted to compile a Jewish history and write certain commentaries" (ἐπεχείρησε μὲν καὶ αὐτὸς Ἰουδαϊκὴν ἱστορίαν συντάξαι καί τινα ὑπομνήματα περιγράφειν), but they dismiss his work(s), noting that Josephus called him a fraud (ἀλλὰ τοῦτον Ἰώσηπος ἐλέγχει ψευσάμενον). The most detailed description of Justus' history, apart from Josephus', is offered by Photius (*Bibl.* 33), who identifies it as a chronology (χρονικόν) and gives the title of the work as "[A Chronicle] of the Kings of the Jews in the form of a genealogy" (ἡ ἐπιγραφὴ Ἰούστου Τιβεριέως Ἰουδαίων βασιλέων τῶν ἐν τοῖς στέμμασιν).[214] Photius also claims that Justus began his work with Moses (ἄρχεται δὲ τῆς ἱστορίας ἀπὸ Μωϋσέως) and continued up through the Herodian dynasty. Photius does not mention any other historical work, which has led some to posit that Justus' discussion of the

212 This digression in *Vita* overlaps notably with *C. Ap.* 1.46–56, which has led some scholars to posit that Justus is also the focus of a second attack. See Laqueur, *Der jüdische Historiker*, 16–21. Identical polemic, however, does not require an identical opponent. So Cohen, *Josephus*, 116–17; Barclay, *Against Apion*, 38–39.

213 For a detailed list of charges levied against Josephus by Justus and vice versa, see Cohen, *Josephus*, 127–28.

214 For the text of Photius, see R. Henry, ed. and trans., *Photius: Bibliothèque* (8 vols.; Paris: Les Belles Lettres, 1959–1977).

war was part of this larger treatise.[215] Photius' title and description, however, do not align well with the depiction of Justus' history presented by Josephus (τὴν ἱστορίαν τῶν πραγμάτων, *Vita* 40).[216] Other ancient authors also associate Justus' history with Moses, specifically his relationship to Egyptian pharaohs and Argive kings.[217] These two references support the statement by Photius that Justus wrote about Moses and imply that his work included chronological elements (cf. Diogenes Laertius, *Vit.* 2.41).

One way to explain this difference is to posit that Josephus and Photius are discussing two different literary works. This is certainly possible and would result in attributing two types of historiographical works to Justus: a (polemic) account of the Jewish war with Rome and a chronology of Jewish kings.[218] Another possibility, though in my opinion less likely, is that the king list mentioned by Photius was a digression embedded within Justus' war history and subsequently excerpted and transmitted independently.[219] Both theories agree that Justus contributed to the writing of Jewish histories, but, due to its fragmented and secondhand nature, little can be said about the way that he engaged with Greek genres.

Antiquities of the Jews

Josephus' largest work, *Antiquities of the Jews* (Ἰουδαϊκῆς ἀρχαιολογίας), was completed around 93/94 CE and chronologically traces the history of the Jewish

215 Photius also refers to Justus' work as ἡ ἱστορία; however, this could be interpreted as "narrative" rather than a statement regarding the work's genre.

216 H. Luther, "Josephus und Justus von Tiberias: Ein Beitrag zur Geschichte des jüdischen Aufstandes" (PhD diss., Universität Halle-Wittenberg, 1910), 51.

217 Syncellus, *Chron.* 73.12–18 (*FGrH* 734 F2–3), citing Eusebius. Cf. Eusebius, *Chron.* 7b; *Praep. ev.* 10.10.15–16. For a detailed discussion of these passages (and others, including those of Sextus Julius Africanus), see C. Milikowsky, "Justus of Tiberias and the Synchronistic Chronology of Israel," in S. J. D. Cohen and J. J. Schwartz, eds., *Studies in Josephus and the Varieties of Ancient Judaism: Louis H. Feldman Jubilee Volume* (AJEC 67; Leiden: Brill, 2007), 103–26.

218 Wacholder (*Eupolemus*, 305, cf. 56–57) claims that Justus' work was modeled on that of Demetrius the Chronographer (see above). Although it is possible, the shared name does not necessitate this position. A comparable example is found in Manetho's *Aegyptiaca*, which is structured on the king lists of Egypt. According to Moyer, this construction by Manetho was a "historiographical strategy that was independent of his Greek predecessors in terms of both the structural principle itself and its chronological function in historiography." Cf. I. S. Moyer, *Egypt and the Limits of Hellenism* (Cambridge: Cambridge University Press, 2011), 103.

219 Lists of officials are not incongruous in ancient histories. Indeed, Josephus provides an extended list of high priests beginning with Aaron (*Ant.* 20.224–251). For a discussion of the title, including references to other theories (which include multiple works attributed to Justus, including one on "Garlands," see Rajak, "Justus of Tiberias," 362–65). *Suda* I 450 mentions that Justus wrote certain commentaries (τινα ὑπομνήματα περιγράφειν), but does not specify on which texts he commentated. There is no additional evidence that he wrote commentaries.

people from creation to 66 CE in twenty volumes.[220] This history is presented by Josephus as being different from the type of history that he wrote in *War* (*C. Ap.* 1.53–56), and apparently no longer superfluous (ἄλλως περιττόν, *BJ* 1.17–18). In *War* Josephus claims to an eyewitness report of a contemporary event, whereas in *Antiquities* the work is a "translation" of ancient texts and records (*Ant.* 1.5).

Important for this discussion is the term that Josephus used to describe his own work: ἀρχαιολογία (*Ant.* 20.259, 267; *Vita* 430 *C. Ap.* 1.1–2, 54, 127; 2.136, 287).[221] In classical antiquity, ἀρχαιολογία was thought to refer to genealogies of heroes and men, the foundations of ancient cities, a list of archons, and so on (Plato, *Hipp. maj.* 285d). However, in the Hellenistic and Roman eras, this term became associated with a type of history that was no longer limited to lists and collections of facts, but recounted the origins of a people from archaic history to the more recent past.[222] Over time, ἀρχαιολογίαι became a recognized literary form with core elements and established reader expectations, a tradition of which Josephus shows awareness through his referencing of previous literary works associated with this genre.[223]

Josephus' discussion of ἀρχαιολογία has led a number of scholars to posit that Dionysius of Halicarnassus' *Roman Antiquities* was the prototype for Josephus' *Antiquities*.[224] Both wrote twenty-volume works that begin with the distant origins of the title nations, narrating the subsequent fortunes that had befallen them, and provide a justification of their subject (although this

220 Cf. H. A. Attridge, "Josephus and His Works," in M. E. Stone, ed., *Jewish Writings of the Second Temple Period: Apocrypha, Pseudepigrapha, Qumran Sectarian Writings, Philo, Josephus* (CRINT 2.2; Philadelphia: Fortress, 1984), 210–11.

221 Josephus also uses ἀρχαιολογία in a more restricted way in *Ant.* 1.5, differentiating it from διάταξιν τοῦ πολιτεύματος.

222 Cf. Polybius, *Hist.* 12.25e.1–7. Varro's *Antiquitates rerum humanarum et divinarum* was an important expression of this genre and was seen as prototypical for subsequent authors (Cicero, *Acad.* 1.8). Cf. A. Momigliano, "Ancient History and the Antiquarian," *JWCI* 13 (1950): 287–89.

223 E.g., *Ant.* 1.5, 94 (Hieronymus the Egyptian wrote *Phoenician Antiquities*), 107–8 (both Greeks and barbarians have written ἀρχαιολογία. Note change of title for Hieronymus, now τὰ Φοινικικά). For a discussion of ἀρχαιολογία, see T. Rajak, "Josephus and the 'Archaeology' of the Jews," *JJS* 33 (1982): 465–77, reprinted in *The Jewish Dialogue with Greece and Rome: Studies in Cultural and Social Interaction* (Leiden: Brill, 2002), 241–55. For genre expectations, see Diodorus, *Bibl.* 1.4.6; Dionysius of Halicarnassus, *Ant. rom.* 1.4.2; 1.8.2; Diogenes Laertius, *Vit.* 7.175.

224 H. St. J. Thackeray, *Josephus: The Man and the Historian* (New York: Ktav, 1967), 56–58; E. J. Bickerman, "Origines Gentium," *CP* 47 (1952): 70–71; R. J. H. Shutt, *Studies in Josephus* (London: SPCK, 1961), 92–101; H. W. Attridge, *The Interpretation of Biblical History in the "Antiquitates Judaicae" of Flavius Josephus* (HDR 7; Missoula, Mont.: Scholars Press, 1976), 43–60; Marincola, *Authority*, 17. Feldman (*Josephus's Interpretation*, 7–12) agrees with this assessment, but also claims that Josephus was influenced by the traditions of Isocrates and Aristotle. For the view of *Antiquities* as apologetic in nature, see Sterling, *Historiography*, 308 (= Oriental historiography); Feldman, *Josephus's Interpretation*, 132; P. Spilsbury, *The Image of the Jew in Flavius Josephus' Paraphrase of the Bible* (TSAJ 69; Tübingen: Mohr Siebeck, 1998), 14–16.

last feature is found in many histories).[225] Other parallels have been noted by scholars, the sum of which suggests that Josephus was aware of the historiographical tradition promoted by Dionysius.[226] Less certain is whether or not Dionysius was a/the literary model for Josephus, although a case could be made to view a direct relationship.[227]

Tessa Rajak has argued that the similarities between Josephus and Dionysius of Halicarnassus are superficial and that "there is no parallel for [*Antiquities*] in the Graeco-Roman world."[228] One of the traditional elements of ἀρχαιολογίαι is the author's retelling of the origin of a people, implying a strong dependence on established myths and legends. Although other historians recognize and employ mythological elements in their ἀρχαιολογίαι (*Ant.* 1.22), this aspect is not embraced by Josephus,[229] who claims that such fabrications were not needed, because, unlike that of the Greeks, the history of the Jews stretched back over five thousand years (πεντακισχιλίων ἐτῶν ἱστορίας) and was well supported by official records (*Ant.* 1.13; 20.259; *C. Ap.* 1.1).[230] This depiction supports Josephus' decision to avoid describing Jewish history in terms of "myth" or "mythology," claiming that ἀσχήμονος μυθολογίας and ψευδῶν πλασμάτων are not to be found in Moses' works (*Ant.* 1.15–16), the contents of which are pure, true, and worthy of reading. Josephus' additional identification of the work as a "political constitution" (διάταξιν τοῦ πολιτεύματος, *Ant.* 1.5) further distances the content from mythical themes.[231] Accordingly, Josephus does not criticize the writings of Moses and his other Jewish sources, but claims to transmit them accurately (*Ant.* 1.17), as they have been faithfully

225 Fortune: Josephus, *Ant.* 1.6 (τίσι χρησάμενοι τύχαις); Dionysius of Halicarnassus, *Ant. rom.* 1.5.1 (τίσι τύχαις χρησάμενοι); justification: Josephus, *Ant.* 1.5; Dionysius of Halicarnassus, *Ant. rom.* 1.2.1–1.3.6.

226 See Sterling, *Historiography*, 284–89.

227 Most recently, J. A. Cowan, "A Tale of Two *Antiquities*: A Fresh Evaluation of the Relationship between the Ancient Histories of T. Flavius Josephus and Dionysius of Halicarnassus," *JSJ* 49 (2018): 475–97.

228 Rajak, "Archaeology," 254.

229 Myth is also critiqued by Greek historians, although often regarding contemporary history and not ἀρχαιολογία. E.g., Polybius, *Hist.* 9.2.1–7; Dionysius of Halicarnassus, *Thuc.* 7. For some allowing of myth in history, see Strabo, *Geogr.* 11.5.3; Lucian, *Hist.* 10.

230 For the benefit of archival resources, see Diodorus Siculus, *Bibl.* 1.4.2–4; Polybius, *Hist.* 12.27.1–7; Livy, *Urba Condita* 6.1.2; *Thoth* 305. On the influence of Eastern authors (Babylonian, Egyptian, Phoenician, Jewish) on the research practices of Greek historians, see G. Coqueugniot, "Scholastic Research in the Archive? Hellenistic Historians and Ancient Archival Records," in S. A. Adams, ed., *Scholastic Culture in the Hellenistic and Roman Eras: Greek, Latin, and Jewish* (Transmissions 2; Berlin: De Gruyter, 2019), 7–29. Cf. Tertullian, *Apol.* 19.5–6.

231 S. Mason, "'Should Any Wish to Enquire Further' (*Ant.* 1.25): The Aim and Audience of Josephus's *Judean Antiquities/Life*," in S. Mason, ed., *Understanding Josephus: Seven Perspectives* (LSTS 32; Sheffield: Sheffield Academic Press, 1998), 80–87.

preserved due to their inspired nature (*C. Ap.* 1.38).[232] This depiction aligns with Josephus' declared motivations for writing: he is not seeking to correct erroneous histories, which were originally written by prophets who witnessed the events (*C. Ap.* 1.37–41), but to make the history of the Jewish people accessible to Greek readers (*Ant.* 1.3, 5; 10.218). This translation project has clear parallels with Manetho, Berossus, Menander the Ephesian (*C. Ap.* 1.73; *Ant.* 8.144), and Lysimachus (*Aigyptiaka*, *C. Ap.* 1.304; 2.236), all of whom are identified by Josephus as literary predecessors. The Josephan parallels with Greco-Roman historians indicate an awareness of his position within the literary landscape as well as his willingness to adopt features that suited his project and reject those that were thought to be unhelpful.[233] Josephus did not present his work as participating in genres determined by prototypical Hellenistic Jewish historians, regarding whom he has little to say (*C. Ap.* 1.218).[234] This is not to say that Josephus did not make use of Jewish historians and other Jewish authors who wrote in Greek. Rather, Josephus does not explicitly associate his work with theirs, implying to his readership a lack of dependence and possibly a different writing tradition.

One aspect in our investigation that is rarely discussed, but is worth considering, is whether or not Josephus' declaration of his work as a translation (μεθηρμηνευμένην γραμμάτων) affects the genre participation of *Antiquities*.[235] Does this claim imply that the genre of the original work is somehow related to the new, "translated" work? Normally, this is thought to be the case, and his claim that he did not add or subtract anything from his source (οὐδὲν προσθεὶς οὐδ' αὖ παραλιπών, *Ant.* 1.17; 10.218; 20.260–261; *C. Ap.* 1.42; LA 310–311) implies both a fidelity and closeness to the original. A strong parallel would be the description of the translation of the law by Pseudo-Aristeas that was incorporated into *Antiquities* (e.g., *Ant.* 12.11–118). In this text, the translation is presented as being of the same kind as the original Hebrew text. Indeed, a majority of ancient translations are not presented as differing in genre from the original.[236] Despite the fact that Josephus' claim is false,[237] the rhetorical presentation parallels that of the Letter of Aristeas and the Greek

232 For a detailed discussion of this claim, see Feldman, "Mikra," 466–70.

233 Attridge, *Interpretation of Biblical History*, 18. For a recent treatment of Josephus' position as a Greco-Roman historian, see M. Friis, *Image and Imitation: Josephus' Antiquities 1–11 and Greco-Roman Historiography* (WUNT 2.472; Tübingen: Mohr Siebeck, 2018).

234 The level of Josephus' knowledge and use of Hellenistic Jewish historians is debated. For a discussion with examples, see Sterling, *Historiography*, 263–84.

235 τὴν μὲν γὰρ ἀρχαιολογίαν, ὥσπερ ἔφην, ἐκ τῶν ἱερῶν γραμμάτων μεθερμήνευκα, *C. Ap.* 1.54; *Ant.* 1.5; 20.261.

236 Adams, "Translating Texts," 154.

237 See Feldman, *Josephus's Interpretation*, 37–46.

translation of the law as well as the wider expectation of literary translation in antiquity, aligning the genre of his work with that of its source text.

Josephus critically distanced his work from some of his sources, aligning his work with Scripture.[238] These comments, although useful for describing his source(s), are not presented as literary models or constraints for his work. The number and diversity of texts available to Josephus require selected excising of material and authorial reshaping to bring it into a cohesive whole that meets with genre and reader expectations.[239] This use of multiple texts is important, especially in contrast to the narrative in the Letter of Aristeas, as it moves the Hebrew texts from models to be emulated to sources to be exploited. This aligns with the way that Josephus described Manetho's history in terms of his translation of Egyptian sacred records, suggesting that acts of translation do not constrain the author's choice of genre.[240]

Josephus' expressed relationship to Scripture has led a number of scholars to view *Antiquities* (at least the first eleven books) as rewritten Scripture.[241] This understanding of *Antiquities* should not be seen in opposition to history, as texts can participate in multiple genres. Some scholars have questioned whether rewritten Scripture is a genre or exegetical process.[242] Josephus' claim of translating Scripture (μεθηρμηνευμένην γραμμάτων, *Ant.* 1.5) brings this debate into sharp relief. Josephus claims to follow Scripture and presents his work as a Greek version of his source text(s). At the same time, Josephus also employs many of the standard formal features of history, thus signaling participation in that genre. In essence, Josephus makes a dual claim: his *Antiquities* is a work of history *and* a representation of Scripture. This dual alignment resists a singular perspective on his work and suggests that Josephus could understand his composition from a plurality of perspectives.

238 For example, Josephus describes the works of Moses as pertaining to laws (*Ant.* 4.198) and philosophy (*Ant.* 1.18; 12.37) and the writings of Solomon as odes and parables (*Ant.* 8.44). On Josephus' sources, see D. R. Schwartz, "Many Sources but a Single Author: Josephus's *Jewish Antiquities*," in H. H. Chapman and Z. Rodgers, eds., *A Companion to Josephus* (Oxford: Wiley-Blackwell, 2016), 36–58.

239 For example, the inclusion of philosophical elements from Moses was thought to undermine the reader's expectation of what a history is supposed to include (*Ant.* 1.18; cf. Dionysius of Halicarnassus, *Pomp.* 6; Lucian, *Hist.* 17).

240 *C. Ap.* 1.228 ὁ γὰρ Μανεθὼς οὗτος ὁ τὴν Αἰγυπτιακὴν ἱστορίαν ἐκ τῶν ἱερῶν γραμμάτων μεθερμηνεύειν ὑπεσχημένος; cf. *C. Ap.* 1.73, which employs μεταφράζω; *FGrH* 609 T9. Some historians speak of translation, but most often these are names and not larger documents (e.g., Berossus F1.5–6; Hecataeus, *FGrH* 264 F25 ll. 27, 32, 45, 48, 54; Diodorus Siculus, *Bibl.* 1.11.2, 4; 1.12.2–3). Cf. P.-A. Beaulieu, "Berossus on Late Babylonian History," *Oriental Studies* (2006): 116–49.

241 Feldman, *Josephus's Interpretation*, 14–73.

242 For a more detailed discussion of rewritten Scripture as a possible genre, see chapter 6 (Joseph and Aseneth).

Steve Mason has claimed a different genre understanding of *Antiquities*, stating that "*Antiquities* is basically history as serial biography."[243] The role of the individual is important for ancient histories, as s/he is the shaper and instigator of events and provides examples of virtue or vice. Theopompus, in his *Philippica*, is thought to be an early example of emphasizing the individual in history, providing deep insight into the motives and feelings of Philip II.[244] This approach was both praised (Dionysius of Halicarnassus, *Pomp.* 6) and censured (Polybius, *Hist.* 8.9.1–8.11.8) by subsequent historians, suggesting that it was a controversial act and represents a nonprototypical genre expression.[245] The biography-like focus on an individual was subsequently seen as an element of history writing.[246] This understanding of the genre of history had a profound impact on subsequent authors. For Josephus, the strong association between history and biography allows for the better integration of scriptural material and his ability to trace the history of the Jewish people through depictions of biblical characters, especially royal and prophetic successions.[247] The association between history and biography is especially relevant for our discussion of Josephus' *Vita*.

Vita

Josephus claims that the *Vita* is an overview of his life's actions (ταῦτα μὲν τὰ πεπραγμένα μοι διὰ παντὸς τοῦ βίου ἐστίν, *Vita* 430; cf. *Ant.* 20.266).[248]

243 S. Mason, *Orientation to the History of Roman Judaea* (Eugene, Ore.: Cascade, 2016), 41; S. Mason, "Josephus as a Roman Historian," in H. H. Chapman and Z. Rodgers, eds., *A Companion to Josephus* (Oxford: Wiley-Blackwell, 2016), 100. Cf. Mason, *History*, 85–87.
244 Cf. Diodorus Siculus, *Bibl.* 17 and the life of Alexander the Great. In 16.95.5, Diodorus defines his discussion of Alexandria in terms of his "accession" rather than "life," thus implying a continuation of the historiographic perspective of the rest of the work. For Diodorus' biographical interests, see *Bibl.* 10.12.1–3. For the embedding of a biography in a history, see L. Prandi, "A Monograph on Alexander the Great within a Universal History: Diodoros Book XVII," in L. I. Hau, A. Meeus, and B. Sheridan, eds., *Diodoros of Sicily: Historiographical Theory and Practice in the "Bibliotheke"* (SH 58; Leuven: Peeters, 2018), 175–85. On the close genre relationship between biography and history, see Adams, *Genre*, 68–115.
245 For discussion, see W. R. Connor, "History without Heroes: Theopompus' Treatment of Philip of Macedon," *GRBS* 8 (1967): 133–54, and the commentary by W. S. Morison, "Theopompos of Chios (115)," in *BNJ*.
246 There were, however, still limits to this overlap. See Plutarch, *Alex.* 1.2; Adams, "Bios," 28.
247 See the discussion on Hermippus above. For discussion of the close connection between biography and history, especially during their early development, see A. Momigliano, *The Development of Greek Biography* (expanded ed.; Cambridge, Mass.: Harvard University Press, 1993), 1–7.
248 E.g., lineage (*Vita* 1–6); education (7–12); marriages and children (414–415, 426–427); Roman citizenship and pension (σύνταξιν χρημάτων) from Vespasian (423); land gifts (422, 425). On autobiographical statements of childhood, see C. B. R. Pelling, "Childhood and Personality in Biography," in C. B. R. Pelling, ed., *Characterization and Individuality in Greek Literature* (Oxford: Oxford University Press, 1990), 221–24. For a discussion of Josephus'

Although the majority of the work recounts his deeds and events in Galilee (28–413), Josephus does not feature in a few sections, but he focuses on other participants and opponents (e.g., Gischala, 43–45; Philip and Varus at Gamala and Ecbatana, 46–61, 179–184; Justus, 336–367). The work as a whole clearly centers on Josephus, providing information about his ancestry (γένος), education (παιδεία), deeds (πράξις), and (most importantly) character (ἦθος).[249]

The dating of *Vita* is tied directly to the dating of *Antiquities* (93/94 CE). However, a major issue for this dating has been the statement by Photius that Agrippa II died in the third year of Trajan's reign (i.e., 100 CE) (τελευτᾷ δὲ ἔτει τρίτῳ Τραϊανοῦ, *Bibl.* 33). As Josephus clearly states that Agrippa II had died by the time Justus published his work (*Vita* 359; cf. 367), this would put the composition, at the earliest, in 101 CE. The longest-lived attempt to save the accuracy of Photius' claim is that of Laqueur, who proposed that Josephus produced two editions of *Antiquities*, one in 93/94 and the other circa 101 CE, citing the two conclusions at the end of *Antiquities* as evidence (20.258 with 267–268 and 20.259–266).[250] The current trend is to take the ending of *Antiquities* as a unified composition, but this does not fully address the issue of dating.[251]

A major scholarly issue in the study of *Vita* is its relationship to *Antiquities*: should *Vita* be considered a distinct work, and so interpreted independently, or does its association with *Antiquities* constrain our understanding of its genre participation? Many scholars (tacitly) view *Vita* independently from *Antiquities* and so classify it as an autobiography.[252] This label, however, implies

programmatic statements regarding his *Vita*, see S. Mason, "An Essay in Character: The Aim and Audience of Josephus' *Vita*," in F. Siegert and J. U. Kalms, eds., *Internationales Josephus-Kolloquium Münster 1997* (Münster: LIT Verlag, 1997), 48–49.

249 For an outline and discussion, see P. V. Varneda, "The Early Empire," in G. Marasco, ed., *Political Autobiographies and Memoirs in Antiquity: A Brill Companion* (Leiden: Brill, 2011), 327–60; S. Mason, ed. and trans., *Flavius Josephus: Life of Josephus; Translation and Commentary* (Leiden: Brill, 2003).

250 Laqueur, *Der jüdische Historiker*, 1–6. Laqueur is followed by M. Gelzer, "Die Vita des Josephus," *Hermes* 80 (1952): 67–90; and A. Pelletier, ed. and trans., *Flavius Josèphe: Autobiographie* (Collection des Universités de France [Budé]; Paris: Les Belles Lettres, 1959), xiii–xiv. For a critique of this view, see T. Frankfort, "La date de l'Autobiographie de Flavius Josèphe et les oeuvres de Justus de Tibériade," *RbPH* 39 (1961): 52–58.

251 For the most recent discussion, see S. Mason, "Josephus' *Autobiography* (*Life of Josephus*)," in H. H. Chapman and Z. Rodgers, eds., *A Companion to Josephus* (Oxford: Wiley-Blackwell, 2016), 59–65. For the claim that Photius is mistaken, see Rajak, "Justus of Tiberias," 361–62.

252 Neyrey argues that Josephus' *Vita* is best interpreted through the genre of encomium. Although he notes important rhetorical parallels, the argument is too narrow and he isolates *Vita* from *Antiquities*. J. H. Neyrey, "Josephus' *Vita* and the Encomium: A Native Model of Personality," *JSJ* 25 (1994): 177–206.

that autobiography was a recognized genre at the time of its composition.[253] The genre of biography continued to change and develop, but *bios* was not the typical term for such self-descriptive works. Rather, *hypomnema*, *commentarius*, and *res gestae* were the dominant labels, and these terms could encompass a wide variety of texts.[254] This diversity has led to uncertainty by a number of scholars about how to classify *Vita*.[255]

The discussion of *Vita* is further complicated by the insufficient number of literary comparators: *Vita* is the only fully extant autobiographical work of this era. The closest parallels are the epitomized autobiography by Nicolaus of Damascus (*FGrH* 90 FF131–139) and the reconstructed works of Sulla and Augustus, although other examples are evident.[256] Greek autobiographies from the Hellenistic era exist in references and fragments (*FGrH* 227–238, although some are debatable, e.g., *FGrH* 232 and 233), but we lack substantial examples to know the full diversity of this literary form and its typical components.[257] The surviving material supports the view that Josephus followed prior literary models, signaling common genre participation through a similar structure to other biographical and autobiographical works and addressing comparable themes.[258]

253 On this point, see C. B. R. Pelling, "Was There an Ancient Genre of 'Autobiography'? Or, Did Augustus Know What He Was Doing?" in C. Smith and A. Powell, eds., *The Lost Memoirs of Augustus* (Swansea: Classical Press of Wales, 2009), 41–64.

254 E.g., letters, histories, inscriptions, oratory, etc. Note Josephus' use of ὑπομνήσω in *Ant.* 20.267. For the classic work on this topic, see G. Misch, *A History of Autobiography in Antiquity* (trans. E. W. Dickes; London: Routledge and Kegan Paul, 1950). See, more recently, A. Riggsby, "Memoir and Autobiography in Republican Rome," in J. Marincola, ed., *A Companion to Greek and Roman Historiography* (BCAW; Malden: Blackwell, 2007), 266–74; A. D. Grojnowski, "Josephus: An Autobiography; A Comparative Analysis of Ancient Literature in the Search for Genre" (PhD diss., King's College London, 2014), 132–53.

255 E.g., Rajak, *Josephus*, 12–13; D. A. Barish, "The Autobiography of Josephus and the Hypothesis of a Second Edition of His Antiquities," *HTR* 71 (1978): 64.

256 Wacholder, *Nicolaus*, 37–51; L. M. Yarrow, *Historiography at the End of the Republic* (Oxford: Oxford University Press, 2006), 67–77; *Suda* N 393. Cf. T. Hägg, *The Art of Biography in Antiquity* (Cambridge: Cambridge University Press, 2012), 195; Cicero, *Brut.* 112, 132.

257 Cf. K. Meister, "Autobiographische Literatur und Memoiren (Hypomnemata) (FGrHist 227–238)," in H. Verdin, G. Schepens, and E. De Keyser, eds., *Purpose of History: Studies in Greek Historiography from the 4th to the 2nd Centuries B.C.; Proceedings of the International Colloquium Leuven, 24–26 May 1988* (Leuven: Orientaliste, 1990), 83–89. For the most recent discussion, see T. Dorandi, "*Ex Uno Fonte Multi Rivuli?* Unity and Multiplicity in Hellenistic Biography," in K. De Temmerman, ed., *Oxford Handbook of Ancient Biography* (Oxford: Oxford University Press, 2020), 137–51; M. S. Williams, "Augustine's Confessions as Autobiography," in K. De Temmerman, ed., *Oxford Handbook of Ancient Biography* (Oxford: Oxford University Press, 2020), 313–28.

258 Contra P. Bilde, *Flavius Josephus between Jerusalem and Rome: His Life, His Works, and Their Importance* (JSPSup 2; Sheffield: Sheffield Academic Press, 1988), 108–10, who rightly identifies *Vita* as autobiographical, but minimizes the role of previous models. For a strong comparison of Josephus' *Vita* and other autobiographies/biographies, especially Tacitus,

An important consideration for this study is whether or not our interpretation of the genre of *Vita* changes if it is viewed as appended to or integrated with *Antiquities*. The use of the term "appendix" for *Vita* can be problematic, as it implies that *Vita* is (potentially) an afterthought and, more importantly, not fully embedded in *Antiquities*.[259] Neither perspective aligns well with the conclusion of *Antiquities*, in which Josephus clearly indicates that his work would close with a description of his lineage and life events (20.262–266), or the ending of *Vita* (430), which he says provides the conclusion to *Antiquities*:

> ταῦτα μὲν τὰ πεπραγμένα μοι διὰ παντὸς τοῦ βίου ἐστίν κρινέτωσαν δ᾽ ἐξ αὐτῶν τὸ ἦθος ὅπως ἂν ἐθέλωσιν ἕτεροι σοὶ δ᾽ ἀποδεδωκώς κράτιστε ἀνδρῶν Ἐπαφρόδιτε τὴν πᾶσαν τῆς ἀρχαιολογίας ἀναγραφὴν ἐπὶ τοῦ παρόντος ἐνταῦθα καταπαύω τὸν λόγον.
>
> These are the events of my whole life; by them let others judge my character as they wish. But giving to you, most excellent Epaphroditus, the whole treatise of [our] antiquities, I here end my narrative.

The reception history of the text strongly suggests that *Vita* did not circulate as a separate work, but traveled with *Antiquities*.[260] These data support the view that the genre label of *Vita* should not be considered in isolation, but as somehow part of *Antiquities*.

The inclusion of autobiographical material is not uncommon in surviving histories and biographies, especially when the author was contemporary with the subject in focus (e.g., Thucydides, Xenophon, and Polybius).[261] These authors do not provide a detailed discussion of their life in their histories, nor are introductory or concluding comments the same as an extended autobiographical discussion.[262] An appropriate comparator is Nicolaus of Damas-

see Cohen, *Josephus*, 101–9, and, most recently and thoroughly, Grojnowski, "Josephus: An Autobiography." In contrast, Dormeyer only identifies biographical predecessors, claiming that Josephus is doing something new. Cf. D. Dormeyer, "Die Vita des Josephus als Biographie eines gescheiterten Herrschers," in F. Siegert and J. U. Kalms, eds., *Internationales Josephus-Kolloquium Dortmund 2002: Arbeiten aus dem Institutum Judaicum Delitzschianum* (Münster: LIT Verlag, 2003), 15–33.

259 Cf. Misch, *Autobiography*, 1.299; Bilde, *Josephus*, 112–13.

260 As evidenced by Eusebius (*Hist. eccl.* 3.9.3–4; 3.10.8) and the manuscript tradition. Cf. Mason, *Life*, xv–xvi.

261 For references and discussion about autopsy in histories, see Marincola, *Authority*, 63–86. Similarly, Plutarch, Lucian, and Galen give personal details in select works as they were deemed to be relevant for the discussion. E.g., Galen, *Lib. prop.* 19.59–60; *Aff. Dig.* 40–41; Lucian, *Somn.*; Eunapius, *Lives* 454; Jerome, *Vir. ill.* 135; cf. Tacitus, *Agr.* 1. On the author's awareness of his actions and their rhetorical purpose, see Whitmarsh, *Greek Literature and the Roman Empire*, 442.

262 E.g., Sallust, *Bell. Cat.* 3–4; Cicero, *Brut.* 301–33. Cf. Misch, *Autobiography*, 1.295–307.

cus' *Concerning His Life and His Education* (Περὶ τοῦ ἰδίου βίου καὶ τῆς ἑαυτοῦ ἀγωγῆς), which is thought to have been placed at the beginning of his *Universal History*.[263] Nicolaus' reference to his *History* in the middle of his autobiography (F135) is thought by Jacoby to exclude the possibility that the latter was a supplement to the former.[264] As a result, the practice of self-discussion exemplified by these authors fits within the broader convention of memorial culture and rhetorical posturing, challenging the rigid divide between autobiography and history.[265]

Highlighting the lack of Greek autobiographies, Wacholder has argued that Nicolaus' *Autobiography* is a synthesis of Greek and Hebrew traditions.[266] Attributing the philosophical and other Hellenic matter in Nicolaus' work to his Greek literary education, Wacholder argues that Nicolaus, during his time with Herod, would have been exposed to first-person reflections and depictions (e.g., Sirach, Psalms, Thanksgiving Psalm), which he claims were literary practices in the East. Wacholder perhaps goes too far in creating a sharp divide between Greek and Eastern literary cultures, as he himself recognizes the diversity of Greco-Roman writing types and the use of first-person examples in philosophical texts. Furthermore, the parallels he draws between Nicolaus and Hillel are not always convincing. Nevertheless, the fact that some of our largest and earliest examples of autobiography come from a Jewish milieu is striking and lends support to this position and to the wider view that genres develop most rapidly through cultural interaction.[267]

263 Misch, *Autobiography*, 1.299. Cf. Stern, *Greek and Latin Authors*, 246–60; M. Toher, "Divining a Lost Text: Augustus' Autobiography and the βίος Καίσαρος of Nicolaus of Damascus," in C. Smith and A. Powell, eds., *The Lost Memoirs of Augustus and the Development of Roman Autobiography* (Swansea: Classical Press of Wales, 2009), 125–44. The originality of this title is unknown. It matches the way that Augustus' biography is discussed (see *Suda* N 393), but both might have come from the pen of the encyclopaedist.

264 Cf. *FGrH* IIC, 289.

265 Mason, *Life*, xxxvi–xli. Cf. Isocrates, *Antid.* 278; Cicero, *Att.* 1.19.10; *Fam.* 5.12.8; *De or.* 2.36; Tacitus, *Agr.* 1.3. Varneda claims that Josephus' "true" autobiography is that dispersed throughout his works and that this was "only of the moment." Varneda, "Early Empire," 327.

This historical perspective is complicated by a narratological approach to texts in which autobiographical statements are not immediately attributable to the author, but to the narrator and the persona that the author creates. Cf. I. J. F. de Jong, R. Nünlist, and A. M. Bowie, eds., *Studies in Ancient Greek Narrative*, vol. 1, *Narrators, Narratees, and Narratives in Ancient Greek Literature* (MneSup 257; Leiden: Brill, 2004); Hau, "Narrator and Narratorial Persona," especially 283–85.

266 Wacholder, *Nicolaus*, 43.

267 Cf. Momigliano, *Development*, 35–38. Since Wacholder, there has been substantial scholarship on autobiography, and the claim that Nicholas and Josephus must have been inspired (solely) by the East is no longer tenable. For the range of scholarly views, see the collection G. Marasco, ed., *Political Autobiographies and Memoirs in Antiquity: A Brill Companion* (Leiden: Brill, 2011).

The close association of both autobiographical works with their respective histories suggests that ancient readers and authors might have seen autobiography as somehow related to the genre of historiography. A number of autobiographical fragments and works identified as *hypomnemata* are associated with the genre of history, even if they are not identified as participating in historiography proper.[268] This flexible association fits well within the larger view that autobiographies in antiquity were not restricted to a specific form but were highly adaptable.[269] Josephus' *Vita* is grounded in rhetorical themes and motifs, which align well with the rhetorical nature of *Antiquities* and ancient historiography at this time.[270] Moreover, the strong apologetic elements (e.g., *Vita* 80–84) and discussion of his character (ἦθος, *Vita* 430) align with the rhetorical thrust of the work. The generic flexibility of autobiographies and their association with history reinforce the view that scholars of Josephus' *Vita* need to recognize its interconnectedness with *Antiquities* and so read *Vita* not only through the lens of autobiography, but also as participating in historiography and rhetoric. By this I am suggesting that we need to consider the broader idea that certain genres were compatible and could be fruitfully joined while retaining some element of independence.

Conclusion

This chapter allows us to make important observations about Jewish historiographical practices. First, Jewish authors throughout the Hellenistic and early Roman eras regularly engaged with the practice of writing histories. From the surviving fragments and texts from the Hellenistic and Roman eras we see that

---

Another issue is his lack of engagement with Latin literary culture and the expectations of Josephus' Roman readers. Although writing in Greek and drawing on Jewish history and literature, Josephus was firmly settled in Rome and was writing with specific Roman readers in mind. This position is most recently articulated by Mason, *Life*, xli; P. Stern, "Life of Josephus: The Autobiography of Flavius Josephus," *JSJ* 41 (2010): 63–93.

Also absent is any reference to autobiographical material from other Eastern cultures. For example, Egypt has a strong tradition of (auto)biographical inscriptions, both in funerary settings (i.e., tombs) and in more public locations (i.e., stelae), in which the major deeds of the pharaoh or leading officials (e.g., Nebneteru, Peftuaneith, Udjahorresne) were recounted (the latter became prominent during the Late Period and the political instability of Egypt). For a more detailed discussion, see M. Lichtheim, *Ancient Egyptian Autobiographies Chiefly of the Middle Kingdom: A Study and an Anthology* (OBO; Göttingen: Vandenhoeck & Ruprecht, 1988).

268 E.g., Plutarch, *Luc.* 1.3; Arrian, *Anab.* 1.1–2; Pyrrhus, *FGrH* 229; Aratus of Sikyon, *FGrH* 231 T1; Ptolemy VIII Euergetes II, *FGrH* 234. Cf. C. Bearzot, "Royal Autobiography in the Hellenistic Age," in G. Marasco, ed., *Political Autobiographies and Memoirs in Antiquity: A Brill Companion* (Leiden: Brill, 2011), 39–40.

269 Misch, *Autobiography*, 1.1; G. Niggl, "Zur Theorie der Autobiographie," in M. Reichel, ed., *Antike Autobiographien: Werke—Epochen—Gattungen* (Cologne: Böhlau, 2005), 1–13; B. Zimmermann, "Anfänge der Autobiographie in der griechischen Literatur," in M. Erler and S. Schorn, eds., *Die griechische Biographie in hellenistischer Zeit* (Berlin: De Gruyter, 2007), 3–9.

270 Mason, "Essay in Character."

Jewish authors participated in history more than any other Greek genre. This consistent engagement is not seen in other genres and suggests that there is something particular about the practice of writing history that resonated with Jewish communities. One explanation could be that history was recognized as a prestige prose genre in the Greco-Roman era and that Jewish authors wanted to engage with this dominant literary form.[271] Perhaps this engagement is a result of the fact that Jewish authors had already been writing histories prior to the Hellenistic era and so felt comfortable continuing that practice.[272] Most certainly, the selection of history related to the authors' view of what that genre represented and the types of values it typically upheld.[273] This could explain why some authors, although writing in Greek, appear to be closer to Jewish history-writing practices, modeling their work on Hebrew or non-Greek prototypes (e.g., Eupolemus).

Second, Jewish authors did not limit themselves to one type of historiography, but participated in a range of subtypes. For example, Demetrius and a number of other Jewish authors are said to have written chronologies.[274] Pseudo-Hecataeus wrote ethnography in the style of Hecataeus, and Eupolemus crafted a history that parallels the works of other minority writers (e.g., Berossus and Manetho). This diversity indicates a wide reading practice among Jews and an appreciation for the diversity of this genre.

Third, the genre of history was adaptable, allowing for the embedding of different literary elements. Demetrius does not limit his work to chronology, but included answers to interpretive questions. Josephus blends (auto)biography and history by incorporating a treatise of his life at the end of his *Antiquities*. Non-Greek literary traditions, especially those stemming from Jewish historiographical practices, are also found in these authors, such as Eupolemus' strong use of Scripture. These examples show the flexibility of the genre and the varied ways that Jewish authors adapted Greek historiography and created new, alternative prototypical works.

Fourth, one important difference between Jewish historians writing in Greek and their Hebrew-writing counterparts is the movement away from anonymity to include clear declarations of authorship.[275] The author and his credentials were of central importance when determining the quality of a

271 For history as the pinnacular prose genre in antiquity, see Adams, *Genre*, 50–53.

272 For genre selection and categories based on the work's relationship to the emotional needs of the author and/or reader, see P. van Tieghem, "La question des genres littéraires," *Helicon* 1 (1939): 97.

273 Cf. Dubrow, *Genre*, 30.

274 E.g., Judas (*FGrH* 261), Thallus (*FGrH* 836), Justus of Tiberias (Photius, *Bibl.* 33), and possibly Eupolemus.

275 A similar practice is adopted by Berossus, who identifies himself at the beginning of his work (F1), in contrast to Mesopotamian chronicle writers.

historical work. This appears to have been recognized by Jewish historians, which led to a change in practice. Interestingly, the notable exceptions to this pattern are works that eventually came to be viewed as scriptural (i.e., 1–4 Maccabees).

Fifth, only one work appears to be pseudepigraphal, Pseudo-Hecataeus' *On the Jews*. This suggests that Jewish authors felt confident about claiming authorship and believed that they had something to contribute to the wider literary and cultural communities (both Greek and Jewish). The genre of history allows individuals from dominated cultures to present their nation from an insider's perspective. In particular, the native's access to original language works is presented as being of the highest importance and allows the author to make a contribution that their monolingual, Greek-speaking counterparts could not (e.g., Josephus, Berossus, Manetho).

8

Jewish Biographers

Biography as a distinct genre in the classical and Hellenistic periods is a growing area of study, with a number of important monographs recently published.[1] Too often New Testament works are excluded from discussions of literary practices in the Greco-Roman period.[2] This artificial scholarly divide is unfortunate, as the Gospels provide important

1 E.g., T. Duff, *Plutarch's Lives: Exploring Virtue and Vice* (Oxford: Oxford University Press, 1999); Hägg, *Art of Biography*; K. De Temmerman and K. Demoen, eds., *Writing Biography in Greece and Rome: Narrative Techniques and Fictionalization* (Cambridge: Cambridge University Press, 2016); K. De Temmerman, ed., *Oxford Handbook of Ancient Biography* (Oxford: Oxford University Press, 2020).

One of the most difficult elements of the study of biography is providing a definition. Many scholars have attempted to do so, but their attempts have not always met with approval. Cf. Momigliano, *Development*, 11; Aune, *New Testament*, 29; C. H. Talbert, *What Is a Gospel? The Genre of the Canonical Gospels* (London: SPCK, 1978), 17; Hägg, *Art of Biography*, 2–3. For a recent discussion of biography, see Adams, "What Are Bioi/Vitae?"

On the relationship between history and biography, see P. Stadter, "Biography and History," in J. Marincola, ed., *A Companion to Greek and Roman Historiography* (BCAW; Malden: Blackwell, 2007), 528–40. On the blurring of genres so that our ability to disambiguate them is questioned, see especially B. Gentili and G. Cerri, *History and Biography in Ancient Thought* (Amsterdam: J. C. Gieben, 1988), *passim*. For the ways that authors took advantage of these connections, see Farrell, "Classical Genre," 388–91.

2 Even before the landmark publication of *What Are the Gospels?* by Richard Burridge in 1992, Greco-Roman biographies were the focus of many New Testament scholars, particularly those engaged in the study of the Gospels. R. A. Burridge, *What Are the Gospels? A Comparison with Graeco-Roman Biography* (3rd ed.; Waco: Baylor University Press, 2018); D. Frickenschmidt, *Evangelium als Biographie: Die vier Evangelien im Rahmen antiker Erzählkunst* (Tübingen: Francke, 1997). P. L. Shuler, *A Genre for the Gospels: The Biographical Character of Matthew* (Philadelphia: Fortress, 1982). For recent critiques of Burridge that draw from linguistic categories, see A. W. Pitts, *History, Biography, and the Genre of Luke-Acts: An Exploration of Literary Divergence in Greek Narrative Discourse* (BIS 177; Leiden: Brill, 2019); Z. K. Dawson, "The Problem of Gospel Genres: Unmasking a Flawed Consensus and Providing a Fresh Way Forward with Systemic Functional Linguistics Genre Theory," *BAGL* 8 (2019): 33–77.

examples of nonprototypical biographies written by members of a minority culture. In this chapter I will examine the Gospels (Mark, Matthew, Luke[-Acts], and John) and the biographies of Philo of Alexandria (*Moses*, *Abraham*, and *Joseph*). As we will see, Philo and the Gospel writers produce different literary expressions and show the diversity of *bioi* in the first century CE.

Gospel of Mark

The Gospel of Mark recounts the final year of Jesus' life (i.e., his ministry and death by crucifixion) and is thought to be the first extant Gospel, written in the late sixties CE.[3] This anonymous composition opens with a declaration by the author, "The beginning of the good news of Jesus Christ, son of God" (Ἀρχὴ τοῦ εὐαγγελίου Ἰησοῦ Χριστοῦ υἱοῦ θεοῦ, 1:1),[4] an opening line that signals the work's topic for the would-be reader.[5] Unlike many individual biographies, Mark does not begin with its principal character or a description of his/her progenitors, but rather opens with a quotation from Jewish Scripture attributed to the prophet Isaiah (1:2–3) and with a contemporary figure, John the Baptist, who prepares both the reader and the characters within the narrative for the arrival of Jesus (1:4–8).[6]

The adult Jesus appears in the narrative at 1:9, but there is little by way of introduction. We learn that he is from Nazareth in Galilee (1:9), that God declares him to be his son (1:9; cf. 1:1), and certain details about his mother and brothers (3:21, 31–35; 6:1–6), but there is no description of Jesus' appearance, nor does Mark provide any information of his birth, childhood, or adolescence. These absences are notable when compared with other prototypical Greek and Latin biographies, as these topics provide opportunities for the author to foreshadow the kind of person the protagonist will become and

3 For the discussion of dating, see A. Y. Collins, *Mark: A Commentary on the Gospel of Mark* (Hermeneia; Minneapolis: Fortress, 2007), 11–14. On the lack of title for the Gospels, see M. Hengel, "The Titles of the Gospels and the Gospel of Mark," in *Studies in the Gospel of Mark* (trans. J. Bowden; London: SCM Press, 1985), 64–84. For convenience, I will refer to the author as Mark. The same practice will be adopted for all of the Gospel authors.

4 On the textual issues of this verse, see T. Wasserman, "The 'Son of God' Was in the Beginning (Mark 1:1)," *JTS* 62 (2011): 20–50. The Greek texts of the Gospels are taken from NA[28].

5 Larsen has recently argued that Mark should not be viewed as a finished text, but as incomplete (i.e., *hypomnemata*). As a result, Matthew and Luke are not individual texts, but are continuations of the same text, which can now be viewed as multiauthored. Although this is intriguing, I am not convinced. M. D. C. Larsen, *Gospels before the Book* (Oxford: Oxford University Press, 2018).

6 S. Moyise, "Composite Citations in the Gospel of Mark," in S. A. Adams and S. M. Ehorn, eds., *Composite Citations in Antiquity*, vol. 2, *New Testament Uses* (LNTS 593; London: Bloomsbury, 2018), 17–25.

indicate the individual's character.[7] At the same time, the suppression of personal details (e.g., mention of earthly father) reinforces a theological perspective: Jesus' parents and ancestors are not indicative of who Jesus truly is; Jesus is God's son. Moreover, Jesus' family members are not determined by genetics, but through shared belief. Both claims subvert a core element of typical *bioi*.

The majority of the work is dedicated to Jesus' ministry (1:14–13:37), in which he teaches, debates, and performs miracles and exorcisms as he travels around Galilee and towards Jerusalem. Mark functions as a host genre, bringing together parables and narrative subunits into a cohesive whole in order to display what he thinks are the most relevant aspects of Jesus' life and career.[8] This space allocation would be expected in a biography, as the individual's famous deeds and sayings form the heart of ancient biographical convention and provide the rationale for why the subject is worthy of remembrance through the composition of a literary work.[9] Mark demonstrates Jesus' superior character by contrasting him with his disciples and antagonists (e.g., Pharisees, chief priests, scribes), showing that Jesus has a divine perspective and the ability to outthink those who are trying to trick him.[10]

A person's nature, however, is best revealed in manner by which s/he faces death,[11] and Jesus' trial and death narrative (14:1–15:47) provide an excellent opportunity for Mark to reinforce Jesus' character. Jesus handles the betrayal from Judas with calmness, unlike one of his disciples, who attacked a member of the arresting party (i.e., the high priest's slave) with a sword (14:47).[12] During his trials by the Jewish leaders and the Roman prefect Pontius Pilate, Jesus displays control under duress by refusing to defend himself against false accusations (14:57–60; 15:3–5). These actions exemplify high moral and philosophical virtues and fit well with the practice of depicting individuals with admirable qualities.

The prominent atypical feature in Mark's Gospel is the manner by which Jesus died: crucifixion. This execution method was often reserved for slaves and enemies of Rome and was considered to be a horrendous form of torture

7 Cf. D. Dormeyer, *Evangelium als literarische und theologische Gattung* (EdF 263; Darmstadt: Wissenschaftliche Buchgesellschaft, 1989), 59–60; Hägg, *Art of Biography*, 85.

8 For the discussion of embedded genres, including the distinction between primary and secondary genres, see M. Bakhtin, "The Problem of Speech Genres," in D. Duff, ed., *Modern Genre Theory* (LCR; London: Longman, 2000), 84–85.

9 For some examples and discussion, see Burridge, *Gospels*, 159–63.

10 E.g., Mark 3:1–6; 7:1–13; 8:11–13; 10:2–9.

11 The standard example in antiquity of a person who accepted the wrongful decision to be executed is Socrates: Plato, *Apology*; Seneca, *Ep*. 24.4–8; 104.22; Plutarch, *Adv. Col.* 18 (*Mor.* 1117e); Lucian, *Peregr*. 12, 37.

12 Jesus' divine foreknowledge of the event (14:18–21) is one possible reason for his emotional control in the moment, although this should not detract from his ability to maintain poise throughout his final day.

and public humiliation.[13] Mark does not detail Jesus' experience on the cross, except his silence in the face of mockery (15:25–32) and his final words: "my God, my God, why have you forsaken me?" (15:34, quoting Ps 21:2 LXX).[14] Recounting a person's last words and actions, especially those of philosophers, was a *topos* in ancient Greek biography, providing an indication of the true character of the individual.[15] Jesus' so-called "cry of dereliction" appears on the surface to undermine the control and integrity he had displayed. However, scholars argue that Jesus' declaration of LXX Ps 21:2 is not one of hopelessness, but of triumph as the Psalm concludes with the speaker's vindication.[16] Mark alludes to a number of elements in Psalm 21,[17] which suggests that the wider text is in focus, but the specific words of Jesus do not mirror the idealized accounts of other martyrs.[18]

Ancient readers who did not have foreknowledge of Jesus' death would likely have been surprised, as an ignominious death often indicated that the person's life was not to be emulated.[19] However, this negative view is offset by other narrative features that show his innocence, an element prominent in the Pilate narrative (15:14). While Jesus was on the cross, Mark mentions a natural phenomenon (darkness, 15:33; cf. Diogenes Laertius, *Vit.* 4.64) as well as supernatural actions at the point of death (the Temple veil torn in two, 15:38), both of which indicate divine observation of the event. Of importance is the testimony of the centurion, who, on seeing how Jesus died, declared, "Surely this man was the Son of God!" (ἀληθῶς οὗτος ὁ ἄνθρωπος υἱὸς θεοῦ ἦν, 15:39). This declaration from a midranking Roman soldier provides the

13 Cf. M. Hengel, *Crucifixion in the Ancient World and the Folly of the Message of the Cross* (trans. J. Bowden; Philadelphia: Fortress, 1977); R. E. Brown, *The Death of the Messiah: From Gethsemane to the Grave; A Commentary on the Passion Narratives in the Four Gospels* (2 vols.; ABRL; Garden City, N.Y.: Doubleday, 1994), 2.945–52; S. A. Adams, "Crucifixion in the Ancient World: A Response to L. L. Welborn," in S. E. Porter, ed., *Paul's World* (PAST 4; Leiden: Brill, 2007), 111–29.

14 For silence as the ideal way to die, see Plato, *Phaed.* 117d.

15 E.g., Bollansée, *Hermippos of Smyrna and His Biographical Writings*, 151–53; E. Kechagia, "Dying Philosophers in Ancient Biography: Zeno the Stoic and Epicurus," in K. De Temmerman and K. Demoen, eds., *Writing Biography in Greece and Rome: Narrative Techniques and Fictionalization* (Cambridge: Cambridge University Press, 2016), 181–99.

16 H. J. Carey, *Jesus' Cry from the Cross: Towards a First-Century Understanding of the Intertextual Relationship between Psalm 22 and the Narrative of Mark's Gospels* (LNTS 398; London: T&T Clark, 2009), especially 171–75.

17 E.g., the dividing of Jesus' clothes by lots (Mark 15:24; Ps 21:19 LXX); the reviling of Jesus by onlookers (Mark 15:28; Ps 21:8–9 LXX).

18 E.g., Socrates (Plato, *Phaed.* 117c–118a); Eleazar (2 Macc 6:30; 4 Macc 6:27–29); the seven brothers (2 Macc 7:6, 9, 11, 14, 16–17, 18–19, 30–38); R. Akiva (b. Ber. 61b).

19 E.g., disloyal slaves (Homer, *Od.* 22.419–504); Antony (Plutarch, *Ant.* 76.1–77.4; cf. *Cleom.* 31.1–6; 37.1–7); Judas (Acts 1:18–19; Matt 27:3–10).

narrator's explicit position: Jesus was wrongfully crucified.[20] Although death by crucifixion is difficult to overlook, the fact (as claimed by Mark) that Jesus was falsely condemned and still accepted his fate with dignity allows the author to maintain that Jesus is someone who is worthy of respect and imitation. Indeed, Jesus himself informed his disciples that they must also be like him in his death (8:34–38), suggesting that Mark, through the words and actions of Jesus, was attempting to transform the perspective of his readers away from dominant cultural values towards those embodied by Jesus.[21]

The biggest difference between Mark's Gospel and other ancient biographies is its ending. Typically, a biography closes with the burial of the protagonist and a brief discussion of his/her tomb and legacy, not with the return of the formerly deceased individual.[22] Mark describes the burial and tomb (15:42–47), but the narrative does not conclude there. Rather, Mark includes an additional scene in which three, named women (Mary Magdalene, Mary the mother of James, and Solome) come to the tomb with spices, but find it disturbed and the body missing (16:1–8). Bodily desecration and pillaging are essentially absent in ancient biographies, as the entombed character is often presented in a very positive light.[23] The same is true in the case of Jesus; his tomb was not looted by robbers, even though this was a real fear in antiquity.[24] Rather, Mark describes a young man dressed in white who informs the women that Jesus is alive and will meet Peter and the disciples in Galilee (16:5–7; cf.

20 The political element of the declaration, in conjunction with 1:1, has not been missed by scholars. Cf. Collins, *Mark*, 764–77.

21 Aune argues that Mark participates in a unique way in the genre of biography. By inverting prototypical features and reader expectations, Mark presents his work as a parody of biography, acting as an antigenre that became the literary model for subsequent depictions of Jesus (i.e., Matthew). D. E. Aune, "Genre Theory and the Genre-Function of Mark and Matthew," in *Collected Essays*, vol. 2, *Jesus, Gospel Tradition and Paul in the Context of Jewish and Greco-Roman Antiquity* (WUNT 1.303; Tübingen: Mohr Siebeck, 2013), 48–51, first published in E.-M. Becker and A. Runesson, eds., *Mark and Matthew I: Comparative Readings; Understanding the Earliest Gospels in Their First-Century Settings* (WUNT 1.271; Tübingen: Mohr Siebeck, 2011), 145–76.

22 Pelling rightly notes that in Plutarch's *Lives* there are a number of examples in which the narrative continues after the death of the principal character. C. B. R. Pelling, "Is Death the End? Closure in Plutarch's *Lives*," in D. H. Roberts, F. M. Dunnand, and D. Fowler, eds., *Classical Closure: Reading the End in Greek and Latin Literature* (Princeton: Princeton University Press, 1997), 228–50.

23 There are examples of bodily desecration, especially for despised individuals (Suetonius, *Cal.* 58–59), but few postburial examples are recorded (e.g., Chariton, *Chaer.* 1.9–10; *Acts of John* 70–71).

24 On curses and fines for disturbing graves, see, for example, *IG* I 217; II[2] 1452, 1815; *CIJ* 1.650; *CIL* 10.2 7136.

14:28). The story concludes abruptly with the women in a state of terror and amazement (16:8), leaving an ending open and unresolved.[25]

Many New Testament scholars see Mark as participating in Greco-Roman biography, but this should not imply that Mark and the other Gospels do not participate in other genres.[26] Unhelpful, in my opinion, is the position that the Gospels are *sui generis*.[27] Although these authors rightly highlight the atypical and unique features of the Gospels, the lack of proposed models and/or parallels is methodologically problematic. Just because aspects in a work are otherwise unattested (e.g., content, time frame, structure, etc.) does not necessitate that the genre was not recognized by ancient readers or that the author did not have different prototypical models which are now lost.

One prominent challenge to the thesis of Mark as biography is the argument of Adela Collins and others, who claim that Mark more closely resembles historical monographs (e.g., Sallust's *Conspiracy of Catiline*).[28] Collins rightly

25 The two additional endings give evidence that ancient readers thought that the ending was too abrupt and/or lacking. For Mark being written in tragic mode and insightful readings of tragic elements in the passion and conclusion, see Jay, *Tragic in Mark*, especially 179–204, 231–61.

26 For an argument of Mark's relationship to Jewish novels based on Mikhail Bakhtin's theory of chronotope, see M. E. Vines, *The Problem of Markan Genre: The Gospel of Mark and the Jewish Novel* (AB 3; Atlanta: SBL, 2002). Tronier has argued that Mark is to be read as an allegorical biography in the vein of Philo. However, as discussed below, Philo does not have one singular approach to biographies. Moreover, there is little in the text to suggest that the author did not want his readers to take the text historically. Cf. H. Tronier, "Markusevangeliets Jesus som biografiseret erkendelsesfigur," in T. L. Thompson and H. Tronier, eds., *Frelsens biografisering* (FBE 13; Copenhagen: Museum Tusculanum, 2004), 237–71. For a recent engagement with gospel genre proposals, see C. S. Keener, *Christobiography: Memory, History, and the Reliability of the Gospels* (Grand Rapids: Eerdmans, 2019), especially 27–67.

27 This position was prominent when form criticism was in vogue, but is no longer widely held. However, some current scholars still use the phrase when discussing the genre of the Gospels within the broader framework of historiography. For older examples, see R. Bultmann, *The History of the Synoptic Tradition* (rev. ed.; trans. J. Marsh; Oxford: Basil Blackwell, 1963), 374; E. Lohse, *The Formation of the New Testament* (trans. M. E. Boring; Nashville: Abingdon, 1981), 119. See recently Becker, *Birth of Christian History*, 71–76. Although placed here, this argument and what follows are relevant for all of the Gospels.

28 A. Y. Collins, *Is Mark's Gospel a Life of Jesus? The Question of Genre* (Père Marquette Lecture in Theology; Milwaukee: Marquette University Press, 1990); A. Y. Collins, "Genre and the Gospels," *JR* 75 (1995): 239–46; Collins, *Mark*, 15–43. For a recent critique of Collins, see D. Konstan and R. Walsh, "Civic and Subversive Biography in Antiquity," in K. De Temmerman and K. Demoen, eds., *Writing Biography in Greece and Rome: Narrative Techniques and Fictionalization* (Cambridge: Cambridge University Press, 2016), 39–42.

Eve-Marie Becker and others have questioned the differentiation of historiographical subgenres and the nature of the biography genre at this time. For Mark's relationship to historiography more broadly, see E.-M. Becker, *Das Markus-Evangelim im Rahmen antiker Historiographie* (WUNT 1.194; Tübingen: Mohr Siebeck, 2006), 51–52, 401–7; Becker, *Birth of Christian History*, 69–76; D. L. Smith and Z. L. Kostopoulos, "Biography, History, and the Genre of Luke-Acts," *NTS* 63 (2017): 390–410.

highlights specific differences between Mark and select Greek texts that are often labeled biographies (e.g., *Life of Homer*, *Life of Aesop*, Philo's *Life of Moses*) and stresses the diversity of this genre. Collins' emphasis on historiography is not without nuance, correctly acknowledging the genre overlap between history and biography by positing "historical biography" as a potential label for Mark.[29] Although I would emphasize the biographical parallels in Mark, Collins' position has merit and provides important insights and counterbalance. The theological perspective of Mark (and the other Gospels) in placing the life of Jesus within the larger narrative of God's interaction with the Jewish people expands the scope of the work beyond that of a typical biography and could be viewed as an example of *macrologia*.

Other scholars argue that Gospel (εὐαγγέλλιον) is a new literary designation.[30] In time, "Gospel" does become used in such a way, with the Gospels (and Acts) acting as prototypical models for subsequent works.[31] However, it is an open question whether or not the author of Mark uses εὐαγγέλλιον in a technical, literary way in his opening (1:1).[32] The subsequent influence of a work and its adoption and adaptation by later authors (e.g., other Gospels and so-called noncanonical gospels) do not automatically confer upon a work (e.g., Mark) genre-generative properties at the time of its creation. Such a position views the work through the lens of readers and subsequent literary history and risks imputing intentionality to the author that may or may not have existed based on future success that could not have been predicted.[33] *Bios* was a flexible genre in the first century CE, and so it is possible that the author of Mark thought that he was doing something new.

When considering the genre of Mark and other Gospels as participating in biography, scholars have not fully engaged with possible non-Greek influences. One reason for this is that there is no surviving individual, discrete work that looks like a biography written in Hebrew/Aramaic.[34] However, this

29 Collins, *Mark*, 32–33.

30 Cf. R. Guelich, "The Gospel Genre," in P. Stuhlmacher, ed., *The Gospel and the Gospels* (Grand Rapids: Eerdmans, 1991), 173–208; J. A. Diehl, "What Is a 'Gospel'? Recent Studies in the Gospel Genre," *CBR* 9 (2011): 171–99.

31 E.g., Justin, *Dial.* 10.2; 100.1; Irenaeus, *Haer.* 3.1.1; Clement, *Strom.* 1.21.

32 There could have been a technical meaning associated with the word in Christian circles (e.g., 1 Thess 1:5; 2:8–9; 3:2; Rom 1:1; 16:25; 1 Cor 9:14, 18; 1 Pet 4:17; Rev 14:6), but it does not appear to function literarily.

33 The evidence from Matthew and Luke also challenges the view that εὐαγγέλλιον is a literary claim, as neither author used the word as a literary designation for his composition: Matthew refers to his work as a βίβλος ("book" or "account," 1:1), and Luke uses the generic διήγησις ("narrative," 1:1). The book of Revelation provides a similar example with regard to the genre of apocalypse. Cf. Aune, *New Testament*, 226–27.

34 The texts at Qumran do not offer a biographical discussion, even for the Teacher of Righteousness. The only biography parallel noted by Manchester's "Database for the Analysis

should not be taken to imply that there was no Jewish biographical tradition. Indeed, rabbinic literature is full of sayings, actions, and anecdotes of Jewish leaders that allow for an understanding of individual lives.[35] These biographical vignettes likely originated with the disciples of the rabbis and were passed down within the school prior to their incorporation into the Talmud, Mishnah, Tosefta, and so on. As a result, we can posit with certainty a preexisting tradition of collecting stories about individuals, although the structure(s) of these stories is not known.[36] The similarities between many of these stories and those in the Gospels (e.g., responses, debates, miracles, etc.), as well as their means of transmission, strongly suggest that the Gospels and rabbinic anecdotes belong to the same tradition of Jewish storytelling.[37] Accordingly, although no rabbinic biography survives, we can see the influence of localized Jewish practice on the composition of Gospel narratives, most prominently in Mark.[38] The Gospels, therefore, although participating in Greek biography, are not exclusively beholden to Greek literary tradition, but evidence an adaption of that genre through influence from its cultural origins and participation in related genres (i.e., history).

Gospel of Matthew

The Gospel of Matthew, although placed first in the New Testament, is thought to have been written later than Mark (i.e., in the last quarter of the first century CE).[39] The strong linguistic similarities among Matthew, Luke, and Mark imply a literary relationship (the Synoptic Gospels), with a majority of scholars

---

of Anonymous and Pseudepigraphic Jewish Texts of Antiquity" (TAPJLA) is the Lives of the Prophets. Some scholars have posited a lost biography based on 1 Macc 9:22 and the reference to the deeds of Judah (τὰ περισσὰ τῶν λόγων Ιουδου). The lack of an extant biography does not undermine the claim by scholars that the Judah material found in 1 and 2 Maccabees is derived from a common biographical source (so Wacholder, *Eupolemus*, 29–32). This is possible, although the claim of a Judas vita, as opposed to another genre (e.g., history), goes beyond the evidence. Cf. K.-D. Schunck, *Die Quellen des I. und II. Makkabäerbuches* (Halle: M. Niemeyer, 1954), 97; Goldstein, *II Maccabees*, 40 n. 89. For similar phraseology, see 1 Kgs 11:41; 14:29; 15:7, etc.

35 On biographical features in rabbinic literature, see P. S. Alexander, "Rabbinic Biography and the Biography of Jesus: A Survey of the Evidence," in C. M. Tuckett, ed., *Synoptic Studies: The Ampleforth Conferences of 1982 and 1983* (JSNTSup 7; Sheffield: JSOT Press, 1984), 19–50. For a critique, see M. J. Edwards, "Gospel and Genre: Some Reservations," in B. C. McGing and J. Mossman, eds., *The Limits of Ancient Biography* (Swansea: Classical Press of Wales, 2006), 51–62.

36 Alexander, "Rabbinic Biography," 24–25.

37 Alexander, "Rabbinic Biography," 41–42.

38 Cf. M. C. Moeser, *The Anecdote in Mark, the Classical World and the Rabbis* (JSNTSup 227; Sheffield: Sheffield Academic Press, 2002).

39 W. D. Davies and D. C. Allison Jr., *A Critical and Exegetical Commentary on The Gospel According to Saint Matthew* (3 vols.; ICC; Edinburgh: T&T Clark, 1988–1997), 1.127–38; U. Luz, *Matthew: A Commentary* (3 vols.; Hermeneia; Minneapolis: Fortress, 2007), 1.41–44 (not discussed but implied by use of sources). For an argument for an earlier date, although

holding the view that Matthew and Luke independently used Mark's Gospel as a source.[40] The major events of Jesus' life in Matthew are similar to those in Mark: Jesus calls disciples (4:18–22), performs miracles (8:1–17), teaches his disciples and the crowds (5:1–7:29; 18:1–20:16), confronts the scribes and Pharisees (12:38; 21:45; 23:1–36), and is betrayed, tried, and crucified (26:1–27:66).[41]

Important differences exist between Matthew and Mark, especially at the beginning and end of the narratives.[42] Matthew opens with an extended genealogy of Jesus (1:1–17), tracing his lineage for 42 generations (3 × 14 generations), through King David (1:1, 6) and back to Abraham (1:1–2), the forefather of the Jewish people. Following this, Matthew offers a detailed account of Jesus' birth, including aspects of his earthly parents (1:19), astrological signs (2:2), scriptural foretelling (2:6, 18), and angelic visitations in dreams (1:20; 2:13, 19). The inclusion of a genealogy and birth narrative suggests that Matthew was not content with the opening of Mark. As these are typical, although not requisite, features of individual biographies, Matthew could be viewed as adapting his primary source (i.e., Mark) to align better with prototypical genre expectations.[43] In particular, the inclusion of portents and divinely given

still after Mark, see R. T. France, *The Gospel of Matthew* (NICNT; Grand Rapids: Eerdmans, 2007), 18–19.

40 For the different views of the relationship among the Synoptic Gospels, see S. E. Porter and B. R. Dyer, eds., *The Synoptic Problem: Four Views* (Grand Rapids: Baker Academic, 2016). The theory one adopts for these data does not affect the question of whether the works participate in biography. Matthew's following of Luke would also support his approval of the inclusion of a birth narrative.

Scholars also posit a sayings source, "Q," that was used by both Matthew and Luke. The *Gospel of Thomas*, another nonnarrative work, provides 114 sayings purported to be from Jesus. Both these texts parallel some gnomic collections in antiquity, particularly those of philosophers (see chapter 4). See Gathercole, *Gospel of Thomas*. On the genre of sayings sources, see C. Heil, "Evangelium als Gattung: Erzähl- und Spruchevangelium," in T. Schmeller, ed., *Historiographie und Biographie im Neuen Testament und seiner Umwelt* (NTOA 69; Göttingen: Vandenhoeck & Ruprecht, 2009), 62–94.

41 Scholars are correct in their identification of different themes, motifs, and aspects of theology between Matthew and Mark. However, these differences do not have substantial influence in determining the genre of the work.

42 For a study of the differences among the Gospels through the lens of biographical composition techniques, see M. R. Licona, *Why Are There Differences in the Gospels? What We Can Learn from Ancient Biography* (Oxford: Oxford University Press, 2017). The prominence and explicit citation of Scripture by the narrator is another important difference from Mark. Cf. Davies and Allison, *Matthew*, 1.32–58; M. J. J. Menken, *Matthew's Bible: The Old Testament Text of the Evangelist* (BETL 173; Leuven: Leuven University Press, 2004).

43 A similar practice of narrative gap filling is evidenced in the so-called infancy gospels (e.g., *Protevangelium of James, Infancy Gospel of Thomas*). Cf. Bockmuehl, *Ancient Apocryphal Gospels*, 55–86.

dreams resonates with contemporary Greek biography practices, as it indicates to the reader that the individual will have a prominent future.[44]

Another major difference is the expansion of Jesus' claim to divinity. In Mark's Gospel, the author states that Jesus was the son of God (Mark 1:1, 9; 15:39). However, in Matthew, although a similar declaration is made at Jesus' baptism (Matt 3:17) and crucifixion (27:54), the divine nature of Jesus is emphasized in the birth narrative and the nature of his conception. Matthew claims that Jesus' mother, Mary, was a virgin and that Jesus was conceived by the Holy Spirit (1:18–25). Philosophical biographies in later antiquity incorporated religious themes and regularly posited divinity as a distinguishing characteristic of the true philosopher.[45] This element was not prominent at the time of the Gospels' composition, however, and is thought to be one of the ways that Matthew and Luke influenced the writing of subsequent intellectual biographies.

Matthew also expands the ending of Mark's narrative. Although there are minor differences in the trial and crucifixion scenes,[46] the major change takes place following Jesus' death, with Matthew providing a more developed, but still open, conclusion. Matthew's narrative has a similar progression, with two Marys (Solome is absent) going to the tomb to apply spices to Jesus' body. However, Matthew reports how the stone was rolled away by an angel (28:2–4). Following the angel's orders, the two Marys begin to return to the disciples. Next, they are met by the resurrected Jesus (28:9–10), whom they worship and who commands them to go and tell his disciples to meet him in Galilee. Following this encounter the scene shifts to the perspective of the guards (whose rationale for guarding the tomb was provided in 27:62–66) and how they and the chief priests began the rumor that Jesus' body was taken by his disciples (28:11–15). The work concludes with the disciples meeting Jesus in Galilee on a mountain and receiving a final instruction from him to go and make disciples of all nations (28:16–20). The narrative ends at this point with no indication of what happened to Jesus or his followers.

44 E.g., Plutarch, *Alex.* 2.3–3.9; *Per.* 6.2–3; *Cic.* 2.1; Suetonius, *Aug.* 94.1–12; Philosotratus, *Vit. Apoll.* 1.5. A large temporal gap remains within the narrative, with Matt 3:1 jumping from Jesus' infancy to his adult ministry. Cf. A. N. Shaw, *Oral Transmission and the Dream Narratives of Matthew 1–2: An Exploration of Matthean Culture Using Memory Techniques* (Eugene, Ore.: Pickwick Press, 2019).

45 P. Cox, *Biography in Late Antiquity: A Quest for the Holy Man* (TCH 1; Berkeley: University of California Press, 1983), 17–18, 43–44; M. J. Edwards, "Birth, Death, and Divinity in Porphyry's Life of Plotinus," in T. Hägg and P. Rousseau, eds., *Greek Biography and Panegyric in Late Antiquity* (TCH 31; Berkeley: University of California Press, 2000), 65.

46 E.g., the expansion of Jesus' prayer in the garden (26:36–46); details about the trial and who was in attendance (e.g., Caiaphas, 26:57); the repentance and death of Judas (27:3–10); the dream given to Pilate's wife (27:19).

Most scholars view Matthew as participating in biography.[47] The addition of a birth narrative and an expanded conclusion suggests that the author of Matthew was not fully satisfied with the shape and purview of Mark's Gospel. It is possible that Matthew saw Mark's Gospel as deficient with regard to its adherence to biographical practices (i.e., lack of birth narrative, genealogy, resurrection appearance), although this is not explicit. Postdeath viewings of the living protagonist are understandably absent in previous biographies, and so some additions by Matthew have no precedent. Nevertheless, as Matthew's Gospel follows the major events of Jesus' ministry and death as established in Mark, it is likely that Matthew saw his work as participating in the same genre as Mark, with Mark as formative, but not fully prototypical in that Matthew addresses aspects that he thought were wanting.[48]

This view should not be taken to imply that Matthew's work is not distinct or that he did not adapt the genre to fit his theological perspective. Matthew's use of Scripture and the interpretation of his protagonist's life through a soteriological frame shape the focus of the work and his presentation of Jesus. Indeed, no other existing Greek biography makes such extended recourse to an authoritative text when discussing their subject.[49] This interplay of authority between the person of Jesus (exhibited through words and deeds) and sacred text results in a work that transcends the typical bounds of biography and allows Matthew to participate in other genres (e.g., commentary, apocalypse, etc.), paralleling the pairing of Scripture and actions found in other Jewish biographical traditions (e.g., rabbis). Similarly, the emphasis on the person, not just as a founder of a philosophical/religious movement or as a model to emulate, but as being inherently different and divinely special (i.e., God's anointed messiah), is also atypical in *bioi*.[50]

Luke-Acts

The Gospel of Luke is an anonymous work thought to have been written in the last quarter of the first century CE.[51] Luke's Gospel situates the narrative in a

47 Few arguments for alternative genres have lasted. Cf. Davies and Allison, *Matthew*, 3.707–18; Shuler, *Genre*; Luz, *Matthew*, 13–15. Genre discussion is notably absent in France, *Matthew*.

48 On the reinforced pairing of words and deeds together in Matthew, with regard to both Jesus and his disciples, see Davies and Allison, *Matthew*, 2.197; 3.714–16.

49 Potter observes that the *bios* allows for direct quotation of documents in a way that the generic rules of narrative history did not. If this is so, then Matthew takes full advantage of this genre element. Cf. D. S. Potter, *Literary Texts and the Roman Historian* (London: Routledge, 1999), 67; Stadter, "Biography and History," 540.

50 Mark, to a lesser degree, is the exception. This is rightly noted by J. Nolland, *The Gospel of Matthew* (NIGTC; Grand Rapids: Eerdmans, 2005), 19, although Nolland goes too far when he says that there is "no sense" in which Matthew's depiction of Jesus' career might sit alongside other biographies.

51 On the dating of Luke-Acts, see F. Dicken, "The Author and Date of Luke-Acts: Exploring the Options," in S. A. Adams and M. Pahl, eds., *Issues in Luke-Acts: Selected Essays* (Piscataway,

specific time in history (1:5) and opens with a description of Jesus' conception and birth (1:5–2:52). Important differences exist between the birth narratives of Matthew and Luke,[52] although the general thrust is similar: Jesus, who was conceived by Mary through the power of the Holy Spirit (1:35) and born in Bethlehem (2:4–7), is a person of importance, one who will do great things in his lifetime.[53] Jesus' distinctive nature is highlighted at the end of this section with an original episode from his childhood (2:41–52): Jesus is found in the Temple in Jerusalem displaying an understanding of Scripture that amazes trained specialists. The "child genius" motif is not uncommon in biographies and helps foreshadow Jesus' adult life, both his ability to teach and to confound Jewish legal experts.[54]

Following the episode in the Temple by the youth Jesus, Luke jumps to Jesus' adult life and his baptism by John the Baptist (3:1–22), beginning with a new chronological orientation (3:1–2). A majority of the work traces the teaching and ministry of Jesus in and around Galilee (4:1–9:50) and on his way to Jerusalem (9:51–21:38). Similar to Matthew and Mark, Luke recounts the Last Supper (22:1–23), the betrayal by Judas (22:47–48), the denial by Peter (22:54–62), the trials by the Jewish leaders (22:63–71) and Pilate (23:1–6, 13), the release of Barabbas (23:18–25), and Jesus' crucifixion (23:32–49) and burial (23:50–56).[55]

Like Matthew, Luke also provides a fuller ending to his Gospel. The post-burial narrative begins with women (now at least five, with three named in 24:10) going to the tomb to apply spices to Jesus' body, which is found to be

N.J.: Gorgias Press, 2012), 7–26. For a second-century date for Acts, see R. I. Pervo, *Dating Acts: Between the Evangelists and the Apologists* (Santa Rosa, Cal.: Polebridge Press, 2006).

52 E.g., the additional narratives of: the birth of John the Baptist to Elizabeth and Zechariah (1:5–25); the circumcision of Jesus on the eighth day and purification (2:21–24); the songs/prayers by Mary (1:46–55), Zechariah (1:67–79), Simeon (2:25–35), and Anna (2:36–40). For a detailed discussion of the changes, see A. T. Lincoln, *Born of a Virgin? Reconceiving Jesus in the Bible, Tradition, and Theology* (Grand Rapids: Eerdmans, 2013), 57–67; R. E. Brown, *The Birth of the Messiah: A Commentary on the Infancy Narratives in the Gospels of Matthew and Luke* (Garden City, N.Y.: Doubleday, 1993).

53 A similar theme is also found in the added birth narrative of John the Baptist. In these paralleled births, the author uses scriptural motifs and stories (e.g., Sarah and Hannah's conceptions) to show the births of John and Jesus as part of God's larger plan for redemption. The close association of these two characters has led some scholars to posit that Luke is engaging with *synkrisis*. Although I agree in the comparison, I would not go as far as to say that this is an example of high-level progymnastic training. Cf. Adams, "Luke and *Progymnasmata*."

54 For examples of brilliant youths, see Jub. 11:18–24; Josephus, *Vita* 8–12; *Ant.* 2.230; Philo, *Mos.* 1.20–24; Plutarch, *Thes.* 6.2; *Cic.* 2.2–4; Philostratus, *Vit. Apoll.* 1.7.1–3; *Setne II* 1.13–14.

55 Some unique features of the passion narrative include Jesus looking at Peter after his denial (22:61); the trial by Herod (23:7–12); Jesus' address to the women when he was on his way to be crucified (23:27–31); the salvation of one of the bandits who was crucified with him (23:39–43).

missing (24:1–3). However, they are greeted by two men in white and given a message for the disciples (24:4–9). The disciples do not believe their message, and so Peter runs to the tomb to see for himself (24:12). The remainder of Luke's Gospel, including Jesus' discussion with two disciples on the road to Emmaus (24:13–35), his sudden appearance to the disciples in Jerusalem (24:36–49), and his ascension into heaven (24:50–53), is unique. These differences between Mark and Luke are important for developing Luke's theology (especially how the Scriptures relate to Jesus, 24:27, 44), but they have minimal influence on our perspective of the work's genre.

On the other hand, two additions in Luke's Gospel have caused scholars to question whether or not Luke participates in biography: the preface in Luke 1:1–4 and the book of Acts. Luke's preface (1:1–4) has been a focus of scholarly activity. Although Loveday Alexander has made a strong case for viewing Luke's prefaces in light of "scientific" (i.e., nonliterary) prefaces in antiquity, a majority of scholars would argue that Luke's preface participates most fully with those of history.[56] Although the parallels that scholars have identified are valid, literary preface writing is not only within the purview of the historian, but was also undertaken by biographers, especially those who were writing collected biographies.[57] More difficult is the absence of biography language or mention of Jesus within the preface. Rather, the preface speaks to the author's methodology, Theophilus' faith, and the subsequent narrative (διήγησις). In contrast, the preface of Acts does invoke *bios* language, opening the second volume of the work with a clear focus on the actions and teachings of Jesus and his disciples and an explicit connection with the Gospel of Luke, "In the first work, Theophilus, I wrote about all the things that Jesus began to do and teach (ποιεῖν τε καὶ διδάσκειν)" (Acts 1:1).[58]

56 Alexander, *Preface*; W. C. van Unnik, "Remarks on the Purpose of Luke's Historical Writing (Luke 1.1–4)," in *Sparsa Collecta: The Collected Essays of W. C. van Unnik* (Leiden: Brill, 1973), 6–15; D. L. Balch, "ἀκριβῶς . . . γράψαι (Luke 1:3): To Write the Full History of God's Receiving All Nations," in D. P. Moessner, ed., *Jesus and the Heritage of Israel* (Philadelphia: Trinity Press, 1999), 229–50; D. P. Moessner, "The Appeal and Power of Poetics (Luke 1:1–4)," in D. P. Moessner, ed., *Jesus and the Heritage of Israel* (Philadelphia: Trinity, 1999), 84–123; D. P. Moessner, "The Lukan Prologues in the Light of Ancient Narrative Hermeneutics," in J. Verheyden, ed., *The Unity of Luke-Acts* (BETL 142; Leuven: Leuven University Press, 1999), 399–417; D. E. Aune, "Luke 1.1–4: Historical or Scientific *Prooimon*?" in A. Christophersen et al., eds., *Paul, Luke and the Graeco-Roman World: Essays in Honour of Alexander J. M. Wedderburn* (JSNTSup 217; London: T&T Clark, 2002), 138–48; Adams, "Luke's Preface."

57 E.g., Plutarch, *Demetr.* 1.1–3; *Alex.* 1.1–3; *Nic.* 1.1–5; Philostratus, *Vit. soph.* 479; Eunapius, *Vit. soph.* 453; Jerome, *Vir. ill. praef.*; Nepos, *praef.* Prefaces are also found in novels, although they are not common (e.g., Longus, *Daphn. praef.* 1–4; Chariton, *Chaer.* 1.1).

58 R. I. Pervo, *Acts: A Commentary* (Hermeneia; Minneapolis: Fortress, 2009), 36. Cf. Plutarch, *Galb.* 2.5; *Pomp.* 8.7; Diogenes Laertius, *Vit.* 2.37.

The larger question, however, is the relationship between Luke and Acts.[59] A majority of scholars argue that Acts is a history (of some form),[60] which often results in assigning separate genre labels to Luke and Acts.[61] Although possible, the implication by the author in the preface of Acts (1:1) is that this work is a continuation of Luke and so would (presumably) participate in the same genre. Scholars need to take this claim seriously when discussing the (dis)unity of Luke-Acts and its genre participation. The book of Acts recounts select events in the early years of the Christian movement by providing a series of vignettes of prominent Christ followers and their engagement (primarily) with those outwith the faith community. The narrative begins with a scene parallel to Luke 24:50–53, in which Jesus talks to his disciples prior to his ascension (Acts 1:1–12). Following the giving of the Holy Spirit at Pentecost (2:1–47), the author recounts the teachings, miracles, travels, and conflicts of Peter and John (3:1–4:23), Stephen (6:8–8:3), Philip (8:4–13, 26–40), Peter by himself (9:32–11:18), and, for the last half of the work, Paul, both by himself and with traveling companions (12:24–15:4; 15:35–28:31).[62]

I have argued that Luke-Acts could be fruitfully viewed as participating in the genre of collected biography, specifically the life of the founder followed by descriptions of the deeds of his disciples.[63] Collected biography had its origins in the Hellenistic period and grew in popularity during the

59 On the question of unity, see, for example: M. C. Parsons and R. I. Pervo, *Rethinking the Unity of Luke and Acts* (Minneapolis: Fortress, 1993); J. Verheyden, "The Unity of Luke-Acts: What Are We Up To?" in J. Verheyden, ed., *The Unity of Luke-Acts* (BETL 142; Leuven: Leuven University Press, 1999), 3–56; P. Walters, *The Assumed Authorial Unity of Luke and Acts: A Reassessment of the Evidence* (SNTSMS 145; Cambridge: Cambridge University Press, 2009).

60 E.g., Aune, *New Testament*, 77–115; Sterling, *Historiography*; C. K. Rothschild, *Luke-Acts and the Rhetoric of History: An Investigation of Early Christian Historiography* (WUNT 2.175; Tübingen: Mohr Siebeck, 2004), 16–23; D. Dormeyer, "Die Gattung der Apostelgeschichte," in J. Frey, C. K. Rothschild, and J. Schröter, with B. Rost, eds., *Die Apostelgeschichte im Kontext antiker und frühchristlicher Historiographie* (Berlin: De Gruyter, 2009), 437–75; D. P. Moessner, *Luke the Historian of Israel's Legacy, Theologian of Israel's "Christ"* (BZNW 182; Berlin: De Gruyter, 2016). For the recent proposal of Acts as prosopography, see Becker, *Birth of Christian History*, 79.

61 Far too many works on this topic exist for specific interaction. For an overview of the genre of Acts and the different proposals, see T. Penner, "Madness in the Method? The Acts of the Apostles in Current Study," *CBR* 2 (2004): 223–93, especially 233–41; T. E. Phillips, "The Genre of Acts: Moving towards a Consensus?" *CBR* 4 (2006): 365–96; S. A. Adams, "The Genre of Luke and Acts," in S. A. Adams and M. Pahl, eds., *Issues in Luke-Acts: Selected Essays* (Piscataway, N.J.: Gorgias Press, 2012), 97–120.

62 For a full accounting of the characters in each passage, see Adams, *Genre*, 125–32.

63 Adams, *Genre*, especially 116–256. Examples of this pairing include Müller, FHG 3.41–42, 45–46, 49–51. Hermippus wrote both *On Isocrates* (F42–44) and *On the Pupils of Isocrates* (FF45–54); Diogenes Laertius' *Vitae* (cf. Adams, *Genre*, 102–8). This is not to discount the historiographical parallels that scholars have identified in Acts, but to emphasize the genre unity of Luke-Acts. For a recent discussion, see Burridge, *Gospels*, I.53–66.

Roman era.[64] A majority of the surviving texts from these eras are fragmentary, but they evidence a diversity of forms (and so prototypical models) and a willingness by ancient authors to experiment with this genre. I argue that a similar perspective was held by Luke, who adopted the collected biography framework, but increased the size and structure of the narrative to better depict the events in the early church.[65] Above I argued that the author of Matthew developed Mark's Gospel through the incorporation of a birth narrative and additional ending scenes. However, he was content to follow Mark in participating in individual biography about Jesus and not recounting the subsequent actions of his disciples. In contrast, Luke developed the biographical focus through the depiction of Jesus' disciples. Luke did not substantially change the biographical portrayal of Jesus, but through the addition of another book (Acts) expanded the scope to go beyond Jesus and trace his legacy through the words and deeds of his disciples. This provides a good example of a Jewish author engaging in *macrologia*. Expanded prose narrative with high levels of cohesion is atypical in Greek collected biographies, but is more commonly associated with histories. Luke's decision to use continuous narrative could be a desire to follow scriptural histories and the way their narratives follow the lives and reigns of Jewish monarchs. Viewed in light of Opacki's theory of royal genres and genre hierarchy, the influence of Jewish Scripture on a Greek genre suggests that Luke had a hierarchy of genres in which native literary forms could exert downward pressure on Greek genres.[66] This implies not only a comparison of genres across culture boundaries, but that the culturally dominant forms (i.e., Greek) might not be viewed as pinnacular compositions by members of a minority community.

Gospel of John

The anonymous Gospel of John was likely composed in the late first or early second century CE.[67] Similar to the Synoptic Gospels above, John recounts the ministry and death of Jesus. However, unlike the other three works, which

64 J. Benecker, "Individual and Collected Lives in Antiquity," in K. De Temmerman, ed., *Oxford Handbook of Ancient Biography* (Oxford: Oxford University Press, forthcoming 2020).

65 Adams, *Genre*, 253–54.

66 Opacki, "Royal Genres," 118–26.

67 For an overview of dating and authorship, see R. E. Brown, *An Introduction to the Gospel of John* (ed. F. J. Moloney; 2 vols.; ABRL; New York: Doubleday, 2003), 1.189–219; C. S. Keener, *The Gospel of John: A Commentary* (2 vols.; Peabody, Mass.: Hendrickson, 2003), 1.81–139. On discussion of the "beloved disciple," see R. Bauckham, "The Beloved Disciple as Ideal Author," *JSNT* 49 (1993): 21–44; H. M. Jackson, "Ancient Self-Referential Conventions and Their Implications for the Authorship and Integrity of the Gospel of John," *JTS* 50 (1999): 1–34.

have direct linguistic connections and a similar outlook, John's Gospel is distinct, both in language and in theological perspective.[68]

The work opens with a prologue (1:1–18) that describes the coming of God's only Son into the world using philosophical and theological terms and images that are echoed throughout the text.[69] This Son is both the creator and the light of the world (1:2–4) and was sent to reveal the Father (1:18) and bring grace and truth to humanity (1:17). Following the prologue, John's narrative parallels the pattern of the other Gospels by beginning with John the Baptist's testimony about Jesus and his baptism (1:19–34) and Jesus' calling of some disciples (1:35–51). Similar to Mark, there is no birth narrative or any discussion of Jesus' early life. John employs substantial family language throughout the narrative, but offers little on Jesus' earthly parents (cf. 1:45; 6:42).[70] Rather, the focus on Jesus' heavenly father (1:14, 18) and the creation of kinship with and among his disciples.[71]

In the heart of the narrative, Jesus is presented as a gifted teacher who is challenged by Jewish leaders (7:45–52; 11:45–53; 12:9–11). Jesus performs "signs" (σημεῖον, e.g., 2:11; 4:54; 6:2; 11:47; 20:30), travels around Galilee, enters Jerusalem to acclamation by the crowds (12:12–19), and, following a lengthy testimony-like discourse during a communal meal (13:31–17:26),[72] is arrested, forced to stand trial before the Jewish leaders (18:19–24) and Pontius Pilate (18:28–19:16), and ultimately crucified (19:17–30).[73] In contrast to the Synoptics, the Jesus in John's Gospel rarely speaks in parables, performs no exorcisms, and has a ministry longer than one year.[74] Rather, John's Jesus speaks

68 For an overview of the possible relationships between John and the Synoptics, see R. Bergmeier, "Die Bedeutung der Synoptiker für das johanneische Zeugnisthema: Mit einem Anhang zum Perfekt-Gebrauch im vierten Evangelium," *NTS* 52 (2006): 458–83.

69 Cf. C. Koester, *Symbolism in the Fourth Gospel: Meaning, Mystery, Community* (2nd ed.; Minneapolis: Fortress, 2003).

70 John evidences the tradition that Jesus came from Nazareth (John 1:45–46; 7:40–42, 52). For other references to Jesus' family, primarily his mother, see 2:1–12; 19:25–27.

71 E.g., John 2:16; 3:35; 5:18–26; 8:19; 10:30, etc. Indeed, πατήρ language is used extensively by Jesus when referring to God (e.g., 4:21–23; 8:27, 41, etc.). On father language in John, see the *Semeia* 95 volume edited by A. Reinhartz, *God the Father in the Gospel of John* (2001).

72 This testimony could begin at 13:31. Cf. A. Dettwiler, *Die Gegenwart des Erhöhten: Eine exegetische Studie zu den johanneischen Abschiedsreden (Joh 13,31–16,33) unter besonderer Berücksichtigung ihres Relecture-Charakters* (FRLANT 169; Göttingen: Vandenhoeck & Ruprecht, 1995); D. F. Tolmie, *Jesus' Farewell to the Disciples: John 12:1–17:26 in Narratological Perspective* (BIS 12; Leiden: Brill, 1995). For a review of positions, see H.-J. Klauck, "Der Weggang Jesu: Neue Arbeiten zu Joh 13–17," *BZ* 40 (1996): 236–50.

73 The trial in the high priest Caiaphas' house is mentioned but not recounted in John. Also omitted is the transfiguration scene.

74 Jesus' ministry is presented as taking about three years, as determined by references to Passovers (2:13; 6:4; 11:55). For John's figurative speech, see his use of παροιμίαι in 10:6; 16:25 and 29.

in metaphors (e.g., the "I am" sayings, 6:35, 48; 8:12; 10:7, 11; 11:25; 15:1) and engages in extended dialogues and discourses (3:1–21; 14:1–17:26).[75] These unique features are important for recognizing John's distinctive theological perspective, but are less significant when considering genre participation.[76]

The Gospel, as it has been received, is regularly read as a biography.[77] However, this position has become more nuanced, especially since the influential article by Harold Attridge "Genre Bending in the Fourth Gospel."[78] Attridge argues that one of the most important features in John is the author's playful use of a range of formal features, placing it within an established tradition of genre mixing and invention that was prominent in the Hellenistic and Roman eras.[79] Scholars have identified fruitful parallels with dramatic literature, suggesting that John might participate in tragedy or comedy by adopting specific motifs and themes.[80] These studies have reinforced the view that the

75 On the unique elements to John's Gospel, in terms of both content and theology, see D. M. Smith, *The Theology of the Gospel of John* (NTT; Cambridge: Cambridge University Press, 1995). On the function of the extended farewell discourse within John and its relationship to Greek literature, see G. Parsenios, *Departure and Consolation: The Johannine Farewell Discourse in Light of Greco-Roman Literature* (NovTSup 117; Leiden: Brill, 2005).

76 One major issue for Johannine studies is the compositional (dis)unity of the work. Scholars have identified duplicate passages and nonchronological arrangements within the narrative, leading many to argue for multiple sources and/or compositional stages. In particular, scholars argue that the double conclusion of John 20 and 21 implies at least a secondary addition to the work, one that was likely not penned by the original author. For an overview of the issues and scholarly positions, see Brown, *Introduction*, 40–89; A. T. Lincoln, "'We Know That His Testimony Is True': Johannine Truth Claims and Historicity," in P. N. Anderson, F. Just, and T. Thatcher, eds., *John, Jesus, and History*, vol. 1, *Critical Appraisals of Critical Views* (SymS 44; Atlanta: SBL, 2007), 179–97. On the differences of Greek style in John 21, see R. E. Brown, *The Gospel According to John* (AB 29; Garden City, N.Y.: Doubleday, 1966), 1077–82.

77 For an argument for John as "historical biography" and an overview of previous positions, see Keener, *John*, 3–34. Cf. Burridge, *Gospels*, 213–32; A. Köstenberger, "The Genre of the Fourth Gospel and Greco-Roman Literary Conventions," in S. E. Porter and A. W. Pitts, eds., *Christian Origins and Greco-Roman Culture: Social and Literary Contexts for the New Testament* (TENTS 9; ECHC 1; Leiden: Brill, 2013), 435–62.

78 H. W. Attridge, "Genre Bending in the Fourth Gospel," *JBL* 121 (2002): 3–21, further developed in H. W. Attridge, "The Gospel of John: Genre Matters?" in K. B. Larsen, ed., *The Gospel of John as Genre Mosaic* (SANt 3; Göttingen: Vandenhoeck & Ruprecht, 2015), 27–45. Attridge uses genre on both the macro (i.e., the whole work) and the localized (i.e., specific pericopes) levels. For a broader introduction to the topic of John and genre, see K. B. Larsen, "Introduction: The Gospel of John as Genre Mosaic," in K. B. Larsen, ed., *The Gospel of John as Genre Mosaic* (SANt 3; Göttingen: Vandenhoeck & Ruprecht, 2015), 13–24.

79 See especially Farrell, "Classical Genre."

80 See especially J.-A. A. Brant, *Dialogue and Drama: Elements of Greek Tragedy in the Fourth Gospel* (Peabody, Mass.: Hendrickson, 2004). On possible use of Euripides' *Bacchae*, see D. R. MacDonald, *The Dionysian Gospel: The Fourth Gospel and Euripides* (Minneapolis: Fortress, 2017). On the topic of irony, see G. W. MacRae, "Theology and Irony in the Fourth Gospel," in R. J. Clifford and G. W. MacRae, eds., *The Word in the World: Essays in Honor of F. L. Moriarty* (Cambridge, Mass.: Weston College, 1973), 83–96; P. N. Anderson, *The Riddles of the Fourth Gospel* (Minneapolis: Fortress, 2011). More recently, Brant has engaged in a similar approach

Gospel of John does not fully conform to prototypical models of biography.[81] There are notable generic affinities that allow the text to be read through such a lens, but the author's practice of playful adaptation encourage scholars to view John's Gospel as a polyphony of genres and recognize elements imported from elsewhere.[82]

Regarding the purpose of this varied text, Attridge argues that the author of John purposefully contrasts his work with that of Luke, adopting the dichotomy of genre that was presented by Plato and Aristotle (i.e., διήγησις versus μιμήσις).[83] This move towards the "dramatic" is not to discredit the historicity of Jesus. Rather, the author of John may not have thought that a purely historiographical narrative sufficiently captured the essence of Jesus or would have properly engaged the reader with the living Word.[84] It is possible that John saw in the production of the Synoptics and other now-lost works a nascent genre and consciously sought to problematize or influence its development. If such a position is adopted, we see a second layer of biographical adaptation by this Jewish author and a further step away from prototypical Greek *bios*.

Gospel Conclusion

Scholars are broadly content to read the Gospels as participating in ancient biography and having literary affiliations with examples found in the Greco-Roman world. Claiming that the Gospels are part of the Greek literary practice of writing lives should not exclude other literary parallels or models. The regular depiction of lives in Jewish Scripture, which the Gospels authors knew and explicitly used, influenced the composition of the Gospels and could have been viewed as exemplaric for their compositions.[85] The Eli-

---

by reading John through the lens of the ancient novel. J.-A. A. Brant, "John among the Ancient Novels," in K. B. Larsen, ed., *The Gospel of John as Genre Mosaic* (SANt 3; Göttingen: Vandenhoeck & Ruprecht, 2015), 157–69.

81 For John as an aretalogical biography, see L. M. Wills, *Quest of the Historical Gospel: Mark, John and the Origins of the Gospel Genre* (London: Routledge, 1997), 10–11, 24. For historiographical elements, see R. Bauckham, "Historiographical Characteristics of the Gospel of John," *NTS* 53 (2007): 17–36.

82 On Johannine "playing" with genre, see K. B. Larsen, *Recognizing the Stranger: Recognition Scenes in the Gospel of John* (BIS 93; Leiden: Brill, 2008); R. Sheridan, "John's Gospel and Modern Genre Theory: The Farewell Discourse (John 13–17) as a Test Case," *ITQ* 75 (2010): 287–99.

83 Plato, *Resp.* 3.393d; Aristotle, *Poet.* 1, 1447a15; 6, 1449b27. Cf. Attridge, "Gospel of John," 33–34.

84 Attridge, "Gospel of John," 38–39. The placement of John in the category of μιμήσις implies a different view of historicity (i.e., movement from the particular [history] towards the universal [poetry], *Poet.* 9, 1451b6–9) following "probability and necessity" (κατὰ τὸ εἰκὸς ἤ τὸ ἀναγκαῖον). Cf. anon., *Treatise on Comedy* 1–2.

85 That the Gospel authors knew and read scriptural texts is clear from the varied citations in their compositions. On the use of Scripture in the Gospels, see R. B. Hays, *Echoes of Scripture in the Gospels* (Waco: Baylor University Press, 2016).

jah narrative contains miracle stories and concludes with a dramatic death scene. The same could be said about the Moses material in the Pentateuch. The book of Nehemiah has an autobiographical character and may show the influence of Persian literary models.[86] To exclude these scriptural narratives from discussion gives the wrong impression that they are not integral to the composition of the works.[87] Although I think that the Gospel authors were influenced by Greco-Roman *bioi*, they did not eschew their sacred texts or features typical of Jewish composition, especially localized oral traditions regarding individuals.[88] Rather, they brought them into contact with a Greek literary form to create distinctive, atypical biographies.

The perceived special nature of Jesus—being "son of God" (all Gospels), born by the Holy Spirit (Matthew and Luke), and/or one with God since the beginning (John)—influenced the makeup of the composition. Although Jesus' ministry and death are presented in words and deeds that he challenges his disciples to emulate (Mark 8:34–38; Matt 16:24–28; 28:19–20; Luke 9:23–27), the actions of Jesus cannot be reproduced, because he has a unique place within the wider narrative of God's redemptive plan, as the authors claim by their invocation of Scripture. Accordingly, although Jesus' life acts as a model,[89] there is no expectation on the part of the authors that the reader would be the same as Jesus. Rather, through the gift of the Holy Spirit, the reader is to follow in the footsteps of the disciples by modeling Jesus to others and spreading the "good news" of what God has accomplished through him (cf. Luke 6:40). The larger worldview expands the scope of these works and could be viewed as an example of *macrologia*. This theological perspective is not found in other, contemporary Greco-Roman biographies, but is an element of a Jewish worldview that has been incorporated into the genre of the dominant culture.

Similarly, the claim that a work participates in biography does not imply that influences from other literary forms are not evident. The close relationship of history and biography allows for historiographical elements to be included

86 Cf. Momigliano, *Development*, 35–37; J. Van Seters, *In Search of History: Historiography in the Ancient World and the Origins of Biblical History* (New Haven: Yale University Press, 1983), 186–87 (for Egyptian influence).

87 On this important point, see L. Alexander, "What Are the Gospels?" in S. C. Barton, ed., *The Cambridge Companion to the Gospels* (Cambridge: Cambridge University Press, 2006), 13–33; Köstenberger, "Genre," 440–44. Some authors, such as Luke, used individuals depicted in Jewish Scripture as literary models for their characters (e.g., the parallels between Elizabeth and Hannah).

88 For example, the Gospel authors (although to a lesser extent the author of Luke) all continue the Jewish tradition of literary anonymity, a practice that was not prominent in Greek and Latin literary circles.

89 Jesus in Luke provides a literary model for the disciples in Acts. See A. C. Clark, *Parallel Lives: The Relation of Paul to the Apostles in the Lucan Perspective* (Carlisle: Paternoster, 2001), 320–41.

easily into biographical works.[90] Likewise, novelistic or tragic elements can be and have been woven into biographies to create a richer literary texture. Each Gospel is a distinct work that has different literary affiliations based on the purpose and desire of the author. Although biography might be the primary genre of participation by the Gospels, no Gospel exactly matches scholarly reconstructions of the "standard" or prototypical *bios*. The creation of such an ideal would not last long in light of the practice of Hellenistic and Roman-era authors to actively experiment with literary composition. As a result, despite the common genre label, we are to expect variation, even among the Synoptic Gospels.

Excursus: Lives of the Prophets

The Lives of the Prophets could also be argued to participate in the genre of collected biography. This work, which is thought to have been written in the first century CE in Palestine, collects biographical information regarding biblical prophets and organizes them sequentially.[91] The work is bracketed by a brief preface and conclusion. The opening informs the reader that the work will cover "the names of the prophets, and where they are from, and where they died and how, and where they lie" (*praef.*), and the ending explains why other prophets are not included in the work and where the reader can go to find them (24:1).

The broad consensus that the work was composed not in Greek but in Hebrew or Aramaic precludes this work from this study.[92] Nevertheless, the increased interest in biographical material on biblical figures (especially origin, tribal affiliation, manner of death, tomb, etc.) enriches our discussion. In particular, the first-century date of the work aligns with the date of composition of the other biographical works discussed in this chapter. This could suggest that the rise in Jewish interest in biography was not solely a Greek-language phenomenon, but was more widely adopted by Jewish authors.[93]

90 Cf. Duff, *Plutarch's Lives*, 18–19; Hägg, *Art of Biography*, 268–72. Polybius, *Hist.* 10.21.8; Plutarch, *Alex.* 1.2; Dionysius of Halicarnassus, *Amm.* 1.3.15; Nepos, *Pel.* 1.1; cf. Lucian, *Hist.* 7 for the distinction between history and encomium.

91 D. R. A. Hare, "The Lives of the Prophets," in *OTP* 2.379–400; Schürer, *History*, 3.1.783–86. Contra D. Satran, *Biblical Prophets in Byzantine Palestine: Reassessing the Lives of the Prophets* (SVTP 11; Leiden: Brill, 1995), 121–28, who argues for a fourth-to-fifth-century CE date.

92 C. C. Torrey, ed. and trans., *The Lives of the Prophets: Greek Text and Translation* (Philadelphia: SBL, 1946), 7. For an argument that some portions are originally Greek, see Hare, "Lives of the Prophets," 380 (with references). This proposal is interesting, as it blurs the boundary between translation and composition, implying that the Greek text as it has come down to us could be viewed as a distinct (although related) text.

93 *Paraleipomena Jeremiou* (= 4 Baruch) is a first–to-second-century CE text that contains biographical elements on the character of Jeremiah. This anonymous text, possibly (but less likely) written in Greek, expands the Jeremianic narrative on the destruction of the first temple

Philo of Alexandria and Ancient Biographies

Philo was a Jewish native of Alexandria who wrote at the beginning of the Roman era.[94] He was thoroughly educated in Greek literature, possessing a deep knowledge of Platonic and Stoic philosophy, and employed an allegorical approach to the interpretation of Scripture.[95] Traditionally, Philo has not been recognized as a biographer by classical scholars, although this oversight is being rectified in recent publications.[96] In this section, we will evaluate *De Vita Mosis*, *De Abrahamo*, and *De Iosepho* through the lens of Greek biography, asking how Philo participated in this genre and adopted it to accommodate his Jewish material, interpretive approach, and larger writing projects.[97]

On the Life of Moses

Philo's *De Vita Mosis* (*On the Life of Moses*) is a two-book, individual biography identified as a βίος (1.1; 2.292), the purpose of which is to make the story of Moses, the greatest and most perfect of individuals, known to outsiders (1.1; cf. *Virt.* 52) and so rectify the intentional oversight of Greek authors (1.2).[98] Philo criticizes educated Greeks who employ their education to compose comedies and licentious fables (κωμῳδίας καὶ συβαριτικὰς ἀσελγείας) and do not

---

and has significant parallels to 2 Baruch and Lives of the Prophets 2:1–19. Cf. Adams, "Jeremiah in the Old Testament Apocrypha."

94 For a fuller discussion about Philo's personal background, see chapter 4.

95 F. Siegert, "Early Jewish Interpretation in a Hellenistic Style," in M. Saebø, ed., *Hebrew Bible / Old Testament: The History of Its Interpretation*, vol. 1, pt. 1, *Antiquity* (Göttingen: Vandenhoeck & Ruprecht, 1996), 163–64. Cf. S. Sandmel, *Philo of Alexandria: An Introduction* (Oxford: Oxford University Press, 1979), 19; Rajak, *Translation and Survival*, 241–42.

96 Cf. B. C. McGing, "Philo's Adaptation of the Bible in His Life of Moses," in B. C. McGing and J. Mossman, eds., *The Limits of Ancient Biography* (Swansea: Classical Press of Wales, 2006), 118; M. J. Edwards, "Biography and Biographic," in M. J. Edwards and S. Swain, eds., *Portraits: Biographical Representation in the Greek and Latin Literature of the Roman Empire* (Oxford: Clarendon, 1997), 229–30. Disappointingly, Philo is essentially absent from Hägg, *Art of Biography*.

97 Philo's *In Flaccum*, as it currently stands, has a number of biographical features and could possibly be read as a tragic biography. The reference to Sejanus at the beginning of the work (§1) and the reference to multiple sufferings at the end (§191) imply that the original was larger and likely included other individuals. Nevertheless, the focus on Flaccus' political life, his downfall (§§146–150), and his tragic death (§§180–190) could be viewed as participating in the genre of biography, even if the work also participates in different genres. For an interesting discussion of the parodied courtroom in *Flaccus*, see Niehoff, *Philo of Alexandria*, 26–28.

98 *Moses*' place in Philo's corpus is undefined and so allows for the possibility to view it as an independent work. Most scholars associate it with Philo's *Exposition*. E.g., Royce, "Works of Philo," 50–51; L. H. Feldman, *Philo's Portrayal of Moses in the Context of Ancient Judaism* (Notre Dame: University of Notre Dame Press, 2007), 19–27. For positive references to Moses in Greco-Roman literature, see L. H. Feldman, "Josephus' Portrait of Moses," *JQR* 82 (1992): 286–88. Niehoff rightly notes that almost all of Philo's treatises are directed at insiders, but *Moses* has a different outlook. Niehoff, *Philo on Jewish Identity*, 13.

use their gifts to preserve a record of virtuous men and praiseworthy lives (ἀγαθῶν ἀνδρῶν τε καὶ βίων ὑφήγησιν, 1.3).[99] By contrasting his biography with Greek comedies and sybaritic tales, Philo communicates to his readers the purpose of his work and how they should approach the text. Philo's use of biographical language (especially 1.3) and reference to an individual at the outset of the work (Μωυσέως τοῦ κατὰ μέν τινας νομοθέτου τῶν Ἰουδαίων, 1.1) encourage the reader to understand that this work is participating in the genre of biography.[100] This reading perspective is further reinforced at the end of the preface by the phrase "I begin where it is necessary to begin" (ἄρξομαι δ' ἀφ" οὗπερ ἀναγκαῖον ἄρξασθαι, 1.5), which implies an awareness of expected literary elements and organizational principles for biographies.

Moses commences with standard biographical *topoi* (e.g., preface, 1.1–4; ancestry, 1.5; appearance, 1.9, 15, 18),[101] chronologically tracing Moses' life as depicted in the Pentateuch. In book 1, Philo presents Moses as a philosopher-king (1.60–62, 148), evoking Platonic and Stoic ideas of "proper" kingship: one who was a νόμος ἔμψυχός τε καὶ λογικὸς ("law incarnate and spoken," 1.162; cf. 1.154; 2.2, 4).[102] In book 2, Philo departs from his chronological framework and switches to a thematic organization, based on Moses' fulfilling of three Jewish offices: lawgiver, high priest, and prophet (2.3, 292).[103] This change in narrative structure allows Philo to return to previously bypassed source material, such as creation, Lot, and Noah when praising Moses as a legislator (2.48–64) and the Red Sea narrative in his discussion of Moses' prophetic nature

99 Niehoff exceeds the evidence when she claims that "*Moses* responds directly to detractors, most probably Apion." Niehoff, *Philo of Alexandria*, 110.

100 Edwards claims that *Moses* is a "commentary on the biblical account" and so not recognized as a biography. This rigid division, however, is no longer supportable. Edwards, "Biography and Biographic," 229.

101 Cf. Adams, *Genre*, 257–60. For the structure of *Moses*, see McGing, "Philo's Adaptation," 134–37.

102 Plato (*Resp*. 5.473c–e; *Ep*. 7.326a–b) claims that it is only through this combination that both a nation and the world will attain peace. Cf. *Mos*. 2.44, in which the other nations would adopt Mosaic law. On the pairing of lawgiver and king, see Plato, *Ep*. 7.332b; *Symp*. 196c. Cf. S. Pearce, "King Moses: Notes on Philo's Portrait of Moses as an Ideal Leader in the Life of Moses," *MUSJ* 57 (2004): 37–74. For Stoic parallels, see E. R. Goodenough, "The Political Philosophy of Hellenistic Kingship," *YCS* 1 (1928): 53–102; H. Clifford, "Moses as Philosopher-Sage in Philo," in A. Graupner and M. Wolter, eds., *Moses in Biblical and Extra-biblical Tradition* (BZAW 372; Berlin: De Gruyter, 2007), 158; Niehoff, *Philo of Alexandria*, 114–15. On the association of king and prophet (μαντικόν) with being wise, see Arius Didymus, *Epit*. 11m (= *SVF* 3.617), 11s.

103 Feldman (*Philo's Portrayal of Moses*, 22–23) continues to propagate the anachronistic, dipartite understanding of biography when he claims that Philo's *Moses* I is basically "Plutarchian" in style, while *Moses* II is "Suetonian." Cf. C. Hywel, "Moses as Philosopher-Sage in Philo," in A. Graupner and M. Wolter, eds., *Moses in Biblical and Extra-biblical Traditions* (BZAW 372; Berlin: De Gruyter, 2007), 151–67.

(2.247–257).[104] The work concludes with the death of Moses (2.288–291), a discussion that would not have been appropriate in book 1, but is core for an individual biography.[105]

The dual structure of Philo's *Moses* resonates with a discussion by Quintilian on the two ways to discuss character: chronologically and thematically (*Inst.* 3.7.15). In the former, one traces the life of the individual through childhood, school, and adulthood, recording important words and deeds. In the latter, words and deeds are also recounted, but examples of virtues are gathered together under specific topics, disrupting chronological flow.[106] The dual nature of Philo's *Moses*, in which the first part of the work is chronological and the second is topical, brings both organizational principles together into one work; a compositional choice that is atypical in extant biographies and represents a unique literary expression.[107]

Philo's *Life of Moses* draws heavily from the Pentateuch for his material (1.4; 2.292),[108] leading some scholars to argue that parts of *Moses* could be understood as rewritten Scripture.[109] These arguments correctly highlight the close parallels between *Moses* and Scripture and Philo's clear dependency. What is less obvious is the view that *Moses* does not also participate in biography. Works regularly participate in multiple genres, and *Moses* can satisfactorily

104 Moses fills similar roles in book 1. For example, Philo states that Moses spoke prophetically when defending the seven daughters of Jethro, the Midianite priest, in 1.57. This, however, contradicts Philo's claim in 2.258 that Moses began his work as a prophet at the Red Sea.

105 For examples, see Adams, *Genre*, 260.

106 For intentional chronological changes in ancient biographies, see Keener, *Gospel of John*, 1.518; C. Cooper, "Phainias' Historiographical and Biographical Method: Chronology and Dramatization," in O. Hellmann and D. C. Mirhady, eds., *Phaenias of Eresus: Text, Translation, and Discussion* (New Brunswick, N.J.: Transaction Publishers, 2015), 235–71.

107 The pairing of chronological life with topical *synkrisis* by Plutarch could be seen as another (albeit different and later) example of this pairing. Quintilian (*Inst.* 3.7.10) recognizes that variety is needed when praising people. On the importance of deeds matching words, see Seneca, *Ep.* 20.1–2.

Geljon and Damgaard suggest that book 2 of *Moses* could be viewed as Moses in writing, with parallels to biographical works of philosophers that discuss an author's literary outputs after recounting their life (e.g., Porphyry's *On the Life of Plotinus*). This is an intriguing suggestion and has some potential. Cf. A. C. Geljon, *Philonic Exegesis in Gregory of Nyssa's "De Vita Moysis"* (BJS 333; SPhiloM 5; Atlanta: Scholars Press, 2002), 37–46; F. Damgaard, "Philo's Life of Moses and 'Rewritten Bible,'" in J. Zsengellér, ed., *"Rewritten Bible" after Fifty Years: Texts, Terms, or Techniques? A Last Dialogue with Geza Vermes* (JSJSup 166; Leiden: Brill, 2014), 235–36.

108 In contrast to the Gospels, which place the life of Jesus within the larger historical narrative of God's redemptive plan, Philo's *Moses* excises biographical elements from a larger composition and stitches them together. This action could be viewed as *brachylogia*.

109 P. Borgen, "Philo of Alexandria: Reviewing and Rewriting Biblical Material," *SPhiloA* 9 (1997): 37–53; Damgaard, "Philo's Life of Moses." With regard to genre, I am not convinced that it is possible to treat book 1 separately from book 2, as is functionally assumed by Damgaard. Niehoff describes Philo as a "biographer in *Midrashic* or exegetical mode." M. Niehoff, "Philo and Plutarch as Biographers: Parallel Responses to Roman Stoicism," *GRBS* 52 (2012): 383.

fulfill criteria for both literary forms. Understanding *Moses* as participating in rewritten Scripture does not take away from viewing *Moses* biographically, but enriches it by recognizing that the work engages with multiple literary constructs and models, providing some rationale for why certain elements of *Moses* differ from standard *bios* features.[110]

Philo's use of allegory in *Moses*, including imagery (1.188–190) and symbolic interpretations (2.115), differs from the composition practices of prototypical Greek biographies. Almost all of his allegorical readings are found in his discussions of the tabernacle and priests in book 2: the numerical significance of the pillars in the tabernacle (2.81–83), the meaning behind the high priest's vestments (2.117–130), and the description of the nuts on Aaron's budding rod (2.180–186).[111] In the chronological depiction of Moses' life, Philo only employs allegory once (i.e., his discussion of the burning bush, 1.65–70; cf. 2.99). Here, Philo does not follow his usual allegorical practice, representing the bush as a representation of the nation's condition at the time and not in a spiritual or theological way (1.67; cf. *Fug.* 161–163). The minimal use of allegory in the first half differentiates Philo's *Moses* from most of his other works (including his other biographies, see below), aligning it more closely with the practice of Greco-Roman biographers, who rarely engage with allegorical interpretations. The inclusion of allegory in book 2 represents a change in approach and parallels, not incidentally, the shift to a topical structure.[112]

Philo's biography is also distinct in its focus on characters and objects beyond the protagonist, such as the content of the law and the collective character of the Hebrew people. In typical individual biographies, the author focuses on the protagonist for the majority of the text; s/he becomes the primary subject who acts or speaks most often and is the center of discussion by other characters.[113] Philo begins with a strong focus on Moses' life (1.1–95). How-

110 Scholars have attempted to interpret *Life of Moses* through different genres: encomium: P. L. Shuler, "Philo's Moses and Matthew's Jesus: A Comparative Study in Ancient Literature," *SPhiloA* 2 (1990): 86–103, followed by Feldman, *Philo's Portrayal of Moses*, 18–19; composite eulogy (narrative eulogy and rhetorical panegyric): A. Priessnig, "Die literarische Form der Patriarchenbiographien des Philon von Alexandrien," *MGWJ* 7 (1929): 143–55; aretalogy: M. Hadas and M. Smith, *Heroes and Gods: Spiritual Biographies in Antiquity* (New York: Harper, 1965), 129–60; biography/philosophical treatise (books 1 and 2, respectively): Geljon, *Philonic Exegesis*, 27, 31.

111 Feldman, *Philo's Portrayal of Moses*, 23.

112 Despite these changes, the unity of the work is not undermined. Cf. Geljon, *Philonic Exegesis*, 44. On *Moses* as an allegory of the migration of the soul, see Damgaard, "Philo's Life of Moses," 240–42.

113 Adams, *Genre*, 125–32; R. A. Burridge, "The Genre of Acts—Revisited," in S. Walton et al., eds., *Readings Acts Today: Essays in Honour of Loveday C. A. Alexander* (LNTS 427; London: T&T Clark, 2011), 11–18; Burridge, *Gospels*, 110–13, 189–93. P. Cox, "Strategies of Representa-

ever, following his depiction of Moses' return to Egypt, Philo dedicates large sections of text to recounting the attitudes of the Hebrew people (e.g., 1.191–195, 227–242), the actions of God (e.g., 1.130–146, 206–209), and the battles between the Hebrew people and the nations along their route (1.239–318). Moses is still part of the account, but at times he appears to take a secondary role to the broader theme of God's redemption of the Jewish people, a feature prominent in Philo's source text.[114]

A similar pattern is found in book 2. Following a brief, secondary preface (2.1–7), Philo recounts Moses' legal achievements, beginning with the content and quality of the law and its translation (2.13–65). Praise of the law naturally highlights the worthiness of the lawgiver (*Mos.* 2.45; Quintilian, *Inst.* 3.7.18; cf. Mal 3:24), but Moses and his actions are not always in view (especially when discussing the translation, 2.25–44). In the section on Moses as priest (2.66–186), a majority of the text is devoted to the tabernacle, its components and dedication, and the selection of the priests and their vestments (2.74–158) and not on Moses specifically. At times, Moses' absence from the narrative is so noticeable that Philo needs to reintroduce him: "Now the leader of the Hebrews, Moses . . ." (ὁ μὲν οὖν ἡγεμὼν τῶν Ἑβραίων Μωυσῆς, 1.243). Philo's use of and adherence to the pentateuchal texts, which have a strong narrative focus on the Hebrew people, is the likely explanation of this divided attention.[115] This difference from typical biographical practice provides evidence of a Jewish author exploiting the flexibility of a Greek genre to accommodate his Jewish source material.

Moses is the only individual properly discussed in the treatise. In fact, only six other individuals are mentioned by name in the narrative: three favorably (Joshua [1.216], Phineas [1.301, 313], Zelophehad [2.234]), and three unfavorably (Chananes, king of the Canaanites [1.250]; Sihon, king of the Amorites [1.258]; and Balak, the king who hired the unnamed Balaam [1.263]).[116] This absence is surprising, as many people alluded to in *Moses* are important to the biblical narrative and are discussed at length in Philo's other treatises (e.g., Jacob and Esau, 1.242; Noah, 2.60). Philo also omits the names of Moses' parents; an atypical decision in a biography, as noble ancestry is an important

tion in Collected Biography," in T. Hägg and P. Rousseau, eds., *Greek Biography and Panegyric in Late Antiquity* (Berkeley: University of California Press, 2000), 244.

114 The best example of this in the first book is the extended focus on Balaam and his three oracles regarding the Hebrew people (1.263–94).

115 For a detailed table of Philo's use of Scripture in *Moses*, see G. E. Sterling, "Thunderous Silence: The Omission of the Sinai Pericope in Philo of Alexander," *JSJ* 49 (2018): 16–20. In particular, Sterling highlights the absence of Sinai and offers a universalizing rationale.

116 Abraham, Isaac, and Jacob are mentioned in God's speech from the burning bush (1.76), but their names are absent when their characters are discussed. Joshua's name is not mentioned in other passages (e.g., scouting the land, 1.234).

indicator of future greatness. Similarly, Aaron, despite being the sole actor in initiating three of the plagues (1.97–112), is referred to only as "Moses' brother."[117]

Despite the fact that his opponents are not named, Moses faces opposition during his career, both from individuals (e.g., Pharaoh, Balam, Korah) and people groups (e.g., Egyptians, Phoenicians, Canaanites). In these contests, Moses is shown to have navigated all challenges successfully. Philo highlights Moses' prowess through *synkrisis* with other *thaumaturges* and magicians who could have become literary comparators.[118] The primary antagonist is Balaam, who is associated with magical arts (1.276, 283, 285), but lacks noble motives and exploits divine dreams and visions for personal gain (1.266, 286).[119] Despite previous success, Balaam's abilities are immediately brought into question when his animal has a divine vision and he, ironically for a seer, sees nothing.[120] Moreover, his character is plagued by failings, and by the end of his vignette he is thoroughly censored, despite having spoken true, divine oracles. Philo's incorporation of encomiastic and rhetorical features supports his praise and censure categories (applied to Moses and Balaam, respectively), allowing Philo to evaluate each individual's character and to establish model lives to emulate and avoid.[121]

The absence of named characters is atypical in ancient biographies, in which authors provide names of secondary individuals for a variety of reasons: to situate the work historically, to fill in narrative details, and/or to provide

117 Cf. Adams, *Genre*, 257–58. Philo does not mention any of Moses' family by name: parents (1.7), sister (1.12, 180), brother (1.97; 2.142), wife (1.59), or sons (1.150; 2.142).

118 Philo, *Hypoth.* 8.6.2; cf. Josephus, *C. Ap.* 2.145; Apuleius, *Apol.* 90; Origen, *Cels.* 5.41, cf. 1.23, 45; 3.5; Strabo, *Geogr.* 16.2.43; Lucian, *Podag.* 173. For the rhetorical function of *synkrisis*, see Theon, *Prog.* 112–115; Ps.-Hermogenes, *Prog.* 18–20; Aphthonius, *Prog.* 42–44; Nicolaus the Sophist, *Prog.* 59–63; Quintilian, *Inst.* 2.4.20–21.

119 Cf. also Korah, *Mos.* 2.275–287. Feldman, *Philo's Portrayal of Moses*, 188–96; G. S. Gasparro, "Mosè e Balaam, *Propheteia* e *Mantiké*: Modalità et segni della rivelazione nel *De Vita Mosis*," in A. M. Mazzanti and F. Calabi, eds., *La rivelazione in Filone di Alessandria: Natura, legge, storia; Atti del VII Convegno di studi del Gruppo italiano di ricerca su Origene e la tradizione alessandrina (Bologna 29–30 settembre 2003)* (BdA 2; Villa Verucchio: Pazzini, 2004), 33–74; T. Seland, "The Expository Use of the Balaam Figure in Philo's *De vita Moysis*," *SPhiloA* 28 (2016): 321–48. For other discussions of Balaam by Philo, see *Cher.* 32–33; *Det.* 71; *Deus* 181; *Conf.* 159; *Migr.* 113–115; and *Mut.* 202.

120 H. Remus, "Moses and the Thaumaturges: Philo's *De Vita Mosis* as a Rescue Operation," *LTP* 62 (1996): 671–72.

121 Remus, "Moses and the Thaumaturges," 671. See Philo, *Mos.* 1.158; cf. Aristotle, *Rhet.* 1.3.3–6 (1358b–1359a), 1.9.1 (1366a), 1.9.32–33 (1367b); Cicero, *Inv.* 2.59.177–78; Ps.-Cicero, *Rhet. Her.* 3.6.11–7.15; Plato, *Gorg.* 483b; Quintilian, *Inst.* 3.7.1. There are many other examples of rhetoric in *Moses*, e.g., speeches in character (i.e., *prosopopoeia*): Moses' parents questioning why they had a child (1.11); Moses before sending the twelve to explore the promised land (1.222–226); Moses about why not to fight with certain people groups (1.244–245); Moses after the victory over Balak (1.322–327); and Moses at the Red Sea (2.251–252).

opponents as literary foils for the protagonist.[122] Nevertheless, withholding names has an important literary effect, as through this practice Philo minimizes any potential comparison with positively viewed characters (e.g., Aaron) and creates a set of "faceless" opponents. In identifying only Moses and refusing to provide other names—names that he clearly had from his use of the LXX—Philo keeps the focus on his protagonist, emphasizing his importance; he is the only one worthy of remembering and therefore modeling one's life after. This helps Philo achieve his intended goal of establishing Moses as the pinnacle of human virtue and achievement (1.3, 154) and rectifying the suppression of his memory (μνήμης) by Greek writers (1.2).[123] This omission further results in different reading experiences; insiders would be able to fill in details from their knowledge of Jewish Scripture, whereas outsiders would not.[124] Nevertheless, the outsider does not need the names of the characters to understand the narrative.[125] Philo makes it clear that Moses is superior to all people (though clearly he is not a god)[126] and as such is to be adopted as an exemplar for all readers in their pursuit of virtue and godly perfection.

On Abraham

Philo's *De Abrahamo* (*On Abraham*) differs from *Moses* in its structure and organizing principles. Unlike *Moses*, which is not explicitly integrated within a specific series, Philo's *Abraham* is part of a larger discussion on Genesis and a continuation of his "former treatise" (i.e., *On the Creation*, *Abr.* 1–2).[127] Philo also expands the scope of the work, going beyond one individual life by recounting the lives of Abraham, Isaac, and Jacob as collected symbols of virtue (*Abr.* 52–54).[128]

122 The practice of omitting names goes beyond the minimal naming of females in Greek biographies (cf. Hägg, *Art of Biography*, 5).

123 Regarding Moses' education, Philo claims that Moses mastered every culture's lore and literature (*Mos.* 1.23–24). Regarding Moses' mind, Philo states, "Whether it was human or divine or a mixture of both, so utterly unlike was it to the majority, soaring about them and exalted to a grander height" (1.27). Philo also describes Moses as having attained the four primary virtues necessary for excellence in lawmaking (2.9–10), "the best of all lawgivers in all countries" (2.12), and a "prophet of the highest quality" (2.188). Cf. *Opif.* 8.

124 It would be expected that Jewish readers would recognize whom Philo was describing. A similar phenomenon is found in Wisdom of Solomon (e.g., 6:22–7:6 and 10:1–21). For discussion see S. Cheon, "Anonymity in the Wisdom of Solomon," *JSP* 18 (1998): 111–19.

125 The absence of names might also be for the ease of non-Jewish readers, who might struggle with Hebrew names and so be distracted from the true focus. McGing, "Philo's Adaptation," 132. Cf. Josephus, *Ant.* 1.129; 2.176; 11.68.

126 Cf. *Mos.* 1.158. For a thorough discussion, see I. W. Scott, "Is Philo's Moses a Divine Man?" *SPhiloA* 14 (2002): 87–111.

127 On *Abraham*'s place in the *Exposition*, see Royse, "Works of Philo," 45–50.

128 For this pairing in other treatises, see *Sobr.* 65; *Congr.* 34–38; *Mos.* 1.76; *Praem.* 24–51, 57–66. For further discussion see S. A. Adams, "Abraham in Philo of Alexandria," in S. A.

Philo does not immediately discuss his titular character. Rather, he begins this treatise with a triad of lives (Enos, Enoch, and Noah), each representing a different aspect of virtue (hope, repentance, and perfection, respectively; *Abr.* 7–47; *Praem.* 13–23). In these vignettes Philo provides minimal details about the individuals' lives from Genesis, choosing instead to emphasize their symbolic value of graded stages of the soul (*Abr.* 47) and to contrast their actions with those of their contemporaries, who pursued evil (*Abr.* 1, 36; cf. *Praem.* 2).[129] In collecting these lives together, Philo moves beyond the individual to a wider interpretation of Scripture, which is more than the sum of each part. Although the triad functions as the model for the second, larger discussion of Abraham, Isaac, and Jacob, this is an atypical way to begin a biography in antiquity.

According to Philo, the patriarchs represent three means by which a soul can acquire virtue—teaching, nature, and practice, respectively (*Abr.* 52)—although each possesses all three qualities (*Abr.* 53).[130] Each character provides a model for a different path to virtue, but Philo highlights the importance of viewing them as a collective: "There is something to be said about them taken as a whole which must not be omitted" (*Abr.* 49). In particular, the characters' genetic relationship offers insight into the nature of virtue and their association with God's name (*Abr.* 50–51), with their lives presenting a "living law" for others to follow (ἔμψυχοι καὶ λογικοὶ νόμοι, *Abr.* 5).[131] This need for viewing the triad as a unified whole encourages the reader to view *Abraham* and the now-lost treatises of *On Isaac* and *On Jacob* as a collected biography in three volumes.

Philo's discussion of Abraham is divided into two unequal parts: right deeds towards God (εὐσέβεια, *Abr.* 60–207; cf. 262–276) and right deeds towards humans (φιλανθρωπία, *Abr.* 208–261).[132] Within this thematic orga-

Adams and Z. Domoney-Lyttle, eds., *Abraham in Jewish and Early Christian Literature* (LSTS; London: Bloomsbury, 2019), 75–92.

129 For a detailed discussion of the theological and philosophical backgrounds to these characters, see Goodenough, *By Light, Light*, 121–52.

130 Cf. Arius Didymus, *Epit.* 5b5.

131 On Philo's particular use of Abraham as *exemplum*, see A. Y. Reed, "The Construction of Subversion of Patriarchal Perfection: Abraham and Exemplarity in Philo, Josephus, and the Testament of Abraham," *JSJ* 40 (2009): 192–95.

132 Termini proposed that the entire work of *De Abrahamo* is structured on piety and humanity; the division of the two Mosaic tablets in *De decalogo*. C. Termini, "The Historical Part of the Pentateuch According to Philo of Alexandria: Biography, Genealogy, and the Philosophical Meaning of the Patriarchal Lives," in N. Calduch-Benages and J. Liesen, eds., *Deuterocanonical and Cognate Literature Yearbook* (Berlin: De Gruyter, 2006), 285. The emphasis on the law is also seen through the connections between *De Abrahamo* and *De opificio mundi* expressed by Philo (*Abr.* 2, 13). For a detailed outline of *Abraham*, its structure and use of Scripture, see D. T. Runia, "The Place of *De Abrahamo* in Philo's Oeuvre," *SPhiloA* 20 (2008): 138–39.

nization, Philo presents Abraham's life in altered chronology.[133] In the first section, Philo broadly follows the events of the Genesis narrative, identifying specific actions of Abraham's life that demonstrate his positive relationship with the divine.[134] The Genesis chronology is especially disrupted when Philo switches to the second section: Abraham's φιλανθρωπία. According to Philo, Abraham's connection with and actions towards Lot, including rescuing him from the four kings, exemplifies his disposition towards other humans (208–244). The discussion of Sarah's death and Abraham's fortitude in overcoming his grief (255–261) provides a transition to the conclusion of the work. Interestingly, Philo does not recount Abraham's death, which would be expected in an individual biography but is less common in collected biographies.[135] The treatise concludes with Philo praising Abraham's faith and calling him "elder" (262–274), aspects that also come from earlier in the Genesis narrative, but are appropriate for a concluding statement.

Philo applies an allegorical reading strategy to each of the events in Abraham's life.[136] This explicit blending of literal and allegorical interpretations is a distinctive aspect of *Abraham* and differentiates it, not only from extant Greek biographies, but also from Philo's *Moses*.[137] This exegetical pairing is regularly found in Philo's *Quaestiones*, suggesting that Philo applied an established interpretive method to the construction of his biography.[138] This not only shows the flexibility of the genre and the ingenuity of the author, but, as far as we can tell, results in a unique expression and structure of a biographical work.

Although Philo draws on Genesis for details about Abraham's life, he is not constrained by a singular interpretation or by the limitations of his source material. Philo provides interpretations that are foreign to his original text and

133 Note the temporal reference by Philo (*Abr.* 89).

134 E.g., leaving Chaldea (60–67), migrating to Egypt (89–98), giving hospitality to the three guests (107–118), the near sacrifice of Isaac (167–177). Major transition breaks include *Abr.* 47, 48, 60, 68, 89, 99, 107, 119, 133, 147, 167, 200, 208, 217, 225, 236, 255, 262 and are often marked with μέν, μὲν οὖν, or μέντοι.

135 Adams, *Genre*, 141, 237–42. It is possible that this scene was included in *Isaac*, as elements of Gen 24–25 are central to Isaac's narrative and were initiated by Abraham. Philo also lacks any discussion of Abraham's birth or childhood. Although often included, this is not required for biographies (e.g., Mark) and fits the narrative in his source material.

136 E.g., *Abr.* 68, 88, 119, 131, 200, 217, and 236. For discussion, see Runia, "Place of *De Abrahamo*," 139–40. The notable exception is the lack of allegorical interpretation for Sarah's death (*Abr.* 262–267).

137 The literal Abraham is absent in most of Philo's corpus. *Quaestiones* contains some material, but there is little expansion of the biblical text. Philo also blends literal and allegorical interpretations of Abraham in *Virt.* 211–219.

138 For discussion of Philo's *Quaestiones*, see chapter 4.

amplifies aspects that are important for his argument.[139] For example, the explicit praising of individuals is prominent, especially at the end of *Abraham*. First, Philo praises the eyes as the dominant sense faculty (*Abr.* 158), highlighting their role in bringing light into the body and for facilitating sight, the most important sense for wisdom and philosophy (*Abr.* 164). Unsurprisingly, Abraham is presented as the object of praise (*Abr.* 178, 191, 217), having lived a virtuous life, achieved a great act of piety (*Abr.* 167–207), and conquered grief (*Abr.* 255). Less expected is the encomium for Sarah (*Abr.* 247–254), as she is not the main character of the work, but is presented as a partner to Abraham and his endeavors.[140] Sarah is named only twice in the entire work (*Abr.* 99, 206), and is subsequently referenced through her relationship with Abraham (i.e., "wife," γυνή) (e.g., *Abr.* 168, 245), even in her encomium. The praising (or criticizing) of individuals is not foreign to Genesis, but Philo extends it and makes it much more explicit.

The withholding of names is another difference from Genesis and applies to all of the characters with whom Abraham engages, not just Sarah. Philo names Isaac once (*Abr.* 201), and this takes place in the interpretation section following the retelling of Genesis (*Abr.* 167–177).[141] Philo does not mention Abraham's ancestors (*Abr.* 62), Pharaoh (*Abr.* 93), Lot (*Abr.* 212, 229), Melchizedek (*Abr.* 235), Hagar (*Abr.* 251–253), or Ishmael (*Abr.* 254), despite recounting their biblical narratives.[142] The only individual besides Abraham whom Philo regularly names is Moses. But here Moses is not presented as a character, but as the author of the source material (*Abr.* 13, 181, 262; cf. 5, 54, 56).[143] The minimizing of references to other characters parallels the practice in *Moses* and focuses the reader's attention on the protagonist.

Philo concludes *Abraham* with biography language: τοιοῦτος ὁ βίος τοῦ πρώτου καὶ ἀρχηγέτου τοῦ ἔθνους ἐστίν (*Abr.* 276).[144] By highlighting the founding role that Abraham had in establishing the Jewish people, Philo

139 In addition, potentially problematic and/or specifically Jewish elements are omitted: Sarah being called Abraham's sister (*Abr.* 93–98), circumcision, and covenant promises.

140 See most recently, Niehoff, *Philo of Alexandria*, 133–41; Adams, "Abraham in Philo," 86–88. Philo also praises Indian women who embrace immolation and so overcome fear of death (*Abr.* 183).

141 Philo mentions Abraham, Isaac, and Jacob as a collective in *Abr.* 51–52, but this is part of the prologue to the collected biography. Israel is also mentioned in *Abr.* 57.

142 Philo does name the Sodomites twice (*Abr.* 133, 226).

143 Philo's references to Moses could imply that his audience would know who he is and so would recognize the authority of the source material. For ancient examples, see Adams, *Genre*, 145–47.

144 Cf. *Opif.* 170. Priessnig ("Die literarische Form") labeled *De Abrahamo* a "theological biography." Sandmel claims that this biography is of "Hellenistic form"; however, he does not further delineate this description. S. Sandmel, *Philo's Place in Judaism: A Study of Conceptions of Abraham in Jewish Literature* (New York: Ktav, 1971), 105–6 n. 14.

reinforces the rationale for why this individual was worthy of a biography; Abraham's deeds and virtuous life provide a perfect model for other seekers of God to emulate (*Abr.* 5, 275–276).[145] The fact that a large portion of the text does not specifically recount episodes of Abraham's life, but allegorically interprets them, does not necessary discount this treatise from participating in biography. The unpacking of anecdotes through explanation was an evolving element of *bioi* and supports the overarching purpose of a biography: to provide examples to emulate and/or avoid.[146] In the case of *Abraham*, Philo claims that his subject will provide instruction and inspiration for the reader's moral improvement (*Abr.* 4), not only by depicting his "words and deeds," but also by discerning the spiritual meaning behind them (*Abr.* 5–6). For Philo, both are important for understanding virtue. As a result, Philo emphasizes that his interpretation of Abraham's narrative is not a "crafted fable" (πλάσμα μύθου, *Abr.* 243), which would undermine the purpose and exemplary nature of Abraham.[147] Rather, Philo claims that these episodes are historical and so could be reproduced by his readers.

Abraham, however, is not the only example of virtue, but is grouped with Isaac and Jacob, who represent spiritual laws endowed with life and reason (*Abr.* 5). The loss of the two subsequent treatises encourages us to hold loosely our understanding of the works' genre. Nevertheless, the intentional grouping of multiple individuals treated in sequence suggests that Philo wrote a collected biography. This literary form is not unique to Philo, but if *Abraham* and its blending of narrative and philosophical discussions are indicative of the two lost works, this collection of three biographies was an important example of the diversity of Jewish and Greek biographies in the Hellenistic and Roman eras.[148]

On Joseph

Philo opens *De Iosepho (On Joseph)* with a reference to his previous trio of biographies (*Ios.* 1), claiming that Joseph represents a fourth type of life, that

145 Philo claims that Abraham filled many roles over his life: sage: *Abr.* 202; *Sobr.* 55–57; prophet: *Somn.* 1.193–195; king: *Abr.* 261; *Mut.* 152; *Virt.* 216. For a further discussion, see Sandmel, *Philo's Place in Judaism*, 168–85; Adams, "Abraham in Philo"; A. Mendelson, *Secular Education in Philo of Alexandria* (Cincinnati: HUC Press, 1982), 62–65.

146 Niehoff, *Philo of Alexandria*, 115–19; Hägg, *Art of Biography*, 76, 314–15.

147 Cf. Philo, *Opif.* 157; *Det.* 125; *Congr.* 61–62; Isocrates, *Antid.* 277; Diodorus Siculus, *Bibl.* 1.67.11; 4.70.1; Plutarch, *Thes.* 28.2; Livy, *Urba Condita* 1. *praef.* 10. In *Mos.* 2.271, Philo uses πλάσμα μύθου as something that would obstruct one's vision of the truth. Cf. Adams, "Fables in Philo."

148 G. E. Sterling, "Philo's *De Abrahamo*: Introduction," *SPhiloA* 20 (2008): 130. Feldman claims that Philo's biographies were "the first Jewish biographies." Feldman (*Philo's Portrayal of Moses*, 23) overlooks the Gospels by stating that after Philo and Josephus' autobiography "we do not find biographies written by Jews until modern times."

of the ideal statesman (*Ios.* 2). *Joseph*, however, does not fit into the original framework established in *Abraham*, as a political life cannot in itself produce a life of excellence, which comes from learning, nature, and practice.[149] Rather, the argument in *Joseph* is that the political life threatens the life of excellence (*Ios.* 9, 36), although with proper training one can resist its influences and lead an upstanding and exemplary life (*Ios.* 40–53, especially 46–48).[150]

In *Joseph*, Philo follows the practice established in *Abraham* by tracing the life of the patriarch and employing a literal-allegorical interpretive pairing.[151] However, in *Joseph* there are important, if minor, differences. First, Philo follows the Genesis chronology much more faithfully. Second, in contrast to the two-part division of *Abraham* (εὐσέβεια and φιλανθρωπία), the structure of *Joseph* is based on the three divisions of statecraft—sheepherding, household management, and self-control (τόν τε ποιμενικὸν καὶ τὸν οἰκονομικὸν καὶ τὸν καρτερικόν, *Ios.* 54). Third, *Joseph* contains fewer allegorical sections (*Ios.* 28–36, 58–79, 125–156), although all follow a literal retelling of the Genesis narrative.[152] Fourth, unlike in *Abraham*, where Philo resolves an issue before providing an allegorical interpretation, the first two allegorical sections in *Joseph* expound a problem that had just been raised prior to recounting its narrative resolution, creating tension within the work. This tension allows Philo to compare the nature of the political world with that of piety and to show how a person of virtue who trusts in God can navigate a potentially compromising situation successfully.[153]

In terms of literary form and style, Philo's tracing of the protagonist's political life from youth to death aligns with prototypical biographies.[154] Philo's structure and use of allegory here are, once again, atypical compared to other Greco-Roman biographies, although the differences are less conspicuous than in *Abraham*. In contrast, Philo appears to make greater use of rhetorical elements in *Joseph*, pairing praise and censure categories for the evaluation of character. In this way, Philo makes use of his authorial freedom to adapt biog-

149 J. M. Bassler, "Philo on Joseph: The Basic Coherence of *De Iosepho* and *De Somniis II*," *JSJ* 16 (1985): 244. Joseph is also missing in the list of persons in *Cher.* 40.

150 Cf. M. Niehoff, *The Figure of Joseph in Post-biblical Jewish Literature* (AGJU 16; Leiden: Brill, 1992), 54–83.

151 Philo also suppresses the names of other characters in the text: brothers (*passim*), Potiphar ("eunuch," *Ios.* 37), Jacob (*Ios.* 163).

152 Niehoff, *Joseph*, 66–78.

153 F. Frazier, "Les visages de Joseph dans le *De Josepho*," *SPhiloA* 14 (2002): 1–30. The focus develops through the three allegorical sections, beginning with a strong emphasis on the political, which gives way to a comparison between reason and irrationality. Bassler, "Philo on Joseph," 247–48.

154 D. T. Runia, "Philo, Alexandrian and Jew," in *Exegesis and Philosophy: Studies on Philo of Alexandria* (Aldershot: Variorum, 1990), 6.

raphy and incorporate other literary features in order to construct his desired portrait.[155]

Moses, *Abraham*, and *Joseph* in *The Exposition of the Law*

One possible challenge to viewing *Moses*, *Abraham*, and *Joseph* as participating in the genre of biography is their inclusion in Philo's larger literary program of *The Exposition of the Law*.[156] Does (or should) our genre understanding change if we situate these works within a larger literary construction? Or, to put it differently, does the association of *Abraham* and *Joseph* with *On the Creation of the World*, *On the Special Laws*, and other expository texts erode our biographical understanding of these treatises?

These questions speak to the issues of genre plurality and embedded genres, topics discussed in chapter 5. Of primary concern for this chapter is whether or not Philo's *Exposition* should be viewed as a cohesive unit that requires genre consistency across treatises and so constrains genre options. The assumption of textual conformity of treatises within a series might be misguided, artificially requiring complete consistency when it is not required. Although modern scholars might question the viability of multiple genres within a series, Philo does not give any indication that his construction was problematic. This implies that Philo had an understanding of his broader composition that was not bound by strict genre conformity or identical models.

One possible explanation as to why genre diversity might have been acceptable to Philo is that he did not see the works as forming a unified whole. This perspective, however, is unlikely and is weakened by his reference to other, nonbiographical works (especially *Abr.* 1–2). More likely is the view that Philo understood his method of alternating literal and allegorical interpretations as being the dominant, unifying element and that other potential genre differences were less important and so did not undermine the unity of the series. The importance of the scriptural text to Philo should also not be underestimated. In following the texts of the Pentateuch closely, Philo allows the source text to determine the shape of his exposition. For instance, Philo's *Abraham* and *Joseph* are structured differently than the other works in the collection (i.e., on the life of individuals). Nevertheless, Philo's dependence on the scriptural text, which limits the purview of each treatise, is similar across the works; *Moses*, *Abraham*, and *Joseph* interpret only the Genesis passages

155 Shuler, "Philo's Moses and Matthew's Jesus," 102–3; Feldman, *Philo's Portrayal of Moses*, 23. Contra Siegert, "Early Jewish Interpretation," 163.

156 Our genre label for *Moses* is less influenced, as Philo does not explicitly place it within a larger literary program. Although see G. E. Sterling, "Philo of Alexandria's *Life of Moses*: An Introduction to the Exposition of the Law," *SPhiloA* 30 (2018): 31–45.

in which their protagonist is in focus. This diversity suggests that a cluster of formal features—in this case a methodological approach outworked through a particular structure and applied to a specific text—can unite multiple works and also provide space for genre variability among texts within a series.[157]

Philo likely modeled his *Exposition* on a work that participated in multiple genres and so viewed his composition as having a literary predecessor. In *Praem.* 1 Philo claims that the writings of Moses, although unified, are of three kinds (ἰδέαι): cosmological, historical, and legal (τήν μὲν περὶ κοσμοποιίας, τὴν δὲ ἱστορικήν, τὴν δὲ τρίτην νομοθετικήν). Philo also presents this view in *Mos.* 2.45–47, although in this section both the cosmological and the historical are joined and classified as history (and/or genealogy).[158] The specific genre divisions of the Pentateuch (i.e., cosmological, historical, and legal) are likely the literary models for Philo in his *Exposition*, with the lives of the patriarchs fulfilling the historical aspect.[159] Overall, the fact that Philo unapologetically presents the Pentateuch as having multiple genres implies that he had a theory of genre that was sufficiently flexible to allow for internal differentiation within a series and even within a work (e.g., Genesis).

Summary

The above discussions allow us to draw some conclusions about Philo's participation in ancient biography. First, in *Moses*, *Abraham*, and *Joseph* Philo displays an awareness of the broad contours of biographies, especially their need to focus on an individual's life and what made him/her worthy of discussion. The worthiness of the subject is directly tied to the purpose of a biography, which is to provide a model for the reader to emulate, a theme that is prominent in Philo's biographies (e.g., *Abr.* 4, 52–55; *Mos.* 1.1–4, 158–159).

Second, Philo recognizes that a biography can be organized in two primary ways, chronologically or thematically. Philo used both in his compositions

157 This perspective also assumes that there might be constraints on formal features (e.g., changes in meter, scope, etc.) for acceptable levels of coherence within the series.

158 A similar tripartite division is seen in Josephus, *Ant.* 1.18. Kamesar has argued that Philo's tripartite division of the Pentateuch is best understood in light of the scholastic literary theory of the Hellenistic age, as is represented by the later works of Diomedes and the *Tractatus Coislinianus*. According to Kamesar, Philo actively adopted Peripatetic theories of genre in order to claim that the Pentateuch was not myth (cf. LA 168; Aristobulus F2.10). The parallels Kamesar develops are plausible and reinforce the view that Philo's genre understanding is not separate from his literary environment. However, Kamesar does not discuss the possible rationale for viewing a collected work as having multiple genres. Kamesar, "Literary Genres," 145–56. Cf. Termini, "Historical Part."

159 The cosmological element corresponds to *On the Creation* and the legislative to *On the Decalogue* and *On the Special Laws*. Cf. A. Kamesar, "Biblical Interpretation in Philo," in A. Kamesar, ed., *The Cambridge Companion to Philo* (Cambridge: Cambridge University Press, 2009), 73–77.

and willingly blended the two when desired (*Moses*). At the macro level, Philo demonstrates knowledge of two different types of biography: individual (*Moses*) and collected (*Abraham*, *Joseph*). Philo's use of both types is important, as it provides one of the earliest examples of a single author using multiple forms of biography and so indicating a plurality of genre models and prototypical exemplars.

Third, Philo's biographies include elements that are not typically witnessed in Greco-Roman *bioi*. The most obvious example of this is Philo's use of allegorical interpretation, with the alternation between the literal retelling of the biblical narrative and its allegorical interpretation used as a major structural element in his *Abraham* and *Joseph*.[160] Another difference is Philo's suppression of names from his scriptural source, which limits the outside reader's ability to grasp the picture of the protagonist fully and to situate the events historically.

Fourth, by including *Abraham* and *Joseph* within a series that incorporated texts that participate in other genres, Philo shows the flexibility of ancient biographies and the way that authors could embed and combine texts at higher organizational levels. This is an important difference from extant collected biographies, whose authors only grouped biographies together to make a larger collection and did not include works of other genres.[161] Overall, Philo's biographies evidence the diversity and fluidity of ancient biography and show that at least one Jewish author was willing to adapt this genre to accommodate his literary agenda.

Conclusion

The biographies discussed in this chapter provide strong examples of different genre expressions and the diversity of Jewish compositions within a genre. All of the authors discussed above incorporated Jewish literary features into their compositions. The role of an authoritative text (i.e., Scripture)—both as a narrative source and as a prophetic text in need of interpretation and authoritatively providing interpretive constraints—is a distinctive feature of Jewish biographies, and its varied use shapes the different narratives. Likewise, the theological perspective of the authors (i.e., their view of God as actively

160 Although allegorical interpretation was a method used by contemporary Greek and Latin scholars, Philo claims that this approach is part of his Jewish heritage for textual interpretation. On this point, see Najman, *Seconding Sinai*, 134; Dawson, *Allegorical Readers*, 73–126.

161 Different aspects of ingenuity are witnessed in the organizational principles of Suetonius' *Lives of the Caesars*, Varro's *Images*, and Nepos' *De viris illustribus*. Cf. G. B. Townend, "Suetonius and His Influences," in T. A. Dorey, ed., *Latin Biography* (London: Routledge, 1967), 80–81; J. Geiger, *Cornelius Nepos and Ancient Political Biography* (HE 47; Stuttgart: Franz Steiner, 1985), 78–93.

engaging with people and seeking to redeem humanity throughout history) moves the focus of the biography beyond the individual.

Unlike history writing, which is found throughout the Hellenistic and Roman eras, all of the extant Jewish biographies come from the first century CE. This concentration is noteworthy, as it suggests that Jewish authors did not previously engage with this genre and that something shifted in their perspective to make participation in biography more desirable. The increased interest in *bios* parallels the rise in biography in the Roman era, suggesting that Jewish authors were influenced by wider literary trends. Jewish authors also participated in different types of biography (individual, collected, embedded autobiography [Josephus' *Vita*]), and at least one author blended literal and allegorical readings. These examples show the diversity of Jewish biographical compositions and imply that Jewish authors did not prioritize, and were not limited to, one type of biography, but explored a range of possible expressions and had a range of prototypical models.

9

Concluding Observations

This chapter represents a synthesis of the previous chapters, in which evidence is brought together in an attempt to address larger questions about how Jewish authors engaged with Greek literary culture and how genre was understood and functioned in antiquity. The observations proposed here are not fully representative of the reality of antiquity. Not only are we limited to authors and texts that have survived, few as they are, we also lack the voices of those who might have adopted alternative positions.[1] Lament as we might, what is offered here is a comprehensive discussion, as can be best determined by the surviving evidence. I argue that, although Jewish authors participated broadly in Greek genres, they were selective in which genres they adopted. These choices are linked to, but not determined by, location, time period, and purpose. Jewish authors did not always align with Greek prototypical models, but had their own core texts and willingly included atypical features if they thought it beneficial. These texts provide insight into the education practices and reading communities of Jews in the Greco-Roman period.

Findings

Greek Influence

The most basic finding of this work is the recognition that some Jewish authors adopted Greek genres and were widely influenced by Greek literary culture. Writing in Greek does not automatically imply adoption of Greek genres or substantial influence of Greek writing practices. Nevertheless, all of the texts

1 I make no attempt to claim uniformity across Jewish authors or among Jewish communities. Communities are not homogeneous, but have a range of outlooks and varying practices of interaction or avoidance. These practices also change over time based on political and historical events.

in this study display awareness of Greek compositional practices and participate, to varying degrees, in recognizable Greek genres.[2]

This engagement was not accidental, nor was it subconsciously done. From the larger corpora of Philo and Josephus to individual works such as Letter of Aristeas, we gain a sense of the genre consciousness of certain Jewish authors, how they sorted genres and texts into categories often based on formal features and purpose, and how these categories related to each other to make a holistic system. Both Philo and Josephus fundamentally divide literature into prose and poetry, thus mirroring the perspective of Greek authors.[3] Each author also assumes that his readers will have a similar, if not identical, expectation of genres, in terms of both form and function. More specifically, Josephus shows a strong awareness of Greek historiographical subgenres (e.g., chronologies, genealogies, ὑπομνήματα) and is able to identify core features, differentiating history from potentially related prose genres, such as encomium (*Ant.* 14.68; *BJ* 1.2) or philosophy (*Ant.* 1.18). Josephus expresses a strong view of the purpose of history and its intention, especially vis-à-vis the recounting of truth. This is shown most forcefully in his polemical statements (e.g., *C. Ap.* 1.57; *Vita* 336–67).

Although explicit genre discussion is limited to a few Jewish authors, evidence of the conscious adoption of Greek genres is clear in many of the authors discussed. Pseudepigraphical attribution of a work to Greek authors (e.g., Hecataeus, Phocylides, Orpheus) shows clear intent on behalf of the author and a strong understanding of ancient literature and could be viewed through the lens of *prosopopoeia*. Similarly, literary emulation and adoption of particular formal features, such as genre-specific meter (e.g., Philo Epicus, Theodotus, Ezekiel), evidence authorial awareness and intentionality. For these Jewish authors, their model writer becomes the prototype for their composition, which suggests that some Jewish authors looked to Greek literature for genre models and actively sought to craft their work in light of Hellenic traditions.

Selective Adoption

Although the full range of Greek genres was open to Jewish writers, we only have evidence for Jewish adoption of certain genres. I have argued in this work that Jewish authors engaged with the Greek genres of epic/epyllion (Philo Epicus, Theodotus), tragedy (Ezekiel), gnomai (Pseudo-Phocylides, Gospel of Thomas), oracula (Pseudo-Orpheus), philosophy (Philo, 4 Maccabees, Letter of Aristeas, Paul), literary letters (Paul, 2 Baruch), commentary (Philo, Aristobulus), novel (Joseph and Aseneth, Artapanus), biography (Philo, Gos-

2 In contrast, there is little engagement with Latin genres by Jewish authors.
3 For specific discussions, see Philo, pp. 90–92; Josephus, pp. 229–39; Aristeas, p. 120.

pel authors, Josephus), and different forms of history (Eupolemus, Pseudo-Eupolemus, Pseudo-Hecataeus, Demetrius the Chronographer, 2 Maccabees/Jason of Cyrene, 3 Maccabees, Justus of Tiberias, Josephus).

Despite this wide engagement, a number of genres were not adopted by Jewish authors (e.g., lyric poetry: Sappho, Alcaeus, Pindar; and erotica: *Anacreontea*). Although the genre of geography was popular in the Hellenistic era (e.g., Eratosthenes, Agatharchides, Strabo), we have no evidence that Jewish authors engaged in such production in Greek. This is not to say that Jewish authors refrained from geographic discussions, but that we have no surviving example of a Jewish-Greek geography. Rather, discussions of place, geology, and natural features are embedded within a larger narrative.[4] The reason for this presumed lack of geographic works is not the sedentary and secluded nature of the Jewish people, but likely that the intended purpose of these works—to educate their readers about interesting flora, fauna, buildings, and peoples from distant lands—did not align with authorial needs. In contrast, many of the surviving Jewish works talk about their own people and educate others through the writing of history, rather than teaching fellow Jews about other people groups.[5] If Jews desired this instruction, the works of Strabo and others may have been thought to be sufficient.

Another genre that was broadly avoided by Jewish authors, so far as we know, is comedy.[6] Comedy writing was revitalized in the late fourth century BCE by the New Comedians Menander, Philemon, and Diphilus, whose influence continued through the Hellenistic era.[7] In subsequent Greco-Roman literature a tradition emerged of writing parodies in order for the author to address certain social and literary issues (e.g., Lucian, *A True Story*; *How to Write History*; Apuleius, *Metamorphoses*). Jewish selection of specific themes, topics, and subjects, often derived from Scripture, could have limited the ways that the material could be expressed. Comedy, farce, and parody might not have been considered appropriate for such topics.[8] Equally possible, given its

4 One possible example could be Philo Epicus' poem on Jerusalem. Too little of the work remains for us to know with certainty, but it is most likely that geographic material was included, but not the primary focus of the work. Cf. M. Sleeman, *Geography and the Ascension Narrative in Acts* (SNTSMS 146; Cambridge: Cambridge University Press, 2009); Z. Safrai, *Seeking Out the Land: Land of Israel Traditions in Ancient Jewish, Christian and Samaritan Literature* (JCPS 32; Leiden: Brill, 2018).

5 Cf. E. Rawson, *Intellectual Life in the Late Roman Republic* (London: Duckworth, 1985), 62–63.

6 This is not to claim that Jewish authors did not write with humor (see Gruen, *Diaspora*, 135–212).

7 Cf. Fantuzzi and Hunter, *Tradition and Innovation*, 404–32.

8 Aune ("Genre Theory," 48–51) has made an interesting argument that Mark's Gospel participated in the parody of Greco-Roman biography. On the negative depiction of farce, see Philo, *Flacc.* 38, 72.

sometimes crude nature, is that the genre of comedy might not have been popular in these authors' communities (cf. Philo, *Mos.* 1.3).

Two Jewish texts could be viewed as participating in the genre of satire.[9] The first is Bel and the Dragon (chapter 6) and the author's humorous critique of idols (Bel 1–22) and the worship of a living dragon (Bel 23–42). The second text is Pseudo-Clement, *Hom.* 4.7–6.25 (chapter 4), in which the author defends Jewish thought and thoroughly critiques the anti-Semite Apion and Greek intellectuals who justify the impiety of the gods through allegorical interpretation (e.g., *Hom.* 4.16; "Encomium of Adultery," 5.9–19).[10] Satire was not a genre in which Greek authors regularly participated, but was considered a Latin genre by the ancients (*Satira quidem tota nostra est*, Quintilian, *Inst.* 10.1.93–95).[11] Jewish participation in satire could evidence the adoption of Latin (i.e., non-Greek) literary models. It could also imply that the genre of satire was more widely participated in by Greek authors than is generally considered.

In light of the perceived preferences for certain genres, it is possible to provide a generalized genre hierarchy of Greek genres for Jewish authors, with the recognition that this hierarchy is not static, but changed over time and differed among communities and individuals.[12] First, at the most basic level, Jewish authors appeared to prefer prose over poetic composition. This is not to claim that Jewish authors did not write poetry or that it was not valued; at the beginning of the Hellenistic era we have some strong examples of Jewish poetry (e.g., Philo Epicus, Theodotus, Ezekiel). This engagement with poetry continued throughout the Greco-Roman period, but prose writing consistently appears more dominant. Epic and tragedy are adopted by ancient authors and of other poetic texts written by Jews, revelatory texts (e.g., Orphica and oracles) also appear to be popular. Many branches of Greek poetry are absent (e.g., iambic, lyric, elegiac, idyll), suggesting a lack of literary interest, though not necessarily a lack of awareness.

9 For the development of satirical characters in Jewish novels, see Wills, "Jewish Novellas Daniel," 224, 229. For the claim that Testament of Abraham is a "satirical novella," see Wills, "Jewish Novellas in a Greek and Roman Age," 142.

10 Adler, "Apion's 'Encomium'"; Paget, *Jews*, 427–92, argues that it is a second-century Jewish writing from Syria.

11 There are a few examples of satirical elements in other genres (e.g., Lycophron reported by Diogenes Laertius, *Vit.* 2.140; Athenaeus, *Deipn.* 2.55d, σατυρικῷ δράματι).

12 Different hierarchies exist in different languages of composition. Similarly, a Greek hierarchy and a Hebrew hierarchy do not necessarily map onto each other, due to issues such as prestige, value, sacredness, importance, etc. What is discussed here is a Greek genre hierarchy based on the evidence of extant texts and fragments of specific genres. This also does not include non-Greek genres written in Greek (e.g., Apocalypse, Testimony, etc.).

Second, within prose genres, history stands as the most important for Jewish authors writing in Greek. Not only do we have the most examples, but these texts stretch almost fully across our period of evaluation. Following history, philosophical/theological compositions appear to have been next in importance. Certain texts are dedicated to specific philosophic topics, and religious issues and ideas are also found in other genres and texts, reinforcing the central position of theology within Jewish literary works. Biography becomes prominent in the first century CE, allowing Jewish authors to blend historical and theological genres with a focus on the life of an individual or group of people. Novelistic writing is also important for Jewish authors in the Hellenistic era, and they also participated in rhetorical composition. This did not take the form of discrete works, but Jewish authors wrote with consideration of rhetorical categories (e.g., Paul, Josephus) and regularly incorporated progymnasmic units in their work (e.g., Aristeas, Philo).

Third, certain genres appear to have been avoided (e.g., geography, comedy, satire), which would imply that they were low on the author's or community's hierarchy. This might not have been the case in antiquity, but it is hard to argue otherwise given the lack of evidence to the contrary.

Many elements influence the placement of genres within a hierarchy and need to be taken into account as best as possible. The specific region or city of the author influences their understanding of the prestige or importance of a genre. Alexandria, with its emphasis on grammatical and text-critical approaches, provides a strong example of how certain literary forms would be more acceptable or prized. Indeed, we see that most of our examples of Greek commentary writing by Jews come from Alexandria. Genre hierarchies also existed in other cultural centers (e.g., Rome, Jerusalem, Pergamum, Babylon) and localized reading communities, and within these locations they differ among individuals, communities, and ethnic groups. As a result, authors in each location, or with a desired audience in these centers, would need to consider reader tastes and preferences when composing.[13]

Cultural and temporal changes also influence genre hierarchies. With the change of power structures and the installation of a new elite (e.g., Ptolemaic, Hasmonean, Roman, etc.) the ordering of literary hierarchy could change, sometimes radically.[14] Although there is no evidence of Hasmonean kings prohibiting or promoting certain genres, a revolutionary change in leadership, especially by individuals with strong ideological positions, can have a

13 E.g., the importance of poetry in Augustan Rome. Cf. M. Citroni, "Poetry in Augustan Rome," in P. E. Knox, ed., *A Companion to Ovid* (Blackwell Companions to the Ancient World; Chichester: Wiley-Blackwell, 2009), 8–25.

14 Cf. Adams, *Genre*, 49–53.

profound effect on composition and the selection of genre.[15] Our lack of evidence in this regard does not allow for detailed discussion, but we need to recognize the pressures faced by authors and the influence exerted by ruling elites, especially in an era that had strong patron–client relationships.[16]

The Temporal Element

The above list of adopted genres implies a sustained engagement with Greek genres. This is not necessarily the case. Jewish adoption of genres changed throughout the Hellenistic and Roman eras, paralleling the fluctuation, development, and popularity of Greek genres more broadly. Because genres are not static, but change and develop over time, as Greek genres changed throughout the Hellenistic era the literary models available to Jewish authors also changed. In addition, Jewish compositions, once created, also function as potential models, influencing the ways that subsequent Jewish authors viewed a genre and its relationship with Greek literary culture. This discussion is further complicated because we are unsure exactly when many of these texts (both Greek and Jewish) were written and what texts have been lost, potentially robbing us of important prototypical models.

The timing of composition needs to be considered, as Jewish preference for participating in certain genres can be limited to specific time periods. Poetic compositions by Jews (i.e., epic/epyllion and tragedy) appear almost exclusively at the beginning of the Hellenistic era.[17] If Theodotus did compose an epyllion, then he would be an early adopter of this genre and part of a growing literary movement. This grouping could indicate that there was a preference for epic among Jewish authors and readers during this time that waned over the centuries.[18] The use of Greek poetic genres could also indicate the type of education these authors received, namely one that was grounded in Homer and the tragedians (see below). Metrical works, such as the *Sentences* of Pseudo-Phocylides and Sibylline Oracles, were written in the first centuries

15 1 and 2 Maccabees have been identified as an example of the renewed importance of scriptural models when engaging in Greek literary compositions. See most recently, Berthelot, *In Search of the Promised Land?* 65–117. For modern examples, in the Stalin era of communist Russia many forms of literature and music were repressed, and in Nazi Germany many authors fled or were heavily censored.

16 E.g., Herod the Great's employing of Nicolaus of Damascus and the latter's composition of a drama on the character of Susanna.

17 This range would be expanded if Sosates is included.

18 Less likely, although possible, is that these surviving poems are not representative of the poetic outputs by Jews in the Hellenistic and Roman eras and that metrical compositions were prominent throughout this time period. Cf. Exod 15:1–18 (Song of Moses); Josephus, *Ant.* 2.346; 4.303.

BCE/CE, so it is clear that some Jewish authors still had the capability to write in dactylic hexameter late in this era.

Jewish biographies, which were written in the first century CE (e.g., Gospels and Philo), also exhibit temporal clustering. This participation parallels the rise in the production of Greek and Latin biographies in the Roman Empire, suggesting that the literary tastes and preferences of Jewish authors and readers were influenced by changes in the wider reading population. The same could be said about Josephus' *Vita* and the rise in examples of autobiography in the first centuries BCE/CE.

History is by far the most important Greek genre for Jewish authors. It was one of the first Greek genres adopted by Jewish writers, and engagement with it continued throughout the Hellenistic era and into the second century CE. However, Jewish writers showed mixed engagement with historiographical trends. Demetrius the Chronographer composed a chronology around the time when major Greeks authors were similarly engaged with this subgenre (e.g., Eratosthenes). On the other hand, a major historical work tracing the origin and development of the Jewish people was not accomplished until late in the first century CE (i.e., Josephus' *Antiquities*), when authors from neighboring ethnic groups, such as the Egyptian Manetho and the Babylonian Berossus, had crafted their texts centuries earlier. This could suggest that the Jewish people were late adopters of this form of historiography, although it is clear that such works continued to be produced in the first century CE (e.g., Apion's *Aigyptiaka*).

Little evidence survives of Jewish participation in Greek genres following the Trajanic revolt. Roman response to the uprisings in Cyrenaica, Egypt, Mesopotamia, and Palestine was severe and no doubt had a substantial impact on the long-term health and even existence of these Jewish communities. Indeed, it is only in the third century that we start to have evidence to support the renewal of the Jewish people in Alexandria.[19] As Alexandria was a prominent location for Jewish composition in Greek, the fallout from the revolt likely contributed to the decline in literary compositions.

Little evidence, however, does not mean no evidence, and fragments and testimonies of Jewish-Greek composition in the second century CE support the argument that some Jewish authors continued to participate in Greek genres after the Trajanic revolt.[20] The dating of texts is constrained by the

19 Horbury, *Jewish War*, 234–35; T. Ilan, "The Jewish Community in Egypt before and after 117 CE in Light of Old and New Papyri," in Y. Furstenberg, ed., *Jewish and Christian Communal Identities in the Roman World* (AJEC 94; Leiden: Brill, 2016), 203–24.

20 Cf. the Apion narrative in Pseudo-Clement's *Homilies*, Joseph and Aseneth, the anonymous Jew mentioned by Origen (*Cels.* 2.28), and Philosabbatius (Epiphanius, *Pan.* 51.8.1).

previous decision that Jews did not write in Greek in the late second century. This study supports the argument that the presumed secession of Jewish composition in Greek after 117 or 136 CE needs to be reconsidered. The assertion that some texts are Christian does not necessarily imply that they were not written by Jewish authors. Scholarly recognition of the slow parting allows for non–mutually exclusive categories.

Adapting Greek Genres

The Hellenistic period was characterized by literary invention and exploration. New genres and subgenres were developed, and existing genres were adapted to suit a new and diverse readership. It is not surprising, therefore, to see Jewish authors engaging with this wider literary trend. Atypical Jewish expressions of Greek genres have been described as "inferior" compositions, implying that the author was not able to attain the pure form of the genre. This critical approach hinders our ability to identify purposeful variation. Bakhtin is correct when he claims that "genres must be fully mastered in order to be manipulated freely" and "the better our command of genres, the more freely we employ them."[21] This perspective of mastery should be adopted when approaching compositions by Jewish authors and other ancients; looking not to see where they might be deficient, but to understand how they might be constructing new genre expressions and prototypical examples.

The primary difference between Jewish works and those of Greek authors is the choice of Jewish material. This is not to imply that Greeks did not write about Jews; some did (e.g., Hecataeus, Alexander Polyhistor). Rather, the selection of a Jewish topic, often taken from Scripture, is one of the distinguishing elements of these texts.[22] Although topic is tied to genre, writing on Jewish topics is not necessarily enough to constitute an adaption of genre. More often, however, it is the author's adoption of a Jewish story that leads to genre changes.[23] If tension arises between the selection of genre and the desired content, Jewish authors, broadly speaking, adapted the genre to fit the content.[24]

21 Bakhtin, *Speech Genres*, 80.

22 This criterion becomes more complicated from the first century CE and the composition of Christian literary works by non-Jewish authors. Cf. Davila, *Provenance*. Determining that some texts were produced by non-Jewish authors would impact our findings of how Jewish authors engaged with Greek literature. However, it would also provide examples of the fluidity and porousness of compositional practices in antiquity.

23 Similarly, a change in topic would also correspond to a change in intended audience (e.g., Sibylline Oracles from Greek to Jewish).

24 The prominent exceptions to this pattern are the works that adopt a Greek author (e.g., Pseudo-Phocylides, Pseudo-Hecataeus, Sibylline Oracles), whose authors are (more) constrained by their choice of persona.

The practice of *macrologia* is a prominent way for Jewish authors to accommodate a biblical narrative or specific worldview. Most prominently, Ezekiel the Tragedian significantly diverges from prescribed features of ancient tragedy, especially, but not exclusively, the expansion of the work's narrative time frame to include most of Moses' life. The authors of the Sibylline Oracles expand the scope of the work, providing a fuller, Jewish perspective of history by situating universal oracular sayings within a Jewish macro-narrative. The Gospels also situate their work within a larger worldview (both in history, but also in an eschatological future) that expands the typical focus of individual biographies. Certain New Testament letters, especially those written by Paul (e.g., Romans, 1 and 2 Corinthians), are substantially longer than nondocumentary letters. The practice of *brachylogia* is also seen in some Jewish compositions, although it is less common. The epyllion was not developed by Theodotus, but he participated in the literary trend. The novella-like septuagintal works (Susanna, Bel and the Dragon) do not have a readily identifiable Greek forerunner but are part of a larger trend in antiquity.

Another way that genres develop is by embedding or "integration": the enclosure of a literary work within another work.[25] Under this definition, the inclusion of the symposia and other rhetorical exercises (e.g., *ekphrasis*, *politeia*, *synkrisis*) in Aristeas may not fully qualify, as the former is not solely a discrete literary form, despite the existence of *symposia* as individual works. On the other hand, the shortened travelogue could be viewed as an embedded genre, modified to fit the new context. Parables within the Synoptic Gospels would be another example of embedding, as the parable is a literary form that could exist independently apart from a Gospel narrative, although parables are rarely found in isolation.[26]

In this study, we find that texts both have individual genres and can be part of a larger collection of texts that may or may not participate in the same genre, raising the question of a unified work being composed of multiple genres. Philo's *Vita Contemplativa* and biographies (*Abraham* and *Joseph*) engage with different levels of genre.[27] Each could be viewed independently as participating in a genre, but their collection in a series or larger work encourages us to

25 The device of a story-within-a-story could also be viewed as embedding and was recognized in antiquity as an established means of expanding a story. This structural feature was employed in Demotic literature (e.g., *The Tales of Prince Setna*), especially *Myth of the Sun's Eye*, which has a series of embedded fables which Thoth tells to Tefnut. The practice is prominent in Apuleius' *Metamorphoses*.

26 For detailed studies of parables in antiquity, see the essays in A. Oegema, J. Pater, and M. Stoutjesdijk, eds., *Parables and Fables in the Graeco-Roman World* (WUNT 1; Tübingen: Mohr Siebeck, forthcoming 2020).

27 See pp. 145–47 (*Contemplativa*) and pp. 289–90 (*Abraham* and *Joseph*).

consider how compositions of different genres can be combined to make a cohesive whole. These multigenre compositions challenge traditional assumptions of a larger work needing to be unified by genre. As they are all from the first century CE, they could represent a development of the idea of genre in antiquity.[28] Josephus' *Vita* could also be considered through the lens of embedding. Josephus claims the need to write about himself, but instead of composing a discrete, freestanding work, he explicitly incorporated his autobiographical discussion into his larger *Antiquities*. History has the ability to integrate smaller genres, but, in the case of *Vita*, the incorporation is not complete. *Vita*, as a biography, was generically compatible with history and so was included, but not fully subsumed, thus providing an example of a Jewish author experimenting with genre integration.

The most common means of adaptation is an author's blending of genres, which is achieved primarily by two means: (1) the author takes a recognizable feature from one genre and incorporates it into another (sometimes pejoratively called "contamination"), or (2) the author combines two or more genres to form an original work. The latter often requires that the blended genres be related (i.e., have some overlap in formal features or similar function), whereas the former can be accomplished with very distinct genres. In our study, some Jewish authors actively blended Greek genres to create a work that resists stereotypical categorization. Demetrius employs standard Greek chronological practices in his *Chronology*, but also incorporates answers to questions that are not temporally focused. Both the *quaestiones* genre and chronological history find their apex in Alexandria scholastic tradition and embody similar approaches to text that make them compatible for generic blending. The embedding of responses to questions and the employment of Greek scholastic methodology are distinct from other chronologies, allowing for the possibility that Demetrius was adapting a Greek genre to better align with his intended purpose and the expectations of his readers.

More complex genre blending is evident in 4 Maccabees. In this work, the author adeptly brings together philosophical, rhetorical, and narrative elements to create a literary work that mixes forms and crosses perceived genre boundaries. In contrast to Demetrius' history, in which the blending of genres is subtle, the seams of genre boundaries are more pronounced in 4 Maccabees. This roughness could indicate a lack of compositional awareness, but this would stand in contrast to the rhetorical sophistication exhibited elsewhere. As a result, we must view the seams as intentional and possibly as evidence of a literary practice that has not been well preserved. Artapanus' work, the

28 The discussion of Luke-Acts could fall in this category (i.e., Luke as participating in biography and Acts in history) depending on how one interprets the evidence.

fragments of which include elements from novel, biography, and history, is another example of the blending of prose genres into one text. A similar blending of philosophy and narrative is witnessed in the Letter of Aristeas, where the author uses an epistolary frame to recount a narrative in which philosophical and cultural questions are asked by non-Jews and answers are provided by Jewish characters. Prioritizing the narrative frame has led scholars to emphasize specific genres. However, a more holistic reading of the work recognizes a sophisticated blend of genres and rhetorical components that resists neat classifications.

In the examples presented above, Jewish authors adapted Greek genres in a variety of ways. Each author, depending on individual needs and circumstances, made changes to known genres, blending them and/or incorporating additional features as required. Although the language of "change" and "adaptation" might be appropriate, caution must be used, as the variations exhibited might not have been viewed as adaptations by ancient readers, but as part of the inherent flexibility of the genres. Such an understanding does not minimize the literary creativity of our Jewish authors, but rather redirects our understanding, allowing us to claim that their knowledge of Greek genres was sufficiently advanced to allow them to explore the full range of genre expressions.

Not all aspects of Jewish genre adaptation are a result of Greek literary prominence; Scripture also influenced Jewish engagement with Greek genres. First, most of the authors studied evidence the use of the Septuagint. The level and methods of engagement with Greek Scripture vary, but many important themes, motifs, and ideas are drawn from the Septuagint. Moreover, a majority of authors took material from Scripture, drawing directly from specific books for events, character details, and literary models. This is most prominently seen in historical and biographical prose compositions (e.g., Philo's *Abraham* and *Moses*; Josephus' *Antiquities*; 1 Esdras), but authors of poetic works also mine biblical texts for narrative details (e.g., Ezekiel's *Exagoge*).

For histories and biographies of contemporary events and people who are not discussed in Scripture, the authors still show a deep awareness of scriptural themes, modeling elements of their works on previous people and events. The Gospels are good examples of this practice, as their authors regularly drew from Scripture for motifs, symbols, and characters that could be thought to prefigure those found in the Jesus narratives.[29] Other historical narratives are less explicitly modeled on Scripture, but still draw from it specific practices or outlooks. For example, the providence of God and his special relationship with

29 E.g., barren women as models for Elizabeth in Luke 1; John the Baptist as a second Elijah (Mark 1:2–3); Jesus as the good shepherd (John 10:1–18, alluding to Ezek 34:11–24).

the Jewish people form the theological underpinning of many Jewish works (e.g., Susanna; 2–4 Maccabees; Gospels).

Jewish authors' membership in multiple cultures represents an important variable in genre adaptation. In this study, we saw an increased probability of variation from prototypical Greek models when the author was participating in a genre for which there was a Jewish analogue. To put it differently, when a Jewish author had multiple prototypical models from which to choose, they were more likely to produce nonprototypical works. The genre of historiography, for example, has Jewish *and* Greek literary models that could have acted prototypically for Jewish authors. The author of 3 Maccabees blends both Jewish and Greek literary features in his treatise. On the one hand, he draws heavily from Jewish texts and appears to have modeled his work on that of 2 Maccabees and the Jew-gentile interaction narratives of Esther and others (e.g., Josephus, *C. Ap.* 2.51–55). At the same time, the author shows a strong awareness of Greek historiography and actively incorporates elements of its practice within his work. In the case of 3 Maccabees, it is not a matter of the Jewish elements being subordinated to Greek literary preferences, or vice versa. Rather, we witness a blending of practices that transcends conceived ethnic lines to create a work that embodies both worlds. A similar blending is witnessed in Philo of Alexandria's commentaries. His compositions are not exact replications of our reconstruction of prototypical Greek commentaries, but appear to have features that are represented in Jewish commentary practices.

One variation by Jewish authors from established Greco-Roman writing practice is anonymity. The expenditure of energy in the creation of a literary work by Greek and Latin authors was predominantly for personal gain and glory. This gain was not (necessarily) financial, but of reputation and prestige, both for the author and for his/her patron(s). In some genres, Jewish authorial attribution is found, especially in Jewish epics and tragedies (Philo Epicus, Theodotus, Ezekiel, etc.). Similarly, authors who appear to be most integrated within the wider Greco-Roman world (e.g., Philo of Alexandria and Josephus) also shun anonymity and actively take ownership of their work.

In contrast, the Jewish practice of anonymity is seen in all four Gospels and a number of historical works (e.g., 1–4 Maccabees).[30] For Greek compositions this choice is atypical, as we lack examples of anonymous biographies or histories written by Greek and Latin authors. This anonymity would have been viewed as problematic for Greek and Latin readers, as one of the primary claims for the importance of a history is the experience, connectedness, participation, and knowledge of its author. This practice, therefore, is almost

30 The epitome of 2 Maccabees is anonymous, although the original was written by Jason of Cyrene.

certainly of Jewish origin and undermines one of the core elements of Greek and Roman historiography. Less surprising are anonymous novels/novellas, especially those that are presented as expansions of Scripture (e.g., septuagintal additions, Joseph and Aseneth), but even in novelistic texts there is little evidence for anonymity within the wider Greco-Roman world.

Equally distinctive is the practice of pseudepigraphy. Of the texts discussed, a sizable portion are pseudepigraphical (e.g., Pseudo-Phocylides; Pseudo-Orpheus; Sibylline Oracles; Poetic Fragments; Pseudo-Hecataeus). This practice is different from anonymity, but is readily found in Jewish compositions, though often in apocalyptic, testimonial, and prophetic texts (e.g., use of Baruch, Enoch, Seth, Abraham, Patriarchs, etc.).[31] The adoption of prominent Greek authors represents a development of this practice, as it results in the appropriation of another culture's writer for the advancement of one's own. This act of cooption signals a power differential and represents the activity of individuals from minority cultures who seek to use the voice of the dominant in specific, often undermining ways.[32]

The Appropriation of Greek Literature

Our wealth of Jewish literature, coupled with few examples from other cultures, might lead us to assume that Jewish authors were distinctive in their engagement with Greek literature. This conclusion, however, should not be adopted without strong caveats. Within Egyptian literary cultures there are parallels between *Oracle of the Potter* and the Sibylline Oracles, suggesting literary fertilization occurred at some point, or the active imitation of Egyptian literature by a Greek author.[33] The *Demotic Chronicle*, *Prophecy of Petesis* (or *Nectanebo's Dream*), *The Myth of the Sun's Eye*, and the translation of *Alexander Romance* into Demotic also evidence literary fertilization in Egyptian compositions.[34]

The most prominent example of genre appropriation by other cultures is the development of historiography by Berossus (*History of Babylonia*) and Manetho (*History of Egypt*). Both of these works are written in Greek and

31 For a nuanced discussion of authorship and composition, especially with regard to "book," see Mroczek, *Literary Imagination*, 86–113.

32 When mentioned, Jewish adoption of Greek cultural heritage was not received warmly. E.g., Plutarch, *Is. Os.* 31 (*Mor.* 363d), cf. Tacitus, *Hist.* 5.2.

33 Cf. The *Oracle of the Lamb*, a Hellenistic-era Demotic text with a similar view of history to the *Oracle of the Potter*, is mediated through prophetic utterances. For other examples and a detailed discussion, see I. Rutherford, "Introduction: Interaction and Translation between Greek Literature and Egypt," in I. Rutherford, ed., *Greco-Egyptian Interactions: Literature, Translation, and Culture, 500 BCE–300 CE* (Oxford: Oxford University Press, 2016), 5–16.

34 Cf. R. Jasnow, "The Greek Alexander Romance and Demotic Egyptian Literature," *JNES* 56 (1997): 95–103.

present the history of their respective countries' native worldviews, traditions, and characters. As a result, they represent alternative views of history in which Greek ideas are challenged through the adoption of a Greek genre. Josephus (and others, e.g., Eupolemus and Lysimachus) was clearly influenced by these authors in the construction of his *Antiquities*, and in doing so followed in the footsteps of writers from other minority cultures. Additional examples of the adoption of Greek genres by minority cultures are evident in the writings of other authors (e.g., Apion, Chaeremon of Alexandria, Isidore of Charax, Philo of Byblos). Although it is outwith the perspective of this study, a comparison of how Jewish authors and writers from other minority cultures adopted Greek genres would be a promising avenue of inquiry for gaining a broader understanding of power dynamics in literary constructions, especially in overlapping locales (e.g., Egypt).

Jewish Contribution to Greek Genres

Although some Jewish authors were influenced by Greek literary works and looked to them as literary models, this relationship was not unidirectional. Certain authors appear to have included nonprototypical features into their Greek compositions and developed distinctive approaches to texts. The *Nachleben* of Paul and Philo of Alexandria demonstrate sustained engagement by and influence on subsequent Christian interpreters. In addition to local features that constitute literary evolution, there are two genres in which Jewish works could be argued to have influenced dominant literary culture: novel and biography.

Our understanding of the ancient novel is derived primarily from seven extant Greek and Latin works.[35] These romances postdate most of our Jewish examples and so raise the possibility that Jewish authors originated this genre, which was subsequently adopted by Greek authors and further developed. This theory, although not without merit, is problematic. Joseph and Aseneth provides our fullest example; however, the author looked primarily to Jewish literature, especially Scripture, for his structure. Joseph and Aseneth does not lack connections with Greek literary elements, but does not take a Greek genre as its prototypical model. Jewish novels may have been instrumental for the development of the Greco-Roman genre, but the evidence is minimal from the major surviving examples. First, there are too few direct ties that bind these works together. There are certain overlapping features and motifs, but these are not sufficiently robust to support direct or indirect influence. Theories

35 Greek: Chariton, *Chaereas and Callirhoe*; Xenophon of Ephesus, *An Ephesian Tale*; Achilles Tatius, *Leucippe and Clitophon*; Longus, *Daphnis and Chloe*; Heliodorus, *An Ethiopian Tale*; Latin: Petronius, *Satyricon*; Apuleius, *Metamorphoses*.

must allow for a much longer evolutionary process or a radical development by a specific author/work. This focused view on Jewish compositions also overlooks possible contributions by other cultures, most notably Egyptian. Egyptian compositions, such as *The Myth of the Sun's Eye*, *Setne Khamwas*, and the narrative in P.Mich. 3378, suggest some sort of literary relationship.[36] A fuller theory of genre development needs to take into account the situated nature of the author and alternative influences.

The influence of Jewish biographies on wider Greek literary practice has a much firmer claim. In particular, the biographical expression provided by the Gospels and Acts strongly influenced the development of this genre in late antiquity, most notably the so-called apocryphal Gospels and apocryphal Acts. This influence is not widespread or even prominent, as many Greek and Latin biographers show no knowledge of the Gospels and Acts and their works do not indicate any literary dependence. However, the Gospels and Acts were the inspiration for many compositions by Christians in the second to fifth centuries CE, the authors of which were almost certainly not Jewish.[37]

In summary, Jewish authors, through their adaptation of established Greek genres (i.e., biography) and, to a lesser extent, their composition of biblically inspired Greek works, contributed to the development of Greek genres. The nature of this relationship is imbalanced, and Jewish authors influenced far less than they were influenced, but it would be inaccurate to say that literary pressure only traveled in one direction (i.e., top-down). As a result, we see in these texts an example of how minority cultures contributed to genre development and the evolution of Greek literary practices.

The Geographic Element

Writing and publishing a book in antiquity was a local and social event.[38] Accordingly, we must consider the place of composition in our interpretation of a work and the author's selection of genre.[39] Although we focused our discussion on the larger issue of genre, we see clear geographic influence on compositional addressee, topic, imagery, intertextual references, social outlook, and

36 Cf. Rutherford, "Greek Fiction and Egyptian Fiction."

37 Cf. the Jewish "anti-gospel," *Toledot Yeshu*, which was originally written in Aramaic.

38 On this point, see R. J. Starr, "The Circulation of Texts in the Ancient World," *Mnemosyne* 40 (1987): 213–23; Selden, "Text Networks."

39 A strong example of the importance of geography for composition is Posidippus, a Greek author who wrote at least 112 epigrams to promote the Ptolemies' imperial self-presentation. Influence from location is also seen in the poems of Callimachus and Theocritus. See S. A. Stephens, "Posidippus's Poetry Book: Where Macedon Meets Egypt," in W. V. Harris and G. Ruffini, eds., *Ancient Alexandria between Egypt and Greece* (Leiden: Brill, 2004), 63–86. For the need to understand local elements (in this case from Alexandria and Egypt) in order to have a thicker interpretation of a text, see Stephens, *Seeing Double*.

language use, to name a few. More attention, therefore, needs to be given to the author's geographic situatedness and the constraints and opportunities each location embodies.[40]

Aristobulus, in his work dedicated to King Ptolemy, employed interpretive approaches prominent in Alexandria, implying that he was presenting an explanation of Scripture in ways that would be recognized and received by its local recipients. Philo's sophisticated use of scholarly genres, such as commentary and ζητήματα, aligns with his residency and education in Alexandria. The literary setting of Aristeas in the Alexandrian court of Ptolemy II and the city's environs supports the view that the work was composed there and tailored to fit that context. Josephus writes in Flavian Rome, and we can identify some of his intended audience (e.g., *Vita* 361–366).[41] Geographic and political situatedness had a direct influence on his rhetorical style of writing and, I argue, his selection of genre. With a desire to communicate with specific individuals and communities, Josephus needed to select genres that would allow him to achieve his goals. From his participation in two subgenres of history, we can assume that he thought that this genre would optimally align with his dual purposes and would be best received by those with whom he wished to communicate.

One challenge to a geographic approach is that an insufficient number of works survive that can be securely tied to specific locales in order to determine the literary specializations, preferences, and/or distinctives of a cultural center. More research needs to be undertaken at a localized level to determine, as best we can, the genre preferences, hierarchies, and local practices that could have influenced composition. For many Jewish authors we do not know where they were located and so are not in a position to determine how geography influenced their compositions. The traditional recourse to Alexandria as an author's provenance, primarily based on the author's ability to compose Greek literary works, is too blunt and fails to recognize how widespread Greek education was in antiquity. Alexandria is a strong option, especially as we know it contained a large Jewish population, some of whom were using their Greek ed-

40 See, most recently, S. Honigman, "The Impact of Locality and Cross-Linguistic Influences on Literary Texts Written in Greek by Jewish Authors," in M. Kramer and M. Leventhal, eds., *Proceedings of the International Conference "Being Jewish, Writing Greek," Cambridge, September 6–8, 2017*, forthcoming. Many thanks to Sylvie Honigman, who shared some prepublished work on this topic. For the localization of Greco-Egyptian literature and its limited readership outside of Egypt, with the notable exception of Egyptian magical texts, see G. Bohak, "The Diffusion of the Greco-Egyptian Magical Tradition in Late Antiquity," in I. Rutherford, ed., *Greco-Egyptian Interactions: Literature, Translation, and Culture, 500 BCE–300 CE* (Oxford: Oxford University Press, 2016), 357–81.

41 Tcherikover, "Jewish Apologetic Literature"; Mason, "Of Audience and Meaning"; Mason, "'Should Any Wish.'"

ucation to produce literary outputs. However, additional evidence needs to be provided to substantiate the claim of why this particular geographic location is the most likely place of composition. Jerusalem also has a strong claim to provenance. Not only did residents undertake translation activities (Colophon of Greek Esther 10:3l, F11), but we see Jewish priests depicted as educated (Letter of Aristeas) and references to a library (2 Macc 2:13–16) and archive (Josephus, *BJ* 2.426–427; 6.354; 7.61); and, in the Roman era, we have evidence of literary patronage (e.g., Nicolaus, cf. Josephus, *Ant.* 16.186). The possibility that certain texts could have been composed in Jerusalem (e.g., 2 Macc; Philo Epicus) further undermines the hegemony of Alexandria.

Jewish Authors and Jewish Topics

Jewish works are often distinguished by topic, specifically religious themes or biblical characters. Some scholars have argued that we lack any example of a purely "secular" writing by a Jew.[42] In this study, I have found no evidence of Jewish authors writing works on what would be considered "non-Jewish" topics. Although it is possible that surviving evidence aligns fully with the historical reality, we should resist the claim that Jewish authors wrote only on Jewish themes and topics or chose to write only religious works. The knowledge of Greek genres exhibited by Jewish authors strongly implies that Jews could have written works on non-Jewish topics, but that these have not survived. The number of fragmentary works from antiquity and the adoption of local (e.g., Greek, Latin, and Egyptian) names by Jews in the Greco-Roman period also suggests that counterevidence may not be recognized.

The explicit inclusion of Jewish topics, especially those that are identified as culturally determinative (e.g., circumcision, Sabbath observance, monotheism), differs among compositions. Some authors do not emphasize these elements (e.g., Greek pseudepigraphic texts), opting to omit or downplay non-Greek perspectives. Other authors highlight the importance of preserving Jewish ethnic markers, presenting their protagonists as true adherents (e.g., 3 and 4 Maccabees). Most Jewish texts fall somewhere along the continuum between these choices.

By presenting Jewish ideas in Greek forms, the authors engage in acts of cultural translation. Some authors repackage traditional stories in Greek genres to make Judaism "palatable" to non-Jews or to present the Hebraic faith and its devotees as culturally sophisticated and worthy of tolerance and respect, if not emulation. The use of Greek forms also affords the opportunity for writers to reappropriate Jewish traditions and make them more relevant to Jews living

42 Fraser, *Ptolemaic Alexandria*, 1.716.

under Greek and Roman rule. This duality of purpose necessitates literary diversity, which is embodied in pluriform genre expressions.

The adoption of Jewish topics by non-Jews, particularly following the rise of Christianity, is significant, as the selection of scriptural content and literary models by non-Jews represents topical innovation and is an important contribution by Jewish authors to the development of Greek literary composition.

Access to Texts and Sources Used

Discussion of literary models and the use of sources raises the question of Jewish authors' access to texts and prototypical exemplars. This is a topic that is often take for granted, but it has substantial implications for how one discusses genre and literary influences. When we say that an author "used" a text, does that mean that they had access to it? Did the author have access to all of the work, part of a work (e.g., book 1 of Herodotus' *History*), or only portions from a work (e.g., *testimonia* or excerpta)? Alternatively, would an author have access to multiple copies/versions (Hebrew and/or Greek) of scriptural texts?

Some scholars assume that ancient authors had access to texts, especially those of the most popular Greek authors (e.g., Homer, Plato, Thucydides, etc.). How Jewish authors accessed texts is rarely discussed, although scholars frequently make recourse to the author's presumed "secular" education (see below). The historical situation and location of the author, should they be known, can assist in determining likely access to texts. For example, because Philo came from a family of phenomenal wealth, it is easier to assume that he had personal copies of certain scriptural texts as well as to some of the works of Homer and Plato. His elite status may have also afforded him access to the Museum and the libraries of other elite individuals. Similarly, Josephus, who wrote in Rome and had prominent patrons, would most likely have had access to texts in Roman libraries and may also have had copies of his own (*Vita* 418). For Jewish authors living in Judaea, access to specific texts is less secure. Although there is some evidence of a library in Jerusalem, we are ignorant of its contents. Similarly, we are not sure who would have had access to such a library. These issues need further research in order to increase our understanding and the level of nuance in our discussion of access to texts.[43]

43 Cf. Houston, *Inside Roman Libraries*, especially his discussion of private book collections. One way to begin to address this issue is to collect the data from all of our Jewish texts (i.e., citations, paraphrases, references, etc.) along with any information about where and when an author wrote. Locations of libraries and other potential text-housing institutions (e.g., synagogues), derived both from treatises and excavations, would also be vital. This information, once compiled in a database, could be used to triangulate the location(s) and potential availability of texts (to the best of our abilities). For ANE collections, see S. W. Crawford, *Scribes and Scrolls at Qumran* (Grand Rapids: Eerdmans, 2019).

One possible method of determining an author's access to texts is by their citations. Although identifying citations and paraphrases is a promising avenue, benefiting from specific textual data, interpretational problems still remain. Does the citation imply access to the whole work, a book, or just the cited lines? Aristobulus, in addition to his use of Scripture, cites a number of Greek writers (Orpheus, fr. 4.5; Aratus, fr. 4.6; Hesiod, fr. 5.13; Homer, fr. 5.14; Linus, fr. 5.16) and references others (Plato and Pythagoras, fr. 3.1; Pythagoras, Socrates, Plato, fr. 4.4). How are we to interpret this evidence? As the citations are grouped together, it has been thought that Aristobulus used an excerpta compiled by someone else. This line of argument, however, only pushes the question back in time and assumes that someone else had access to texts.

A further challenge to our inquiry is that Jewish compositions in the Hellenistic and Roman eras often lack explicit engagement with Greek and Latin authors. In some genres, it is difficult to determine whether the authors engaged with specific non-Jewish works (e.g., biography, novel). Historians show an increased willingness to engage with Greek compositions, but even here many authors refrain from identifying their sources, both Jewish and non-Jewish. This has some precedent in Greek history composition, especially the avoidance of other authors with whom the historian disagreed (e.g., Polybius, *Hist.* 5.33.1–3; cf. Josephus and his mention of Justus of Tiberias, *Vita* 336–367). This practice, however, frustrates our ability to determine the author's access to texts.

One pattern that emerged in this study was the relationship between the genre of the literary composition and the types of texts the work engaged or emulated. The poetic works from chapters 2 and 3 have strong similarities with the works of Homer, Hesiod, and the tragedians, but show essentially no engagement with history and prose authors. In contrast, mention of and engagement with poets is limited in historical works, even though it is clear that some authors had familiarity with them. Josephus, in his histories, made substantial reference to other prose works, especially histories and *hypomnemata* from non-Greek authors, but mentions poets only in his *Apion*. Eupolemus gives indirect evidence that the works of Herodotus, Hecataeus, and Ctesias were available and being read in Judaea during the mid- to late second century BCE. Philo, in his commentaries, draws heavily from Plato and other philosophical works, and the authors of the Gospels of Matthew and Luke, and possibly that of John, all made use of Mark. By raising these examples, I am not claiming that ancient authors *only* used works that were similar in genre to their composition; clearly Jewish authors could and did draw from a range of texts.[44]

44 For example, Philo cites Homer and other Greek poets many times. Cf. Lincicum, "Preliminary Index."

Rather, these authors appear to engage most regularly and deeply with works that are closest in genre to their own. This finding is not surprising, as authors needed not only to situate their composition within the larger literary world, but also to be familiar with prototypical works in order to compose a work of that genre successfully. The correlation between works cited and the genre of the work, even if it is not strong, supports the claim that more attention should be given to this feature in future discussions of genre.

The major exception to this discussion is the authors' use of Jewish Scripture, which for most of them does not align generically with their composition. As all of the authors investigated in this study composed their works in Greek, it is not surprising to see that most of them engaged with the Greek rather than the Hebrew versions of Scripture (when such differentiation can be determined).[45] Imputing an ability by the author to read and access the Hebrew text requires an extra layer of assumption by the scholar. Although most of the authors discussed in this study show evidence of using a Greek translation of Scripture, some of the earliest Jewish authors (e.g., Philo Epicus, Theodotus) show little evidence of Septuagint use, which raises the question of their access to this text and its dissemination at the time of their writing, especially if both are writing in Judaea.[46] An alternative interpretation of the data is that the Septuagint was not viewed as prototypical, which raises the question of its standing within the community. Is this evidence of a lower view of Greek Scripture? If so, this indicates a fluidity of Jewish religious and ethnic identity in the period. Thus, "genre" is an access point into that larger historical question of adaptation and inculturation.

I am not implying that all authors had access to the same Greek (or Hebrew) version or that they exclusively used the Greek translation. Scholars now recognize that there was pluriformity of texts in antiquity, for both Greek and Hebrew versions.[47] The discussion of the different authors provides further evidence of textual plurality. By this I mean that the scriptural text reconstructed for each author rarely conforms fully to our (also reconstructed) Septuagint. Rather, most authors display a mix of features that would imply a text version that has not survived.[48] We have no idea how many Greek translations circu-

45 Cf. J. Joosten, "The Origin of the Septuagint Canon," in S. Kreuzer, M. Meiser, and M. Sigismund, eds., *Die Septuaginta—Orte und Intentionen* (WUNT 1.361; Tübingen: Mohr Siebeck, 2016), 688–99, especially 695.

46 This is not to imply that they used the Hebrew version, but that there is insufficient evidence to claim LXX use.

47 L. I. Lied and H. Lundhaug, eds., *Snapshots of Evolving Traditions: Jewish and Christian Manuscript Culture, Textual Fluidity, and New Philology* (Berlin: De Gruyter, 2017); Selden, "Text Networks" (especially regarding translations).

48 For example, Ezekiel the Tragedian follows the text of our Septuagint at some points (e.g., Exod 14:25), but not at others (e.g., Exod 1:5). Similarly, the Greek citations of Aristobulus do

lated in the Hellenistic and early Roman eras or even if our authors were able to create their own. Each author in this study, therefore, provides a unique window into this epoch and a data point on the types and nature of scriptural texts. Complicating this discussion is the possibility that an author had multiple versions of a text or knew of competing variations. The likeliness of this situation is highly dependent on the author's access to large numbers of texts (i.e., a library). Should an author have multiple versions, s/he can prioritize the narrative of a preferred version over that of another. As a result, the variety of texts should be a caution against claims of conformity and deviance.

Education Systems

All of the authors discussed in this volume had some level of Greek education, although we do not know its specific nature. Some authors hint at their Greek education through personal discussion, but these declarative statements are rare and do not give us a clear picture of the depth, methods, texts, and intensity of the training.[49] The lack of explicit discussion by the authors forces us to infer from their texts what level of training each author attained. This approach has inherent problems, the most obvious being that one (sometimes fragmentary) work may not accurately represent the author's writing ability and/or level of education. Authors can write in different registers and tailor their work to fit specific models. In the case of Jewish authors, this model could be the Septuagint, the imitation of which would not showcase their level of education in Homer or classical authors.

Certain authors, based on their compositions, likely attained the highest levels of education, among whom we would include Jewish epic writers (Philo Epicus, Theodotus), authors who wrote larger works under a Greek pseudonym (Aristeas, Pseudo-Phocylides, Pseudo-Orpheus), Ezekiel the Tragedian, Philo of Alexandria, and Josephus. Other Jewish authors, such as Paul, Eupolemus, Demetrius, and the authors of the Gospels, Joseph and Aseneth, and 2–4 Maccabees, also likely had substantial Greek education, although their level of attainment is debated.[50] Higher levels of education are to be expected from ancient authors whose work has survived, presumably because inferior works were not considered to be worth the effort to preserve. As a result, the evidence base for discussing Greek education undertaken by Jews is skewed.

---

not conform neatly to the LXX, but suggest a different translation and/or access to a Hebrew text. See Adams, "Aristobulus."

49 E.g., Josephus, *Ant.* 20.262–263; *Vita* 8–12 (Jewish education modeled on Greek paideia); Philo, *Congr.* 14–18, 74–80.

50 Cf. Adams, "Luke and *Progymnasmata*"; Schellenberg, *Rethinking Paul's Rhetorical Education.*

The author's location feeds into the wider discussion of Greek education and geography. Education settings were not equal, with quality and opportunities differing among locations (rural/urban) and also within locations, due to differences in social class and wealth.[51] Pedagogical practices also changed over time, following the trends and demands of society and local preferences.[52] Scholars who study education in antiquity have rightly highlighted the importance of Homer and other pinnacular authors as exemplars for students.[53] Less consideration has been given to the types of texts and literary models that would have been employed within Jewish communities in their Greek education. No doubt for some communities there would have been little or no difference from "standard" Greek education, and Jewish students would have learned Homer alongside their non-Jewish classmates. This would almost certainly be the case at the beginning of the Hellenistic era, when only Greek literary works would have been available. Over the centuries, however, a growing diversity of Greek-language literary works, especially from Jewish authors, would have afforded the possibility of alternative models from which to learn.

Some surviving Jewish texts imply a school setting; the *Sentences* of Pseudo-Phocylides provides a strong example. The use of gnomologies and similar collections of aphorisms was common in Greek philosophical and literary education and so would have been known to the author.[54] Although specific Jewish cultural markers are absent, Pseudo-Phocylides' gnomologia provide strong moral advice, using the linguistic features that would have been appropriate for a sixth-century BCE author (e.g., dactylic hexameter and Ionic morphology). This work indicates not only that its Jewish author had sufficient mastery of sixth-century language in order to create this document, but also that other Jews were interested and actively learned this style of Greek. Some of the surviving treatises of Philo of Alexandria are also thought to be educationally orientated.[55] Each series (*Exposition, Allegorical Commentary, Questions and Answers*) has a specific intended audience in mind and is written for different levels of expertise. Unlike gnomologia, which were given to students even at the lower level, Philo's treatises are not elementary, but presume a knowledgeable reader, one familiar with grammar and philosophy.

51 Cribiore, *Gymnastics*, 18.

52 One change was the rise in rhetorical education throughout the Hellenistic era, which became dominant in the Roman era. Cf. Kennedy, *Art of Rhetoric*; M. C. Parsons and M. W. Martin, *Ancient Rhetoric and the New Testament: The Influence of Elementary Greek Composition* (Waco: Baylor University Press, 2018), 1–15.

53 Morgan, *Literate Education*, 67–73; Cribiore, *Gymnastics*, 194–97; H. I. Marrou, *A History of Education in Antiquity* (trans. G. Lamb; London: Sheen and Ward, 1956), 161–63.

54 Cribiore, *Gymnastics*, 179, 202; Morgan, *Literate Education*, 120–25.

55 Sterling, "'School of Sacred Laws'"; Sterling, "Philo's School"; Adams, "Philo's *Questions*."

The widespread knowledge of Scripture evidenced by Jewish authors could also be viewed as evidence for the use of the Septuagint as a school text. I am not arguing for the view that the Greek text was used as a crib to understand Hebrew,[56] or that it would have been used exclusively, but that Jewish teachers may have presented the Septuagint as a literary model from which to learn alternative genres and different registers of Greek. Such a situation could explain the prominence of the Septuagint in Jewish compositions, in terms of both content and language.[57] Also relevant is the author's wider community. Knowledge of the Septuagint is not limited to the classroom, but is provided in the synagogue or home. Both of these locations need to be considered when asserting the possibility of the Septuagint as a school text.

The prominence of the Septuagint is highlighted by the diminished role that Homer and other Greek authors have in Jewish compositions, especially those written in the latter part of the Hellenistic era and whose authors did not adopt a Greek pseudonym. Clearly some Jewish authors had a good understanding of Greek authors and texts, but the diversity of compositions could imply variation in education practices within different communities. As literary education functioned as a form of cultural indoctrination, it would not be surprising if some non-Greeks (including, but not limited to, the Jewish people) felt some unease with the content of the curriculum and created a bespoke program of study with alternative texts. There is little surviving evidence for this from the Hellenistic era, although in the following centuries certain Christian educators would acknowledge this tension and develop a Greek curriculum based on texts with appropriate theological and philosophical ideas.[58] In such cases,

56 Cf. A. Pietersma, "A New Paradigm for Addressing an Old Question: The Relevance of the Interlinear Model for the Study of the Septuagint," in J. Cook, ed., *Bible and Computer: The Stellenbosch AIBI-6 Conference; Proceedings of the Association Internationale Bible et Informatique "From Alpha to Byte," 17–21 July, 2000* (Leiden: Brill, 2002), 337–64; S. P. Brock, "Aspects of Translation Technique in Antiquity," *GRBS* 20 (1978): 69–87. For inter- and intralingual translation in Greek education, see Adams, "Translating Texts," 148–50.

57 L. Rydbeck, *Fachprosa, vermeintliche Volkssprache und Neues Testament: Zur Beurteilung der sprachlichen Niveauunterschiede im nachklassischen Griechisch* (SGU 5; Uppsala: Berlingska Boktryckeriet, 1967); A. Wifstrand, *Epochs and Styles* (ed. and trans. L. Rydbeck and S. E. Porter; WUNT 1.179; Tübingen: Mohr Siebeck, 2005).

58 Cf. Jerome, *Ep.* 107; Basil, *Reg. Fus.* 15 (PG 31.952–57); Pachomius, *Reg. praef.* 139–140. For Scripture as school texts (e.g., Greek Psalms, Matthew, and Paul), see R. Cribiore, "Literary School Exercises," *ZPE* 116 (1997): 60. For a text of Romans as a Greek-Coptic school exercise (P. Mich. 926), see E. M. Husselmann, "A Bohairic School Text on Papyrus," *JNES* 6 (1947): 129–51. H.-G. Nesselrath, "Die Christen und die heidnische Bildung: Das Beispiel des Sokrates Scholastikos (*hist. eccl.* 3,16)," in J. Dummer and M. Vielberg, eds., *Leitbilder der Spätantike—Eliten und Leitbilder* (Stuttgart: Franz Steiner, 1999), 79–100; S. Rappe, "The New Math: How to Add and Subtract Pagan Elements in Christian Education," in Y. L. Too, ed., *Education in Greek and Roman Antiquity* (Leiden: Brill, 2001), 405–32; L. I. Larsen, "Monastic Paideia and Textual Fluidity in the Classroom," in L. I. Lied and H. Lundhaug, eds., *Snapshots of Evolving Traditions:*

Jewish works that model Greek genres—including, but not limited to, pseudepigraphic works—could have had a mediating function within the education system, providing a sufficiently suitable text in terms of content and form.

Authorial knowledge of Hebrew was discussed briefly in a few places in this study. Although this is topic is not central to my argument, it is closely tied to our understanding of Jewish educational practices and our authors' access to texts. Translations of Hebrew and Aramaic Scriptures and other documents provide evidence that some Jews were educated in at least two languages, but it is also clear that many diaspora Jews did not have (strong) knowledge of Hebrew (e.g., Sir. *praef.*).[59] Although this statement is broadly true, nuance is needed, as each author needs to be understood through their own work(s). A good example of this would be Eupolemus, who shows an awareness of Greek translations of the Hexateuch and other books, but also appears to depend on the Hebrew texts of Kings and Chronicles (or at the very least an alternative Greek version). Other authors, such as Aristobulus, Matthew, Paul, Josephus, and the translators of the Septuagint (including the grandson of Joshua Ben Sira), also display knowledge of Hebrew.[60] This blending of source languages demands that we be sensitive to the variety of possible texts available to authors, not only in Judaea, but wherever Jewish authors wrote.

Scholars regularly focus on the author for insights into the ancient education system. Also important, I would argue, is considering the readership of these texts. Unnuanced claims that Jewish authors *only* or *always* wrote for fellow Jews are problematic. The selection of Greek as the language of composition automatically places the authors' works in a larger culture setting.[61] Whereas Hebrew and to a lesser extent Aramaic works could be viewed as purposefully limited to a Jewish readership, the use of Greek indicates that these authors provided an opportunity for their works to be understood and

Jewish and Christian Manuscript Culture, Textual Fluidity, and New Philology (Berlin: De Gruyter, 2017), 146–77; C. Hezser, "The Torah versus Homer: Jewish and Greco-Roman Education in Late Roman Palestine," in M. R. Hauge and A. W. Pitts, eds., *Ancient Education and Early Christianity* (LNTS 533; London: Bloomsbury, 2016), 5–24.

59 For a detailed study of Jewish and Egyptian documentary translation techniques, highlighting similarities between surviving Demotic documents and the Septuagint, see J. K. Aitken, "The Septuagint and Egyptian Translation Methods," in W. Kraus, M. N. van der Meer, and M. Meiser, eds., *XV Congress of the International Organization for Septuagint and Cognate Studies: Munich, 2013* (SCS 64; Atlanta: SBL, 2016), 269–93.

60 Contra Wacholder (*Eupolemus*, 253), who claims that "Eupolemus is the only Graeco-Jewish writer whose knowledge of Hebrew seems attested."

61 Greek would have been the primary or only language for many ancient Jews, and so the element of intentional selection would be lessened. For bilingual writers (e.g., Josephus), the choice of Greek is meaningful. Cf. M. Janse, "Aspects of Bilingualism in the History of the Greek Language," in J. N. Adams, M. Janse, and S. Swain, eds., *Bilingualism in Ancient Society: Language Contact and the Written Text* (Oxford: Oxford University Press, 2002), 340–41.

read outwith the Jewish populous. A broader question, and one that differs depending on the author, is whether or not the writer had an expectation that their work would be read and engaged by a wider audience. In some cases, this desire, or the narrative construct of it, is explicitly made by the author (e.g., Josephus, *BJ* 1.16; Aristobulus, *apud* Eusebius, *Praep. ev.* 8.9.38), whereas in other cases the desired audience needs to be inferred from the work's contents.

In order to understand challenging syntax and deep theoretical arguments, one needs to have been educated to a certain level. Philo Epicus' work is very difficult to read and demands an extensive education to interpret it. The different recensions of Pseudo-Orpheus, especially the addition of new lines and the "correcting" of other lines, indicate that this work was being read by Jews and that a number of its readers had sufficient Greek education both to read and to compose in hexameter. The readers of Philo of Alexandria needed to have had a substantial education in order to understand his treatises. Although we do not know who Philo's contemporary readers were, we do know that subsequent readers, such as Clement of Alexandria and Origen, were thoroughly educated and thought highly of his work.[62] This suggests that Philo's original readers were also highly educated, not only in Jewish literature, but also in Greek philosophy. These examples help us to recognize that behind every author there was a group of readers who would be sufficiently educated in order to read and appreciate the text. As a majority of Jewish works composed in Greek appear to have anticipated a Jewish readership, we can posit with reasonable confidence that in the locations where these texts were written there was a sufficiently large literary community.[63]

Going Forward

The above discussions highlight the "what" findings of this book and are important for understanding how Jewish authors participated in Greek genres during the Hellenistic and Roman eras. More difficult to explain are the "why" questions: Why did these authors do what they did, and what did they think they were doing? Why did they adopt Greek genres? Why did they create atypical examples? Why are different genres used at different times in the Hellenistic era? Answers to these questions and others are more difficult to answer,

62 See the study by D. T. Runia, *Philo in Early Christian Literature: A Survey* (CRINT; Assen: Van Gorcum, 1993).

63 Many Jewish authors wrote for social and literary elites: Aristobulus dedicated his text to King Ptolemy (Eusebius, *Praep. ev.* 8.9.38); Josephus wrote for his Flavian patrons and sent his work to Agrippa (*Vita* 361–367). Although we do not know the intended audience of Philo Epicus' work, the extreme use of the Greek language limits its audience to all but the most educated.

as they go beyond empirical evidence, assigning perceived motivations to authors that are derived from select elements of surviving texts.

Motivations at the macro level are easier to divine, especially in light of the large sampling of authors that has survived. These authors show a sustained effort over the centuries to engage with Greek literary culture, indicating that at least part of the motivation was to have a larger audience for their work, specifically from other ethnic groups, both dominant (e.g., Romans, Greeks) and subordinate (e.g., Egyptians, Babylonians, etc.). Writing in Hebrew would not have accomplished this, and so these authors were required to adopt Greek as their language of communication. Similarly, composing works in Greek but avoiding Greek genres would also have alienated potential outside readers.

Discussions of individual authors benefit from a broad understanding of the literary trends, educational practices, and reading communities in antiquity. By isolating individual works, scholars risk missing wider compositional trends and could impute originality to a more common practice. I argue that a holistic study offers insights otherwise not identified. For the fullest picture of antiquity, the findings identified above need to be compared to studies of other minority cultures in the Greek and Roman eras. These findings are also relevant to modern contexts in which the need for knowledge of English, the colonizing and now-dominant language of trade and politics, redefines individuals' relationship with their native language and the choice of language and genre in which to write.

BIBLIOGRAPHY

Primary

Aucher, J. B., trans. *Philonis Judaei: Paralipomena Armena*. Venice, 1826.

Bastianini, G., and D. N. Sedley, eds. and trans. "Commentarium in Platonis *Theaetetum*: PBerol.inv. 9782." In *Corpus dei Papiri Filosofici greci e latini*, pt. 3, *Commentary*. Florence: Olschki, 1995: 227–562.

Bedrosian, R., trans. *Eusebius' Chronicle: Translated from the Original Aramaic*. SAT. Long Branch: self-published, 2008.

Bergk, T., ed. *Poetae Lyrici Graeci*. Vol. 2. 4th ed. Leipzig: Teubner, 1883.

Bernabé, A., ed. *Orphicorum et Orphicis similium testimonia et fragmenta: Poetae Epici Graeci*. Pars II, fasc. 1. Bibliotheca Teubneriana. Munich: K. G. Saur, 2004.

Bernard, A., trans. *La prose sur pierre dans l'Égypte hellénistique et romaine*. 2 vols. Paris: Éditions du CNRS, 1992.

Bollansée, J., ed. "Hermippos of Smyrna." In *FGrH* IVA.3. Leiden: Brill, 1999.

Burchard, C., ed. *Joseph und Aseneth: Kritisch herausgegeben von Christoph Burchard mit Unterstützung von Carsten Burfeind und Uta Barbara Fink*. PVTG 5. Leiden: Brill, 2003.

Cohn, L., I. Heinemann, and W. Theiler, eds. *Philo von Alexandria: Die Werke in deutscher Übersetzung*. 7 vols. Berlin: De Gruyter, 1909–1964.

Colomo, D., and D. Obbink, eds. "P.Oxy. 5348, Ezekiel Ἐξαγωγή." In P. J. Parsons and N. Gonis, eds., *The Oxyrhynchus Papyri LXXXIII*. London: Egypt Exploration Society, 2018: 14–19.

Colson, C. H., trans. *Philo*. 10 vols., 2 supps. LCL. Cambridge, Mass.: Harvard University Press; London: William Heinemann, 1929.

Cotton, H. M., et al., eds. *Corpus Inscriptionum Iudaeae/Palaestinae*. Berlin: De Gruyter, 2010–.

Conybeare, F. C., ed. *Philo: About the Contemplative Life*. Oxford: Clarendon, 1895.

de Cenival, F., trans. *Le Mythe de l'Oeil du Soleil: Translittération et Traduction avec Commentaire Philologique.* DS 9. Sommerhausen: Zauzich Verlag, 1988.

Derron, P., trans. *Pseudo-Phocylide: Sentences.* Collection des Universités de France (Budé). Paris: Les Belles Lettres, 1986.

Diehl, E., ed. *Anthologia Lyrica Graeca.* 3 vols. Leipzig: Teubner, 1949–1952.

Diels, H., and W. Schubart, eds. *Anonymer Kommentar zu Platons Theatet (Papyrus 9782).* Berlin: Weidmann, 1905.

Dindorf, L., ed. *Historici Graeci minores.* 2 vols. Leipzig: Teubner, 1870–1871.

Dumas, F., ed., and P. Miquel, trans. *De Vita Contemplativa.* PAPM 29. Paris: Éditions du Cerf, 1963.

Dupont-Sommer, A. *Le quatrième livre des Machabées: Introduction, traduction et notes.* Paris: H. Champion, 1939.

Erbse, H., ed. *Scholia Graeca in Homeri Iliadem: Scholia vetera.* 7 vols. Berlin: De Gruyter, 1969–1988.

Fink, U. B., ed. *Joseph und Aseneth: Revision des griechischen Textes und Edition der zweiten lateinischen Übersetzung.* FSBP 5. Berlin: De Gruyter, 2008.

Frick, C., ed. *Chronica Minora: Collegit et Emendavit.* Leipzig: Teubner, 1892.

Geffcken, J., ed. *Die Oracula Sibyllina.* GCS 8. Leipzig: Hinrichs, 1902.

Gifford, E. H., ed. and trans. *Eusebius of Caesarea: Praeparatio Evangelica.* Oxford: Clarendon, 1903.

Gow, A. S. F., ed. and trans. *Theocritus.* 2 vols. Cambridge: Cambridge University Press, 1950.

Grayson, A. K., ed. and trans. *Assyrian and Babylonian Chronicles.* TCS 5. Locust Valley, N.Y.: Augustin, 1975.

Gurtner, D. M., ed. and trans. *Second Baruch: A Critical Edition of the Syriac Text, with Greek and Latin Fragments, English Translation, Introduction, and Concordances.* JCTCRS. London: T&T Clark, 2009.

Hanhart, R., ed. *Septuaginta: Vetus Testamentum Graecum.* Vol. IX.3, *Maccabaeorum liber III.* 2nd ed. Göttingen: Vandenhoeck & Ruprecht, 1980.

Henry, R., ed. and trans. *Photius: Bibliothèque.* 8 vols. Paris: Les Belles Lettres, 1959–1977.

Hollis, A. S., ed. *Callimachus, "Hecale": Edited with Introduction and Commentary.* 2nd ed. Oxford: Clarendon, 2009.

Horbury, W., and D. Noy, eds. *Jewish Inscriptions of Graeco-Roman Egypt.* Cambridge: Cambridge University Press, 1992.

Jasnow, R., and K.-T. Zauzich, eds. and trans. *The Ancient Egyptian Book of Thoth: A Demotic Discourse on Knowledge and Pendant to Classical Hermetica.* 2 vols. Wiesbaden: Harrassowitz, 2005.

Kappler, W., and R. Hanhart, eds. *Maccabaeorum liber II.* Vol. IX.2. 3rd ed. Göttingen: Vandenhoeck & Ruprecht, 2008.

Kern, O. *Orphicorum fragmenta.* Berlin: Apud, 1922.

Kouremenos, T., K. Tsantsanoglou, and G. Parássoglou, eds. *The Derveni Papyrus*. STCPF 13. Florence: Olschki, 2006.

Kühn, C. G., ed. *Claudii Galeni Opera Omnia*. Leipzig: C. Cnobloch, 1821–1833.

Kuhn, T., ed. and trans. *Die jüdisch-hellenistischen Epiker Theodot und Philon: Literarische Untersuchungen, kritische Edition und Übersetzung der Fragmente*. Vertumnus 9. Göttingen: Vandenhoeck & Ruprecht, 2012.

Layton, B., ed. *Nag Hammadi Codex II*. Leiden: Brill, 1989.

Lloyd-Jones, H., and P. Parsons, eds. *Supplementum Hellenisticum*. Berlin: De Gruyter, 1983.

MacPhail, J. A., Jr., ed. and trans. *Porphyry's "Homeric Questions" on the "Iliad."* TUK 36. Berlin: De Gruyter, 2011.

Malherbe, A. J. *Ancient Epistolary Theorists*. SBLSBS 19. Atlanta: Scholars Press, 1988.

Manetti, D. "Heliodorus, *Chirurgumena*." In A. Carlini and M. G. Calvini, eds., *Papiri letterari greci della Bayerische Staatsbibliothek di Monaco di Baviera*. Stuttgart: Teubner, 1986: 19–25.

Moore, C. A., trans. *Daniel, Esther, and Jeremiah: The Additions*. AYBC. New Haven: Yale University Press, 1995.

Mras, K., ed. *Eusebius' Werke*. Vol. 8, *Die Praeparatio evangelica*. Die griechischen christlichen Schriftsteller. 43.1 and 43.2. 2nd ed. Berlin: Akademie Verlag, 1982.

Müller, K., ed. *Geographi Graeci Minores*. 2 vols. Paris: A. Firmin Didot, 1882.

Niese, B., ed. *Flavii Iosephi opera*. 7 vols. 1885. Reprint, Berlin: Weidmann, 1955.

Noy, D., H. Bloedhorn, and W. Ameling, eds. *Inscriptiones Judaicae Orientis*. 3 vols. TSAJ 99, 101, 102. Tübingen: Mohr Siebeck, 2004.

Parry, D. W., and E. Tov, with G. I. Clements, eds. *The Dead Sea Scrolls Reader*. 2nd ed., rev. and expanded. 2 vols. Leiden: Brill, 2014.

Pelletier, A., ed. and trans. *Flavius Josèphe: Autobiographie*. Collection des Universités de France (Budé). Paris: Les Belles Lettres, 1959.

———, ed. and trans. *Lettre d'Aristée à Philocrate: Texte critique, traduction et notes*. SC 89. Paris: Éditions du Cerf, 1962.

Petit, F., ed. *Quaestiones in Genesim et in Exodum, Fragmenta Graeca: Introduction, texte critique et notes*. PAPM 33. Paris: Éditions du Cerf, 1978.

Philonenko, M., ed. and trans. *Joseph et Aséneth: Introduction, texte critique, traduction et notes*. StPB 13. Leiden: Brill, 1968.

Rehm, B., ed. *Die Pseudoklementinen*. Vol. 1, *Homilien*. 3rd ed. Updated by G. Strecker. GCS 42. Berlin: Akademie Verlag, 1992.

Rose, V. *Aristotelis qui ferebantur librorum fragmenta*. Stutgardiae: B.G. Teubner, 1967.

Russell, D. A., and D. Konstan, eds. and trans. *Heraclitus: Homeric Problems*. WGRW 14. Atlanta: SBL, 2005.

Sodano, A. R., ed. *Porphyrii quaestionum Homericarum liber i*. Naples: Giannini, 1970.

Spiegelberg, W., ed. *Die sogenannte Demotische Chronik des Pap. 215 der Bibliothèque Nationale zu Paris nebst den auf der Rückseite des Papyrus stehenden Texten*. Leipzig: Hinrichs, 1914.

Stählin, O., and L. Früchtel, eds. *Clemens Alexandrinus*. Vol. 2, *Stromata Buch I–VI*. 3rd ed. GCS 52. Berlin: Akademie Verlag, 1960.

Stephens, S. A., and J. J. Winkler, eds. and trans. *Ancient Greek Novels: The Fragments; Introduction, Text, Translations, and Commentary*. Princeton: Princeton University Press, 1995.

Stern, M., ed. *Greek and Latin Authors on Jews and Judaism*. 3 vols. Jerusalem: Israel Academy of Sciences and Humanities, 1974–1984.

Tarrant, H., ed. and trans. *Proclus: Commentary on Plato's "Timaeus."* Vol. 1, *Book 1: Proclus on the Socratic State and Atlantis*. Cambridge: Cambridge University Press, 2007.

Thackeray, H. St. J., trans. *Josephus: Wars*. LCL. Cambridge, Mass.: Harvard University Press, 1956.

Torrey, C. C., ed. and trans. *The Lives of the Prophets: Greek Text and Translation*. Philadelphia: SBL, 1946.

Tragan, P.-R., ed. *Josep i Asenet: Introduccio, text grec revisat i notes*. Literatura Intertestamenaria Supplementa 4. Barcelona: Ed. Alpha, 2005.

Trapp, M. B., ed. *Greek and Latin Letters: An Anthology with Translation*. Cambridge: Cambridge University Press, 2003.

van der Horst, P. W., ed. and trans. *Chaeremon: Egyptian Priest and Stoic Philosopher; The Fragments, Collected and Translated with Explanatory Notes*. Leiden: Brill, 1984.

Verbrugghe, G. P., and J. M. Wickersham, ed. and trans. *Berossos and Manetho, Introduced and Translated: Native Traditions in Ancient Mesopotamia and Egypt*. Ann Arbor: University of Michigan Press, 1996.

Wasserstein, A., ed. and trans. *Galen's Commentary on the Hippocratic Treatise Airs, Waters, Places: In the Hebrew Translation of Solomon ha-Me'ati*. Jerusalem: Israel Academy of Science and Humanities, 1982.

Wehrli, F., ed. *Hermippos der Kallimacher: Die Schule des Aristoteles*. Supp. vol. 1. Basel: Schwabe, 1974.

West, M. L., ed. *The Orphic Poems*. Oxford: Clarendon, 1983.

———, ed. *Theognidis et Phocylidis Fragmenta et Adespota quaedam Gnomica*. Berlin: De Gruyter, 1978.

Wevers, J. W., ed. *Genesis*. Vol. 1. Vetus Testamentum Graecum. Auctoritate Academiae Scientiarum Gottingensis editum. Göttingen: Vandenhoeck & Ruprecht, 1974.

White, H., trans. *Appian: Greek Texts with Facing English Translation*. LCL 4. Cambridge, Mass.: Harvard University Press, 1912–1913.

Wieneke, J., ed. *Ezechielis Iudaei poetae Alexandrini fabulae quae inscribitur Ἐξαγωγή fragmenta*. Münster: Aschendorff, 1931.

Ziegler, J., O. Munnich, and D. Fraenkel, eds. *Susanna, Daniel, Bel et Draco*. Vol. XVI.2. 2nd ed. Göttingen: Vandenhoeck & Ruprecht, 1999.

Secondary

Adams, S. A. "Abraham in Philo of Alexandria." In S. A. Adams and Z. Domoney-Lyttle, eds., *Abraham in Jewish and Early Christian Literature*. LSTS. London: Bloomsbury, 2019: 75–92.

———. *Baruch and The Epistle of Jeremiah: A Commentary on the Greek Text of Codex Vaticanus*. SEPT. Leiden: Brill, 2014.

———. "Crucifixion in the Ancient World: A Response to L. L. Welborn." In S. E. Porter, ed., *Paul's World*. PAST 4. Leiden: Brill, 2007: 111–29.

———. "Did Aristobulus Use the LXX for His Citations?" *JSJ* 45 (2014): 1–14.

———. "Fables in Philo of Alexandria: λόγος, μῦθος, and παραβολή." In A. Oegema, J. Pater, and M. Stoutjesdijk, eds., *Parables and Fables in the Graeco-Roman World*. WUNT 1. Tübingen: Mohr Siebeck, forthcoming 2020.

———. *The Genre of Acts and Collected Biography*. SNTSMS 156. Cambridge: Cambridge University Press, 2013.

———. "The Genre of Luke and Acts." In S. A. Adams and M. Pahl, eds., *Issues in Luke-Acts: Selected Essays*. Piscataway, N.J.: Gorgias Press, 2012: 97–120.

———. "How Should We Reconstruct the Historical Paul? Review Essay of Thomas Phillips' *Paul, His Letters, and Acts*." *Journal for the Study of Paul and His Letters* 1 (2011): 93–100.

———. "Jeremiah in the Old Testament Apocrypha and Pseudepigrapha." In J. Lundbom, C. A. Evans, and B. Anderson, eds., *The Book of Jeremiah: Composition, Reception, and Interpretation*. VTSup 178. FIOTL. Leiden: Brill, 2018: 359–78.

———. "Luke, Josephus, and Self-Definition: The Genre of Luke-Acts and Its Relationship to Apologetic Historiography and Collected Biography." In S. E. Porter and A. W. Pitts, eds., *Christian Origins and Hellenistic Judaism: Social and Literary Contexts for the New Testament*. TENTS 10. Leiden: Brill, 2013: 439–59.

———. "Luke and *Progymnasmata*: Rhetorical Handbooks, Rhetorical Sophistication, and Genre Selection." In M. R. Hauge and A. W. Pitts, eds., *Ancient Education and Early Christianity*. LNTS 533. London: Bloomsbury, 2016: 137–54.

———. "Luke's Preface (1.1–4) and Its Relationship to Greek Historical Prefaces: A Response to Loveday Alexander." *JGRChJ* 3 (2006): 177–91.

———. "Paul's Letter Opening and Its Relationship to Ancient Greek Letters: A Study in Epistolary Presence." In S. E. Porter and S. A. Adams, eds., *Paul and the Ancient Letter Form*. PAST 6. Leiden: Brill, 2010: 33–55.

———. "Philo's *Questions* and the Adaptation of Greek Literary Curriculum." In J. Zurawski and G. Boccaccini, eds., *Second Temple Jewish "Paideia" in Context*. BZNW 228. Berlin: De Gruyter, 2017: 167–84.

———. "Sympotic Learning: Symposia Literature and Cultural Education." In J. Norton, L. Askin, and G. Allen, eds., *Bookish Circles: Varieties of Adult*

Learning and Literacy in the Greco-Roman Mediterranean and the Early Church. WUNT 1. Tübingen: Mohr Siebeck, forthcoming 2020.

———. "Translating Texts: Contrasting Roman and Jewish Translation Practices." In S. A. Adams, ed., *Scholastic Culture in the Hellenistic and Roman Eras: Greek, Latin, and Jewish*. Transmissions 2. Berlin: De Gruyter, 2019: 147–67.

———. "What Are Bioi/Vitae? Generic Self-Consciousness in Ancient Biography." In K. De Temmerman, ed., *Oxford Handbook of Ancient Biography*. Oxford: Oxford University Press, 2020: 21–35.

Adams, S. A., and S. M. Ehorn. "Composite Citations in Early Christian Manuscripts." In S. E. Porter, D. I. Yoon, and C. S. Stevens, eds., *Paratextual Features of New Testament Papyrology and Early Christian Manuscripts*. TENTS. Leiden: Brill, forthcoming 2020.

Adler, M. *Studien zu Philon von Alexandreia*. Breslau: Marcus, 1929.

Adler, W. "Alexander Polyhistor's *Peri Ioudaiôn* and Literary Culture in Republican Rome." In S. Inowlocki and C. Zamagni, eds., *Reconsidering Eusebius: Collected Papers on Literary, Historical, and Theological Issues*. VCS 107. Leiden: Brill, 2011: 225–40.

———. "Apion's 'Encomium of Adultery': A Jewish Satire of Greek Paideia in the Pseudo-Clementine *Homilies*." *HUCA* 64 (1993): 15–49.

Ahearne-Kroll, P. "Joseph and Aseneth and Jewish Identity in Greco-Roman Egypt." PhD diss., University of Chicago, 2005.

Aitken, J. K. "The Septuagint and Egyptian Translation Methods." In W. Kraus, M. N. van der Meer, and M. Meiser, eds., *XV Congress of the International Organization for Septuagint and Cognate Studies: Munich, 2013*. SCS 64. Atlanta: SBL, 2016: 269–93.

Aitken, J. K., and L. Cuppi. "Proverbs." In J. K. Aitken, ed., *The T&T Clark Companion to the Septuagint*. London: Bloomsbury, 2015: 341–55.

Albl, M. C. *"And Scripture Cannot Be Broken": The Form and Function of the Early Christian Testimonia Collections*. NovTSup 96. Leiden: Brill, 1999.

Alexander, L. "The Living Voice: Scepticism towards the Written Word in Early Christian and Greco-Roman Texts." In D. J. A. Clines, S. E. Fowl, and S. E. Porter, eds., *The Bible in Three Dimensions: Essays in Celebration of Forty Years of Biblical Studies in the University of Sheffield*. JSOTSup 87. Sheffield: JSOT Press, 1990: 221–47.

———. *The Preface to Luke's Gospel: Literary Convention and Social Context in Luke 1.1–4 and Acts 1.1*. SNTSMS 78. Cambridge: Cambridge University Press, 1993: 34–41.

———. "What Are the Gospels?" In S. C. Barton, ed., *The Cambridge Companion to the Gospels*. Cambridge: Cambridge University Press, 2006: 13–33.

Alexander, P. S. "Epistolary Literature." In M. E. Stone, ed., *Jewish Writings of the Second Temple Period: Apocrypha, Pseudepigrapha, Qumran Sectarian Writings, Philo, Josephus*. CRINT 2.2. Philadelphia: Fortress, 1984: 579–96.

———. "Rabbinic Biography and the Biography of Jesus: A Survey of the Evidence." In C. M. Tuckett, ed., *Synoptic Studies: The Ampleforth Conferences of 1982 and 1983*. JSNTSup 7. Sheffield: JSOT Press, 1984: 19–50.

———. "Retelling the Old Testament." In D. A. Carson and H. G. M. Williamson, eds., *It Is Written: Scripture Citing Scripture*. Cambridge: Cambridge University Press, 1988: 99–120.

Allison, D. C., Jr. *Testament of Abraham*. Berlin: De Gruyter, 2003.

Alon, G. "The Halakah in the Teaching of the Twelve Apostles (Hebrew)." In *Studies in Jewish History in the Times of the Second Temple, the Mishnah and the Talmud*. 2nd ed. Tel Aviv: Hakibbutz Hameuchad, 1967: 274–94.

Anderson, G. *Ancient Fiction: The Novel in the Graeco-Roman World*. London: Croom Helm, 1984.

Anderson, H. "3 Maccabees." In *OTP* 2.509–29.

———. "4 Maccabees: A New Translation and Introduction." In *OTP* 2.531–64.

Anderson, P. *The Riddles of the Fourth Gospel*. Minneapolis: Fortress, 2011.

Appelbaum, A. "A Fresh Look at Philo's Family." *SPhiloA* 30 (2018): 93–113.

Arrighetti, G. "Hypomnemata e scholia: Alcuni problemi." *MPL* 2 (1977): 49–67.

Athanassiadi, P., and M. Frede. *Pagan Monotheism in Late Antiquity*. Oxford: Oxford University Press, 1999.

Atkins, W. H. *Literary Criticism in Antiquity: A Sketch of its Development*. Vol. 1, *Greek*. Cambridge: Cambridge University Press, 1934.

Attridge, H. W. *The Epistle to the Hebrews: A Commentary on the Epistle to the Hebrews*. Hermeneia. Philadelphia: Fortress, 1989.

———. "Fragments of Pseudo-Greek Poets." In *OTP* 2.821–30.

———. "Genre Bending in the Fourth Gospel." *JBL* 121 (2002): 3–21.

———. "The Gospel of John: Genre Matters?" In K. B. Larsen, ed., *The Gospel of John as Genre Mosaic*. SANt 3. Göttingen: Vandenhoeck & Ruprecht, 2015: 27–45.

———. "Historiography." In M. E. Stone, ed., *Jewish Writings of the Second Temple Period: Apocrypha, Pseudepigrapha, Qumran Sectarian Writings, Philo, Josephus*. CRINT 2.2. Philadelphia: Fortress, 1984: 157–84.

———. *The Interpretation of Biblical History in the "Antiquitates Judaicae" of Flavius Josephus*. HDR 7. Missoula, Mont.: Scholars Press, 1976.

———. "Josephus and His Works." In M. E. Stone, ed., *Jewish Writings of the Second Temple Period: Apocrypha, Pseudepigrapha, Qumran Sectarian Writings, Philo, Josephus*. CRINT 2.2. Philadelphia: Fortress, 1984: 185–232.

Aufrère, S. H. "About Strategies and Objectives of Metatextuality." In S. H. Aufrère, P. S. Alexander, and Z. Pleše, eds., *On the Fringes of Commentary: Metatextuality in Ancient Near Eastern and Ancient Mediterranean Cultures*. OLA 232. Leuven: Peeters, 2014: 3–85.

Aune, D. E. "Genre Theory and the Genre-Function of Mark and Matthew." In *Collected Essays*, vol. 2, *Jesus, Gospel Tradition and Paul in the Context of Jewish and Greco-Roman Antiquity*. WUNT 1.303. Tübingen: Mohr Siebeck, 2013: 25–56. First published in E.-M. Becker and A. Runesson, eds., *Mark and Mat-*

thew I: Comparative Readings; Understanding the Earliest Gospels in Their First-Century Settings. WUNT 1.271. Tübingen: Mohr Siebeck, 2011: 145–76.

———. "Luke 1.1–4: Historical or Scientific *Prooimon*?" In A. Christophersen, B. Longenecker, J. Frey, and C. Claussen, eds., *Paul, Luke and the Graeco-Roman World: Essays in Honour of Alexander J. M. Wedderburn*. JSNTSup 217. London: T&T Clark, 2002: 138–48.

———. *The New Testament in Its Literary Environment*. LEC 8. Philadelphia: Westminster, 1987.

———. "Romans as a *Logos Protreptikos*." In K. P. Donfried, ed., *The Romans Debate*. Rev. and expanded ed. Peabody, Mass.: Hendrickson, 1991: 278–96.

Avenarius, G. *Lukians Schrift zur Geschichtsschreibung*. Meisenheim: Hain, 1956.

Baines, J., and C. Eyre, "Four Notes on Literacy." In J. Baines, ed., *Visual and Written Culture in Ancient Egypt*. Oxford: Oxford University Press, 2007: 63–94.

Baker, C. "A 'Jew' by Any Other Name?" *JAJ* 2 (2011): 152–80.

Bakhtin, M. *The Dialogic Imagination: Four Essays by M. M. Bakhtin*. Edited by M. Holquist. Translated by C. Emerson and M. Holquist. Austin: University of Texas Press, 1981.

———. "Discourse in the Novel." In M. Holquist, ed., *The Dialogic Imagination: Four Essays by M. M. Bakhtin*. Translated by C. Emerson and M. Holquist. Austin: University of Texas Press, 1981: 259–422.

———. "Epic and Novel: Toward a Methodology for the Study of the Novel." In M. Holquist, ed., *The Dialogic Imagination: Four Essays by M. M. Bakhtin*. Translated by C. Emerson and M. Holquist. Austin: University of Texas Press, 1981: 3–40.

———. "The Problem of Speech Genres." In D. Duff, ed., *Modern Genre Theory*. LCR. London: Longman, 2000: 82–97.

———. *Speech Genres and Other Late Essays*. Translated by V. W. McGee. Austin: University of Texas Press, 1986.

Balch, D. L. "ἀκριβῶς . . . γράψαι (Luke 1:3): To Write the Full History of God's Receiving All Nations." In D. P. Moessner, ed., *Jesus and the Heritage of Israel*. Philadelphia: Trinity Press, 1999: 229–50.

———. "Attitudes towards Foreigners in 2 Maccabees, Eupolemus, Esther, Aristeas, and Luke-Acts." In A. J. Malherbe, F. W. Norris, and J. W. Thompson, eds., *The Early Church in Its Context: Essays in Honor of Everett Ferguson*. NovTSup 90. Leiden: Brill, 1998: 22–47.

Barbu, D. "Artapan: Introduction Historique et Historiographique." In P. Borgeaud, T. Römer, and Y. Volokhine, eds., *Interprétations de Moïse: Égypte, Judée, Grèce et Rome*. JSRC 10. Leiden: Brill, 2010: 3–23.

Barclay, J. M. G., trans. *Flavius Josephus: Against Apion, Translation and Commentary*. Leiden: Brill, 2007.

———. *Jews in the Mediterranean Diaspora: From Alexander to Trajan (323 BCE–117 CE)*. Edinburgh: T&T Clark, 1996.

———. "Josephus' *Contra Apionem* as Jewish Apologetics." In A.-C. Jacobsen, J. Ulrich, and D. Brakke, eds., *Critique and Apologetics: Jews, Christians and Pagans in Antiquity*. ECCA. Frankfurt am Main: Peter Lang, 2009: 265–82.

———. "Josephus v. Apion: Analysis of an Argument." In S. Mason, ed., *Understanding Josephus: Seven Perspectives*. LSTS 32. Sheffield: Sheffield Academic Press, 1998: 194–221.

Bar-Ilan, M. "Illiteracy in the Land of Israel in the First Centuries C.E." In S. Fishbane and S. Schoenfeld, with A. Goldschläger, eds., *Essays in the Social Scientific Study of Judaism and Jewish Society*, vol. 2. Hoboken, N.J.: Ktav, 1992: 46–61.

Barish, D. A. "The Autobiography of Josephus and the Hypothesis of a Second Edition of His Antiquities." *HTR* 71 (1978): 61–75.

Bar-Kochva, B. *The Image of the Jews in Greek Literature: The Hellenistic Period*. Berkeley: University of California Press, 2010.

———. *Judas Maccabaeus: The Jewish Struggle against the Seleucids*. Cambridge: Cambridge University Press, 1989.

———. *Pseudo-Hecataeus, "On the Jews": Legitimizing the Jewish Diaspora*. HCS 21. Berkeley: University of California Press, 1996.

Barnes, T. D. "The Sack of the Temple in Josephus and Tacitus." In J. Edmondson, S. Mason, and J. Rives, eds., *Flavius Josephus and Flavian Rome*. Oxford: Oxford University Press, 2005: 129–44.

Baron, C. A. *Timaeus of Tauromenium and Hellenistic Historiography*. Cambridge: Cambridge University Press, 2012.

Barzanò, A. "Giusto di Tiberiade." *ANRW* 2.20.1 (1987): 337–58.

Bassler, J. M. "Philo on Joseph: The Basic Coherence of *De Iosepho* and *De Somniis II*." *JSJ* 16 (1985): 240–55.

Bauckham, R. "The Beloved Disciple as Ideal Author." *JSNT* 49 (1993): 21–44.

———. "Historiographical Characteristics of the Gospel of John." *NTS* 53 (2007): 17–36.

Baumbach, M. "Borderline Experiences with Genre: The Homeric *Hymn to Aphrodite* between Epic, Hymn and Epyllic Poetry." In M. Baumbach and S. Bär, eds., *Brill's Companion to Greek and Latin Epyllion and Its Reception*. Leiden: Brill, 2012: 135–48.

Baumbach, M., and S. Bär. "A Short Introduction to the Ancient Epyllion." In M. Baumbach and S. Bär, eds., *Brill's Companion to Greek and Latin Epyllion and Its Reception*. Leiden: Brill, 2012: ix–xvi.

Bearzot, C. "Royal Autobiography in the Hellenistic Age." In G. Marasco, ed., *Political Autobiographies and Memoirs in Antiquity: A Brill Companion*. Leiden: Brill, 2011: 37–85.

Beaulieu, P.-A. "Berossus on Late Babylonian History." *Oriental Studies* (2006): 116–49.

Beavis, M. A. "Philo's Therapeutai: Philosopher's Dream or Utopian Construction?" *JSP* 14 (2004): 30–42.

Becker, E.-M. “Artapanus ‘Judaica’: A Contribution to Early Jewish Historiography.” In N. Calduch-Benages and J. Liesen, eds., *History and Identity: How Israel's Later Authors Viewed Its Earlier History*. Berlin: De Gruyter, 2006: 297–320.

———. *The Birth of Christian History: Memory and Time from Mark to Luke-Acts*. AYBRL. New Haven: Yale University Press, 2017.

———. *Das Markus-Evangelim im Rahmen antiker Historiographie*. WUNT 1.194. Tübingen: Mohr Siebeck, 2006.

Benecker, J. “Individual and Collected Lives in Antiquity.” In K. De Temmerman, ed., *Oxford Handbook of Ancient Biography*. Oxford: Oxford University Press, forthcoming 2020.

Ben Zeev, M. P. *Diaspora Judaism in Turmoil, 116/117 CE: Ancient Sources and Modern Insights*. Leuven: Peeters, 2005.

Berger, K. “Hellenistische Gattungen im Neuen Testament.” *ANRW* 2.25.2 (1984): 1031–432.

Bergmeier, R. “Die Bedeutung der Synoptiker für das johanneische Zeugnisthema: Mit einem Anhang zum Perfekt-Gebrauch im vierten Evangelium.” *NTS* 52 (2006): 458–83.

Bernays, J. *Ueber das phokylideische Gedicht: Ein Beittrag zur hellenistischen Literatur*. Berlin, 1856.

Bernstein, M. J. “4Q252: From Re-written Bible to Biblical Commentary.” In *Reading and Re-reading Scripture at Qumran*. 2 vols. STDJ 107. Leiden: Brill, 2013: 1.92–125.

———. “Introductory Formulas for the Citation and Re-citation of Biblical Verses in the Qumran Pesharim: Observations on a Pesher Technique.” *DSD* 1 (1994): 30–70.

———. “‘Rewritten Bible’: A Generic Category Which Has Outlived Its Usefulness?” *Textus* 22 (2005): 169–96.

Berrin, S. L. *Pesher Nahum Scroll from Qumran: An Exegetical Study of 4Q169*. STDJ 53. Leiden: Brill, 2004.

Berthelot, K. “Hecataeus of Abdera and Jewish ‘Misanthropy.’” *BCRFJ* 19 (2008): n.p.

———. *In Search of the Promised Land? The Hasmonean Dynasty between Biblical Models and Hellenistic Diplomacy*. Translated by M. Rigaud. JAJSup 24. Göttingen: Vandenhoeck & Ruprecht, 2018.

Betegh, G. *The Derveni Papyrus: Cosmology, Theology, and Interpretation*. Cambridge: Cambridge University Press, 2004.

Bhabha, H. *The Location of Culture*. London: Routledge, 1994.

Bickerman, E. J. “The Jewish Historian Demetrios.” In J. Neusner, ed., *Christianity, Judaism and Other Greco-Roman Cults: Studies for Morton Smith at Sixty; Part 3: Judaism before 70*. Leiden: Brill, 1975: 72–84.

———. *The Jews in the Greek Age*. Cambridge, Mass.: Harvard University Press, 1988.

———. “Origines Gentium.” *CP* 47 (1952): 65–81.

———. "Zur Datierung des Pseudo-Aristeas." *ZNW* 29 (1930): 280–98.

Bilde, P. "*Contra Apionem* 1.28–56: An Essay on Josephus' View of His Own Work." In E.-M. Becker, M. H. Jensen, and J. Mortensen, eds., *Collected Studies on Philo and Josephus*. SANt 7. Göttingen: Vandenhoeck & Ruprecht, 2016: 105–20.

———. *Flavius Josephus between Jerusalem and Rome: His Life, His Works, and Their Importance*. JSPSup 2. Sheffield: Sheffield Academic Press, 1988.

Bird, M. F. *1 Esdras: Introduction and Commentary on the Greek Text in Codex Vaticanus*. SEPT. Leiden: Brill, 2012: 141–89.

Bloch, H., ed. *Abhandlungen der griechischen Geschichtsschreibung*. Leiden: Brill, 1956.

Bloch, R. *Jüdische Drehbühnen: Biblische Variationen im antiken Judentum*. TrC 7. Tübingen: Mohr Siebeck, 2013.

———. "Part of the Scene: Jewish Theater in Antiquity." *JAJ* 8 (2017): 150–69.

Boccaccini, G. "La sapienza dello Pseudo-Aristea." In A. Vivian, ed., *Biblische und judaistische Studien: Festschrift für Paolo Sacchi*. Frankfurt am Main: Peter Lang, 1990: 143–76.

Bockmuehl, M. *Ancient Apocryphal Gospels*. Interpretation. Louisville: Westminster John Knox, 2017.

———. "The Dead Sea Scrolls and the Origin of Biblical Commentary." In R. Clements and D. R. Schwartz, eds., *Text, Thought, and Practice in Qumran and Early Christianity: Proceedings of the Ninth International Symposium of the Orion Center for the Study of the Dead Sea Scrolls and Associated Literature, Jointly Sponsored by the Hebrew University Center for the Study of Christianity, 11–13 January, 2004*. STDJ 84. Leiden: Brill, 2009: 1–29.

Bogaert, P.-M. *Apocalypse de Baruch: Introduction, tradition du Syriaque et commentaire*. SC 144 and 145. Paris: Éditions du Cerf, 1969.

Bohak, G. *Ancient Jewish Magic: A History*. Cambridge: Cambridge University Press, 2008.

———. "Asenath's Honeycomb and Onias' Temple: The Key to 'Joseph and Asenath.'" In D. Assaf, ed., *Proceedings of the Eleventh World Congress of Jewish Studies, Division A: The Bible and Its World*. Jerusalem: Magnes Press, 1994: 163–70.

———. "The Diffusion of the Greco-Egyptian Magical Tradition in Late Antiquity." In I. Rutherford, ed., *Greco-Egyptian Interactions: Literature, Translation, and Culture, 500 BCE–300 CE*. Oxford: Oxford University Press, 2016: 357–81.

———. *"Joseph and Aseneth" and the Jewish Temple in Heliopolis*. EJL 10. Atlanta: Scholars Press, 1996.

Bollansée, J. *Hermippos of Smyrna and His Biographical Writings: A Reappraisal*. SH 35. Leuven: Peeters, 1999.

Bömer, F. "Der Commentarius: Zur Vorgeschichte und literarischen Form der Schriften Caesars." *Hermes* 81 (1953): 210–50.

Bonazzi, M. "The Commentary as Polemical Tool: The Anonymous Commentator on the *Theaetetus* against the Stoics." *Laval Théologique et Philosophique* 64 (2008): 597–605.

Borchardt, F. "How Bel and the Serpent Went from Addition to Edition of Daniel." *CBQ* 80 (2018): 409–28.

———. "Reading Aid: 2 Maccabees and the History of Jason of Cyrene Reconsidered." *JSJ* 47 (2016): 71–87.

Borgen, P. "Man's Sovereignty over Animals and Nature According to Philo of Alexandria." In T. Fornberg and D. Hellholm, eds., *Texts and Contexts: Biblical Texts in Their Textual and Situational Contexts: Essays in Honor of Lars Hartman*. Oslo: Scandinavian University Press, 1995: 369–89.

———. "Philo of Alexandria: A Critical and Synthetical Survey of Research since World War II." *ANRW* 2.21.1 (1984): 98–154.

———. *Philo of Alexandria: An Exegete for His Time*. NovTSup 86. Leiden: Brill, 1997: 80–101.

———. "Philo of Alexandria: Reviewing and Rewriting Biblical Material." *SPhiloA* 9 (1997): 37–53.

Borgen, P., and R. Skarsten. "*Questiones et solutiones*: Some Observations on the Form of Philo's Exegesis." *SPhiloA* 4 (1976–1977): 1–16.

Bourgel, J. "Brethren or Strangers? Samaritans in the Eyes of Second-Century B.C.E. Jews." *Bib* 98 (2017): 382–408.

Bowie, E. L. "The Greek Novel." In S. Swain, ed., *Oxford Readings in the Greek Novel*. Oxford: Oxford University Press, 1999: 39–59.

———. "The Readership of Greek Novels in the Ancient World." In J. Tatum, ed., *The Search for the Ancient Novel*. Baltimore: Johns Hopkins University Press, 1994: 435–59.

Bowker, G. C., and S. L. Star. *Sorting Things Out: Classification and Its Consequences*. Cambridge, Mass.: MIT Press, 1999.

Boyarin, D. "Midrash in Hebrews / Hebrews as Midrash." In G. Gelardini and H. W. Attridge, eds., *Hebrews in Context*. AJEC 91. Leiden: Brill, 2016: 15–30.

Braginskaya, N. V. "'Joseph and Aseneth' in Greek Literary History: The Case of the 'First Novel.'" In M. P. F. Pinheiro, J. Perkins, and R. Pervo, eds., *The Ancient Novel and Early Christian and Jewish Narrative: Fictional Intersections*. ANS 16. Groningen: Barkhuis, 2012: 79–105.

Brant, J.-A. A. *Dialogue and Drama: Elements of Greek Tragedy in the Fourth Gospel*. Peabody, Mass.: Hendrickson, 2004.

———. "John among the Ancient Novels." In K. B. Larsen, ed., *The Gospel of John as Genre Mosaic*. SANt 3. Göttingen: Vandenhoeck & Ruprecht, 2015: 157–69.

Braun, M. *History and Romance in Graeco-Oriental Literature*. Oxford: Basil Blackwell, 1938.

Braune, S. "How to Analyze Texts That Were Burned, Lost, Fragmented, or Never Written." *Symploke* 21 (2013): 239–55.

Breitenstein, U. *Beobachtungen zu Sprache, Stil und Gedankengut des Vierten Makkabäerbuchs*. Stuttgart: Schwabe, 1978.

Brenk, F. E. "'In Learned Conversation': Plutarch's Symposiac Literature and the Elusive Authorial Voice." In J. R. Ferreira, D. F. Leão, M. Troster, and P. B. Dias, eds., *Symposion and Philanthropia in Plutarch*. Coimbra, Portugal: Classica Digitalia, 2009: 51–61.

Brock, S. P. "Aspects of Translation Technique in Antiquity." *GRBS* 20 (1978): 69–87.

Broggiato, M. "Beyond the Canon: Hellenistic Scholars and Their Texts." In G. Colesanti and M. Giorgano, eds., *Submerged Literature in Ancient Greek Culture: An Introduction*. Berlin: De Gruyter, 2014: 46–60.

Brooke, G. J. "The Genre of 4Q252: From Poetry to Pesher." *DSD* 1 (1994): 160–79.

———. "Genre Theory, Rewritten Bible, and Pesher." *DSD* 17 (2010): 332–57.

———. "Qumran Pesher: Towards the Redefinition of a Genre." *RevQ* 10 (1981): 483–503.

———. "Rewritten Bible." In L. H. Schiffman and J. C. VanderKam, eds., *Encyclopedia of the Dead Sea Scrolls*. 2 vols. Oxford: Oxford University Press, 2000: 2:777–81.

———. "Thematic Commentaries on Prophetic Scripture." In M. Henze, ed., *Biblical Interpretation at Qumran*. Grand Rapids: Eerdmans, 2005: 134–57.

———. "Types of Historiography in the Qumran Scrolls." In G. J. Brooke and T. Römer, eds., *Ancient and Modern Scriptural Historiography*. BETL 207. Leuven: Leuven University Press, 2007: 211–30.

Brown, R. E. *The Birth of the Messiah: A Commentary on the Infancy Narratives in the Gospels of Matthew and Luke*. Garden City, N.Y.: Doubleday, 1993.

———. *The Death of the Messiah: From Gethsemane to the Grave; A Commentary on the Passion Narratives in the Four Gospels*. 2 vols. ABRL. Garden City, N.Y.: Doubleday, 1994.

———. *The Gospel According to John*. AB 29. Garden City, N.Y.: Doubleday, 1966.

———. *An Introduction to the Gospel of John*. Edited by F. J. Moloney. 2 vols. ABRL. New York: Doubleday, 2003.

Brown-deVost, B. *Commentary and Authority in Mesopotamia and Qumran*. JAJSup 29. Göttingen: Vandenhoeck & Ruprecht, 2019.

———. "The Compositional Development of Qumran Pesharim in Light of Mesopotamian Commentaries." *JBL* 135 (2016): 525–41.

Brownlee, W. H. *The Midrash-Pesher Habakkuk*. Missoula, Mont.: Scholars Press, 1977.

Buitenwerf, R. *Book III of the Sibylline Oracles and Its Social Setting*. SVTP 17. Leiden: Brill, 2003.

Bull, R. J. "A Note on Theodotus's Description of Shechem." *HTR* 60 (1967): 221–28.

Bultmann, R. *The History of the Synoptic Tradition*. Rev. ed. Translated by J. Marsh. Oxford: Basil Blackwell, 1963.

Bunge, J. G. "Untersuchungen zum zweiten Makkabäerbuch: Quellenkritische, literarische, chronologische und historische Untersuchungen zum zweiten Makkabäerbuch als Quelle syrisch-palästinensischer Geschichte im 2. Jh. v. Chr." PhD diss., University of Bonn, 1971.

Burchard, C. "Joseph and Aseneth." In *OTP* 2.177–247.

———. "Joseph et Aseneth: Questions actuelles." In *Gesammelte Studien zu Joseph & Aseneth*. SVTP 39. Leiden: Brill, 1996: 223–61.

———. *Untersuchungen zu Joseph und Aseneth: Überlieferung—Ortsbestimmung*. WUNT 1.8. Tübingen: Mohr Siebeck, 1965.

Burgess, J. S. *The Tradition of the Trojan Women and the Epic Cycle*. Baltimore: Johns Hopkins University Press, 2001.

Burgess, R. W. "Another Look at Sosates, the 'Jewish Homer.'" *JSJ* 44 (2013): 195–217.

Burridge, R. A. "The Genre of Acts—Revisited." In S. Walton, T. E. Phillips, L. K. Pietersen, and F. S. Spencer, eds., *Readings Acts Today: Essays in Honour of Loveday C. A. Alexander*. LNTS 427. London: T&T Clark, 2011: 3–28.

———. *What Are the Gospels? A Comparison with Graeco-Roman Biography*. 3rd ed. Waco: Baylor University Press, 2018.

Burton, A. *Diodorus Siculus, Book I: A Commentary*. Leiden: Brill, 1972.

Bwarshi A. S., and M. J. Reiff. *Genre: An Introduction to History, Theory, Research, and Pedagogy*. West Lafayette, Ind.: Parlor Press, 2010.

Cairns, F. *Generic Composition in Greek and Roman Poetry*. Edinburgh: Edinburgh University Press, 1972.

Campbell, D. A. *Framing Paul: An Epistolary Biography*. Grand Rapids: Eerdmans, 2014.

Campbell, J. G. "'Rewritten Bible' and 'Parabiblical Texts': A Terminological and Ideological Critique." In J. G. Campbell, W. J. Lyons, and L. K. Pietersen, eds., *New Directions in Qumran Studies: Proceedings of the Bristol Colloquium on the Dead Sea Scrolls, 8–10 September 2003*. LNTS 52. London: T&T Clark, 2005: 43–68.

———. "Rewritten Bible: A Terminological Reassessment." In J. Zsengellér, ed., *"Rewritten Bible" after Fifty Years: Texts, Terms, or Techniques? A Last Dialogue with Geza Vermes*. JSJSup 166. Leiden: Brill, 2014: 49–82.

Carey, H. J. *Jesus' Cry from the Cross: Towards a First-Century Understanding of the Intertextual Relationship between Psalm 22 and the Narrative of Mark's Gospels*. LNTS 398. London: T&T Clark, 2009.

Carmignac, J. "Le document de Qumrân sur Melkisédek." *RevQ* 7 (1969): 342–78.

Cervelli, I. "Questioni Sibilline." *Studi Storici* 4 (1993): 895–1001.

Chadwick, H. "Florilegium." *RAC* 7 (1960): 1131–59.

Chankowski, A. S. "Les souverains hellénistiques et l'institution du gymnase: Politiques royales et modèles culturels." In O. Curty and M. Piérart, eds., *L'huile et l'argent: Gymnasiarchie et évergétisme dans la Grèce hellénistique: Actes du colloque tenu à Fribourg, du 13 au 15 octobre 2005, publiés en l'honneur du Prof. Marcel Piérart à l'occasion de son 60ème anniversaire*. Paris: De Boccard, 2009: 95–114.

Chapman, H. H. "'By the Waters of Babylon': Josephus and Greek Poetry." In J. Sievers and G. Lembi, eds., *Josephus and Jewish History in Flavian Rome and Beyond*. JSJSup 104. Leiden: Brill, 2005: 121–46.

Chapman, H. H., and Z. Rodgers, eds. *A Companion to Josephus*. Oxford: Wiley-Blackwell, 2016.

Charlesworth, J. H. *The Pseudepigrapha and Modern Research with a Supplement*. SCS 75. Atlanta: Scholars Press, 1981.

Cheon, S. "Anonymity in the Wisdom of Solomon." *JSP* 18 (1998): 111–19.

Chesnutt, R. D. *From Death to Life: Conversion in Joseph and Aseneth*. JSPSup 16. Sheffield: Sheffield Academic Press, 1995.

Cheung, L. L. *The Genre, Composition and Hermeneutics of the Epistle of James*. PBM. Milton Keynes: Paternoster, 2003.

Christesen, P. *Olympic Victor Lists and Ancient Greek History*. Cambridge: Cambridge University Press, 2007.

Chyutin, M. *Tendentious Hagiographies: Jewish Propagandist Fiction BCE*. LSTS. London: T&T Clark, 2011.

Citroni, M. "Poetry in Augustan Rome." In P. E. Knox, ed., *A Companion to Ovid*. Blackwell Companions to the Ancient World. Chichester: Wiley-Blackwell, 2009: 8–25.

———. "Quintilian and the Perception of the System of Poetic Genres in the Flavian Age." In R. R. Nauta, H. van Dam, and H. Smolenaars, eds., *Flavian Poetry*. MneSup 270. Leiden: Brill, 2005: 1–19.

Clancy, F. "Eupolemus the Chronographer and 141 BCE." *SJOT* 23 (2009): 274–81.

Clark, A. C. *Parallel Lives: The Relation of Paul to the Apostles in the Lucan Perspective*. Carlisle: Paternoster, 2001.

Classen, C. J. "Satire—The Elusive Genre." *Symbolae Osloenses* 63 (1988): 95–121.

Clemens, R., and T. Graham. *Introduction to Manuscript Studies*. Ithaca: Cornell University Press, 2007.

Clifford, H. "Moses as Philosopher-Sage in Philo." In A. Graupner and M. Wolter, eds., *Moses in Biblical and Extra-biblical Tradition*. BZAW 372. Berlin: De Gruyter, 2007: 151–67.

Cohen, R. "Genre Theory, Literary History, and Historical Change." In D. Perkins, ed., *Theoretical Issues in Literary History*. Cambridge, Mass.: Harvard University Press, 1991: 85–113.

———. "History and Genre." *New Literary History* 17 (1986): 201–18.

Cohen, S. J. D. "History and Historiography in the *Against Apion* of Josephus." *History and Theory* 27 (1988): 1–11.

———. *Josephus in Galilee and Rome*. Leiden: Brill, 1979.

———. "Sosates, the Jewish Homer." *HTR* 74 (1981): 391–96.

Colie, R. *The Resources of Kind: Genre Theory in the Renaissance*. Edited by B. K. Lewalski. Berkeley: University of California Press, 1973.

Collins, A. Y. "Aristobulus." In *OTP* 2.831–42.

———. "Genre and the Gospels." *JR* 75 (1995): 239–46.

———. *Is Mark's Gospel a Life of Jesus? The Question of Genre*. Père Marquette Lecture in Theology. Milwaukee: Marquette University Press, 1990.

———. *Mark: A Commentary on the Gospel of Mark*. Hermeneia. Minneapolis: Fortress, 2007.

Collins, J. J. *The Apocalyptic Imagination: An Introduction to Jewish Apocalyptic Literature*. 2nd ed. Grand Rapids: Eerdmans, 1998. 3rd ed. Grand Rapids: Eerdmans, 2016.

———. *Between Athens and Jerusalem: Jewish Identity in the Hellenistic Diaspora*. 2nd ed. Grand Rapids: Eerdmans, 2000.

———. "The Development of the Sibylline Tradition." *ANRW* 2.20.1 (1987): 421–59.

———. "The Epic of Theodotus and the Hellenism of the Hasmoneans." *HTR* 73 (1980): 91–104.

———. "The Jewish Transformation of Sibylline Oracles." In *Seers, Sibyls, and Sages in Hellenistic-Roman Judaism*. Leiden: Brill, 1997: 181–97.

———. *Jewish Wisdom in the Hellenistic Age*. Edinburgh: T&T Clark, 1997.

———. "Joseph and Aseneth: Jewish or Christian?" In J. J. Collins, ed., *Jewish Cult and Hellenistic Culture: Essays on the Jewish Encounter with Hellenism and Roman Rule*. JSJSup 100. Leiden: Brill, 2005: 112–27.

———. "Life after Death in Pseudo-Phocylides." In F. García Martínez and G. P. Luttikhuizen, eds., *Jerusalem, Alexandria, Rome: Studies in Ancient Cultural Interaction in Honour of A. Hilhorst*. JSJSup 82. Leiden: Brill, 2003: 75–86.

———. "Powers in Heaven: God, Gods, and Angels in the Dead Sea Scrolls." In J. J. Collins and R. A. Kugler, eds., *Religion in the Dead Sea Scrolls*. Grand Rapids: Eerdmans, 2000: 1–28.

———. *The Sibylline Oracles of Egyptian Judaism*. DS 13. Missoula, Mont.: Scholars Press, 1974.

———. "Wisdom Reconsidered, in Light of the Scrolls." *DSD* 4 (1997): 265–81.

Collins, N. L. "Ezekiel, the Author of the *Exagoge*: His Calendar and Home." *JSJ* 22 (1991): 201–11.

Connor, W. R. "History without Heroes: Theopompus' Treatment of Philip of Macedon." *GRBS* 8 (1967): 133–54.

Conte, G. B. *Latin Literature: A History*. Translated by J. B. Solodow. Revised by D. Fowler and G. W. Most. Baltimore: Johns Hopkins University Press, 1994.

Cook, J. "The Dating of Septuagint Proverbs." *ETL* 69 (1993): 383–99.

———. *The Septuagint of Proverbs: Jewish and/or Hellenistic Proverbs? Concerning the Hellenistic Colouring of LXX Proverbs*. VTSup 69. Leiden: Brill, 1997.

Cooper, C. "Phainias' Historiographical and Biographical Method: Chronology and Dramatization." In O. Hellmann and D. C. Mirhady, eds., *Phaenias of Eresus: Text, Translation, and Discussion*. New Brunswick, N.J.: Transaction Publishers, 2015: 235–71.

Cooper, J. M. *Pursuits of Wisdom: Six Ways of Life in Ancient Philosophy from Socrates to Plotinus*. Princeton: Princeton University Press, 2012.

Coqueugniot, G. "Scholastic Research in the Archive? Hellenistic Historians and Ancient Archival Records." In S. A. Adams, ed., *Scholastic Culture in the Hellenistic and Roman Eras: Greek, Latin, and Jewish*. Transmissions 2. Berlin: De Gruyter, 2019: 7–29.

Corley, J. "Searching for Structure and Redaction in Ben Sira." In A. Passaro and G. Bella, eds., *The Wisdom of Ben Sira: Studies on Tradition, Redaction, and Theology*. DCLS 1. Berlin: De Gruyter, 2008: 21–48.

Corti, M. *An Introduction to Literary Semiotics*. Translated by M. Bogat and A. Mandelbaum. Bloomington: Indiana University Press, 1978.

Côté, D. "Rhetoric and Jewish-Christianity: The Case of the Grammarian Apion in the Pseudo-Clementine *Homilies*." In P. Piovanelli and T. Burke, eds., *Rediscovering the Apocryphal Continent: New Perspectives on Early Christian and Late Antique Apocryphal Texts and Traditions*. WUNT 1.349. Tübingen: Mohr Siebeck, 2015: 369–90.

Cousland, J. R. C. "Reversal, Recidivism, and Reward in 3 Maccabees: Structure and Purpose." *JSJ* 31 (2003): 39–51.

Cowan, J. A. "A Tale of Two *Antiquities*: A Fresh Evaluation of the Relationship between the Ancient Histories of T. Flavius Josephus and Dionysius of Halicarnassus." *JSJ* 49 (2018): 475–97.

Cox, P. *Biography in Late Antiquity: A Quest for the Holy Man*. TCH 1. Berkeley: University of California Press, 1983.

———. "Strategies of Representation in Collected Biography." In T. Hägg and P. Rousseau, eds., *Greek Biography and Panegyric in Late Antiquity*. Berkeley: University of California Press, 2000: 209–54.

Crawford, S. W. *Rewriting Scripture in Second Temple Times*. Grand Rapids: Eerdmans, 2008.

———. "The 'Rewritten Bible' at Qumran: A Look at Three Texts." *Eretz-Israel* 26 (1999): 1–8.

———. *Scribes and Scrolls at Qumran*. Grand Rapids: Eerdmans, 2019.

Creech, D. A. "'The Lawless Pride: Jewish Identity in the Fragments of Eupolemus." *ASE* 29 (2012): 29–51.

Crenshaw, J. L. *Old Testament Wisdom: An Introduction*. Rev. ed. Louisville: Westminster John Knox, 1998.

Cribiore, R. *Gymnastics of the Mind: Greek Education in Hellenistic and Roman Egypt*. Princeton: Princeton University Press, 2005.

———. "Literary School Exercises." *ZPE* 116 (1997): 53–60.

Croce, B. *Cultura e vita morale*. 2nd ed. Bari: Laterza & Figli, 1936.

———. *Ultimi saggi*. Bari: Laterza & Figli, 1963.

Croy, N. C. *3 Maccabees*. SEPT. Leiden: Brill, 2006.

Crump, M. M. *The Epyllion from Theocritus to Ovid*. Oxford: Blackwell, 1931.

Daise, M. "Samaritans, Seleucids, and the Epic of Theodotus." *JSP* 17 (1998): 25–51.

Damgaard, F. "Philo's Life of Moses and 'Rewritten Bible.'" In J. Zsengellér, ed., *"Rewritten Bible" after Fifty Years: Texts, Terms, or Techniques? A Last Dialogue with Geza Vermes*. JSJSup 166. Leiden: Brill, 2014: 233–48.

Davies, J. "Religion in Historiography." In A. Feldherr, ed., *The Cambridge Companion to Roman Historians*. Cambridge: Cambridge University Press, 2009: 166–80.

Davies, R. B. "Reading Ezekiel's *Exagoge*: Tragedy, Sacrificial Ritual, and the Midrashic Tradition." *GRBS* 48 (2008): 393–415.

Davies, W. D., and D. C. Allison Jr.. *A Critical and Exegetical Commentary on The Gospel According to Saint Matthew*. 3 vols. ICC. Edinburgh: T&T Clark, 1988–1997.

Davila, J. R. *The Provenance of the Pseudepigrapha: Jewish, Christian, or Other?* JSJSup 105. Leiden: Brill, 2005.

Dawson, D. *Allegorical Readers and Cultural Revision in Ancient Alexandria*. Berkeley: University of California Press, 1992.

Dawson, Z. K. "The Problem of Gospel Genres: Unmasking a Flawed Consensus and Providing a Fresh Way Forward with Systemic Functional Linguistics Genre Theory." *BAGL* 8 (2019): 33–77.

DeConick, A. D. *The Original Gospel of Thomas in Translation: With a Commentary and New English Translation of the Complete Gospel*. LNTS 287. London: T&T Clark, 2006.

———. *Recovering the Original Gospel of Thomas: A History of the Gospel and Its Growth*. LNTS 286. London: T&T Clark, 2005.

de Crom, D. "The *Letter of Aristeas* and the Authority of the Septuagint." *JSP* 17 (2008): 141–60.

Deissmann, A. *Bible Studies*. Translated by A. Grieve. Edinburgh: T&T Clark, 1901.

———. *Light from the Ancient East: The New Testament Illustrated by Recently Discovered Texts of the Graeco-Roman World*. 4th ed. Translated by L. R. M. Strachan. London: Hodder and Stoughton, 1927.

———. "Das vierte Makkabäerbuch." In E. Kautzsch, ed., *Die Apokryphen und Pseudepigraphen des Alten Testaments*. 2 vols. Hildesheim: Georg Olms, 1900: 2.149–76.

de Jong, I. J. F. "Narratological Theory on Narrators, Narratees, and Narrative." In I. J. F. de Jong, R. Nünlist, and A. M. Bowie, eds., *Studies in Ancient Greek Narrative*. Vol. 1, *Narrators, Narratees, and Narratives in Ancient Greek Literature*. MneSup 257. Leiden: Brill, 2004: 1–10.

———. *Narratology and Classics: A Practical Guide*. Oxford: Oxford University Press, 2014.

de Jong, I. J. F., R. Nünlist, and A. Bowie, eds. *Studies in Ancient Greek Narrative*. Vol. 1, *Narrators, Narratees, and Narratives in Ancient Greek Literature*. MneSup 257. Leiden: Brill, 2004.

Del Fabbro, M. “Il commentario nella tradizione papiracea.” *SPap* 18 (1979): 69–132.

Delling, G. “Einwirkungen der Sprache der Septuaginta in ‘Joseph and Aseneth.’” *JSJ* 9 (1978): 29–56.

Denis, A.-M. *Introduction à la Littérature Religieuse Judéo-Hellénistique*. Turnhout, Belgium: Brepols, 2000.

Depew, M. “ἰαμβεῖον καλεῖται νῦν: Genre, Occasion, and Imitation in Callimachus, frr. 191 and 203Pf.” *TAPA* 122 (1992): 313–30.

Depew, M., and D. Obbink. “Introduction.” In M. Depew and D. Obbink, eds., *Matrices of Genre: Authors, Canons, and Societies*. CHSC 4. Cambridge, Mass.: Harvard University Press, 2000: 1–14.

Derrida, J. “The Law of Genre.” *Critical Inquiry* 7 (1980): 55–81. Reprinted with revisions in D. Attridge, ed., *Acts of Literature*. London: Routledge, 1992: 221–52.

deSilva, D. A. “The Author of 4 Maccabees and Greek *Paideia*: Facets of the Formation of a Hellenistic Jewish Rhetor.” In J. Zurawski and G. Boccaccini, eds., *Second Temple Jewish “Paideia” in Context*. BZNW 228. Berlin: De Gruyter, 2017: 205–38.

———. *4 Maccabees*. Sheffield: Sheffield Academic Press, 1998.

———. *4 Maccabees: Introduction and Commentary on the Greek Text of Codex Sinaiticus*. SEPT. Leiden: Brill, 2006.

———. *Introducing the Apocrypha: Message, Context, and Significance*. 2nd ed. Grand Rapids: Baker Academic, 2018.

De Temmerman, K., ed. *Oxford Handbook of Ancient Biography*. Oxford: Oxford University Press, forthcoming 2020.

De Temmerman, K., and K. Demoen, eds. *Writing Biography in Greece and Rome: Narrative Techniques and Fictionalization*. Cambridge: Cambridge University Press, 2016.

de Troyer, K. *Rewriting the Sacred Text: What the Old Greek Texts Tell Us about the Literary Growth of the Bible*. TCSt 4. Atlanta: SBL, 2003.

———. “Zerubbabel and Ezra: A Revived and Revised Solomon and Josiah? A Survey of Current 1 Esdras Research.” *CBR* 1 (2002): 30–60.

Dettwiler, A. *Die Gegenwart des Erhböten: Eine exegetische Studie zu den johanneischen Abschiedsreden (Joh 13,31–16,33) unter besonderer Berücksichtigung ihres Relecture-Charakters*. FRLANT 169. Göttingen: Vandenhoeck & Ruprecht, 1995.

Devitt, A. J. *Writing Genres*. Carbondale: Southern Illinois University Press, 2004.

De Vos, B. “The Role of the *Homilistic* Disputes with Appion.” *VC* 73 (2019): 54–88.

Dhont, M. “The Appreciation of Jewish Literature in the Hellenistic Era: The Case of Eupolemus.” Presented at SBL Boston, November 2017.

Dicken, F. “The Author and Date of Luke-Acts: Exploring the Options.” In S. A. Adams and M. Pahl, eds., *Issues in Luke-Acts: Selected Essays*. Piscataway, N.J.: Gorgias Press, 2012: 7–26.

Dickey, E. *Ancient Greek Scholarship: A Guide to Finding, Reading, and Understanding Scholia, Commentaries, Lexica, and Grammatical Treatises, from Their Beginnings to the Byzantine Period.* Oxford: Oxford University Press, 2007.

———. *The Colloquia of the Hermeneumata Pseudodositheana*. 2 vols. CCTC. Cambridge: Cambridge University Press, 2012–2015.

———. "The Sources of Our Knowledge of Ancient Scholarship." In F. Montanari, S. Matthaios, and A. Rengakos, eds., *Brill's Companion to Ancient Greek Scholarship*, vol. 1, *History, Disciplinary Profiles*. Leiden: Brill, 2015: 459–514.

Diehl, J. A. "What Is a 'Gospel'? Recent Studies in the Gospel Genre." *CBR* 9 (2011): 171–99.

Dihle, A. "Zur hellenistischen Ethnographie." In *Grecs et barbares.* Entretiens sur l'Antiquité classique 8. Geneva: Fondation Hardt, 1961: 207–39.

Dillery, J. *Clio's Other Sons: Berossus and Manetho*. Ann Arbor: University of Michigan Press, 2015.

———. "Manetho." In T. Whitmarsh and S. Thomson, eds., *The Romance between Greece and the East*. Cambridge: Cambridge University Press, 2013: 38–58.

———. "Putting Him Back Together Again: Apion Historian, Apion Grammatikos." *CPhil* 98 (2003): 383–90.

Dillon, J. *The Middle Platonists*. London: Duckworth, 1977.

Dimant, D. "Qumran Sectarian Literature." In M. E. Stone, ed., *Jewish Writings of the Second Temple Period: Apocrypha, Pseudepigrapha, Qumran Sectarian Writings, Philo, Josephus*. CRINT 2.2. Philadelphia: Fortress, 1984: 483–550.

———. "Use and Interpretation of Mikra in the Apocrypha and Pseudepigrapha." In M. J. Mulder, ed., *Mikra*. Assen: Van Gorcum, 1988: 379–419.

DiTommaso, L. *The Book of Daniel and the Apocryphal Daniel Literature.* SVTP 20. Leiden: Brill, 2005.

Dixon, R. M. W. *The Rise and Fall of Languages*. Cambridge: Cambridge University Press, 1997.

Docherty, S. *The Jewish Pseudepigrapha: An Introduction to the Literature of the Second Temple Period.* London: SPCK, 2014.

———. "*Joseph and Aseneth*: Rewritten Bible or Narrative Expansion?" *JSJ* 35 (2004): 27–48.

Doering, L. *Ancient Jewish Letters and the Beginnings of Christian Epistolography.* WUNT 1.298. Tübingen: Mohr Siebeck, 2012.

Doran, R. "The High Cost of a Good Education." In J. J. Collins and G. E. Sterling, eds., *Hellenism in the Land of Israel.* Notre Dame: University of Notre Dame Press, 2001: 94–115.

———. "Jason's Gymnasion." In H. W. Attridge, J. J. Collins, and T. H. Tobin, eds., *Of Scribes and Scrolls: Studies on the Hebrew Bible, Intertestamental Judaism and Christian Origins*. Lanham, Md.: University Press of America, 1990: 99–109.

———. "The Jewish Hellenistic Historians before Josephus." *ANRW* 2.20.1 (1987): 246–97.

———. "Ps.-Eupolemus." In *OTP* 2.873–76.
———. *2 Maccabees: A Critical Commentary.* Hermeneia. Minneapolis: Fortress, 2012.
———. "2 Maccabees and 'Tragic History.'" *HUCA* 50 (1979): 107–14.
———. *Temple Propaganda: The Purpose and Character of 2 Maccabees.* CBQMS 12. Washington, D.C.: Catholic Biblical Association, 1981.
Dorandi, T. "*Ex Uno Fonte Multi Rivuli?* Unity and Multiplicity in Hellenistic Biography." In K. De Temmerman, ed., *Oxford Handbook of Ancient Biography.* Oxford: Oxford University Press, 2020: 137–51.
———. "Le commentaire dans la tradition papyrologique: Quelques cas Controversés." In M.-O. Goulet-Cazé, ed., *Le commentaire entre tradition et innovation, Actes du Colloque international de l'Institut des Traditions textuelles (Paris et Villejuif, 22–25 septembre 1999).* Paris: Vrin, 2000: 15–28.
Dormeyer, D. *Evangelium als literarische und theologische Gattung.* EdF 263. Darmstadt: Wissenschaftliche Buchgesellschaft, 1989.
———. "Die Gattung der Apostelgeschichte." In J. Frey, C. K. Rothschild, and J. Schröter, with B. Rost, eds., *Die Apostelgeschichte im Kontext antiker und frühchristlicher Historiographie.* Berlin: De Gruyter, 2009: 437–75.
———. "Die Vita des Josephus als Biographie eines gescheiterten Herrschers." In F. Siegert and J. U. Kalms, eds., *Internationales Josephus-Kolloquium Dortmund 2002: Arbeiten aus dem Institutum Judaicum Delitzschianum.* Münster: LIT Verlag, 2003: 15–33.
Dörrie, H., and H. Dörries. "Erotapokriseis." *RAC* 6 (1966): 342–70.
Doty, W. G. *Letters in Primitive Christianity.* Philadelphia: Fortress, 1973.
Dougherty, C., and L. Kurke, "Introduction." In C. Dougherty and L. Kurke, eds., *The Cultures within Ancient Greek Culture: Contact, Conflict, Collaboration.* Cambridge: Cambridge University Press, 2003: 1–19.
Dreyer, O. "Luseis." *KP* (1975): 832–33.
Droge, A. J. *Homer or Moses? Early Christian Interpretation of the History of Culture.* Tübingen: Mohr Siebeck, 1989.
Dubischar, M. "Survival of the Most Condensed? Auxiliary Texts, Communications Theory, and Condensation of Knowledge." In M. Horster and C. Reitz, eds., *Condensing Texts—Condensed Texts.* Stuttgart: Steiner, 2010: 39–68.
Dubrow, H. *Genre.* Critical Idiom 42. London: Methuen, 1982.
Duff, D. "Introduction." In D. Duff, ed., *Modern Genre Theory.* LCR. London: Longman, 2000: 1–24.
Duff, T. *Plutarch's Lives: Exploring Virtue and Vice.* Oxford: Oxford University Press, 1999.
Dunn, J. D. G., ed. *The Cambridge Companion to St. Paul.* Cambridge: Cambridge University Press, 2003.
Earl, D. "Prologue-Form in Ancient Historiography." *ANRW* 1.2 (1972): 484–856.
Edmunds, L., and R. W. Wallace, eds. *Poet, Public, and Performance in Ancient Greece.* Baltimore: Johns Hopkins University Press, 1997.

Edwards, M. J. "Biography and Biographic." In M. J. Edwards and S. Swain, eds., *Portraits: Biographical Representation in the Greek and Latin Literature of the Roman Empire*. Oxford: Clarendon, 1997: 228–34.

———. "Birth, Death, and Divinity in Porphyry's Life of Plotinus." In T. Hägg and P. Rousseau, eds., *Greek Biography and Panegyric in Late Antiquity*. TCH 31. Berkeley: University of California Press, 2000: 52–71.

———. "Gospel and Genre: Some Reservations." In B. C. McGing and J. Mossman, eds., *The Limits of Ancient Biography*. Swansea: Classical Press of Wales, 2006: 51–62.

Ehrensperger, K. *Paul at the Crossroads of Cultures: Theologizing in the Space Between*. LNTS 456. London: Bloomsbury, 2013.

Ehrman, B. D. *Forgery and Counterforgery: The Use of Literary Deceit in Early Christian Polemics*. New York: Oxford University Press, 2013.

Ellingworth, P. *The Epistle to the Hebrews: A Commentary on the Greek Text*. NIGTC. Grand Rapids: Eerdmans, 1993.

Ellis, E. E. "Biblical Interpretation in the New Testament Church." In M. J. Mulder, ed., *Mikra: Text, Translation, Reading and Interpretation of the Hebrew Bible in Ancient Judaism and Early Christianity*. CRINT 2.1. Philadelphia: Fortress, 1988: 691–725.

Emmet, C. W. "The Third Book of Maccabees." In *APOT* 1.155–73.

Engberg-Pedersen, T. "Philo's *De vita contemplativa* as Philosopher's Dream." *JSJ* 30 (1999): 40–64.

Erbse, H. "Über Aristarchs Iliasausgaben." *Hermes* 87 (1959): 275–303.

Fallon, F. "Theodotus." In *OTP* 2.785–93.

Fantham, E. *Roman Literary Culture: From Cicero to Apuleius*. Baltimore: Johns Hopkins University Press, 1996.

Fantuzzi, M. "Epyllion." In *BNP* 4.1170–72.

Fantuzzi, M., and R. L. Hunter. *Tradition and Innovation in Hellenistic Poetry*. Cambridge: Cambridge University Press, 2004.

Farrell, J. "Classical Genre in Theory and Practice." *New Literary History* 34 (2003): 383–408.

Feder, F. "The Legend of the Sun's Eye: The Translation of an Egyptian Novel into Greek." In S. T. Tovar and J. P. Monferrer-Sala, eds., *Cultures in Contact: Transfer of Knowledge in the Mediterranean Context; Selected Papers*. Cordoba: Oriens Academic, 2013: 3–12.

Felber, H. "Die demotische Chronik." In A. Blasius and B. U. Schipper, eds., *Apokalyptik und Ägypten: Eine kritische Analyse der relevanten Texte aus dem griechisch-römischen Ägypten*. OLA 107. Leuven: Peeters, 2002: 65–111.

Feldman, L. H. "The Influence of Greek Tragedians on Josephus." In A. Ovadiah, ed., *The Howard Gilman International Conferences I: Hellenic and Jewish Arts*. Tel Aviv: RAMOT, 1998: 51–80.

———. *Josephus and Modern Scholarship (1937–1980)*. Berlin: De Gruyter, 1984.

———. *Josephus's Interpretation of the Bible*. Berkeley: University of California Press, 1998.

———. "Josephus' Portrait of Moses." *JQR* 82 (1992): 285–328.

———. *Philo's Portrayal of Moses in the Context of Ancient Judaism*. Notre Dame: University of Notre Dame Press, 2007.

———. "Use, Authority and Exegesis of Mikra in the Writings of Josephus." In M. J. Mulder, ed., *Mikra: Text, Translation, Reading and Interpretation of the Hebrew Bible in Ancient Judaism and Early Christianity*. CRINT 2.1. Philadelphia: Fortress, 1988: 455–518.

Fernández Delgado, J. A. "Paráfrasis homéricas en papiros, tablillas y óstraka." *EC* 15 (2011): 3–45.

Finkelberg, M. "Elitist Orality and the Triviality of Writing." In C. Cooper, ed., *Politics of Orality*. MneSup 280. OLAC 6. Leiden: Brill, 2007: 293–305.

Finlay, M. I. *The World of Odysseus*. New York: Viking Press, 1965.

Fishbane, M. "The Qumran Pesher and Traits of Ancient Hermeneutics." In A. Shinan, ed., *Proceedings of the Sixth World Congress of Jewish Studies*. 4 vols. Jerusalem: World Union of Jewish Studies, 1977: 1:97–114.

Fitzmyer, J. A. *Tobit*. CEJL. Berlin: De Gruyter, 2002.

Fletcher, M. *Reading Revelation as Pastiche: Imitating the Past*. LNTS 571. London: Bloomsbury, 2017.

Flint, P. W. "The Prophet David at Qumran." In M. Henze, ed., *Biblical Interpretation at Qumran*. Grand Rapids: Eerdmans, 2005: 158–67.

Fountoulakis, A. "Greek Dramatic Conventions in Ezekiel's *Exagoge*." *Platon* 48 (1996): 88–112.

Fowler, A. *Kinds of Literature: An Introduction to the Theory of Genres and Modes*. Oxford: Oxford University Press, 1982.

Fraade, S. D. "Early Rabbinic Midrash between Philo and Qumran." In M. L. Satlow, ed., *Strength to Strength: Essays in Appreciation of Shaye J. D. Cohen*. Providence: Brown Judaic Studies, 2018: 281–93.

———. *From Tradition to Commentary: Torah and Its Interpretation in the Midrash Sifre to Deuteronomy*. Albany: State University of New York Press, 1991.

———. "Rewritten Bible and Rabbinic Midrash as Commentary." In C. Bakhos, ed., *Current Trends in the Study of Midrash*. Leiden: Brill, 2006: 59–78.

Frahm, E. *Babylonian and Assyrian Text Commentaries: Origins of Interpretation*. GMTR 5. Münster: Ugarit-Verlag, 2011.

France, R. T. *The Gospel of Matthew*. NICNT. Grand Rapids: Eerdmans, 2007.

Frankfort, T. "La date de l'Autobiographie de Flavius Josèphe et les oeuvres de Justus de Tibériade." *RbPH* 39 (1961): 52–58.

Fraser, P. M. *Ptolemaic Alexandria*. 3 vols. Oxford: Clarendon, 1972.

Frazier, F. "Les visages de Joseph dans le *De Josepho*." *SPhiloA* 14 (2002): 1–30.

Freudenthal, J. *Alexander Polyhistor und die von ihm erhaltenen Reste jüdischer und samaritanischer Geschichtswerke*. Books 1 and 2 of *Hellenistische Studien*. Breslau: Skutsch, 1874–1875.

———. *Die Flavius Josephus beigelegte Schrift über die Herrschaft der Vernunft (IV Makkabäerbuch), eine Predigt aus dem ersten nachchristlichen Jahrhundert*. Breslau: Skutsch, 1869.

Frickenschmidt, D. *Evangelium als Biographie: Die vier Evangelien im Rahmen antiker Erzählkunst*. Tübingen: Francke, 1997.

Friedländer, M. *Geschichte der jüdischen Apologetik als Vorgeschichte des Christentums*. Zürich: Schmidt, 1903.

Friesen, C. J. P. *Reading Dionysus: Euripides' "Bacchae" and the Cultural Contestations of Greeks, Jews, Romans, and Christians*. STAC 95. Tübingen: Mohr Siebeck, 2015.

Friis, M. *Image and Imitation: Josephus' Antiquities 1–11 and Greco-Roman Historiography*. WUNT 2.472. Tübingen: Mohr Siebeck, 2018.

Frow, J. *Genre*. 2nd ed. London: Routledge, 2015.

———. "'Reproducibles, Rubrics, and Everything You Need': Genre Theory Today." *PMLA* 122 (2007): 1626–34.

Gabba, E. "True History and False History in Classical Antiquity." *JRS* 71 (1981): 50–62.

Gabbay, U. "Akkadian Commentaries from Ancient Mesopotamia and Their Relation to Early Hebrew Exegesis." *DSD* 19 (2012): 267–312.

Gager, J. G. "Pseudo-Hecataeus Again." *ZNW* 60 (1969): 130–39.

Gambetti, S. "Some Considerations on Ezekiel's *Exagoge*." *JAJ* 8 (2017): 188–207.

Gamble, H. Y. *Books and Readers in the Early Church: A History of Early Christian Texts*. New Haven: Yale University Press, 1995.

Garstad, B. "Thallos (256)." In *BNJ*.

Gartner, H. A. "Zetema." *DNP* 12 (2002): 778–79.

Gasparro, G. S. "Mosè e Balaam, *Propheteia* e *Mantiké*. Modalità et segni della rivelazione nel *De Vita Mosis*." In A. M. Mazzanti and F. Calabi, eds., *La rivelazione in Filone di Alessandria: Natura, legge, storia; Atti del VII Convegno di studi del Gruppo italiano di ricerca su Origene e la tradizione alessandrina (Bologna 29–30 settembre 2003)*. BdA 2. Villa Verucchio: Pazzini, 2004: 33–74.

Gathercole, S. *The Composition of the Gospel of Thomas: Original Language and Influences*. SNTSMS 151. Cambridge: Cambridge University Press, 2012.

———. *The Gospel of Thomas: Introduction and Commentary*. TENTS 11. Leiden: Brill, 2014.

Gauger, J.-D. *Authentizität und Methode: Untersuchungen zum historischen Wert des persich-griechischen Herrscherbriefs in literarischer Tradition*. SGA 6. Hamburg: Kovač, 2000.

———. "Zitate in der jüdischen Apologetik und die Authentizität der Hekataios-Passagen bei Flavius Josephus und im Ps. Aristeas-Brief." *JSJ* 13 (1982): 6–46.

Geffcken, J. *Komposition und Entstehungszeit der Oracula Sibyllina*. Leipzig: Hinrichs, 1902.

Geiger, J. *Cornelius Nepos and Ancient Political Biography*. HE 47. Stuttgart: Franz Steiner, 1985.

Geljon, A. C. *Philonic Exegesis in Gregory of Nyssa's "De Vita Moysis."* BJS 333. SPhiloM 5. Atlanta: Scholars Press, 2002.
Gelzer, M. "Die Vita des Josephus." *Hermes* 80 (1952): 67–90.
Genette, G. *Palimpsests: Literature in the Second Degree.* Translated by C. Newman and C. Doubinsky. Lincoln: University of Nebraska Press, 1997.
Gentili, B., and G. Cerri. *History and Biography in Ancient Thought.* Amsterdam: J. C. Gieben, 1988.
Gera, D. L. *Judith.* CEJL. Berlin: De Gruyter, 2014.
Gerber, C. *Ein Bild des Judentums für Nichtjuden von Flavius Josephus: Untersuchungen ze seiner Schrift Contra Apionum.* Leiden: Brill, 1997.
———. "Des Josephus Apologie für das Judentum: Prolegomena zu einer Interpretation von C 2:145ff." In J. U. Kalms and F. Siegert, eds., *Internationales Josephus-Kolloquium Brüssel 1998.* Münster: LIT Verlag, 1999: 251–69.
Giblet, J. "Eupolème et l'historiographie de Judaïsme hellénistique." *ETL* 39 (1963): 539–54.
Gibson, R. K., and A. D. Morrison. "Introduction: What Is a Letter?" In R. Morello and A. D. Morrison, eds., *Ancient Letters: Classical and Late Antique Epistolography.* Oxford: Oxford University Press, 2007: 1–16.
Goeken, J. "Orateurs et sophists au banquet." In B. Wyss, R. Hirsch-Luipold, and S.-J. Hirschi, eds., *Sophisten im Hellenismus und Kaiserzeit: Orte, Methoden und Personen der Bildungsvermittlung.* STAC 101. Tübingen: Mohr Siebeck, 2017: 83–97.
Goff, M. "Qumran Wisdom Literature and the Problem of Genre." *DSD* 17 (2010): 286–306.
Goldhill, S. "Genre." In T. Whitmarsh, ed., *The Cambridge Companion to the Greek and Roman Novel.* Cambridge: Cambridge University Press, 2008: 185–200.
Goldstein, J. A. "Jewish Acceptance and Rejection of Hellenism." In E. P. Sanders, A. I. Baumgarten, and A. Mendelson, eds., *Jewish and Christian Self-Definition.* 2 vols. Philadelphia: Fortress, 1981: 2.64–87.
———, trans. *II Maccabees: A New Translation with Introduction and Commentary.* AB 41A. Garden City, N.Y.: Doubleday, 1983.
Goodenough, E. R. *By Light, Light: The Mystic Gospel of Hellenistic Judaism.* Amsterdam: Philo Press, 1969.
———. "The Political Philosophy of Hellenistic Kingship." *YCS* 1 (1928): 53–102.
———. *The Politics of Philo Judaeus: Practice and Theory.* New Haven: Yale University Press, 1938.
Goodman, M. "Josephus' Treatise *Against Apion.*" In M. Edwards, M. Goodman, and S. Price, with C. Rowland, eds., *Apologetics in the Roman Empire: Pagans, Jews, and Christians.* Oxford: Oxford University Press, 1999: 45–58.
Grabbe, L. L. *Etymology in Early Jewish Interpretation: The Hebrew Names in Philo.* BJS 115. Atlanta: Scholars Press, 1988.
———. "Jewish Identity and Hellenism in the Fragmentary Jewish Writings in Greek." In P. Gray and G. R. O'Day, eds., *Scripture and Traditions: Essays on*

Early Judaism and Christianity in Honor of Carl R. Holladay. NovTSup 129. Leiden: Brill, 2008: 21–32.

Grant, R. M. *Greek Apologists of the Second Century*. London: SCM Press, 1988.

Gregory, A. F., and C. M. Tuckett. "New Editions of Non-canonical Gospels." *Theology* 111 (2008): 178–84.

Grilli, A. *Il problema della vita contemplativa nel mondo greco-romano*. Rome: Fratelli Bocca, 1953.

Grojnowski, A. D. "Josephus: An Autobiography; A Comparative Analysis of Ancient Literature in the Search for Genre." PhD diss., King's College London, 2014.

Groß-Albenhausen, K. "Bedeutung und Function der Gymnasien für die Hellenisierung Ostens." In D. Kah and P. Scholz, eds., *Das hellenistische Gymnasion*. WGW 8. Berlin: Akademie Verlag, 2004: 313–33.

Gruen, E. S. *Diaspora: Jews amidst Greeks and Romans*. Cambridge, Mass.: Harvard University Press, 2002: 124–25.

———. *Heritage and Hellenism: The Reinvention of Jewish Tradition*. Berkeley: University of California Press, 1998.

———. "Jews and Greeks as Philosophers: A Challenge to Otherness." In *The Construct of Identity in Hellenistic Judaism: Essays on Early Jewish Literature and History*. DCLS 29. Berlin: De Gruyter, 2016: 133–52.

———. "The Twisted Tales of Artapanus: Biblical Rewritings as Novelistic Narrative." In *The Construct of Identity in Hellenistic Judaism: Essays on Early Jewish Literature and History*. DCLS 29. Berlin: De Gruyter, 2016: 437–50.

Gudeman, A. "Λύσεις." *PW* 13 (1927): 2511–29.

Guelich, R. "The Gospel Genre." In P. Stuhlmacher, ed., *The Gospel and the Gospels*. Grand Rapids: Eerdmans, 1991: 173–208.

Gutman, Y. *The Beginnings of Jewish-Hellenistic Literature* (in Hebrew). Jerusalem: Mosad Byaliḳ, 1958.

———. "Philo the Epic Poet." *ScrHier* 1 (1954): 36–63.

Gutzwiller, K. "Introduction." In K. Gutzwiller, ed., *The New Posidippus: A Hellenistic Poetry Book*. Oxford: Oxford University Press, 2005: 1–16.

Hacham, N. "The *Letter of Aristeas*: A New Exodus Story?" *JSJ* 36 (2005): 2–20.

———. "The Third Century BCE: New Light on Egyptian Jewish History from the Papyri." In M. M. Piotrkowski, G. Herman, and S. Dönitz, eds., *Sources and Interpretation in Ancient Judaism: Studies for Tal Ilan at Sixty*. AJEC 104. Leiden: Brill, 2018: 130–42.

———. "3 Maccabees and Esther: Parallels, Intertextuality, and Diaspora Identity." *JBL* 126 (2007): 765–85.

Hadas, M. *Aristeas to Philocrates (Letter of Aristeas)*. New York: Harper and Brothers, 1951.

———. *Hellenistic Culture: Fusion and Diffusion*. New York: Columbia University Press, 1959.

———. *The Third and Fourth Books of Maccabees*. New York: Harper, 1953.

Hadas, M., and M. Smith. *Heroes and Gods: Spiritual Biographies in Antiquity*. New York: Harper, 1965.

Hägg, T. *The Art of Biography in Antiquity*. Cambridge: Cambridge University Press, 2012.

Halliday, M. A. K. *An Introduction to Functional Grammar*. 3rd ed. Revised by Christian M. I. M. Matthiessen. London: Edward Arnold, 2004.

Halliday, M. A. K., and R. Hasan. *Language, Context and Text: Aspects of Language in a Social-Semiotic Perspective*. Geelong, Australia: Deakin University, 1985.

Hare, D. R. A. "The Lives of the Prophets." In *OTP* 2.379–400.

Harrington, D. J. "Palestinian Adaptations of Biblical Narratives and Prophecies." In R. A. Kraft and G. W. E. Nickelsburg, eds., *Early Judaism and Its Modern Interpreters*. Philadelphia: Fortress, 1986: 239–58.

Harrison, S. J. *Generic Enrichment in Virgil and Horace*. Oxford: Oxford University Press, 2007.

Hartner, M. "Hybrid Genres and Cultural Change: A Cognitive Approach." In M. Basseler, A. Nünning, and C. Schwanecke, eds., *The Cultural Dynamics of Generic Change in Contemporary Fiction: Theoretical Frameworks, Genres and Model Interpretations*. ELCH 56. Trier: Wissenschaftlicher Verlag Trier, 2013: 163–82.

Hartog, P. B. *Pesher and Hypomnema: A Comparison of Two Commentary Traditions from the Hellenistic-Roman World*. STDJ 121. Leiden: Brill, 2017.

Hata, G. "Is the Greek Version of Josephus' 'Jewish War' a Translation or a Rewriting of the First Version?" *JQR* 66 (1975): 89–108.

Hau, L. I. "Narrator and Narratorial Persona in Diodoros' *Bibliotheke* (and Their Implications for the Tradition of Greek Historiography)." In L. I. Hau, A. Meeus, and B. Sheridan, eds., *Diodoros of Sicily: Historiographical Theory and Practice in the Bibliotheke*. SH 58. Leuven: Peeters, 2018: 277–301.

Hays, R. B. *Echoes of Scripture in the Gospels*. Waco: Baylor University Press, 2016.

Heath, J. "Ezekiel Tragicus and Hellenistic Visuality: The Phoenix at Elim." *JTS* 57 (2006): 23–41.

Heil, C. "Evangelium als Gattung: Erzähl- und Spruchevangelium." In T. Schmeller, ed., *Historiographie und Biographie im Neuen Testament und seiner Umwelt*. NTOA 69. Göttingen: Vandenhoeck & Ruprecht, 2009: 62–94.

Heinemann, I. "Therapeutae." *PW* 5a (1934): 2337–38.

Hengel, M. "Anonymität, Pseudepigraphie und 'Literarische Fälschung' in der jüdisch-hellenistischen Literatur." In K. von Fritz, ed., *Pseudepigraphie*, vol. 1. Entretiens sur l'antiquité classique 18. Geneva: Hardt, 1972: 229–308.

———. *Crucifixion in the Ancient World and the Folly of the Message of the Cross*. Translated by J. Bowden. Philadelphia: Fortress, 1977.

———. *Judaism and Hellenism: Studies in Their Encounter in Palestine during the Early Hellenistic Period*. Translated by J. Bowden. 2 vols. Philadelphia: Fortress, 1974.

———. "The Titles of the Gospels and the Gospel of Mark." In *Studies in the Gospel of Mark*. Translated by J. Bowden. London: SCM Press, 1985: 64–84.

Henrichs, A. *Die "Phoinikika" des Lollianos*. PTA 14. Bonn: R. Habelt, 1972.

Hernadi, P. *Beyond Genre: New Directions in Literary Classifications*. Ithaca: Cornell University Press, 1972.

Herr, M. D. "Midrash." In M. Berenbaum and F. Skolnik, eds., *Encyclopaedia Judaica*, vol. 14. 2nd ed. Detroit: Macmillan Reference, 2007: 182–85.

Herrero de Jáuregui, M. *Orphism and Christianity in Late Antiquity*. Sozomena 7. Berlin: De Gruyter, 2010.

Hezser, C. *Jewish Literacy in Roman Palestine*. TSAJ 81. Tübingen: Mohr Siebeck, 2001.

———. "'Joseph and Aseneth' in the Context of Ancient Greek Erotic Novels." *FJB* 24 (1997): 1–40.

———. "Rabbis as Intellectuals in the Context of Graeco-Roman and Byzantine Christian Scholasticism." In S. A. Adams, ed., *Scholastic Culture in the Hellenistic and Roman Eras: Greek, Latin, and Jewish*. Transmissions 2. Berlin: De Gruyter, 2019: 169–85.

———. "The Torah versus Homer: Jewish and Greco-Roman Education in Late Roman Palestine." In M. R. Hauge and A. W. Pitts, eds., *Ancient Education and Early Christianity*. LNTS 533. London: Bloomsbury, 2016: 5–24.

Hicks-Keeton, J. *Arguing with Aseneth: Gentile Access to Israel's Living God in Jewish Antiquity*. Oxford: Oxford University Press, 2018.

Hildary, R. *Rabbis and Classical Rhetoric: Sophistic Education and Oratory in the Talmud and Midrash*. Cambridge: Cambridge University Press, 2018.

Hinds, S. "Epic Essentialism from Macer to Statius." In M. Depew and D. Obbink, eds., *Matrices of Genre: Authors, Canons, and Societies*. CHSC 4. Cambridge, Mass.: Harvard University Press, 2000: 221–44.

Hock, R. F. "The Rhetoric of Romance." In S. E. Porter, ed., *Handbook of Classical Rhetoric in the Hellenistic Period (330 B.C.–A.D. 400)*. Leiden: Brill, 2001: 445–65.

Hoffmann, F., and J. F. Quack. *Anthologie der demotischen Literatur: Einführungen und Quellentexte zur Ägyptologie*. Berlin: LIT Verlag, 2018.

Hoffmann, P. "What Was Commentary in Late Antiquity? The Example of Neoplatonic Commentators." In M. L. Gill and P. Pellegrin, eds., *A Companion to Ancient Philosophy*. Oxford: Blackwell, 2006: 597–622.

Hölbl, G. *A History of the Ptolemaic Empire*. Translated by T. Saavedra. London: Routledge, 2001.

Holladay, C. R. *Fragments from Hellenistic Jewish Authors*. 4 vols. SBLTT 20, 30, 39, 40. SBLPS 10, 12, 13, 14. Atlanta: Scholars Press, 1983–1996.

———. "The Portrait of Moses in Ezekiel the Tragedian." In G. MacRae, ed., *SBLSP 1976*. Missoula, Mont.: Scholars Press, 1976: 447–52.

———. "Pseudo-Orpheus: Tracking a Tradition." In A. J. Malherbe, F. W. Norris, and J. W. Thompson, eds., *The Early Church in Its Context: Essays in Honor of Everett Ferguson*. NovTSup 90. Leiden: Brill, 1998: 192–220.

———. "The Textual Tradition of Pseudo-Orpheus: Walter or Riedweg?" In H. Cancik, H. Lichtenberger, and P. Schäfer, eds., *Geschichte—Tradition—Reflection: Festschrift für Martin Hengel zum 70. Geburtstag*. 3 vols. Tübingen: Mohr Siebeck, 1996: 1.159–80.

Hollis, A. S. "The Hellenistic Epyllion and Its Descendants." In S. F. Johnson, ed., *Greek Literature in Late Antiquity: Dynamism, Didactism, Classicism*. Aldershot: Ashgate, 2006: 141–57.

Honigman, S. "The Impact of Locality and Cross-Linguistic Influences on Literary Texts Written in Greek by Jewish Authors." In M. Kramer and M. Leventhal, eds., *Proceedings of the International Conference "Being Jewish, Writing Greek," Cambridge, September 6–8, 2017*. Forthcoming.

———. "Literary Genres and Identity in the *Letter of Aristeas*: Courtly and Demotic Models." In C. R. Katz, N. Hacham, G. Herman, and L. Sagiv, eds., *A Question of Identity: Formation, Transition, Negotiation*. Berlin: De Gruyter Oldenbourg, 2019: 223–44.

———. *The Septuagint and Homeric Scholarship in Alexandria: A Study in the Narrative of the "Letter of Aristeas."* London: Routledge, 2003.

———. *Tales of High Priests and Taxes: The Books of the Maccabees and the Judean Rebellion against Antiochos IV*. Berkeley: University of California Press, 2014.

Hooley, D. M. *Roman Satire*. Oxford: Blackwell, 2007.

Horbury, W. *Jewish War under Trajan and Hadrian*. Cambridge: Cambridge University Press, 2014.

Horgan, M. P. *Pesharim: Qumran Interpretations of Biblical Books*. CBQMS 8. Washington, D.C.: Catholic Biblical Association of America, 1979.

Horster, M., and C. Reitz. "'Condensation' of Literature and the Pragmatics of Literary Production." In M. Horster and C. Reitz, eds., *Condensing Texts—Condensed Texts*. Stuttgart: Steiner, 2010: 3–14.

Houston, G. W. *Inside Roman Libraries: Book Collections and Their Management in Antiquity*. Chapel Hill: University of North Carolina Press, 2014.

Hudson, R. A. *Sociolinguistics*. CTL. Cambridge: Cambridge University Press, 1980.

Hughes, J. *Secrets of the Times: Myth and History in Biblical Chronology*. JSOT 66. Sheffield: Sheffield Academic Press, 1990.

Humphrey, E. M. *Joseph and Aseneth*. GAP. Sheffield: Sheffield Academic Press, 2000.

Hunter, R. "Ancient Readers." In T. Whitmarsh, ed., *The Cambridge Companion to the Greek and Roman Novel*. Cambridge: Cambridge University Press, 2008: 261–71.

———. "History and Historicity in the Romance of Chariton." *ANRW* 2.34.2 (1994): 1055–86.

———. "The Letter of Aristeas." In A. Erskine and L. Llewellyn-Jones, eds., *Creating a Hellenistic World*. Swansea: Classical Press of Wales, 2011: 47–60.

Husselmann, E. M. "A Bohairic School Text on Papyrus." *JNES* 6 (1947): 129–51.

Hywel, C. "Moses as Philosopher-Sage in Philo." In A. Graupner and M. Wolter, eds., *Moses in Biblical and Extra-biblical Traditions*. BZAW 372. Berlin: De Gruyter, 2007: 151–67.

Ilan, T. "The Jewish Community in Egypt before and after 117 CE in Light of Old and New Papyri." In Y. Furstenberg, ed., *Jewish and Christian Communal Identities in the Roman World*. AJEC 94. Leiden: Brill, 2016: 203–24.

———. *Lexicon of Jewish Names in Late Antiquity*. 4 vols. TSAJ. Tübingen: Mohr Siebeck, 2002–2012.

Inowlocki, S. *Eusebius and the Jewish Authors: His Citation Technique in an Apologetic Context*. AJEC 64. Leiden: Brill, 2006.

Jackson, H. M. "Ancient Self-Referential Conventions and Their Implications for the Authorship and Integrity of the Gospel of John." *JTS* 50 (1999): 1–34.

Jacob, C. "Questions sur les questions: Archéologie d'une pratique intellectuelle et d'une forme discursive." In A. Volgers and C. Zamagni, eds., *Erotapokriseis: Early Christian Question-and-Answer Literature in Context*. CBET 37. Leuven: Peeters, 2004: 25–54.

Jacobson, H. "Artapanus Judaeus." *JJS* 57 (2006): 210–21.

———. *The Exagoge of Ezekiel*. Cambridge: Cambridge University Press, 1983.

———. "Ezekiel's *Exagoge*, One Play or Four?" *GRBS* 43 (2002/3): 391–96.

———. "Two Studies on Ezekiel the Tragedian." *GRBS* 22 (1981): 167–78.

Jacoby, F. "Eupolemos." *PW* 11 (1907): 1226–29.

———. "Hekataios aus Abdera." *PW* 7 (1912): 2750–69.

———. "Über die Entwicklung der griechischen Historiographie und den Plan einer neuen Sammlung der griechischen Historikerfragmente." *Kilo* 9 (1909): 80–123.

Jakobson, R. "The Dominant." In L. Metejka and K. Pomorska, eds., *Readings in Russian Poetics: Formalist and Structuralist Views*. Cambridge, Mass.: MIT Press, 1971: 82–87.

Jamieson, K. M. "Antecedent Genre as Rhetorical Constraint." *Quarterly Journal of Speech* 61 (1975): 405–15.

Janse M. "Aspects of Bilingualism in the History of the Greek Language." In J. N. Adams, M. Janse, and S. Swain, eds., *Bilingualism in Ancient Society: Language Contact and the Written Text*. Oxford: Oxford University Press, 2002: 332–90.

Jarecsni, J. "The 'Epitome': An Original Work or a Copy? An Analysis of the First Eleven Chapters of the Epitome of Caesaribus." *ACD* 33 (1997): 203–14.

Jasnow, R. "Between Two Waters: The Book of Thoth and the Problem of Greco-Egyptian Interaction." In I. Rutherford, ed., *Greco-Egyptian Interactions: Literature, Translation, and Culture, 500 BCE–300 CE*. Oxford: Oxford University Press, 2016: 317–56.

———. "The Greek Alexander Romance and Demotic Egyptian Literature." *JNES* 56 (1997): 95–103.

Jassen, A. P. "The Pesharim and the Rise of Commentary in Early Jewish Scriptural Interpretation." *DSD* 19 (2012): 363–98.

Jay, J. "The Problem of the Theater in Early Judaism." *JSJ* 44 (2013): 218–53.

———. *The Tragic in Mark: A Literary-Historical Interpretation.* HUT 66. Tübingen: Mohr Siebeck, 2014.

Johnson, S. R. "3 Maccabees." In J. K. Aitken, ed., *T&T Clark Companion to the Septuagint.* London: Bloomsbury, 2015: 292–305.

———. *Historical Fictions and Hellenistic Jewish Identity: Third Maccabees in Its Cultural Context.* HCS 43. Berkeley: University of California Press, 2004.

Jones, F. S. "The Pseudo-Clementines." In M. Jackson-McCabe, ed., *Jewish Christianity Reconsidered: Rethinking Ancient Groups and Texts.* Minneapolis: Fortress, 2007: 285–304.

———. "The Pseudo-Clementines: A History of Research." *Second Century* 2 (1982): 1–33, 63–95.

Joosten, J. "The Origin of the Septuagint Canon." In S. Kreuzer, M. Meiser, and M. Sigismund, eds., *Die Septuaginta—Orte und Intentionen.* WUNT 1.361. Tübingen: Mohr Siebeck, 2016: 688–99.

———. "The Original Language and Historical Milieu of the Book of Judith." In *Collected Studies on the Septuagint.* FAT 83. Tübingen: Mohr Siebeck, 2012: 195–209.

Jordan, M. D. "Ancient Philosophic Protreptic and the Problem of Persuasive Genres." *Rhetorica* 4 (1986): 309–33.

Joseph, J. E. *Language and Identity: National, Ethnic, Religious.* New York: Palgrave Macmillan, 2004.

Jourdan, F. *Poème judéo-hellénistique attribute à Orphée: Production juive et reception chrétienne.* Paris: Les Belles Lettres, 2010.

Kamesar, A. "Biblical Interpretation in Philo." In A. Kamesar, ed., *The Cambridge Companion to Philo.* Cambridge: Cambridge University Press, 2009: 65–91.

———. *Jerome, Greek Scholarship, and the Hebrew Bible: A Study of the "Quaestiones Hebraicae in Genesim."* Oxford: Oxford University Press, 1993.

———. "The Literary Genres of the Pentateuch as Seen from the Greek Perspective: The Testimony of Philo of Alexandria." *SPhiloA* 9 (1997): 143–89.

Kasher, A. "Hecataeus of Abdera on Mosollamus the Jewish Mounted Archer (Contra Apionem 1.200–204)." In H. Cancik, H. Lichtenberger, and P. Schäfer, eds., *Geschichte—Tradition—Reflexion: Festschrift für Martin Hengel zum 70. Geburtstag.* 3 vols. Tübingen: Mohr Siebeck, 1996: 1:147–58.

———. *The Jews in Hellenistic and Roman Egypt.* TSAJ 7. Tübingen: Mohr Siebeck, 1985.

Kechagia, E. "Dying Philosophers in Ancient Biography: Zeno the Stoic and Epicurus." In K. De Temmerman and K. Demoen, eds., *Writing Biography in Greece and Rome: Narrative Techniques and Fictionalization.* Cambridge: Cambridge University Press, 2016: 181–99.

Keddie, G. A. "Solomon to His Friends: The Role of Epistolarity in Eupolemus." *JSP* 22 (2013): 201–37.

Keddie, G. A., and J. MacLellan. "Ezekiel's *Exagoge* and the Politics of Hellenistic Theatre: Mosaic Hegemony on a Ptolemaic Model." *JAJ* 8 (2017): 170–87.

Keener, C. S. *Christobiography: Memory, History, and the Reliability of the Gospels*. Grand Rapids: Eerdmans, 2019.

———. *The Gospel of John: A Commentary*. 2 vols. Peabody, Mass.: Hendrickson, 2003.

Kennedy, G. *The Art of Rhetoric in the Roman World, 300 B.C.–A.D. 300*. Princeton: Princeton University Press, 1972.

Kerenyi, K. *Die griechische-orientalische Romanliteratur in religionsgeschichtlicher Beleuchtung*. Tübingen: Mohr, 1927.

Kister, M. "Wisdom Literature and Its Relation to Other Genres: From Ben Sira to Mysteries." In J. J. Collins, G. E. Sterling, and R. A. Clements, eds., *Sapiential Perspectives: Wisdom Literature in Light of the Dead Sea Scrolls*. STDJ 51. Leiden: Brill, 2004: 13–47.

Klauck, H.-J. *Ancient Letters and the New Testament: A Guide to Context and Exegesis*. Waco: Baylor University Press, 2006.

———. *4 Makkabäerbuch*. *JSHRZ* 3.6.

———. "Hellenistiche Rhetorik im Diasporajudentum: Das Exordium des vierten Makkabäerbuchs (4 Makk 1.1–12)." *NTS* 35 (1989): 451–65.

———. "Der Weggang Jesu: Neue Arbeiten zu Joh 13–17." *BZ* 40 (1996): 236–50.

Klawans, J. "The Pseudo-Jewishness of Pseudo-Phocylides." *JSP* 26 (2017): 201–33.

Klęczar, A. *Ezechiel Tragik i jego dramat Exagoge Wyprowadzenie z Egiptu*. AST 1. Kraków-Mogilany: Enigma Press, 2006.

Klotz, D. "Who Was with Antiochos III at Raphia? Revisiting the Hieroglyphic Versions of the Raphia Decree (CG 31008 and 50048)." *CdE* 87 (2013): 45–59.

Klotz, F., and K. Oikonomopoulou. "Introduction." In F. Klotz and K. Oikonomopoulou, eds., *The Philosopher's Banquet: Plutarch's Table Talk in the Intellectual Culture of the Roman Empire*. Oxford: Oxford University Press, 2011: 1–31.

Koester, C. *Symbolism in the Fourth Gospel: Meaning, Mystery, Community*. 2nd ed. Minneapolis: Fortress, 2003.

Kohn, T. D. "The Tragedies of Ezekiel." *GRBS* 43 (2002/3): 5–12.

Konstan, D., and R. Walsh. "Civic and Subversive Biography in Antiquity." In K. De Temmerman and K. Demoen, eds., *Writing Biography in Greece and Rome: Narrative Techniques and Fictionalization*. Cambridge: Cambridge University Press, 2016: 26–43.

Koskenniemi, E. *Greek Writers and Philosophers in Philo and Josephus: A Study of Their Secular Education and Educational Ideals*. Philo 9. Leiden: Brill, 2019.

Kosmin, P. J. "Seleucid Ethnography and Indigenous Kingship: The Babylonian Education of Antiochus I." In J. Haubold, G. B. Lanfranchi, R. Rollinger, and J. M. Steele, eds., *The World of Berossos: Proceedings of the 4th International Colloquium on "The Ancient Near East between Classical and Ancient Orien-*

tal Traditions," Hatfield College, Durham 7th–9th July 2010. CO 5. Wiesbaden: Harrassowitz Verlag, 2013: 199–212.

Köstenberger, A. "The Genre of the Fourth Gospel and Greco-Roman Literary Conventions." In S. E. Porter and A. W. Pitts, eds., *Christian Origins and Greco-Roman Culture: Social and Literary Contexts for the New Testament*. TENTS 9. ECHC 1. Leiden: Brill, 2013: 435–62.

Kotlińska-Toma, A. *Hellenistic Tragedy: Texts, Translations and a Critical Survey*. BCSM. London: Bloomsbury, 2015.

Kraemer, R. "Monastic Jewish Women in Greco-Roman Egypt: Philo Judaeus on the Therapeutrides." *Signs* 14 (1989): 342–70.

———. *When Aseneth Met Joseph: A Late Antique Tale of the Biblical Patriarch and His Egyptian Wife, Reconsidered*. Oxford: Oxford University Press, 1998: 224–44.

———. "Women's Authorship of Jewish and Christian Literature in the Greco-Roman Period." In A.-J. Levine, ed., *"Women Like This": New Perspectives on Jewish Women in the Greco-Roman World*. EJL 1. Atlanta: Scholars Press, 1991: 221–42.

Kratz, R. G. "Text and Commentary: The *Pesharim* of Qumran in the Context of Hellenistic Scholarship." In T. L. Thompson and P. Wajdenbaum, eds., *The Bible and Hellenism: Greek Influence on Jewish and Early Christian Literature*. Durham: Acumen, 2014: 212–29.

Kraus, C. "Ezechiele Poeta Tragico." *RFIC* 96 (1968): 164–75.

Kraus, C. S. "Introduction: Reading Commentaries/Commentaries as Reading." In R. K. Gibson and C. S. Kraus, eds., *The Classical Commentary: Histories, Practices, Theory*. Mnemosyne 232. Leiden: Brill, 2002: 1–27.

Krivoruchko, J. G. "Judeo-Greek." In L. Kahn and A. D. Rubin, eds., *Handbook of Jewish Languages*. BHL. Leiden: Brill, 2016: 194–225.

Kroll, W. *Studien zum Verständnis der römischen Literatur*. Stuttgart: Metzler, 1924.

Kuch, H. "Funktionswandlungen des antiken Romans." In H. Kuch, ed., *Der antike Roman: Untersuchungen zur literarischen Kommunikation und Gattungsgeschichte*. Berlin: Akademie Verlag, 1989: 52–81.

Küchler, M. *Frühjüdische Weisheitstraditionen: Zum Fortgang weisheitlichen Denkens im Bereich des frühjüdischen Jahweglaubens*. OBO 26. Freiburg: Universitätsverlag, 1979.

Kugel, J. L. *The Idea of Biblical Poetry: Parallelism and Its History*. New Haven: Yale University Press, 1981.

———. *In Potiphar's House: The Interpretive Life of Biblical Texts*. San Francisco: HarperSanFrancisco, 1990.

Kuiper, K. "De Ezechiele poeta Judaeo." *Mnemosyne* 28 (1900): 237–80.

———. "Le poète juif Ezéchiel." *REJ* 46 (1903): 161–77.

Kurfess, A. "Homer und Hesiod im 1 Buch der Oracula Sibyllina." *Phil* 100 (1956): 147–53.

Lafargue, M. "The Jewish Orpheus," in P. J. Achtemeier, ed., *SBLSP 1978*, 2 vols. Missoula, Mont.: Scholars Press, 1978: 2:137–44.

Lakoff, G. *Women, Fire, and Dangerous Things: What Categories Reveal about the Mind.* Chicago: University of Chicago Press, 1987.

Lamedica, A. "Il Papiro di Derveni come commentario: Problemi formali." In A. H. S. El-Mosalamy, ed., *Proceedings of the XIXth International Congress of Papyrology, Cairo 2–9 September 1989.* 2 vols. Cairo: Ain Shams University, 1992: 1:325–33.

Lanfranchi, P. *L'Exagoge d'Ezéchiel le Tragique: Introduction, texte, traduction et commentaire.* SVTP 21. Leiden: Brill, 2006.

———. "The Exagoge of Ezekiel the Tragedian." In V. Liapis and A. K. Petrides, eds., *Greek Tragedy after the Fifth Century: A Survey from ca. 400 BC to ca. AD 400.* Cambridge: Cambridge University Press, 2018: 125–46.

———. "Ezéchiel le Tragique et la question du théâtre juif ancien." *Cahiers du Judaïsme* 14 (2003): 18–24.

———. "Il sogno di Mose nell'exagoge di Ezechiele il Tragico." *Materia giudaica* 8 (2003): 105–12.

Lange, A. "From Literature to Scripture: The Unity and Plurality of the Hebrew Scriptures in Light of the Qumran Library." In C. Helmer and C. Landmesser, eds., *One Scripture or Many? Canon from Biblical, Theological, and Philosophical Perspectives.* Oxford: Oxford University Press, 2004: 51–107.

Lange, A., and Z. Pleše. "Derveni—Alexandria—Qumran: Transpositional Hermeneutics in Greek Culture." In S. H. Aufrère, P. S. Alexander, and Z. Pleše, eds., *On the Fringes of Commentary: Metatextuality in Ancient Near Eastern and Ancient Mediterranean Cultures.* OLA 232. Leuven: Peeters, 2014: 89–160.

Langslow, D. R. "The *Epistula* in Ancient Scientific and Technical Literature, with Special Reference to Medicine." In R. Morello and A. D. Morrison, eds., *Ancient Letters: Classical and Late Antique Epistolography.* Oxford: Oxford University Press, 2007: 211–34.

Laqueur, R. *Der jüdische Historiker Flavius Josephus: Ein biographischer Versuch auf neuer quellenkritischer Grundlage.* 1920. Reprint, Darmstadt: Wissenschaftliche Buchgesellschaft, 1970.

Larsen, K. B. "Introduction: The Gospel of John as Genre Mosaic." In K. B. Larsen, ed., *The Gospel of John as Genre Mosaic.* SANt 3. Göttingen: Vandenhoeck & Ruprecht, 2015: 13–24.

———. *Recognizing the Stranger: Recognition Scenes in the Gospel of John.* BIS 93. Leiden: Brill, 2008.

Larsen, L. I. "Monastic Paideia and Textual Fluidity in the Classroom." In L. I. Lied and H. Lundhaug, eds., *Snapshots of Evolving Traditions: Jewish and Christian Manuscript Culture, Textual Fluidity, and New Philology.* Berlin: De Gruyter, 2017: 146–77.

Larsen, M. D. C. *Gospels before the Book.* Oxford: Oxford University Press, 2018.

Lauer, S. "*Eusebes Logismos* in IV Macc." *JJS* 6 (1955): 170–71.

Laurand, V. "La Contemplation chez Philon d'Alexandrie." In T. Bénatouïl and M. Bonazzi, eds., *Theoria, Praxis, and the Contemplative Life after Plato and Aristotle*. Leiden: Brill, 2012: 121–38.

Le Boulluec, A. "La place des concepts philosophiques dans la réflexion de Philon sur le plaisir." In C. Lévy, ed., *Philon d'Alexandrie et le langage de la philosophie*. Monothéismes et philosophie. Turnhout: Brepols, 1998: 129–52.

Lebram, J. C. H. "Die literarische Form des vierten Makkabäerbuches." *VC* 28 (1974): 81–96.

Lee, J. A. L. *The Greek of the Pentateuch: Grinfield Lectures on the Septuagint, 2011–2012*. Oxford: Oxford University Press, 2018.

Lelyveld, M. *Les Logia de la vie dans l'Évangile selon Thomas: À la recherche d'une tradition et d'une redaction*. NHMS. Leiden: Brill, 1987.

Lewy, H. "Hekataios von Abdera περὶ Ἰουδαίων." *ZNW* 31 (1932): 117–32.

Lichtheim, M. *Ancient Egyptian Autobiographies Chiefly of the Middle Kingdom: A Study and an Anthology*. OBO. Göttingen: Vandenhoeck & Ruprecht, 1988.

———. *Late Egyptian Wisdom in the International Context: A Study of Demotic Instructions*. OBO 52. Göttingen: Vandenhoeck & Ruprecht, 1983.

Licona, M. R. *Why Are There Differences in the Gospels? What We Can Learn from Ancient Biography*. Oxford: Oxford University Press, 2017.

Lied, L. I., and H. Lundhaug, eds. *Snapshots of Evolving Traditions: Jewish and Christian Manuscript Culture, Textual Fluidity, and New Philology*. Berlin: De Gruyter, 2017.

Lightfoot, J. L. *The Sibylline Oracles: With Introduction, Translation, and Commentary on the First and Second Books*. Oxford: Oxford University Press, 2007.

Lim, T. H. "Biblical Quotations in the Pesharim and the Text of the Bible—Methodological Considerations." In E. D. Herbert and E. Tov, eds., *The Bible as Book: The Hebrew Bible and the Judaean Desert Discoveries*. London: British Library, 2002: 71–79.

———. *Holy Scripture in the Qumran Commentaries and Pauline Letters*. Oxford: Clarendon, 1997.

———. *Pesharim*. CQS 3. London: Sheffield, 2002.

Lincicum, D. "Philo's Library." *SPhiloA* 26 (2014): 99–114.

———. "A Preliminary Index to Philo's Non-biblical Citations and Allusions." *SPhiloA* 25 (2013): 139–67.

Lincke, K. F. A. "Phokylides und die Essener." *Die Grenzboten* 68 (1909): 128–38.

———. *Samaria und seine Propheten: Ein religionsgeschichtlicher Versuch; Mit einer Textbeilage, die Weisheitslehre des Phokylides*. Tübingen: Mohr Siebeck, 1903.

Lincoln, A. T. *Born of a Virgin? Reconceiving Jesus in the Bible, Tradition, and Theology*. Grand Rapids: Eerdmans, 2013.

———. "'We Know That His Testimony Is True': Johannine Truth Claims and Historicity." In P. N. Anderson, F. Just, and T. Thatcher, eds., *John, Jesus, and History*, vol. 1, *Critical Appraisals of Critical Views*. SymS 44. Atlanta: SBL, 2007: 179–97.

Link, H. *Rezeptionsforschung: Eine Einführung in Methoden und Probleme*. 2nd ed. Stuttgart: Kohlhammer, 1980.

Linton, G. L. "Reading the Apocalypse as Apocalypse: The Limits of Genre." In D. L. Barr, ed., *The Reality of Apocalypse: Rhetoric and Politics in the Book of Revelation*. SymS 39. Atlanta: SBL, 2006: 9–41.

Lloyd-Jones, H. "The Pride of Halicarnassus." *ZPE* 124 (1999): 1–14.

Lohse, E. *The Formation of the New Testament*. Translated by M. E. Boring. Nashville: Abingdon, 1981.

Lundon, J. "Homeric Commentaries on Papyrus: A Survey." In S. Matthaios, F. Montanari, and A. Rengakos, eds., *Ancient Scholarship and Grammar: Archetypes, Concepts and Contexts*. TCSup 8. Berlin: De Gruyter, 2011: 159–79.

Luther, H. "Josephus und Justus von Tiberias: Ein Beitrag zur Geschichte des jüdischen Aufstandes." PhD diss., Universität Halle-Wittenberg, 1910.

Luz, U. *Matthew: A Commentary*. 3 vols. Hermeneia. Minneapolis: Fortress, 2007.

MacDonald, D. R. *The Dionysian Gospel: The Fourth Gospel and Euripides*. Minneapolis: Fortress, 2017.

Machiela, D. A. "Once More, with Feeling: Rewritten Scripture in Ancient Judaism—A Review of Recent Developments." *JJS* 61 (2010): 308–20.

MacRae, G. W. "Theology and Irony in the Fourth Gospel." In R. J. Clifford and G. W. MacRae, eds., *The Word in the World: Essays in Honor of F. L. Moriarty*. Cambridge, Mass.: Weston College, 1973: 83–96.

Mader, G. *Josephus and the Politics of Historiography: Apologetic and Impression-Management in the "Bellum Judaicum."* MneSup 205. Leiden: Brill, 2000.

Magness, J. *The Archeology of Qumran and the Dead Sea Scrolls*. Grand Rapids: Eerdmans, 2002.

Manetti, D., and A. Roselli. "Galeno commentatore di Ippocrate." *ANRW* 2.37.2 (1994): 1529–635.

Manitius, K. *In Arati et Eudoxi Phaenomena commentariorum libri tres*. Leipzig: Teubner, 1894.

Marasco, G., ed. *Political Autobiographies and Memoirs in Antiquity: A Brill Companion*. Leiden: Brill, 2011.

Marincola, J. *Authority and Tradition in Ancient Historiography*. Cambridge: Cambridge University Press, 1997.

———. "Beyond Pity and Fear: The Emotions of History." *Ancient Society* 33 (2003): 285–315.

———. "Genre, Convention, and Innovation in Greco-Roman Historiography." In C. S. Kraus, ed., *The Limits of Historiography: Genre and Narrative in Ancient Historical Texts*. Leiden: Brill, 1999: 281–324.

Marrou, H. I. *A History of Education in Antiquity*. Translated by G. Lamb. London: Sheen and Ward, 1956.

Martin, D. B. *The Corinthian Body*. New Haven: Yale University Press, 1995.

Martin, J. R. "Analysing Genre: Functional Parameters." In F. Christie and J. R. Martin, eds., *Genre and Institutions: Social Processes in the Workplace and School*. London: Cassell, 1997: 3–39.

Martin, J. R., and D. Rose. *Genre Relations: Mapping Culture*. London: Equinox, 2008.

Martin, M. W., and J. A. Whitlark. *Inventing Hebrews: Design and Purpose in Ancient Rhetoric*. SNTSMS 171. Cambridge: Cambridge University Press, 2018.

Mason, S. "The *Contra Apionem* in Social and Literary Context: An Invitation to Judean Philosophy." In L. H. Feldman and J. R. Levison, eds., *Josephus' "Contra Apionem": Studies in Its Character and Contexts with a Latin Concordance to the Portion Missing in Greek*. AGJU 34. Leiden: Brill, 1996: 187–228.

———. "An Essay in Character: The Aim and Audience of Josephus' *Vita*." In F. Siegert and J. U. Kalms, eds., *Internationales Josephus-Kolloquium Münster 1997*. Münster: LIT Verlag, 1997: 31–77.

———, ed. and trans. *Flavius Josephus: Life of Josephus; Translation and Commentary*. Leiden: Brill, 2003.

———. *Flavius Josephus on the Pharisees: A Composition-Critical Study*. Leiden: Brill, 1991.

———. *A History of the Jewish War, A.D. 66–74*. Cambridge: Cambridge University Press, 2016.

———. "Jews, Judaeans, Judaizing, Judaism: Problems of Categorization in Ancient History," *JSJ* 38 (2007): 457–512.

———. "Josephus as a Roman Historian." In H. H. Chapman and Z. Rodgers, eds., *A Companion to Josephus*. Oxford: Wiley-Blackwell, 2016: 89–107.

———. "Josephus' *Autobiography* (*Life of Josephus*)." In H. H. Chapman and Z. Rodgers, eds., *A Companion to Josephus*. Oxford: Wiley-Blackwell, 2016: 59–74.

———. "Of Audience and Meaning: Reading Josephus' *Bellum Judaicum* in the Context of a Flavian Audience." In J. Sievers and G. Lembi, eds., *Jewish History in Flavian Rome and Beyond*. JSJSup 104. Leiden: Brill, 2005: 71–100.

———. *Orientation to the History of Roman Judaea*. Eugene, Ore.: Cascade, 2016.

———. "'Should Any Wish to Enquire Further' (*Ant.* 1.25): The Aim and Audience of Josephus's *Judean Antiquities/Life*." In S. Mason, ed., *Understanding Josephus: Seven Perspectives*. LSTS 32. Sheffield: Sheffield Academic Press, 1998: 64–103.

Matusova, E. "Allegorical Interpretation of the Pentateuch in Alexandria: Inscribing Aristobulos and Philo in a Wider Literary Context." *SPhiloA* 22 (2010): 1–51.

———. *The Meaning of the Letter of Aristeas: In Light of Biblical Interpretation and Grammatical Tradition, and with Reference to Its Historical Context*. FRLANT 260. Göttingen: Vandenhoeck & Ruprecht, 2015.

Mayhew, R. *Aristotle's Lost "Homeric Problems": Textual Studies*. Oxford: Oxford University Press, 2019.

McConnell, S. *Philosophical Life in Cicero's Letters*. CCS. Cambridge: Cambridge University Press, 2014.

McGing, B. C. "Philo's Adaptation of the Bible in His Life of Moses." In B. C. McGing and J. Mossman, eds., *The Limits of Ancient Biography*. Swansea: Classical Press of Wales, 2006: 113–40.

Meister, K. "Autobiographische Literatur und Memoiren (Hypomnemata) (FGrHist 227–238)." In H. Verdin, G. Schepens, and E. De Keyser, eds., *Purpose of History: Studies in Greek Historiography from the 4th to the 2nd Centuries B.C.; Proceedings of the International Colloquium Leuven, 24–26 May 1988*. Leuven: Orientaliste, 1990: 83–89.

Mendels, D. "'Creative History' in the Hellenistic Near East in the Third and Second Centuries BCE: The Jewish Case." *JSP* 2 (1988): 13–20.

———. "Hellenistic Writers of the Second Century BCE on the Hiram–Solomon Relationship." *Studia Phoenicia* 5 (1986): 445–55.

———. *The Land of Israel as a Political Concept in Hasmonean Literature: Recourse to History in Second Century B.C. Claims to the Holy Land*. Tübingen: Mohr Siebeck, 1987.

Mendelson, A. *Secular Education in Philo of Alexandria*. Cincinnati: HUC Press, 1982.

Menken, M. J. J. *Matthew's Bible: The Old Testament Text of the Evangelist*. BETL 173. Leuven: Leuven University Press, 2004.

Merkelbach, R. *Roman und Mysterium in der Antike*. Munich: C. H. Beck, 1962.

Merriam, C. U. *The Development of the Epyllion Genre through the Hellenistic and Roman Periods*. Studies in Classics 14. Lewiston, N.Y.: Edwin Mellen Press, 2001.

Milikowsky, C. "Justus of Tiberias and the Synchronistic Chronology of Israel." In S. J. D. Cohen and J. J. Schwartz, eds., *Studies in Josephus and the Varieties of Ancient Judaism: Louis H. Feldman Jubilee Volume*. AJEC 67. Leiden: Brill, 2007: 103–26.

Millar, F. "The Background to the Maccabean Revolution: Reflections on Martin Hengel's 'Judaism and Hellenism.'" *JJS* 29 (1978): 1–21.

Misch, G. *A History of Autobiography in Antiquity*. Translated by E. W. Dickes. London: Routledge and Kegan Paul, 1950.

Mittmann-Richert, U. "Demetrios the Exegete and Chronographer." In I. H. Henderson and G. S. Oegema, eds., *The Changing Face of Judaism, Christianity, and Other Greco-Roman Religions in Antiquity: Presented to James H. Charlesworth on the Occasion of His 65th Birthday*. SJSHRZ 2. Gütersloh: Gütersloher Verlagshaus, 2006: 186–209.

Modrzejewski, J. M. *The Jews of Egypt from Ramses II to Emperor Hadrian*. Translated by R. Cornman. Philadelphia: Jewish Publication Society, 1995.

Moeser, M. C. *The Anecdote in Mark, the Classical World and the Rabbis*. JSNTSup 227. Sheffield: Sheffield Academic Press, 2002.

Moessner, D. P. "The Appeal and Power of Poetics (Luke 1:1–4)." In D. P. Moessner, ed., *Jesus and the Heritage of Israel*. Philadelphia: Trinity, 1999: 84–123.

———. "The Lukan Prologues in the Light of Ancient Narrative Hermeneutics." In J. Verheyden, ed., *The Unity of Luke-Acts*. BETL 142. Leuven: Leuven University Press, 1999: 399–417.

———. *Luke the Historian of Israel's Legacy, Theologian of Israel's "Christ."* BZNW 182. Berlin: De Gruyter, 2016.

Momigliano, A. *Alien Wisdom: The Limits of Hellenization*. Cambridge: Cambridge University Press, 1975.

———. "Ancient History and the Antiquarian." *JWCI* 13 (1950): 285–315.

———. *The Development of Greek Biography*. Expanded ed. Cambridge, Mass.: Harvard University Press, 1993.

———. "From the Pagan to the Christian Sibyl." In A. C. Dionisotti, A. Grafton, and J. Kraye, eds., *The Uses of Greek and Latin: Historical Essays*. London: Warburg Institute, 1988: 3–18.

———. "The Second Book of Maccabees." *CP* 70 (1975): 81–88.

Montanari, F. "Gli *Homerica* su papiro: Per una distinzione di generi." In *Studi di filologia omerica antica*, vol. 2. Pisa: Giardini, 1995: 69–85.

———. "Hypomnema." In *BNP* 6.641–43.

Moore, C. A. "On the Origins of the LXX Additions to the Book of Esther." *JBL* 92 (1973): 382–93.

———. "Towards the Dating of the Book of Baruch." *CBQ* 36 (1974): 312–20.

Mor, M. *The Second Jewish Revolt: The Bar Kokhba War, 132–136 CE*. BRLJ 50. Leiden: Brill, 2016.

Morgan, K. A. "Plato." In I. J. F. de Jong, R. Nünlist, and A. M. Bowie, eds., *Studies in Ancient Greek Narrative*. Vol. 1, *Narrators, Narratees, and Narratives in Ancient Greek Literature*. MneSup 257. Leiden: Brill, 2004: 357–76.

Morgan, T. *Literate Education in the Hellenistic and Roman Worlds*. CCS. Cambridge: Cambridge University Press, 1999.

Morison, W. S. "Theopompos of Chios (115)." In *BNJ*.

Morris, J. "The Jewish Philosopher Philo." In E. Schürer, *The History of the Jewish People in the Age of Jesus Christ (175 BC–AD 135)*. Revised and edited by G. Vermes, F. Millar, M. Black, and M. Goodman. 3 vols. Edinburgh: T&T Clark, 1973–1987: 3.2.809–70.

Morrison, G. "The Composition of II Maccabees: Insights Provided by a Literary *Topos*." *Bib* 90 (2009): 564–72.

Motzo, R. B. "Il rifacimento greco di 'Ester' e il 'III Macc.'" In *Saggi di storia e letteratura giudeo-ellenistica*. Florence: F. Le Monnier, 1924: 272–90.

Moyer, I. S. *Egypt and the Limits of Hellenism*. Cambridge: Cambridge University Press, 2011.

Moyise, S. "Composite Citations in the Gospel of Mark." In S. A. Adams and S. M. Ehorn, eds., *Composite Citations in Antiquity*, vol. 2, *New Testament Uses*. LNTS 593. London: Bloomsbury, 2018: 16–33.

Mroczek, E. *The Literary Imagination in Jewish Antiquity*. Oxford: Oxford University Press, 2016.

Mülke, M. *Aristobulos in Alexandria: Jüdische Bibelexegese zwischen Griechen und Ägyptern unter Ptolemaios VI. Philometor*. ULG 126. Berlin: De Gruyter, 2018.
———. "Die Epitome—das bessere Original?" In M. Horster and C. Reitz, eds., *Condensing Texts—Condensed Texts*. Stuttgart: Steiner, 2010: 69–89.
Murphy, R. E. *The Tree of Life: An Exploration of Biblical Wisdom Literature*. 3rd ed. Grand Rapids: Eerdmans, 2002.
Murray, O. "Aristeas and Ptolemaic Kingship." *JTS* 18 (1967): 337–71.
———. "Hecataeus of Abdera and Pharaonic Kingship." *JEA* 56 (1970): 141–71.
———. "Hellenistic Royal Symposia." In P. Bilde, T. Engberg-Pedersen, L. Hannestad, and J. Zahle, eds., *Aspects of Hellenistic Kingship*. Aarhus: Aarhus University Press, 1996: 16–27.
———. "Philosophy and Monarchy in the Hellenistic World." In R. Rajak, S. Pearce, J. K. Aitken, and J. Dines, eds., *Jewish Perspectives on Hellenistic Rulers*. HCS 50. Berkeley: University of California Press, 2007: 13–28.
Najman, H. "The Idea of Biblical Genre: From Discourse to Constellation." In J. Penner, K. M. Penner, and C. Wassen, eds., *Prayer and Poetry in the Dead Sea Scrolls and Related Literature: Essays in Honor of Eileen Schuller on the Occasion of Her 65th Birthday*. STDJ 98. Leiden: Brill, 2012: 307–22.
———. *Seconding Sinai: The Development of Mosaic Discourse in Second Temple Judaism*. JSJSup 77. Leiden: Brill, 2003.
Nawotka, K. *The Alexander Romance by Ps.-Callisthenes: A Historical Commentary*. MneSup 399. Leiden: Brill, 2017.
Nelles, W. "Historical and Implied Authors and Readers." *Comparative Literature* 45 (1993): 22–46.
Nesselrath, H.-G. "Die Christen und die heidnische Bildung: Das Beispiel des Sokrates Scholastikos (*hist. eccl.* 3,16)." In J. Dummer and M. Vielberg, eds., *Leitbilder der Spätantike—Eliten und Leitbilder*. Stuttgart: Franz Steiner, 1999: 79–100.
Neubert, L. "Inventing Jason of Cyrene? 2 Maccabees and the Epitome." In F. Avemarie, P. Bukovec, S. Krauter, and M. Tilly, eds., *Die Makkabäer*. WUNT 1.382. Tübingen: Mohr Siebeck, 2017: 187–207.
Neyrey, J. H. "Josephus' *Vita* and the Encomium: A Native Model of Personality." *JSJ* 25 (1994): 177–206.
Nickelsburg, G. W. E. "The Bible Rewritten and Expanded." In M. E. Stone, ed., *Jewish Writings of the Second Temple Period: Apocrypha, Pseudepigrapha, Qumran Sectarian Writings, Philo, Josephus*. CRINT 2.2. Philadelphia: Fortress, 1984: 89–156.
———. *1 Enoch 1: A Commentary on the Book of 1 Enoch, Chapters 1–36; 81–108*. Hermeneia. Minneapolis: Fortress, 2001.
Niebuhr, K.-W. *Gesetz und Paränese: Katechismusartige Weisungsreihen in der frühjüdischen Literatur*. WUNT 2.28. Tübingen: Mohr Siebeck, 1987.
Niehoff, M. R. "Commentary Culture in the Land of Israel from an Alexandrian Perspective." *DSD* 19 (2012): 442–63.

———. *The Figure of Joseph in Post-biblical Jewish Literature*. AGJU 16. Leiden: Brill, 1992.

———. "A Jewish Critique of Christianity from Second-Century Alexandria: Revisiting the Jew Mentioned in *Contra Celsum*." *JECS* 21 (2013): 151–75.

———. *Jewish Exegesis and Homeric Scholarship in Alexandria*. Cambridge: Cambridge University Press, 2011.

———. "Philo and Plutarch as Biographers: Parallel Responses to Roman Stoicism." *GRBS* 52 (2012): 361–92.

———. *Philo of Alexandria: An Intellectual Biography*. AYBRL. New Haven: Yale University Press, 2018.

———. *Philo on Jewish Identity and Culture*. TSAJ 86. Tübingen: Mohr Siebeck, 2001.

———. "The Phoenix in Rabbinic Literature." *HTR* 89 (1996): 245–65.

———. "Questions and Answers in Philo and Genesis Rabbah." *JSJ* 39 (2008): 337–66.

Niggl, G. "Zur Theorie der Autobiographie." In M. Reichel, ed., *Antike Autobiographien: Werke—Epochen—Gattungen*. Cologne: Böhlau, 2005: 1–13.

Nikiprowetzky, V. *Le commentaire de l'Écriture chez Philon d'Alexandrie: Son caractère et sa portée; Observations philologiques*. ALGHJ 11. Leiden: Brill, 1977.

———. "L'exégèse de Philon d'Alexandrie dans le *De Gigantibus* et le *Quod Deus*." In D. Winston and J. Dillon, eds., *Two Treatises of Philo of Alexandria: A Commentary on De Gigantibus and Quod Deus Sit Immutabilis*. BJS 25. Chico: Scholars Press, 1983: 5–75.

———. *La troisième Sibylle*. ÉB 9. Paris: Mouton, 1970.

Nimis, S. A. "The Novel." In G. Boys-Stones, B. Graziosi, and P. Vasunia, eds., *Oxford Handbook of Hellenic Studies*. Oxford: Oxford University Press, 2009: 617–27.

———. "The Prosaics of the Ancient Novel." *Arethusa* 27 (1994): 387–411.

Nolland, J. *The Gospel of Matthew*. NIGTC. Grand Rapids: Eerdmans, 2005.

Norden, E. *Die antike Kunstprosa vom VI. Jahrhundert v. Chr. bis in die Zeit der Renaissance*. Leipzig: Teubner, 1923.

Nünlist, R. *The Ancient Critic at Work: Terms and Concepts of Literary Criticism in Greek Scholia*. Cambridge: Cambridge University Press, 2009.

Oegema, A., J. Pater, and M. Stoutjesdijk, eds., *Parables and Fables in the Graeco-Roman World*. WUNT 1. Tübingen: Mohr Siebeck, forthcoming 2020.

Opacki, I. "Royal Genres." In D. Duff, ed., *Modern Genre Theory*. LCR. London: Longman, 2000: 118–26.

Paget, J. C. "Jewish Christianity." In W. Horbury et al., eds., *Cambridge History of Judaism*, vol. 3, *The Early Roman Period*. Cambridge: Cambridge University Press, 1999: 731–75.

———. *Jews, Christians, and Jewish Christians in Antiquity*. WUNT 1.251. Tübingen: Mohr Siebeck, 2010: 383–425.

Pardee, D. *Handbook of Ancient Hebrew Letters*. SBLSBS 15. Chico: Scholars Press, 1982.

Parente, F. "The Impotence of Titus, or Flavius Josephus's *Bellum Judaicum* as an Example of 'Pathetic' Historiography." In J. Sievers and G. Lembi, eds., *Josephus and Jewish History in Flavian Rome and Beyond*. JSJSup 104. Leiden: Brill, 2005: 45–69.

———. "The Third Book of Maccabees as Ideological Document and Historical Source." *Henoch* 10 (1988): 143–82.

Parke, H. W. *Sibyls and Sibylline Prophecy in Classical Antiquity*. London: Routledge, 1988.

Parker, V. "The Letters in II Maccabees: Reflections on the Book's Composition." *ZAW* 119 (2007): 386–402.

Parsenios, G. *Departure and Consolation: The Johannine Farewell Discourse in Light of Greco-Roman Literature*. NovTSup 117. Leiden: Brill, 2005.

Parsons, M. C., and M. W. Martin. *Ancient Rhetoric and the New Testament: The Influence of Elementary Greek Composition*. Waco: Baylor University Press, 2018.

Parsons, M. C., and R. I. Pervo. *Rethinking the Unity of Luke and Acts*. Minneapolis: Fortress, 1993.

Patterson, S. J. *The Gospel of Thomas and Jesus*. FFRS. Sonoma: Polebridge Press, 1993.

———. "Wisdom in Q and Thomas." In L. G. Perdue, B. Brandon, and W. J. Wiseman, eds., *In Search of Wisdom: Essays in Memory of John G. Gammie*. Louisville: Westminster John Knox, 1993: 187–221.

Pearce, S. "King Moses: Notes on Philo's Portrait of Moses as an Ideal Leader in the Life of Moses." *MUSJ* 57 (2004): 37–74.

Pelletier, A. *Flavius Josèphe, Adaptateur de la Lettre d'Aristée: Une réaction atticisante contre la koinè*. ÉC 45. Paris: Klincksieck, 1962.

Pelling, C. B. R. "Childhood and Personality in Biography." In C. B. R. Pelling, ed., *Characterization and Individuality in Greek Literature*. Oxford: Oxford University Press, 1990: 213–44.

———. "Is Death the End? Closure in Plutarch's *Lives*." In D. H. Roberts, F. M. Dunnand, and D. Fowler, eds., *Classical Closure: Reading the End in Greek and Latin Literature*. Princeton: Princeton University Press, 1997: 228–50.

———. "Was There an Ancient Genre of 'Autobiography'? Or, Did Augustus Know What He Was Doing?" In C. Smith and A. Powell, eds., *The Lost Memoirs of Augustus*. Swansea: Classical Press of Wales, 2009: 41–64.

Penner, T. "Madness in the Method? The Acts of the Apostles in Current Study." *CBR* 2 (2004): 223–93.

Pépin, J. *La tradition de l'allégorie de Philon d'Alexandrie à Dante: Études historiques*. Paris: Études Augustiniennes, 1987.

Perrin, N., and C. W. Skinner, "Recent Trends in *Gospel of Thomas* Research (1989–2011), Part II: Genre, Theology and Relationship to the Gospel of John." *CBR* 11 (2012): 65–86.

Perrone, L. "Sulla preistoria delle 'quaestiones' nella letteratura patristica: presupposti e sviluppi del genere letterario fino al IV sec." *Annali di storia dell'exegesi* 8 (1991): 485–505.

Perry, B. E. *The Ancient Romances: A Literary-Historical Account of Their Origins*. Berkeley: University of California Press, 1967.

———. "The Egyptian Legend of Nectanebus." *TAPA* 97 (1966): 327–33.

Pervo, R. I. *Acts: A Commentary*. Hermeneia. Minneapolis: Fortress, 2009.

———. *Dating Acts: Between the Evangelists and the Apologists*. Santa Rosa, Cal.: Polebridge Press, 2006.

———. "Joseph and Asenath and the Greek Novel." In G. MacRae, ed., *SBLSP 1976*. Missoula, Mont.: Scholars Press, 1976: 171–81.

———. *Profit with Delight: The Literary Genre of the Acts of the Apostles*. Minneapolis: Fortress, 1987.

Petersen, A. K. "Rewritten Bible as a Borderline Phenomenon—Genre, Textual Strategy, or Canonical Anachronism?" In A. Hilhorst, E. Puech, and E. Tigchelaar, eds., *Flores Florentino: Dead Sea Scrolls and Other Early Jewish Studies in Honour of Florentino García Martínez*. JSJSup 122. Leiden: Brill, 2007: 285–306.

Petrovic, I. "Rhapsodic Hymns and Epyllia." In M. Baumbach and S. Bär, eds., *Brill's Companion to Greek and Latin Epyllion and Its Reception*. Leiden: Brill, 2012: 149–76.

Pfeiffer, R. *History of Classical Scholarship: From the Beginnings to the End of the Hellenistic Age*. Oxford: Clarendon, 1968.

Pfeiffer, R. H. *History of New Testament Times: With an Introduction to the Apocrypha*. New York: Harper and Brothers, 1949.

Philippson, L. M. *Ezechiel des jüdischen Trauerspieldichters Auszug aus Egypten und Philo des aelteren Jerusalem*. Berlin, 1830.

Phillips, M. S. "Histories, Micro- and Literary: Problems of Genre and Distance." *NLH* 34 (2003): 211–29.

Phillips, T. E. "The Genre of Acts: Moving towards a Consensus?" *CBR* 4 (2006): 365–96.

Pietersma, A. "A New Paradigm for Addressing an Old Question: The Relevance of the Interlinear Model for the Study of the Septuagint." In J. Cook, ed., *Bible and Computer: The Stellenbosch AIBI-6 Conference; Proceedings of the Association Internationale Bible et Informatique "From Alpha to Byte," 17–21 July, 2000*. Leiden: Brill, 2002: 337–64.

Pitts, A. W. *History, Biography, and the Genre of Luke-Acts: An Exploration of Literary Divergence in Greek Narrative Discourse*. BIS 177. Leiden: Brill, 2019.

Porter, J. I. *The Origins of Aesthetic Thought in Ancient Greece: Matter, Sensation and Experience*. Cambridge: Cambridge University Press, 2010.

———. *The Sublime in Antiquity*. Cambridge: Cambridge University Press, 2016.

Porter, S. E., and S. A. Adams, eds. *Paul and the Ancient Letter Form*. PAST 6. Leiden: Brill, 2010.

Porter, S. E., and B. R. Dyer, eds. *The Synoptic Problem: Four Views*. Grand Rapids: Baker Academic, 2016.

Potter, D. S. *Literary Texts and the Roman Historian*. London: Routledge, 1999.

———. *Prophecy and History in the Crisis of the Roman Empire: A Historical Commentary on the Thirteenth Sibylline Oracle*. OCM. Oxford: Clarendon, 1990.

Pouderon, B. "Aux origines du Roman pseudo clémentin: Prototype païen, refonte judéo-héllénistique, remaniement chrétien." In F. S. Jones and S. C. Mimouni, eds., *Le judéo-christianisme dans tous ses états: Actes du Colloque de Jérusalem 6–10 juillet 1998*. Paris: Éditions du Cerf, 2001: 231–56.

———. "Flavius Clemens et le Proto-Clément juif du Roman pseudo-clémentin." *Apocrypha* 7 (1996): 63–97.

Prandi, L. "A Monograph on Alexander the Great within a Universal History: Diodoros Book XVII." In L. I. Hau, A. Meeus, and B. Sheridan, eds., *Diodoros of Sicily: Historiographical Theory and Practice in the "Bibliotheke."* SH 58. Leuven: Peeters, 2018: 175–85.

Preuner, E. "Inschriften aus Akarnanien." *MDAI* 27 (1902): 330–52.

Price, R. M. "Implied Reader Response and the Evolution of Genres: Transitional Stages between the Ancient Novels and the Apocryphal Act." *HTS* 53 (1997): 909–38.

Priessnig, A. "Die literarische Form der Patriarchenbiographien des Philon von Alexandrien." *MGWJ* 7 (1929): 143–55.

Pummer, R. "Genesis 34 in Jewish Writings of the Hellenistic and Roman Periods." *HTR* 75 (1982): 177–88.

———. *The Samaritans: A Profile*. Grand Rapids: Eerdmans, 2016.

Pummer, R., and M. Roussel. "A Note on Theodotus and Homer." *JSJ* 13 (1982): 177–82.

Quack, J. F. *Einführung in die altägyptische Literaturgeschichte*. Vol. 3, *Die demotische und gräko-ägyptische Literatur*. 2nd ed. Münster: LIT Verlag, 2009.

Radice, R. *La filosofia di Aristobulo e i suoi nessi con il "De mundo" attribuito ad Aristotele*. Temi metafisici e problemi del pensiero antico, Studi e Testi 33. Milan: Vita e pensiero, 1994.

Rajak, T. "Josephus and the 'Archaeology' of the Jews." *JJS* 33 (1982): 465–77.

———. *Josephus: The Historian and His Society*. 2nd ed. London: Duckworth, 2002.

———. "Judaism and Hellenism Revisited." In *The Jewish Dialogue with Greece and Rome: Studies in Cultural and Social Interaction*. Leiden: Brill, 2002: 3–10.

———. "Justus of Tiberias." *CQ* 23 (1973): 345–68.

———. "*Paideia* in the Fourth Book of Maccabees." In G. J. Brooke and R. Smithuis, eds., *Jewish Education from Antiquity to the Middle Ages: Studies in Honour of Philip S. Alexander*. AJEC 100. Leiden: Brill, 2017: 63–84.

———. *Translation and Survival: The Greek Bible of the Ancient Jewish Diaspora*. Oxford: Oxford University Press, 2009.

Rappe, S. "The New Math: How to Add and Subtract Pagan Elements in Christian Education." In Y. L. Too, ed., *Education in Greek and Roman Antiquity*. Leiden: Brill, 2001: 405–32.

Rawson, E. *Intellectual Life in the Late Roman Republic*. London: Duckworth, 1985.

Reardon, B. P. *Courants littéraires grecs des IIe et IIIe siècles après J.-C.* Paris: Les Belles Lettres, 1971.

Redford, D. B. *Pharaonic King-Lists, Annals and Day-Books: A Contribution to the Study of Egyptian Sense of History*. SSEA 4. Mississauga: Benben, 1986.

Reed, A. Y. "The Construction of Subversion of Patriarchal Perfection: Abraham and Exemplarity in Philo, Josephus, and the Testament of Abraham." *JSJ* 40 (2009): 185–212.

———. "Job as Jobab: The Interpretation of Job in LXX Job 42:19b–e." *JBL* 120 (2001): 31–55.

Reinhartz, A., ed. *God the Father in the Gospel of John*. *Semeia* 95 (2001).

Remus, H. "Moses and the Thaumaturges: Philo's *De Vita Mosis* as a Rescue Operation." *LTP* 62 (1996): 665–80.

Reynolds, L. D., and N. G. Wilson. *Scribes and Scholars: A Guide to the Transmission of Greek and Latin Literature*. 4th ed. Oxford: Oxford University Press, 2013.

Riaud, J. "Les Thérapeutes d'Alexandrie dans la tradition et dans la recherche critique jusqu'aux découvertes de Qumran." *ANRW* 2.20.2 (1987): 1189–295.

Richards, E. R. *Paul and First-Century Letter Writing: Secretaries, Composition and Collection*. Downers Grove: IVP, 2004: 59–93.

———. *The Secretary in the Letters of St. Paul*. WUNT 2.42. Tübingen: Mohr Siebeck, 1991.

Riedweg, C. *Jüdisch-hellenistische Imitation eines orphischen Hieros Logos: Beobachtungen zu OF 245 und 247 (sog. Testament des Orpheus)*. CM 7. Tübingen: Gunter Narr, 1993.

Riggsby, A. "Memoir and Autobiography in Republican Rome." In J. Marincola, ed., *A Companion to Greek and Roman Historiography*. BCAW. Malden: Blackwell, 2007: 266–74.

Robbins, V. K. "Progymnastic Rhetorical Composition and Pre-Gospel Traditions: A New Approach." In C. Focant, ed., *Synoptic Gospels: Source Criticism and the New Literary Criticism*. BETL 110. Leuven: Leuven University Press, 1993: 111–47.

Robinson, J. M., and H. Koester. *Trajectories through Early Christianity*. Philadelphia: Fortress, 1971.

Roetzel, C. *Paul: The Man and the Myth*. Minneapolis: Fortress, 1999.

Rohde, E. *Der griechische Roman und seine Vorläufer*. 4th ed. Hildesheim: Olms, 1876.

Rosenmeyer, P. A. *Ancient Epistolary Fictions: The Letter in Greek Literature*. Cambridge: Cambridge University Press, 2004.

Rosenmeyer, T. G. "Ancient Literary Genres: A Mirage?" *Yearbook of Comparative and General Literature* 34 (1985).

Rösler, W. *Dichter und Gruppe: Eine Untersuchung zu den Bedingungen und zur historischen Funktion früher griechischer Lyrik am Beispiel Alkaios*. Theorie und Geschichte der Literatur und der schönen Künste 50. Munich: Fink, 1980.

Rothschild, C. K. *Luke-Acts and the Rhetoric of History: An Investigation of Early Christian Historiography*. WUNT 2.175. Tübingen: Mohr Siebeck, 2004.

Royse, J. R. "Further Greek Fragments of Philo's *Quaestiones*." In F. E. Greenspan, E. Hilgert, and B. L. Mack, eds., *Nourished with Peace: Studies in Hellenistic Judaism in Memory of Samuel Sandmel*. SPHS. Chico: Scholars Press, 1984: 143–53.

———. "The Original Structure of Philo's *Quaestiones*." *SPhiloA* 4 (1976–1977): 41–78.

———. "The Works of Philo." In A. Kamesar, ed., *The Cambridge Companion to Philo*. Cambridge: Cambridge University Press, 2009: 32–64.

Runia, D. T. "Further Observations on the Structure of Philo's Allegorical Treatises." *VC* 41 (1987): 105–38.

———. "Philo, Alexandrian and Jew." In *Exegesis and Philosophy: Studies on Philo of Alexandria*. Aldershot: Variorum, 1990: 1–18.

———. *Philo in Early Christian Literature: A Survey*. CRINT. Assen: Van Gorcum, 1993.

———. "Philonic Nomenclature." *SPhiloA* 6 (1994): 1–27.

———, ed. and trans. *Philo of Alexandria: On the Creation of the Cosmos According to Moses; Introduction, Translation, and Commentary*. PACS 1. Leiden: Brill, 2001.

———. "Philo of Alexandria and the Greek *Hairesis* Model." *VC* 53 (1999): 117–47.

———. *Philo of Alexandria and the "Timaeus" of Plato*. Leiden: Brill, 1986.

———. "The Place of *De Abrahamo* in Philo's Oeuvre." *SPhiloA* 20 (2008): 133–50.

———. "Secondary Texts in Philo's *Quaestiones*." In D. M. Hay, ed., *Both Literal and Allegorical: Studies in Philo of Alexandria's "Questions and Answers on Genesis and Exodus."* BJS 232. Atlanta: Scholars Press, 1991: 47–79.

———. "The Structure of Philo's Allegorical Treatise *De Agricultura*." *SPhiloA* 22 (2010): 87–109.

———. "The Structure of Philo's Allegorical Treatises: A Review of Two Recent Studies and Some Additional Comments." *VC* 38 (1984): 209–56.

———. "The Theme of Flight and Exile in the Allegorical Thought-World of Philo of Alexandria." *SPhiloA* 21 (2009): 1–24.

Rutherford, I. "Greek Fiction and Egyptian Fiction: Are They Related and, if So, How?" In T. Whitmarsh and S. Thompson, eds., *The Romance between Greece and the East*. Cambridge: Cambridge University Press, 2013: 23–37.

———. "Introduction: Interaction and Translation between Greek Literature and Egypt." In I. Rutherford, ed., *Greco-Egyptian Interactions: Literature, Transla-*

tion, and Culture, 500 BCE–300 CE. Oxford: Oxford University Press, 2016: 1–39.

———. "Kalasiris and Setne Khamwas: How Greek Literature Appropriated an Egyptian Narrative-Motif." *JHS* 117 (1997): 203–9.

Rydbeck, L. *Fachprosa, vermeintliche Volkssprache und Neues Testament: Zur Beurteilung der sprachlichen Niveauunterschiede im nachklassischen Griechisch*. SGU 5. Uppsala: Berlingska Boktryckeriet, 1967.

Ryholt, K. "A Demotic Version of Nectanebo's Dream (P. Carlsberg 562)." *ZPE* 122 (1998): 197–200.

———. "Nectanebo's Dream or The Prophecy of Petesis." In A. Blasius and B. U. Schipper, eds., *Apokalyptik und Ägypten: Eine kritische Analyse der relevanten Texte aus dem griechisch-römischen Ägypten*. OLA 107. Leuven: Peeters, 2002: 221–41.

Sachs, A. J., and D. J. Wiseman. "A Babylonian King List of the Hellenistic Period." *Iraq* 16 (1954): 202–211.

Safrai, Z. *Seeking Out the Land: Land of Israel Traditions in Ancient Jewish, Christian and Samaritan Literature*. JCPS 32. Leiden: Brill, 2018.

Samely, A., P. S. Alexander, R. Bernasconi, and R. Hayward. *Profiling Jewish Literature in Antiquity: An Inventory, from Second Temple Texts to the Talmuds*. Oxford: Oxford University Press, 2013.

Sandmel, S. *Philo of Alexandria: An Introduction*. Oxford: Oxford University Press, 1979.

———. *Philo's Place in Judaism: A Study of Conceptions of Abraham in Jewish Literature*. New York: Ktav, 1971.

Satran, D. *Biblical Prophets in Byzantine Palestine: Reassessing the Lives of the Prophets*. SVTP 11. Leiden: Brill, 1995.

Schedtler, J. P. J. "Perplexing Pseudepigraphy: The Pseudonymous Greek Poets." *JAJ* 8 (2017): 69–89.

Schellenberg, R. S. *Rethinking Paul's Rhetorical Education: Comparative Rhetoric and 2 Corinthians 10–13*. ECL 10. Atlanta: SBL, 2013.

Schepens, G., and S. Schorn. "Verkürzungen in und von Historiographie in klassischer und hellenistischer Zeit." In M. Horster and C. Reitz, eds., *Condensing Texts—Condensed Texts*. Stuttgart: Steiner, 2010: 395–433.

Schironi, F. "Greek Commentaries." *DSD* 19 (2012): 399–441.

Schlatter, A. *Jason von Kyrene: Ein Beitrag zu seiner Wiederherstellung*. Munich: C. H. Beck, 1891.

Schmidt, W. *Untersuchungen zur Fälschung historischer Dokumente bei Pseudo-Aristaios*. Bonn: Habelt Verlag, 1986.

Schnabel, P. *Berossos und die babylonisch-hellenistische Literatur*. Leipzig: Teubner, 1923.

Schoene, A. "Eusebi Gbronicorum libri duo." In *Göttingische gelehrte Anzeigen*. Göttingen: Dieterichschen, 1875.

Scholz, P. "Elementarunterricht und intellektuelle Bildung im hellenistischen Gymnasion." In D. Kah and P. Scholz, eds., *Das hellenistische Gymnasion*. WGW 8. Berlin: Akademie Verlag, 2004: 103–28.

Schreckenberg, H. *Bibliographie zu Flavius Josephus*. ALGHJ 1. Leiden: Brill, 1968.

Schröter, J. *Erinnerung an Jesu Worte: Studien zur Rezeption der Logienüberlieferung in Markus, Q und Thomas*. WMANT 76. Neukirchen-Vluyn: Neukirchener, 1997.

Schubert, P. *Form and Function of the Pauline Thanksgiving*. BZNW 20. Berlin: Töpelmann, 1939.

Schunck, K.-D. *Die Quellen des I. und II. Makkabäerbuches*. Halle: M. Niemeyer, 1954.

Schürer, E. *The History of the Jewish People in the Age of Jesus Christ (175 BC–AD 135)*. Revised and edited by G. Vermes, F. Millar, M. Black, and M. Goodman. 3 vols. Edinburgh: T&T Clark, 1973–1987.

Schwartz, D. R. "Josephus on His Jewish Forerunners (*Contra Apionem* 1.218)." In S. J. D. Cohen and J. J. Schwartz, eds., *Studies in Josephus and the Varieties of Ancient Judaism: Louis H. Feldman Jubilee Volume*. AJEC 67. Leiden: Brill, 2007: 195–206.

———. "Many Sources but a Single Author: Josephus's *Jewish Antiquities*." In H. H. Chapman and Z. Rodgers, eds., *A Companion to Josephus*. Oxford: Wiley-Blackwell, 2016: 36–58.

———. "Philo, His Family, and His Times." In A. Kamesar, ed., *The Cambridge Companion to Philo*. Cambridge: Cambridge University Press, 2009: 9–31.

———. *2 Maccabees*. CEJL. Berlin: De Gruyter, 2008.

Schwartz, S. "How Many Judaisms Were There? A Critique of Neusner and Smith on Definition and Mason and Boyarin on Categorization." *JAJ* 2 (2011): 208–38.

———. *Josephus and Judean Politics*. CSCT 18. Leiden: Brill, 1990.

Scott, I. W. "Is Philo's Moses a Divine Man?" *SPhiloA* 14 (2002): 87–111.

Seland, T. "The Expository Use of the Balaam Figure in Philo's *De Vita Moysis*." *SPhiloA* 28 (2016): 321–48.

Selden, D. "Genre of Genre." In J. Tatum, ed., *The Search for the Ancient Novel*. Baltimore: Johns Hopkins University Press, 1994: 39–64.

———. "Text Networks." *Ancient Narrative* 8 (2010): 1–23.

Sevrin, J.-M. "Remarques sur le genre litteraire de *l'Évangile selon Thomas* (II,2)." In L. Painchaud and A. Pasquier, eds., *Les textes de Nag Hammadi et le problème de leur classification: Actes du colloque tenu à Québec du 15 au 19 septembre 1993*. BCNH 3. Leuven: Peeters, 1995: 263–78.

Sharifian, F. *Cultural Conceptualisations of Language: Theoretical Framework and Applications*. Philadelphia: John Benjamins, 2011.

Shaw, A. N. *Oral Transmission and the Dream Narratives of Matthew 1–2: An Exploration of Matthean Culture Using Memory Techniques*. Eugene, Ore.: Pickwick Press, 2019.

Sheppard, A. "Proclus' Place in the Reception of Plato's *Republic*." In A. Sheppard, ed., *Ancient Approaches to Plato's Republic*. London: University College London, 2013: 107–16.

Sheridan, R. "John's Gospel and Modern Genre Theory: The Farewell Discourse (John 13–17) as a Test Case." *ITQ* 75 (2010): 287–99.

Shuler, P. L. *A Genre for the Gospels: The Biographical Character of Matthew*. Philadelphia: Fortress, 1982.

———. "Philo's Moses and Matthew's Jesus: A Comparative Study in Ancient Literature." *SPhiloA* 2 (1990): 86–103.

Shutt, R. J. H. "Letter of Aristeas." In *OTP* 2.7–34.

———. *Studies in Josephus*. London: SPCK, 1961.

Siegert, F. "Early Jewish Interpretation in a Hellenistic Style." In M. Saebø, ed., *Hebrew Bible / Old Testament: The History of Its Interpretation*, vol. 1, pt. 1, *Antiquity*. Göttingen: Vandenhoeck & Ruprecht, 1996: 130–97.

Sievers, J. *The Hasmoneans and Their Supporters: From Mattathias to the Death of John Hyrcanus I*. SFSHJ 6. Atlanta: Scholars Press, 1990.

Simkovich, M. Z. "Greek Influence on the Composition of 2 Maccabees." *JSJ* 42 (2011): 293–310.

Simpson, R. S. *Demotic Grammar in the Ptolemaic Sacerdotal Decrees*. Oxford: Griffith Institute, Ashmolean Museum, 1996.

Sinding, M. "After Definitions: Genre, Categories, and Cognitive Science." *Genre* 35 (2002): 181–219.

Sleeman, M. *Geography and the Ascension Narrative in Acts*. SNTSMS 146. Cambridge: Cambridge University Press, 2009.

Sluiter, I. "The Dialectics of Genre: Some Aspects of Secondary Literature and Genre in Antiquity." In M. Depew and D. Obbink, eds., *Matrices of Genre: Authors, Canons, and Society*. Cambridge, Mass.: Harvard University Press, 2000: 183–203.

Smith, D. L., and Z. L. Kostopoulos. "Biography, History, and the Genre of Luke-Acts." *NTS* 63 (2017): 390–410.

Smith, D. M. *The Theology of the Gospel of John*. NTT. Cambridge: Cambridge University Press, 1995.

Snell, B. "Die Iamben in Ezechiels Moses-Drama." *Glotta* 44 (1966): 25–32.

———. *Szenen aus griechischen Dramen*. Berlin: De Gruyter, 1971.

Sørensen, S. L. "Identifying the Jewish Eupolemoi: An Onomastic Approach." *JJS* 66 (2015): 24–35.

Spanoudakis, K. *Philitas of Cos*. MneSup 229. Leiden: Brill, 2002.

Sperber, D., and D. Wilson. *Relevance: Communication and Cognition*. Oxford: Blackwell, 1986.

Spilsbury, P. *The Image of the Jew in Flavius Josephus' Paraphrase of the Bible*. TSAJ 69. Tübingen: Mohr Siebeck, 1998.

Stadter, P. "Biography and History." In J. Marincola, ed., *A Companion to Greek and Roman Historiography*. BCAW. Malden: Blackwell, 2007: 528–40.

Standhartinger, A. *Das Frauenbild im Judentum der hellenistischen Zeit: Ein Beitrag anhand von "Joseph und Aseneth."* AGJU 26. Leiden: Brill, 1995.

———. "Recent Scholarship on *Joseph and Aseneth* (1988–2013)." *CBR* 12 (2014): 353–406.

Stanton, G. N. "Evidence in the Pseudo-Clementic Writings for Jewish Believers in Jesus." In O. Skarsaune and R. Hvalvik, eds., *Jewish Believers in Jesus*. Peabody, Mass.: Hendrickson, 2008: 305–24.

Starr, R. J. "The Circulation of Texts in the Ancient World." *Mnemosyne* 40 (1987): 213–23.

Steiner, P. *Russian Formalism: A Metapoetics*. Ithaca: Cornell University Press, 1984.

Stephens, S. A. "Commenting on Fragments." In R. K. Gibson and C. S. Kraus, eds., *The Classical Commentary: Histories, Practices, Theory*. Mnemosyne 232. Leiden: Brill, 2002: 67–88.

———. *The Poets of Alexandria*. London: I. B. Tauris, 2018.

———. "Posidippus's Poetry Book: Where Macedon Meets Egypt." In W. V. Harris and G. Ruffini, eds., *Ancient Alexandria between Egypt and Greece*. Leiden: Brill, 2004: 63–86.

———. *Seeing Double: Intercultural Poetics in Ptolemaic Alexandria*. HCS 37. Berkeley: University of California Press, 2003.

———. "Who Read Ancient Novels?" In J. Tatum, ed., *The Search for the Ancient Novel*. Baltimore: Johns Hopkins University Press, 1994: 405–18.

Sterling, G. E. "From the Thick Marshes of the Nile to the Throne of God: Moses in Ezekiel the Tragedian and Philo of Alexandria." *SPhiloA* 26 (2014): 115–33.

———. *Historiography and Self-Definition: Josephos, Luke-Acts, and Apologetic History*. NovTSup 64. Leiden: Brill, 1992.

———. "Philo of Alexandria's *Life of Moses*: An Introduction to the Exposition of the Law." *SPhiloA* 30 (2018): 31–45.

———. "Philo's *De Abrahamo*: Introduction." *SPhiloA* 20 (2008): 129–31.

———. "Philo's *Quaestiones*: Prolegomena or Afterthought." In D. M. Hay, ed., *Both Literal and Allegorical: Studies in Philo of Alexandria's "Questions and Answers on Genesis and Exodus."* BJS 232. Atlanta: Scholars Press, 1991: 99–123.

———. "Philo's School: The Social Setting of Ancient Commentaries." In B. Wyss, R. Hirsch-Luipold, and S.-J. Hirschi, eds., *Sophisten im Hellenismus und Kaiserzeit: Orte, Methoden und Personen der Bildungsvermittlung*. STAC 101. Tübingen: Mohr Siebeck, 2017: 121–42.

———. "Platonizing Moses: Philo and Middle Platonism." *SPhiloA* 5 (1993): 96–111.

———. "The School of Moses in Alexandria: An Attempt to Reconstruct the School of Philo." In J. Zurawski and G. Boccaccini, eds., *Second Temple Jewish "Paideia" in Context*. BZNW 228. Berlin: De Gruyter, 2017: 141–66.

———. "'The School of Sacred Laws': The Social Setting of Philo's Treatises." *VC* 53 (1999): 148–64.

———. "Thunderous Silence: The Omission of the Sinai Pericope in Philo of Alexander." *JSJ* 49 (2018): 1–26.

Stern, M., and O. Murray. "Hecataeus of Abdera and Theophrastus on Jews and Egyptians." *JEA* 59 (1973): 159–68.

Stern, P. "Life of Josephus: The Autobiography of Flavius Josephus." *JSJ* 41 (2010): 63–93.

Stern, S. "Qumran Calendars and Sectarianism." In T. H. Lim and J. J. Collins, eds., *The Oxford Handbook to the Dead Sea Scrolls*. Oxford: Oxford University Press, 2010: 232–53.

Stewart, E. J. "Ezekiel's *Exagoge*: A Typical Hellenistic Tragedy?" *GRBS* 58 (2018): 223–52.

———. *Greek Tragedy on the Move: The Birth of a Panhellenic Art Form, c. 500–300 BC*. Oxford: Oxford University Press, 2017.

Stirewalt, M. L., Jr. "The Form and Function of the Greek Letter-Essay." In K. P. Donfried, ed., *The Romans Debate*. Rev. and expanded ed. Edinburgh: T&T Clark, 1991: 147–71.

———. *Paul, the Letter Writer*. Grand Rapids: Eerdmans, 2003.

Stone, M. E. *Ancient Judaism: New Visions and Views*. Grand Rapids: Eerdmans, 2011.

Stowers, S. K. "4 Maccabees." In J. L. Mays, ed., *The HarperCollins Bible Commentary*. San Francisco: HarperSanFrancisco, 2000: 844–55.

———. *Letter Writing in Greco-Roman Antiquity*. LEC 5. Philadelphia: Westminster Press, 1986.

Strecker, G. *Das Judenchristentum in den Pseudoklementinen*. 2nd ed. Berlin: Akademie Verlag, 1981.

Strugnell, J. "Notes on the Text and Metre of Ezekiel the Tragedian's 'Exagoge.'" *HTR* 60 (1967): 449–57.

Stuckenbruck, L. *1 Enoch 91–108*. CEJL. Berlin: De Gruyter, 2008: 60–62.

Swales, J. *Genre Analysis: English in Academic and Research Settings*. Cambridge: Cambridge University Press, 1991.

Taatz, I. *Frühjüdische Briefe: Die paulinischen Briefe im Rahmen der offiziellen religiösen Briefe des Frühjudentums*. NTOA 16. Göttingen: Vandenhoeck & Ruprecht, 1991.

Tait, J. "Egyptian Fiction in Demotic Greek." In J. R. Morgan and R. Stoneman, eds., *Ancient Fiction: The Greek Novel in Context*. London: Routledge, 1994: 203–22.

Talbert, C. H. *What Is a Gospel? The Genre of the Canonical Gospels*. London: SPCK, 1978.

Talshir, Z. *1 Esdras: A Text Critical Commentary*. SCS 50. Atlanta: SBL, 2001.

———. *1 Esdras: From Origin to Translation*. SCS 47. Atlanta: SBL, 1999.

Taylor, J. E., and P. R. Davies. "The So-Called Therapeutai of *De vita contemplativa*: Identity and Character." *HTR* 91 (1998): 3–24.

Taylor, J. E. *Jewish Women Philosophers of First-Century Alexandria: Philo's "Therapeutae" Reconsidered*. Oxford: Oxford University Press, 2003.

Taylor J. E., and D. Hay. "Astrology in Philo of Alexandria's *De Vita Contemplativa*." *ARAM Periodical* 24 (2012): 56–74.

Tcherikover, V. A. "Jewish Apologetic Literature Reconsidered." *Eos* 48 (1956): 169–93.

———. "The Third Book of Maccabees as a Historical Source of Augustus' Time." *ScrHier* 7 (1961): 1–26.

______. *Hellenistic Civilization and the Jews*. Translated by S. Applebaum. New York: Atheneum, 1977.

Terian, A. "The Priority of the *Quaestiones* among Philo's Exegetical Commentaries." In D. M. Hay, ed., *Both Literal and Allegorical: Studies in Philo of Alexandria's "Questions and Answers on Genesis and Exodus."* BJS 232. Atlanta: Scholars Press, 1991: 29–46.

Termini, C. "The Historical Part of the Pentateuch According to Philo of Alexandria: Biography, Genealogy, and the Philosophical Meaning of the Patriarchal Lives." In N. Calduch-Benages and J. Liesen, eds., *Deuterocanonical and Cognate Literature Yearbook*. Berlin: De Gruyter, 2006: 265–97.

Thackeray, H. St. J. *Josephus: The Man and the Historian*. New York: Ktav, 1967.

Thiessen, M. "Aseneth's Eight-Day Transformation as Scriptural Justification for Conversion." *JSJ* 45 (2014): 229–49.

Thissen, H.-J. "Lost in Translation? Von Übersetzungen und Übersetzern." In H.-W. Fischer-Elfert and T. S. Richter, eds., *Literatur und Religion im Alten Ägypten—Ein Symposium zu Ehren von Elke Blumenthal*. Stuttgart: Hirzel, 2011: 125–63.

Thomas, J. *Der jüdische Phokylides: Formgeschichtliche Zugänge zu Pseudo-Phokylides und Vergleich mit der neutestamentlichen Paränese*. NTOA 23. Göttingen: Vandenhoeck & Ruprecht, 1992.

Thomas, S. I. *The "Mysteries" of Qumran: Mystery, Secrecy, and Esotericism in the Dead Sea Scrolls*. Atlanta: SBL, 2009.

Thompson, E. M. *An Introduction to Greek and Latin Palaeography*. Oxford: Clarendon, 1912.

Thyen, H. *Der Stil der jüdische-hellenistischen Homilie*. Göttingen: Vandenhoeck & Ruprecht, 1955.

Tiede, D. L. *The Charismatic Figure as Miracle Worker*. SBLDS 1. Missoula, Mont.: Scholars Press, 1972.

Tilg, S. "On the Origins of the Modern Term 'Epyllion': Some Revisions to a Chapter in This History of Classical Scholarship." In M. Baumbach and S. Bär, eds., *Brill's Companion to Greek and Latin Epyllion and Its Reception*. Leiden: Brill, 2012: 29–54.

Todorov, T. *The Fantastic: A Structural Approach to a Literary Genre*. Translated by R. Howard. Ithaca: Cornell University Press, 1975.

———. *Genres in Discourse*. Translated by C. Porter. Cambridge: Cambridge University Press, 1990.

———. "The Origin of Genres." In D. Duff, ed., *Modern Genre Theory*. LCR. London: Longman, 2000: 193–209.

Toher, M. "Divining a Lost Text: Augustus' Autobiography and the βίος Καίσαρος of Nicolaus of Damascus." In C. Smith and A. Powell, eds., *The Lost Memoirs of Augustus and the Development of Roman Autobiography*. Swansea: Classical Press of Wales, 2009: 125–44.

Tolmie, D. F. *Jesus' Farewell to the Disciples: John 12:1–17:26 in Narratological Perspective*. BIS 12. Leiden: Brill, 1995.

Too, Y. L. "The Walking Library: The Performance of Cultural Memories." In D. Braund and J. Wilkins, eds., *Athenaeus and His World: Reading Greek Culture in the Roman Empire*. Exeter: University of Exeter Press, 2001: 111–23.

Toohey, P. *Epic Lessons: An Introduction to Didactic Poetry*. London: Routledge, 1996.

Townend, G. B. "Suetonius and His Influences." In T. A. Dorey, ed., *Latin Biography*. London: Routledge, 1967: 79–111.

Trobisch, D. *Die Entstehung der Paulusbriefsammlung: Studien zu den Anfängen christlicher Publizistik*. NTOA 10. Göttingen: Vandenhoeck & Ruprecht, 1989.

Trojahn, S. *Die auf Papyri erhaltenen Kommentare zur Alten Komödie: Ein Beitrag zur Geschichte der antiken Philologie*. BzA 175. Munich: Saur, 2002.

Tromp, J. "The Formation of the Third Book of Maccabees." *Henoch* 17 (1995): 311–28.

Tronier, H. "Markusevangeliets Jesus som biografiseret erkendelsesfigur." In T. L. Thompson and H. Tronier, eds., *Frelsens biografisering*. FBE 13. Copenhagen: Museum Tusculanum, 2004: 237–71.

Tuplin, C. "Berossus and Greek Historiography." In J. Haubold, G. B. Lanfranchi, R. Rollinger, and J. M. Steele, eds., *The World of Berossos: Proceedings of the 4th International Colloquium on "The Ancient Near East between Classical and Ancient Oriental Traditions," Hatfield College, Durham 7th–9th July 2010*. CO 5. Wiesbaden: Harrassowitz Verlag, 2013: 177–97.

Turner, E. G. *Greek Manuscripts of the Ancient World*. Princeton: Princeton University Press, 1971.

Tynyanov, Y. "On Literary Evolution." In L. Metejka and K. Pomorska, eds., *Readings in Russian Poetics: Formalist and Structuralist Views*. Cambridge, Mass.: MIT Press, 1971: 66–78.

Tynyanov, Y., and R. Jakobson. "Problems in the Study of Literature and Language." In L. Metejka and K. Pomorska, eds., *Readings in Russian Poetics: Formalist and Structuralist Views*. Cambridge, Mass.: MIT Press, 1971: 79–81.

Ulf, C. "Rethinking Cultural Contacts." *Ancient West and East* 8 (2009): 81–132.

Ullmann, L., and J. Price. "Drama and History in Josephus' *Bellum Judaicum*." *Scripta Classica Israelica* 21 (2002): 97–111.

Uusimäki, E. "Local and Global: Philo of Alexandria on the Philosophical Life of the Therapeutae." *Henoch* 40 (2018): 298–317.

van der Horst, P. W. "Greek in Jewish Palestine in the Light of Jewish Epigraphy." In *Japheth in the Tents of Shem: Studies on Jewish Hellenism in Antiquity*. BET 32. Leuven: Peeters, 2002: 9–26.

———. "The Interpretation of the Bible by the Minor Hellenistic Jewish Authors." In M. J. Mulder, ed., *Mikra: Text, Translation, Reading and Interpretation of the Hebrew Bible in Ancient Judaism and Early Christianity*. CRINT 2.1. Philadelphia: Fortress, 1988: 519–46.

———. "Moses' Throne Vision in Ezekiel the Dramatist." *JJS* 34 (1983): 21–29.

———. "Philo and the Rabbis on Genesis: Similar Questions, Different Answers." In A. Volgers and C. Zamagni, eds., *Erotapokriseis: Early Christian Question-and-Answer Literature in Context*. CBET 37. Leuven: Peeters, 2004: 55–70.

———. "Philosabbatius, a Forgotten Early Jewish Philosopher." *JJS* 69 (2018): 256–61.

———. "Pseudo-Phocylides on the Afterlife: A Rejoinder to John J. Collins." *JSJ* 35 (2004): 70–75.

———. "Pseudo-Phocylides and the New Testament." *ZNW* 69 (1978): 187–202.

———. "Pseudo-Phocylides Revisited." *JSP* 3 (1988): 3–30.

———. *The Sentences of Pseudo-Phocylides*. SVTP. Leiden: Brill, 1978.

van Henten, J. W. "Datierung und Herkunft des Vierten Makkabäerbuches." In J. W. van Henten, H. J. De Jonge, P. T. van Rooden, and J. W. Wesselius, eds., *Tradition and Re-interpretation in Jewish and Early Christian Literature*. Leiden: Brill, 1986: 136–49.

———. *The Maccabean Martyrs as Saviours of the Jewish People: A Study of 2 and 4 Maccabees*. JSJSup 57. Leiden: Brill, 1997.

van Henten, J. W., and R. Abusch. "The Jews as Typhonians and Josephus' Strategy of Refutation in *Contra Apionem*." In L. H. Feldman and J. R. Levison, eds., *Josephus' "Contra Apionem": Studies in Its Character and Contexts with a Latin Concordance to the Portion Missing in Greek*. AGJU 34. Leiden: Brill, 1996: 271–309.

van Henten, J. W., and F. Avemarie. *Martyrdom and Noble Death: Selected Texts from Graeco-Roman, Jewish and Christian Antiquity*. London: Routledge, 2002.

Van Seters, J. *In Search of History: Historiography in the Ancient World and the Origins of Biblical History*. New Haven: Yale University Press, 1983.

van Tieghem, P. "La question des genres littéraires." *Helicon* 1 (1939): 95–101.

van Unnik, W. C. "Remarks on the Purpose of Luke's Historical Writing (Luke 1.1–4)." In *Sparsa Collecta: The Collected Essays of W. C. van Unnik*. Leiden: Brill, 1973: 6–15.

Varneda, P. V. "The Early Empire." In G. Marasco, ed., *Political Autobiographies and Memoirs in Antiquity: A Brill Companion*. Leiden: Brill, 2011: 315–62.

Verheyden, J. “The Unity of Luke-Acts: What Are We Up To?” In J. Verheyden, ed., *The Unity of Luke-Acts*. BETL 142. Leuven: Leuven University Press, 1999: 3–56.

Vines, M. E. *The Problem of Markan Genre: The Gospel of Mark and the Jewish Novel*. AB 3. Atlanta: SBL, 2002.

Vinson, S. “Good and Bad Women in Egyptian and Greek Fiction.” In I. Rutherford, ed., *Greco-Egyptian Interactions: Literature, Translation, and Culture, 500 BCE–300 CE*. Oxford: Oxford University Press, 2016: 245–66.

Vogt, E. “Tragiker Ezechiel.” In *JSHRZ* 4.3, 113–34.

Volk, K. *The Poetics of Latin Didactic: Lucretius, Vergil, Ovid, Manilius*. Oxford: Oxford University Press, 2002.

Wacholder, B. Z. *Eupolemus: A Study of Judaeo-Greek Literature*. HUMC 3. Cincinnati: Hebrew Union College Press, 1974.

———. *Nicolaus of Damascus*. UCPH 75. Berkeley: University of California Press, 1962.

———. “Philo (The Elder).” In M. Berenbaum and F. Skolnik, eds., *Encyclopedia Judaica*, vol. 16. 2nd ed. Detroit: Macmillan Reference, 2007: 58.

———. “Pseudo-Eupolemus’ Two Greek Fragments on the Life of Abraham.” *HUCA* 34 (1963): 83–113.

Waitz, H. *Die Pseudoklementinen: Homilien und Rekognitionen; Eine quellenkritische Untersuchung*. Leipzig: Hinrichs, 1904.

Walbank, F. W. “History and Tragedy.” *Historia* 9 (1960): 216–34.

———. *Polybius*. SCL 42. Berkeley: University of California Press, 1972.

Wallace-Hadrill, A. *Rome’s Cultural Revolution*. Cambridge: Cambridge University Press, 2008.

Walter, N. “Fragmente jüdisch-hellenistischer Epik: Philon, Theodotos.” In *JSHRZ* 4.3, 135–72.

———. *Fragmente jüdisch-hellenistischer Historiker*. *JSHRZ* 1.2.

———. “Fragmente jüdisch-hellenisticher Exegeten: Aristobulos, Demetrios, Aristeas.” In *JSHRZ* 3.2, 257–99.

———. “Pseudepigraphische jüdisch-hellenistischer Dichtung: Pseudo-Phokylides, Pseudo-Orpheus, Gefälschte Verse auf Namen griechischer Dichter.” In *JSHRZ* 4.3, 173–276.

———. *Der Thoraausleger Aristobulos*. Berlin: Akademie Verlag, 1964.

———. “Zu Pseudo-Eupolemus.” *Kilo* 43/45 (1965): 282–90.

Walters, P. *The Assumed Authorial Unity of Luke and Acts: A Reassessment of the Evidence*. SNTSMS 145. Cambridge: Cambridge University Press, 2009.

Wan, S.-K. “Philo’s *Quaestiones et solutiones in Genesim*: A Synoptic Approach.” In E. H. Lovering, ed., *SBLSP 1993*. Atlanta: Scholars Press, 1993: 22–53.

Wasserman, T. “The ‘Son of God’ Was in the Beginning (Mark 1:1).” *JTS* 62 (2011): 20–50.

Wassmuth, O. *Sibyllinische Orakel 1–2: Studien und Kommentar*. AJEC 76. Leiden: Brill, 2011.

Wasyl, A. M. *Genres Rediscovered: Studies in Latin Miniature Epic, Love Elegy, and Epigram of the Roman-Barbaric Age*. Kraków: Jagiellonian University Press, 2011.

Węcowski, M. "Homer and the Origins of the Symposion." In F. Montanari and P. Ascheri, eds., *Omero tremila anni dopo*. Rome: Edizione di Storia e Letteratura, 2002: 625–37.

Weima, J. A. D. *Paul the Letter Writer: An Introduction to Epistolary Analysis*. Grand Rapids: Baker Academic, 2016.

Wellek, R., and A. Warren. *Theory of Literature*. 3rd ed. Harmondsworth: Penguin, 1982.

Wente, E. *Letters from Ancient Egypt*. Atlanta: SBL, 1990.

West, M. L. "Phocylides." *JHS* 98 (1978): 164–67.

———. *Studies in Greek Elegy and Iambus*. Berlin: De Gruyter, 1974.

West, S. "*Joseph and Asenath*: A Neglected Greek Romance." *CQ* 24 (1974): 70–81.

White, J. *Light from Ancient Letters*. Philadelphia: Fortress, 1986.

Whitmarsh, T. *Beyond the Second Sophistic: Adventures in Greek Postclassicism*. Berkeley: University of California Press, 2013.

———. "The Birth of a Prodigy: Heliodorus and the Genealogy of Hellenism." In R. Hunter, ed., *Studies in Heliodorus*. Cambridge: Cambridge Philological Society, 1998: 93–124.

———. *Greek Literature and the Roman Empire: The Politics of Imitation*. Oxford: Oxford University Press, 2001.

———. "Joseph et Aseneth: Erotisme et Religion." In C. Bost Pouderon and B. Pouderon, eds., *Les hommes et les dieux dans l'ancien roman: Actes du colloque des Tours, 22–24 octobre 2009*. Lyon: Maison de l'Orient et de la Méditerranée, 2012: 237–52.

———. *Narrative and Identity in the Ancient Greek Novel: Returning Romance*. Cambridge: Cambridge University Press, 2011.

Whitters, M. F. *The Epistle of Second Baruch: A Study in Form and Message*. JSPSup 42. Sheffield: Sheffield Academic Press, 2003.

Wifstrand, A. *Epochs and Styles*. Edited and translated by L. Rydbeck and S. E. Porter. WUNT 1.179. Tübingen: Mohr Siebeck, 2005.

Williams, D. S. "Josephus and the Authorship of IV Maccabees: A Critical Investigation." PhD diss., Hebrew Union College, 1987.

———. "Recent Research in 2 Maccabees." *CBR* 2 (2003): 69–83.

Williams, M. H. *Jews in a Graeco-Roman Environment*. WUNT 1.312. Tübingen: Mohr Siebeck, 2013.

Williams, M. S. "Augustine's Confessions as Autobiography." In K. De Temmerman, ed., *Oxford Handbook of Ancient Biography*. Oxford: Oxford University Press, 2020: 313–28.

Williamson, R., Jr. "Pesher: A Cognitive Model of the Genre." *DSD* 17 (2010): 336–60.

Wills, L. M., ed. and trans. *Ancient Jewish Novels: An Anthology*. Oxford: Oxford University Press, 2002.
———. *Judith: A Commentary on the Book of Judith*. Hermeneia. Minneapolis: Fortress, 2019.
———. *The Jew in the Court of the Foreign King: Ancient Jewish Court Legends*. HDR 26. Minneapolis: Fortress, 1990.
———. *The Jewish Novel in the Ancient World*. Ithaca: Cornell University Press, 1995.
———. "The Jewish Novellas Daniel, Esther, Tobit, Judith, Joseph and Aseneth." In J. R. Morgan and R. Stoneman, eds., *Greek Fiction: The Greek Novel in Context*. London: Routledge, 1994: 223–38.
———. "Jewish Novellas in a Greek and Roman Age: Fiction and Identity." *JSJ* 42 (2011): 141–65.
———. *Quest of the Historical Gospel: Mark, John and the Origins of the Gospel Genre*. London: Routledge, 1997.
Wilson, W. T. *The Mysteries of Righteousness: The Literary Composition and Genre of the Sentences of Pseudo-Phocylides*. TSAJ 40. Tübingen: Mohr Siebeck, 1993.
———. *The Sentences of Pseudo-Phocylides*. CEJL. Berlin: De Gruyter, 2005.
Winston, D. "Aristobulus from Walter to Holladay." *SPhiloA* 8 (1996): 155–66.
———. "Philo and the Hellenistic Jewish Encounter." *SPhiloA* 7 (1995): 124–42.
Wise, M. O. *Language and Literacy in Roman Judaea: A Study of the Bar Kokhba Documents*. AYBRL. New Haven: Yale University Press, 2015.
Wiseman, T. P. "Lying Historians: Seven Types of Mendacity." In C. Gill and T. P. Wiseman, eds., *Lies and Fiction in the Ancient World*. Austin: University of Texas Press, 1993: 122–46.
Wittgenstein, L. *Philosophical Investigations*. Translated by G. E. M. Anscombe. Oxford: Basil Blackwell, 1967.
Wolff, E. "Quelques précisions sur le mot 'Epyllion.'" *RevPhil* 62 (1988): 299–303.
Woodman, A. J. *Rhetoric in Classical Historiography*. London: Croom Helm, 1988.
Wright, B. G., III. "Joining the Club: A Suggestion about Genre in Early Jewish Texts." *DSD* 17 (2010): 289–314.
———. *The Letter of Aristeas: "Aristeas to Philocrates" or "On the Translation of the Law of the Jews."* CEJL. Berlin: De Gruyter, 2015.
Wright, J. L. "Remember Nehemiah: 1 Esdras and the *Damnatio Memoriae Nehemiae*." In L. S. Fried, ed., *Was 1 Esdras First? An Investigation into the Priority and Nature of 1 Esdras*. AIL 7. Atlanta: SBL, 2011: 145–63.
Wright, M. *The Lost Plays of Greek Tragedy*. Vol. 1, *Neglected Authors*. London: Bloomsbury, 2016.
Yarrow, L. M. *Historiography at the End of the Republic*. Oxford: Oxford University Press, 2006.
———. "How to Read a Diodoros Fragment." In L. I. Hau, A. Meeus, and B. Sheridan, eds., *Diodoros of Sicily: Historiographical Theory and Practice in the "Bibliotheke."* SH 58. Leuven: Peeters, 2018: 247–74.

Young, D. "Ps.-Phocylides." In A.-M. Denis, ed., *Fragmenta Pseudepigraphorum quae supersunt graeca*. Leiden: Brill, 1970: 149–56.

Zahn, M. M. "Genre and Rewritten Scripture: A Reassessment." *JBL* 131 (2012): 271–88.

———. "Talking about Rewritten Texts: Some Reflections on Terminology." In H. von Weissenberg, J. Pakkala, and M. Marttila, eds., *Changes in Scripture: Rewriting and Interpreting Authoritative Traditions in the Second Temple Period*. BZAW 419. Berlin: De Gruyter, 2011: 93–119.

Ziegler, K. *Das Hellenistische Epos: Ein Vergessenes Kapitel Griechischer Dichtung*. 2nd ed. Leipzig: Teubner, 1966.

———. "Tragoedia." *PW* 6A.2 (1937): 1899–2075.

Zimmermann, B. "Anfänge der Autobiographie in der griechischen Literatur." In M. Erler and S. Schorn, eds., *Die griechische Biographie in hellenistischer Zeit*. Berlin: De Gruyter, 2007: 3–9.

Zuntz, G. "Aristeas Studies I: 'The Seven Banquets.'" *JSS* 4 (1959): 21–36.

INDEX OF MODERN AUTHORS

INDEX OF ANCIENT LITERATURE

1. Scripture

A. Jewish Scripture

B. Old Testament Apocrypha

C. New Testament

2. Jewish Literature (texts ordered by abbreviation)

3. Christian Literature

4. Greco-Roman Literature

5. Ancient Near Eastern Literature

6. Papyri, Codices, and Inscriptions